All information in the narrative sections of this book is from newspaper archives, magazine articles, personal interviews, police case files, and is a matter of public record.

Any rumor or conjecture is typically identified as such within these sections.

Although actual interview quotes from the 1966 case file are used, some dialogue is imagined for dramatic or revelatory effect, while remaining consistent with the characters and events as portrayed.

The author's summations are his subjective opinion based on the evidence as stated in the narrative, and do not represent an accusation against any person living or dead.

All images are used under the public domain with fair use, unless otherwise noted or part of the author's collection.

Also by JT Townsend

Queen City Gothic...

Cincinnati's Most Infamous Murder Mysteries

Queen City Notorious...

Cincinnati's Most Sensational Murder Cases

SUMMER'S ALMOST GONE

The Bricca Family Murders... The Most Notorious Cold Case in Cincinnati History

J.T. TOWNSEND

True Crime Detective Press
Cincinnati, Ohio 45215
513-315-6512
jtesch@cinci.rr.com
www.jttownsend.com

First published by TCD Press 9/14/18

ISBN: 978-1-64440-939-8 Hard Cover
ISBN: 978-1-64440-940-4 Soft Cover

Printed in the United States of America
Cincinnati, Ohio

This book is dedicated to Gerald John, Linda Jayne, and Deborah Ann...

Author Unknown

Now summer goes
And tomorrow's snows
Will soon be deep,
And the sky of blue
Which summer knew
Sees shadows creep.

As the gleam tonight
Which is silver bright
Spans ghostly forms,
The winds rush by
With a warning cry
Of coming storms.

So the laurel fades
In the snow-swept glades
Of flying years,
And the dreams of youth
Find the bitter truth
Of pain and tears.

Through the cheering mass
Let the victors pass
To find fate's thrust,
As tomorrow's fame
Writes another name
On drifting dust...

"Adultery is not a crime, it's an amusement."

Kathleen Winsor

"I don't think sex has much to do with morals. It's more a compulsion – like murder."

Alice Thomas Ellis

"People insist upon reading their own minds, their own characteristics, into the plans of a murderer. Because they never take a risk, they forget that frightful risks are taken daily, and that criminals succeed in their plans because of their daring."

Edmund Pearson

"One sin, I know, another doth provoke; Murder's as near to lust as flame to smoke."

William Shakespeare

"Women seem wicked, when you're unwanted..."

Jim Morrison

Mr. and Mrs. Adolph Bulaw

request the honour of your presence

at the marriage of their daughter

Linda Jayne

to

Mr. Gerald John Bricca

on Saturday, the twenty-fifth of November

at four o'clock

St. Anne Church

Barrington, Illinois

TABLE OF CONTENTS

Adolph Bulaw ready to escort his daughter Linda down the aisle.

PREFACE: A VERY COLD CASE

"There is something ominous at the heart of these murders – a motive so twisted that the line between passion and insanity was obliterated."

JT Townsend 2012

September 25th, 2016

The Gerald Bricca family was murdered in their home fifty years ago tonight. It was an unbelievable crime – hideous, unexpected, baffling. A crime destined to become the most notorious and obsessive cold case in Cincinnati history.

On that long ago September day, we were horrified by the blaring Bricca headlines. Jerry, his wife Linda, and their young daughter Debbie were found stabbed to death on Greenway Avenue in the city's Bridgetown neighborhood. Striking between the 4th and 5th slayings of the "Cincinnati Strangler" in 1966, the Bricca killer plunged a city already on edge into the abyss.

A half century later, this shocking crime still haunts anyone who dares evoke it. The Bricca mystery lingers in cobwebs and survives on whispers. It's a terminal case with a fading pulse.

Why does it still echo five decades later? Better still, why conjure up this gruesome crime at all? Why not let it fall victim to time and memory?

Some say it's an investigation that became a sinister stalemate after detectives got the break they were craving. Others remember a prominent suspect who lawyered up and lived the rest of his life under a cloud of unrelenting suspicion.

But mostly, it's a community still burdened by this gothic wickedness against all that was good and decent in a conservative Midwestern city. When ordinary people are confronted with evil, we depend on certain justice and swift retribution. Yet Bricca defies our comfortable expectation that killers are always captured, victims will be avenged, and justice aligns with the truth.

If you read my Bricca chapter in **Queen City Gothic**, you are aware of my passion for solving this case. Of all the local unsolved murders I have studied, this is the one that goes bump in the night in my head. My passion to unearth the truth of this crime has spanned almost 80% of my life.

I was just shy of 13 in September of 1966, entering the strange new world of junior high school and puberty. We had a serial killer on the loose. The city was simmering, waiting – just like with the Boston Strangler three years earlier.

Then a beautiful family is viciously slain, and I finally felt afraid. A faceless killer could enter any house and massacre any family just like my own.

Eventually my dread eased into curiosity, then significance, then pursuit, and lastly obsession.

It came to a climax in November 2014, when the Hamilton County Sheriff's Department granted me access to the Bricca case file. This startling consent changed everything – and opened the door for this book.

So why now, after a half century has passed? Can I rewind this stained history without lancing old wounds? Will my unique perspective skewer long held beliefs, and alter the opinions of those who know everything and nothing?

Opening up any cold case is daunting. Evidence is lost, buried, or forgotten. Contradiction and hearsay muddy the waters. The truth is elusive, shrouded, or shameful.

Who is left alive to interview? And whom do you trust out of those survivors? Is their agenda at odds with yours? As detectives like to say: "You can't put toothpaste back in the tube."

I caution any reader who believes they already know this story. The Bricca file is awash with information that never saw the light of print – evidence that might staunch the rumors that police "screwed up the crime scene" or "covered up for the suspect."

As an armchair detective stalking a legendary murder mystery, I am not shackled by presumption of innocence and reasonable doubt. In my purview ALL evidence is admissible – hearsay, rumors, gossip, undertones, tangents. Objectivity never solved a murder case. You have to get down in the gutter.

I merely flirt with the law. It all comes down to probability for me – who IS the most probable killer.

I must step beyond the case file and the evidence. What I narrate here is the reality for me. There is no finite truth when no one was there to record it. I've had to recreate scenes and imagine dialogue based on my consummate knowledge of this story and its cast of characters. Our concept of historical certainty must always travel through someone. This is MY version of it.

I confess that CSI type forensics do not excite me. I'm a circumstantial evidence guy who tingles when occurrence meets coincidence. I get excited hearing about the suspect's companions or cohorts. Are there rumors of rancor? Is this idolatry or adultery?

Contrary to popular belief, circumstantial evidence is not a chain that snaps when one link breaks. It is a rope with many strands. Cut away some fiber and you still have a strong rope.

Police and prosecutors often hone in on a suspect and build a case around him while ignoring others. Armchair detectives, however, have no hidden agenda, no boss to impress, no case backlog, and no stake in the solution.

But I DO have a stake with Bricca. I plan to drive it through the heart of this undead case.

As Sherlock Holmes memorably said: "When you eliminate the impossible, what remains, however improbable, is the truth." With this overdue excavation of the Bricca murders, I will jettison the unworkable and the implausible until we arrive at the probable truth.

For those of us who preserved this slaughtered family in our memory, it will never be too late to learn that truth. There looms one huge, lasting question? Who killed the Briccas?

A moment of silence please, for Gerald John Bricca, Linda Jayne Bulaw Bricca, and Deborah Ann Bricca, murdered 50 years ago tonight...

PRELUDE: A MEMORY OF THE FUTURE

Wednesday September 21st 1966

She is late, terrified and drunk.

At nearly 10:30 PM, Linda knows she's in trouble. Jerry's car sits in the driveway – she can't believe he's home early from that stag party. Why? He was with his boss, who always stays for last call. Linda had hoped to already be in bed asleep.

Now, on top of everything else that has transpired this week, she would have to face him.

Even in her bewildered, intoxicated state, Linda understands that something has to give. This thing is coming to an inescapable head. But she's three sheets to the wind, smelling of liquor, unable even to think clearly – why does it have to be tonight? And on the last day of summer?

Her mother keeps telling her to stick it out with Jerry. Yet tonight's events have made that impossible now.

As she lurches out of the car, her fear becomes palpable, like an icy hand clutching her heart. Whom could she confide in? And would they believe her?

Linda Bricca is certain of only one thing. Everything has changed.

But at least nobody died...

Thursday September 29th 1966

My mother says I'll have nightmares if I keep reading this stuff.

Lizzie Borden and Jack the Ripper. Agatha Christie and Alfred Hitchcock. True crime and fictional mysteries. I just can't get enough.

Yet I am a normal 7th grader. I love baseball and Batman. I grew taller this summer, and suddenly girls are fascinating. A new mystery to explore.

But things are crazy in this city right now. Not only is The Cincinnati Strangler on the prowl, but that nice family in Bridgetown just got murdered in their own home. It's like my nightly tales have jumped off the pages.

I lay my book aside and head downstairs. My mother, brother and sister are watching the evening news. My father has just headed out the back door to haul the garbage cans to the curb.

The TV blares that the city is on high alert and urges everyone to start locking their doors. I peer outside – it has gotten dark quickly. I can hear the rain hissing.

My father returns, and my mother calls out, "Don't forget to bring the cats inside." No reply.

As we turn back to the news, I hear that Jerry Bricca was killed shortly after taking out the garbage. In the rain! I call out, "Dad, are you okay?"

No answer. A harrowing chill crawls up my spine.

My father steps into the room. Only it's NOT him! There's a tall man dressed in black holding a long knife. Jack the Ripper! No, wait...It's the Bricca killer!

We all cower there, powerless to move. His evil, impassive face seems sculpted from granite. As his blade descends in a deadly arc, my screams are entombed. I'm frozen. Like in a dream.

Abruptly I am jolted awake by my mother's voice calling from the stairway. "You're going to be late for school."

I am soaked with sweat – and something any boy older than a toddler will never admit to...

Email: April 5th 2012

Dear Mr. Townsend:

When I was younger, across my room and above my bed was a portrait of a young girl. She was beautiful, and I would always ask my mom who it was. She would reply that it was Debbie, my guardian angel. I knew that she had died, but I never asked how and was never told.

About two years ago my grandmother told me of the murders. I was shocked... I never thought something like that could be lurking in our family history. But when I tried to question my mother or my grandmother, they would always turn me away.

I somehow feel the need to find out what could have happened and know more about my family. I hope you can and will help me...

Email: March 3rd, 2016

JT:

You are treading in some murky water with the Briccas. But do not fear where this mystery may lead. You are too bright for the darkness to take you...

The Epicenter... the back of the Bricca house (right) as seen from the Lawrence/Greencrest “catwalk.”

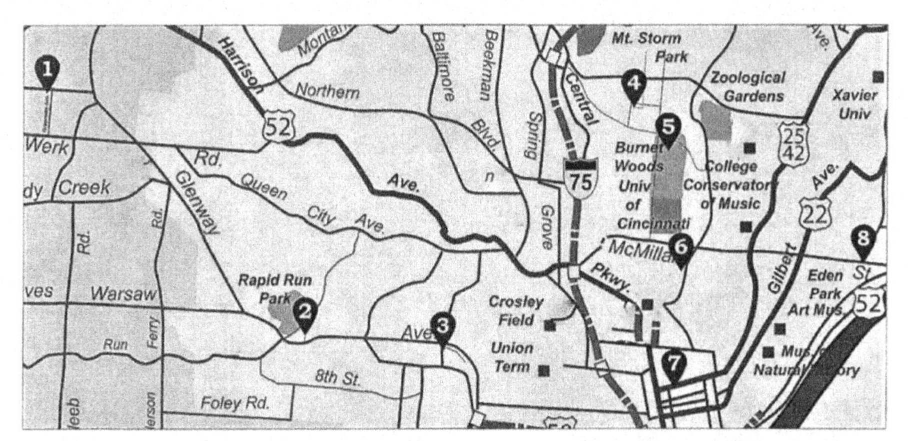

1. Bricca family murder scene
2. Lois Dant murder scene
3. Barbara Bowman murder scene
4. Alice Hochhausler murder scene
5. Jeannette Messer murder scene
6. Rose Winstel murder scene
7. Lulu Kerrick murder scene
8. Emogene Harrington murder scene & Krecco and Hinners assault scenes

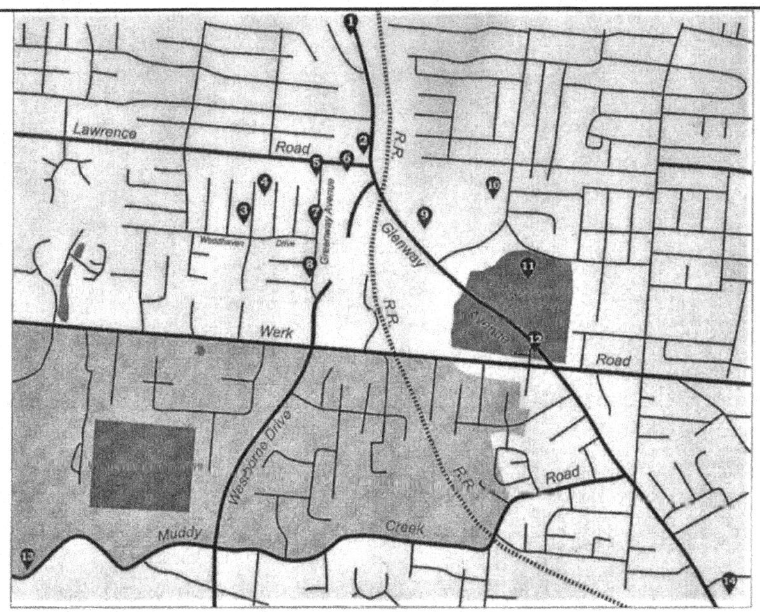

1. Larry Foppe's Hi Lo Deli
2. Lou's Greenacre Deli
3. Woodhaven Swim Club
4. Larry Foppe's House
5. Gerald Bricca House
6. Western Bowl
7. Linda Zeff's House
8. Hyacinth Mailbox
9. Glenway Animal Hospital
10. Jim Cannon's House
11. Western Hills Plaza
12. Werk Rd. Shell Station
13. Crescent Bow Archery Club
14. Stanley Keller's Clinic

Just something
to remember
Be good!
Lin

Linda Bricca pictured in early September 1966 (with her personal note on the back), just a few weeks before she was murdered.

CHAPTER ONE

SMALL TOWN CITY

"You're so earnest about morality that I hate to think how essentially immoral you must be underneath."
Sinclair Lewis, "Babbitt"

APRIL-JUNE 6TH 1966

Sunday, April 3rd

She sauntered through the concourse, a coquettish glide more coy than brazen, tossing her raven hair in a way that ignored and invited the eyes of men.

Under sleek green slacks the young woman's hips rocked, undulating deftly like a scale settling its balance. Her stride was carefree yet somehow aloof, as if she was hoarding her energy for more important motions.

She gazed up at the echoing rafters of the Cincinnati Gardens, housing the Shrine Circus on this weekend before Easter. Ah, the circus. A childhood haven for all her hopes and schemes. She smiled, remembering how she threatened to run away from home as a teenager just to feed the animals.

The young woman enjoyed visiting this place. From the distinctive athletic figures adorning the brick and limestone facing to the cavernous ten story high ceiling, the "Gardens" was the hub of Cincinnati entertainment. There were no interior columns to obstruct the view, and the venue known for perfect sightlines and hollow acoustics had witnessed a diverse history.

From orchestras to rodeos, musicals to roller derby, the "Gardens" booked them all, even hosting the Beatles and presidential candidate Richard Nixon. Professional wrestling was thriving there, with grapplers such as "The Sheik", "Gorgeous George", and "Dick the Bruiser" gracing the match day placards. The rest of the 1966 schedule included everything from ice follies to dirt track auto racing.

None of that mattered to her – except the circus.

The Shrine Circus would travel to over 120 cities in 1966. Over the years many stars appeared in the Shrine, including Clyde Beatty, the Flying Wallendas, and Emmett Kelly.

Yet now it looked like a shabby carnival.

As she meandered through the ugly, fluorescent suffused auditorium, the air was thick with the odor of rank hot dogs, stale popcorn, dead cigars, and sickly disinfectant. The circus men were no better than scruffy, itinerant carnival denizens – the women were hard-faced, wary and rasping.

Not the magical world she remembered. It was more like the distorted underbelly of a child's fantasy, harsh and cheerless.

She gravitated toward the animals, and the man picked up on her immediately. As this stunning brunette gazed up at his elephants, Marion Earl Grubbs inclined his head, watching her.

The 51-year-old trainer retained the rough, brooding exterior of a small time grifter who had exceeded his depth. His angled lips, long teeth and skewed nose aligned as mismatched parts. He looked like a desultory ranch hand, hard drinking and haphazard.

But Grubbs possessed a sixth sense about women, and something about the way this one's tan sweater adhered to the jut of her breasts forced a smile that declined to reach his narrow eyes.

She was speaking to him, her voice hushed and musical. "Are these your elephants?"

"Yes, Ma'am," he mumbled. "That big bull is Tusker."

"He's a male?" She was incredulous. "What happens if he goes into musth? His eyes wavered – she had stumped him. "You know, if he gets horny. He could do some damage".

"What's that word again?" he stammered, face reddening.

She fixed him in her gaze. "Do you need help taking care of them? I have experience."

"You do, now?" he drawled, regaining his composure.

She laughed, quick and light, but flattering. She knew the type – a guy who spoke in hot whispers about gaudy conquests that never happened. "I've worked with all kinds of animals." His eyes involuntarily raced up and down her body, and her blush was genuine yet friendly.

Grubbs took a shot. "My wife probably wouldn't like it."

The brunette smiled and flicked her eyes around the enclosure. "Is she here? I'd love to meet her."

"She's back home in Canton. We just had our first child in March." Grubbs grinned sheepishly. "Of course, she's a tad bit younger than this old dog."

If he expected flattery for his deprecation he was mistaken. She stepped forward, so that only a folding table was separating them, and her smile invited him into some unknown conspiracy. The animal trainer experienced the luminous intensity of her eyes, sapphire moons with mysteriously golden crevices in them.

Grubbs recalled something his mother had said about women like this. "She may be spoiled, but she was never spared."

"My name is Linda," she whispered. "Is there somewhere we can go and talk this over?"

Monday, April 4th

On the last morning of her life, 58-year-old Lois Dant was engaged in her normal Monday chore of doing the laundry, singing softly to herself as she waited for her husband to come home.

Spring had arrived, full of eternal hope and wrapped in the promise of wonder.

Lois had been married for 30 years to Frank Dant. The retired couple lived in a modest one bedroom flat on the first floor of 1210 Rutledge Avenue, part of a sprawling apartment complex in Cincinnati's Price Hill neighborhood. From her window Lois could see Glenway Avenue, a hectic artery coursing through the heart of the West Side. On this brisk, sunlit day, the Glenway corner was filled with bustling workers and inattentive neighbors.

Rutledge was a narrow street of multiple dwellings and duplexes, mostly inhabited by younger families where both husband and wife worked. Those likely to be observant were at their jobs, while older residents stayed inside on a day where the temperature would not reach 60.

The Dants were a devoutly religious couple who went to Mass together every day except Monday, when 66-year-old Frank would stay behind and supervise the counting of the Sunday collection. Monday morning was the only time of the week the Dants were ever apart, and Lois always used this brief interlude for the laundry.

Shortly after 10 AM she was hanging some stockings over the shower curtain rod when the phone rang. Lois was delighted to hear her Cousin Ruth's voice on the line. The two women settled in for a lengthy chat.

"Have you heard from Susan?" Ruth asked, knowing how proud Lois was of their only daughter, who lived in California.

"She is taking her final vows for the Sisterhood of Charity. Oh Ruth, did you ever imagine she would really become a nun?" Lois sounded both pleased and amazed.

"You and Frank raised her right." Ruth soothed. "She had the discipline to take this on. Is she coming back to visit afterwards?"

"Yes!" Lois exhaled. "Sometime in June. She hasn't been home in six years. Frank is thrilled beyond words." Lois paused. "I wonder what's keeping him at church."

As the two women chattered on, a stranger entered the building foyer and hovered near the Dant's door, marked with a gold numeral 1. An odd, musky odor began to pervade the hallway.

A moment later, Lois interrupted her cousin. "There's somebody at the front door."

"She put down the phone," her cousin would later say. "I could hear the voices, but couldn't distinguish any words."

Lois came back to the phone, clearly puzzled. "It was someone looking for the caretaker. They always mistake our apartment for his because we're the first door they come to."

They talked a few more minutes but were again interrupted. "There's the door again," Lois said. "Maybe he's back. I'll talk to you later."

Ruth hung up the phone. But her cousin would never call back.

Lois Dant walked the five short steps to the front door...

FRANK DANT WAS RUNNING late.

He had waited longer for the generous pre-Easter Sunday donation at St. William's Church to be counted. Usually home by ten on Mondays, it was 10:20 when Dant left the church and turned onto Glenway Avenue for the half mile ride home. He stopped to deposit the collection at a nearby bank on his way.

At 1210 Rutledge, two upstairs neighbors heard strange noises from the first floor. The morning stillness was punctured by a man's voice

Lois was on the phone with her cousin in her first floor apartment when the killer knocked on her door twice.

around 10:15, followed by a brief commotion. One witness said later that she heard "a startled cry or an excited yell. Then I heard a door slam. I looked down the stairs but saw nothing."

Another resident came part way down and listened. She was certain it was the Dant's door she heard. She told her husband after returning upstairs, but neither of them investigated further.

Around 10:30 Frank arrived home. He parked his car in the garage behind the building, and went to the laundry room where he expected to find his wife. Lois wasn't there, but their laundry was hanging on the lines. He climbed the rear stairway leading to the back door of his apartment, knocked several times and rang the doorbell. Getting no answer, he tried his key and was surprised to find the door bolted from the inside.

Concerned now, he hurried around to the front entrance, letting himself in with the key. Nothing could have prepared him for the horrific scene he encountered.

The ravaged body of his wife was splayed out on the living room floor. Her black polka dot house dress had been ripped down the front with such force the buttons popped. Her underwear was torn off, and she was posed with her legs spread-eagled. Wound tightly around her neck was one of her nylon stockings.

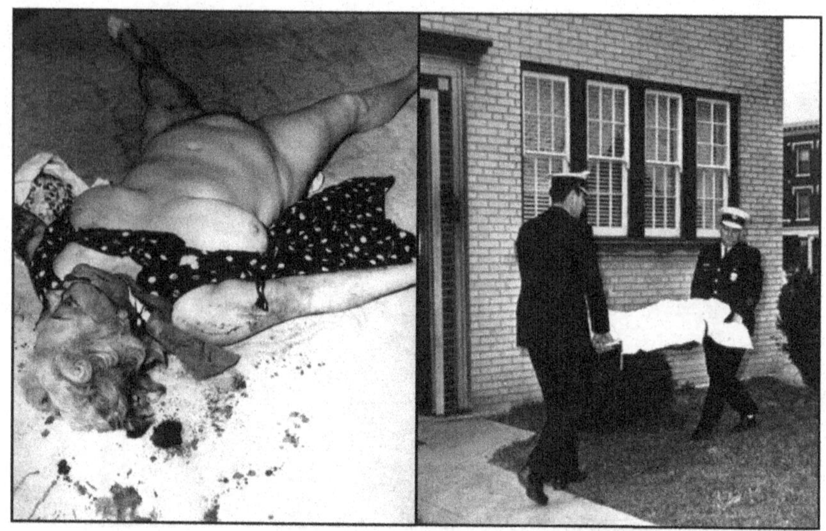

Lois Dant was murdered on Monday morning, during the only time of the week she was known to be home alone.

She had been struck a crushing blow to the left side of her face, which lay in a spreading pool of blood. An autopsy would reveal subdural hematoma and contusions of the brain. Cause of death was strangulation – she had been raped as she lay dying next to the sofa. There were signs of a struggle, and the killer inflicted several fierce blows to finally subdue her.

A tall, strong woman, Lois Dant had fought hard for her life...

Thursday, April 7th

Linda Bricca sat in the doctor's waiting room, leafing through an old copy of Look Magazine, her heart beating through her chest.

Coming from the West Side, the eight mile drive to Clifton had jangled her nerves. Rush hour traffic across the viaduct moved like a glacier and jay-walking students around the University of Cincinnati had delayed her arrival for the 4:00 PM appointment.

A few older women in the waiting room stole furtive glances at the attractive brunette, wondering why she was there. This young woman appeared slender and taut. She was lovely in an elusive, unsettled way, with spacious eyes that never stopped zooming.

Finally the nurse took Linda into an exam room. There was no small talk – a quick check showed her temperature and weight were normal, but her blood pressure was running amok.

When Dr. Mark Upson entered the room, he was briefly startled by the female sitting there. A smoothly handsome man nearing 50, Upson didn't see many patients who looked like her. It was four months since her last visit, and he had forgotten the effect she had on him. He shuffled her chart with a hint of nervousness.

"I've got the blood work." He kept his eyes at bay. "Your thyroid is low, and I'm going to prescribe Cytomel once a day. That should help alleviate that sluggish feeling you complained about.

"Wouldn't hypothyroidism contribute to my weight gain?"

Upson was impressed. He checked the chart. "We have you at 5 feet 5 inches tall and 128 lbs. The Tri-Presate I prescribed last time is keeping your weight under control. Are you still taking the Hydo-Diuril for fluid retention?"

Linda scowled. "Yes, but my legs still feel heavy and bloated. And that's not the worst of it. My heart is like a racehorse."

"Well, your blood pressure IS high." Upson stepped forward and took her pulse, silently counting while trying to ignore her wafting perfume. "Resting pulse 115...hmm." He abruptly dropped her wrist and moved away from her. "Do you have time to take a short test while you're here?"

A half hour later Upson came back in as Linda was buttoning her olive colored blouse. She turned, and again he was unsettled by the explicit, almost vulnerable way she regarded him.

"That EEG you just took shows a rapid heart rate that originates above the ventricles." He coughed, yet she remained silent. "My diagnosis is Paroxysmal Tachycardia."

Her eyes flashed. "My father-in-law is a doctor, and I understand Tachycardia. What is that other word?"

"Paroxysmal. It means from time to time, like episodes."

She summoned a smile for the first time. "So it's nothing to worry about?"

"The symptoms like you experienced today are sometimes alarming, but I would not consider it by itself to be hazardous."

"Why do I have it? I'm not even 24 yet." Now she inhaled, and he noticed her breasts were trembling.

"I'm not sure, Mrs. Bricca. It's a nervous condition, and can be aggravated by mental or physical stress." Dr. Upson removed his glasses. "Has there been anything bothering you lately?"

AT THAT VERY MOMENT across town, Jerry Bricca pulled into the parking lot of Dr. James DeFranco. The 28-year-old Monsanto engineer was in a hurry – his 4-year-old daughter was with him, and he was not happy.

Linda called around lunchtime to inform him she had an "emergency" appointment with Dr. Upson and he would have to take Debbie to her 4:30 appointment with Dr. DeFranco. Jerry was steamed – she had spent most of that week at the circus, and now she dropped this on him at the last minute. She knew he was swamped at work and was flying out tomorrow on business.

Sitting next to him, Debbie let out a thin cough. She had been having some sort of allergic reaction the last few weeks and her throat was bothering her.

"We're here, sweetheart. Are you doing okay?"

His daughter looked up at him with Linda's eyes, opened her mouth and pointed. "It hurts there. You said I could have ice cream after we saw the man."

Jerry marveled at her poise and maturity. *Barely out of nursery school and she's talking like a 4th grader.* And just like her mother, she never forgets any promise he makes.

"Then we'll have it!" he said in a magical voice. He got out of the car, came around and scooped her up in his arms. "What flavor?" She just stared at him, as if he didn't know it was chocolate. Just like Linda.

Jerry had first taken her to DeFranco in late March, after Linda and Debbie returned from Florida. He thought she may have picked up a bug down there, yet her sore throat was lingering. Now Jerry wondered if she was allergic to their rabbits – Debbie had been outside playing with them now that spring was here.

DeFranco took one look at Jerry and scolded him. "You looked wiped out. Should I check YOU over?

Jerry flashed a weak grin. "We've got a new water line installation at the plant. I worked all through last night and today."

The doctor gave an appreciative whistle and started checking the child. Debbie's throat was inflamed, but it was no better, no worse than last time. Definitely not a virus – there were signs of an allergy. The child's eyes were rheumy, with a thin discharge.

Still looking at Debbie, DeFranco said "Just how many animals do you have in that menagerie on Greenway?" He smiled, and glanced back at the father when no answer came.

Jerry Bricca was still sitting up – fast asleep.

Friday, April 8th

Lt. Colonel Jacob W. Schott was tall and iron jawed handsome, with a flair for keeping his good side to the camera. If central casting needed a Gary Cooper type to play the top cop, Jake Schott would have garnered the lead.

He was a straight shooter, his speech peppered with outdated slang and brittle humor. Schott had a habit of squinting his left eye when something didn't add up. His men joked privately that he was always looking down the barrel of a gun.

When Cincinnati Police Chief Stanley Schrotel named his 50-year-old lieutenant the Crime Bureau Commander in early March, he picked the rising star of the division. With Schrotel hinting about early retirement, Jake Schott could become chief this year.

But even an experienced officer like Schott couldn't fathom how the tribulations of 1966 would play out.

Lois Dant had been found raped and strangled in Price Hill on Monday, and his detectives were not getting any traction. While his statements to the press were optimistic, privately he was whistling in the dark.

Schott knew good police work rarely solved this kind of crime. Their typical homicide was the "smoking gun" variety, the killer known to the victim and often captured at the scene. Their primary job was to collect evidence to build a case rather than solve one. When the killer was a stranger to the victim, the chances of an arrest were remote.

This morning Schott was huddled with Safety Director Henry Sandman, a veteran homicide cop and Schrotel's former right hand man. The other Dant investigators had filed out after the briefing, leaving them to ponder the Rutledge Avenue murder.

"It all comes down to the cousin," Sandman was saying. "If she's right about the timing, it means the killer knocked on Dant's door twice." He shook his head. "Can you believe it was the only time of the week when the husband was known to be gone?"

Schott exhaled the dregs of his cigar. "So he asks for the caretaker the first time, and suggests her husband show him the way. When he finds out she's alone, he comes back and does her."

Sandman flipped through the cousin's interview. "Yet she was adamant Dant expressed no concern or fear about this man. Too bad she didn't give her a description." He gazed at Schott, the unspoken question hanging between them.

"You think she would have told her cousin if it was a black man?"

Sandman nodded. "This is the West Side. A Negro wandering around those apartments on a Monday morning would be cause for alarm. But the murder itself – we've seen this before."

"So Dant is connected with Walnut Hills?" Jake Schott couldn't ignore the obvious. The press was already speculating about a maniac on the loose...

THE TERROR HAD BEGUN on October 12th 1965.

Elizabeth Kreco, a 65-year-old widow, was leaving the Verona Apartments in Walnut Hills to meet her daughter for lunch. A short, slightly built black man wearing dark clothing and sunglasses approached her in the courtyard. He quietly explained that he was reporting for work and looking for the caretaker.

It was a sun drenched day under a cobalt blue sky. Any momentary fear Liz may have felt quickly vanished. Glancing at her watch, she offered to show him the janitor's basement quarters.

Once down there he quickly looped a cord around her neck, dragged her into a small bathroom and slammed her head into the wall. As he threw her onto the dingy floor, the intruder tightened the cord and choked her until she passed out.

As Elizabeth Kreco lay unconscious, the man raped her, rifled her purse of $13, and fled into the bright and bustling October afternoon, leaving her for dead.

She was found an hour later dazed but alive, with the ligature still hanging from her neck. It was a Venetian blind cord double knotted at both ends, a hint of premeditation that the attacker had planned to murder her.

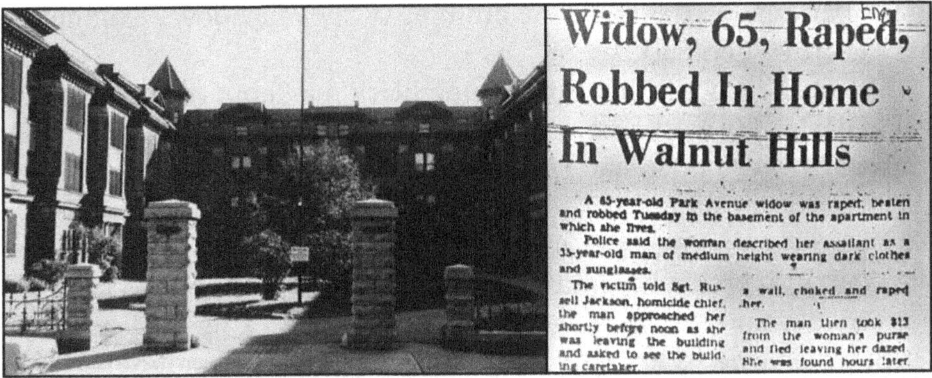

Widow, 65, Raped, Robbed In Home In Walnut Hills

A 65-year-old Park Avenue widow was raped, beaten and robbed Tuesday in the basement of the apartment in which she lives.

Police said the woman described her assailant as a 35-year-old man of medium height wearing dark clothes and sunglasses.

The victim told Sgt. Russell Jackson, homicide chief, the man approached her shortly before noon as she was leaving the building and asked to see the building caretaker.

a wall, choked and raped her.

The man then took $13 from the woman's purse and fled leaving her dazed. She was found hours later.

Elizabeth Kreco was attacked while showing a man where the caretaker's office was in the basement of her building.

At General Hospital in serious condition, Kreco described her assailant as a male Negro, between 35 and 40, 5 feet 5 inches tall and about 150-160 lbs. There was a suggestion of a mustache, but his sunglasses had rendered his face anonymous.

Elizabeth Kreco never recovered from her injuries. She would die a year later.

On October 21st, two more women were attacked in Walnut Hills. Just after 11 AM, a 32-year-old housewife was confronted in her basement by a black man in his early 30's, about 5-10 and 155 pounds. He tried to throttle her, but fled when she screamed.

Around 8 PM, a 16-year-old high school girl was accosted on Windsor Avenue, two blocks from where Kreco was nearly murdered nine days earlier. A stocky black man sauntered over and asked directions before grabbing her and clamping his hand over her mouth. He whispered, "I'll kill you if you scream, " and then struck her flush in the face with what felt like the butt of a gun.

The teenager lay motionless on the sidewalk, face throbbing while she feigned unconsciousness. When the attacker touched her blouse she shrieked "Help!" He grabbed her purse and took off down the street. She later described him as 40 years old, around 5-7 and muscular, with a thick mustache. An all-night hard target search of the area failed to flush him out.

Four days later Walnut Hills was again the scene of a hit-and-run assault. On October 25th around 7 PM, 39-year-old Margie Helton left her job at the Baldwin Piano Company on Gilbert Avenue. As she walked to the parking lot, daylight was draining away as shadows lengthened over nearby Eden Park.

When she reached her car a young black man appeared and joined her in the lot. He was short and thin, around 20, with a goatee and wearing a narrow brimmed hat. He politely asked for directions to Dorchester Street.

But as she opened her car door he moved in, slamming her against the door and forcing her into the front seat. "This is a robbery. Give me your money and you won't get hurt," he hissed, reeking of alcohol.

She managed to hand over ten dollars. The man then hopped into the back seat and put a rope around her neck. She screamed several times, her flailing hand hitting the car horn. He cursed, and she felt the cord slacken. As he scrambled out she leaned on the horn, the blare resounding through the darkening lot as the sound of his running footsteps faded.

Using a cord as the weapon convinced some detectives that Helton's assailant was the same man who raped Mrs. Kreco.

There had been four serious attacks on women in Walnut Hills in just 13 days. The victims were brought in to scrutinize mug shots of known sexual offenders, but none of them were recognized.

Cincinnati police were non-committal about any common thread in this October onslaught. There was some concern, yet they believed the incidents were random and unrelated. The varying descriptions suggested several black strong arm robbers preying on defenseless white victims.

November passed with no new attacks. But in early December an ill wind would churn through the Queen City...

December 2nd, 1965 – April 7th, 1966

Just after 1 PM December 2nd, Emogene Harrington eased her station wagon along the curb in front of the Clermont Apartments at 1404 East McMillan Street. Mrs. Harrington, age 56, had just returned home from the Hyde Park Kroger store, where she always shopped every Thursday at noon.

The wife of Dr. Paul Harrington, an internationally known University of Cincinnati aerospace scientist, Emogene was herself an educated

Emogene Harrington parked her station wagon (right) at the curb and went looking for the janitor to help with the groceries.

woman, small and friendly with dark hair. Their three married daughters all lived out of town.

Mrs. Harrington was in the habit of asking the janitor to help carry in her groceries. It's not known whether she returned to her apartment before trying to locate him. What is certain is that she ventured into the gloomy basement of the Clermont to look for him.

Around 1:20 PM, janitor Eugene Waugh was in the basement when he saw a pair of legs sticking out the restroom door. Stepping inside, he discovered the body of a woman lying on her back. The lighting was so dim and her features so contorted that Waugh failed to recognize her.

When police arrived, the distraught janitor learned the dead woman was his favorite tenant Emogene Harrington, lying face up on the floor of the dank toilet room with her legs spread wide apart. A length of yellow clothes line knotted at both ends was looped around her neck. Her clothing was in disarray; her dress was pulled up and her underwear discarded nearby. Strewn around the body were her hat, car keys and one shoe.

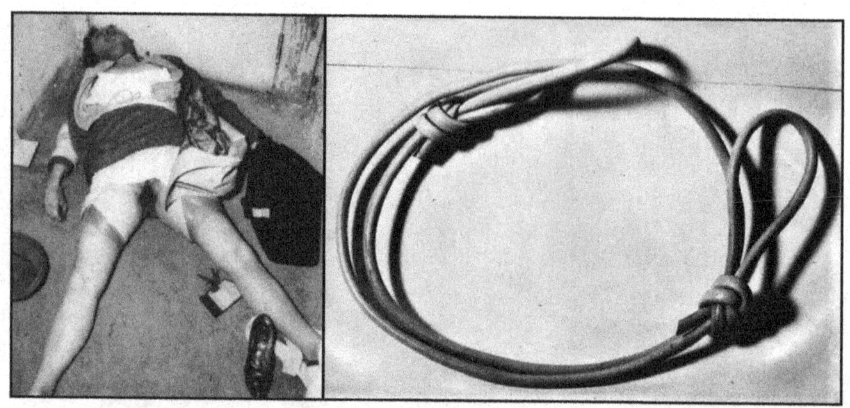

Somewhere in the dark basement of the Clermont Apartments, Emogene Harrington met her killer.

She had been struck in the face, raped, robbed and strangled. Propped against the wall was her purse with a broken strap and contents scattered nearby. Her billfold was missing – it was later determined she'd received $21 in change from her shopping trip.

Coroner Frank Cleveland attributed her death to strangulation, time of death shortly before the janitor found her at 1:20 PM. A check of residents confirmed no one had seen or heard Mrs. Harrington or anyone else enter the building during the last hour.

It was the 5th attack on a Walnut Hills woman in the past two months. This time detectives had a murder scene to process. When then detective Henry Sandman arrived on the scene, he theorized that the killer was the same man who battered and violated Elizabeth Kreco in October. The double knotted cords were almost identical, the buildings only four blocks apart, and their basements a similar maze of dark and twisting corridors.

Sandman admitted it was conjecture, but the press latched on to the idea that there might be a strangler at large in Cincinnati. Meanwhile, the homicide squad canvassed the neighborhood, rounded up known sexual predators, and sent boxes of evidence to the FBI.

They found a resident in a neighboring building who saw a suspicious black man in their basement about 20 minutes before the murder. A passing truck driver had seen a similar man outside the Clermont just after 1 PM. But these leads had wilted by nightfall.

One week after the crime, the Cincinnati Reds traded All-Star slugger Frank Robinson to the Baltimore Orioles, pushing the unsolved killing of Emogene Harrington off the front page.

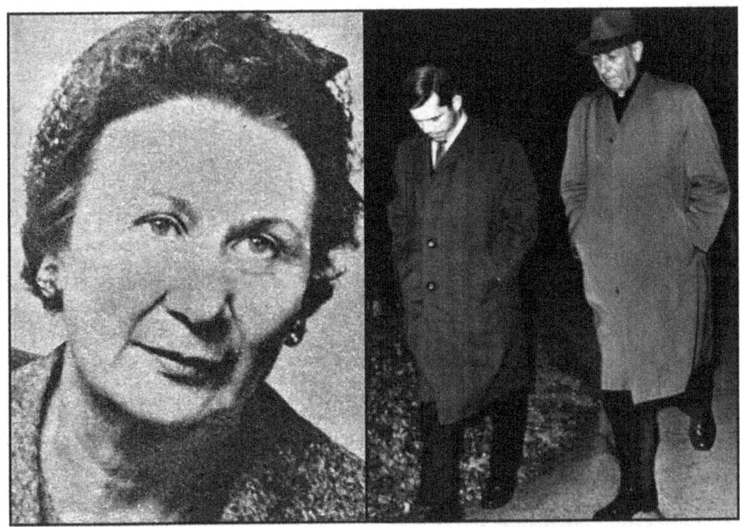

Emogene was the wife of a UC aerospace scientist (2nd picture on left) and the mother of three grown daughters.

On December 17th, a 20-year-old secretary was ambushed on her way to work and forced at knifepoint to climb the stone stairway connecting Elsinore Place with Mt. Adams. The young black man pulled her up the narrow, steep staircase, a crumbling wino haven littered with bottles and stinking of urine, and then raped her in a wooded area off Ida Street.

On January 16th, a doctor's wife said an intruder attempted to choke her with a cord in the basement of her North Avondale home. This was the third attack in the Avondale/Walnut Hills area in the last three months by an intruder using a cord – the other two had resulted in a near fatal rape and a murder. This time the victim was unhurt except for welts on her neck from the ligature, a frayed black shoestring that was recovered at the scene.

Two days later 46-year-old Helen Smith was cleaning a vacant apartment in Walnut Hills when a black man wearing a trench coat suddenly lunged up the basement steps toward her. She scurried from the building and yelled to a neighbor, who called police. Within minutes 20 carloads of cops were dispatched to the area.

The coverage of Helen Smith's scary encounter was aggressive, a large headline in the *Enquirer* blaring **New Fears Raised By 'Phantom'**. The press had granted the first nickname to the shadowy figure stalking

Walnut Hills, and detectives felt "phantom" was no misnomer – their quarry seemed to vanish after each attack.

On Monday the 24th, Mrs. Bonnie Catoe, age 37, told police she saw a black man wearing a ski mask enter her building on Park Avenue in Walnut Hills. Her shouts frightened him off. Police noted the proximity of this incident to the Verona Apartments, scene of the Kreco assault three months earlier.

Irene Peck was attacked on March 1st around 11 PM as she returned from a Walnut Hills store. A young black man jumped from behind a car on Kemper Lane and knocked the 77-year-old woman to the sidewalk. He began to choke her while dragging her into a nearby lot, but she was able to scream and attract a pedestrian, causing the attacker to bolt. Mrs. Peck was treated and released, but could not embellish her meager description of the "black youth".

Detectives were reluctant to link this one with the earlier Walnut Hills incidents. In truth, they were reluctant to commit to any theory about the recent crime wave. As the cold, frustrating winter dissolved into a windy Cincinnati spring, the Emogene Harrington case jacket was filed under Unknown Killer...

So here they sat on April 8th, Jake Schott and Henry Sandman, two weary lawmen who could not dismiss their gut feelings.

Similarities to the Walnut Hills cases were there – mostly daylight attacks on elderly women in the basements of old apartment buildings. Lois Dant had been doing laundry in her basement shortly before being murdered. The crippling blow to the head and the ensuing rape all fit the pattern.

Yet Lois Dant's killer did not bring his own ligature, and the timing suggested prior knowledge of her husband being gone. She hadn't been robbed, but it was possible Frank Dant's arrival prevented that. Rather than a blitz style attack, this murder revealed a blend of planning and audacity not seen previously.

Hidden beneath all the interviews was a sketchy description of a black man seen leaving the area via a taxi cab parked in the convenience store lot across the street from the Dant apartment.

The common denominator was a black assailant. Yet the age ranged from early 20's to mid-40's, the height estimated as between 5 foot 4 to

6 feet, the build described from thin to heavy, the moustache sometimes there, sometimes not. Despite these discrepancies, Homicide Sergeant Russ Jackson reminded the press that this might be expected from a traumatized victim or a confused eyewitness.

The tighter timeline made Schott and Sandman reluctant to link this West Side murder to the earlier crimes in Walnut Hills. When asked about the connection, Jake Schott told the press that "the difference is not great enough to eliminate the possibility that the same man was responsible" for the murders of Harrington, Dant, and the attempt on Elizabeth Kreco.

Residents of Price Hill were drawing their own conclusions. Huddled behind her locked door, one woman told a reporter she was aware of the Walnut Hills crimes. "But who would think this kind of thing would happen in Price Hill?" she moaned. "They're always downtown or over on the other side of town."

Indeed, the brutal rape-strangulation of Lois Dant had staggered the West Side, as if some dark specter from the East Side had leached over the viaducts and into their little slice of heaven.

Like any community dealing with a horrendous crime, they were praying for protection and hoping for a clear motive. Yet this killer's arbitrary selection defied their rational perspective – the one insisting that decent, law abiding people can control their own fate.

Still, even random evil must be perfect. Or depend on the imperfections of others...

Saturday, April 9th

Susan Keller was becoming anxious.

It was past 10:00 PM on Easter Eve, and Linda Bricca was not home yet. The 18-year-old babysitter assumed she would be back by nine in time to put Debbie to bed.

Susan had been babysitting for the family at 3381 Greenway Avenue for over two years, mostly at the behest of her good friend Linda Zeff, a Bricca neighbor who was their primary sitter.

Her friend warned her that Linda Bricca was always running late and could be a bit "fickle" when it came to her child. Still, Susan liked the attractive housewife, so much younger than other mothers in the Bridgetown neighborhood. Mrs. Bricca was only five years older than her and Linda Zeff – she was like a big sister, a confidante on boys and other charms of girlish angst.

But the faint spring sun had long since dipped from sight along Greenway, and a trace of moonlight suffused the blackness of the sky. Susan looked out the dining room window, where another brick split level house sat twenty feet away. Beyond that another. Beyond that rows of them, snaking out along the dense, commonplace streets of Cincinnati's West Side.

Susan had been alternating with Linda Zeff the last few days so Mrs. Bricca could attend the Shrine Circus. Apparently she'd met someone in one of the animal acts – she told Susan she was helping take care of a baby elephant and two young monkeys.

Susan put Debbie to bed around 9:30 PM and then called Linda Zeff, who was out. She called her boyfriend Mike, cancelling their date to meet at McDonalds. Now she waited, feeling that classic babysitter conundrum – boredom that nothing ever happens yet fearful that something will.

Just after 11 PM the ringing phone sliced through her uneasy reverie. Susan answered with a breathless "Hello?"

"Susan, its Linda Bricca. Has my husband called?"

The babysitter could barely hear her through the mingling of clamorous voices and background din. "No, he hasn't," she replied.

"He's coming in on a plane from Chicago. When he calls, tell him to take a cab home from the airport. We just now finished taking down the tents but I'm having car trouble and I can't pick him up." There was a pause as Linda spoke to someone else. "Susan, can you stay a little longer?"

"Sure Mrs. Bricca, uh, I mean Linda." She giggled and listened for a response, but the woman was already gone.

Jerry Bricca never did call, arriving home by cab just before midnight. The young husband was robust and muscular, with close-cut brown hair. Susan thought he was handsome, in a blunt, dangerous way. She couldn't read him like she could Linda.

"Your wife called. She was having car trouble at the circus."

Jerry regarded her with more resignation than surprise. She watched him descend to the lower level, and heard the dogs yapping as he brought them in from the back yard. A few minutes later he came back up, looking absolutely wasted. As Saturday night became Easter Sunday, he sat down in his tasteful living room to scan a stack of newspapers. "How much do I owe you?"

Why hadn't he used the word we? "Oh, your wife already paid me, sir. But I did stay three hours over."

He fished in his pants and came up with four singles. "Thank you, Susan." His eyes were sunken, face taut and tedious. "She said car trouble?"

"Yes. And that she was helping take down the tents."

His lips twitched as if to speak, but thought better of it and gave her a ragged smile. Then Jerry Bricca turned back to his paper.

Susan said goodnight and walked out the front door at 12:05 AM, her vision suddenly hazy from the bracing night air. The wind had picked up. As she neared her car she saw them.

Linda Bricca's blue station wagon was parked behind her car, but she was leaning on the passenger side of another auto idling between her car and the corner, talking to the driver. Susan heard her distinctive peal of laughter, and she saw a masculine silhouette behind the wheel of a red car, maybe a Chevy convertible.

Linda saw her and waved, then said something to the driver, who pulled away from the curb as Linda started toward her. She caught a glimpse of his bony, angular face, but that was all.

"Susan, I'm sorry for being..." was all Linda managed before stopping short, her eyes moving beyond the teenager.

Jerry had come out the front door and was standing on his front walk. As Linda walked up to him, Susan heard him indignantly exclaim, "Who was that?"

Linda moved toward him on the darkened walkway, speaking in the same soothing voice Susan heard her use with Debbie. "That was the man who started my car. He followed me to make sure I got home all right."

As Susan opened her car door, she heard Jerry curse. She watched Linda walk past him and towards the house. As she drove away, she remembered scenes like this between her and Mike. Badgering each other, making furtive promises, weepy scenes of reproach and forgiveness.

In the first hour of Easter, good Catholic girl Susan Keller found herself wondering if Linda Bricca would find absolution and redemption before dawn...

Monday, April 11th

One week after the Lois Dant was murdered, an *Enquirer* article heightened the growing fear among its readers. Easter weekend saw three home invasions in three different neighborhoods with one common thread – black intruders menacing white women.

In the Hyde Park neighborhood on Saturday afternoon, 14-year-old Carolyn Richter was home alone when she saw a man standing at the foot of the basement stairs, a light skinned black man wearing a leather coat and a green baseball cap. She quickly locked the door – he banged on it and tried to force it open. When police arrived they found a basement window wide open.

Around 1 AM Sunday morning, Reva Watson of Northside was asleep on her living room couch when a prowler entered her apartment through an unlocked kitchen window. The 31-year-old secretary awoke to his footsteps moving toward her, but feigned sleep as a young black man rifled her purse, pocketed her $26 in cash, and left through the same window.

Finally, Virginia Blaurock, age 43, was sleeping in her Westwood bedroom about 3 AM Sunday when she was violently awakened by a man trying to pull her out of bed. Her husband, sleeping in an adjoining room, responded to her screams and chased the intruder out the open front door. In the darkened house neither could be certain, but they thought the trespasser was a black man.

Sgt. Russell Jackson personally investigated all three reports and downplayed any link to the Dant slaying. This was the normal volume of intruder reports on any given weekend, so there was no cause for alarm.

But his tepid promises couldn't quell the anxiety and suspicion gushing over the Queen City. Especially in Price Hill, a neighborhood perched sharply on one of the city's seven hills and connected to downtown by a chain of ancient viaducts stretching across the Mill Creek industrial valley. Price Hill is the epicenter of the "West Side", the corner of the Midwestern Bible and Rust Belts, a bastion of staunch German Catholic Republican conservatism that is the marrow of Cincinnati's backbone.

Interstate 75 is the line of demarcation between the city's west and east sides, and never the twain shall meet. The west side is blue collar; the east side is executive. The west is Hudepohl beer and chili; the east

Strangulation Shocks Victim's Neighborhood

Quiet Rutledge Avenue was in a state of shock Monday as news of the murder of Mrs. Lois Dant spread down the street from Glenway Avenue to Rapid Run Park.

"Sure, you hear about these things happening," said a woman huddled be-

Rutledge Avenue, with a few [illegible] of multiple, dwellings—apartment buildings and duplexes. Most of the neighborhood people are either retired or both husband and wife work and live in efficiency apartments.

from Versailles, Ind., and we've been the best of friends since I moved in.

"Their lovely daughter, Sue Ann, is supposed to take her final vows next year and she was allowed to come home for three days this summer.

"Lois was very excited about it. It would have

said Mrs. Robert Wolfert, also of 1219 Rutledge.

"I felt like the [illegible] was going to collapse under me. I didn't know the lady but there are a lot of us on this street who don't know each other. Many of us work and you don't really get to know your neighbors when

The murder of Lois Dant occurred in the predominantly white West Side neighborhood of Price Hill.

is white zinfandel and lobster. The west is bowling and bingo; the east is golf and garden parties.

West-Siders spare no expense on sunglasses because downtown workers are driving into the sun on their commute to and from the job. They also brag about the fresh air that wafts in from Indiana, pristine until it travels through the factory smoke and manufacturing waste sitting below them.

People who live on the West Side rarely think of moving someplace else. It's not unusual for several generations of a family to live on the same block, families that traditionally support local merchants by keeping their money on the hill. As a largely Catholic district, churches play an integral role in their lives, from first communion wafers to quaffing beer at a festival. Residents are more likely to identify their neighborhood as a parish than by the street they live on.

In 1966, the only thing missing from Price Hill was black people. This was a white's only enclave, far removed from the terrible crime spree in racially mixed Walnut Hills. A black man wandering through Price Hill couldn't do so with impunity. His very presence would elicit cold stares, rude questions, and nasty harassment.

When some blacks moved into Lower Price Hill, a depressed area at the bottom of Eighth and State streets, white residents on The Hill revoked the area from Price Hill despite the boundary lines. For them it became part of the West End, an impoverished black section wind burned by rapid white flight.

Race was on the minds of Schott and Sandman after their Monday morning briefing on the Dant case. In addition to the three weekend reports of black prowlers, they were checking out a report of a woman threatened in Price Hill that morning. Mrs. Katherine Loth had surprised a black man skulking around her basement around 9 AM. The intruder ran off when she yelled at him – her husband rushed to the basement but saw no one.

Sandman had just received lab results on hairs found in Lois Dant's hand and pubic hair from the rape – preliminary indications suggested both samples were from a white man. Semen from the rape was found to be blood type "O", but no racial determination could be made. They had already questioned six known white sex offenders from the Price Hill area with no luck.

A week later their investigation had slowed down to the walking pace of a beat cop knocking on doors. The word "standstill" was not being used, but Schott had earlier responded to media questions with a glum reply: "Nothing New."

Questions thrived. Why would a cautious woman with three locks and a peephole open her door to a stranger? What had the assailant hit her with to cause such severe facial fractures? Did Frank Dant arrive while the attacker was still in the apartment?

And how had the killer targeted Lois Dant during the only time of the week she was known to be alone...

Friday, April 15th

Jerry Bricca was with his friend Dan at Lil's Cottage Grill in Addyston, just up the road from the sprawling Monsanto complex. After a particularly rough morning at work, they were taking their time over lunch and Dan was nursing a beer. He had something to tell Jerry but was in no hurry. As his friend chattered on about work problems, Dan wondered how he could get the words out.

At 38 Dan was ten years older, yet was Jerry's closest friend at the plant. He and his wife often socialized with the Briccas, including a bridge party Linda had hosted the week before Easter.

That party was the turning point for his wife. Linda had pestered her about seeing their sick bird, but Pat demurred, saying "I don't like sick animals." Dan humored their hostess and went upstairs to see the ailing parakeet while Pat remained with Jerry, who rolled his eyes over his wife's devotion to their pets. "Linda would keep an entire zoo here if I would let her," Jerry had said.

Later Debbie came down and kissed the guests goodnight. Pat couldn't believe how casual Linda was with her child, letting Jerry put her to bed rather than tucking in her beautiful 4-year-old. And Linda confided to Pat between bridge hands that having a young child was preventing her from doing the things she was "passionate" about, like "working with baby animals at the circus."

Pat also told Dan about Linda's behavior at the Monsanto Wives Club. Linda went to the meetings for the last year and a half, but being younger than the other wives she didn't seem to fit in. The fact that she was prettier and thinner than the others had provoked gossip among the more traditional women.

Linda would sometimes tell off color jokes, usually about married couple's sex lives, always greeted with nervous titters. And she was blunt, having told several wives that she didn't like them.

Just this past Monday Linda had called the entire club out. Frustrated with the planning for a party at Western Bowl, she sat there quietly fuming. Pat knew she wasn't a bowler, but didn't expect what came next.

"Why doesn't this club try to do something useful?" Linda huffed as Pat winced. "We should be working to help homeless or abused animals". In the stony silence that followed, Linda grabbed her coat and walked out, saying she "didn't like being out at night."

When she left the wives took potshots at the "stuck up former airline stewardess." Pat said nothing, having heard most of it before in private conversation. Now here were 25 women venting about their Monsanto black sheep housewife.

Then one of them spilled something that startled Pat. "I'm pretty sure I saw Linda in the Walgreens getting some sleeping pills," the woman had said. "And the guy with her certainly wasn't Jerry."

Dan looked across at his friend, who had stopped talking when he realized Dan was lost in thought. They were in a high backed booth in the corner, removed from the other Monsanto workers, some of them already celebrating the end of the work week. Jerry leaned forward and shot Dan an inquisitive look.

Linda Bulaw and Jerry Bricca in high school.

"Hey, Jerry, you mentioned the four of us going out tomorrow?" Dan cleared his throat. "Well here's the thing. Pat thinks we need to back off on this foursome. You know, not get together as often."

The young engineer nodded – he seemed to be expecting this. "Well, Linda and Pat do have completely different interests." He lowered his eyes and picked at the remains of his lunch.

"Jerry, please understand. Pat likes Linda. But it's not just the age difference. Pat and the other women in the wives' club like bowling, playing cards and bake sales at the school. With Linda, all she seems to talk about is animals. And that's OK." Dan chuckled to break the tension. "Pat says she's never met anyone who that loved animals as much as her."

Jerry glowered in exasperation, a look Dan had seen before when a job at the plant wasn't going right. "Dan, you don't know the half of it. She brought home some bear trainer for supper once. Some seedy guy with an animal act at the Western Hills Shopping Center, sitting at our dinner table with Debbie. Can you imagine it? And Dan, this fellow made our friend Jim Cannon look like a prince."

Dan laughed – Jim Cannon was Jerry's nemesis at work. Jerry had that Stanford image, while Cannon was strictly community college. "Maybe you should have Cannon over for dinner?"

Jerry didn't share in the joviality. "She was at the Shrine Circus all last week, taking care of a baby elephant and some monkeys. She strikes up a conversation with a perfect stranger, talking to these carny people about their animals. Pretty soon she's working for free while Debbie spends all day with a babysitter! She even put Debbie in that nursery school last year to try for a job at the zoo."

"Is there something else going on?" Dan hesitated. "I mean between you two? In the bedroom?" His inflection suggested that any man to man sexual confidence would be kept. Jerry's change in coloration gave Dan the answer he'd already guessed. His eyes were haggard yet spellbound. Underneath his petulance, his friend was holding back a wave of frustration and anger.

"That's just it Dan." Jerry Bricca seemed embarrassed, but then spiked him with a baleful stare. "There is NOTHING going on between us..."

April-May

As April coasted toward May, the virgin splendor of spring was undeniable. The sullen, soggy early April air was now pungent with a rhapsody of flavors and colors.

But there was something else in mid-flight. The early 1960's glacial pace of socio-cultural change was picking up steam by the second quarter of 1966. A conflux of racial problems, Vietnam War protests, the youth culture, and sexual freedom sustained a turbulent national backdrop to the drama playing out in the Queen City.

While the country bickered over political issues like civil rights and an unpopular war, a 50-year-old gynecologist and his female research associate completed an unprecedented scientific study for their highly anticipated book. William Masters and Virginia Johnson had been observing married couples having sex in their St. Louis laboratory for over a decade, charting respiration, measuring heart rates, and recording reactions to stress and stimulation.

On April 18th their landmark book *Human Sexual Response* hit the bookstores. Calling marital sex problems "the most important cause of divorce," their advice coincided with the rise of formerly taboo sexual behaviors like oral sex, infidelity, and "swinging."

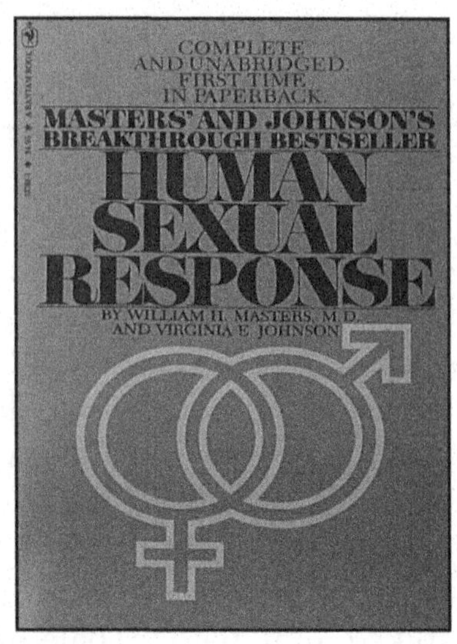

The marriage of sexuality with pornography had roiled the psyche of staid Cincinnati since the 1950s. This flood of sexual indulgence ricocheted in an *Enquirer* editorial – **Women's Defense Against Rapists** fueled the mounting fears of the weaker sex.

It reminded women that their best defensive weapon was to "scream at the top of her lungs and keep on screaming." This PSA ended with an empowering promise: "Any woman can be a formidable adversary for a rapist if she reacts properly."

The numbers showed an upward spiral in all sexual offenses, including molestation, indecent exposure, and "licentious liberties." Rapes had doubled from the previous year. Meanwhile, treatment and therapy for sexual offenders judged to be criminally insane remained a "highly controversial" subject in Cincinnati.

President Johnson declared that the passage of the two momentous Civil Rights Acts now marked the end of the "Negro quest for liberty and equality, and the beginning of the search for true brotherhood with the white majority." The president summed up the challenges facing Americans when he said: "A nation that aspires to greatness cannot be a divided nation with whites and Negroes entrenched behind barriers of mutual suspicion and fear."

That same week the Supreme Court cleared the way for the Federal government to try those believed responsible for the murder of three civil rights workers in 1964. The "Mississippi Burning" case decision, involving the deaths of "freedom riders" Andrew Goodman, Michael Schwerner and James Chaney, became the first step toward reforming "southern justice."

The most explosive issue in race relations was on a collision course with the Supreme Court in the aptly named "Loving vs. Virginia" case. In 1965, a Virginia court upheld a state law forbidding interracial marriages. The case was being appealed by Mildred Loving, a black woman, and Richard Loving, a white man, who'd been sentenced to a year in prison for marrying each other.

The irony was tragic – interracial couples could not marry in certain states, while white supremacists had a license to kill blacks in the Deep South.

Unrest over Civil Rights and the Vietnam War was threatening to turn the summer of 1966 into a season of violent resistance.

During the first week of May, the government announced that the total number of American combat deaths in Vietnam had exceeded 3,000. Escalation was written all over the grim statistics – 100 soldiers killed every week, more killed in the first four months of 1966 than the total for all of 1965, and a projected year end casualty figure of 6,000 killed in action.

In Cincinnati, the month of May was thankfully quiet, with no new attacks on either side of the city. But racial fires were flaring.

Leonard Ball, Chairman of the Cincinnati Congress on Racial Equality (CORE), promised more local protests while pleading for restraint: "As long as you have a system that refuses to acknowledge the wrongs that are daily inflicted on minorities, then you are going to have unrest and discontent. But we must continue to have non-violent demonstrations."

The Queen City had yet to see any racial violence, perhaps because of what Mark Twain once said: "When the end of the world comes, I want to be in Cincinnati because it's always 20 years behind the times." The city often seemed out of step – was this time warp the sign of deeper problems?

Author Sinclair Lewis had used Cincinnati as the model for his 1922 novel *Babbitt*, and the city proudly wore the badge of social conservatism ever since. Cultural values were sacrificed for business success and that tenacious sense of decorum. Boasting was impolite, sexuality was quashed, and public exhibition had better be restrained.

There has always been a persistent civility in Cincinnati. It is a hustling yet orderly place. Citizens obey "Don't Walk" signs, queue up in polite single file lines, and beg pardon with a "please". Catholic influence, German heritage, and Republican politics had melded into a charming province nestled along the leafy hills of the Ohio River valley.

But as the world churned into 1966, the "city of seven hills" had become an island, exiled from the forces of change. Cincinnati was a cloistered, spinster city, a somnolent little burg with only meager ripples of vibrancy.

It was a town that listens but doesn't hear – if they want your opinion they'll give it to you. Change only happens through erosion of the opposition. Opponents are never convinced, just outlived.

The Queen City remained a reticent community with a collective memory that ran long and deep. The footprints were everywhere...

Monday, June 6th

It was Debbie Bricca's 4th birthday, and her mother Linda was stressed out.

For one thing it was Monday, and Jerry had flown out that morning on business. After a tepid celebration last night, he was gone before the sun came up, leaving Linda without a babysitter in sight. Monday was always tough for that.

Debbie was a loving and obedient child, not yet in kindergarten but sounding like a third grader. Unlike her own upbringing, Linda never spoiled her daughter. She put Debbie on equal footing with their two dogs, Thumper and Dusty, telling her "they are your sisters." That raised some eyebrows on Greenway Avenue.

Linda was cursed with self-awareness. At age 23 the mirror affirmed she was attractive, and her youth distanced her from the older house wives. Linda thought that every husband on the street was secretly in love with her. Or lusting after her – one in particular had been bothering her lately.

She suspected the neighbor women honed their twitching tongues to the sharpest point when discussing her. Same thing with the Monsanto wives. But she was not bothered by gossip, superstition or faith, and when she made up her mind she never changed it. Other women on Greenway probably thought she was isolated, but in her mind she was merely insulated.

So here they were at the Western Hills Shopping Center, the largest of the newly sprouting strip malls along Glenway Avenue. Linda drove slowly through the parking lot, so she could see the reflection of her car in the large department store windows, just like the cruising teenagers did on weekends.

They parked in the rear, where several small rides were permanent fixtures. As they took a spin on the Merry-Go-Round, the June sun darted out from behind a cloud. The sky turned a metallic shade that began to press on Linda's temples. She was suddenly aware of the dry, dusky scent of baked blacktop.

Though only four years old, beautiful, precocious Debbie Bricca talked and acted like a much older child.

She gathered Debbie up and they strolled inside. "Best to get the cake last, baby," she cooed. "So we won't have to carry it around." Linda was saddened to see no animal acts, but there were other distractions. She stopped in the Walden Bookstore and the Hallmark Shop, where she purchased a card for her friend in Florida. She lingered a moment in Globe Records, which she considered "the coolest place" in the mall.

Somewhere between McAlpin's and Kroger Linda realized her billfold was missing from her purse. Fighting the flood of panic, she retraced her steps back to the McAlpin's counter where she'd purchased a scarf on sale. The clerk remembered the billfold but hadn't seen what Linda did with it.

She grabbed Debbie and made a bee-line for the parking lot. Linda sped the mile back home, slipping through a red light onto Lawrence before bolting onto Greenway, tires screeching against the curb. Telling Debbie to play in the front yard, she rushed inside and called her two banks, putting a stop on the credit cards.

Her jauntiness from the mall was gone, replaced by the familiar melancholy descending like a weight. She lay down on the living room couch with a cold towel on her forehead, feeling the fluid seeping into in her legs. She had already taken her medication this morning – now she dived into her purse and took another pill.

Around 3 PM the Cincinnati Police station called. Her billfold had been found on Glenway near Werk Road, her twenty dollar bill and credit cards missing. An officer brought it by a short time later.

By then Linda had already started writing in the card to "Petie."

She had some things to get off her chest, and there was no one up here who compared to her Florida friend. But the venting was difficult to put into words. She struggled, finally writing that "things with Jerry have gotten worse", and it was the "things they left unsaid" that were "the reason for his mounting distress." Linda promised to write her a long letter soon, to "tell you what had happened, because I cannot even begin to recount it now."

As Linda Bricca sealed and stamped the envelope, a montage of her Florida "vacation" began rolling through her mind.

In early February Jerry had driven her and Debbie to Ft. Lauderdale, ostensibly to visit her maternal grandparents. Jerry left a week later to resume working, but his wife and child did not return with him.

Everyone understood that it was a trial separation. For Linda, it was the first taste of real freedom in over four years of marriage. The beautiful weather and nearby beach were intoxicating, and her grandparents loved babysitting Debbie. On Linda's third day there they introduced her to their neighbors James and Eva Evans.

Soon Linda was over there every day with Eva, a 40ish housewife who looked younger and was called "Petie" by her friends. She swam in the Evans pool and helped Petie with her dogs. The two women spent time shopping and going to the beach. On several occasions they went to the dog track with James, a handsome, suntanned man who ran his own business.

These were tranquil days for Linda – no Jerry, a regular babysitter for Debbie, an engaging friend who seemed like an older sister. Linda eventually began to confide in Petie, telling her that she was "fed up with sex" and was going to leave Jerry because she "had all I can take of him." At the time Petie advised her to think it over before doing anything rash.

But then she was thrown together with Ed Clark, an ex-New Jersey cop who was boarding at the Evans house during the winter months. Lean and agile, he had a broad, feline face that appeared unblemished by feeling or intellect. Watching him strut along the beach with lanky grace did something to her equilibrium that Linda preferred not to confess to Petie.

One night in mid-March still glowed for Linda, even three months later. She hadn't actually slept with him, but a stealthy, poignant sexual episode had transpired while Petie and James were asleep. It was thrilling, passionate and fleeting, because a week later Clark went back to New Jersey.

Feeling bereft, Linda poured out her heart to Petie, questioning whether she could ever return home again. She and Jerry were growing apart, with Jerry standing up to her about her obsessive involvement with animals and veterinarians.

Petie was silent for a moment, before looking deep into Linda's eyes. "Do you want to lead him by the nose or by the hand?"

A few days later she called Jerry. He came down as soon as possible, loaded up their Volkswagen, and brought his family back home to 3381 Greenway Avenue.

In the midst of her Florida daydream, Linda had dozed off on the couch. Suddenly she felt one of the dogs tugging at her sleeve. Moving the cloth from her eyes, she saw instead that it was her daughter, with sad eyes as big as saucers.

"You forgot my birthday cake," said Debbie Bricca...

Linda Bulaw transferred from Barrington High to Elgin High for her senior year so she could graduate at age 17.

CHAPTER TWO

SILENT NOONS

"They have their silent noons, tearful nights, angry dawns..."
Carly Simon

JUNE 10TH - AUGUST 16TH 1966

Friday, June 10th

June was busting out all over in the Queen City. The pungent, waxy spring air had vacated the Ohio River valley, also known as "allergy alley", to be replaced by dry summer aromas.

May had offered a respite from the mysterious "phantom" believed to have strangled two women and attacked several others since October. Yet on Saturday morning June 4th, a downtown area assault grabbed the attention of Cincinnati Police.

61-year-old Mary Teppe was cutting through an alley near her apartment on East McMicken at 3 AM when a black man approached and asked directions. As she turned to point the way, he slipped a ligature around her neck and choked her until she passed out. When she came to the contents of her purse were scattered in the alley and her wallet containing $8 was missing.

She described her assailant as a short, slightly built black man in his 20's, tallying with the Walnut Hills perpetrator who often asked directions before attacking his victims. Detectives were reluctant to link this attack to their homicides, but privately they were bracing for another murder.

Yet ordinary citizens were beginning to kick back, sitting on their porches and admiring those early summer evenings when the sky became pearl gray and it got dark so gradually you barely noticed. Kids counted cars as the streetlights came on, orderly and predictable, just like the city itself.

There was something dull yet comforting about it.

On Friday morning June 10th, Jeannette Messer rose in darkness and began her morning routine. The 56-year-old widow lived in a brick four-family on Jefferson Avenue, just east of the Burnet Woods entrance in Cincinnati's Clifton neighborhood. She had moved there three years ago when her husband died unexpectedly – her son was in the navy and her married daughter lived on the West Side.

After breakfast, at 5:45 AM she snapped the leash on her small terrier "Judy" and headed out for their daily Burnet Woods walk. She saw neighbor Josie Chambers bringing her newspaper in.

Josie bid her good morning. "Are you stopping by for coffee?"

Jeannette smiled. "Don't I always?"

"Are you sure it's safe to be walking this girl in the park before sunup?" Josie tried to keep her tone light.

Jeannette heard it all before. Her friend had been warning her against this pre-dawn hike, citing the attacks against women in nearby Walnut Hills. She replied that their neighborhood was a safe area. "Judy is plenty of protection. You know I got her as a puppy right after I moved here – after Henry died."

Josie let it go. "I'll see you soon. Looks like a beautiful day coming up."

With a wave of her hand, Jeannette moved off down Jefferson. The sun was barely creasing the horizon behind her, as city lights flickered off like dying orbs. She was wearing a blue and green plaid dress with red strips under a white and tan sweater with brown moccasins. A few minutes later Jeannette arrived at the north entrance of the park.

Burnet Woods is a city park near the University of Cincinnati, 90 lush acres featuring a fishing lake, a historic bandstand, playgrounds, shelters, picnic areas and hiking trails. The small museum also housed the Wolff Planetarium – the oldest one west of the Allegheny Mountains. It is one of Cincinnati's oldest parks, less than a mile from the Cincinnati Zoo and Botanical Gardens.

As Jeannette walked down the mild slope into the park, she recognized some of the regular dog walkers in the fading gloom. Judy pulled her ahead toward the familiar stone steps next to the Nature Center, and she descended into a grassy area flanked by a swing set and a stone shelter. Straight ahead was the Chipmunk Trail, with another set of stone steps that led up to Clifton Avenue.

The dog stopped at the bottom of the steps, ears pricked up, sniffing the air. The owner caught a whiff of a strange, musky odor. Puzzled, Jeannette Messer tugged the leash and began the slow climb away from the sun's first rays and into the darkened woods...

Clifton resident Fred Scheurle, age 65, was also walking his dog that morning in Burnet Woods. At 6:15 AM he ascended the Chipmunk trail, a mere fifteen minutes after Jeannette Messer.

As he reached the midpoint landing he spotted someone on the ground to the south of the stairway, partially obscured by a clump of brush. He assumed the figure lying face down was a tramp sleeping one off. As he moved away, his dog began jerking at the leash and barking furiously. He took a closer look, and saw a small black and white terrier tied to a tree just beyond the nearly naked person on the ground.

Approaching the silent animal, he could see it was trembling. Scheurle walked his dog back to the park bandstand and flagged down a patrol car. "There's a bum sleeping up that trail in his underwear," he told the officer.

They quickly learned the person on the ground was no transient. Just before 6:30 AM, she was confirmed as a homicide victim. Police noted the name on the dog's collar tag and saw that the owner was Jeannette Messer.

On the scene as the sun arched into the sky, Jake Schott did not spare the grisly details for the gathering press. The killer attacked Mrs. Messer on the trail landing, striking her a brutal blow to the head with an object Schott speculated was "the size of a two-by- four". She was then dragged about forty feet off the trail, leaving a swathe of blood and flattened grass between the landing and where she was found. All her clothing had been ripped off, and a man's tie was still knotted around her neck. The coroner would later confirm that she was raped.

When asked about her dog, Schott frowned. "When she needed it most, the dog allowed itself to be tied to a tree."

Schott was already thinking back to the Harrington and Dant murders. If this was the same killer, he had become more daring – a dawn attack in a public park with witnesses nearby. Messer was also beaten more severely than the other two, as if the killer was somehow personally involved with the victim.

Jeannette Messer entered the trail entrance to the left of the pavilion and shortly thereafter met her killer.

"Is this one related to the other two?" a *Post* reporter queried, as if reading the veteran detective's thoughts.

"Too early to tell, fellas." But Schott's mind was spinning.

Back on Jefferson Avenue, Josie Chambers had become concerned. Her friend never failed to stop off at her next door apartment for coffee after walking Judy in the park. Her failure to do so this morning was most baffling. At 7 AM she went next door to see what was keeping Jeannette. But now there were two policemen standing there, looking grim.

Josie tried to speak, but her hand was already clasped over her mouth in shock...

June 11th – 12th

Jay Bulaw was just two years older than his sister Linda, but their age gap had always seemed wider to him.

When his parents brought Linda home from the hospital in January 1943, Jay was three months past his second birthday – old enough to understand something had changed. His new sister was promptly moved

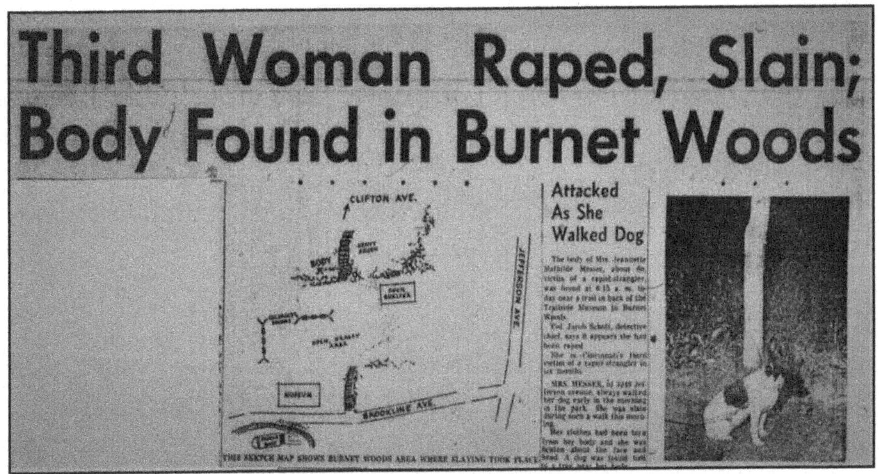

Third Woman Raped, Slain; Body Found in Burnet Woods

Attacked As She Walked Dog

The third rape-strangulation was audacious, as the killer took his victim in a popular city park.

into the choice bedroom next to his parents, and with each passing year Jay realized she was their favorite.

By the time their brother Brian belatedly came along in 1956, the tension between Jay and Linda was tangible. Jay was set to enter the family welding business and was content to remain in the Chicago area. Linda had no such designs.

She had graduated high school a year early, and the Elgin High yearbook listed her senior ambition as "to be a professional office girl." Linda harbored a secret dream – to become a veterinarian, or own a clinic and have vets working for her. But at age 19 life had derailed her plans.

Yet on this balmy June afternoon in Barrington Hills, Illinois, brother and sister were sharing a beer and trying to make amends. Linda was visiting their parents, and surprised Jay by offering to help him with a patio remodel project. As she handed him tools and hauled away debris, they slowly began to clear the air.

At one point he asked her if she still had the "family heirloom". She laughed, knowing he was talking about the carving set. The elaborate handle of the six inch knife, with its mysterious "Rajba Bros. India" inscription, had been their plaything when the adults weren't around. They had made up elaborate stories about the knife's history and bestowed strange, supernatural powers upon it. When Mrs. Bulaw gave the set to Linda shorty after her marriage to Jerry, Jay had chafed about it at the time.

"We still have it," Linda replied. But we keep it put away so Debbie won't play with it." Their eyes met in a shared giggle at the irony. "Jerry uses it more than I do."

"Is he still taking his medication?" Jay instantly regretted the question. This was a real wedge between her and Jerry.

"He better be." Linda took a long pull on her can of Carling, like it was a liquid salve for a blistered soul.

When the project was completed brother and sister vowed to put their differences aside. And that was the last time Jay saw Linda...

JUNE BULAW WATCHED HER daughter putter around her old room.

She recognized those vast blue eyes, moments before intent on the task, yet now staring off as if planning an escape.

Linda was packing for her trip home. Her mother was grateful for the visit – this time Linda had confided in her more openly.

She talked about Florida, admitting the trip to see her grandparents was a trial separation. June remembered Linda's anguished call in February, when she was on the verge of leaving Jerry. She had urged her daughter to relax, enjoy the sunshine, and think things over. In late March, Linda called her again and said she was going "to stay with Jerry no matter what happened."

June stood there in her kitchen, nursing a cup of coffee as daylight drained away in Barrington Hills. None of Linda's earlier relationships had been serious. Until Erwin.

She met him while selling magazine subscriptions for a high school promotion. One memorable day in November 1959, 16-year-old Linda called on Seegers Industries, a machine tool shop owned by Erwin Seegers Sr. and managed by his son Erwin Jr. Adolf and June Bulaw had been close friends with the Seegers family for over twenty years.

Erwin Jr. had not laid eyes Linda since she was in grade school. Now the 30-year-old company president was charmed by the burgeoning beauty of the high school junior. She laughed and joked while trying to sell him a subscription, but he changed the subject and asked if she liked to ski. They talked about it, and then Erwin offered to teach her.

Erwin drove her home that afternoon, and the next day he showed up at the Bulaw house and took Linda skiing.

June was astounded at how quickly things took off. Erwin began calling at their house almost daily to see Linda. He was always a perfect gentleman, and they were genuinely fond of this young man they'd known for two decades. He was kind and considerate with their daughter, always taking Linda to nice places and never keeping her out past their curfew.

In early March, June and Adolph went to Florida for several weeks. Linda was now 17, and planning to graduate early from high school in May. June saw her accelerating her life, as if she could close the gap between her and Erwin. When Linda set her mind on something she always followed through on it.

June had hired a woman to stay at the house and watch over Linda and 4-year-old Brian. With Adolf's blessing, she gave her daughter a set of rules that limited her dates with Erwin to one per week while they were gone.

Upon their return home June got a full report from the nanny. Linda abided by the rules yet exploited some loopholes. Since there was no rule about breakfast, Erwin came to the house every morning to eat with Linda before driving her to school. He would then pick her up after school and bring her home.

June was not pleased with this blatant ruse, and asked Adolf to intervene. She was unsettled by the whole thing, so Ad called Erwin and told him their 14-year age difference was "too disturbing."

But incredibly, Erwin brought his parents to the Bulaw house in early April and declared his honorable intentions by proposing to Linda in front of all of them. Suspicion turned to joy for both families, and preparations began for a June wedding right after Linda's graduation. Invitations were sent out, and by late May some of the wedding gifts had arrived. June had never seen her young daughter so radiant with joy and anticipation.

One week before the nuptials it all fell apart.

Erwin wrote Linda a maudlin note, saying he had "changed his mind" and wanted to "call the wedding off." She immediately called him, becoming first hysterical and then nauseated over the phone. When a worried Erwin arrived to check on her, Adolph Bulaw angrily threw

Linda Bulaw met Erwin in 1959 (left), but after he called off the wedding she became aloof and withdrawn (right).

him out of the house, only to have Linda turn on her father, screaming "I could have got him back!"

June Bulaw sipped her coffee, shivering over the events of six years past, a day that had transformed everything.

After being jilted Linda hovered between wounded pride and blatant shock for several weeks. At night she rippled between restless stupors and sodden sleep. Just when June was ready to call the doctor, her daughter returned to a semblance of life.

Linda mechanically walked through her graduation ceremony and immediately enrolled in college full time. Surfacing from her emotional eclipse, Linda was a picture of determination tinged with bitterness. She didn't date, socialize, or have any other activities outside of school. June saw it as a misguided attempt to grow up in a hurry and return to Erwin's world.

However, in early September Linda found out Erwin had married someone else over Labor Day weekend. Linda again became distraught – June kept an eye on her daughter and held her breath.

Within a few weeks Linda met a boy her age named Chuck and started dating him. He was fun and athletic and made her laugh. Linda liked him a great deal, and June could see her heart thawing.

But it never had a chance. After dating for six weeks, Chuck was killed in an auto accident. His death shattered Linda's brittle spirit. The day of his funeral she experienced a complete nervous breakdown. June pulled her out of college, and they went to Florida and stayed with her parents for five months. When they returned to Chicago in March Linda got a job as a stewardess for United Airlines.

Thinking back on those unbridled days, June was amazed at the twists and turns Linda's life had taken by the time she turned 18. As she hugged her daughter goodbye, she again urged her to stand by her husband. Linda kissed her on the cheek but said nothing.

Later that night it came to her once again, a misty remembrance from her daughter's childhood and her love for animals.

Their family dog had died. Adolph buried it in the backyard, but little Linda had dug it up. This went on all day, until after the fifth burial Linda came into the house carrying the dead animal.

June brushed the tears from her baby girl's eyes. "Sweetheart, we buried him so he would go to heaven. If you keep digging him up, he won't go to heaven."

She never forgot her daughter's reply. "Would you leave me in the ground if I died?" answered six-year-old Linda Jayne Bulaw.

Monday, June 13th

Cigarettes were stubbed out as Chief Stanley Schrotel strode into the conference room. The stale air hummed with anticipation. Veteran detectives hadn't seen him chair a homicide squad meeting since the 1956 murder of Hyde Park socialite Audrey Pugh **(Queen City Gothic Chapter 7)**.

Schrotel, his white hair set off by dynamic blue eyes, looked around the room and pierced them with a gaze of matchless intensity. The man's persona inspired complete attention.

The Chief usually had no problem delegating to his command staff. For him, it was simply a matter of utility. He liked to talk about "being bitten by the efficiency bug" during training with J. Edgar Hoover at the FBI academy after the war.

Stan Schrotel came up through the ranks as a college graduate, working some of the city's biggest murder cases in the 1940's before becoming the youngest ever Cincinnati Police Chief in 1951 at age 37. During the next 15 years he transformed the CPD from a cumbersome, crony-laden relic into a contemporary model for efficient and effective law enforcement.

He let everyone know that the old methods were out. They would do everything by the numbers. And there would be no more dubious confessions obtained in sweltering, cloistered rooms.

By June of 1966, Schrotel had earned a law degree and listed the following accomplishments on his resume: Current President of the International Association of Police Chiefs; Former adviser to JFK's Committee on Youth Crime; and lecturer at the FBI National Academy (requested by Hoover). He'd also appeared on the cover of *Life Magazine* for a feature on the CPD.

Schrotel became a real legend in his own time. Like any good CEO, he promoted the best people without fear of being overshadowed by them. This earned him loyalty, an emotional, elusive quality that not every leader commands.

So when Schrotel stepped into the morning briefing detectives understood the import. Three rape-strangulations in six months had ripped the chief away from his big picture planning.

Lt. Colonel Jake Schott, certain to be Schrotel's successor, had assigned 14 detectives full-time to the Messer homicide. All were present, along with Safety Director Henry Sandman, when Schott turned the meeting over to his boss.

The idea of a "serial killer" was daunting to cops with no frame of reference. There were no FBI profiles, no psychological experts, and few documented cases. Cincinnati detectives already researched the Boston Strangler, and were aware this type of killer often let long periods of time elapse between murders.

Plus there were other forces at work besides the "phantom" roaming the Queen City, and Schrotel was painfully aware of them.

Earlier that year President Johnson had called crime "a sore on the face of America". Insisting it was the product of other afflictions in American society, Johnson proposed fighting crime with a strong dose of "Great Society" programs emphasizing less poverty and more education: "Plainly laws are less likely to command the respect of those forced to live at the margins of society."

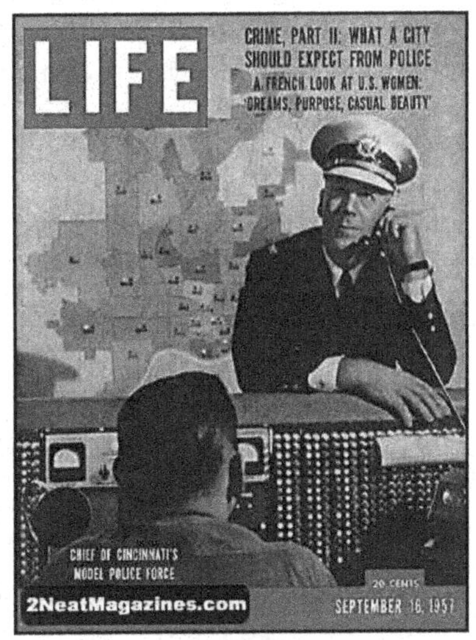

Yet LBJ's sociological perspective was an abomination to Cincinnati cops, from those walking a beat all the way up to the Chief. And just now someone whispered to Schrotel that the Supreme Court had ruled for the plaintiff in Miranda vs. Arizona, a landmark decision that suspects must be advised of their rights against self-incrimination when arrested.

But that would be another meeting for another time. Schrotel quickly got down to business. "What do we have on Messer?"

Schott nodded towards lead detective Eugene Moore. "We combed the area with rakes," Moore began. "We found the necktie used as a ligature and a partial footprint in the mud near her body. It might not be the killer's, but we took a cast of it anyway. We've interviewed twelve known sexual offenders who were around the Clifton area on Friday morning – so far nothing on that. We've been canvasing Burnet Woods for witnesses, and have a report of a two-tone Chevy parked near the crime scene around 6 AM."

"What about the FBI testing?" Schrotel inquired.

"We sent the ligature, the victim's clothing, hair, blood and semen samples. The hair was short, black and curly, similar to what we found on Harrington and the Kreco woman last October. We should have results by tomorrow. We also found her purse and the wallet was missing."

Schott spoke up. "Harrington was also robbed, but Dant wasn't, correct?

Moore nodded. "This was not a botched robbery." He looked at the coroner's report. "Both cheek bones and several ribs fractured. In the others the blow to the head was just to take them down. This looks more personal."

Sandman piped in. "What are the links to Harrington and Dant?"

Moore touched on the obvious ones – strangulation with an improvised ligature, the ages of the victims, the rape committed as they were dead or dying.

Schrotel cleared his throat. "The press is giving us favorable coverage. But they are hounding us to make the call. Do we have a single killer? Or three unrelated murders?"

He picked up the morning *Enquirer* and read from their editorial: "Somewhere in this city of a half million there must be someone who knows something that could lead to the arrest of the rapist-strangler who killed his third victim early Friday morning in Burnet Woods." The chief's sapphire eyes swept the room. "Perhaps they have already decided for us."

He then read several headlines from over the weekend:

- **Mad Strangler Catches Widow Strolling Alone**
- **The Strangler...Who, What, Why?**
- **Fear Gripping Women While Strangler Roams**

The chief knew the terror coursing through the city was not a reporter's imagination. It was tangible and pervasive – increased sales of locks and guns, decreased night life, and thousands of calls to their tip line by concerned citizens.

He also knew how important their next press conference would be. A mad dog killer would reinforce vigilance, but he believed it would also create suspicion bordering on isolation. This level of fear would erode social bonds and fracture the informant network that police counted on to catch criminals.

"What about manpower?" Schrotel always wanted the numbers.

"We've added eight more men to the 14 already working Messer," Schott replied. "The legwork is grueling, especially checking out all those cars," referring to a two tone Chevy seen in Burnet Woods that morning. "We've already checked out 150 with no luck."

Schrotel turned to his number two man. "We'll wait for the FBI analysis before we make the call on this, and you will meet the press the day after." He appraised his team with an earnest glint. "Let's get to work, gentlemen."

ON TUESDAY THE FBI results arrived, confirming the hairs found on Jeannette Messer were consistent with a "negro male" like the Harrington

Mad Strangler Catches Widow Strolling Alone

Fear gripped Cincinnati anew Friday as the mad rapist-strangler claimed his third victim.

This time the killer struck at dawn in heavily wooded Burnet Woods.

His victim was Mrs. Jeannette M. Messer, 56, a widow who lived at 3249 Jefferson Ave.

She was walking her small fox terrier along a leafy path when the killer struck, bludgeoning her, then assaulting and strangling her.

... his area of activity, Colonel Schott added.

Mrs. Messer was initially struck so hard she was never able to offer any resistance, said Colonel Schott. She was first struck by an instrument about the size of a two-by-four. Both cheek bones were fractured. She was then dragged 40 feet where she was strangled and then raped.

Colonel Schott also had advice for women who may have to be alone. "Be careful not to expose yourself to unnecessary risk. In this case Mrs. Messer was attacked in an isolated area. ... versity of Cincinnati and just north of Good Samaritan Hospital.

The body was found by Fred Scheurle, 65, 3205 Bishop St. Mr. Scheurle was also walking his dog when he discovered the body and reported it to police. A park caretaker said he had seen Mrs. Messer walking her dog in the park for the past three years. He said he had spoken to her a few times, but had nevered learned her name.

A dark blue and red Paisley tie was used for the strangulation. Several foot-... ing. Solid cl... lacking in th... cases, he add...

On April ... Dant, 58, was ... and strangled ... floor apartm... Hill. She was ... nylon stockin... beaten with a ...

Last Decemb... of a Universi... nati professo... gene D. Harri... found rap... in the dimly ... ment of her ... apartment b... was killed w... cord looped a...

After the third murder in six months, the press seemed to have decided there was only one killer.

slaying. Hair found on Lois Dant came back "inconclusive", but Schott felt he had enough to go public with the single killer theory.

An unexpected bonus came from the analysis of semen from a vaginal swab, which identified Messer's killer as having type "O" blood. Yet an attempt by Schott to check blood bank records for type "O" black men with criminal records would eventually be thwarted by the local branch of the NAACP.

On Wednesday June 15th, Jake Schott did not waver at his press conference. "Jeannette Messer's killer is the same man who raped and strangled the other two women. The man is a maniac. There cannot be three of them."

Over shouted questions Schott speculated that the killer was a black man. The next day the *Enquirer* ran a story with this provocative headline: **Negro Killed Three Women, Police Say.**

A few days later, an *Enquirer* interview cast doubt on the single killer theory.

Retired police captain Patrick Hayes was 82, described as "one of the last of the old-time cops." This colorful sleuth was looking back on a half century of famous cases, including his arrest of serial poisoner Anna Marie Hahn in 1937. He also helped capture Lindbergh Trent in 1938 **(Queen City Notorious Chapter 5)** and Tony Treat in 1942 **(QCN Chapter 6)**, two infamous "sex morons" who murdered children.

Speculating on the murder of Jeannette Messer, Hayes wondered if she knew her killer. "Why would a stranger beat her up," he demanded. "He wanted to make damn sure she wouldn't talk. They need to start looking at her friends, who she talked to, who she's been out with." Sitting on his porch, Hayes was itching to be involved in one of Cincinnati's biggest manhunts ever.

"I don't think the killings are connected," the old captain declared. "I'll be damned if I do..."

Thursday, June 23rd

Lisa awakened to a rapid swirl of air just after midnight, as if someone was moving swiftly through the darkened bedroom. She had only a moment to glimpse a figure crossing her field of vision, before blackness descended in a violent arc.

At 9:30 AM the next morning, Joyce Bowe returned to the basement apartment in Seattle's Queen Anne Hill district that she shared with her two roommates. All three women were attractive, 20-year-old airline stewardesses. She had stayed the night with a friend "on the spur of the moment" – the sway of small human choices. Joyce was surprised to find the door unlocked and a light burning in the living room.

Odd that her roommates were sleeping in on a Thursday, she thought to herself. When they didn't respond to her "Good morning, sleepyheads!" she glanced in their bedroom and turned on the light. Joyce was horrified. "I looked at Lonnie and didn't believe my eyes," she told detectives. "Then I started to wake Lisa and she was in the same state."

Stewardess Still Critical; Police Searching for Clues

SEATTLE (AP) — An attractive airline stewardess was in critical condition in a hospital today, unaware that her roommate had been killed by an assailant who entered their basement apartment and beat both girls brutally.

Killed in the attack that occurred Thursday was Lonnie Trumbull. In critical condition with multiple fractures of the skull was Lisa Wick. They were found by another roommate, Joyce Bowe, who had spent Tuesday night with friends.

All three were 20, all were from Portland, Ore., and all had graduated from a United Air Lines' training school just six weeks ago.

Det. Sgt. Herb Arnold said a blood-stained piece of wood three inches square and 18 inches long found in a nearby vacant lot was believed to have

LONNIE TRUMBULL
. . . beaten to death

LISA WICK
. . . critical

Despite rumors that Linda Bricca knew the two stewardesses, they were in high school during her short stint with UAL.

Flight attendants Lisa Wick and Lonnie Trumbull were sprawled in their twin beds, their heads and faces torn asunder from a savage bludgeoning. Lisa was drawing ragged breaths and moaning – the plucky blonde would survive. Doctors would credit the heavy curlers she wore to bed with saving her life.

But Lonnie was dead. The coroner said later that the pretty brunette lived for at least 45 minutes after the attack.

The apartment was not ransacked, and the victim's purses were intact. The weapon was found in a nearby vacant lot, a blood spattered, hair matted piece of wood 3" square by 1-1/2 feet long.

Investigators learned that Lonnie was dating a King County Deputy Sheriff, who saw her that afternoon and called her around 10 PM as she and Lisa were getting ready for bed. All three roommates were from Portland, Oregon, and had only started working for United Airlines six weeks previously.

"The girls have been in Seattle such a limited time; we don't know whether it was an acquaintance or a prowler," Captain Paul Lee told the press. The SPD homicide chief could not say when Lisa Wick would be able to give a statement. "She's in a coma, and they may operate to relieve pressure on her brain. Chances are she will have no memory of the attack."

The investigation quickly ran aground. United Airlines offered a $10,000 reward, destined to go unclaimed. The horrific attack on the two flight attendants was picked up on the national news wire, but did not run in the Cincinnati papers.

After undergoing emergency brain surgery, Lisa Wick endured a slow and painful recovery. On July 15th, she broke through weeks of confusion as she described her assailant – a white man about 30, 5-10 and 165 lbs. with thinning blonde hair.

Several months later their best suspect took his own life – the son of the building's landlord. A search of his apartment uncovered a scrapbook of newspaper clippings about the case.

More than two decades later, Seattle detectives journeyed to Florida to ask condemned serial killer Ted Bundy about the 1966 attack on Wick and Trumbull. Bundy was employed at a drugstore stocking shelves four blocks away from the crime scene, and investigators knew the bludgeoning of sleeping females fit his MO in the 1978 FSU Chi Omega murders.

Even this eerie glimmer would fade. There was no evidence other than his possible proximity, and more than twenty years later they could not ascertain if he was even working that night. Despite copping to 30 murders just before his electrocution, Bundy repeatedly denied involvement in the Seattle case.

SEVERAL DAYS AFTER THE attack on Lonnie and Lisa, Linda Bricca received a letter from her mother containing a Chicago article about the crime. Scrawled across the top of her note was this unnerving question: "Did you know them?"

She did not. The two victims did not become stewardesses until April, a full five years after Linda graduated from her own training class in 1961. And by that November she was engaged and no longer working for the airline. She had no connection whatsoever to Lonnie Trumbull and Lisa Wick.

But this shocking crime gave her pause, especially with the Strangler lurking about. Linda gave an involuntary shudder as she read details about the two young women, one murdered and one maimed, girls much like she had been five years ago.

She folded up the clipping and put it away, ruminating on her eight months flying the friendly skies. She had loved the job, and was upset when United terminated her that November after she became nauseous on a flight out of Seattle.

Her supervisor understood that her spell of vomiting was not food poisoning, but she never voiced what Linda already knew.

It was morning sickness...

June 23rd – July 13th

Despite a robust investigation by the Cincinnati homicide squad, investigators had no viable clues in the killings of Emogene Harrington, Lois Dant, and Jeannette Messer.

Schott told Schrotel that only an eyewitness would move the investigation forward. So these veteran cops were forced to wait for the next murder attempt and hope someone sees it.

On June 23rd a promising lead fizzled out. Detectives quizzed a 43-year-old hospital orderly who'd been seen in Burnet Woods around midnight, about six hours before the Messer murder. He was a former patient at Rollman Psychiatric Institute who was drinking that day and had no memory of anything.

A pair of his pants sent to the FBI for testing came back negative for blood and hair. Plus he was white man who didn't fit the prevailing theory of a black killer. Police finally cut him loose.

With the headline **Negro Killed Three Women** still hanging like an inflammatory shadow, the Cincinnati summer arrived like a bonfire fueled by the nationwide cycle of bigotry, poverty and pain.

As the Messer investigation dwindled, racial stories from Klan senate hearings to violent riots dominated the news, and it would play out all summer: frustrated whites, agitated blacks, and the misery of daily

Negro Killed Three Women, Police Say

After a careful evaluation, Cincinnati Police announced that a lone wolf black killer was on the loose.

life in the ghetto, where drugs, alcohol and idleness became the rationale for despair.

But other middle class black people were making great strides beyond civil rights, becoming more educated, earning better money, and seeking better things. Rising above the squalor and desperation their parents had experienced, many blacks were defiantly refusing to be pushed around anymore.

On July 4th, the Congress of Racial Equality adopted a resolution calling for an end to "non-violence" in the civil rights movement. This new stance put CORE directly at odds with the more restrained NAACP, further splitting the uneasy truce between militants calling for defiance in the face of moderates hoping for persuasion.

After the CORE announcement, NAACP director Roy Wilkins addressed the escalating "Black Power" movement in no uncertain terms: "The trouble with black power is it implies anti-white, and we can't have anything to do with that. We are loathe to talk about it."

In Cincinnati, this belligerent dogma was unsettling conservative citizens fearful of an unknown black man killing white women. Backlash was conspicuous around the city, especially on the West Side, the most segregated section of Cincinnati.

With a black suspect being sought as the strangler, one *Enquirer* columnist implied that the killer was "using the kind of JUNGLE tactics that are pushing up crime rates in the United States."

AT THE MONSANTO PLANT at the western edge of the county, thoughts of racial strife never entered the mind of Jerry Bricca. Dedicated to his job and obsessed with every detail of it, if he was concerned about social conditions he never let it show.

Born in San Francisco, Jerry was a high school honor student and a standout swimmer before moving on to Stanford, where he graduated in 1960 with a BS in Chemical Engineering. Always a high achiever, he had worked a significant amount of hours at the Monsanto plant in Addytson since being transferred here from Seattle in November 1963.

Although only 5-9, Jerry kept in shape and with his crew cut could pass for a college wrestler. As he walked through Building 7, his neck and biceps bulged underneath his crisp white shirt and tie.

Jerry's boss, 30-year-old Ted Anderson, was cutting through the plant and saw his best engineer grabbing lunch from the company vending machines. Ted caught his eye and gave Jerry a rueful glance – eating on the run was becoming a habit for him.

It wasn't helping his demeanor either. Known around Monsanto as a temperamental perfectionist, Jerry had made progress in controlling his short fuse. Yet Ted could see stress stamped across Jerry's face as he wolfed down a pastry and gulped some coffee.

Anderson knew Jerry didn't get along with his previous boss, and had told others he was ready to leave the company. But since Ted took over plant engineering Jerry had stayed on, and the two men fostered a good working relationship. Although they didn't socialize much, Ted felt like they were getting closer. Jerry even confided in him about a medical condition, assuring his boss that as long as he took his medication he could control his temper.

Ted walked toward Jerry, but stopped when he saw Jim Cannon approaching. Cannon engaged Jerry in a brief conversation, and Ted could see Jerry struggling to maintain his composure. Both men reported to him – he was well aware of their mutual animosity.

Cannon was working in Building 7, having transferred over a few weeks back. Ted had implored Jerry to help him get acclimated, but these guys were like oil and water. Cannon was a volatile ladies man who would fly off the handle one minute and be cool as a cucumber the next. His working style clashed with Jerry's – Cannon could not see past the project at hand and refused to plan ahead. Jerry was meticulous, believing that an efficient design would cause fewer problems down the road.

Ted Anderson watched as the two men separated, and saw their enmity for what it was. Jerry was collegiate with his approach. Cannon was strictly night school.

Was there something more going on? The two of them had been quite frosty since that company cookout at Anderson's house in June. Cannon had been hitting on Linda Bricca the whole time while Jerry was talking shop with another engineer. At one point Cannon drunkenly grabbed Linda's arm and tried to kiss her on the mouth. Jerry had walked over and calmly told him to "bug off."

Cannon moved near the grill but continued quaffing his cocktail and eyeing Linda. At one point Cannon started riding her about her passion for animals. "You treat your dogs like human babies,"

Anderson heard Linda's angry retort. "You don't know a damn thing about animals!" That seemed to shut him up.

But he saw Jerry Bricca grab a burger off the grill and heard him whisper to Cannon: "If you don't leave my wife alone, I'm ready to kick your ass."

July 13th – July 14th

1966 had not started well for Richard Speck. And the shit was about to hit the fan.

The lanky, tattooed drifter was flying high on this sweltering July night in Chicago. Rawboned and ugly, his pockmarked face was dominated by a long, cruel nose. Coiling on his left arm was the most ominous tattoo of all: Born to Raise Hell.

Speck was simmering with dark emotions. Bitter, lonely and penniless, he haunted dimly lit bars, stoking his anger with booze and pills while flashing his knife around in macho displays.

He had been fired from his merchant seaman job on July 2nd and put ashore on Lake Michigan, about 50 miles east of Chicago. Later that day, three young women vanished from a lakefront park a mile from where Speck landed. They were never seen again. Two weeks later, with his name splashed across front page headlines, there were rumors Speck had killed these three women also.

Destitute and desperate, Speck landed another cargo ship assignment on July 13th – but lost it to a sailor with more seniority. Instead of shipping out, he bought a pint of Thunderbird and gulped it down with some reds. A block from the Maritime Union Hall he staked out a spot in Louella Park. While sipping from a water fountain, he stared at some townhouses only one hundred feet away. Behind one of them he spied a pretty girl in a yellow dress.

Speck passed the night on a park bench, and spent Wednesday July 14th binging on uppers and cheap whiskey in various dives near Louella Park. By evening he was in free fall, wandering the streets and playing with his knife.

His thoughts careened to his ex-wife Shirley. During their brief, tumultuous marriage in Texas, his constant suspicions about Shirley's infidelity only intensified his contempt and mistrust for women. He saw them all as the classic Madonna-Whore paradox, a fixation that made him loathe any woman low enough to have sex with him. They were all sluts.

As Richard Speck ambled back to Louella Park, there was lava flowing through his veins...

INSIDE THE TOWNHOUSE AT 2319 East 100th Street, student nurse Corazon Amurao was preparing for bed, along with five of her other housemates. She was one of three Philippine graduate nurses living there with five American student nurses – their townhouse was one of three nursing residences in the complex.

Amurao was blessed with a profound presence of mind, a calmness that masked a keen perception about people. Along with uncanny luck, these qualities would save her life tonight.

Awakened by a knock on her bedroom door just before 11 PM, Amurao was confronted by Speck, reeking of alcohol and brandishing a gun. He quickly roused the other women, herded them into a back bedroom and told them he "needed money."

Amurao noted his soft voice and watery eyes – he seemed kind, yet she was on guard.

As Speck calmly talked to the startled nurses, 22-year-old Gloria Davy was sitting outside in a parked car with her fiancé. Gloria was a stunning, raven haired woman that men noticed. Coming from a wealthy family, she was determined, confident and a trifle spoiled.

When a tipsy Gloria entered the front door at 11:20 PM and went upstairs, the pretty brunette walked into the vortex of Richard Speck's savage vision. She instantly reminded him of his wife – Speck would

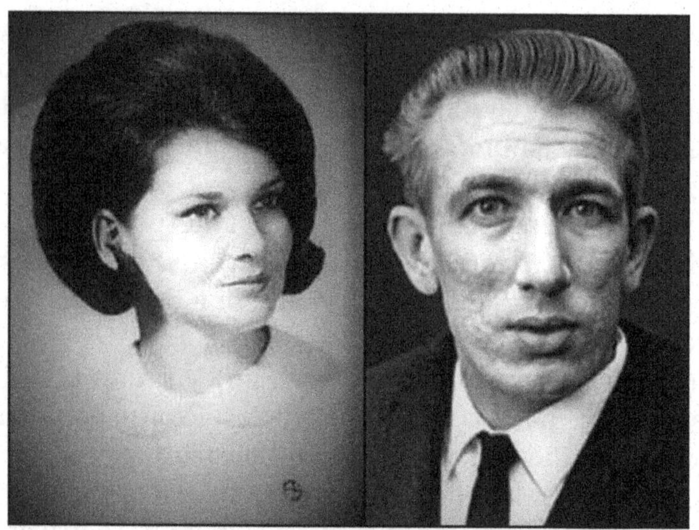

Gloria Davy bore a striking resemblance to Speck's ex-wife, which may have turned a simple burglary into a mass murder.

later say Davy was a "dead ringer for Shirley" and that "she was flirting with me."

From that moment on, Speck's behavior became more agitated, and the presence of Gloria Davy would veer this crime from a mere burglary into something brutal and inexplicable.

In the 52 years since this horrendous crime, one question remains. Why did the women fail to resist Speck? They had opportunities to mount an attack, and the three Philippine nurses were ready to fight him. But the American girls took a calculated risk, either out of fear or disbelief. They reasoned that by remaining calm they would lull this intruder away from his primary motive of rape. A false sense of security told them that one man could not rape that many women – much less kill them. But none of them grasped the effect Davy was having on Speck.

The dark-haired beauty could have been Shirley's sister, and his icy calm was melting into rage.

He first took Pamela Wilkening into a front bedroom and began to strangle her. At that moment, the eighth and final nurse arrived home with a friend who was spending the night. Suzanne Farris had enticed Mary Ann Jordan with the promise of air conditioning, a choice by Jordan that proved fatal. Surprised by their arrival, Speck quickly killed all three girls with brutal knife thrusts.

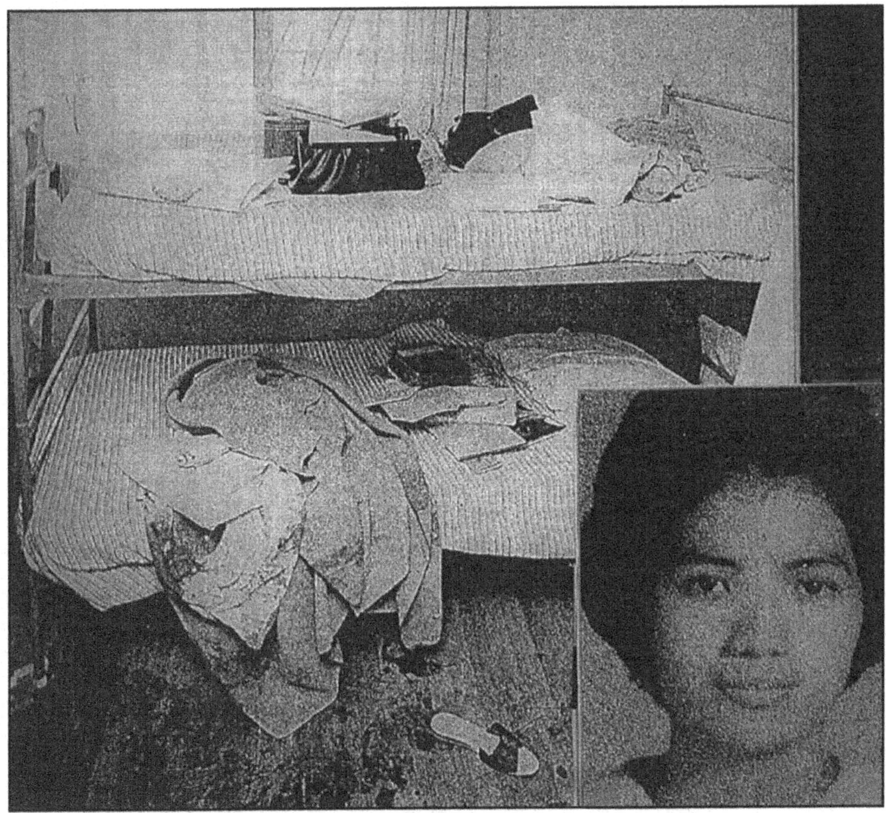

Lone survivor Corazon Amurao hid under a bed as Speck slaughtered the eight other nurses.

As he continued to lead the other nurses to their doom, Speck missed Corazon Amurao hiding under the bed because his focus was on Gloria Davy. The autopsy would show she had been raped, sodomized with an unknown object, and strangled. According to Amurao, Speck saved her for last, raping Davy on the very bed she was hiding under.

When the lone survivor gave the alarm the next morning, eight young nurses lay savagely murdered in the townhouse, stabbed, strangled and left weltering in their own blood. The headlines for such an unparalleled slaughter were epic. When Speck was arrested several days later after a suicide attempt, the entire country gazed at pictures of this pathetic loser and grappled with the big question: Why?

The blitz of alcohol and drugs had eaten away the remnants of Speck's self-control. But it was the sight of Gloria Davy that cracked his last vestige of sanity. Her resemblance to his hated ex-wife warped him from a drunken burglar into an inhuman killer...

THE SUNDAY AFTER RICHARD Speck's arrest in Chicago, Betty Meyer was sitting on her front porch, reading the paper with a cigarette dangling from her lips. As she learned more about the killer of the eight student nurses, Linda Bricca was on her driveway, washing her car in a pair of snug tennis shorts.

She mused about her attractive neighbor, at least ten years younger than any other wife on this side of Greenway. Linda was like a big girl playing house. It was hard to believe some of the things she said, such as Jerry making $35,000 a year.

Linda looked up from her chore and waved to Betty, who noticed two husbands doing yard work across the street and eyeing Linda as she moved around the car, hosing it off and bending down in those shorts. On an airless July afternoon like this one, Linda didn't seem concerned that her outfit was getting wet.

Betty puckered her lips and tossed her cigarette. She grudgingly liked Linda, but the kid was gorgeous and knew it – she basked in the idea that every man in the neighborhood was in love with her.

Earlier that spring she was certain Jerry and Linda weren't going to make it. That vacation in Florida was a thinly disguised separation that Betty saw coming a mile away. Over cocktails Linda had confided that Jerry was pushing for another child, which Linda did not want, even while she begged him to adopt more pets.

Her love for animals was unwavering even as her passion for Jerry cooled. She told Betty she didn't enjoy sex with him, and that she would just get him worked up and then tell him to forget it.

Linda had brought some dirty jokes home from Florida and gave them to her to read, but Richard Meyer had handed them back with an icy reply that "we do not read those types of jokes."

Betty saw Debbie come out to the driveway, but Linda sent her back inside. She was not a very loving mother, almost acting like the child spoiled her fun. But she got her way most of the time with Jerry. Every so often he would put his foot down, like last year when she wanted to go to Europe with her parents and Jerry gave a firm NO.

Linda strolled into Betty's yard, water still dripping off her face. They started to chat, and Betty marveled at her pretty neighbor's manner. Her voice was hearty, often on the brink of laughter. But was she ever really laughing WITH you?

"Well, they caught the man who killed those eight nurses in Chicago," Betty scowled, showing Linda the picture of Richard Speck on the front page. "My God, what he did to those poor girls. The electric chair is too good for this creep."

When the news about the murdered nurses had first hit the papers, Betty told Linda that the class picture of victim Gloria Davy resembled the one taken of her when she became an airline stewardess. Linda had then studied Davy's picture for several minutes without comment.

Now Linda took the paper from her hands and looked at the baleful picture of Richard Speck for a full ten seconds. Then she fixed Betty with those huge blue eyes.

"I feel sorry for him..."

Mid-July

Around lunchtime, Gloria Weyman left her house on Lawrence Road and felt the July humidity pressing down.

It was a cloudless day of glaring heat, where you saw what looked like puddles of water on the street that vanished when you got up close.

Gooey, black tar bubbles boiled up on the pavement in the summer sun. Some kids were breaking them with their bare feet, and Gloria heard them wail with delight as the ruptured pustules released a sharp, metallic odor that jolted their noses.

She glanced across the street and was relieved her strange neighbor wasn't in his front yard – nor was his work truck parked in the side lot of Western Bowl, which bordered her property.

Some in the neighborhood believed he was shell-shocked from the Korean War. Gloria often saw him just standing there, grunting and groaning as people walked past. On one strange, sleepless night, she had looked out her window at 4 AM and saw him crawling around his yard on all fours before he sprang up and dashed inside.

Gloria was walking over to see her young friend Linda Bricca, who hadn't been around for morning coffee lately. Ever since Jerry bought her that car she was not her usual chatty self. Gloria's pretense was to return a book, but her visit was really about the whispers other wives were sharing about their pretty neighbor.

Gloria could see why Linda's freshness and candor attracted men to her. But was she really as sexually audacious as the rumors suggested?

Linda had always confided in her. Gloria knew all about her relatives in Florida and her time as an airline stewardess. Linda also talked about meeting a fellow when she was in New York and all the expensive places he took her and extravagant gifts he bought her. Gloria wasn't surprised – she knew that Linda was used to fine living because her parents were somewhat wealthy.

Then Linda confessed that she would switch her schedule to stay longer with this man. Gloria was shocked, but tried not to show it. Linda was just 18 years old in 1961, single and adventurous. Still she prattled on about spending several days with this man, whom she referred to as Ed.

Then there was her marriage to Jerry. They'd only known each other four months before their hasty wedding. One time Linda mentioned the date of their marriage and Debbie's birth date in the same sentence, only to realize they were not nine months apart – she turned red and quickly changed the subject.

She liked Linda, but 40ish Gloria struggled to accept the younger woman's contradictions. She was overly opinionated but too immature to back it up. She was obsessed with animals, yet unable to make friends with women. She was nervous about their family finances, yet believed she could handle any situation.

Linda once claimed that she had a nervous breakdown sometime before her marriage to Jerry. For Gloria this had a ring of truth to it. Her mind reeled as she reviewed some of Linda's strange tales, and Gloria floundered for a metaphor to describe her.

As she turned the corner onto Greenway Avenue, she could see Linda's blue station wagon in the Bricca driveway. Gloria came up the short walk, rang the doorbell, and then turned her back to wave at Joan Janszen across the street.

There was a surge of movement and a deafening thump behind her. Linda's two dogs had launched themselves at the screen door. They were mixed breeds, a poodle and a dachshund, not large but hostile to anyone standing on their front porch. They continued to propel themselves at the door as Gloria backed down the steps.

Linda appeared from the kitchen, called the dogs off with a ready command, offered a mild rebuke, and joined Gloria on the porch. She was wearing stylish shorts and a blue sleeveless top, showing off tanned, toned arms. Her hair was pulled back, not the French Roll that Gloria was used to.

"What a pleasant surprise." Linda's voice had a peculiar, lilting quality, her cadence speckled with an underlying energy. "I was just thinking about you the other day."

"Well, I wanted to return your book." Gloria handed her the copy of "Born Free."

Linda held the book as if it was a spider, and her eyebrows knitted to question marks. "Oh, I meant for you to keep it. I have other copies. Did you enjoy it?"

Gloria was not much of a reader, and stammered for a polite response. "I loved, uh, the ending, you know, that Elsa recognized them after more than a year. It was beautiful."

Linda gave her a blank smile, but was quickly interrupted by a commotion in her living room. Debbie had stepped on one of the dog's toes, and it was yelping. Linda went inside, and Gloria was astounded to hear her say "I've told you to be careful with them. They are not our pets. They are your sisters."

As Gloria looked on, Linda made Debbie kiss the dog's toe. Gloria blanched, but recovered as Linda came back onto the porch.

"It would be nice to have a governess," she said airily. "You could play with the kid when you wanted to without having to do any of the dirty work." Linda quickly segued into a monologue about her animals, and how much money they spent on shots for the rabbits and the fencing for the hutch. Gloria listened politely until the phone rang, and then bade Linda a quick goodbye.

A faint breeze stirred the sultry air as she turned the corner onto Lawrence. She was almost home when she saw his truck parked at Western. And there he was – her across the street neighbor.

Tall and husky, he stood in his short, sloping yard staring at Gloria, waving his hands in that way that always frightened her...

Monday, August 1st

The brooding, burly ex-marine had just murdered the two most important women in his life.

Around midnight he showed up at his mother's apartment, saying his house was too hot and he needed to sleep in her air-conditioned living room. She was happy to see him, but when she turned her back he choked her into unconsciousness before stabbing her in the heart. He placed her body on her bed and covered her with a blanket before heading back home.

Now standing over his wife as she lay sleeping in their bed, the young husband pulled out a bayonet and stabbed her in the chest four times, and then pulled the sheet up over her naked body.

It was 3 AM. There was no turning back now. Charles Whitman was on his final mission.

It was a clear, cloudless Monday morning of simmering heat as he rode the elevator to the top of the University of Texas at Austin main building with a footlocker full of weapons and supplies. Whitman had no future. Knowing full well he would never leave the tower alive, he was a dead man walking.

When he reached the 28th floor with his cargo dolly, Whitman was accosted by receptionist Edna Townsley, who was filling in for someone else today. Whitman quickly bludgeoned her with his rifle butt, so viciously that her skull was fractured.

As Whitman hid the dying woman's body behind a desk, two young visitors came down from the observation deck. Don Walden and Cheryl Botts, later called "the luckiest couple in Austin", were unaware of the violence that had occurred moments before. They were unnerved by the husky stranger brandishing two rifles, but Cheryl managed to say "Hi." Whitman smiled and cheerfully replied, "Hi, how are you?" As they left Cheryl warned Don not to step in the brownish-red stain on the carpet, not knowing it was Edna Townsley's blood.

When they were gone Whitman tried to barricade the stairwell but was again interrupted, this time by a luckless family heading for the observation deck. Springing into action, he fatally shot 15-year-old Mark Gabour and his aunt Marguerite Lamport on the stairwell. Mark's 18-year-old brother Mike and his mother Mary Gabour were critically wounded, but managed to tumble down the stairs and out of range for Whitman to finish them off.

Whitman told a psychiatrist that he fantasized about shooting people from the tower three months before he did it.

Finally, at 11:48 AM, 25-year-old Charles Whitman opened fire from the clock tower and rained death down upon the peaceful campus. His first victim was a pregnant student, who was wounded and lost her baby – moments later he fatally shot her boyfriend as he bent over her. Whitman killed 10 more people and wounded 32 others before three police officers and a civilian stormed the deck and took him out 96 minutes later.

Dazed by the second sensational mass murder in a little over two weeks, the nation regarded Speck and Whitman as alien beings. Their rampages had no precedent to allow the average person to grasp them.

Investigators in Austin soon realized that Whitman's onslaught could have been much worse. The unplanned murders of Townsley, Gabour, and Lamport delayed the start of his sniper attack. By the time Whitman began shooting the scheduled class change had just ended, leaving far fewer targets visible below him. His body count would certainly have escalated were he not hindered by killing the three victims in the tower.

Why did this melancholy former marine reach the breaking point? Consumed by personal failures, financial troubles, and hatred for his father, Whitman had begun to fantasize about shooting people from the

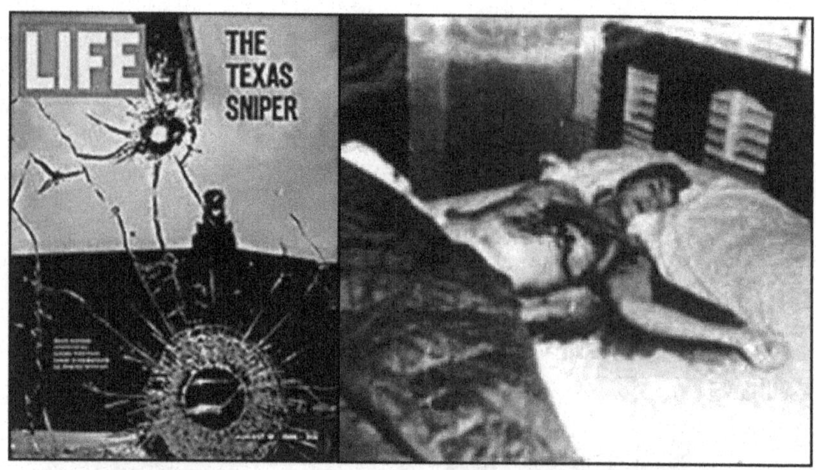

By the time Whitman barricaded himself on the tower observation deck, he had already killed his mother and his wife (right).

tower the previous April, when he told a psychiatrist about his twisted vision of becoming a sniper.

All he needed was a catalyst. The final push over the edge.

So he killed his mother Margaret and his wife Kathy, both of whom he loved dearly. In his misshapen mind, he was eliminating the pain and retribution that his bloody Armageddon would surely cause them...

August 2nd – 12th

In early August, an article in *Datebook Magazine* exploded into a national furor. Everyone from teeny boppers to grandparents was talking about the profane remarks made by Beatle John Lennon.

Quoting an interview he gave to the British press in March, stunned readers read this statement from the Fab Four's leader:

> **Christianity will go. It will vanish and shrink. I needn't argue about that; I'm right and I'll be proved right. We're more popular than Jesus now; I don't know which will go first – rock 'n' roll or Christianity...**

Datebook printed this quote on the cover of its August issue, and controversy quickly erupted, mostly in the Bible Belt states. Some southern radio stations banned Beatle music entirely, while others scheduled bonfires to burn Beatle records and pictures.

Local radio station WSAI, co-sponsor of the Beatles upcoming August 20th concert at Crosley field, said that they would keep playing Beatle records. One disc jockey speculated that Lennon's quote "was just an example of British satirical humor...I don't believe they meant the statement like it sounded. Most people who have met the Beatles have nothing but high praise for them."

They finally took the stage on Sunday August 21st, after the concert was cancelled the previous night due to a torrential downpour. Disappointed teens had thrown away their Saturday tickets only to see Lennon, in an amazing PR move, announce that they would come back to play the next day.

Beatles All Wet but They'll Be Back Today read the *Enquirer* headline, even though they had a show in St. Louis that night – this would be the only time they performed two concerts in different cities on the same day. The Cincinnati show went on, although most of their eleven song set was drowned out by the din of screaming teenage girls.

Eight days later the Beatles gave their final concert at Candlestick Park in San Francisco. George Harrison summed up their frustration with touring: "Our music is no longer being heard."

CARPOOLING TO WORK ON a sticky August Friday, it is doubtful Jerry Bricca had given the Beatles a moment's thought.

The following Wednesday Jerry and his family were flying to San Francisco for the wedding of his sister. With only three work days left until a three week vacation, the young engineer was consumed with numerous objectives he must accomplish before he could feel relaxed on the trip.

Jerry Bricca was an obsessive-compulsive before the term came into vogue. As a process engineer at the Monsanto plant, it was his job to be fixated with details. The guys in product development could be creative – but when you're responsible for insuring the means of production, belief in your own precision was paramount. To keep the factory humming, he was in pursuit of methods that were both cost effective and time efficient.

On this day Jerry was riding with another young engineer named Richard, who liked his colleague but didn't really know him. The strapping young man sitting next to him was friendly enough, but in other ways he was inscrutable, almost a sphinx.

Jerry mostly talked about work and seldom attended company social functions. He never talked about his home life, not even to complain as many Monsanto husbands did. Richard was surprised last year when Jerry first mentioned he had a daughter. But he did like to reminisce about his college days and the family hunting trips of his youth in California.

Richard glanced over at Jerry, who was chewing his lip and staring straight ahead. "So Monday's your last day before the trip?"

"We fly out noon Wednesday, so I'll probably come in Tuesday for a last walk through." Jerry frowned and looked out the window. "Those pipefitters Cannon hired are not getting the job done. I've to do it myself." He snorted in disgust.

Richard heard talk about Jerry's confrontation with Jim Cannon at the company picnic in July. These two guys never liked each other, yet they had been downright surly since then. And Cannon had been transferred to Jerry's department just last week.

"He still upset about the transfer?"

"I'm not sure why. He's in my old job now, but the money's the same and the hours are better. I think he was in love with his old job title – Supervisory Engineer. Like it gave him some status."

Richard nodded. "The way that guy treats women at the office. I can't decide whether he's a flirt or a clown. Funny thing is some of them seem to like it."

As they pulled into the Monsanto north parking lot, Jerry chose his words carefully. "He is relentlessly inappropriate." Richard's remark lingered as he entered his office. Cannon was incompetent and unsuitable, and he was making it tough on everybody.

Karen Campton and Ruth Bernard were standing near Jerry's cubicle chatting. It was just after 8 AM, and the technical secretaries, both in their late 20's, were savoring that final cup of coffee. Their jobs were challenging, and went far beyond the typical typing and filing of regular clerks. They did a fair share of technical groundwork for the plant engineers.

Jerry stopped and wished them good morning. "Did either of you watch The Munsters last night? It was hilarious."

Karen started to nod and laugh, but Ruth just looked at him. "I don't get that show – can you explain it to me? Are they really monsters, or is it just a satire?"

Jerry smiled and changed the subject. "Has Jim Cannon been bothering either of you?" He cleared his throat and looked away. "And I don't mean with work."

Karen chuckled. "I've played putt-putt golf with him and his buddies a few times. He knows better than to try that stuff with me. Besides, he's just a harmless goof. Except when he's drinking."

Jerry blinked. "Well, just let me know if he does something that makes you uncomfortable."

Karen let out a hearty laugh. "Remember Pat Hay? Reddish-blonde, heavy-set, moved to West Virginia last year?" Well...he gave her a birthday present in front of everyone, and when she opened it there was some skimpy lingerie. She turned five shades of red while all the men busted out laughing. Someone said she went right to her supervisor and complained."

"What does his wife think of all this?" Ruth asked.

"Doesn't bother her anymore. They split." Karen looked at Jerry. "Don't take this the wrong way. He's a hopeless cad, but he's funny. He's a good mixer at these stuffy company parties."

Jerry merely frowned and sat down at his desk as Karen went over to her section. Ruth turned and smiled at Jerry, his face buried in a schematic drawing. She was two years younger than him, married with a young child. Her duties often took her to the lab, but there was no office space there so her cubicle had been next to Jerry's since last summer.

Ruth enjoyed admitting to herself that Jerry was handsome. She had a harmless crush on him, with something brotherly mixed in. She'd been warned about his temper but had yet to see it.

Most of all, she felt protected working near him. The man was no wimp – he was extremely well built, like a weight lifter. Yet even more than his obvious physical strength, Jerry possessed that aura of confidence combined with stability. And Ruth knew he had the goods to back it up.

In the suspicious, transforming and sometimes unbalanced world of 1966, Ruth understood that Jerry Bricca would always come out a winner...

Sunday, August 14th

"Someone call for a cab?"

Amid the drunken din of the Lark Café, Barbara Bowman heard the voice, picked up her purse and wobbled off the bar stool. It was 2:00 AM Sunday morning, and she had reached her limit of alcohol and the money to pay for it.

Ray and a few of the regulars begged her to stay. Barbara was the only single female left at the bar, and at age 31 was both attractive and shapely. Not to mention tipsy. She gazed at the blurred, eager faces of her horny drinking buddies, waved goodbye, and followed the cabby to the curb.

Her black-rimmed glasses fogged up as she slid inside the humid cab. Rain was beginning to fall, and the shift from the smoky, raucous bar to the heavy, wet air and the dank vehicle was disorienting. *Why did she have those last two drinks?*

Barbara murmured her address on Grand Place in Price Hill, and the young, black driver started the fare and rumbled his Yellow Cab away from the curb. He was thin with a wispy goatee, a beret slanting rakishly off the side of his head. She attempted some polite conversation as they left Clifton and headed for the viaduct to Price Hill, but he seemed occupied with the dispatcher.

Then he looked in the rear view mirror and they briefly locked eyes. He had a sly, unsettling way of peering at her, similar to some other men she had encountered. As if they knew something about her.

She lay back on the seat, closed her eyes, and retreated into a dreamlike state. As the cab travelled toward the West Side, Barbara Bowman felt secure in her metal cocoon, shielded from the drizzling darkness.

She thought about going back to work Monday, riding that ordinary bus among the dreary little women on their daily missions. They wore their morality like righteous beggars, judging her when they had no right. Yet she was a woman just as they were – and they all shared a destiny against which virtue was no protection.

As she began to doze on the sour smelling leather seat, her last thought was that she shouldn't drink so much.

A block away from her apartment the cab took a sickening swerve and jolted her awake. She smelled the bitter, sweaty odor of the driver as he crawled over the front seat and enveloped her. She felt the rope

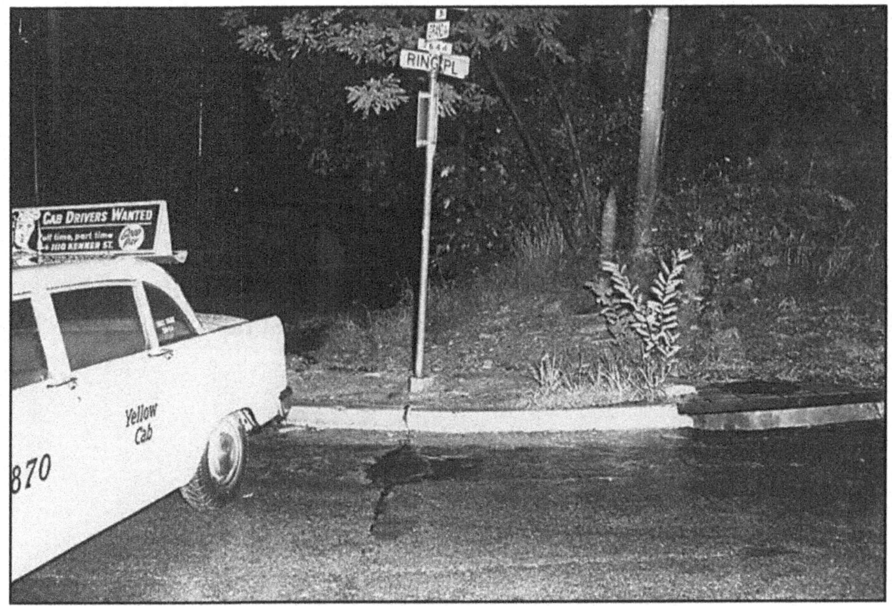

The taxi driver ran over a fleeing Barbara Bowman and then stabbed her to death by the sewer grate.

around her neck, and heard the pelting rain as darkness washed over her.

Was she dreaming? From somewhere far away she heard a woman's voice. "Can you tell us how to get to Sunset?" Barbara rose up in the back seat, like breaking the surface moments before drowning, and gulped the air. She saw two women in another car staring at her as they drove away.

The driver ignored them, crawled back into the front seat and started the cab. Dazed and disjointed, Barbara Bowman mashed the door handle down, tumbled out onto the wet pavement, and began staggering away from the cab toward Ring Place. If she could just turn that corner she knew there were friendly houses to rescue her.

Running now, she frantically ditched her high heels and tossed her purse and glasses along the road. The rain was coming down in sheets. Stumbling, she groped her way toward the warm lights.

But the cab had turned around and was bearing down on her! Barbara tried to scream, but her throat was raw and closed. As she reached the intersection, the cab was looming behind her.

She managed a final croak of "help" as she hopped onto the curb, but the demonic car lurched off the road and mowed her down. Barbara heard her right ankle snap, but felt no pain as she fell across the sewer grate at the corner of Ring and Grand.

The cab stopped a few feet past her. Barbara felt the warm rain on her face, and had a fleeting thought about the child she gave up so long ago. Her daughter would be 13 now – was she happy?

Her final vision was of the cab driver with the knife. As he hovered over her, she felt the rain wash away her fears, just before the drenching August night closed down upon her...

Linda Bulaw became a stewardess for United Airlines in April 1961 and met Jerry Bricca three months later.

CHAPTER THREE

CHERISH IS THE WORD

"They are not long, the days of wine and roses."

Ernest Dowson

AUGUST 15TH - SEPTEMBER 18TH 1966

August 17th

Dolores Bricca ignored the chatter around the dinner table and concentrated on her daughter-in-law Linda. There had been much discussion in her household about Jerry's marriage to his beautiful, headstrong wife, especially during Linda's "vacation" in Florida.

Dolores had raised her eldest child to be a free thinker who stood up for himself. Yet during her Cincinnati visit in April, she saw the change in Jerry. Perhaps the separation had finally cowed him, because now he let Linda do whatever she wanted and rarely spoke up about it. Dolores tried to ignore it – both of them were blithely green at life, so why should marriage be any different?

Her husband Elmer was giving an expansive welcome to the whole family, as plates were passed around amidst polite laughter. Her daughter Joan was to be married on the 27th, and Dolores was gratified to have all four of her children together again in San Francisco. But as she gazed at Linda across the table Dolores could see trouble brewing.

And there it was. During a lull, little Debbie began to speak, and Linda held her finger to her lips so her daughter could command everyone's attention. She was an articulate child, and now she babbled on gaily about something their dogs did before they left for the trip. Linda had indulged her before with no protests from Jerry, and Debbie would expect everyone to listen to her.

Elmer cleared his throat loudly, and directed his remarks to Linda. "At my dinner table, the adults will do the talking and the children will speak only when spoken to." It was a rule they had abided by growing up, and Dr. Bricca was still a stickler about it.

"Don't you think that's being rude?" Linda glanced at Jerry sitting there, his face no longer beaming. Everyone else was suddenly intent on their plates with frightened neutrality. Debbie looked at her mother, clearly confused.

"Children should be seen and not heard." For Elmer, this closed the discussion.

"Don't give me your tired platitudes!" Linda's large eyes flashed and her nostrils flared. "This isn't the 1940's anymore. If Debbie has something to say, then what's the harm?"

"What you do in your home is your business." Dr. Bricca's voice frosted over with icy calm. "We do things a bit differently out here."

"I thought I was a guest in your home?" Without another word she left the table and stalked out of the room.

By the time dessert was served Linda returned and apologized. Yet another dark cloud hovered. Dr. Bricca and his sons were talking about the hunting lodge, and Dolores braced herself for an outburst. Jerry tried to flank it, saying he and Linda were not going on the family hunting trip because she did not like to see animals hurt. Linda's eyes were darting at the mere mention of it.

Dr. Bricca put down his fork with some emphasis, and addressed his eldest son. "Gerald, the caretaker at the lodge has always been very fond of you. He told me last week he was looking forward to seeing you. Look, you are out here for your sister's wedding and she wants you to go hunting with us, just like we did when you were boys. This is a family tradition, after all."

Linda started to speak, looked at Jerry and stayed silent. Dr. Bricca smiled for the first time. "As our guest, we are willing to go three-quarters of the way to meet your wishes. Perhaps to keep harmony you could go the other quarter to meet us."

Linda squinted at his math. "For me to condone the killing of helpless animals is way more than one fourth of a compromise." She rose from the table, and Jerry followed her into the living room. Everyone at the table could hear their vehement whispers.

A few minutes later they came back. Linda spoke in a tremulous voice. "Since I will NOT participate in the hunting, it won't hurt me if

Elmer and Dolores Bricca (right) were all smiles at Jerry and Linda's wedding, but there was friction during the San Francisco trip.

Jerry goes." She seemed on the verge of tears. "I won't stand in the way of Jerry enjoying his family tradition – one last time."

There were after dinner drinks, and Joan regaled everyone with niceties about her wedding just a week away. Jerry's siblings eventually left, and he, Linda and Elmer retired for the night.

Dolores sat in her living room as the house quieted down. Like she often did while alone, she pulled out their family photo albums and reminisced.

Her children were growing up and away from her. Jerry was married five years now and in Cincinnati for three. Robert had been married more than a year, and his wife was expecting their first child in October. Joan was to wed Stephen Freeman next Saturday, and Elmer Jr. was keeping company with a lovely girl named Barbara. Dolores Bricca was certain that their nuptials would be planned for next year.

She realized these old photographs were her lifeblood. And the older she got, the more attuned she became to those visual cues in the fading images. She could travel back in time to when the memory was born, recalling the sights, sounds, and smells, the little things one took for granted, drifting back there in the mists.

Dolores paused on a casual snapshot of Linda and Jerry from the brief time they were dating. Jerry wore his usual broad smile, but Linda seemed to be pouting. Their hurried marriage a few months later had unsettled everyone. Although they sported a façade of happiness, she and Elmer were in the dark about their married life in Cincinnati.

Dolores Bricca gazed once more at the frozen image of her future daughter-in-law, and came to a stark realization. "I don't know anything about her," she whispered into the empty room...

August 18th – 20th

The Cincinnati Strangler had struck again. Or had he?

Four days after Barbara Bowman was slain, a crime the *Enquirer* called "the most bizarre in city history", detectives were confounded by the case they caught in the early morning hours of August 14th. Despite a wealth of physical evidence and several eyewitnesses, the investigation was stalled.

The irony was burning Jake Schott. The killer had left both murder weapons at the scene – the knife and the stranded cab with a broken trans-axle sustained when Bowman was run over. There was a report from the Yellow Cab Company that a car was stolen from their West End lot, and the disabled metal hunk at the corner of Ring and Grand was indeed that vehicle.

The victim's movements on the night of her death were bookended. Her downstairs neighbor shared a drink with her at 7 PM in her apartment on Warsaw Avenue, before Barbara heard a honk and ran out to a car driven by a young couple. Less than eight hours later she lay dying in a rain swept gutter a block away from the china cats and leafy ferns adorning her modest dwelling.

Investigators were favored with a well-documented timeline between those two events. From 8 PM to 2 AM she was perched on a stool at the Lark Café in Clifton, a neighborhood bar owned by former Cincinnati Red's player Clyde Vollmer. Barbara was popular there, and many of the regulars saw her that night. The 31-year-old secretary was sitting with her two friends and being plied with drinks by men milling around the bar area.

Killer's Methods Called Most Bizarre In City History

BY DAVE HOOD
Of The Enquirer Staff

The usual quiet of Sunday was shattered in the neighborhood of Grand Avenue and Ring Place, Price Hill—and it was the same in the area of 2909 Warsaw Ave—where, suddenly and without warning, vicious and violent death had occurred in the rainy hours before dawn.

her, either by name or physical description.

Police considered the manner of Miss Bowman's murder to have been the most bizarre and complex within the memory of veteran officers.

Strangulation, or an attempt at it . . . multiple fractures inflicted when she

they still do not know where the woman entered the cab.

And as the investigation was pressed, police believed they had new cause to dig in: "Col. Jacob Schott, Chief of Detectives, said a taxicab driver had reported he had picked up a young Negro "out of breath, nervous, and in a hurry" as the driver returned from Price

The city had never dealt with a crime quite like the "hit and run" stabbing of 31-year-old Barbara Bowman.

Just after 2:00 a short black man entered the café and called out "Cab!" Barbara was seen leaving by the front door and entering the cab – witnesses said she was only mildly intoxicated.

According to his radio transmissions, the driver went west on McMillan and then crossed the Western Hills Viaduct. He turned south on State Street and paralleled the Mill Creek until arriving on Warsaw Avenue. At that time of night detectives calculated it to be a 15 minute drive.

After going past her stop the driver attacked Bowman around 2:20. She broke away and ran toward Ring Place. Her glasses, purse, and shoes were strewn along Grand Avenue, mute testament to her desperate dash from the cab, which careened after her and ran her down, shattering her right ankle. As Barbara lay helpless in the pelting rain, the driver jumped out and stabbed her seven times in the neck.

His stolen cab immobilized, the killer ran up Ring Place, ditching more evidence along the way. A neighborhood resident found the dying victim at 2:30, minutes after the killer had finished her off.

Just before 3 AM, a drenched and breathless black man hailed a cab about a mile from the crime scene. This driver, also black, was suspicious of his agitated fare and feared he might be robbed. The passenger had scooted over so he could not be seen in the rear view mirror, rasping

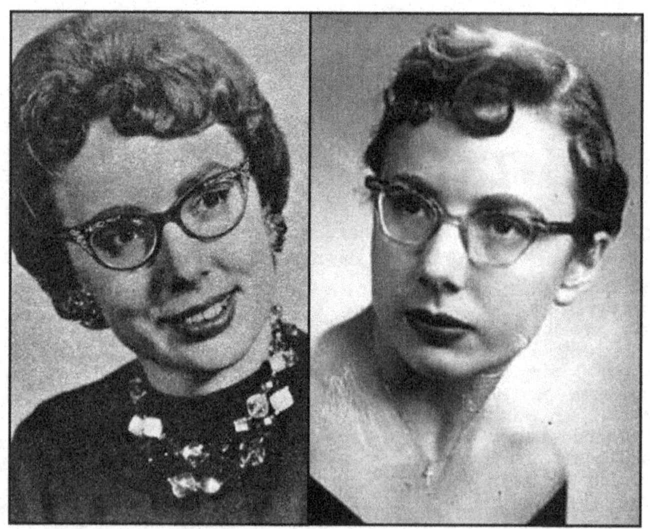

The papers could not reconcile Barbara's sweet high school image (left) with the single adult woman drinking in a bar until 2 AM.

that he wanted to go to Brighton corner. Yet the strange man jumped out before his stop, throwing two soaked $1 bills to the driver.

And there the trail ended...

A COMPOSITE DRAWING OF THE suspect was making the rounds without any hits, and the aggressive roundup of short, slender black cab drivers had netted nothing but the ire of local civil rights groups.

Yet protests of racial profiling went unheard, given the rising anxiety felt by Queen City residents. Barbara Bowman was the fourth victim since December 1965, and the first three murders had been linked to a single killer. As summer waned, Cincinnati was in the thrall of an unknown fiend, just like Boston three years before.

CPD detectives were split on linking this latest slaying to their killer. Bowman was much younger than the previous victims, and she had not been sexually assaulted. This killer's "bizarre" methods did not fit the strangler's pattern of blitz style attacks.

Sgt. Russ Jackson learned that the bootleg driver had called Yellow Cab dispatch and picked up legitimate fares – Barbara Bowman was his ninth. Other passengers gave the same description as the Lark patrons – a small, thin black man in his late 20's. Jackson was amazed that their suspect was willing to show himself to other riders and the regulars at the café.

Their unidentified driver matched the description of the man who attacked Liz Kreco the previous October. And Barbara's killer did attempt to choke her with a knotted piece of cord found in the taxi's back seat. In their final evaluation, investigators linked Barbara Bowman with the other three victims.

But the press pointed out that their grisly deaths were all they had in common. Unlike matronly mothers Emogene Harrington, Lois Dant, and Jeannette Messer, Barbara was a single woman who apparently put herself in harm's way. Drinking in a male dominated bar at 2 AM on a Sunday morning, the young secretary's lifestyle did not merit sympathy from the parochial Queen City of1966.

Despite her reputation as a quiet, religious girl, there were rumors that she was sexually promiscuous and had given birth to an illegitimate child in high school.

In an interview with the *Enquirer*, her landlord jumped to her defense. "She was a conservative girl," explained Cliff Sizer. "She never missed a week's rent, and she was a very desirable tenant – clean, neat and a nice person. She went to church twice a week, even while working a full-time job."

Sizer wept recalling the dark haired girl with the big glasses. "She was a very lonely person. She just wanted some affection."

August 26th

Linda Bricca stood naked in front of the mirror in her in-law's spacious San Francisco home.

Jerry was out with his parents and siblings – Linda had not been invited. She knew only the immediate family was taking Joan to lunch, for her last time as a single woman. Linda was looking forward to tonight's rehearsal dinner.

But she was upset about a change in their sleeping arrangements. With more out of town guests arriving, Jerry informed her they would have to stay at his aunt's house for several days, starting tonight. Linda fumed but said nothing. Now she desperately needed some time to herself.

At 5-5 and 125 pounds, Linda would be the envy of any young housewife. But she was still retaining fluids in her legs, and had avoided wearing shorts on this trip, despite the warm bay area weather. Except for Linda, no one else would think her legs were anything but shapely.

Linda gazed at her 23-year-old body, grimacing at the faint stretch marks. *What was she thinking, getting pregnant so young?* This was not the course she had planned for her life.

She had enjoyed the stewardess life – especially the stopovers in New York City. But meeting Jerry on a flight changed all that. He had invited her to a party at his apartment house in Seattle where he lived with some male grad students. Linda took some other stewardesses with her, and they all had a great time. Suddenly, Linda had redirected her life into Jerry's world.

She hadn't counted on getting pregnant so quickly.

When she told Jerry, Linda made it clear that she would not force him into marriage. She was adamant about it, because she was unsure about Jerry. They already had sexual problems just three months into the relationship. Yet Jerry swore that he loved her, and proposed marriage that very moment.

She turned sideways to the mirror and felt her belly. Her period was overdue by several weeks – in her mind she was officially "late". It had happened twice this year without consequence. Linda smiled ruefully at her reflection: *Third time the charm?*

She didn't want another child, or so she thought. Perhaps she just didn't want another child in Cincinnati?

She had grown to hate living with Jerry in that Midwestern burg, and their relationship was teetering. Perhaps a change of scenery would make all the difference? He was interviewing for that job at Standard Oil next week, after the wedding. She found herself excited by the prospect. Could they make it here in San Francisco?

She ran her hands over her abdomen. Should she tell him now?

Better to wait until after the wedding. Linda didn't want to upstage Joan right before the biggest day of her life...

JERRY'S MIND WAS WANDERING while at lunch with his family. The restaurant was noisy, and he strained to hear Joan and his brothers talking about tomorrow's big day. As he looked down at his plate, he caught his mother staring at him.

Jerry Bricca's smiling personality and pensive mood as captured during his Stanford days.

What to do about Linda? One minute playfully carefree, the next darkly tempestuous. She was always a bit erratic, but it was flaring up on this trip.

After Linda's argument with his father at the arrival dinner last week, his younger brothers cornered him for "the talk." Robert and Elmer Jr. had always looked up to Jerry, giving their words even more weight now. Neither could understand why he allowed Linda to do whatever she wanted. Robert reminded Jerry that "you always had a mind of your own."

Elmer went even further, at one point shouting "How can you let her walk on you like this? You were never like this when you were living at home."

Mrs. Bricca asked Jerry if his food was all right, and he made a show of picking at it. Linda's extended Florida stay that spring had not fooled his mother. Shortly after his wife returned home Dolores Bricca had made the trip out to Cincinnati and stayed for a week.

She later confided to Jerry that she was shocked by just how little of substance they had. "You have a good job with a nice income," she had scolded him out of Linda's earshot. "I can't understand what you two do with all your money. Why are you always broke?"

Jerry gave her the same refrain. "Linda spends a lot of money on our pets and their care. She also donates to animal shelters."

One embarrassing afternoon his mother took him to a men's store and bought him a new suit. Dolores was appalled that his best one was two years old and no longer fit her strapping son. They came back with Jerry wearing the new suit – Linda bestowed a polite roll of her eyes but said nothing.

Jerry knew his family's concerns with his wife were not his biggest problem. Their marriage was in trouble for three reasons.

His medication had unpleasant side effects – it created painful sexual issues for him and Linda was turned off even talking about it. He was privately considering ditching the pills.

Her friendship with the people at the vet clinic was another obstacle, specifically her relationship with the head doctor. Now she was talking about going to work there. But if he landed the Standard Oil job that would be easily settled when they moved back San Francisco.

The third challenge was hurtful and cruel, and Jerry had a few sleepless nights over it. Because just before their trip, Linda had told him she did NOT want any more children...

August 27th

As Chief Schrotel walked out of the squad room, detectives seated at the conference table seemed to exhale as one. Cigarettes glowed with the big guy gone, and the 11 by 22 foot colorless room closed down on them again. It was smallish for sixteen cops, but its importance could not be measured.

Rumors were on the wing about Schrotel. A man of his stature would always be a candidate for a high profile career in a larger city – scuttlebutt had the chief up for the top jobs in Chicago and Philadelphia. Schrotel's friendship with Hoover prompted others to speculate he was in line for something big at the FBI.

Sgt. Russ Jackson wasn't buying it – there was no way the chief would abandon Cincinnati with a killer on the prowl and the force stretched so thin. He looked around at the tired Saturday morning faces, seasoned homicide investigators facing a challenge with no guidelines. Every man there recognized that they were up against a cunning criminal who moved like a phantom.

Jake Schott allowed himself an ashen smile. "You heard the man. Asses and elbows. Let's try to be the elbows this time."

"Was the chief serious about the whistles," someone asked, referencing Schrotel's deal with the Kroger Company to hand out 10,000 whistles to women customers. "How can they blow a whistle when they're being strangled?"

Jackson stifled any laughter. "It can't hurt. When Jack the Ripper was killing in London all the officers carried whistles."

Schott turned the briefing over to Jackson who checked off the action items from that week. The *Enquirer* police reporter was allowed in at this point. George Lecky was working on a feature, and the "Strangler" was the only game in town.

While the lack of evidence in the three rape-strangulations was challenging, the wealth of it in the Bowman case was cause for optimism. Eugene Moore repeated that they had the murder knife, the taxi cab, and a dozen witnesses.

Cab #870 had been stolen from the Yellow Cab lot on Kenner around 10 PM – their keys would work in all the vehicles. Barbara's killer was also familiar with driver procedure and radio operations, as he was able to "short-stop" calls by radioing the dispatcher and saying he would "take all calls in his vicinity."

Although the quality was poor, a tape recording of the driver's dialogue with the dispatcher was a significant clue. He was heard responding with call number "186" while picking up eight fares before Bowman at the Lark. Jackson had contacted an acoustical engineer at a New Jersey lab to analyze the tape with a "voice spectrogram" of their killer for comparison to any suspects.

A list was compiled of over 150 former cab drivers who were black, ages 25-40, short and slightly built. Special attention was paid to those with criminal records, and scores of them were being hauled in for lineups. Schrotel had warned them civil rights groups were watching these dragnets of "suspicious" black men closely.

Yet so far they had zilch, and Jackson was concerned about discrepancies in the suspect's description. There was no agreement on how he was dressed, and there was confusion over whether he had facial hair.

Most disappointing were two women who had actually interrupted the attack on Bowman by asking the driver for directions. Jackson looked at them askance – married women with husbands in Vietnam looking for

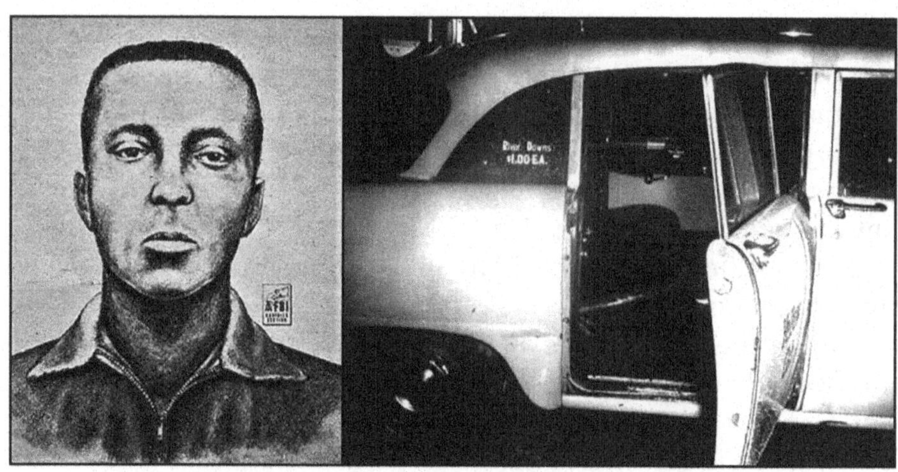

An FBI artist made this composite sketch of the cab driver who picked up Barbara Bowman and attacked her in this back seat.

a party at 2:30 AM Sunday morning? They claimed the darkness and the rain had hindered their vision, yet he felt they were holding back. Several times they asked to make sure their names were not in the papers.

Schrotel had called in a favor with the FBI, who sent their top sketch artist to Cincinnati. His composite drawing had been circulated in the Brighton Corner area of the West End, where the soaked passenger picked up near the Bowman murder was last seen by the Parkway cab driver.

The reporter asked for an update on the August 24th attack on a Corryville woman. The 35-year-old mother had just returned to her Mulberry Street home and was folding laundry when a man burst into the room, picked up her clothesline from the floor and began to choke her with it. She bit the intruder on the chest several times and kicked him before passing out.

"Was this the Strangler?" George Lecky wanted to know.

"She's given us two different descriptions," Jackson sighed. "First he was a short, slightly built, black man, but older than our suspect. "Yesterday she claimed he was younger but taller, like 6-3, which doesn't match our guy either."

"What about the clothesline?"

"The garrote was improvised, just like our three murders. But this attack was nothing like Harrington, Dant, or Messer. I don't think this is our guy."

"Well, do you have a good suspect? Lecky's question was hopeful. "Our readers want to know."

"We are working on the case daily, but the older it gets the fewer leads we have." Jackson replied. "Some leads just fade, others are from crackpots."

"Come on, Russ. Give me something."

Jackson picked up the printout of the 150 black ex-cab drivers. "I won't comment on the Strangler cases at this time." He paused, choosing his words for maximum effect. "But I'd stake my career that Barbara Bowman's killer is on this list."

August 27th

Marilyn Norton was enjoying the wedding reception for Jerry's sister and her new husband. The after party was in full swing with over two hundred friends and relatives attending. There was music and dancing – the song "Cherish" by the Association was climbing the charts, and was now playing a slow dance as couples relaxed from the celebratory music played earlier.

Marilyn was Jerry's first cousin and had known him since they were kids growing up in San Francisco. They were the same age and had always been close – she had no brothers of her own, and Cousin Jerry was the next best thing.

Sipping a white wine, Marilyn's thoughts turned to Jerry's wife. Everyone had noticed Linda earlier on the dance floor, boogying to the Supremes' "You Can't Hurry Love", currently the number one song in the country. Her dancing could be a bit wild, especially when she was a little soused.

Marilyn was still pondering what Linda told her earlier after swearing her to strictest confidence. Apparently her period was overdue and she might be pregnant.

Linda insisted having another child was Jerry's idea. "My enthusiasm certainly doesn't match his," she confided. Debbie had come so early. Now Linda wanted to explore her passion for animals, and "another child this soon would be too much." For Marilyn, it was an extraordinary conversation.

Yet watching Linda dancing, she looked like a stick compared to the other wives. If she was pregnant it sure wasn't showing.

Based on family rumblings since Linda's Florida "vacation", Marilyn wondered just how often they were intimate. Several years ago Linda told her about being treated for frigidity – somehow she and Jerry were not "compatible" in the bedroom.

Marilyn thought back to 1961, when Jerry was working in Seattle while living in an apartment complex populated with young college graduates. His July letter spoke of meeting a "beautiful woman named Linda" who had been dating some of the other "boys" who lived there and attending the weekend parties. Now the other guys were upset with Jerry, because he had "wound up with Linda."

Then there was his abrupt marriage. The family was aware of Linda's pregnancy and how morning sickness had ended her airline job. Soon she was living with Jerry as a 19-year-old wife and mother, in a neighborhood where all the other housewives were in their mid-30s. The theme of her loneliness was pervasive.

Marilyn recalled that strange visit four months after Debbie was born. She and her husband were on their honeymoon in the Pacific Northwest, and had stopped in one day to visit Jerry and Linda at their Seattle home.

The mood was weird from the moment they arrived, as if they had walked into the middle of something. Linda and Jerry seemed ill at ease, and soon Linda became extremely uncomfortable. When they asked to see the baby, a look of alarm crossed her face. She wouldn't let them go into the bedroom and refused to bring the baby out. Marilyn became exasperated while Jerry remained silent.

Linda finally said they could go out the front door, walk to the rear of the house and look through the bedroom window at her. Marilyn gave Jerry an incredulous look. They humored Linda and went to view the baby from the window, leaving shortly thereafter.

Linda was still on the dance floor, this time with Jerry. Marilyn thought her behavior seemed out of character – the way she clung to him, as if she was afraid to let him out of her sight.

But with others on this trip Linda acted cold and aloof. People chalked it up to her being shy, but Marilyn could see through that ploy. Linda was just bored with everyone in San Francisco. She felt superior to other people and was dismayed when she was not treated as someone special. Marilyn knew that Linda had an upper-middle class upbringing, but she had married into the equally well-to-do family of Dr. Elmer Bricca.

She noticed the changes in Jerry this time. He had always been o outgoing, enjoying parties with his circle of friends, an engaging talker who truly enjoyed interacting with different people. Marilyn's mother had remarked to her several days ago that her nephew's personality changed drastically when Linda was in the room.

Marilyn agreed. When Linda left Jerry by himself, he became talkative and jovial – like the Jerry she used to know. When she returned he would withdraw and become strangely quiet.

When Marilyn asked Jerry about their social life back in Cincinnati, he admitted sheepishly that they "did not go out very often, and rarely had company." He gave the excuse that "Linda was sick quite a bit" and would "always complain about bad headaches." Jerry whispered that "she has to lay down a lot."

Her reverie was disturbed as Jerry and Linda plopped down at her table. They were flushed from the energetic dancing, and Jerry had downed at least four mixed drinks since the reception started. They looked like the picture of happiness, and Marilyn's heart softened toward Linda.

"Cousin Jerry?" she asked in mock seriousness. "Wouldn't it be nice if you moved back to San Francisco with Linda and Debbie?"

"I'd love to come back," he replied earnestly. "I'm interviewing next week with Standard Oil for a job here."

"That's wonderful!" Marilyn gushed. "How do you feel about that, Linda?"

It was a dangerous question. Their marriage was in jeopardy from the events of earlier this year. And Linda was known to be candid about her discontentment.

"I wouldn't mind at all," she replied, tossing her raven hair. "I would like living out here in California."

Marilyn looked at her in mild amazement, but Jerry did a complete double take. He immediately peppered her with startled questions. "Since when did you want to move to San Francisco?"

Marilyn had a fleeting thought – *she hasn't told him about her pregnancy worries.*

Jerry now seemed completely sober as he clasped her hand in his. "Why have you never told me this before?

August 29th

It was a soggy Monday afternoon, and the Cincinnati Homicide Squad was at the crossroads in the Bowman investigation. Two weeks after

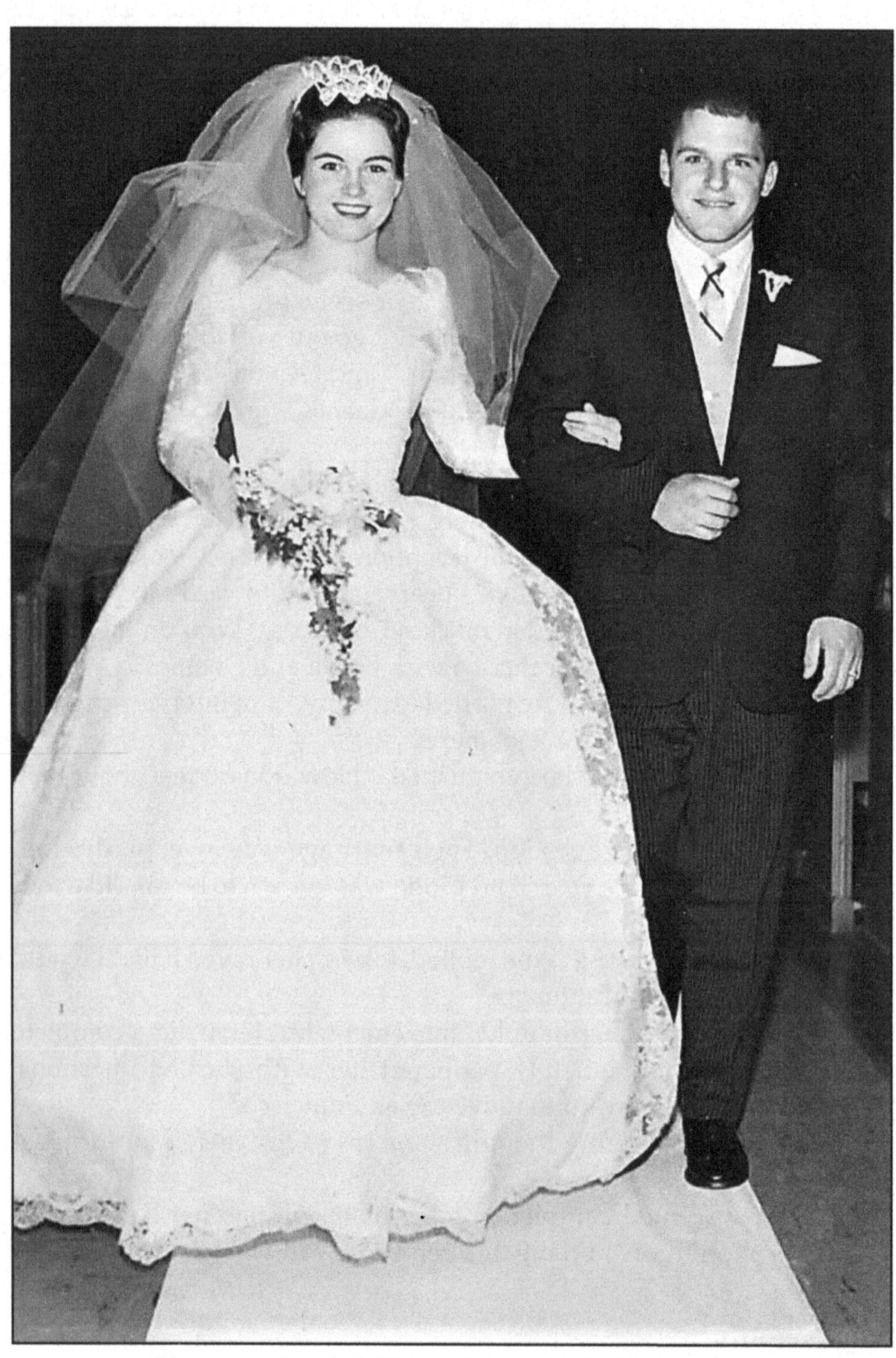

Linda was already 2-1/2 months pregnant when she and Jerry married in Chicago on November 25th, 1961.

the young secretary was mowed down with a stolen cab and stabbed to death in a rain swollen gutter, their case was crashing against the rocks.

Jackson and Moore were candid with Jake Schott. The three strangulation-murders had gone cold. Manpower was being transferred to Bowman – now their best chance to nab the killer.

They had kept some details from the press, a standard practice to weed out false confessions. There was a strangulation attempt in the cab – the coroner found ligature marks around her neck. The killer first tried with Barbara's necklace, which broke, before using a piece of cord to throttle her. The cord was recovered in the cab, and its uncommon design made it a valuable clue.

Media coverage gave readers the idea that detectives were reluctant to connect Bowman with the other three murders. But inside the cramped, smoky air of the squad room, there was no doubt. Barbara's killer was the man they had been looking for since December, and they were certain he would kill again.

Going over old ground in the Bowman case, Jackson and Moore kept coming back to two witnesses. Cab driver Sol Thompson had picked up a shady, rain-soaked man in lower Price Hill about 45 minutes after the murder. And Eileen Aultz interrupted the attack on Bowman by stopping to ask the cab driver for directions. After taking their statements the morning of August 15th, today Jackson sent Detective Rutledge out to interview them one more time.

Mrs. Aultz was reluctant to get involved from the start. She and her girlfriend Charlotte were young, bored housewives with soldier husbands in Vietnam. After some casual barhopping, they were out cruising for a party a friend had told them about. Now they were key witnesses in a high profile murder investigation.

With Charlotte driving and rain pouring down, about 2:15 AM they pulled up alongside a cab stopped on Grand Avenue about a half mile north of Warsaw, facing south in the northbound lane. When Aultz asked directions, she was no more than three feet away from the passenger side of the cab.

Q: What did you see?
A: Well, we saw this colored man in the back seat, sort of laying down.
Q: What did you say?
A: We asked where this street was, but he didn't answer.

Q: What did he do?
A: He climbed into the front seat, and as he got up I noticed this girl rise up from the back and I said to Charlotte, "My God, that's a white woman!"
Q: Was there a light on in the cab?
A: The cab was completely dark.
Q: You saw the white girl sit up...did she have her eyes open?
A: I couldn't tell. I never saw her face.
Q: Was she screaming or making any noise?
A: No. Then I saw her go back down.
Q: Did the driver ever look at you?
A: No, not directly. He looked frightened.
Q: He was laying down before he climbed over the seat?
A: Yeah, like he had been on top of the woman.
Q: Would you be able to recognize him again if you saw him.
A: I'm not sure.

Further questioning revealed that the women drove back up Grand Avenue "about 15 minutes later" and saw a police car parked near the cab sitting at the Ring Place intersection. They assumed the couple "had been caught." They drove on unaware that Barbara Bowman was dying in the gutter...

CAB DRIVER SOLOMON THOMPSON'S second interview was visual – detectives brought a photo lineup of likely suspects.

They had crosschecked them against a list of short, slightly built Yellow Cab drivers discharged in the last five years whose names were marked "not to be rehired for any reason." Then they asked the dispatchers to listen to the tapes of the bootleg driver and pick likely suspects from the list.

Meeting at Thompson's West End home, Rutledge was impressed by the older black man's willingness to help. Before looking at the photos, they reviewed his statement about his strange passenger the night Bowman was killed.

In an astounding coincidence, Rutledge learned Thompson had taken a fare to Price Hill and driven right past the disabled cab on Grand Avenue. Doubling back, he was flagged down by a policeman at Ring Place.

Thompson checked the cab for a trip sheet but couldn't find it. He called on the radio for a Yellow supervisor, and left the scene around 2:55 AM.

Thompson dropped his next fare on Mistletoe Street at 3:15 AM. The rain was pouring now, and he heard a whistle. Seeing no one, as he stopped his cab the rear door opened and a "male Negro" got in. Thompson was instantly on guard. The man was "rough looking and drenched," skulking around an "all-white neighborhood." He asked to go to Baymiller Street in the West End, and tossed two soaked $1 bills on the front seat.

While crossing the Western Hills viaduct, Thompson asked the man to move over in the backseat "so I could keep an eye on him." When they got to Bank Street, his passenger saw a police car and jumped out – Thompson watched him run off between two houses.

Sol Thompson was an excellent witness. Jackson and Moore felt he might be the key to breaking the case. Now Rutledge pulled out six photographs from their profile. All these men had criminal records, some for assault and battery. He told Thompson to take his time, and pull out any photo that resembled the suspect.

He eliminated the first one as "too old" and the next as "too heavy". A third man "was not dark enough". But he liked the picture of Charles Edward Thomas, calling him "a strong look-alike". Thomas had a lengthy record of larceny arrests, yet Thompson stopped short of identifying him.

Sol looked at the last two pictures, and said they were "definitely not the man" in his cab that night. One was Alfred Walker.

The other one's name was hard to forget. Posteal Laskey, Jr...

August 30th

Jack Liljeberg leaned back in his chair and studied the earnest young man seated on the other side of his desk.

Jack was Vice President of Engineering at Standard Oil in San Francisco. In his early 40's, he liked being involved in the hiring process, especially when an exceptional candidate came along.

This square-jawed, crew-cut 28-year-old Stanford graduate before him fit the bill. Jerry Bricca had been with Monsanto since 1960, first in Seattle and then Cincinnati. His work history was excellent, showing upward progress in job titles – Liljeberg felt they must be grooming him for bigger things.

The department manager was impressed during the initial interview, and sent him up to the VP's office for an in-depth screening. Liljeberg had spent four hours with Bricca, giving him a plant tour and reviewing his qualifications.

"So why do you want to leave Monsanto?" Liljeberg always paid close attention to what a candidate said about his current employer.

"I grew up in San Francisco and my family still lives here. We agreed Cincinnati is not the best place for our family at this point in our lives." Jerry grinned. "We really need a change of scenery."

Liljeberg checked his notes. "All we have right now is one plant engineering job – same money you're making now. Of course, we have room for advancement and like to promote from within."

For the first time the young man frowned. "A lateral move won't work. I told my wife I'm NOT leaving Monsanto unless it's a step up." He kept his eyes fixed on the VP.

Liljeberg smiled. "We may have a good position for you in late October. In fact, I think it would be a better fit for your expertise. Can you wait until then?"

"Are you offering me the job?"

"It technically isn't available yet to offer," the VP replied. "There are some fine details to be worked out. But we are very impressed with your qualifications. If you can be patient, I' will have an offer of employment sent to you by October 1st." Liljeberg rose and extended his hand. "I trust my handshake will be good enough for now. And I hope you can wait that long."

The young engineer's smile returned as the two men shook hands. "No problem," beamed Jerry Bricca. "A month is not too long to wait for a whole new life."

George Fox and his wife Joyce lived about an hour south of San Francisco in Sunnyvale, and were delighted when Jerry and Linda drove down for dinner at their home. George and Jerry were fraternity brothers at Stanford and had stayed in touch since graduation. Also there were former fraternity mates and Sunnyvale residents Jerry Reinhart and Jack McCullough.

Jerry and Linda seemed happy together, yet Joyce found her aloof and withdrawn. George and Jerry were both engineers, often speaking in a technical dialect that Joyce found hard to decipher. Now the four men were talking a mix of current work problems and humorous college tales, and Joyce caught Linda stifling a yawn.

They first met four years ago, when Linda was still the blushing, teenage bride, yet Joyce was amazed at how little she had changed. She did not mix well with this dinner party group at all, still the shy, bored woman-child who had a hard time making friends. Joyce could not remember Linda ever mentioning any close girlfriends, either in Seattle or Cincinnati.

While the men chattered on she freshened her guest's cocktail. And after some light banter, Linda started to open up.

"Are your health issues improving?" Joyce was aware of Linda's repeated doctor visits.

"I think this is the best I've felt since we've been married." Linda showed a rare smile. "Jerry wants another child, and I finally feel like I'm physically ready for it."

"Are you getting used to Cincinnati?"

Linda gave her a perplexed look before the words came in a gush. "Jerry wants to move back here. We really don't like living in the Midwest. I hate our neighborhood – all our neighbors are older and I have nothing in common with them."

"Jerry should talk to George about getting on at his company. It's a great place to work. With George as a reference he would be hired for sure."

"Well, Jerry does like his job at Monsanto, and he likes the company." Linda gazed at Joyce and touched her hand. "He won't leave Cincinnati unless he can better himself."

As the evening wore on and the cocktails flowed, everyone was getting loose. Jerry Reinhart was almost as close with Jerry as George was, and he had seen Jerry and Linda several times in the past five years. Now as inebriated laughter filled the Fox living room, Reinhart took a long hard look at the beautiful wife of his former college chum.

There was no outward sign of problems, yet Reinhart thought they were having difficulties. He always compared other couples with his own stable marriage, and got the impression the Briccas were not as happy as they tried to make other people believe.

Around midnight, Linda seemed to come out of her shell. George asked about their pets back in Cincinnati, and Jerry's reticent wife

Jerry Bricca (2nd row left) and George Fox (2nd row right) were close friends and fraternity brothers at Stanford.

became animated while talking about their two dogs, launching into a tipsy monologue about pets she had growing up and circus animals she'd seen as a child. She even joked that she had run away to join the circus just to feed the animals.

At one point she glanced at Jerry, looking for a signal that she might be dominating the conversation with animal stories.

"Do you still go to the circus?" George Fox asked.

Linda gave Jerry a long look, and then returned George's smile. "I take good care of my furry babies." She took a long sip of her drink. "In fact, we have an extremely good vet back home."

Reinhart saw Jerry visibly react to this remark, and Linda quickly changed the subject. Yet the laughter vanished, and Reinhart sensed a profound change in attitude between them.

Within a few minutes Jerry stood up and announced that they were leaving...

September 5th – 12th

On September 5th, the hard-working city founded by German immigrants took a much deserved break to celebrate Labor Day – and to bid farewell to the tumultuous summer of 1966.

Against a national setting of war protests and race riots, the Queen City was confronting its own racial turmoil and a mysterious killer. With vacations spent and children returning to school, people in Cincinnati were looking to escape the culture shift that was sweeping both coasts.

In a year that had already seen cult hits *Batman* and *Dark Shadows* debut, the networks were rolling out promising new TV shows in September. The first episode of *Star Trek* would air on the 8th, followed by *The Green Hornet* and *The Time Tunnel* the next night. On September 12th America met *The Monkees*, while spy thriller *Mission: Impossible* launched on the 17th.

It was another golden age of American television. *Bonanza* was the top rated show, followed by *Gomer Pyle, The Lucy Show, Andy Griffith,* and *Batman*. Quality dramas like *The Fugitive, Combat,* and *Peyton Place* were returning after several seasons and many devoted fans. This year also saw fan favorites like *The Donna Reed Show, Perry Mason,* and *The Dick Van Dyke Show* finish their successful runs.

The big screen had its share of diversions as well, with ticket prices averaging around $1.25.

Shockingly sensual movies like *Who's Afraid of Virginia Woolf* and *A Man and a Woman* challenged American sexual mores that summer, but the top grossing film of the year was *The Bible*. This Labor Day weekend *Fantastic Voyage* with comely Raquel Welch and *Alfie* with rakish Michael Caine were still riding high after their August 24th debuts.

The number one song that week was *You Can't Hurry Love* by the Supremes, followed by *Yellow Submarine, Sunshine Superman, See You in September,* and *Summer in the City*. *Cherish* checked in at number 14, on its way to being the top hit later in the month. Other songs with suggestive titles like *Wild Thing, Hanky Panky,* and *Lightning Strikes* were also getting steady radio play.

With gasoline hovering around 32 cents per gallon, the muscular Chevrolet Impala was the most popular car with sales topping one million vehicles, while the sporty Ford Mustang and the bulbous VW Beatle each sold about a half million. Average cost of a new car was $2,653 – no small expense considering average household income was $6,899 per year.

In sports, the Baltimore Orioles were rampaging through the American League on their way to winning the pennant and the World Series behind former Cincinnati slugger Frank Robinson, who won the AL Triple Crown

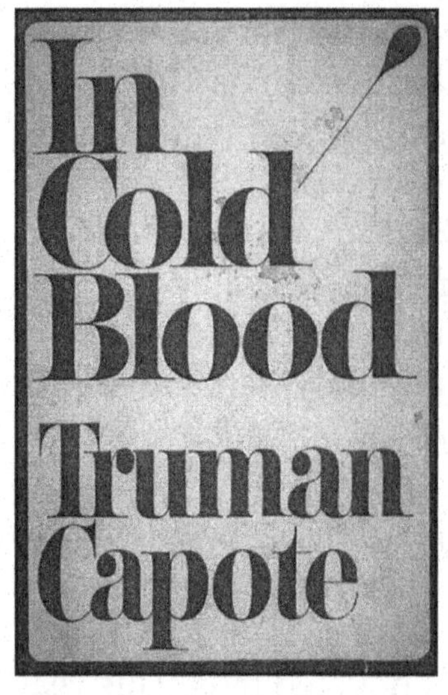

and proved that he was not "an old 30" when he was traded the previous December.

And in literature, Truman Capote's *In Cold Blood* would be serialized in the Cincinnati *Enquirer* beginning September 12th. This "non-fiction novel" genre bender chronicled the killing spree of two psychopathic drifters in 1959 Kansas. Capote blended the facts and reporting of a real murder case with eerie reenactments and the somber, moody tone of a fictional work.

Given the mood in Cincinnati, *Enquirer* editors must have debated not running a serialization about a family being murdered. They went ahead – within weeks they would regret it...

THERE WERE OTHER OMINOUS signs as summer ebbed. A recent Gallup poll identified racial problems as the biggest domestic issue facing the American people, overshadowing Vietnam, economic inflation, and the rising crime rate.

Race riots flickered throughout the Midwest around the Labor Day weekend. Just fifty miles north of Cincinnati, insurgence landed like a bomb in Dayton, Ohio. Police there eventually blocked all 12 bridges leading into the riot torn west end, snarling traffic on major Ohio highways.

A new voice was roaring from the radical wing of the civil rights movement, mostly silent since the assassination of Malcolm X in February, 1965. Stokley Carmichael had become chairman of the Student Nonviolent Coordinating Committee in May, and the 25-year-old former "Freedom Rider" was already a pivotal figure in the fledgling Black Power movement.

Unlike Martin Luther King, Carmichael considered nonviolence to be a tactic rather than an underlying principle, and he criticized civil rights leaders who called for the integration of black people into the white middle-class mainstream.

The September 5th *Enquirer* printed excerpts from his fiery speech the previous day in a Harlem church, and his militant views certainly upset many white residents reading their morning paper.

"This country is moving to destroy black people," he shouted to waves of applause. "WE cannot afford to be part of the American system. We have to destroy Western Civilization...this country is anti-black, and we must be against the things they're for."

Carmichael also called Vietnam "a filthy, racist war," and chided black people for abandoning their culture. "You are ashamed to get up and say that James Brown has more musical genius than Bach, Beethoven, and Mozart put together." He implored them to practice self-reliance and personal discipline, urging them to turn their backs on "government hand-outs."

"We don't want to take over this country," he exhorted the crowd. "We just want to get white people off our backs!"

None of his rhetoric was playing well in traditional, dignified Cincinnati. Especially when there appeared to be a black villain ravaging elderly white mothers...

IN THE CINCINNATI HOMICIDE squad room, a diminishing number of detectives were still pursuing Barbara Bowman's slayer, whom they believed had murdered three other women. Yet as each crime receded back into the calendar, manpower shifted back to the daily round of assaults, robberies, and property crimes.

On Wednesday September 7th, shock waves echoed through the Cincinnati Police division. Chief Stanley Schrotel announced he was retiring at 52 to work for the Kroger Company as director of security for their huge twenty state grocery store operation.

It was the right move for the ever logical Schrotel. Now he could collect his pension and his new salary in the private sector. It was a sweet deal for the man who molded the Cincinnati force into a model for competence and efficiency while becoming a national figure and a local icon.

An *Enquirer* editorial captured the civic pride mixed with sadness over losing such a stellar public servant: "It is part of the American tradition to believe that no man is indispensable...but Stanley Schrotel was as close as any man is apt to get. That this particular moment should have been chosen for his retirement is a genuine community misfortune...the only loser is the city of Cincinnati."

Speculation around the squad room had Jake Schott becoming chief. The tall, good-looking Schott had a John Wayne quality that could serve him well during this time of trouble in river city.

On Monday night September 12th, detectives caught a big break.

Mrs. Margaret McHone, a 25-year-old white woman, was returning to her Walnut Hills apartment with groceries when she was accosted by a young black man.

"Does someone named Curtis live here?" He looked to be in his early 20's, and seemed nervous.

"No, I don't know anybody of that name." When she turned away he grabbed her around the neck and clamped a hand over her mouth. He struck her several times while wrestling her to the floor. Screaming loudly, she managed to break loose as the man escaped out the front door of the building.

The Strangler detail rushed to the scene. Within minutes, officers arrested Arnold Eugene Hill sitting in his car two blocks away from the attack. Mrs. McHone identified him as her assailant, and Hill was booked for assault and battery.

With this arrest, the mood lightened in the squad room. Their Hall of Fame manager was leaving, but at least they were back in the ballgame.

Friday, September 16th

The Bricca family had returned from San Francisco just after Labor Day. Jerry was back working his exhaustive schedule at Monsanto, and Linda resumed her aimless existence as a housewife on Greenway Avenue.

Their marriage seemed to be a stacked deck with wild cards dealing. Had Jerry told Linda about his job offer? Had she told him about her possible pregnancy?

This morning Nettie Caudell stopped to chat with Linda as she puttered around the yard. Nettie had a genuine affection for her youthful neighbor. Linda was always nice to her and kept Debbie clean and well dressed, even if she was a bit of a perfectionist.

Unlike other wives on the street, Nettie did not believe Linda had a boyfriend. She seemed indifferent to men. Plus she was SO devoted to her animals – both dogs slept with her every night, probably at Jerry's expense on the living room sofa.

She never saw the young couple being affectionate. Nor did she see Linda ever pick up Debbie to hug or kiss her.

Nettie had learned to take Linda's stories with a grain of salt. She knew Linda didn't have two years of college, and didn't believe she once worked for a man who trained bears for the circus. Tales from her brief airline career sounded a bit self-serving. Linda once mentioned helping "break up a drug ring" during that time, but she refused to offer any details and Nettie had discounted it.

The women chatted pleasantly, and Linda gave Nettie some cursory details about the wedding in San Francisco before abruptly changing the subject.

"I want to get another dog. But Jerry wants to have another child before we get another dog." Linda looked at her for sympathy.

Nettie was taken aback and tried to deflect the tone. "You still have your parakeet, don't you?"

Linda scrunched her face. "She died right after we got back. I still can't understand why. I called the head vet at the Zoo about it – he's a parakeet expert. Did you know I worked for him while I was going to school?

Nettie smiled and nodded, wondering where this was going.

Linda gave her a solemn gaze. "If anything happened to Jerry or me, I wouldn't be concerned about Debbie being taken care of. But I would be worried about what happens to the dogs..."

ART NAGEL HAD NEVER seen Jerry Bricca so steamed.

The young engineer had just checked the work his pipefitters did on 2nd shift and was plainly irritated. "Those two guys, Patrick and Terry, were loafing on the job last night! Jerry's eye twitched briefly. "It looks like they did two hours of work in eight hours!"

Nagel quickly checked his roster. "They're not my guys – probably subcontractors. Talk to either Cannon or Yankowski."

Bricca scowled upon hearing Cannon's name. "I'll take it up with John first." He strode back toward the office.

John Jarvis worked under Jerry Bricca and acted as his foreman at times. They were the same age, yet their co-workers knew John thought Jerry had "hung the moon." Some even snickered that John had his lips firmly planted on Jerry's ass.

"John, those pipe fitters in 7 just laid down on the job." Jerry had his temper under control, but Jarvis could see he was still perturbed. "Do you have anyone to spare that could finish it?"

"I will Monday," replied Jarvis. "Can it wait until then?"

Jerry sighed. "Probably. I'll give you my notes on it after I talk to Yankowski. I'd like to resolve it without Cannon's involvement."

John could see his friend was frazzled. "Hey, it's getting close to noon. You wanna grab lunch at the Cottage?"

"No time." Jerry was already on the move. "I'll just get something from the vending machines."

Around 4 PM Jerry called John and asked to meet at Lake Edwards for a beer. Upon arrival Jarvis saw that Jerry was sitting with John Yankowski and Ted Bowling – as he sat down he could feel tension at the table. Apparently Jerry had put a letter in Yankowski's file complaining about the poor quality of the sub-contractors he hired for the Building 7 project.

Jerry kept saying it was nothing personal, but Yankowski was pissed. Yet with John Jarvis there, he swallowed his anger and quietly sipped the beer that Jerry had bought for him...

AROUND 9 PM THAT night, Betty Haas heard the phone ring in her Cleves home. Her husband had started back working 2nd shift at Monsanto. He'd been on days the previous two weeks, and the strange late night calls had ceased.

With some trepidation, the pretty, 26-year-old housewife rose from her couch, picked up the receiver, and listened.

At first there was silence, just like the other times. Then that vaguely familiar voice came on. "Your husband has to work until 4 AM tonight, so can I come over?

"I've got a pretty good idea who you are." Betty tried to keep her voice steady. "I know you work at Monsanto with him."

The caller ignored the warning. "You are very pretty. And when I've seen you around you're always dressed so nice."

"Maybe I'll skip Monsanto and just call the police." The voice sounded like Jim Cannon, or maybe Ted Bowling. They worked in her husband's building, and she met them earlier that summer at the company picnic. Both of those guys were bad news.

"I've admired your figure for a long time." Now the voice sounded different to Betty, and she became afraid. When he made the first vulgar suggestion she slammed the receiver down...

Sunday, September 18th

Sunday was looking like a bad day for Sgt. Russ Jackson.

Arnold Eugene Hill, their promising Strangler suspect, had been officially eliminated the previous afternoon. Though guilty of the

September 12th assault on Margaret McHone, Hill could not be linked to any of the four unsolved murders. Bowman witnesses failed to identify him, and he was incarcerated when Emogene Harrington and Lois Dant were murdered in December and April.

Jackson had continued to parade black suspects in front of cabby Sol Thompson and the Lark patrons without any luck. More than a month since Barbara Bowman was run down and stabbed to death, their investigation was a stagnant pond.

Just before noon, a report came in about a possible homicide in the Mt. Washington area of eastern Cincinnati.

The negligee-clad body of Nancy Lou Haffner, a 26-year-old proofreader, was found that morning in her disordered apartment on Beechmont Avenue. The attractive blonde was face up on a bloodstained newspaper next to an overturned coffee table and a broken drinking glass. There was caked blood on her ankles, possibly from the jagged pieces of the glass.

After viewing the scene, Jackson felt some evidence pointed to accidental death from a fall and some suggested foul play. A woman who lived in the apartment complex next door reported seeing a man running from Haffner's building and entering a "big late model car" about 12:30 AM Sunday morning.

Haffner was eight months pregnant, and a male associate was being questioned about her background. She had been active in Civil Air Patrol missions, and was a licensed flight instructor working part-time at Lunken Airport.

Eventually, after questioning another man who had casually dated her, the police could not make a case for homicide. On September 24th the coroner ruled Nancy Haffner died from an "accidental fall" brought on by a liver ailment that was aggravated by her pregnancy and medication she was taking. The autopsy revealed extensive necrosis of the liver and a fractured skull consistent with a fall.

Despite some odd circumstances, her family accepted the official ruling and the case was closed.

AROUND NOON ON THAT Sunday, news of an astonishing, dreadful crime fanned out from Chicago across the country.

Valerie Percy, one of the blonde and blue eyed 21-year-old twin daughters of Republican Senatorial candidate Charles Percy, had been bludgeoned and stabbed to death that morning in the family mansion in Kenilworth, Illinois. With the high profile crimes of Speck and Whitman still resonating, this audacious home invasion murder in a swank neighborhood was an instant media sensation.

It began just after 5 AM in "Windward", the Percy manor hugging the Lake Michigan shoreline, when Lorraine Percy was awakened by the sound of moaning from down the hall. Without turning on any lights, she went to Valerie's bedroom door and was startled to see a shadowy figure bending over the struggling form of her step-daughter. The intruder quickly shined his flashlight beam into Mrs. Percy's face, momentarily blinding her, before bolting past her down the stairway and out the patio door toward the lake.

Mrs. Percy retreated to her bedroom and woke her husband, who turned on the upstairs lights and activated the siren alarm on the roof. She called the police and then a doctor neighbor, saying she thought Valerie was still alive.

But when Kenilworth patrol officers arrived within minutes, they found Valerie Percy dead from a dozen stab wounds in her breasts, throat, and abdomen. She had also been struck two terrible blows to the left side of her head with a heavy instrument, most probably the flashlight the intruder was carrying.

Valerie resisted the attack and fought hard, sustaining defensive wounds on her fingers, hands, and knees. But she had perished within minutes, drowning in her own blood on her own bed.

The sadistic slaying of a senatorial candidate's daughter would completely overwhelm the eleven man Kenilworth police force – they had no detectives, and didn't seem to need any. This was the first murder ever recorded in the wealthy suburb of 3000 people.

The killer entered the house by cutting out a glass pane in a patio door around 5:10 AM. He moved stealthily through the living room and up the stairway, not waking the Percy's Labrador retriever in the garage. He moved past the Percy's bedroom without disturbing them and went directly to Valerie's room.

Two trails of footprints were found between the nearby beach and the patio. Kenilworth Chief Robert Daley said both sets were made "by the same person" and they were "definitely man-sized." Valerie's killer had invaded and fled the Percy house from the Lake Michigan shoreline.

The murder Charles Percy's daughter Valerie remains unsolved – prime suspect Fred Malchow was killed running from police.

Loraine Percy gave police a hazy description of the man – dark hair, about 5-foot-8 and 160 pounds, and wearing a checkered shirt. Along with the footprints, he had left five bloody palm prints on the banister and a black leather glove outside the mansion.

There were immediate press allegations of a compromised crime scene, overmatched cops, and an inept investigation. Certainly mistakes were made within the first hours of finding Valerie's body.

Perhaps out of deference to a powerful political clan, standard methods to preserve the crime scene were not employed and the family was treated with extreme deference.

A Chicago homicide detective was called in to consult, but the Kenilworth PD retained jurisdiction despite pressure to involve the Illinois Bureau of Investigation. This was a puzzling murder, the kind that would baffle even big city cops.

The brutality of the attack on Valerie indicated a personal motive – she had been battered almost beyond recognition. Other characteristics of intruder crimes were missing, as nothing was stolen and she had not been raped. This killer had gone directly to Valerie's room after passing two other bedrooms, including one where her twin sister Sharon was sleeping.

After eight days of wrangling, the Illinois State police and the FBI took over the investigation. Experienced investigators began looking at jilted boyfriends and political enemies. But by the time Charles Percy won the election in November, the trail was cold.

The investigation eventually focused on a gang of home invasion robbers working in elite neighborhoods, including Fred Malchow, who would later tell an associate that he killed Valerie Percy. Malchow died in 1967 after falling from a railroad trestle while fleeing police in Pennsylvania.

In Cincinnati that Sunday, most residents had learned of the Percy murder by the time the 6 PM news came on. For a city already in the grip of a mysterious killer, the vicious slaying of a candidate's daughter in her own bedroom must have felt like a violation of trust – as if no one was truly safe.

Linda Bricca heard the news, and the location of the Percy murder must have echoed – she had grown up in the Chicago suburb of Barrington Hills, which mirrored the affluence of Kenilworth and was only 27 miles west of the lake side enclave.

There are unconfirmed reports Linda told several people in the last week of her life that she knew Valerie Percy and had gone to high school with her. But Linda attended Barrington until transferring to Elgin for her senior year, while Valerie graduated from New Trier High School in Northfield three years later.

In reality, there was no evidence to connect the Percy crime to a nasty triple homicide that would rock Cincinnati one week later.

Yet like the Percy murder in Chicago, the approaching Queen City outrage was also destined to remain unsolved more than a half century later...

The last week of her life, Debbie Bricca was shuttled between multiple babysitters because Linda began her new job.

CHAPTER FOUR

LATE HARBINGERS

"And then it started like a guilty thing, upon a fearful summons..."
William Shakespeare

SEPTEMBER 19TH – SEPTEMBER 24TH, 1966

Monday, September 19th

As the last week of their lives began, Jerry, Linda, and Debbie Bricca appeared to be, as they would soon be memorialized, the ideal middle class family. There were no outward signs that anything was wrong with this narrative.

But upon closer scrutiny of their Monday through Saturday timeline, the catalyst for the events of Sunday night September 25th is lurking within this period. By that fateful Sunday morning, sinister, relentless forces were already moving against them.

Something irretrievable happened. An action taken for safety may have been perceived as a threat. The reaction paints or pushes someone into a deadly corner.

The consequence would be murder...

If there was any doubt we were dealing with a jarring culture shock in 1966, a Monday press conference in New York officially introduced the "free love generation."

Timothy Leary announced the formation of the League for Spiritual Discovery, which he called a new "psychedelic religion." Leary described their goal as follows: "We seek to find the divinity within and to express this revelation in a life of glorification and the worship of God. These ancient goals we define in the metaphor of the present — **turn on, tune in, drop out**."

His mantra would sweep both coasts, but it was greeted with shock and despair by the conservative Cincinnati press. The same day an article deplored the increase in boys wearing "unusual length and bizarre hairstyles" in high schools around the city. A proposal to ban long-haired lads was already before a school board committee considering "suspensions for those in violation."

But the Queen City had more serious concerns on this Monday than the flood of shaggy male students.

After a weekend of violence, Councilman John Held called for a full investigation into the surging crime rate. Held called for hiring up to 300 additional cops to help "the shorthanded police department." He said the investigation would "determine what is needed to halt violence in homes, streets, parks, and highways."

He didn't have to mention the Cincinnati Strangler – the unknown slayer of four women was casting a long shadow over city politics as summer took a final curtain call...

SHORTLY AFTER NOON ON that Monday, Linda Bricca walked into the Glenway Animal Hospital to pay a bill.

Jerry's wife had been a client at this clinic since they moved here in November 1963 – she took Thumper and Dusty there since it was convenient. The GAH was a half mile from their house on Greenway, located between the Lawrence and Werk Road intersections of Glenway Avenue.

GAH was owned and operated by Dr. Fred Leininger, a respected 36-year-old veterinarian who opened the clinic in 1957. Linda had told several neighbors that she was "bothering" Leininger about "a part-time job."

After some conversation between the two, Linda went back to the Doctor's private office, leaving Debbie to play in the lobby. Linda knew the couple who worked there had just returned to grad school and that Leininger had advertised for a receptionist. Now an impromptu job interview was taking place. Leininger agreed to hire her until he could find a new couple to live in the clinic's apartment.

At 12:50 PM, Helen Wulsekuhl showed up for an interview for the receptionist job. She was sent there by the Unemployment Bureau – Leininger had posted the opening there as well. A married woman in her 50's, Mrs. Wulsekuhl arrived and noticed a small girl playing

The Glenway Animal Hospital was founded in 1959 by Dr. Fred Leininger in Bridgetown.

outside the door of the clinic. At 1 PM she saw the doctor escort a smiling brunette woman to the front door, where she took charge of the child.

Helen introduced herself to Leininger. He hesitated, and then awkwardly apologized – the position had just been filled.

Seeing pictures of the murdered family ten days later, Helen was positive the woman and child victims were the two people she'd seen at the Glenway Animal Hospital on Monday September 19th.

At 3 PM, Linda Bricca placed a call to Jerry's boss at Monsanto. Ted Anderson had talked with her a few times before, but now she sounded a little breathless. Jerry was in Danville, Illinois for the day, looking at equipment with several Monsanto engineers.

"Do you know what time Jerry will be back home today?" she asked. "I have this job tonight and I might need a babysitter."

Anderson was puzzled by the call and unsure what to say. "I don't know when they'll be back. There's some bad weather out there. You should probably get a sitter just to be safe."

Around 5 PM Jerry called Linda from Danville. Weather had cancelled his flight, scheduled to arrive at Greater Cincinnati airport at 5:30 PM. He told her they were driving back instead, and that he he wouldn't be home until after 9 PM.

At 6 PM, Linda began her part-time receptionist job at the Glenway Animal Hospital. The clinic had evening hours on Monday, and she was scheduled to work until 9 PM.

A half hour later, a young couple named Steve and Valinda Westman arrived at the GAH to apply for the live-in caretaker jobs. Linda asked them to wait for the doctor – when Leininger came out he did not introduce them to her. He showed them the apartment in the rear of the clinic while talking about their duties.

They hit it off well, and Leininger hired them on the spot. He said they could start the next day, but after some discussion they decided to begin work on Thursday the 22nd and move into the apartment at that time. When the Westmans left Linda Bricca smiled at them but didn't speak.

It had been a long day for Jerry Bricca, and now he was facing a four hour car ride back home. That morning their flight to Danville was diverted to Chicago because of a storm system. Jerry knew some good places to eat there, and he took the other engineers to a steak house downtown. After lunch they all bought tickets on an Ozark flight to Champagne, and then drove to the Danville.

Jerry was supposed to attend a training program at Monsanto at 7 PM, and he was disappointed because it was the second session of a two-part program. He tried to catch a few winks in the car as Glenn Ritchie drove toward Cincinnati.

Ritchie dropped Jerry in front of his residence around 10:15 PM, turned around in the next driveway, and drove back by Jerry's house on the opposite side of the street. Taking a quick look back he didn't see Jerry, but his car was in the driveway with a dark station wagon behind it.

There were no lights on. 3381 Greenway was pitch black...

Tuesday, September 20th

It was a rainy Tuesday in the Queen City, and *Enquirer* readers buzzing over Timothy Leary's comments were greeted with yet another culture shift, this time on the silver screen.

Inspired by salty language in the hit movie "Who's Afraid of Virginia Woolf", the Motion Picture Association of America announced a new code for film production. New movies would either be classified "G" for general release or "M" for "mature audiences". Ten new standards would now be applied in rating a film, including whether "evil, sin, crime, and violence" were justified and if there was "indecent or undue exposure of the human body."

Dodging raindrops with Debbie, Linda Bricca was in a rush. As she waltzed into the Sears store on Glenway just after noon, clerk Jerry Hicks recognized her as the attractive housewife who bought some white paint on Saturday. Hicks recalled that she was friendly yet fussy about the way he mixed the white.

Linda asked if the parchment color she had ordered was in yet – Hicks checked, and told her they would have it on Thursday. She sighed, said she was "in a hurry", and ordered another gallon of the white, with careful instructions on the mixing. She seemed preoccupied, and was not talkative like before.

When she left Hicks watched her going out the door. She was a looker all right, but he was not just ogling her. It seemed odd to him that she was not holding her child's hand.

Within the next hour Linda must have dropped Debbie off at a babysitter, because she arrived at the GAH for work at 1:30 PM. Dr. Leininger had scheduled her to work a split shift until 4 PM, and then come back after dinner from 6:30 PM-8 PM.

Linda had barely clocked in when Leininger was surprised by the arrival of Steve and Valinda Westman at the clinic. Steve, age 20, and his 21-year-old wife had been hired the previous day after touring the facility. They had asked to start on Thursday, but here they were on Tuesday ready to move into the clinic apartment.

Whether this was a miscommunication or Leininger was confused about what he told them on Monday is unclear. The apartment was being cleaned and refurbished and wasn't ready yet. So the Westmans agreed to start work on Thursday instead. Leininger told them they would work six days a week, with Sundays off so Steve could preach at a Northern Kentucky Church.

As they walked back into the lobby, Leininger looked at Linda for a moment, and then told the Westmans they could have Wednesdays off as well, so Linda could work on those days.

AT THE MONSANTO PLANT, Jerry and John Jarvis were having coffee with the foreman whose men were doing the pipe fitting for Jerry's project. Jarvis was there to mediate, as Jerry and 54-year-old Stan Drahman had

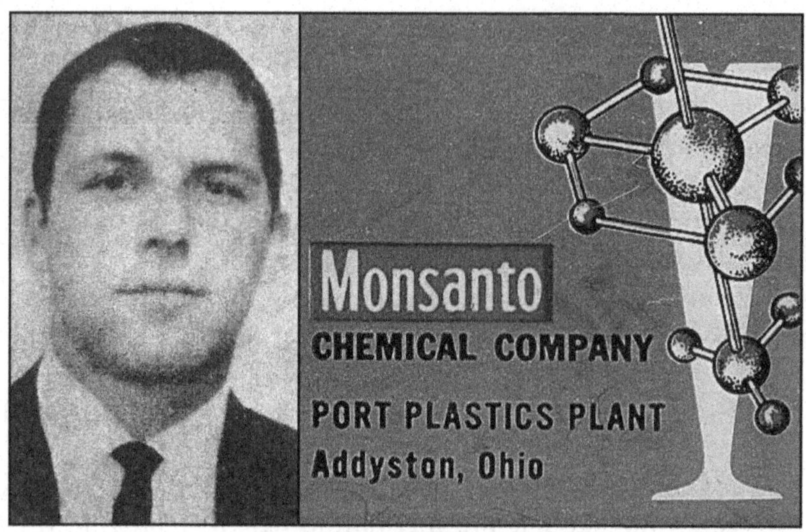

Jerry Bricca was a rising star at the Cincinnati Monsanto plant, but he was also looking to relocate to San Francisco.

gotten into a heated argument after Jerry discovered his men "laying down on the job." Jarvis heard the two had almost come to blows early Saturday morning. He knew Jerry had a temper and often came to the plant at odd hours to check on work.

Drahman and Jerry offered apologies, the foreman pointing to the 3 AM time of their dispute as an indication everyone was frustrated and cranky – nothing said should be taken personally. Jerry agreed this was just a normal conflict between construction and engineering over the best way to do an installation. As they sipped coffee in the break room, Jerry began talking about his vacation in California.

The two men shook hands and the matter seemed settled. Jarvis was pleased by the peaceful resolution but still concerned about his friend. Jerry was working ungodly hours and seemed distracted by something. The only breaks he took were to inhale snacks from the vending machines.

Back in the Bricca neighborhood, the Tuesday rain showed no sign of letting up. Kids were back in school, and neighbors were more watchful as autumn was moving in.

Around 4 PM Gale Griswold looked out her window and saw the man. She lived on Childs Avenue, a half mile from the Bricca house. Around 1 PM she had noticed him near her house. Now there he was again, standing in the same spot even though the rain was pelting down.

He was a white man in his mid-twenties, obviously not a neighborhood resident. Tall with a thin build, he had longish dark hair and was wearing odd boots – she thought they looked like something the Beatles would wear.

This guy was way out of place here, she thought. *What on earth was he doing, just standing there getting soaked?*

Wednesday, September 21st

A *New York Times* article warned that the "White Backlash" was frightening liberal Democratic candidates. And as the civil rights movement began to blend with the anti-war protestors, conservative voters were threatening to let their ballots do the talking.

There were two flashpoints – black families moving into white neighborhoods and the growing violence of the protest movement.

The term "White Flight" was coined to describe the Caucasian exodus to the suburbs. But more concerning was militancy among young blacks mutating into race riots. Some liberals were now sounding like southern conservatives as they condemned the demonstrations and charged that "communist subversives" had infiltrated the civil rights movement.

New York congressman Adam Clayton Powell summed up the new "Black Power" movement with this telling quote: "These are a new breed of cats. They hiss A. Phillip Randolph. They boo Martin Luther King. They even picket my church."

BEFORE THIS DAY WAS over the seeds of murder would be sown.

Just before 9 AM, Linda Bricca arrived at 3313 Greenway to drop off Debbie. Linda was working a split shift that day at the GAH, and told Estelle Zeff she would pick Debbie up at noon.

Estelle's daughter, 18-year-old Linda, was the Bricca's primary babysitter and a sometime confidante of Linda Bricca, who was only five years older than the recent high school graduate. The younger Linda was drawn to the lovely housewife the moment they met.

In an interview with this writer, Linda Zeff told me that "Linda Bricca was pretty, classy and sweet...always stylishly dressed. She seemed so much older than me."

Young Linda began to emulate her as she became comfortable with the family. She described Jerry as "powerfully built", and appreciated it when he helped with her math homework. One day after talking about animals, Linda gave her a copy of "Born Free" to read, telling her it was "a great book."

Linda Zeff had been babysitting Debbie since 1964, when she was referred by another sitter because of her affinity for dogs. The Bricca dogs were aggressive with everyone outside the family and didn't like the previous sitter. Yet they quickly bonded with Linda Zeff, who returned the affection in a way that impressed Linda Bricca and earned her trust.

Linda would usually babysit Debbie at the Bricca home, while her mother would watch the child at the Zeff home.

Estelle Zeff would remember two things about Debbie that morning. The clever youngster wanted to play in Linda's room, but Estelle warned her that it was a mess. "I want to be a mess just like her," she cheerfully replied.

And later, for some unknown reason, Debbie asked Mrs. Zeff to call her Carol...

A HALF MILE AWAY, LINDA Bricca was working at GAH just past 1 PM when another veterinarian entered the clinic.

Dr. Herman Rehder was a 36-year-old Columbus native who attended Ohio State Vet School with Dr. Leininger. He was "Fred's relief vet", and had stopped by to see if he was needed to fill in the following week when Leininger would be on a hunting trip As Rehder strolled in, Fred and Linda Bricca were sitting at the desk talking, and the Doctor introduced his new receptionist to Dr. Rehder. After a few minutes Leininger went to treat an animal and Rehder had a conversation with Linda, which he later remembered as mostly small talk.

"Do you like working here?" he asked the striking brunette.

"This is only my third day, but it's like a dream come true." Linda gushed. I've always wanted to work with animals. Doc might let me assist him on procedures when I get some experience."

Rehder frowned but moved on. "What does your husband do?"

"He works at Monsanto. I'm curious, what does Fred, uh, Doc pay you for this relief work?" Rehder reluctantly cited a figure, and Linda gave a low whistle. "Pipe fitters working for my husband at the plant make more than that!"

Rehder would say later they spoke for twenty minutes, and claimed he didn't discuss anything personal with Linda Bricca. When leaving Rehder said he'd see her the week of October 3rd.

As Rehder walked out of the clinic, Linda Bricca knew nothing about the skeletons in his closet. We don't know if Fred Leininger filled her in later that day. Because although he appeared outwardly normal, Dr. Herman Rehder was hiding a dark, secretive past, one that dated back to his veterinary school days.

Was it mere coincidence they met on that fateful Wednesday? Because it's mind boggling that such a physically dangerous, sexually unstable individual had somehow crossed paths with Linda Bricca at this point in her life.

A life that would end just five days later...

Wednesday, September 21st

The mild Wednesday had turned into a brittle evening by the time Virginia Hinners took her place in the office of the New Thought Unity Center in Walnut Hills. The 46-year-old secretary was preparing to record the mid-week service in the church. A large congregation was in attendance, and the minister wanted to get the choir's selections on the church tape recorder.

Just after 8 PM, a short, thin black man entered the side door and asked about getting a job. Virginia sent him in search of the custodian, whose office was in the basement.

"Can you take me down there?" he asked.

"I'm sorry, but I'm getting ready to turn on this tape machine and record the service." She could hear the reassuring sounds of people settling into the chapel.

The man went down the stairs to the basement but returned a few minutes later, saying he knocked on the custodian's door without getting an answer.

Virginia was busy, and her toned showed it. "Well, I'm sorry but I can't leave the office. Did you knock on the right door?" He looked away and remained silent. In profile she saw he had a wispy goatee, which seemed to disappear when he faced her.

Virginia got up from behind her desk, walked out of the office to the stairway railing and leaned over to point at the door. The man was right next to her, and she noticed a pungent smell – body odor mixed with something else. She quickly moved back to the office as he went down the stairs.

Shortly afterwards he came back again. His voice was soft, with a slight rasp. "I saw a man come in a door at the other end of the basement. I believe he's the janitor. Can you go down there with me and talk to him?"

"I've already told you I can't leave right now!" She paused, and then lowered her voice. "Why don't you come back in the morning around 9:30?" Virginia grabbed a prayer pamphlet and wrote the custodian's name on it. "I'm sure he can talk to you then."

The man hesitated. "Well...won't you go down with me? I'm a little bit afraid, and maybe you could talk to this man."

Virginia could hear the service beginning. "I'm sorry, but I can't do it now." She offered her first smile. "Why don't you come back?"

He walked out of the office, and Virginia turned on the recorder and resumed typing. Her back was to the exterior door, and several minutes later she felt a presence nearby. She swung around in her chair, and the man was behind her with his hands outstretched.

She jumped up and backed away from him. Blunt awareness that he really wasn't a job seeker trickled over her in a cold sweat. His demeanor changed completely. Before he was respectful and soft spoken, but now he grabbed her arms and drew her into him.

Virginia pushed him back and pleaded "Don't do that." He bent her arm behind her back and forced her towards the outside door. She managed to hook her foot against it so he couldn't open it.

It was then he began to whisper the words Virginia would never forget to her dying day. "Do you want what the others got?" he hissed. "Do you want what the others got? Don't scream. Don't scream. I'll slit your throat. I'll slit your throat."

Failing to get her out the door, he hit her across the temple and threw her into the desk. "Now you're going to get it," he muttered, whacking Virginia on the chin, knocking Virginia to the floor.

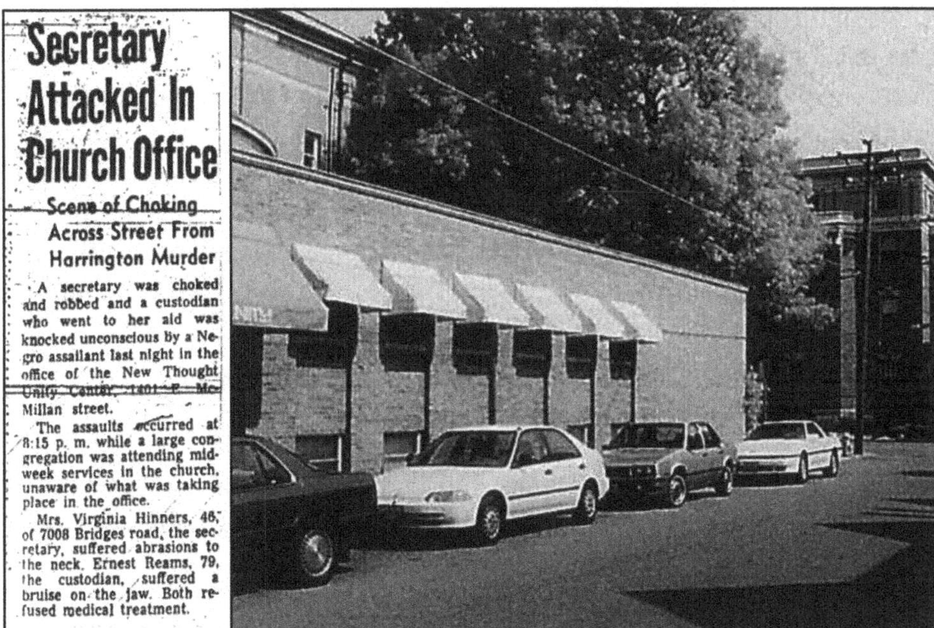

Secretary Attacked In Church Office

Scene of Choking Across Street From Harrington Murder

A secretary was choked and robbed and a custodian who went to her aid was knocked unconscious by a Negro assailant last night in the office of the New Thought Unity Center, 1401 E. McMillan street.

The assaults occurred at 8:15 p. m. while a large congregation was attending midweek services in the church, unaware of what was taking place in the office.

Mrs. Virginia Hinners, 46, of 7008 Bridges road, the secretary, suffered abrasions to the neck. Ernest Reams, 79, the custodian, suffered a bruise on the jaw. Both refused medical treatment.

The Hinners assault was across the street from the scene of the Harrington murder in December 1965.

"Please don't hurt me," she begged, but he picked her up and threw her against the wall. He got behind her and began choking her with his shirt sleeve – Virginia could feel herself blacking out.

At that moment the custodian entered the office. Ernest Reams, age 79, heard the commotion and had gone up to investigate. The intruder threw Virginia aside and attacked the older man, brutally pounding him and knocking him to the floor.

Instead of running away, he came back at Virginia. "What do you want?" she gasped. "If you want money I'll give it to you." He grabbed her purse, rifled her wallet of $28, and threw her face down on the floor. Then he casually strolled out and into the night.

Reams recovered and called the police, and within five minutes several officers responded. Mrs. Hinners suffered facial bruises and neck abrasions, while Reams had a bruised jaw and a possible concussion – both of them refused medical treatment. Virginia was able to give an accurate description of the attacker, eerily similar to what the Bowman witnesses had depicted in August.

That he claimed to be looking for work resonated with the cops. The perpetrator of last October's attack on Elizabeth Kreco at the nearby Verona Apartments had asked her to guide him to the custodian's basement office.

There was one more coincidence – staring the Cincinnati cops right in the face.

The New Thought Unity Church was across the street from 1404 East McMillan, where Emogene Harrington had been strangled last December 2nd in the basement of the Clermont Apartments...

September 21st

While Virginia Hinners revealed the details of her harrowing assault to responding officers, Jerry Bricca was nursing a few drinks during a "stag party" at River Downs with his boss Ted Anderson.

Jerry had been in St. Louis that day, flying back on a private plane with Ted and stopping by the party on the way home. He was weary from the travel, but Linda was working at the clinic, and an empty house didn't sound appealing.

Ted noticed Jerry seemed preoccupied – he was neither unwinding from their trip nor joining in the raucous fun of the bachelor party. The guy was all business – he never discussed his home life and rarely went out with people from Monsanto.

Ted Anderson was concerned about Jerry, a rising star who knew how to make the boss look good. Yet he was a perfectionist with a bit of a temper. Lately he had seemed more in control, but maybe he was just holding it in – and the cork was too tight.

Anderson already did damage control when he took over the department last year. Jerry was candid in his first meeting with his new boss, saying "I'm ready to quit if things don't change." Ted had assured him that his own management style was nothing like his old boss, and implored Jerry to give him a chance to prove it.

So with rumors flying about Jerry looking for greener grass, Ted was making a conscious effort to get closer to him. He was only a few years older than Jerry, and he hoped going to this bash together would cement their relationship.

Anderson was aware of the friction between Jerry and the pipe fitter's foreman from Friday. Yet Jerry's part of the overall project started today, and Ted had received good reports about the replacement crew and their progress.

Anderson happily told Jerry that Jim Cannon was on vacation that Friday and through the following Tuesday. Cannon was currently working in their department, and the tension between the two men was exhausting – Jerry could really use the break.

Amid the din of the party, Ted leaned close to Jerry and asked, "Are you having a good time."

Jerry finished off his third gin and tonic, checked his watch, and then turned to his boss. "I'm outta here. My wife gets off work at 9 PM. I need to be there when she gets home..."

BETTY MEYER WAS STARTING to get antsy.

Linda Bricca's next door neighbor was a last minute replacement when her babysitter canceled. Betty reluctantly agreed to watch Debbie from 6-9 PM, Linda's evening hours at the clinic. Her husband was working second shift at General Electric that night, and Betty had three sons at home ages 14, 10, and 6. Watching Debbie was not how she'd planned to spend her evening.

So here it was going on 9:30 PM and Linda was nowhere in sight. Debbie was playing with her youngest son, but the kids were starting to get cranky. Looking out her front door, Betty noticed the Bricca house was still dark. Linda had mentioned something about Jerry going to River Downs from the airport and she wasn't expecting him home until late.

The temperature had dipped into the 50s as Betty stood on her porch in the fresh night air and had a smoke, keeping watch for Linda's station wagon. She mused about her new job – working at the clinic wasn't going to help her flagging marriage to Jerry. Linda seemed to think that particular veterinarian could do no wrong.

Betty couldn't really fault Linda's fascination with animals. She was just weird about it sometimes. Like before their vacation last year, when Linda brought over two tiny wooden coffins, telling Betty she was leaving her rabbits with Dr. Leininger. She'd given him instructions to call the Meyer house if the rabbits died – so the Doctor could bring their bodies over and put them in the coffins!

Just recently, Linda's parakeet died and she kept it in their freezer until her father came down from Chicago with a special metal box made at his welding company. Linda then wrapped the dead bird in a monogramed towel and made Jerry dig a six foot deep hole to bury the box in.

By 10:20 PM Debbie was asleep on the Meyer's living room couch. Betty he glanced out the window. Still no sign of Linda.

A few minutes later there was a loud rap at the front door. Betty opened it to reveal a clearly agitated Jerry Bricca, who strode past her to look at Debbie on the couch. He spoke without turning toward Betty.

"Where is she?" His tone was deliberately measured, but she could tell he'd been drinking. Jerry's short sleeve shirt revealed his muscled torso and heaving chest.

"I guess she's still at work," Betty offered halfheartedly. "She did say the clinic closed at 9 PM."

Jerry turned and glared at her. "It's almost 10:30. I'm going over there."

"Why don't you sit here with me and have a drink instead." Betty knew Jerry and what buttons could be pushed, so her request wasn't a question. "Dick will be home soon from work," she added. "I'm sure he'll need a cocktail."

"He's on second this week?" The mention of work seemed to soothe Jerry. "I'll have a gin and tonic."

Betty was mixing it when Linda appeared in the doorway. Her expression upon seeing Jerry was remarkable and unknowable, a mixture of satisfaction and dread. Betty watched Linda gather herself – she'd seen this before, but now there was something askew as Linda frothed into the room, words coming in torrents.

Jerry wasn't having it. "Why are you so late picking up Debbie?"

"Well, we had something happen at the clinic right before closing. I had to stay and help the Doc."

Jerry laughed. It wasn't a pretty sound.

Linda struggled to regain her composure. "Someone brought a cat in that had been hit by a car, and Doc's assistant was already gone. So you see I had to stay and help him work on the cat." Her voice wavered. "We worked damn hard trying to save that cat, but it died." She turned to Betty. "Could you please fix me a double?"

Jerry's eyes softened. Linda was profoundly affected by animal deaths. He smiled for the first time, crossed the room to embrace her, but stopped short. "Why is there whiskey on your breath?"

Linda averted her eyes. "We were both upset about the cat. Fred, uh, Doc got a bottle from his desk and suggested we sit down and have a drink."

Either the lighting had changed – or Jerry had. The gentleness vanished from his face, and he no longer looked harmless.

"I should go over there and beat him up!" Jerry sauntered out the front door and went next door to his house, as Betty and Linda watched him from the Meyer's porch. Standing next to her, Betty realized Linda was more blotto than Jerry.

At 11 PM Jerry came back over, and without a word took his wife and child back home. That night, while Linda slept with her two dogs, Jerry bedded down on the living room couch, finally drifting off into a woozy slumber with a belly full of undigested anger...

Thursday, September 22nd

On Thursday, Cincinnati City Council went on the offensive. Armed with statistics for August, one councilman told the *Enquirer* "the crime rate in the city is skyrocketing."

Year to date showed a 15% increase in violent offenses like murder, robbery, assault and rape from over the same time period in 1965. And there was a killer on the rampage. So the *Enquirer* announced a three part series called **"Spotlight on Danger"** beginning on Saturday the 24th.

Readers were still buzzing about a feature in the previous day's edition: **"Terror – 'Phantom Roommate' Of Local Women"**. With "cocked ears" and behind "bolted doors", female residents were living in dread. Reporter Margaret Josten captured the mood:

> **Cincinnati women find it easy to pinpoint the time when fear became a part of everyday life. Several said Tuesday they began double-bolting doors and listening for strange footfalls after April 4th – the day Mrs. Lois Dant was murdered in her Price Hill apartment.**
>
> **One told how she sets up an elaborate pyramid of pots and pans just inside her apartment so the slightest movement at the door will precipitate a terrible clatter. "From what I've read about this murderer he may be smart enough to get a key," she said.**

Cocked Ears And Bolted Doors

Terror—'Phantom Roommate' Of Local Women

By MARGARET JOSTEN
Of The Enquirer Staff

Cincinnati women find it easy to pinpoint the time when fear became a part of everyday life.

Several said Tuesday they began double-bolting doors and listening for strange footfalls after April 4—the day Mrs. Lois Dant was murdered in her Price Hill apartment.

Mrs. Dant was the second victim of the phantom rapist-strangler. The first was a space scientist's wife, slain in the basement of a Walnut Hills apartment building. The third, a widow walking her dog in Burnet Woods.

"The first death was shocking," observed Mrs. Nathan Gilbert, Bond Hill. "But after Price Hill, this (being watchful) became the thing to do."

Mrs. Gilbert added that she had not only installed extra bolts on all the doors of their home, but that she never leaves the house these days, even to walk the dog, without making sure all the doors are locked.

"I'm very surprised to know this is my reaction," she added in a wry tone.

Mrs. Gilbert was among dozens of Cincinnati women heartily endorsing Councilman John E. Held's proposal to investigate violence here with an eye to getting remedies. All queried felt Cincinnati's police force was undermanned and underpaid.

Mrs. Armel Hooker, manager of a large apartment house in Walnut Hills where many elderly women live, said the tenants refused to open their doors after 6:30 or 7 p.m., whenever it gets dark.

To get into this particular apartment house one must have a key to the outer door, another to get from the lobby to the hallway. Each apartment door carries three locks.

Mrs. Hooker told how a boy, 13 or 14 years old, had followed a girl into the lobby and grabbed her. He had done the same thing several times, she recalled.

"Now I see him on the street wearing a big leather jacket with 'Frankie, The Great Lover' written across the back of it," said Mrs. Hooker. She wondered why he was out on the streets.

Mrs. Laura Bangs, Delhi, said "everybody is afraid."

Even her children, she added, are afraid to go into the basement alone to get soft drinks. "One goes along with the other to see if somebody is hiding behind the steps."

Miss Bobbie Franzreb, a legal secretary, said she wouldn't go into her basement without her dog—"just a mutt, not a police dog."

If police pay raises were put into a bond issue, Miss Franzreb said she was "sure" the public would approve.

"We have a good police force now, but there don't seem to be enough around," she said. "Every time a policeman—or a fireman—goes out, his life is in jeopardy. Younger boys are not going into this work because it is underpaid."

Both Miss Franzreb and Mrs. Gilbert thought there should be more police cruising in trouble neighborhoods. Miss Franzreb asked that bus stops be better lighted.

One of the many women who telephoned Mr. Held Tuesday lived across the street from Christ The King Church, only a few steps from Mt. Lookout Square.

She told Mr. Held she was afraid to walk down to the square to buy a newspaper in the daytime.

The Mt. Lookout woman also said there had been "incidents" in the neighborhood that had not been reported to police.

An elderly woman living on the far end of Price Hill called to tell him she refused to open her door these days.

Several women who live alone expressed fear at even having their names appear in the newspaper.

One told how she sets up an elaborate pyramid of pots and pans just inside her apartment so the slightest movement at the door will precipitate a terrible clatter.

"From what I've read about this murderer he may be smart enough to get a key," she said.

Having a killer on the prowl in Cincinnati generated feverish coverage for frightened women.

With the crime numbers trending badly and women huddling nervously, the environment was ideal for two political objectives. City council would get their crime study, and Cincinnati Police would get more cops on the street.

It was a perfect storm – and the biggest story in town...

TED ANDERSON WAS SITTING in his office that morning when Jerry Bricca walked in and plopped down, fatigue stamped across his face. As Ted listened, Jerry began to unburden himself, confiding about his personal life for the first time ever.

"How long did you stay last night?" Jerry asked.

"Till 11:30 – and I'm paying for it." Ted flashed a conspiratorial leer. "There were guys still getting hammered when I left."

"Well, I got home at 9:30 and my house was dark. My wife was still working at that clinic." Jerry's disgust was evident. "I sat there in the dark for 45 minutes, but she never showed. So I go next door to pick up Debbie, and our neighbor hasn't heard from her either."

"When did she start working there?" Anderson flashed back to his Monday call from Linda.

"Monday, when I was in St. Louis. She's been bugging the guy for months to get some part time hours."

"So what happened?"

"She finally showed up at the Meyers around 10:30, and she was really stewed. Claimed she had a drink with the doctor." Jerry set his jaw and began to grind his teeth.

Ted wasn't sure what to say – Linda was attractive but he knew nothing about her. "So is everything OK?"

"Yeah," Jerry waved his hand, leaving out that he had threatened to "beat up" Dr. Leininger. "She assumed I would be "getting loaded", as she calls it, at the party until at least 11 PM, so there was no reason to hurry home." He snorted. "Turned out she was more loaded than I was."

Jerry then steered the conversation back to work problems, but Ted Anderson saw that his star player was deeply troubled by the games of last night...

At noon, Linda Bricca picked Debbie up from the Zeff house where Estelle was watching her since 9 AM. "Please remind Linda that she's watching Debbie at my house from 1-4," she said.

"She can't make it by one," Estelle replied. "But I have her key – I'll be there at 1 PM to watch Debbie."

Linda Bricca frowned. "Just leave the dogs in the back yard."

She was seen shortly afterwards in a cocktail lounge at the Western Hills Plaza buying lunch for Debbie and herself.

Around 12:30 PM Linda returned to the Sears store to pick up her beige paint. This was Jerry Hicks third interaction with her and Debbie since Saturday. As she was leaving she told Hicks "my husband is doing some painting this weekend."

At 1 PM she dropped Debbie off at her home. Estelle was there, and Linda said she'd be back by 4 PM. Linda Zeff was used to babysitting Debbie in the Bricca home, yet this was the first time Estelle had been inside 3381 Greenway.

A few minutes later, Linda Bricca walked into the Hi-Lo Deli on Glenway. Owner Larry Foppe rang up her purchases consisting of wine and some snacks, and Linda paid with a check. She was a familiar customer to Foppe, who was used to seeing Debbie with her – this time she was alone.

Around 4:15 PM Linda arrived home to relieve Linda Zeff, who had taken over for her mother at 2:45. They talked for ten minutes or so, yet Linda Zeff would later say that Linda seemed distracted and anxious for her to leave.

As Zeff said goodbye at 4:30, Linda Bricca whispered something that startled the younger woman: *"If the phone ever rings and it's a man, don't tell them where I am."* With that cryptic request hanging in the air, Linda

Zeff walked out the front door, then turned and waved to Linda Bricca standing on the porch.

It was the last time the younger Linda would see her beautiful neighbor...

Just after 5 PM Linda Bricca called the Zeff home and asked if either Linda or her mother could watch Debbie from 7-9 PM that night. She had been called in to work for Dr. Leininger, and Jerry was in a training session at Monsanto. Neither Zeff was available.

When investigators looked at this later, they realized Glenway Animal Hospital hours were only 9-noon on Thursdays. Why would Linda lie about the reason for needing the sitter? It's not known whether she got one for that night, but it wasn't because she was working at the GAH.

At 7:15 PM, Vera Richardson was working at the Western Hills Answering Service when she took a call from Linda Bricca for Dr. Leininger, whose phone automatically rang at the service whenever his clinic was closed. Linda seemed anxious, and requested that Dr. Leininger call her immediately. Richardson would log it in the Doctor's book as an "emergency call".

Around 7:30 PM Linda Zeff drove past her house and saw a young girl walking up to the Bricca front door. She soon forgot about the girl, but there was one thing she couldn't get out of her mind. Something her mother said when Linda showed up at the Bricca house to relieve her from watching Debbie that afternoon.

"Thank God you're here," Estelle told her only daughter. *"I have to leave. There's something wrong in this house. Something evil..."*

Friday, September 23rd

Fall officially started at 6:43 this morning – the "long, hot, summer" of discontent slipped into autumn without missing a beat. In Cincinnati, residents were looking at moderate temperatures, with a high in the mid-60s.

At Monsanto, Jerry Bricca was still upset about the "loafing" pipe fitters loafing from the previous Friday night. He sought out Art Nagel, who was concerned about losing sub-contracting work at Monsanto – Jerry's opinion carried some weight. Nagel's conciliatory tone seemed to help matters, and they parted ways with Art believing that everything was smoothed over.

Just after 10 AM the new receptionist at the Glenway Animal Hospital took a call from Linda Bricca. This was Valinda Westman's second day on the job, and although she'd met Mrs. Bricca they had not worked together. Valinda wasn't sure what to make of the slender, classy brunette who seemed obsessed with animals.

"Did I by chance leave one of Debbie's books there?" Linda's voice was pleasantly detached.

Valinda barely had time to answer when Dr. Leininger appeared in the lobby, the child's book in his hand. "Tell her I'll drop it off on my way home for lunch." He turned and went back to his office.

"He said he'd bring it by at lunchtime." Valinda wanted to ask a question about the files, but Linda merely thanked her and hung up.

At 10:30 AM Linda Bricca dialed the Shell station at the corner of Werk and Glenway. Donald Sebastian knew both Jerry and Linda as frequent customers – now Linda said her car wouldn't start.

Sebastian took their tow truck and was there in five minutes. He jumped it, but battery terminals were corroded. Linda fluttered a smile and said she'd bring it over after she got Debbie dressed.

At 11:15 AM she brought the car in. Sebastian gave the battery a full charge and removed the dirt and corrosion. He had her car ready in 15 minutes – Linda was grateful for the quick service, telling Don she had to take Debbie somewhere for an appointment. He watched them drive away around 11:30 AM.

Back on Greenway, Linda Bricca walked across the street to see Nettie Caudell. It was a few minutes before noon, and Linda asked if she could watch Debbie while she went to pay some bills. Nettie loved the child, and was only too happy to oblige. Linda thought she'd be back in about ninety minutes.

Dr. Fred Leininger left his clinic at noon sharp and drove the half mile to the Bricca house. He pulled up along the curb, and noticed Debbie playing in the front yard. He left his car and strolled up the front walkway to knock on the door.

Then he stopped halfway – Debbie was watching him, with those same huge blue eyes that her mother possessed. Leininger turned and handed her the book with the knowing smile that adults give to children. "Here you go, Debra."

The child regarded the book with a grave expression beyond her years, and then gazed up at the veterinarian.

"Thanks, Uncle Fred."

September 23rd

Fred Leininger did not go home for lunch. He and his friend Robert Girten met at the Crescent Bow Club archery range on Muddy Creek Road, a remote section of Bridgetown about two miles from his clinic. The sky was a vivid blue, with languid white clouds swimming by on the cusp of autumn.

They were eating their lunch about 1 PM when Girten saw a blue station wagon pull up. An attractive young woman got out and walked over to their picnic table. Girten noticed Leininger was immediately on edge, although he tried to hide it. He introduced her as "Linda, the girl who is working for me." She smiled yet hardly glanced at Robert.

For several minutes she watched them finish eating, their conversation speckled with long silences. Girten thought his friend seemed upset by her presence at the range, which was a guy's only hangout for Leininger and his fellow bow hunters.

She asked Doc if she could follow them around on the course, and he mumbled "If you want to." Linda starting asking questions as they moved from target to target, but Fred seemed indifferent to answering them. When she complimented him on a particularly good shot, Girten saw Leininger turn away and smirk.

Finally she just shut up. Girten was uneasy with this awkward scene – he felt like a third wheel. He finished the course ahead of Leininger, put his gear in this car and bade his friend farewell.

They had a brief conversation about their upcoming hunting trip the week of October 3rd. Several months ago Robert had made reservations at a hunting lodge in Pennsylvania for Leininger and two friends – these four were regular lunching buddies at David's Buffet or The Wagon Wheel.

Robert Girten pulled out onto Muddy Creek and headed north toward Werk Road, where his business was located. When he left that secluded archery range, no other members were on the course.

Fred Leininger and Linda Bricca were alone there...

Back in the Woodhaven subdivision, residents began to notice strangers wandering their streets and cul-de-sacs.

Around 3 PM on Moonridge Drive, Minnie Green answered the door to find an odd man standing there. He did not identify his company, but offered to come in and show her how he would clean her furnace. She brusquely refused him entrance and closed the door. Looking outside a few minutes later, she saw he had moved slowly down the sidewalk toward Lawrence Road.

Something told her this guy didn't belong on her street. Mrs. Green described him as short, between 35-40, dark hair and wearing a white shirt and dark pants.

Just after 4 PM, Arthur Miller of Biscayne Avenue was confronted by a man at his door who asked if he needed his furnace cleaned. Miller described him as 6 feet tall, about 170 pounds, and "very dirty." The man seemed lost, disoriented, and possibly drunk, asking Miller several times where the nearest bus stop was. He directed the man to Lawrence Avenue and closed the door.

Miller made a report to the Green Township police – a man in this condition shouldn't be knocking on doors and startling people.

Minnie Green told of her encounter the following week. This was after the events of Sunday night September 25th, when every strange vagrant or weird wanderer became an urgent matter.

Linda Bricca was late picking up Debbie – it was after 3 PM when she finally showed up. She apologized profusely to Nettie Caudell, saying that her car battery died while running errands and she had walked to the Shell station at Werk and Glenway. They were able to drive to the car's location and start it.

As she walked Debbie back home Linda smiled to herself. Nettie was so nice to watch Debbie, and for a moment Linda felt guilty about lying to her. She had indeed gotten a jump for her car, but that was around 10:15 in the morning.

The trick was not to lie more than you had to...

Saturday, September 24th

On Saturday morning *Enquirer* readers were confronted with the first installment of **Spotlight on Danger**. If Queen City residents weren't already terror stricken because of the Strangler, now they were being asked to confess what else was scaring them.

> **Our news columns have reported the crimes at length that roused City Council to action. Now you're invited to tell where you think dangers lurk, using the clip-out form furnished below. We'll study your replies carefully and report what we've learned... it's your city and your safety we speak of. Join now with the Enquirer to shine the spotlight of public concern on danger, and help us make Cincinnati "The Safest City in America."**

At 9 AM that morning the phone rang in the Bricca house. Jerry grabbed it, much to Linda's chagrin.

It was Dr. Fred Leininger, calling to offer Linda a permanent position as part-time receptionist at his clinic. He spoke briefly with Jerry, and Leininger said later their conversation was "cordial". If it wasn't, the two people who could dispute it were not alive to do so.

Linda came on the line and enthusiastically accepted the job. She would work every Wednesday until the end of the year. Leininger later claimed this was the last time he ever spoke to her.

Jerry went to work a short time later. Working weekends was nothing new for him. But why this dedication to a job he might be leaving soon? Was he avoiding something unpleasant at home?

At noon, Linda Bricca walked into the J & J Food Market to buy rib eye steaks. Butcher Harry Caldwell picked out some nice ones with minimal fat, wrapped them up and marked them with a red pencil. They chatted amiably for a minute or so before Linda paid by check and left with her daughter.

Between 12:30-2 PM two witnesses would later claim to have seen Linda Bricca riding with a man – one on Lawrence and the other on Schwartz Avenue near Glenmore. Since Jerry Bricca was at work, the driver was not her husband.

Cheryl Rehling would later describe the car as a light green or gray foreign car. She knew it was Linda from meeting her at neighborhood parties, and said Linda was sitting very close to the man. Cheryl saw this same car in the Bricca drive later that day.

Between 2:30-3 PM Joan Janszen noticed Linda washing her car in the driveway. Shortly after that Betty Meyer came home and saw Linda finishing up her car and putting it in the garage.

Around this same time, a Mrs. Bode reported a prowler at her home on Greencrest Court, which was almost directly behind the Bricca house on Greenway. She had returned home to find a young man sitting on her porch smoking cigarettes. She ignored him and entered her house, but when he asked to use her phone she slammed the door in his face. Mrs. Bode later found cigarette butts and torn up magazines in her bushes.

Around 4 PM another unusual man knocked on the door of the Keifler home on North Glen Road, less than a mile from the Bricca house. Mr. Keifler encountered a man about 40 years old, with thinning hair and wearing an army field jacket. He claimed to represent the AH Furnace company and was there for a scheduled cleaning. Keifler turned him away and watched him leave on foot.

Overly suspicious, he checked out the company and found they didn't exist.

Eventually, physical evidence would indicate that Linda Bricca had sexual intercourse with a man sometime during this Saturday afternoon or early evening. The fact that Jerry was working during this time was telling enough.

But even rudimentary forensic testing from 1966 would confirm that this man had a different blood type than her husband...

September 24th

Clouds began to move in that evening, as fledgling autumn stretched amid yawning shadows.

Autumn, when everything was clean. The hot, sticky life of summer was almost gone, and soon lush bursting leaves would curl into rich reds and golds, gathered for bonfires and drifting smoke, signaling crisp and poignant beginnings.

People staying in on this Saturday night were enjoying new seasons of their favorite programs. Variety shows like *Jackie Gleason* and *Lawrence Welk* were there for the older folks, while the *Hollywood Palace* featured the Lovin' Spoonful performing their hit *Summer in the City*.

Get Smart and *Gunsmoke* had their devoted fans as well. The NBC movie was *The Last Sunset*, a western starring Rock Hudson and Kirk Douglas.

ABC was running persistent promos for their Sunday night "Big Movie Event", the television premiere of *Bridge on the River Kwai* starring Alec Guinness and William Holden and sponsored by the Ford Motor Company.

Just before midnight, CBS would air *The Girl in the Black Stockings*, staring Lex Barker, Ann Bancroft, and the curvaceous Mamie Van Doren. Definitely not for prime time, this 1957 B movie noir thriller was about a lawyer investigating a movie starlet's murder. With the kids in bed, the movie trailer boasted "She was every inch a teasing, taunting, 'come-on' blonde...and she made every inch pay off!"

Outside on Greenway Avenue life was slackening. Yet an unspeakable crime was evolving in the darkness, its final destination only 24 hours away. This was a street with lynx-eyed neighbors – anything observed from now on would have significance later.

Mr. and Mrs. Emmitt Baldwin were getting ready to go to a wedding reception. They were the Briccas next door neighbors to the north, the second house from the Lawrence corner. Linda and Jerry had planned to go to the reception with them, but Jerry got called into work and Linda said she wouldn't go without her husband. Mrs. Baldwin was touched by her loyalty, telling Linda "that's the kind of girl you are."

Around 7 PM their son Dan stopped by their house to pick up a flashlight. Backing out of this parent's driveway, he noticed a light green or gray car parked in the Bricca's driveway. In the gathering dusk it looked like a foreign model to him.

Around 9 PM three young friends were standing on Greenway talking. Janice Buell, Larry Abbott, and Dave Mair were students at Oak Hills High School and they'd just left Mair's house, across the street from the Bricca residence.

Janice was facing the street when she saw a familiar looking car emerge from the shadows heading south. Under muted street lights it looked brown or burgundy, similar to her boyfriend's car. She yelled out "Hey, Mike!" and the driver slowed down to stop. Janice jogged over, a smile spreading over her 17-year-old face.

Yet when she got close her smile vanished. There were two men in the car, neither one a high school student. The driver made a move to open his door, and Janice backed away saying "sorry, my mistake."

The car drove away and disappeared over the slight ridge on north Greenway...

AROUND 9:30 PM LINDA Bricca received a phone call from her mother. Linda had called her several times during the week, and June Bulaw was beginning to worry about her only daughter. She knew only too well just how tenuous and fragile her marriage was.

Linda had complained about the return of Jerry's temper, which she blamed on "not taking his medication". At one point she blurted out that she wanted to take Debbie and move back home to Chicago. June suggested she try to work through their problems, especially if they were planning to move to San Francisco.

On this night June sensed no angst coming from her daughter. She was excited about going to work for Dr. Leininger, who had offered her a regular Wednesday job that morning. Linda eagerly explained that she was working to get more experience with treating animals. In a rush of words, she regaled June with tales of working at the clinic on Monday, Tuesday, and Wednesday, going into sweeping detail about the receptionist job and all the operations she "assisted the Doc" to perform.

June and her husband Adolph were preparing to go out of town on Monday. Linda wished them a safe trip, and made her mother promise to call the day they got back. As she hung up with her daughter's voice lingering, June believed Linda sounded happy.

Yet moments later, she found herself wondering if her daughter was hiding something with her clash of words. Because June had heard it again – that implacable tinge of fear in Linda's voice...

HAMILTON COUNTY SHERIFF'S DEPUTY Ray Hoffbauer clocked out at 11:15 PM and headed west on Hamilton Avenue toward his home in Delhi. He was still in uniform but driving his own car, a gray 1950 Plymouth four door sedan.

It was a clear night growing sharp around the edges. The young deputy put a jacket on as he crossed over Colerain Avenue and entered the West Side of Cincinnati.

At 11:45 he turned left onto Greenway from Lawrence, stopping his car momentarily to mail a letter for his wife. The mailbox was on the same side of the street as the Bricca house, in front of the first house from the corner. As he left the car, he looked across the street and observed the neon aura emanating from Western Bowl, whose Saturday night leagues were legendary and never ended before midnight.

His supervisor always told him to be on the lookout for anything odd or usual, even while off duty. And as Ray went to drop the letter in the box, there he was – someone who just didn't belong.

He saw "an individual just standing there, in front of the next house over", which was the Baldwin home. Ray quickly cataloged the guy. He was early 20's, about 5-10, and wearing a light beige jacket. But what really drew his attention was the young man's posture – he appeared to be standing at attention by a sign post, just staring at the Bricca house.

The guy was about 25 feet away, and to Hoffbauer something didn't seem right. Mentally back on the job, he startled the subject by asking "What are you doing there?"

Ray would always remember the answer, the strange inflection, the flawless diction. "I am waiting for a friend," the stranger replied.

Ray turned away to mail the letter. He later would say his "eyes were off the subject" for about ten seconds.

But when he turned back, the man was gone...

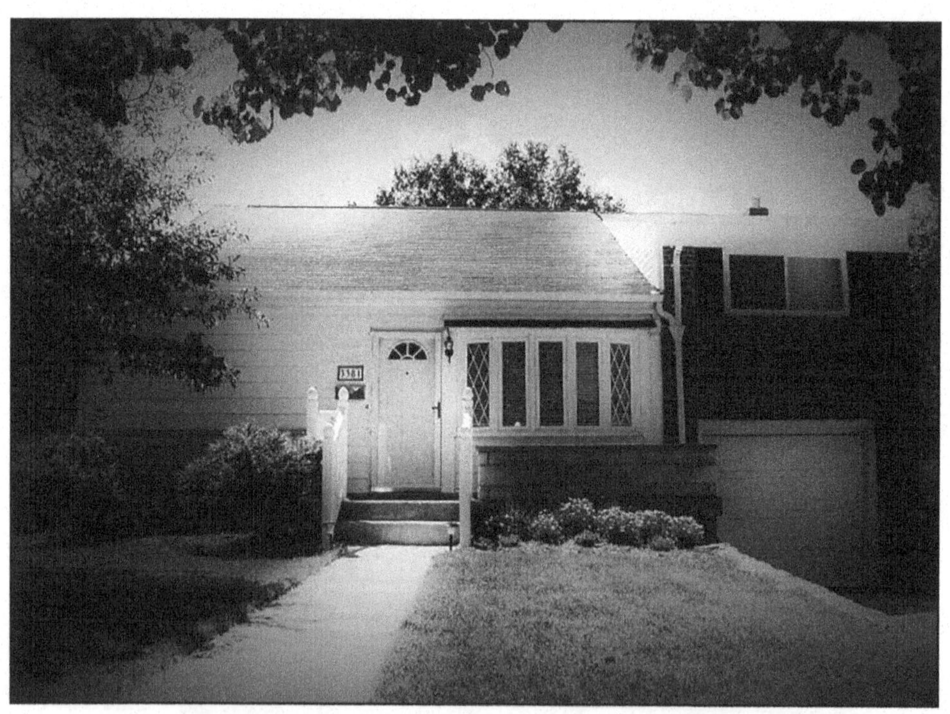

Before September 25th, 1966, the Bricca house on Greenway looked no different from thousands of others on the West Side.

CHAPTER FIVE

CERTAIN SHADOWS ON THE WALL

"Between the idea and the reality... between the motion and the act... falls the shadow."

TS Eliot

SUNDAY, SEPTEMBER 25TH, 1966

Dawn

Thousands of people who woke up on this particular morning would be dead by nightfall.

Disease, accidents, homicides, heart attacks and the blight of age would claim many victims on this day who would be quietly mourned and privately put to rest. Some would say they had gone to a better place – although the living were in no hurry to get there.

Like that old blues song says – everyone wants to go to heaven, but no one wants to die.

On the last day of their lives, Jerry, Linda, and Debbie Bricca awoke to tepid fall temperatures and a blanket of clouds. An intermittent rain would fall throughout the day. This September Sunday would be a portent that summer was almost gone.

Soon leaves would be drifting down in the Ohio River Valley, and light morning frosts would tint the oaks and maples red and yellow against vibrant blue skies. It was Linda Bricca's favorite time of the year, and this morning she had every reason to anticipate endless October wonders.

Tonight she was looking forward to the broadcast premiere of *Bridge on the River Kwai,* but not without misgivings. Ed Sullivan was countering the hit movie with headliners The Supremes, who would perform *You Can't Hurry Love* and a medley of five other songs, including *I Hear a Symphony* and *Stranger in Paradise.*

Ethel Merman was also on Sullivan, ready to belt out a few Irving Berlin tunes to lure older viewers away from the 1957 masterpiece that

Sunday September 25th dawned damp and drizzly.

won seven academy awards. NBC was hoping their top rated "Bonanza" followed by "The Andy Williams Show" would hold their loyal viewers as well.

With increasing chances of rain being forecast, it looked like a good night for Linda to stay in and wear a path to the TV while manually "channel surfing" the stellar Sunday night lineup. Plus she used her TV time to catch up on laundry.

She knew her marriage had entered a precarious phase. Would living with Jerry in San Francisco really be different than living with him here? Of course the environment would be better, but it wouldn't fix what was wrong.

Because our future is securely hidden from all of us, people often advocate taking a leap of faith because "life is short". For Linda Bricca, her life was ready to move beyond its margins, and she had summoned up the courage to make it happen. Life for her would never be short – it would be the longest thing she could do.

She had no inkling that her future was now measured in hours, that disaster would soon strike her family. She could not imagine that their names would hold citizens spellbound for months and years to come.

The crime would take on a life of its own, rippling out from the epicenter to the whole West Side and spilling into the city of Cincinnati and beyond. Peace of mind would take flight, as people eyed each other and pondered what primal thoughts existed in the minds of their neighbors or hid behind the faces of strangers.

And there would be deeper fears scavenging the Greenway neighborhood, qualms and pangs whispered in corners between husbands and wives.

Investigators would scrutinize every aspect of this Sunday, wringing every last drop of information while reconstructing the victim's movements and compiling reports of suspicious people within a mile radius of 3381 Greenway Avenue.

The investigation would eventually spread into many pathetic corners, like a random twister that exposes and scatters the pitiful refuse from dank city cellars...

Morning

In the early hours of that Sunday, the blemished oval of the waxing moon turned gray as it slipped in and out of the clouds like a beacon on cobwebbed seas.

As Saturday night blended into Sunday morning, with West Side families safely tucked away, there were doubtless many lonely, boozy assignations and tawdry trysts nearing completion. The lure of sex in the small hours of the weekend was powerful, and illicit couplings took flight on the night wing.

Those on the outside could not conceive it, and those on the inside could not convey it. Love after midnight – a true unknown.

Around 1:30 AM, 23-year-old Donna Nixon was struggling to stay awake at her babysitting job on Woodhaven Drive, less than a half mile from the Bricca house.

Mr. and Mrs. Kesse were at a cocktail party, and had warned her they might be out late. Cocktail parties were the life blood of the adult social scene in the 1960s, and the Woodhaven subdivision was no different. People here were considered "light drinkers" if they limited themselves to only 3-4 mixed drinks at one sitting.

Fighting the urge to nod off, Donna stood up and looked out the living room picture window of the terracotta colored brick ranch house.

She could see the Woodhaven Swim Club, which had closed for the season just after Labor Day. Across the street was a row of brick split levels, with postage stamp lawns and the typical driveway beginning at street level and ending in a sunken garage.

There was rapid movement to her left, and Donna saw a young man in the driveway, very close to the house. She stepped away from the window and watched as he skulked toward the round glow spilling from the nearby street light.

He looked to be in his twenties with dark hair, a tall, thin man wearing black pants and a beige jacket. He began pacing back and forth under the light. He appeared to be talking to himself, almost like he was screwing up his courage, his hand gestures imploring.

Donna was mesmerized watching him. After about five minutes he left, walking past the swim club and out of her view. She thought about calling the police, but was he really prowling?

When the Kesse's returned home around 2:30 AM, they were met by a clearly shaken Donna Nixon holding a kitchen knife in her hand. She told them about the man she saw – and that she discovered someone had fooled with the door.

Mrs. Kesse was not shocked. She had been bothered by prowlers for the last month, awakened by strange noises from the yard. When she told Donna about finding some scratches on the front doorknob, the babysitter left the house quickly, vowing to herself that she would never return.

ON THE LAST MORNING of his life, Jerry Bricca arrived at Monsanto around 7:30 AM. It was not unusual for the young engineer to work on Sundays – he would often travel the 11 mile round trip several times while putting in 2-3 hour stints.

Today he forgot to sign in on the personnel sheet, but the guard at the gate would later verify he was there. Jerry also saw John Jarvis, who reminded him that he had not signed in. Jerry stayed about an hour before leaving, telling Jarvis was going to church.

Jerry was next seen at St. Aloysius Gonzaga Church on Bridgetown Road attending the 9 AM Mass. Father Joseph Hageman recognized the burly, clean cut young man from previous Sundays, although he was not in their parish. He was always alone, and Hageman briefly

Rain showers would be sporadic all during the day.

wondered why he'd stopped attending Our Lady of Lourdes in his own parish.

A credit card slip would confirm that Jerry stopped in for gas around 10:30 at the Werk Road Shell station – the same place that worked on Linda's car Friday. Attendant Russ Older later said he didn't recall waiting on Jerry or seeing his vehicle that morning.

At 10:50 AM, Bricca neighbor Dick Janszen saw Jerry getting out of his car in front of his house and waved hello.

Janszen was 38 years old, with four children all older than Debbie Bricca, a more typical demographic for Greenway families. The Janszen home abutted the back parking lot of Western Bowl, and Dick was an avid kegler like many of the West Siders who flocked to the big bowling mecca at the corner of Glenway and Lawrence. Janszen bowled up to five times a week while maintaining an over 200 average, and was the emergency sub when a league bowler didn't show. On a moment's notice he could walk through his back yard and be rolling frames within minutes.

Janszen crossed the street to chat, kidding Jerry about "being up so early on a Sunday." Jerry smiled and admitted he was "an early bird", and told Janszen he was just coming back from church.

Janszen would later tell investigators that Jerry was dressed in dark pants and a dark sports shirt – the same clothing he would be found dead in. And he confirmed that this was the last time he saw any of the Bricca family alive...

Mid-Day

The temperature nudged 50 around noon, and the rain started up again. There was a 40% chance of precipitation all day in the greater Cincinnati area, with higher chances on the West Side.

At 12:10 PM the phone rang in the Walgreen's Pharmacy at the Western Hills Plaza. Mr. Neisel took the call from Linda Bricca for a refill of her HydroDiuril, which she took for her fluid retention issues. Neisel told her it would be ready after 3 PM.

Around the same time Jerry was seen at the J & J Market by butcher Vernon Ward, ordering some lunch meat and bread like he was getting ready to brown bag it. Ward was used to seeing Jerry, who did more of the meat purchasing than his wife.

At 12:25 PM Jerry returned to work at Monsanto, this time signing in with the guard. He left four hours later, and this was the last time, officially, that he worked at Monsanto.

He could have slipped back into the plant after 7 PM without the guard seeing him. Yet Jerry was flying out to the Monsanto facility in Nitro, West Virginia early Monday morning. It is doubtful he would make a third trip to Monsanto on a Sunday night.

There is no record that anyone interacted with Jerry that afternoon at Monsanto. The factory was not running and only the most dedicated office drones would be spending a Sunday afternoon there. Unless they had a reason to avoid being home.

These long hours on the job were nothing new for Jerry Bricca, who worked evenings, weekends, and holidays without complaint. So why was this man sitting on a verbal job offer from Standard Oil in San Francisco busting his tail at Monsanto as the last afternoon of his life drained away?

At around 3:30 PM there was a strange sighting on Greenway Avenue, about a quarter mile south of the Bricca house. A woman calling herself Emily Stout reported seeing a nude man on the sidewalk, standing in the light rain. Discarded at the time, this tip took on greater significance after the murders were discovered.

But by that time Emily Stout was nowhere to be found.

At the Cincinnati homicide squad, Sgt. Russ Jackson was showing photo lineups to Virginia Hinners and Ernest Reams, the victims of the Wednesday night melee at the New Thought Unity Center in Walnut Hills. Hinners and Reams had come in both Saturday and Sunday after taking several days off to heal from their traumatic encounter.

Reams was knocked out before getting a good look at his assailant, and merely shrugged with each successive image. However, Mrs. Hinners had conversed with her attacker several times over a period of at least ten minutes, and she felt strongly that she would recognize him again.

Jackson was counting on her, because the proximity of her assault to the December 1965 murder of Emogene Harrington could not be overlooked. This man had even asked for the caretaker, just like Elizabeth Kreco's assailant in Walnut Hills the previous October. If Hinners could identify her attacker, Jackson was certain the Strangler would be dropped.

They were bearing down on the one year anniversary of the October 12th 1965 attack on Kreco. Jackson tried to interview her several times without success – but she had never recovered from the horrific injuries inflicted upon her.

Elizabeth Kreco would die the following month, never officially added to the Strangler's body count. The unknown killer's first victim was destined to be forgotten.

Afternoon

Around 4 PM residents on Lawrence Avenue noticed two subjects going door to door.

One remembered talking to two clean cut young men dressed in suits taking a survey for a church – he said they did nothing to arouse suspicion. They were also seen on Greenway, but it's not known if they knocked on the Bricca door or if Linda answered it. Despite a plea from the police, they never came forward.

Other than a single report of Linda Bricca calling in a prescription to Walgreens around noon, there is no record of anyone seeing her or interacting with her on the last day of her life.

Often a killer or a victim will do something the day of the crime that doesn't seem related – but is completely out of character. Something this person has never done before. Yet there is virtually no insight into Linda as her final hours ticked away.

When recreating a murder timeline, the quirks of arbitrary movement and the flukes of witness observation offer a narrow margin for detectives. People around 3381 Greenway had no reason to be more sharp-eyed today than any other day. The circle of time and events swirled randomly, some briefly touching while others barely missed colliding.

Whatever Linda was up to on this drizzly day can only be speculated. No babysitters were engaged, no phone calls received, no sightings of the pretty brunette on Greenway or around the business district.

Someone must have interacted with Linda Bricca in the hours before she and her family were slain. There had to be some type of a secret assignation.

Perhaps a dry run for murder...

JERRY BRICCA SIGNED OUT at the Monsanto gate at 4:25 PM and placed his helmet and safety glasses on the passenger seat of his gray Volkswagen. He had worked four hours, and began driving the long rise from Addyston toward Bridgetown. The rain had dissipated, and he made good time getting to Glenway Avenue.

Some newspaper accounts would later place him working until 8:30 PM that night. But this was at odds with his known movements between 4:30-7 PM.

He was next seen around 4:40 PM at the Walgreens in Western Hills Plaza picking up Linda's prescription. The pharmacist would later confirm that Jerry was alone, and chatted with him only briefly since they were getting ready to close.

At 5:30 PM, Betty Hardig was driving to an evening church service when she saw her neighbor, a man named Hinkley, walking across the Western Bowl parking lot. Mrs. Hardig lived on Green Acres court, the next street over from Lawrence and only a quarter mile from the Bricca house.

She knew that Hinkley had recently been released from prison and was living with his mother. She was uneasy having him right next door, and kept an eye peeled when he was on the move.

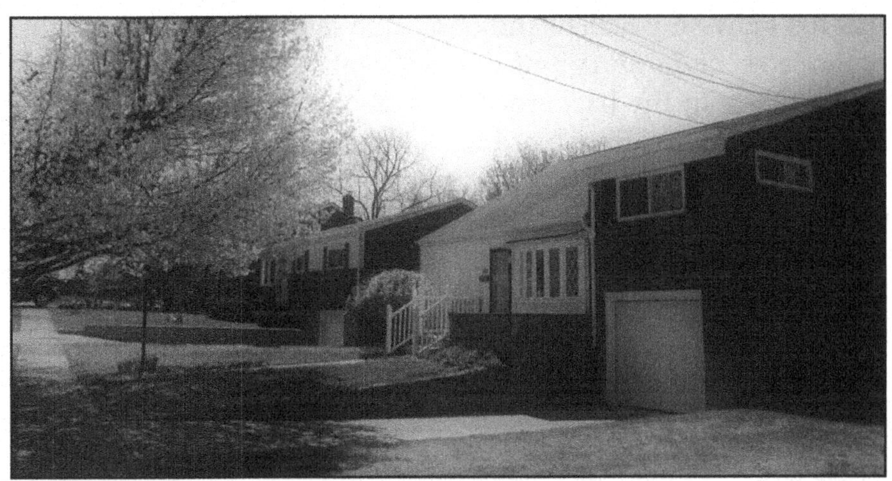

There were brief peaks of sun late in the afternoon.

Sometime between 6-7 PM, Steve and Valinda Westman returned to the Glenway Animal Hospital for the night after spending the day in Northern Kentucky. They had begun working at the clinic on Thursday and moved into the apartment that same day.

The Westmans had left the clinic around 8 AM that morning, and were planning to return around 10 PM. But since they were new on the job, Steve decided an earlier return would be better.

To their knowledge, no one else entered the clinic at any time that night.

JERRY BRICCA WAS HOME at 6:45 PM when his co-worker Glenn Ritchie called. The two men were flying out to the West Virginia plant Monday morning and needed to make arrangements. Ritchie was a year older than Jerry, and they'd known each other since Jerry transferred here in 1963.

Most of that time they worked at different plants doing the same job – almost all of their communication was by phone. But the last three months Ritchie had worked on a project in Jerry's building, and the young engineers developed a friendly rapport.

To Glenn Ritchie, the last known person to have called the Bricca number, Jerry seemed relaxed, and joked about "the Sunday work hours" he put in. He detected no fear or stress in his voice.

"I don't have my ticket handy," Ritchie said. "When is our flight?"

"Just a second." Jerry put down the phone. Ritchie later said he heard nothing in the background for about 30 seconds. Nor did he hear Jerry speak to anyone or be spoken to. He listened to the silent house at the other end until Jerry came back on. "It says 8:15 AM. How about I pick you up at your place 6:30 sharp? We can take my car to the airport."

"I appreciate that Jerry." Glenn Ritchie replied. "I'll drive the next time."

"Works for me," said Jerry Bricca. "See you soon."

Twilight

This dreary day officially became a desolate night at 7:31 PM, the veiled sun vanishing over an invisible horizon and cuing harder rain showers. Events of this night would soon recede into the foggy unknown, and for weeks afterwards the descending darkness would fill West Siders with apprehension.

Residents of the Woodhaven subdivision would rack their memory for anything or anyone out of place in the vicinity of 3381 Greenway Avenue. But on this wet evening people were dashing about and not paying close attention.

Just before 8 PM the rain briefly subsided, and Oscar Martz rushed out to give his dachshund a quick walk. Martz lived nine houses south from the Briccas – he either walked the dog on Woodhaven or Greenway.

Tonight he started on the east side of Greenway, strolling up to the Lawrence corner before returning on the west side of the street, placing him directly in front of the Bricca house. He did not see any unusual cars or persons during this walk, and as the rain started up again he hurried home.

Before heading out his wife had reminded him that *The Bridge on the River Kwai* was starting at 8 PM. Like people all over the country, Greenway residents were settling in to watch the world premiere of the Oscar winning movie. It was the perfect weekend extender on a rainy night, with the jolt of Monday morning alarm clocks just ten hours away.

This premiere was sponsored by Ford, and the auto giant placed a full page ad in TV Guide, topped with NOW, KWAI: *8 PM, ABC*

As the sun went down all evidence suggests Jerry, Linda and Debbie were at home.

Channel 2,6,12, in color. A great show, a television first. William Holden, Alec Guinness, and Jack Hawkins, directed by David Lean. And another great show, another television first. The 1967 Ford Motor Company cars; starring Mustang, Fairlane, Falcon, Mercury, Thunderbird, Lincoln Continental and introducing...Cougar. Are you ready for that double bill?

ABC had paid Columbia Pictures $2 million for the rights for two showings of the 1957 film, and reaped $1.8 million in commercials from Ford on the first night. By the time the movie ended at 11:10 PM, an estimated 60 million viewers (a 38.3 rating and a 61 share) had tuned in to watch "Kwai," at that time the largest audience ever to watch a feature film on TV.

TV Guide featured the movie with a half page "close-up" blurb: *In the Ceylonese jungle during World War II, a battalion of British war prisoners, working on the "death railroad," is ordered to build a strategic bridge over the River Kwai. Pierre Boulle's screenplay (adapted from his novel) focuses on Colonel Nicholson, the stiff-necked British commanding officer, and Colonel Saito, the Japanese prison-camp commandant, who faces death if the bridge is not completed on schedule...*

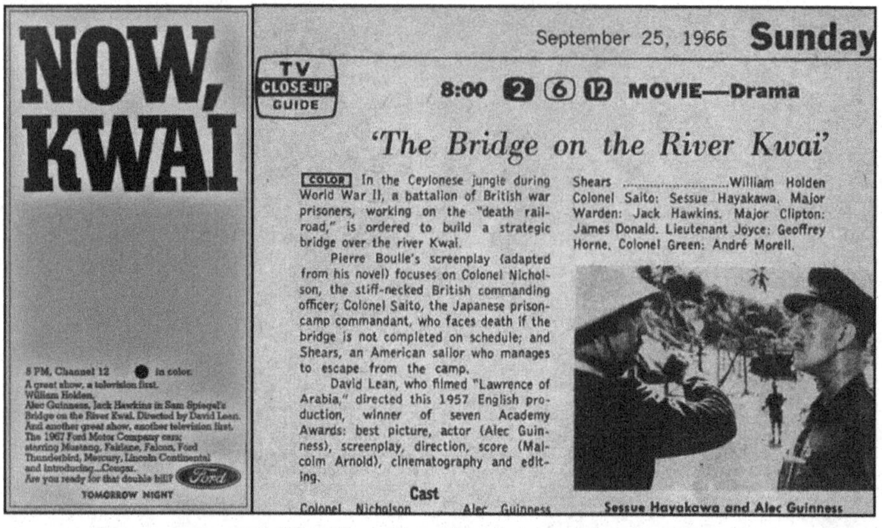

NOW, KWAI

8 PM, Channel 12 ● in color.
A great show, a television first.
William Holden,
Alec Guinness, Jack Hawkins in Sam Spiegel's
Bridge on the River Kwai. Directed by David Lean.
And another great show, another television first.
The 1967 Ford Motor Company cars;
starring Mustang, Fairlane, Falcon, Ford
Thunderbird, Mercury, Lincoln Continental
and introducing...Cougar.
Are you ready for that double bill?
Ford
TOMORROW NIGHT

September 25, 1966 **Sunday**

TV CLOSE-UP GUIDE

8:00 2 6 12 MOVIE—Drama

'The Bridge on the River Kwai'

COLOR In the Ceylonese jungle during World War II, a battalion of British war prisoners, working on the "death railroad," is ordered to build a strategic bridge over the river Kwai.

Pierre Boulle's screenplay (adapted from his novel) focuses on Colonel Nicholson, the stiff-necked British commanding officer; Colonel Saito, the Japanese prison-camp commandant, who faces death if the bridge is not completed on schedule; and Shears, an American sailor who manages to escape from the camp.

David Lean, who filmed "Lawrence of Arabia," directed this 1957 English production, winner of seven Academy Awards: best picture, actor (Alec Guinness), screenplay, direction, score (Malcolm Arnold), cinematography and editing.

Cast

Colonel Nicholson .... Alec Guinness
Shears .... William Holden
Colonel Saito: Sessue Hayakawa. Major Warden: Jack Hawkins. Major Clipton: James Donald. Lieutenant Joyce: Geoffrey Horne. Colonel Green: André Morell.

Sessue Hayakawa and Alec Guinness

The premiere of "Kwai" on Sunday night September 25th drew the largest TV audience ever for a feature film.

As the opening credits for Kwai rolled, things were winding down inside the Bricca house. Their TV set was tuned to the movie on channel 12 – Linda was folding some towels with Debbie on the couch. If Jerry was sitting there for the start of the movie, he must have become restless, because he would be seen running an errand sometime before 9 PM.

It's possible he slipped out earlier than 8 PM and made a quick stop at Monsanto, perhaps some final preparation or missing documentation for his West Virginia trip Monday morning. Either way, he was back inside the house just after 9 PM.

Linda probably switched over to the Sullivan show during Kwai's opening to catch Diana Rose and the Supremes cooing their top hit *You Can't Hurry Love*, the former number one song in the country until being eclipsed by The Association's *Cherish* the day before.

When she turned back to the movie, at morning assembly Colonel Nicholson orders his officers to stay behind when the enlisted men are sent off to work. The previous day Japanese commandant Colonel Saito, played brilliantly by Sessue Hayakawa, told them all prisoners were to work on the railroad bridge over River Kwai regardless of rank, Geneva Convention be damned.

When Nicholson doesn't relent, Saito slaps him across the face with his copy of the conventions, summons a jeep with a machine gun in the back, and threatens to have all the British officers shot. Nicholson still refuses to back down, so Saito says he will count to three and open fire.

Major Clipton, the British medical officer, quickly intervenes and warns Saito. *"There are too many witnesses! You'll never get away with calling it a mass escape! Most of those men can't walk...Is this your soldier's code? Murdering unarmed men?"* Saito backs down, the tension subsides, and ABC breaks for their first Ford commercial. In millions of homes across the country, viewers bolted for the kitchen and the bathroom, or maybe flipped over to Ed Sullivan.

But in the Bricca home, Major Clipton's warning hung in the air like an uncanny echo flowing through the rooms, a foreshadowing of events already unfolding.

"There are too many witnesses..."

Evening

As her customers diminished on a damp Sunday night, Mrs. Ruby Grayson glanced at the clock. It was 8:45 PM, 15 minutes until closing time at the United Dairy Farmers store on Glenway Avenue, where she was the only clerk on duty. She lived close by, and was hoping to get home and catch the last half of the movie.

The door opened and a familiar face walked in. Ruby knew Jerry Bricca as a routine customer who bought milk there for the last several years. Tonight he was alone and not wearing a jacket on this rainy evening. In the past he sometimes had Debbie with him, but Ruby had never met Jerry's wife.

They bantered momentarily as Ruby rung him up for three half gallons of milk and a quart of orange juice. She smiled, chiding him for not wearing a coat. Then the strapping young man strolled out the door with a friendly wave of his hand.

As she began wiping down the counters for the last time tonight, Ruby mused about Jerry. The guy worked ungodly hours, yet he always put a smile on her face when he came in.

That man is a real gentleman, Ruby said to herself. *Squeaky clean. He would never do anything out of the way.*

At 8:50 PM, Greenway resident George Ditullio left a party at the Burris residence, two doors south of the Bricca house. He walked across the street to his house at 3370, turned on his porch light, and hauled his garbage cans to the curb. The rain was picking up a little, so George didn't loiter. He thought he saw both of the Bricca's cars, with Jerry's parked on the street in front of the house.

His wife Janet left the party a few minutes before 9 PM and hurried across the street. She also saw the Bricca automobiles, but didn't notice other cars parked nearby or anything unusual.

But then again, neither of them had reason to be watching for signs of a nasty crime rapidly approaching from out of the gloom.

Minutes later, the clock struck 9 PM – zero hour at 3381 Greenway. The turbulence of this night was cresting into the climax of a lethal passion play...

MRS. JOAN JANSZEN WAS walking her Chihuahua on Greenway, her head down against the obstinate mist.

As she passed the Bricca house she was startled by a figure in their driveway, emerging from the darkness. Stifling a scream, she recognized her neighbor Jerry Bricca standing by his garbage cans. They greeted each other, but Jerry was brusque and in no mood to chat. Joan watched him trudge into his garage, dressed as if he had just come home from work.

Joan would later insist: "I know it was Jerry. If it had been a stranger, everybody on the street would have heard me screaming." She was the last person outside his house to see Jerry Bricca alive.

Moments later Emmett Baldwin, the Bricca's next door neighbor to the north, took his garbage cans to the curb. He saw Joan Janszen, her rain coat pulled tight around her neck, cross the street with her dog and head towards her front door. Hearing movement to his right, he turned and saw Jerry Bricca walking back into his garage. Baldwin saw Jerry's cans at the curb – the Bricca house was mostly dark, except for the garage light.

Baldwin, a meteorologist with the National Weather Bureau, had an eye for detail, and he was certain the man he saw enter the Bricca garage was Jerry. As he went back into his house, Baldwin noticed that Bricca bathroom window was open.

A minute later, Mrs. Edith Kesse was driving north on Greenway when she observed a black 1965 Chevrolet with a lone male driver cruising slowly past the Bricca house towards Woodhaven.

Around 9:05 PM, a neighbor to the rear saw something odd. Helen Zambatis lived on Greencrest, and her back yard abutted the Bricca property. She had known the family since 1963 and engaged in many back fence chats with Linda, although she hadn't seen much of her this summer. Helen always got a kick out of the younger couple, who usually ran around their yard barefoot and often didn't have dinner until 8 or 9 PM.

At the critical time on this night in question, Helen had the best vantage point for viewing the back of the Bricca house – the killer's likely point of entry. Her house sat on a small knoll and she could look down into the Bricca yard.

It was her young son's bedtime, and his room was on the back side of their house. Helen pulled open the drapes as she tucked him in, and her eyes swept the Bricca back yard. She could see that the TV in their lower level was on, which was odd, because she usually couldn't see their set at all.

She realized later that the only way she could see into the Bricca TV room was if their back door was wide open.

Darkness

Mary Alice Baldwin was sitting in the living room of her home at 3387 Greenway. It was a few minutes after 9 PM, and she heard Emmett coming in through the garage after taking the garbage out. He entered his den and went back to his reading. Mary Alice knew not to bother her husband when he was absorbed in a book.

She took pride in being an old-style housewife. Three months ago the *Enquirer* profiled her in a feature headlined **The Woman Behind The Man**. The caption under her photo read "Mrs. Emmett Baldwin, wife of Cincinnati's chief meteorologist, has helped and encouraged her husband in his career of weather forecasting."

Mary Alice had refused to marry Emmett unless he returned to work for the federal government as a weatherman. He lost that position two years previously in 1933, when FDR instituted the Economy Act requiring all unmarried men in Federal service be laid off, and was languishing as a pharmacist. With their engagement hanging in the balance, Emmett wired his old boss and was soon working as a weatherman again – this time a married one.

MRS. EMMETT E. Baldwin, wife of Cincinnati's chief meteorologist, has helped and encouraged her husband in his career of weather forecasting.
—Enquirer Photo
Weatherman With Charts
. . . Mr. Baldwin now in charge of bureau

Bricca neighbors Emmett and Mary Alice Baldwin heard some unusual noises between 9:15-9:45 PM.

They moved to Cincinnati in 1956, and in 1964 Emmett was given the top job: Chief Meteorologist in charge of the Cincinnati Weather Bureau. But the *Enquirer* profile focused on Mary Alice, who represented the stalwart and faithful West Side wife. With feminism escalating on both coasts, she was the embodiment of traditional values still flourishing in the heartland.

Mary Alice told the reporter that "Emmett has always been my first consideration. I always have dinner ready the minute he walks in the door." And she gave him plenty of space. "I feel that a man needs a certain amount of privacy...we were always taught at home to respect the head of the house. To me, Emmett's word is law."

As Mary Alice reflected on her small measure of local fame, she had no idea of the infamy ascending next door, twenty feet away from her, separated by two brick walls and a narrow strip of grass.

Shortly after Emmett came in she heard a noise, like someone bumping into a tree or brushing against a shrub. She looked outside and saw that the Bricca's bathroom window was open.

Mary Alice was getting ready for bed around 9:30 PM when she heard a thumping noise coming from the south. Peering out her window, she noticed the Bricca bathroom window was closed but now their master bedroom window was part way open.

Evidence suggests the killer or killers entered this back door sometime between 9:15-9:30 PM that night.

She thought this was odd given the rainfall. But she soon drifted off to sleep, blissfully unaware of the carnage unfolding nearby...

At 9:15 PM, Charles Herbig was stopped on Glenway at the Lawrence traffic light when a dark blue Pontiac or Chevy pulled up beside him. Glancing at the driver, Herbig thought the guy appeared "really nervous". He was a white man, mid 30's with short dark hair. As the light turned green, the car did a jackrabbit onto Lawrence, putting it less than a quarter mile from the Bricca house.

Just before 9:30 PM, Lou Theuer waited on Richard Meyer at Lou's Greenacres Food and Beverage. The deli was at the corner of Glenway and Lawrence, and Theuer was familiar with all the nearby residents. Meyer was a regular who always bought lunchmeat for his upcoming work week.

When Meyer returned home at 9:30, he saw Jerry's garbage cans were out. He noticed their kitchen light was on, yet he didn't see anyone around the Bricca house. Meyer went inside and sat down to watch the rest of the movie with his wife Betty.

As Meyer entered his house, Edith Kesse was driving south on Greenway, where earlier she'd seen a car driving slowly past the Bricca house. Now here it was again, the dark Chevy or Pontiac with a male driver cruising north on Greenway. She watched the car almost stop near the Bricca house before she went over the rise towards her home on Woodhaven.

Edith was already on edge. Her babysitter Donna had been frightened by a prowler around 1:30 AM that morning, and she'd seen a similar dark car trolling on Woodhaven just before that incident. Edith herself heard odd noises in her yard at night several times recently, and later found scratches on her doorknobs.

At 10:15 PM a strange visitor interrupted a wedding shower at a house on Moonridge Drive – a half mile from the Bricca house.

Anne Wippel was there along with four other couples and a few single women. When she moved away from the group to look out front window, a woman startled her by walking onto the porch and peering in at the party. She locked eyes with Mrs. Wippel, who quickly called the hostess over.

Alma Schreck answered the door and inquired of the woman, who appeared confused and distressed. She told Mrs. Schreck she would give her $5 to call a Yellow cab to pick her up. Alma told her husband, prompting him and another man to go out and talk to this woman. They advised her that she could catch a bus at the Lawrence intersection, and their weird caller left.

They would later describe her as mid-50's, about 5-7, with dishwater blonde hair and wearing a full length raincoat with a plastic bonnet.

While working at Shillito's department store the following week, Anne Wippel heard about the Sunday night murders and flashed back to the strange woman on her friend's porch. She even told her boss about the woman's unusual demeanor.

It was like she was frightened by something and running away from it...

Nightfall

Most businesses along the Glenway corridor were closed by now, but the Hi-Lo Beverage Depot was still open at 10:30 PM. The store was just north of the Glenway and Lawrence intersection, a half mile from the Bricca house.

Owner Larry Foppe worked there seven days a week, from 8 AM until 11 PM every day. He was a gregarious man who enjoyed bantering with his customers, but they were scarce on this wet night. Foppe began to close up so he could get out of there early.

The door swung open, and one of his regulars came rushing in. Foppe recognized him but the man looked askew. He was normally distinguished looking, but tonight he appeared unkempt.

The man shot Foppe a furtive look – Larry saw the color rising in his cheeks. He attempted to use the pay phone, became flustered, and then hurried back out into the rainy night.

Larry Foppe had never seen this guy acting so peculiar...

BACK ON GREENWAY, AROUND 10:35 PM Ruth Hemmer put her poodle in their fenced back yard. Her house was a brick and frame tri-level identical to the Bricca house and only five doors south of it.

A few minutes later the dog began barking in an excited tone. Ruth went back out and saw her dog baring its teeth and looking to the north, as if something or someone was in one of those yards. Their back yard was lighted, and Ruth thought she saw some movement behind the Bricca house, but the rain was picking up again and her perspective was hazy at best.

About the same time, Mary Alice and Emmett Baldwin were lying in bed when they heard a strange noise – they would later say it sounded like "something falling". Their bedroom was only twenty feet from the Bricca bedroom, and they were certain the sound came from there. This was the third time between 9:00-10:30 PM that they heard noises from next door.

Yet these sounds were not distinct, and on a wet night when neighbors were darting out and dragging their trash cans to the curb, one would expect to hear various splashes, clatters, and thuds. Greenway was the ideal shortcut for the denizens of Western Bowl to cut through to Werk Road, and at this hour was still awash with hasty figures and wet vehicles.

At 11:00 PM Jean Skinner drove past the Bricca house on her way home from work. Jean lived next door to Ruth Hemmer, and both women worked in the Rodeo Room at Western Bowl. It was raining hard and she didn't notice anything unusual.

The Baldwins were in their bedroom (right), only 15-20 feet away from the Bricca house as the murders went down.

At 11:01 PM, INSIDE the Bricca house and all across America, *Bridge on the River Kwai* was sounding the death knell. In a final act rivaling Hamlet for the intensity of climactic bloodshed, the characters saw fate roaring towards them with swift certitude.

As Colonel Nicholson marvels over the completed bridge, a monument to HIS ingenuity and dedication, the team of commandos moves in to destroy it as a train carrying Japanese soldiers and dignitaries makes the very first crossing.

British Major Warden, US Navy Commander Shears, and Canadian Lieutenant Joyce reach the river in time to plant explosives on the bridge towers under cover of darkness. Yet the next morning Nicholson spots the wire connecting the explosives to the detonator, and he and Colonel Saito investigate. The commandos are shocked to see a British officer betray their plot.

Joyce breaks cover and stabs Saito to death. Nicholson yells for help and tries to prevent Joyce from getting to the detonator. Joyce implores Nicholson to stop, telling him he is a British officer with orders to destroy the bridge. When Joyce is killed by Japanese fire, Shears swims across the river, only to be fatally wounded as he reaches Nicholson.

Recognizing the dying Shears, Nicholson cries out "What have I done?" Warden then fires his mortar, mortally wounding Nicholson.

The colonel stumbles towards the detonator and collapses on the plunger just in time to blow up the bridge and send the train hurtling into the river below.

As the lights and sounds from the movie flickered into the Bricca TV room, their house had become part of the other world. Violence had flashed out, feverish yet precise, cleaving flesh from spirit, leaving certain shadows on the wall.

In the final shot, Major Clipton surveys the carnage on the River Kwai. Earlier he had warned Saito against gunning down British officers, imploring him that *"There are too many witnesses!"*

Now Clipton can only shake his head and whisper. *"Madness! Madness."*

Night

Kristy Crawley had watched most of the movie while also working on a letter to her boyfriend. The 18-year-old was staying the summer with the Bachman family on Hyacinth Terrace, a cul-de-sac off the west side of Greenway. She was enjoying spending time with her aunt, uncle, and cousins in Cincinnati.

After reading it over several times, Kristy finished the letter at 11:15 PM. It was an important communiqué – they had been apart all summer, but his letters were short and lacking affection. She felt they were at a turning point, and had poured out heart on paper.

With everyone else asleep, Kristy peered out the front door and saw the rain had subsided. With the letter sealed, she wanted to get it in the mailbox. And she was in luck – there was a box at the corner of Greenway and Hyacinth with a 10 AM pickup.

Kristy dashed down the street in flip flops, splashing puddles and smiling with anticipation over mailing THIS letter, which she was certain would have the desired effect. It apparently did – Kristy wed her boyfriend the next year, and is still married to him today.

As she neared the corner a figure on the left caught her eye.

It was a white male, striding south on Greenway on her side of the street. She wasn't sure why she paused, but she remained in the shadows as he crossed Hyacinth. Something about his purposeful gait spooked her. She would later describe him as about 5-10, long dark hair, white shirt and suit coat but no tie.

Only after he passed out of sight did she approach the box and drop the letter in it. Returning to her Uncle's home, she soon forgot about the lone man on Greenway. Three days later her memory was revived when the big story hit the paper.

That man was just a quarter mile from the Bricca house when she observed him...

WESTERN BOWL IS THE unquestioned hub of the Glenway Avenue corridor. And close proximity to the Bricca house would make it a focal point in the coming investigation.

Lovingly called "The Tomb of the Unknown Bowler", the massive building at 6383 Glenway offered an astounding 68 lanes along with a nursery, two restaurants, several bars, and even a night club, combining the best of bowling, games, food, drink and entertainment in a way that made it the "go to" West Side destination. In 1966 it was the place to be, always full of people from early morning until late night.

The place could be garish and loud, but low ceilings absorbed the noise and the vivid lighting gave it an air of constant excitement. The bars were always crowded, and the pool room was smoky and mysterious, the soft thwack of balls smacking each other contrasting with the crash of bigger balls into pins.

There was entertainment beyond the average bowling alley. The Rodeo Room booked celebrities of all kinds, from Phyllis Diller to Robert Goulet to Joey Bishop. The Surf Club had a more intimate atmosphere, and would be dogged by rumors of afterhours gambling and prostitution in the 1970s.

Western's day care center in the basement hosted children while their parents bowled. It was often wall to wall kids down there with usually only two or three women to supervise.

On this night, the Sunday evening mixed couples league was winding up about 11:10 PM. The rain had slackened as Robert Reicheld and his wife walked out to the back parking lot. Between 11:20-11:25 PM they turned left out of Western Bowl onto Lawrence before taking another left onto Greenway.

As Reicheld neared the dip in the road before Greenway rises, he saw a car parked in front of the Bricca residence, facing south. To Reicheld it

An aerial shot of Western Bowl shows Greenway Avenue and a portion of the Bricca house on the extreme left.

looked like a 1963 Falcon, a light green color that almost appeared white when his lights hit it.

As he slowed down to pass the car, he and his wife observed a white male getting into the driver's side door. As their headlights captured him, he looked up with a startled, frightened look on his face. They would later describe him as early 20s, about 5-8 and 150lbs, with medium length light brown hair, wearing Khaki pants and a white shirt with the tail hanging out.

There were no other cars parked on this section of Greenway. As Reicheld swung out to pass this automobile another car was speeding down the rise going north, so he quickly pulled back to give it room. He and his wife both remarked it was unusual that this was the only auto parked on the north end of Greenway.

When interviewed the following week, Reicheld was asked how he knew the Falcon was in front of the Bricca residence. He said it was parked by the third house from the corner on the west side where the street takes a dip – which is in fact the Bricca house.

Leaving Western Bowl just moments after the Reichelds, Ray McAdams was behind them as he hung a left on Greenway.

As he approached the dip in the road, he too saw the parked vehicle, which looked green or white to him. Slowing down to let up the northbound vehicle past on the narrow street, McAdams came right behind the car and glimpsed a slender, young woman getting into the passenger side.

He was taken aback by the "frightened expression" on her face. He also saw two subjects sitting in the front seat, who appeared to be male based on their size.

As McAdams climbed the short rise of Greenway, he noticed no other cars parked on the street between Lawrence and Woodhaven. He hit Westbourne Avenue just behind Bob Reicheld and his wife, and put the people he had seen out of his mind.

Investigators love it when two witnesses can verify something independently of each other. But what did these men really see? Both were adult males in their 30's, just leaving their bowling league, and had probably knocked back a few beers while rolling their frames. Perhaps their headlights merely startled three innocent people getting into their car.

Except that on this night, these unknown subjects were observed in front of a house where a grisly crime had just been committed...

Midnight

Even in the light of what we know now, many of these witness accounts are frustrating. Some people in the vicinity of 3381 Greenway were extremely close by when the murders occurred, but through fate or circumstance just missed seeing something incriminating, or at least suspicious.

By the time they came forward, precious details had ebbed from their memories, the sights and sounds of another night fading in their mind's rear view mirror, drifting deeper into the gray matter.

As the clock neared midnight, human activity on Greenway evaporated into the darkness. The street was hushed, empty. The rain diminished and the wind swirled dead leaves mingled with careless debris along the bleak avenues and gloomy blocks.

The muffled, pulsing of a distant train throbbed like an underground heart, cracking its skin. It was the hour when everyone's guilty conscience returns to its house.

Just after midnight, the Ervin Hall family was returning from the Ferguson Hills Drive-In. They turned left onto Greenway, where they lived at 3216. The kids were asleep in the back, and his wife was drowsy. But Ervin saw the car parked near the house – third one from the corner where the road dipped. It was a 1964 red Chevy Impala – Ervin recognized the make and year because his neighbor down the street had a blue one. For no reason at all, he made a mental note of the license plate number.

But Hall wouldn't recognize the significance until weeks after the horrific events of this night were discovered. By that time the license number had muddled in his memory.

As Sunday slipped into Monday, Larry Foppe lay awake in his bed, his wife and children fast asleep in their home on Harmony Lane, about a half mile from the Bricca house.

Foppe was still contemplating his odd encounter with that customer just before closing. He had mentioned it to his wife, telling her this man's behavior, including the timing of his visit on a Sunday night, was completely out of character.

It unnerved him, and Foppe closed up right after his edgy patron departed. Turning left onto Greenway, he thought he saw the familiar sight of Jerry Bricca's car parked in front of his house – and there was another car he didn't recognize parked behind it.

Linda was a semi-regular customer, and Foppe knew this was their house. The other car looked blue in color, but it was raining hard and he didn't give it much thought. By the time Foppe got home a few minutes later at 10:45 PM, it was really pouring down.

Now the relentless rain had stopped, and Larry Foppe stared at the darkened ceiling in his bedroom, his mind still racing. What was going on with that guy tonight?

He normally had a polished appearance, but tonight he wore a tattered sport coat that didn't match his pants, and he kept his left hand jammed in his pocket. He seemed frayed around the edges, looking like he hadn't shaved and with his clothes hanging loose.

He had asked to use the pay telephone without greeting Larry, even though they knew each other. Foppe noticed his hands were shaking. For some reason he was unable to make his call – when Larry asked if anything was wrong, the man threw off a cryptic comment about being on an emergency call, and then stalked out the door. The whole encounter had lasted about three minutes.

Foppe already had some opinions about this man, and had heard some rumors. It was easy to pick up gossip at the Hi-Lo, where alcohol was sold long after other stores had closed.

This man had always taken a friendly yet superior attitude toward Larry, even though both of them owned a business in the Glenway corridor. Larry in turn thought him to be furtive and oddly repellent, despite his professional demeanor. Yet he was a good customer who came in three to four times a week, a man who had excellent taste in wine and champagne.

But the guy always managed to irk Larry, acting like he was connected to powerful people – as if he could get anything done he wanted. He often hinted of vague yet brilliant plans.

As Larry Foppe drifted off to sleep, his last thought was something like *you're no better than me, Fred Leininger...*

Neighbors Richard Meyer and Richard Janszen emerge from the Bricca house after identifying the bodies.

CHAPTER SIX

THE LISTENING HOUSE

"Truth will come to light; murder cannot be hid long."
William Shakespeare

SEPTEMBER 26TH – 28TH, 1966

Monday, September 26th

The rains of Sunday tapered off sometime after midnight.

Just after 1 AM, waitress Sarah Luskey saw a bloodstained man try to board a downtown Cincinnati bus. She didn't see any cuts on him, yet he appeared to have blood on his left hand and his shirt, and kept his right hand jammed in his pocket. The man asked the driver for directions to Bond Hill and then left the bus.

She would later describe him as a white man about 35, with brown hair and a dark complexion, wearing a black trench coat.

Enquirer route man Bob Holzschuh turned onto Greenway from Lawrence about 2:15 AM. The first house on the west side of the street did not subscribe, but the next four did. Holzschuh tossed the Bricca's copy on their driveway and moved on. He didn't notice anything unusual at 3381 Greenway.

That paper would become a bone of contention. Holzschuh was certain he didn't skip the Bricca house, yet it went missing from that driveway and caused speculation about who had taken it and why.

Across the city inhabitants were rousing from their beds to face the drudge of another Monday morning. Work, school, chores and errands were awaiting countless Queen City residents.

As he headed out to work at 5:15 AM, next door neighbor Richard Meyer noticed the Bricca's back patio lights were still on – he'd never seen that before. Their kitchen light was burning, but the rest of the house looked dark. Meyer knew Jerry was an early to work kind of guy. Maybe he was off today?

Meyer recalled the previous Wednesday night when Linda was late picking up Debbie and finally showed up drunk – "three sheets to the wind" according to his wife. She said that Jerry was furious with her, and Richard had not spoken to either of them since.

Meyer drove to work wondering – did he really know them? There was that remark Linda made last spring, saying it was a good thing she came home from Florida "because I would have become an alcoholic if I hadn't."

Richard Meyer liked "the kids", as others on their end of Greenway called the Bricca family. Yet he knew his wife Betty could only take so much of Linda...

At 5:30 AM a Lawrence Road resident saw a fancy red sports car parked in the rear lot of Western Bowl. He had never seen this rare vehicle in the neighborhood before.

Florence Hines was arriving early for her shift at Walgreens, and while sitting in her car applying makeup she noticed a white car parked in the Western Hills Plaza lot, which seemed odd since none of the stores were open yet. Standing nearby was a man holding what appeared to be a large paper bag.

Hines watched him for several minutes before going into Walgreens. The man wasn't doing anything suspicious, but she felt compelled to mention his presence to the pharmacist, who speculated he was working on this car. When she looked outside at 9 AM, the man and his car were gone.

Another suspicious subject was observed at 9 AM, this one at least five miles from the Bricca house.

Art Tenhunfeld was manning his filling station on Delhi Road when a guy walked in looking like death, claiming he'd been in a fight and asking where he could get a drink. He had large bruises on his cheeks and his left ear was bleeding profusely.

This guy was acting weird, so Tenhunfeld followed him outside and took down his license number. He had a good relationship with the County deputies, and always kept his eyes open for anyone at his station who seemed out of place.

Just before the guy pulled away, Tenhunfeld looked into his car and saw a snub-nosed revolver lying on the man's car seat...

September 26th

Around 10:30 AM the phone rang on Mary Bailey's desk. The young woman from Rising Sun, Indiana worked as an assistant to several engineers in Monsanto Building 7. On this fall Monday with the sun finally peeking out after that dreary weekend, Mary gave silent thanks that Jim Cannon was still on vacation.

The caller asked for Jerry Bricca. Mary checked her log. "He might be out of town for the day. "May I ask who is calling?"

"This is Richard Meyer. I'm Jerry's next door neighbor." There was a pause, and Mary could tell he was choosing his words carefully. "Could you...uh...ask him to call me sometime today?"

"Does he have your number?"

"He has my home number. But feel free to give him my work number." She heard him exhale deeply.

Mary jotted the digits and put an attention slip on Jerry's desk, wondering why Jerry's neighbor would call him at work. Soon her thoughts drifted back to Jim Cannon.

He had a great sense of humor, but he acted way too familiar with the women and would try to mess around if no supervisors were around. When Mary was at the filing cabinet he would suddenly appear, trying to reach around her on the pretext of getting a file. But she was wise to him.

Since Cannon was working in her office the last two weeks he had toned down his act. Whenever Jerry was around he would become downright stand-offish.

RICHARD MEYER DID WHAT his wife asked. Betty had called him at work, concerned about the lack of activity at the Bricca house.

Their cars were there, and the garbage cans were still out after the 6:30 AM pickup. As he hung up the phone, Richard Meyer went back to work, assuming there was a simple explanation. Someone probably picked Jerry up on the way to the airport. Linda was either sleeping in or working at the clinic. He put it out of his mind.

Glenn Ritchie, Jerry's traveling companion to the Nitro, WV Monsanto plant, was also concerned about his young colleague.

After talking with him at 6:45 PM last night, Glenn was surprised when the normally reliable Jerry failed to pick him up at 6:30 AM and drive to the airport as planned. Ritchie tried his house three times between 6:45-6:50 AM with no answer. He figured either something happened at the plant and Jerry couldn't make the trip, or Jerry misunderstood him and had already gone ahead to the airport.

But he was not at the airport. As Ritchie boarded his flight, he wondered why Jerry hadn't called him about the change in plans. No show, No call was out of character for Jerry Bricca.

At the Glenway Animal Hospital that morning, Steve and Valinda Westman began their first full week of employment. They had started the previous Thursday, worked Friday and Saturday, and spent most of Sunday in northern Kentucky. They were settling into the clinic apartment while learning to become veterinary assistants.

This morning Dr. Leininger approached Valinda and offered to give the Westman's an additional day off besides Sunday. This seemed odd to her, since he had already said that "Linda would be working on Wednesdays." Valinda said they didn't have a preference, and Leininger again suggested Wednesday.

"You remember Mrs. Bricca?"

"Yes, she was working here the day you hired us." Valinda had also talked to her on the phone Friday when she called about the book her daughter left there.

"Well, why don't we make it Wednesday then?" Leininger said.

"That's fine with Steve." Valinda replied.

The Doc seemed a little muddled. "She...uh, Mrs. Bricca has been wanting to work here for a long time. I've...already offered her the Wednesdays...uh, and I'll start training her this week." He paused, shaking his head. "Linda likes animals so well that I believe she would have worked here for free."

At 4:30 PM the *Cincinnati Post* carrier tossed the Monday late addition on the Bricca driveway. There were no other papers on the driveway. He noticed the garbage cans were still by the street when all the others on Greenway had been taken in.

Minutes later Richard Meyer arrived home and picked up his *Post* from his driveway. He saw that Jerry's car hadn't moved all day from the curb, and those cans were still out there. He went inside and asked Betty if she had seen the Bricca dogs in the yard today. She hadn't, which was unusual, but she was also running errands through the middle part of the day.

Glenn Ritchie arrived home from his day trip to WV and immediately called Jerry Bricca's home phone to find out why he had bailed. He tried him first at 6 PM, and then ten minutes later – but the phone just kept on ringing. He thought momentarily about going over there, but Glenn had never been to Jerry's house before and didn't know the family socially.

Besides, he knew last minute changes were the rule rather than the exception at Monsanto. All the engineers worked long hours, but none of them were on a particular time schedule.

Something must have come up, Glenn reasoned, as he put the receiver down. *We'll get it straightened out tomorrow.*

Tuesday, September 27th

The *Enquirer* had asked readers to weigh in on the spate of violence plaguing Cincinnati in a feature called "Spotlight on Danger". Some residents offered constructive suggestions, while others just vented – people were either incensed or afraid.

Under the headline **Worried Public Wants More Protection**, the lead comment summed up the mounting frustration:

> **A crime is a crime, a thug is a thug, a killer is a killer, a rapist is a rapist, whether they are an adult or a so-called juvenile...let the punishment fit the crime and let the police use their guns, clubs and dogs.**

Many of the dangers cited involved "poorly-paid policemen hampered by the Supreme Court", a shortage of patrolmen walking their beats, and "molly-coddled juvenile offenders" taking advantage of "lax curfew enforcement."

Tuesday dawned dreary around the edges, a repeat of Sunday's weather. As Dick Meyer was leaving for work, he noticed the Bricca patio light was still on. Backing out of his driveway he saw their garbage cans, standing vigil by the curb next to Jerry's car, which hadn't budged since Meyer saw it Monday morning.

Their garage door was closed, so he couldn't tell if Linda's blue station wagon was in there. As he drove off down Greenway, Richard Meyer made a mental note to call Betty at lunchtime in hopes she had seen either Jerry or Linda.

JUST AFTER 8 AM Glenn Ritchie rolled into Monsanto and made several attempts to reach Jerry Bricca at his office – he never answered and no one picked up to take a message. Ritchie still didn't give it much thought. Jerry was often out of the plant where he could not be reached by telephone.

At 8:30 Dr. Carroll Rolfes called the Glenway Animal Hospital. His dog swallowed a mothball and became violently ill on Monday night, and knowing Dr. Leininger personally he called him at home. Leininger had given him instructions over the phone.

On Tuesday morning the dog was no better. Dr. Rolfes asked his wife to call the clinic and tell Dr. Leininger that he was bringing the dog in on his way to work. Yet Leininger told her he was swamped and there was no one to watch the dog.

She relayed this to Rolfes, who thought Leininger's response was out of character for him.

A FEW MINUTES AFTER 12 noon, a Cincinnati Water Works meter reader arrived at the Bricca house on his regular Bridgetown route.

Al Shelton parked his white Oldsmobile in front of 3381 Greenway and walked up the driveway, past the Tuesday *Enquirer* delivered that morning, lying next to the Monday *Post*. As usual, he went around to the back of the house, opened the gate, and knocked on the lower level door. The lady of the house would usually open the garage door – the meter was just inside there.

There was no answer, and Shelton peered in the large window to the right of the door. He saw that the two dogs were in the room. Since the bigger one was always hostile with him, he didn't lean in the door to call out. The TV set was on, and the volume was turned up. Maybe she couldn't hear him because of it.

As Shelton went back to the front of the house, he heard and then noticed a swarm of flies outside the back bedroom windows.

Meter reader Al Shelton looked in the back window but had no idea of the horror inside the Bricca bedrooms above him.

When he knocked on the front door there was no answer there either. He thought about pushing it open and calling out per CWW procedure. The door was closed, but he didn't try it. If he had, he would have found it unlocked, just like the back door.

He went around to the back one more time, just in case the housewife there now. She wasn't, but as he looked in the window he saw the dogs still sitting there. That was odd, because they always ran at the door when he knocked any other time.

Yet now they were barely moving. And the room was in disarray – Shelton thought he even saw some feces on the floor.

He marked an estimated reading on his sheet and moved on down Greenway. But as looked back at the house, Al Shelton was still wondering what had gotten into those two dogs...

September 27th

At 1:10 PM Robert Schwartz checked his book at Windcrest Kennels, confirming that Linda Bricca hadn't shown up for her 1:00 PM appointment to have her dog groomed. She hadn't called to cancel either, which was not like her.

He flipped back and noted her previous visit was on March 31st. Schwartz remembered she had just returned from Florida, telling him the dog service was "really bad down there."

Schwartz took pride in his longtime customers and his reputation as a first rate groomer. He knew Mrs. Bricca was very particular about her dogs, driving 30 miles roundtrip to Springfield Township for Dusty, her poodle-cocker mix. She'd been coming there twice a year since 1964, and he was certain she would call to reschedule.

Just before 4:30 PM, *Post* route man Charles Beherns delivered the Bricca's afternoon paper. He noticed both his Monday paper and the Tuesday *Enquirer* on the Bricca front walk.

And as far as he could see, this was the only house on Greenway with garbage cans still out...

ANYONE READING THAT AFTERNOON paper got a sobering update on the City Council's "War-on-Crime" agenda. The committee crunched the numbers – the financial toll of crime was $15 million annually, but would increase as more cops were mobilized.

The committee agreed to focus on solving the problem of crime rather than getting bogged down documenting the causes, as Councilman John Held reiterated that the crime probe should exclude any racial overtones or partisan politics.

With the threat of the "Strangler" looming over the city, assaults on local women were fervently reported. The Tuesday *Post* featured stories about two downtown attacks.

On Monday afternoon, 61-year-old Lottie Willhoit was grabbed in an apartment hallway on Logan Street by a slender black man who seized her about the neck and placed his hand over her mouth. When she screamed he broke off the assault and fled.

That night, a 27-year-old woman was accosted about a half mile from the Willhoit attack. Verna Hickman was walking home at 11:50 PM when a black man in his mid-20's asked her for directions before grabbing her and throwing her down on the pavement. Her shouts brought a resident who chased the assailant off.

Also on Tuesday, a 42-year-old woman was sentenced to six months in jail for falsely claiming to be a victim of the Cincinnati Strangler. Mrs. Mildred Wethington alleged that a man tried to throttle her with a rope in the early morning hours of August 26th. Coming just eleven days after the Barbara Bowman slaying, a police contingent of at least 30 officers had responded to her Dana Avenue home and spent several hours searching the area.

Mrs. Wethington later told officers she made the story up to get attention from her children. In defending his harsh sentence for a false report, Judge Robert Wood said "There is already too much hysteria and police have too much work to do on legitimate cases."

THE OAK HILLS HIGH School PTA meeting had a special visitor. Hamilton County Deputy Sheldon Kroner was working the room, distributing petitions started by a Green Township housewife calling for a manpower increase for the County Sheriff's patrol. From 7-9 PM Kroner, voted Cincinnati "policeman of the year" in 1961, spread the word that staffing levels were not keeping pace with the recent upsurge in crime.

Just 90 minutes after the meeting ended the West Side would be rocked by the discovery of a brutal crime. On Wednesday, Kroner would tell the *Enquirer*: "It's a heck of a thing to say, but I think my message might have gone over better tonight."

At 3377 Greenway, Betty Meyer arrived home from a meeting and told her husband Richard that something was wrong at the Bricca house. The garbage cans were still out, and Betty heard their dogs wailing. Meyer made a quick run to Lou's Deli, noticing the continued lack of activity at his neighbor's house.

When he returned about 10 PM, Betty met him at the front door. "I called them three times while you were gone. No one answered. You need to go over there and see if everything is all right with them..."

September 27th

Richard Meyer turned around and headed down his front walk, took a left and moved past his own driveway. He was in no hurry, watching the Bricca house as he arrived at their front walk.

The clouds had slowly dissolved in the darkness, uncovering a watchful moon shimmering like a silver dollar, a moon that would be full by tomorrow night. Stars were dusting the black ceiling of sky.

For no reason at all, Meyer began to whistle. He thought he saw a shape in their window, but it was just the play of moonlight.

Cutting across to the driveway, Meyer opened the garage door just enough to confirm that Linda's blue station wagon was parked inside. On the curb, Jerry's VW hadn't moved for two days.

Meyer picked up the three newspapers and laid them down on the front porch. He rang the doorbell three times, and stood there for several minutes, listening – it sounded like the TV was on. Normally the sound of the doorbell would drive the Bricca dogs wild. But tonight their house was hushed.

Meyer didn't want to jump to conclusions – the family could be out of town. Moving quickly now, he went back to his house and asked Betty to call Linda Zeff. Perhaps she was taking care of the dogs while they were out of town.

Linda said she hadn't seen them since she babysat Debbie on Thursday. Betty asked if she had a key to their house, but Linda had given it back to them when they returned from San Francisco.

Betty asked if Linda could come to their house. "Something seems to be wrong there..."

DICK MEYER HAD GONE across the street to check with Richard Janszen. It was now 10:15 PM, and behind the Janszen house Meyer could see the lights from Western Bowl, their parking lot packed with cars. It seemed like a normal Tuesday night at the popular west side hub, and Meyer felt momentarily reassured. This was a nice neighborhood – there had to be a simple explanation.

When Janszen answered the door Meyer's cool vanished. "Something is wrong across the street," he said, gesturing with his head. "They're not answering the phone or the door, garbage and newspapers still out. We need to check it out."

"Is Linda's car in the garage?" Janszen asked, gauging his neighbor's worried look.

"Yes." Meyer inhaled sharply. "I think we ought to break in."

Janszen grabbed his arm. "Before we do that, we should call Monsanto. They could be out of town, you know?"

"When was the last time you saw any of them?"

"I saw Jerry Sunday morning." Janszen said. "He said he had just been to church, and was heading back to work."

Meyer went in with Janszen and they dialed Monsanto. The guard connected them to someone in Jerry's building, but he knew nothing about his schedule and couldn't give them any information.

Their concern multiplying by the minute, the two men went back across the street and met Linda Zeff and her father Joseph walking over in response to Betty's anxious phone call. Linda was pale and drawn. "If they were leaving town she would have told me," the young babysitter confirmed. "Something must be wrong in there."

While Janszen waited in the Bricca front yard, Linda, Joe Zeff, and Meyer walked around to the back door. Looking in the window to the TV room, Linda's heart sank – the television set was on but no one was watching. And the dogs. She had never seen them like that. Just lying there, like they were comatose.

In a recent interview with this writer, Linda Zeff recalled the sight, "The dogs were just sitting there, which was totally unlike them. I think they were drugged."

They came back around to the front of the Bricca house. Linda was distressed and breathing heavily. Meyer and Zeff went to the front door, with Linda right behind them, while Janszen remained on the sidewalk. Meyer rang the doorbell several more times – again there was no answer, but this time he heard a dog bark.

"Let's try the door and see if it's unlocked." Zeff said to Meyer.

Dick Meyer opened the door about eight inches. "Lin, are you in there? Lin, can you hear me?" He opened the door wider to about three feet, holding it at arm's length.

Then it came rushing out – the unmistakable stench of decaying flesh. "My God," Meyer whispered. "Somebody's dead in there."

Linda confirmed it to me. "I was right behind them. The smell was overpowering...I just knew they were dead."

Meyer stood in the doorway without entering the house. The television set in the lower level was on, the volume loud enough to be heard upstairs. From his vantage point he could see into the master bedroom on the right. Squinting in the dim light, he turned on his flashlight and shined it towards the bedrooms. He saw what he later said looked like someone's foot or hand on the floor.

He closed the door and stared at Joseph and Linda Zeff, his eyes dark and distant. "Don't touch anything or go in there. I'm calling the police!"

September 27th

Joe Zeff and his daughter hurried off the porch and joined Dick Janszen on the front sidewalk. No one said anything as they waited for Meyer to come back out.

Linda Zeff was starting to hyperventilate. The dogs' demeanor had spooked her – she loved those animals, and they loved her. Getting along with Linda Bricca's pets was a prerequisite for baby-sitting there, and she took great pride that this elegant woman trusted her with her human and animal children.

But that smell was her breaking point. She thought back to the last time she saw Linda, and the last thing she said on Thursday: *"If the phone ever rings and it's a man, don't tell them where I am."*

Meyer came out of his house and said Green Township constables were on their way. Linda Zeff moved away from the three men, trying to staunch the flood of emotions. Her mother's puzzling remark about babysitting in the Bricca house that Thursday echoed in her mind: *"I have to leave. There's something wrong in this house, something evil..."*

JOSEPH ZEFF WAS CONFRONTING his own demons.

On Sunday morning, April 16th, 1961 he had called the police under similar circumstances when he couldn't reach his sister Goldie. Unanswered phone calls brought him to her house in Price Hill, and the lack of response to his knocks was alarming.

When a police officer broke in the locked back door, they found Goldie and her husband James Cunningham lying underneath a bedspread in the ransacked house. They had been stabbed to death with a screwdriver – the killer had moved the bodies to the bedroom, posed them in an embrace, and then covered them up.

Family friend Jack Rauss was eventually arrested and convicted **(Queen City Notorious Chapter 10)** for the crime. Now Joe Zeff was standing in front of the Bricca house, waiting for the police. He had a bad feeling in 1961, and 5-1/2 years later he recognized the same, creeping awareness that a motionless house could be concealing a crime of terrible import.

18-year-old Linda Zeff (left) was the Bricca family's primary babysitter and a confidante to 23-year-old Linda Bricca (right).

As the Green Township patrol car pulled up, Linda Zeff became hysterical. The constables were responding to a call of "unknown trouble" – Joe Zeff gave them a quick statement. He confirmed the lack of activity reported by Meyer. He told them he didn't know Jerry or Linda Bricca by sight, but had met Debbie when she was at his house with his wife.

With that, Joe wrapped an arm around a tearful Linda, and they slowly walked back toward their home, an unlucky 13 doors south of the Bricca house. As they trudged down the street, Joseph Zeff's memory drifted back towards his murdered sister...

AT 3381 GREENWAY, PATROLMEN Ray Smith and Richard Anderson were talking with Meyer and Janszen. Meyer was a war veteran – he knew what death smelled like. Janszen told them his wife had spoken to Jerry Bricca Sunday night while he was taking out the garbage, but no one had seen any family member since then.

There was brief speculation about carbon monoxide poisoning, but the four men standing in front of the house agreed it was probably something more sinister. Telling the neighbors to stay back, the officers advanced toward the Bricca front door.

This 2016 image shows Richard Meyer's view as he looked in the Bricca front door on September 27th, 1966.

As they pushed it open, they could hear the flies buzzing, even on a cool night like this. The smell of decay was overpowering – Smith pulled out a handkerchief to cover his face. The house was quiet – except for the television and the hum of the insects.

Moving across the living room, the officers saw someone's legs on the floor of the master bedroom. They climbed the seven step stairway to the third level, crouched down, and crossed the narrow hallway to bedroom door.

A woman dressed in negligee and housecoat was lying face up on top of a man lying face down between the bed and the wall. There was a huge bloodstain on the bed. The woman's hair was fanned out and her breasts were exposed, the left one dotted with stab wounds. The man had been gagged with a pair of socks, and from what they could see his features were bloody and contused.

Anderson stepped back out, stifling the urge to vomit. As he entered the smaller bedroom on the back of the house, he saw a young child lying stretched out in the middle of the room, as if she'd been dragged from under the bed or out of the closet. Her pajama top was stained with blood.

He called to his partner, who groaned when he saw the girl. She couldn't have been more than five years old. Her thin body looked pathetic lying there, like she was just discarded refuse.

Both officers' mouths hung open. The stench was bad enough, but the hideous, surreal tableau in the bedrooms struck them dumb.

Smith broke the spell. "Let's get out of here and call it in."

They had just stumbled onto the most sensational triple homicide in Cincinnati history. And for everyone that this case would touch in the coming months, years, and decades, nothing would ever be the same.

This crime would get under their skin – a vile shard that could not be extracted...

September 27th

Bob Sweeney got the call around 10:50 PM as he was getting ready for bed.

An industrial salesman by day, he was a member of the Mack Volunteer Fire Department, on call to respond to the various calamities that befell Green Township residents. From cats in trees to bizarre suicides, at age 26 Bob had seen his share of trouble.

On this night he was asked to respond to a "suspicious circumstance" at 3381 Greenway – he was given strict instructions "not to enter the house if the police were not there yet." Since he lived only a mile away, Bob decided to drive directly to the scene without stopping at the Mack firehouse, arriving at 11:05 PM

About the same time, Sweeney's supervisor Robert Weitzel got a call about "unknown trouble" at the Greenway address. Weitzel was the fire officer in charge, holding the rank of Lieutenant at the age of 24 – he would serve 48 years with the Mack VFD, the last 38 as chief. Like his friend Bob Sweeney, Bob Weitzel had no hint of the horror that awaited first responders.

Weitzel quickly arrived at the firehouse on the corner of Bridgetown and Ebenezer Roads. After checking with the other assembling volunteers, they responded with a "heavy rescue unit".

Sweeney knew this was "no ordinary run" when he saw the various police agencies already at the scene, including several Hamilton County Deputies. A Green Township constable met him outside, telling him that "we've got three dead people in there." He requested they bring spotlights to illuminate the scene and high powered fans to "blow the smell out of the house."

By the time the heavy rescue unit manned by Weitzel arrived at the Bricca home, the rain had dissipated and a wispy fog was drifting in. Greenway and Lawrence residents attracted by the commotion were perched in the cone of their porch lights and hovering on the sidewalk in hushed conversation.

The Mack Volunteer Fire Department vehicle was state of the art, ready to handle traffic collisions, passenger extrication, building collapses, and flood rescues. Their special equipment included the Jaws of Life, generators, winches, hi-lift jacks, cranes, cutting torches, and circular saws – items not on standard fire trucks.

Bob Sweeney arrived back at the scene with the spotlights and fans. Soon 3381 Greenway Avenue was roped off and lights were flaring over the small brick house and scalding the yard, casting shadows over curious neighbors on the sidewalk, giving their faces a bluish tinge. The big industrial fans hummed and whirred, flushing out the flies and pumping the putrefied air into the street.

Bob Weitzel stepped inside the Bricca house and was knocked back. In a personal interview, he recalled the night of September 27th 1966 like it was yesterday. "You never, ever forget that smell. And it was right at the front door." Weitzel saw the "big green flies" swarming the screens and heard the "drone of their buzzing", knowing that these flies were the type "that gather around meat."

Weitzel and Sweeney took a look in the upstairs bedrooms, neither man crossing the thresholds. Sweeney noticed the male victim was quite brawny, and whispered to Weitzel that he "must have been ambushed." A large piece of tape almost obscured his bloody face. He was dressed in a sport shirt and slacks, but was not wearing shoes.

The female victim was wearing a low cut nightgown under her housecoat, and her breasts were exposed. She was lying on her left side, her body covering the head and shoulders of the male victim. She had visible stab wounds in the chest, neck and head.

Neither man lingered at the door of the child's room. Weitzel had a 2-year-old daughter, and the sight of this tiny murdered girl wearing white pajamas and one red sock was too much to bear.

THE CRIME SCENE QUICKLY became a bedlam of cops, firemen, EMT's, and non-authorized personnel.

Detective Gerald Taylor was the ranking officer from the Hamilton County Sheriff's Department, but Green Township had yet to relinquish jurisdiction. A Cincinnati homicide detective had flashed his badge and was also wandering through – the location was only a few blocks beyond the city limits, and Taylor was certain they would want the case.

Already things were out of his control. Everyone was walking through the house. He saw a fireman pick up Jerry's briefcase lying on a table in the TV room before realizing it was evidence.

Taylor made several calls to his supervisor Lt. Herb Vogel, the head of the County criminal investigation division. Vogel was "of weight", and had the authority to assume control from Green Township. But Taylor's boss was dealing with his own family emergency at the moment, and his home phone went unanswered.

Bob Sweeney remembers the confusion. "The whole house was contaminated and compromised from the beginning," he recalled. "Too many people walking around and picking up things." And Sweeney was stunned by the lack of protocol: "We should have called the coroner right away."

Bob Weitzel went even further in our interview: "No way should we have been allowed in there. This was a crime scene, a homicide. It was not a suicide. No way should firemen be in there as long as we were." Weitzel estimated that "there were around 15-20 people inside during the first hour.

Taylor tried to ignore the trespassers and do his job. He brought back Meyer and Janszen to walk through the house and make the identification of the slain family.

An *Enquirer* photo of the two Richards exiting the Bricca house indelibly captured the mood. Dick Meyer with his arms tightly folded, looking sick to his stomach. Dick Janszen with his hands jammed in his pockets, eyes cast downward from the popping flashbulbs. Between the two men is Bob Weitzel, a dazed expression on his young face.

With the identification complete, about 11:25 PM Taylor and Sgt. Koeninger of Green Township began taking crime scene photos of the victims and all the rooms. Drawers in the bedrooms and living room were pulled out and ransacked, while next to a large bloodstain on the bed laid Jerry Bricca's empty billfold.

With the crowd swelling outside, an *Enquirer* reporter collared the distraught Richard Meyer as he left the scene. His face pale and shining in the garish lights, the neighbor gave the press their first sound bite. "My God, I can hardly remember what I saw. It's just like a fog now. I knew what it was as soon as I opened the door. Nothing smells like that. I remember it from World War II."

The reporter pressed him for details. "Can you tell us what you saw in there?"

Richard Meyer inhaled the night air, and then broke into tears. "My God, what they did to that baby!"

September 27th

At 11:40 PM the phone rang again in Lieutenant Herb Vogel's house in Mt. Washington, the eastern most community within Cincinnati city limits.

It had been a tough day for Hamilton County's top criminal investigator. He had just arrived home from the hospital with his wife and daughter, injured that afternoon in a car accident. Phyllis Vogel sustained a broken nose and a gashed knee, while 7-year-old Coletta suffered a broken left arm and facial lacerations.

Vogel was spent. He had just tucked them in, and his head was ready to hit the pillow. But the insistent peal of the phone roused him from his stupor. Calls to his house at this hour meant trouble.

It was Sgt. Bell from County, informing him of the triple homicide at 3381 Greenway Avenue in Bridgetown. The husband, wife, and child were the victims, and the crime scene was swarming with people and still unsecured.

Vogel broke the news to his wife, and told her he might not be back that night. He couldn't know that he'd just caught the case of a lifetime, and that he wouldn't be home for three days.

The crime scene was twenty miles away from Vogel's residence. With limited freeways in 1966, his travel time would approach one hour. Belting down a quick cup of coffee, the caring husband and devoted father who'd just brought home his injured wife and daughter headed back out into the night as a homicide detective.

Herb Vogel had joined the County Sheriff's Department in 1952 following a short stint as a motorcycle patrolman with the Cincinnati Police. At 35 he was a young Lieutenant, a soft spoken, muscular man and a fitness fanatic. He worked for Sheriff Dan Tehan, an elected official, and Vogel understood that the higher he moved up the chain of command, the more politics he would have to deal with.

Homicide was always in Vogel's blood. He had spent countless hours poring over autopsies and medical journals, teaching himself the basics of pathology. He learned how to approach murder like a challenging puzzle, and knew how gratifying it was to solve the most heinous of crimes.

Driving west on deserted streets, Herb Vogel was already conjecturing about what awaited him at 3381 Greenway Avenue...

BACK AT THE CRIME scene, neighbors and strangers collected on the sidewalk, drawn by the police cars and emergency vehicles blocking the street. The crowd seemed deadened, almost frozen. The hollow faces of the cops and firemen plodding in and out of the house were enough to stifle any questions.

Scant details were leaking out to those gathered at the north end of Greenway. Residents had learned that this was a multiple murder – a crime at once vicious and mysterious.

Inside the house something had to be done about the dogs. Thumper and Dusty were whining in the TV room, which needed to be secured. The SPCA was called around 11:15 PM, and soon after animal control officer Bernard Tigges arrived at the scene.

The *Enquirer* photographer captured Bernie bringing out Thumper, the smaller cocker spaniel, and stepping into the harsh lights. He's wearing dark clothing and a somber expression – the dog looks hungry and miserable.

Some rumors would involve those dogs, strangely silent during the 48 hours before the discovery and now meek and docile. Their normal aggression should have been heightened after two days without food and fresh water. Why weren't they barking and snapping at all the strangers wandering around?

In an interview before his death, Bernie Tigges could only speculate about the dog's condition. Had they been drugged? He felt it was

SPCA officer Bernard Tigges was called to the crime scene to remove the Bricca dogs.

possible, but no testing was done, as the dogs were turned over to Linda Bricca's mother the next day.

He had a perspective on the activity inside the murder house. "The officers were all told to keep it 'hush hush', and there was no talking at the crime scene at all." He heard a cop warn them "not to discuss any details, even among themselves."

Tigges confirmed that everyone there was "very subdued", saying it "wasn't like any other crime scene that I had been to before. There were so many people from all different agencies there."

Joining the crowd outside were two Monsanto employees who worked with Jerry Bricca. Art Nagel heard the news on the radio at 11:15 PM, and recognized the address immediately. He called Tom Olding, who came by his house and took Nagel and his wife to the scene around 11:30 PM.

Nagel and Jerry had argued the previous week about the lazy pipefitters, but he liked the young engineer and was shocked to hear his death confirmed when they arrived at the Bricca house.

The radio report and the 11:00 PM breaking news story commenced a flurry of activity regarding the dead family. Richard Franks, the Monsanto real estate agent for transfers, called the county around

11:25 PM with all the contact information for Jerry and Linda's families. The Bricca's insurance agent had already called 15 minutes earlier with a list of insured valuables, including a fur cape and two cameras, in case they had been stolen.

At around 11:45 Olding saw a familiar face among the cluster of people standing vigil. It was Jim Cannon, Monsanto engineer and sometime nemesis of Jerry Bricca. Both men knew the irrepressible Cannon and the stoic Bricca were like oil and water.

Cannon saw them and came. "What has happened?" he asked.

Olding told him Jerry Bricca and his family had been killed.

"Is this his house?" Cannon queried.

"Yes," replied Olding. "Did you hear about it on the radio?"

Cannon gave no reply, and the four of them stood behind the ropes exchanging shocked whispers as they watched the now tainted and stained Bricca house.

Nagel's wife stared at Cannon. "So how did you find out?"

"I was driving by, just like you."

Tom Oldham spoke up. "But we heard about it on the radio."

Cannon shifted his feet. "Well, I saw the red lights from Glenway." He volunteered that he'd been on vacation since Friday.

Olding would later tell investigators that he and Nagel didn't see the flashing lights until they were on Lawrence. And he was certain that Cannon knew where Jerry Bricca lived, because his house was less than a mile away, and Jim had carpooled with Jerry a few times several years back.

INSIDE THE HOUSE, BOB Sweeney was amazed at the number of personnel still roaming the rooms and examining possible evidence. Everyone was looking for the murder weapon, thinking the bloody knife must be concealed somewhere within the crime scene. He noticed the Cincinnati detective in a hushed conference with Gerald Taylor – were they debating who should have final jurisdiction?

Sweeney walked outside to clear his head. Looking at Linda's car in the garage and Jerry's out by the curb, a thought struck him. He went to a deputy standing on the driveway and blurted "Maybe you should look in the car gas tank for the weapon?"

The deputy scowled and dismissed him. "Mind your own job and let us do ours."

Sweeney didn't give up. "Shouldn't somebody call the coroner?" But the deputy had turned away. He and Bob Weitzel went back inside the house.

At exactly 12:42 AM, a deputy stood in the living room and shouted "Everyone who is not with County get out now!"

Lieutenant Herbert Vogel had arrived on the scene...

Wednesday, September 28th

It was almost 1 AM, and Richard Meyer was beside himself. He and Betty sat in their living room, the flashing red lights flickering shadows on their walls. Meyer was drained, his mind depleted and his will shattered.

He'd seen his neighbors lying dead in their own blood. He held it together when identifying Jerry and Linda, yet when he saw the little one splayed out in her room he'd lost it. Meyer's youngest son was six, and he could still remember when his teenage daughter was four years old, the final age Debbie Bricca would ever be.

Now sitting here, more than two hours later with the throng still outside, Meyer knew what he'd seen next door would never leave him, an indelible image burned into his brain.

A figure stepped onto his porch, and they heard a tapping at the door. A detective flashed his badge, showing he was from the Cincinnati Police. He asked if he could use their phone. As Meyer and his wife sat there, the detective called his supervisor at CPD and vented for several minutes about the lack of protocol at the crime scene, calling it "a circus."

When he said that Vogel had just arrived, Meyer saw him listen, nod, and say "Well, it's their case now."

The Cincinnati cop, later identified as a Sgt. Rutledge, thanked them and walked out, leaving Richard Meyer to wrestle with his fresh demons...

NEXT DOOR AT 3381 Greenway, Herb Vogel affirmed the County's authority over this grisly crime and locked down the house. Rumors triggered from this night would persist for decades – that the crime scene was hopelessly compromised within the first two hours, tainting or obliterating any useful physical evidence.

Yet the reality of 1966 homicide investigation implies that all crime scenes suffered some degree of contamination. Overlapping duties and a lack of specialization insured that officers on the scene would continually duplicate actions others had already taken.

Moving his deputies to the living room, Vogel did a quick study of the murder rooms with Detective Gerald Taylor. Calls had gone out to other County detectives, who began arriving bleary eyed just after 1 AM for their appalling wake-up call.

Using a tape recorder, Vogel and Taylor began to dictate a detailed description of the murder scene, while Sgt. Herb Bell delegated tasks to the deputies, including canvassing of the neighborhood for possible witnesses. Now more than two hours after the victims were found, a sense of order and precision settled over these quiet, deathly rooms.

Based on a preliminary examination and the lack of activity at the house since Monday morning, Vogel felt they had been dead at least 36 hours. Taylor grimaced. "It smells like 48." Vogel agreed, knowing full well their best chance of solving a crime was to "get a hook" in the first 48 hours.

Some of his detectives were baseball fans, looking for easy outs. "Will the case be a grounder or a whodunit?" some would ask. Vogel knew right away that this investigation was the World Series.

The County didn't have the luxury afforded large urban departments like the city of Cincinnati, where support staff, lab technicians, and other investigative tools were in abundance. Vogel had 12 detectives allocated to cover all crimes within Hamilton County limits, turning each man into a "jack of all trades" who tried to crack everything from simple vandalism up to a nasty homicide.

These men were not murder specialists. Their investigative training was a playbook, directing them to take an inventory of potential suspects who had a close association or a frequent interaction with the victims. Beyond the obvious family members, they were looking for mutual interests, financial dealings, romantic rivalry, sexual fixation or just plain bad blood.

Was this a crime for gain – or one driven by passion?

VOGEL AND TAYLOR STOOD in the master bedroom, contemplating the murdered bodies of Jerry and Linda Bricca. Few pieces of evidence are more eloquent than a crime scene corpse. With proper interpretation the dead victims can speak more effectively than any living witness.

Vogel's initial report, typed up from his recorder, captures the crime scene in dispassionate fashion:

Linda Bricca: Well-nourished female white, approx. 24 yrs. old, weighing about 135# – long black hair. Blue house coat, trimmed in gold with a zipper in front. Zipper only halfway down and found in down position. A pale blue thin night gown was worn under the robe. No shoes or socks. Front of night gown was pulled down to expose breasts. Hands were partly closed. Strand of hair apparent in right hand. No on top of right breast. Gaping wounds in upper chest, at sternum, left pectoral, side of neck, wound over right eye, wound over right temple, hemorrhaging from nose.

Even with the exposed breasts, Vogel noted her panties were in place and didn't appear to have been pulled up by the killer.

Gerald Bricca: Well-nourished male white, approx. 28 yrs. old, weighing about 185# – dark hair cut short. Long sleeve plaid sport shirt, dark gray slacks, dark socks, defense wounds seen on either hand. Bloody towel no shoes. Gold wedding band on left hand. Tear in back of shirt about 10″ from belt line, near middle of back. At least four stab wounds in back. No indication of defense wounds on hands. Hands open; fingers slightly bent. White tape on jaw and left cheek. Face bloody with contusions. Socks stuffed in mouth.

Vogel, a well-built man himself, was stunned by Jerry's muscular physique – almost like that of a college wrestler.

Debbie Bricca: On her stomach with head turned left...wearing white nightgown and one red knee length sock. A small stuffed animal was just beyond her outstretched hand. Other sock on bed along with small blood stain. Four stab wounds penetrated her body and left cut marks in the rug. Body position consistent with dragging.

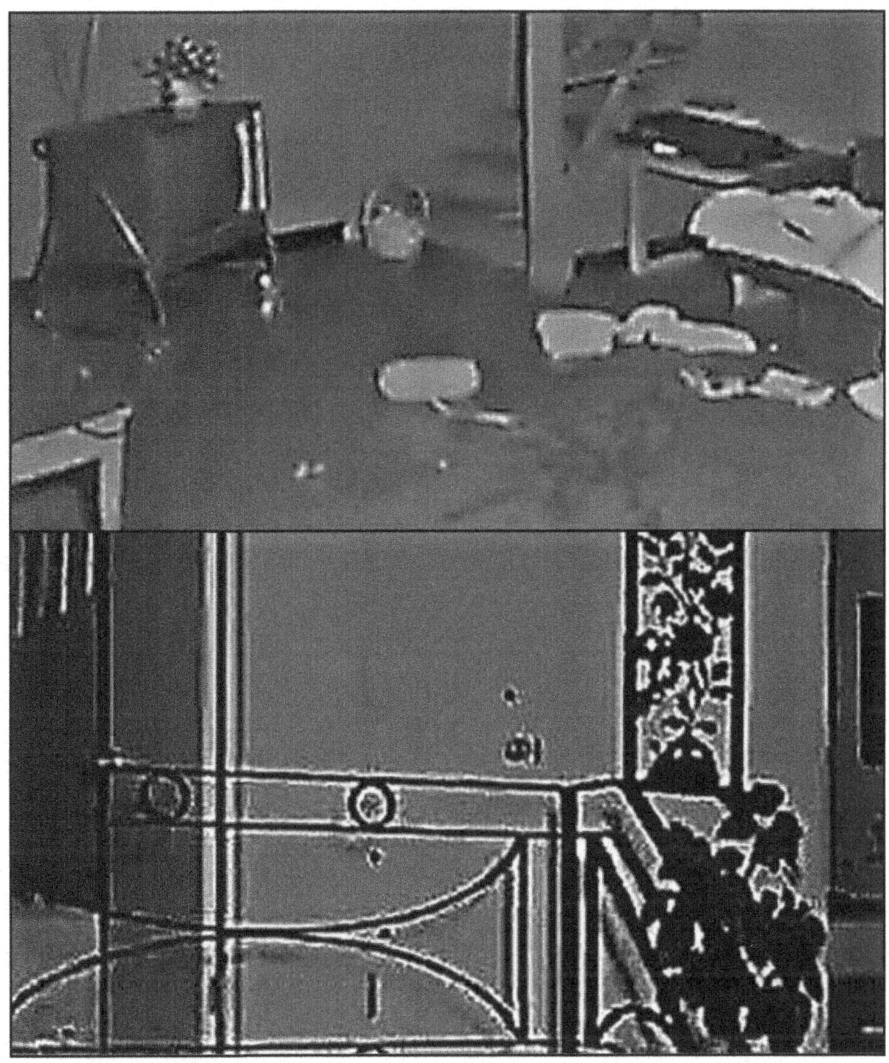

Pictures taken the night of the discovery show the TV room in disarray and the doors to both murder bedrooms.

Vogel's youngest daughter was six – two years older than the dead child before him.

There was no evidence of a struggle or defensive wounds. The large number of knife thrusts in a confined area indicated that the adult victims were not resisting when they were killed. The furniture was in place and no lamps were knocked over, yet almost all the drawers were pulled out.

The blood evidence in the 13′ x 11′ master bedroom was vexing. Both bodies were found between the wall and the bed in the northeast corner, lying in large pools soaked through the rug-pad to the floor. There was no back-spatter on the walls, which would have indicated wild thrusts with castoff blood. There were two large pools on the bed sheet along with a smaller spot in between.

I have viewed the crime scene photographs, taken with a speed graphic flash camera that delivered stark black and white images. But they could not replicate the full color reality and olfactory nightmare confronting the cops in 1966.

The pictures of Debbie are hard to look at. Her arms are straight over her head, like she was dragged from under the bed or out of the closet, as she is halfway between them. The flashing knife went all the way through her frail, defenseless body.

Jerry's shoulders and back are beneath Linda's body – he was stabbed while on the floor, an extremely tight space to kill someone in. He was trapped, but again no defensive wounds. He's face down, arms at his side but positioned as if they were behind his back from a ligature. There's a massive hematoma over his left eye, and the facial contusions suggest a severe beating. The piece of tape holding the socks in his mouth obscures his right cheek.

Linda is lying at a right angle across Jerry's body, partially on her left side and back, completely covering his head and shoulders. Her head is on the rug and her hair is fanned out towards the door. Her housecoat is halfway unzipped, and her negligee is low cut and skimpy. Her breasts are exposed, which at first glance would indicate a sex crime. Her hands are partly clenched, with what appears to be a strand of hair in her right hand. She is barefoot with a bloody nose, but no defensive wounds.

Vogel's report describes the master bedroom in great detail – a "Hollywood" type king size bed, a nightstand with 13 books in the lower section and a vase with plastic flowers on top. A picture of a fat clown and a small dog smelling his foot - white leatherette chair with small splatters of blood on the lower right front.

Another picture hung on the west wall over the night stand. In the lower right corner was a clown labeled "Glad".

But this picture was dominated by a crying clown – labeled "Sad."

September 28th

Deputies canvassed the neighborhood into the early morning hours, knocking on doors and rousing residents who weren't already standing outside the Bricca house.

The north end of Greenway was a surreal montage, flooded with dumbfounded people, the murder house seared by the glare of klieg lights, casting thick shadows that hung like curtains.

I recently interviewed a West Side woman who was standing outside 3381 Greenway in the hours after the discovery. She and her husband were visiting her parents, and when they stopped at the Woodhaven and Greenway corner they could see the flashing red lights. They parked on Greenway and walked up to where the police had the street roped off.

As they stood there, she estimated the crowd to be about 50 people. From time to time a cop or an EMT would come out the front door, gasping for breath and rushing into the side yard. She saw some of them bending over, as if they were vomiting.

One of them told her husband what was going on. As word spread the mood became grim. "No one standing there believed something like this could happen in Bridgetown," she told me.

They left after about an hour. Half a century later, the memory of that horrible night is forever a part of her personal legacy.

INSIDE THE HOUSE THINGS settled into a routine – if there was such a thing in a home with three murdered corpses.

They were hamstrung because the killers had a 48 hour head start. Leads were drifting, memories fading, people straining to recall anything from a rapidly receding timeline.

So Vogel delayed calling the coroner, ignoring suggestions from the EMT's and Green Township officers, now milling around in the Bricca front yard. The crime scene photos had been taken and rushed in for processing, yet Vogel wanted to visually preserve the dreadful reality for as long as possible.

He had studied crime scene preservation, and knew the Locarde theory by heart: "Every criminal leaves something of himself at the crime scene and takes something from the scene with him."

Like most homicide commanders, Vogel owned a copy of the Paul Kirk's *Crime Investigation: Physical Evidence and the Police Laboratory.* Kirk came into prominence after the wrongful conviction of Dr. Sam Sheppard in 1954, and was considered the father of modern blood stain analysis. His work had influenced a whole new generation of detectives.

Kirk's bedrock principal was unequivocal and unyielding:

> **Wherever the criminal steps, whatever he touches, whatever he leaves, even unconsciously, will serve as silent evidence against him. This is evidence that does not forget. Physical evidence cannot be wrong; it cannot perjure itself; it cannot be wholly absent. Only its interpretation can err. Only human failure to find it, study and understand it can diminish its value.**

The coroner could wait a little longer.

With a female victim there's an 80% chance the motive is sexual. Linda had been killed on the bed, which was in disarray, and then thrown on top of her husband. Her breasts were exposed, but this may have resulted from being flung in a low cut negligee.

Vogel realized the sex angle could take over the case and shift the focus away from the evidence. Already he heard some of his men couching lurid speculations about the dead woman. But they would have to wait until the coroner took body cavity swabs to determine if Linda Bricca had been raped.

The ransacking of the drawers looked staged. Vogel was familiar with killers who would fake a burglary to disguise an emotional connection to the victim.

Any detective could observe a crime scene and dish out conjecture about the actions of a killer or a victim. Vogel wanted this investigation to mirror the evidence and establish probability based on comparable crimes.

Yet there was nothing in his experience that could parallel this malicious, unspeakable deed...

OUTSIDE THE CRIME SCENE, Mack Volunteer Firemen Bob Sweeney and Bob Weitzel were packing it up. It was just before 2 AM, and Weitzel's crew had been there for almost three hours after responding to a call of "unknown trouble."

Weitzel took all the equipment back to firehouse, and everyone sat there in stunned silence. Sweeney heard some loose talk about the female victim but ignored it. He was sapped and devastated. Seeing the little girl's body had shaken his very faith in humanity.

Bob finally arrived home at 3 AM, only to find he was locked out. He pounded on the back door, but his wife did not answer it. It was the first time he had ever been locked out, and an irrational panic rose within him. He lived in a tri-level house, just like the Bricca family. And he was locked out!

He smashed the window and unchained the door. *My God, I'm breaking into my own house!* Going up the stairs to the next level, he saw his wife standing at the top, holding a large kitchen knife.

"Where have YOU been? Her words came in a gushing torrent. "I've been worried sick about you!" "Why didn't you call me?

Sweeney had never seen her so "steaming mad." Then he told her about it, and her eyes got big. He spared her the gory details, but the rapid change in her demeanor said enough. The fear that had mutated into anger was once again fear.

It was a bizarre ending to a ghastly night for Robert Sweeney.

AT 3381 GREENWAY AVENUE, the coroner was finally notified at 2:30 AM by Township patrolman Ray Smith. When the van rolled up, there were still spectators strewn along the sidewalk.

This dwelling was no longer just a charnel house. It was now the focus of curiosity and sensation, the fascination of extreme horror against a backdrop of suburban respectability.

On this awful night of September 27th, 1966, only one thing was certain – these murders would seize the West Side imagination as a crime beyond all other crimes. Amid flourishing rumors of evidence lost, bungled or buried, or persistent allegations of incompetence or deception, there remained THIS CRIME of shocking atrocity, as inexplicable as it was repulsive. A triple murder that was at once vicious and cowardly, calculated and fiendish.

So through the night others joined in the vigil, furtive human traffic intent on a small frame and brick house, as the ghostly pre-dawn fog began to filter through the trees before vanishing...

THE CINCINNATI ENQUIRER

KENTUCKY EDITION

126TH YEAR NO. 173 — THURSDAY MORNING, SEPTEMBER 29, 1966 — PRICE 10 CENTS—HOME DELIVERED 50¢ A WEEK

Neighbors Think Bricca Killer No Stranger

BY MARGARET JOSTEN, Of The Enquirer Staff

Deborah Bricca

Mrs. Linda Bricca

Gerald Bricca

'Maniac' Hunted

Fingerprints Slim Clue In Murder Of 3

Sewer Checked For Murder Weapon

. . . County Detective Rudy McKinney makes fruitless search

Bombs, Looting Rock San Francisco

Erhart Says Bonn Can't Buy U. S. Weapons

Tentative Truce Averts American Airlines Strike

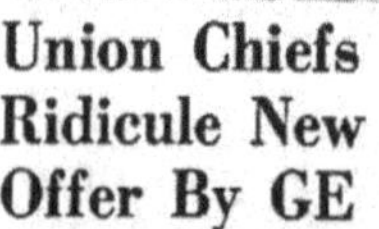

Union Chiefs Ridicule New Offer By GE

Hurricane Inez Will Hit Hispaniola

New Cars Are Out

Saudi Arabia Deal Confirmed

Top Of The News

Inside The Enquirer

State And Nation

World-Wide

Washington

Index

Today's Weather

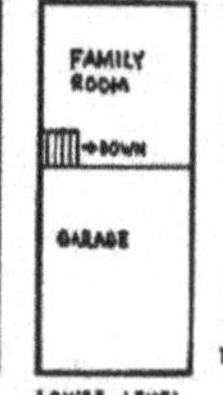

The *Enquirer* devoted most of their Thursday front Page to the mysterious triple homicide.

CHAPTER SEVEN

MURDER AT LARGE

"Behold, I send you forth as sheep amidst the wolves."
Matthew 10:16

SEPTEMBER 28TH – SEPTEMBER 30TH, 1966

Wednesday, September 28th

A rumor is just a premature fact.

It's a saying among homicide detectives, reminding them objectivity only goes so far in solving a case. Sometimes you have to get down in the gutter and knock on a few coffins. And nothing is more subjective than the word on the street.

By early morning Wednesday, news of the murders was seeping through the West Side. Papers were late hitting driveways, because when the story broke just before 11 PM, the *Enquirer* staff stayed past midnight and re-set their entire front page.

The hideous narrative was spreading like an infection.

In type large enough to herald a major disaster, Queen City residents glowered through breakfast with **Family Of Three Knifed To Death; Rape Is Suspected.** To a city already trembling in the Strangler's wake, the slaughter of this young family in their own home was a visceral jolt.

> **A man, his wife, and their four-year-old daughter were found stabbed to death late Tuesday in a home in the fashionable section of Green Township... Police said Mrs. Linda Bricca, 25, apparently was raped and her husband Jerry and daughter Debbie were mutilated... The site swarmed with neighbors and others who invaded the area shortly before midnight. Police refused newsman permission to inspect the home.**

The *Enquirer* article had a rushed feel, with sketchy quotes, vague details, and erroneous info churned out from reporters chasing the juiciest murder story of the year on a skintight deadline.

Richard Meyer was quoted several times, along with a Monsanto official who called Jerry Bricca a "friendly, conscientious engineer". For the first of many times, Linda Bricca was referred to as a "former airline stewardess."

The number of stab wounds inflicted would not be determined until after the coroner's report. The reporter noted that "no weapon had been found," and that "the home had been burglarized."

City Council member Phil Collins was reached at home shortly after the murders were discovered. Grim faced, he told the reporter that "if my wife is any indication of the public reaction to this thing, well, she's just petrified."

Already that morning, the inevitable first suspect was the unknown subject being called the Cincinnati Strangler.

ON THE NORTH END of Greenway anxiety was intense. Some fathers stayed home from work, including Richard Janszen and Richard Meyer. The Bricca neighbors were still reeling from their ghastly tour inside the murder house eight hours earlier.

In the Janszen home, Dick and Joan's four children awoke to an unreal landscape across the street. As they came down for breakfast, their mother sat down daughter Mary, age 12, along with her three younger brothers, telling them they weren't going to school today because their bus couldn't get down the street. Then she told them why.

Mary stayed inside, but Jim, Gus and Jerry, ages 11, 10, and 6, perched on their front porch openmouthed and watched the activity at the Bricca house. Jim already knew something was up when the flashing police cars woke him around midnight. He had seen the crowd gathering, bleached white by the massive spotlights.

Just that summer he and his brothers had peddled their bikes daily to the Woodhaven Swim Club, except when they were at Western Bowl, whose parking lot abutted the Janszen backyard. In a recent interview, Jim Janszen recalled that "we lived at Western Bowl...even collected the empty beer bottles for money." That back parking lot was often empty and made a great blacktop baseball field for Jim and his friends.

CINNATI ENQUIRER

EDNESDAY MORNING, SEPTEMBER 28, 1966 PRICE 10 CENTS—HOME DELIVERED 50c A WEEK

FAMILY OF THREE KNIFED TO DEATH; RAPE IS SUSPECTED

The *Enquirer's* first story of the crime implied that a sexual assault was the motive for the murders.

Now sitting on the porch with his brothers, Jim sensed that his carefree boyhood in Bridgetown was forever tainted.

Their parents were in shock. Joan was the last person to see Jerry Bricca alive other than the killer or killers. Richard Janszen witnessed what had been done to the family. Both were trying to process the enormity of what had occurred across the street.

Yet they could not foresee the aggravation and misfortune it would bring to the Janszen household.

Later that morning, Joan told Richard their dog had been barking furiously around 4 AM Monday. The dog never barked while inside unless someone was cutting through their yard. With their children gaping at the defiled house across the street, they had to consider the unthinkable – that the killer parked in the Western Bowl back lot and used their yard to access and flee the crime scene.

Joan talked to her children throughout the day, shielding them from gossip without trying to avoid their questions. She was a good listener, and according to Jim she could be "a good interrogator. People wanted to confide in her. She truly knew everything that was happening on that street."

Dick Janszen was another matter. From the moment he stepped out of the Bricca house and into the spotlights last night, he was inescapably

3381 Greenway Avenue on Wednesday morning as detectives continued to work the crime scene.

transformed. He said nothing about the crime to his children that morning. Or ever.

That it happened less than 100 feet from their front door was eerie and unknowable, the ultimate test of the soul's defense mechanism. It was calm clashing with hysteria, survival against evil. For Richard and Joan Janszen, fate had skipped over them and dealt the black card across the street, shattering their illusions that things happen for a reason.

Or that a person can control their own destiny...

Susan Keller was getting ready for work. The Bricca's babysitter had heard on the radio last night about the triple murder of a family on Greenway. Her first thought was about her friend Linda Zeff, the the only child of two parents on Greenway. Her late night call to their house had gone unanswered.

Suddenly she heard a yell from their front yard. Looking out her open window, Susan saw her younger sister holding the morning paper and staring at the front page. She looked up, saw Susan, and cried out "Oh God, It was the Briccas!"

At the Monsanto plant Ruth Bernard parked near building 7 and strolled in to work. The woman who shared a cubicle wall with Jerry Bricca hadn't heard anything during the night or read a morning paper. Her attention was immediately drawn to the crowd of people gathered in the engineering department.

Before she could even ask, someone blurted out that Jerry Bricca and his family had been murdered.

When I interviewed her in 2016, she recalled that dark Wednesday at Monsanto. "Everyone was gathered around talking – in a state of shock. When I heard it I got an immediate migraine headache, the first and last one I ever had."

Ruth said it felt "like someone had stabbed her brain. I loved Jerry Bricca, but it was more like an infatuation. He was as cute as could be. He talked about his daughter but never his wife."

Now she was struggling to breathe, the florescent office lights searing her eyes. Though she'd never met Jerry's family, "I kept picturing what was done to the little girl."

Feeling the bile rising in her throat, Ruth ran to the restroom.

September 28th

By mid-morning rumors were whirling. The adult victims were an alluring wife and a workaholic husband, and the phrase "former airline stewardess" was grist for that mill.

At 9 AM Vogel called a meeting with his 12 detectives, telling them that robberies, car thefts, and assaults would be investigated by the uniforms. If you were in "plain clothes" you were on Bricca.

Knowing they had caught an overwhelming murder case, the detectives were anxious to push off in the right direction. But those 48 hours between murder and discovery were an obstacle.

Their bullpen was now the murder room – just like the Cincinnati PD "Strangler" squad room. Vogel laid out the ground rules:

Sergeant Bell will catalog all the leads and tips. Every scrap of information runs through this room, with relevance and priority assigned later. We'll use a cross-referenced lead card file, and narrow down the information and circulate it. Phone calls

will be logged and eliminated when possible. Evidence will be accessed and categorized.

Vogel didn't share a conclusion he'd already drawn – the victims knew their killer. Or killers – he wasn't ready to address that one either until he read the coroner's report.

He told his men the killer was familiar with the house, almost comfortable there. So they would be moving from the center outward. The first level was the victims' inner circle, including neighbors, friends, relatives, co-workers, babysitters, and visitors. Farther out were regular delivery people like mailmen, paper boys, meter readers, milk and bread trucks. At the edge were the periodic on-site workers – cleaning services, tree-trimmers, landscapers. ALL would have to be checked.

Hopefully, they would compile a list of suspects – only then could they expedite the process of elimination and narrow the list. They would delve deeper into anyone not immediately cleared, then more canvassing, checking, considering.

"We have to get to know the Briccas inside out," Vogel said. "There could be a random link between this murdered family and something that happened years ago."

Which meant keeping an ear to the ground for gossip. In court, hearsay rules are in place to staunch rumors – people may only testify to what they saw, not what they heard from someone else. Yet in a murder investigation, allegations about something a dead person said were always coveted.

A murder is rarely solved by wild speculation. Anyone linked to the victims must be methodically tracked down, while every fact would be gathered with sweat and examined with persistence.

Because one fact is worth a hundred theories.

But this was still 1966. The science of forensic evidence collection was in its infancy. There was no staff of scene videographers, print men, blood experts, or hair/fiber analyzers. DNA was a vagrant fantasy from a high school biology class

Lt. Herb Vogel gave his first press conference at noon standing in front of the Bricca house. Exhaustion creased his face as he gave the first official details of the murders. The man charged with capturing the

A weary Herb Vogel gave his first press conference in the front yard of the Bricca house.

killers was wearing a white short sleeved shirt, tie cinched tight against his neck. Sunlight glinted off his black glasses and dark crew cut.

Vogel had that Midwestern reticence, answering with sparse words, never offering too much or adding any more. Being an ex- athlete helped. He was a team player, always fair-minded, and upheld his integrity no matter the game.

Reporters would learn in the months ahead that he never dominated any dialogue. A predatory listener, he would cherry pick comments and slowly shift the discussion to his own concerns.

Already the questions had a sexual overtone. Vogel denied the early reports that Linda was raped – "criminal assault has not been confirmed, I don't know where you got that." He gave a brief background on the adult victims before retreating into a neutral zone, using the disclaimer "I can't say at this point" repeatedly during the ten-minute conference.

He remained close-lipped about suspects, but didn't shy away from sharing details with the press. Certain specifics would be held back as "polygraph keys" to trip up those who might falsely confess.

"I am inclined to believe whoever did it came in the back basement door into the family room," Vogel announced. "It could have been a revenge killing, a sex attack, or a robbery." He mentioned that a carving knife was missing from a set kept in the Bricca dining room.

He turned to walk back into the murder house, queries echoing behind him. Once inside, he checked in with Sgt. Bell and learned they were being inundated with calls.

Vogel would see it all during this marathon investigation. A torrent of phone calls from oddballs, cranks, buffs, and jokers. An avalanche of letters from publicity stalkers, speculators, shakedown artists. People saddled with their ignorant, incessant opinions. Not to mention those who knew the killer personally.

Detective Gerald Taylor warned him. "You can't escape the sex angle. The woman was wearing a low cut negligee, she was attacked on the bed, and her breasts were exposed.

Vogel sighed. "We'll know soon enough if she was raped. Coroner's report should be over any time now."

Taylor flashed a pale smile. "With sex crimes it's always easy to trash the female victim, or partially blame them." He nodded his head toward the front yard where reporters still clustered. "Their readers like a little sex with their mystery."

"I can't judge Linda," Vogel replied, surprised to be using her first name. "Not after what we saw last night. No one deserves that."

September 28th

The FBI criminal classification manual lists 48 different types of homicide. This unwieldy catalog is broken down into six distinct categories of homicide:

- **Personal cause: acts ensuing from interpersonal aggression, including domestic homicide.**
- **Group cause: cult/extremist murders, hostage situations, and group excitement homicide.**

- **Third party: a contract killing usually for gain but sometimes for personal reasons.**
- **Felony murder: a criminal enterprise or a homicide during the commission of another crime.**
- **Sexual homicide: a lust murder usually committed by an offender in the 20-35 age group.**
- **Sociopathic killings: random or planned stranger murders with or without a specific victimology.**

The Bricca case would spawn countless theories from each category. Contract murder, sexual homicide and revenge murder were the most popular, but alternative speculations would ultimately include a drug murder, sadism, and a killer cult.

The crime scene suggested the killer knew the family – no forced entry, no signs of struggle, and no defensive wounds. Other than a few strange thumps, neighbors heard no sounds of distress.

That missing carving knife may have been in a dining room drawer found standing open – or displayed in plain sight. The knife's wooden scabbard was also gone, but the matching fork was there. If the carving set was hidden and the knife was the murder weapon, this would indicate someone familiar with the house.

The Briccas' two dogs, usually aggressive toward strangers and protective of Linda, were found locked in the lower level TV room and weren't heard barking Sunday night. Richard Meyer told police the dogs "had the run of the house" yet confirmed Jerry put them in the basement when they had company.

The third victim also suggested the killer knew the family. There aren't many scenarios where the elimination of a 4-ear-old child is necessary. Debbie was most likely murdered because she knew the man who killed her parents.

Crime scene analysis indicated the probability that an "organized offender" was involved: the control of the dogs and the two adults, the use of ligatures, the killer remaining at crime scene, the staging of the robbery, and removal of incriminating evidence all suggested the Bricca killer was a cool and callous customer.

It is said that every good mystery has a wild card. Was there hidden evidence or a surprise suspect waiting in left field?

SHORTLY AFTER LUNCH VOGEL was handed the Coroner's report.

Frank Cleveland was elected county coroner in 1964. By 1966 he had received mostly high marks, but during his 30-year tenure allegations of lax security, workers drinking on duty, and attendants abusing corpses would eventually force him from office.

With Taylor looking over his shoulder, Vogel quickly found what he was looking for. "They got semen out of her."

"How did it get there?" Taylor asked. "Force or consent?"

"He's calling it rape." Vogel read further. "But here he's saying she had 'recent intercourse' before the slaying. What does he mean by recent? 24 hours? We need a clarification on this."

Whether Linda had been raped or merely had consensual intercourse was one more paradox in this baffling case. That sperm would be tested for blood type – all they could expect in 1966.

They were getting affirmation from neighbor wives that Linda Bricca was attractive and flaunted it. Vogel realized she was the youngest, prettiest housewife on that end of Greenway, so he took it in stride. Yet Linda's behavior was important as it related to motive, and would quickly become a fertile field of inquiry.

The public already had a preconceived notion of what the Bricca killer looked like. The killing of the little girl had curdled many a stomach that morning, and the unknown slayer took on monstrous qualities across the city.

How did Vogel and Taylor envision him? Could he be a stalker who had some casual interaction with Linda, like a grocery store bag boy or a route truck driver? Or a lust murder, with the killer living a fantasy about having a relationship with the victim?

Was it a criminal enterprise like burglary that crossed over into sexual homicide? Sneaking into a stranger's home in the dead of night, coupled with the uncertainty of who will be there, can be an erotically charged experience for some robbers.

Just after lunch, Taylor and detective Charles Nagel headed over to Monsanto to gather information from Jerry's employer. Vogel had the rest of his squad going over the Bricca's personal phone book. Every single number would be called, and whoever answered would be asked to explain why they were in there.

Gerald Taylor was in his mid-30s and had a reputation as a "Dapper Dan". The number two man had come up through the department with

After scouring the house into Wednesday morning, detectives searched the back yard that afternoon.

Vogel and remained his sounding board. Always impeccably dressed, the college educated Taylor was believed by some to be a bit self-absorbed with his own career trajectory.

"Charley" Nagel was in his mid-40s, considered by many to be a criminal's worst enemy. He was low key yet tenacious, a short and stocky WWII combat veteran with a large family. A colleague told me that "Nagel was a Columbo type guy. He was always one step ahead, and could never be tripped up."

Interview #1 was with William Holub, the Monsanto Personnel Manager. He told them Jerry had "an excellent record" but would not elaborate. Holub set them up for interviews with Jerry's supervisor and closest co-workers.

If there was any work friction or professional rivalry hidden in Jerry Bricca's Monsanto career, they were going to ferret it out.

September 28th

As the afternoon stretched, West Side residents waited for the Cincinnati *Post* to hit their driveways. The area was throbbing with speculation about the murders, and the *Post* deadline allowed more time than the *Enquirer* to develop the breaking story.

Another blaring headline greeted readers: **Bridgetown Couple, Child 4, Stabbed to Death in Home.** The sub-headline "Sock Stuffed in Mouth of Husband" was one of those little, grisly details that Vogel had considered holding back from the press.

Lieutenant Robert Bradford was quoted several times. Bradford would not actively investigate the Bricca case, instead serving more as a quality control advisor. He said that Jerry Bricca worked all through Saturday night at Monsanto and didn't return home until Sunday morning at 9:30 AM. Bradford admitted he was bewildered by the lack of resistance put up by the victims.

"We have no strong leads as far as I know," Bradford said. "The house was processed last night and this morning, and the yard will be processed today. We don't know if anything is missing – we need to find someone who knew what was in the house."

Richard Meyer and Richard Janszen told the *Post* about their Tuesday evening of wondering, worrying and revulsion. Emmett Baldwin confirmed that he saw Jerry walking back up his driveway after taking his garbage cans out. "Mrs. Bricca was very attractive," he said. "She was a former airline stewardess. The little girl was beautiful – just a doll."

On Greenway Avenue things began to quiet down. Small clusters of people were nestled on the sidewalk, talking quietly and looking sideways at the house. Some gawkers in cars cruised the scene. There were toys strewn in driveways, but on this Wednesday children were not playing with them.

The house was still roped off as detectives combed the yard for clues. The backyard was enclosed by four foot tall steel and wire fence – the reason Linda was rarely seen walking her dogs. Inside the fence was a long rabbit hutch covered with a tarp. There was a half-moon concrete block patio extending out from the back door, and in the back northwest corner was a new swing set with a slide.

The murder night was a wet one, but any footprints left by the killer would have been tracked over by the meter reader and the worried neighbors. If there was any physical evidence collected from the outdoor search, or mud tracked in by the killers, those details were never made public.

At Monsanto, Taylor and Nagel were interviewing some of Jerry's stunned co-workers.

Will Rist had given Jerry a lift to work several times in March, but didn't know him well, and was surprised to learn about his wife and daughter, since Jerry never mentioned them.

Glenn Ritchie recounted his conversation with Jerry regarding their Monday morning trip to West Virginia. He was peeved when Bricca didn't pick him up as planned, but Ritchie assumed a work emergency changed his schedule. But it was odd that Jerry didn't call him. Ritchie tried him Monday night and Tuesday morning without success. He'd known Jerry for three years, but had "never been to the Bricca house or socialized with the family in any way."

Jerry's boss Ted Anderson was genuinely shaken up during his interview. Anderson had worked hard to keep him at Monsanto despite the young engineer's frustration. He was determined to hold on to one of his top men. Yet he'd only socialized with Jerry twice, the first time at an office Christmas party last year. He met Linda that night but knew nothing about her.

Jerry never spoke about his home life – with one notable exception. On the Thursday morning before the murders, he'd opened up about an incident the previous night. The two men had gone to a bachelor party at River Downs, but when Jerry got home his wife was gone and his house was dark. Eventually Linda had walked in drunk next door where the neighbors were watching Debbie, and Jerry had made a scene.

He tried to play it off like it was nothing serious, yet Anderson could tell he was still angry about it. The fact that this private man shared this personal episode with his boss was completely out of character for Jerry Bricca.

Before leaving, Taylor and Nagel stopped by William Holub's office to thank him. Holub checked his Sunday personnel sheet and saw that Jerry Bricca was there around 7:30 AM on the morning of his death. He stayed for two hours and left to go to church.

Jerry later returned to Monsanto and signed in at 12:25 PM. Exactly four hours later he signed out. And this was the final time Jerry Bricca was at work.

That they knew of...

September 28th

Herb Vogel watched his men going through the Bricca's personal phone book. Every name was being catalogued on a lead card and assigned to detectives for follow-up. It was homicide investigation 101 – always start close. If you worked with Jerry, did Linda's hair, or babysat Debbie you were going to be interviewed.

He had checked in with his wife several times, relieved that she and his daughter were recovering comfortably after their Tuesday afternoon car accident. Phyllis Vogel told me that she "knew he wouldn't come home for quite a while."

Vogel had been turning the case over in his brain all day – pondering, venturing, and smoking out theories. How could no stone remain unturned if these early trails were strewn with an avalanche of rocks? They would have to root around in the underbrush and flush out the hidden debris of murder.

This crime had no perspective in Vogel's experience to draw from. But if he felt overmatched he never showed it.

BACK AT MONSANTO, TAYLOR and Nagel were going through Jerry Bricca's desk. His phone numbers were all for companies connected with work. They checked with the operator about personal calls Jerry may have received – there were only occasional ones from his wife.

Everyone was asked about girl friends or women Jerry might have been seeing. Some expressed surprise at this question – Jerry was "just not that type of person." His co-workers could not imagine him involved in any adulterous conduct.

John Jarvis worked for Jerry, and they would sometimes go to the nearby Cottage Inn for a sandwich and a beer. Lately Jerry was so swamped that Jarvis had seen him grabbing lunch from the vending machines.

Jarvis was visibly upset during the interview, a combination of grief over Jerry and shock at being interrogated about him. Ruth Bernard told me that Jarvis "adored Jerry and followed him around like a puppy. I rarely saw one without the other. Jerry was polished, and John idolized him for that."

John Jarvis didn't know anything about Jerry's personal life, and insisted he had never been to his home.

By the end of Wednesday, the shock and confusion of the crime scene became as quiet as the grave.

Taylor and Nagel then spoke with Dan Subtelny, who was the closest to Jerry of anyone at the plant. Investigators would eventually interview him and his wife three times.

They had socialized with Jerry and Linda on many occasions, everything from playing Bridge to seeing a live show. Dan had been in the Bricca house often in the first part of the year, but not since July. The two husbands had agreed that Pat Subtelny and Linda didn't have enough in common to mingle regularly.

Subtelny was able to flesh out the persona of Linda Bricca. So far she had been described by everyone as "beautiful", as if this were her only asset. Now detectives were learning that her personality did not always match her looks.

Dan's wife had told him about Linda's behavior at the Monsanto Wives Club. Bake sales and bowling leagues didn't excite her, and she couldn't understand why the other wives didn't care about helping homeless animals. Linda quit going to the meetings around February when she went to stay with her grandparents in Florida.

Dan had commiserated with Jerry over beers about his mercurial wife. Apparently Linda would seek out any circus or animal act in the area and ingratiate herself with the trainers. She would work for free with strangers, some of whom seemed rather disreputable.

Jerry was an avid swimmer in high school and college, and had joined the Woodhaven Swim Club that summer.

He remembered how upset Jerry was when Linda invited an itinerant bear trainer to their home for dinner. And he recalled Jerry's anger over Linda's obsession with the Shrine Circus in April. She'd become friendly with a few elephant trainers and spent every day that week at the Cincinnati Gardens, often staying well into the night, which wreaked havoc with Jerry's work schedule and strained their network of babysitters.

Dan had never seen Jerry or Linda inside Western Bowl – the Bricca's main activities being his work, his swimming, and her animals. They belonged to the Woodhaven Swim Club, and Dan mentioned that Jerry was a powerful swimmer who won numerous trophies in high school and college.

Leaving Monsanto by mid-afternoon, Taylor and Nagel checked off three more leads based on items found in the Bricca home – an airline ticket, a note about carpet, and a prescription filled Sunday.

The William Butler Travel Agency had procured Jerry's ticket for his Charleston trip that Monday. They handled all Monsanto travel, but only dealt with their purchasing department and didn't know Jerry Bricca. The note was traced to National Carpet, but the owner had no record of ever selling them carpet.

The prescription had been phoned in by Linda on Sunday, and Jerry picked it up around 4:30 PM, about five hours before the murders. The pharmacist indicated he was alone at the time.

HAVING COMPLETED PRELIMINARY INTERVIEWS with Jerry's employer, Taylor and Nagel had one more stop that Wednesday – Linda Bricca's employer. They arrived at the Glenway Animal Hospital just before 5 PM to talk with Dr. Fred Leininger.

Checking his records, Leininger stated he had been treating the Bricca animals since their first office visit on November 9th, 1963, He showed one house call in November, 1965 when he treated a rabbit and a parakeet. When asked, the doctor stated this was the only time he had been in the Bricca home.

So how did Linda Bricca come to work there?

According to Leininger, at noon on Monday September 19th she came there with Debbie to pay a bill and the two were talking. "She had been bothering me for some time inquiring about a job," the doctor recalled. "She loved working with animals and had always dreamed of working in a Veterinarian's office."

The couple he employed had just left, so they agreed Linda would work there until he hired someone. She worked there Monday thru Wednesday, and the new couple started on Thursday the 20th. He agreed to let them have Wednesdays off and that "Mrs. Bricca would work part time and come in on Wednesdays only."

Leininger volunteered that he had dropped by the Bricca house on Friday the 23rd "to return a book that Mrs. Bricca's daughter left at the office." When he arrived Debbie was playing in the front yard, so he handed her the book. Leininger "did not go in the house, and I did not see Mr. or Mrs. Bricca at this time."

The interview lasted ten minutes. Taylor and Nagel headed back to headquarters, still puzzling over Leininger's demeanor during the interview. Cops had a name for it – inappropriate effect.

Unlike others that day, he asked them no questions about the murders. They would learn later that Linda Bricca had called the clinic and specifically asked for Leininger to bring the book – which he neglected to mention.

Gerald Taylor could not get Leininger out of his head. His speech was stilted with imposing words that made him seem clinical and aloof.

And there were the things he didn't express, like shock over the murders or sadness for the victims.

In Taylor's view, pretense clung to Leininger like a second skin...

Thursday, September 29th

Late on that Wednesday night, 24 hours after their daughter, son-in-law and granddaughter were found murdered, Mr. and Mrs. Adolph Bulaw were meeting with County investigators.

They had flown in that afternoon from their vacation in Arkansas. As the meeting ran past midnight, the Bulaw's confided some intimate details of Jerry and Linda's marriage, including Linda's Florida retreat/separation.

Vogel kept his tone restrained, but he didn't have much time to respect their grief. He later told the press that they learned "some very interesting things about their married life" but would not elaborate. This quote, hinting of romantic intrigue, would stir up the talk all around the West Side.

All three men I interviewed who were inside the crime scene heard the rumor that Linda was having an affair with a local veterinarian. Bob Weitzel and Bob Sweeney first heard it at the Mack Fire Department building.

SPCA officer Bernard Tigges, who removed the dogs from the crime scene and knew the local vets, remembered that within days "everyone was talking about her affair with Fred Leininger". Anyone associated with the local clinics had apparently caught it.

Jerry's co-worker Ruth Bernard heard it at Monsanto within days. And Judith Bush Hemmer, who lived five doors down from the Bricca family, told me her mother-in-law believed that Linda Bricca had strayed outside her marriage.

Ultimately the shadow of adultery became a total eclipse. Talk of Key Clubs, swingers, and swappers hurtled around the West Side. The sexual aura that permeated the murders was seen by conservative residents as a sign of spiritual and moral bankruptcy.

For others, the whispers were too delectable to ignore...

ON THURSDAY MORNING THE Cincinnati *Enquirer* ran five articles pertaining to the Bricca case.

FBI May Help Police Hunt in Murder of 3 was one hopeful headline, with the sub heading **'Maniac Sought'**. "A large box of items from the Bricca home," including clothing, bed sheets and the hair samples were being sent to their Washington lab today.

Coroner Cleveland verified that "Mrs. Bricca was raped", even though Herb Vogel believed she merely had "recent intercourse." Cleveland also speculated about the "penetrative head wounds" on the two adults, suggesting they were not caused by a knife.

The front page headline left no doubt where the investigation was headed: **Neighbors Think Bricca Killer No Stranger**. Another article on page 44 asked the question: **Did Murderer Know Briccas? Indications Say He Did.** The control of the dogs, the lack of struggle or defensive wounds, and the missing carving knife pointed to a killer known to the family.

These revelations were a mixed blessing for Bridgetown neighborhood. On one hand residents could take comfort that this crime was not the handiwork of some random fiend.

Yet they had to worry that a killer was walking among them...

WITH NO ARREST IN the "Cincinnati Strangler" murders, reports of suspicious black men prowling the predominantly white West Side kept rolling in.

A young black man was seen running across Greenway towards the Western Bowl parking lot on Monday at 7:30 AM. Someone saw "a colored man" going through garbage cans on Sharlene Drive (1.5 miles from crime scene) later that day. A tip about a black man sitting in a car at Westbourne and Werk (0.5 miles) several mornings quickly died – he turned out to be a construction worker.

A report of a strange black man at Western Bowl prompted detectives to see if any of their "colored employees" did not show for work on Monday or Tuesday. After checking "both white and Negro" workers, all were accounted for at work on those days.

Murders Spur Plea for Police headlined an *Enquirer* story about housewives signing petitions to increase the size of the Hamilton County Sheriff's patrol. Terrified women up and down Greenway were talking about the lack of protection, one of them quoted as saying that "police are scarce out here."

This article also fleshed out the lives of the victims. Joan Janszen, the last person to see Jerry, remembered the Briccas as "lovely people, very fine, very genteel. The little girl was just as courteous and refined. She talked like an adult."

Jerry Bricca attended a catholic high school in San Francisco and received a chemical engineering degree from Stanford. He had been with Monsanto since 1960 and transferred to their Port Plastics Division in Addyston in 1963 – the article erroneously said he was in charge of in-plant operations there. Neighbors said Jerry was devoted to his career, working long hours and sometimes staying on the job for 24 hours at a time.

Linda Bricca, described as "beautiful" by all who knew her, graduated from Elgin High School near Chicago and had attended the National College of Education in Illinois. The former Linda Bulaw met Jerry while working as a stewardess for United Airlines.

Also in that *Enquirer* was an article headlined **7 Murders Here in 10 Months – All of Them Unsolved**. Cincinnati police were still investigating the murders of four women – the juxtaposition of "The Strangler" with "The Maniac" was extraordinary, causing yet another surge of fear.

Richard Meyer, who found the bodies, lamented that residents could no longer leave their doors unlocked. He mentioned that his wife had seen a "strange man walking back and forth" in front of the Bricca house the previous Thursday. "She wondered about him, but says she couldn't identify his face now."

Meyer was still shaken. "This happened only 15 feet from us. It could have been our house."

A patrolman standing outside the roped off Bricca house gave *Enquirer* crime reporter Margaret Josten the sound bite of the day. Herb Vogel had earlier complained that Greenway was a street where "outsiders" were likely to go unnoticed. Now the street cop cut to the chase. "This is the kind of street where everybody knows it in five minutes if a man takes a strange woman into his house."

He flashed a baleful grin. "But let something like this happen and they haven't seen anything."

September 29th

Back at the County murder room, detectives were putting the finishing touches on an aggressive interview schedule.

Their burgeoning file of "lead cards" came from two sources – people who had contact with the Briccas and phone tips from possible witnesses. The information blitz was already stretching them thin – by the end of the week it would swamp them.

Some neighbors were identified because of their peculiar actions on the murder night. Other callers claimed to have found the weapon. There were aspiring suspects, crazy informants, and childishly scrawled postcards. The phone lines burned with strident denials, false confessions, and anonymous calls.

Once the liars and the attention seekers were eliminated, anything remotely promising was typed up on a lead card, prioritized by Vogel or Bell, and assigned to a detective team to gather background and schedule an interview.

Working the theory that the victims knew their killer, the Bricca's network of primary friends and secondary associates became paramount. Everyone has hidden human friction in their lives – this time it may have led to murder.

It's astounding to find how many toes you've stepped on or people you've rubbed the wrong way. We all suffer slights and affronts, face quarrels and outbursts – most quickly pass. Until that one day when you're confronted by someone who let it fester.

Most people get killed over small things – humiliation, disrespect, snubs and slurs. Or avarice over a few dollars.

Gerald Taylor and Charlie Nagel's first interview on Thursday was Waterworks meter reader Al Shelton. He had attempted to read the Bricca's meter on Tuesday at noon, but received no answer to his repeated knocks. The dogs were in the lower level, but for the first time ever did not react to him.

The detectives left the interview wishing he had tried harder to read the Bricca meter. If Shelton had found the bodies at noon they would have an eleven hour head start on where they were now.

Taylor and Nagel next interviewed the two newspaper delivery men. *Enquirer* carrier Bob Holzschuh was positive that he delivered the Bricca paper at 2:15 AM Monday morning. Since that paper was missing, they had to consider that killer was still in the house and used it to wrap evidence. With the garbage cans due to be picked up around

Bricca Family Slayer Wielded Murder Knife Over 20 Times

The slayer of the Bricca family wielded his death knife more than 20 times in snuffing out the lives of the young Bridgetown family.

Reports from the Hamilton County coroner's office and county police show that:

Slain family's neighbors recall the "little things." Picture of possible slaying knife—Both on Page 38.

level home at 3381 Greenway avenue, Bridgetown.

VOGEL SAYS his office has been flooded with calls

a matching fork were given to the Bricca's as a gift about a year ago. He says the set apparently was kept on top of a china cupboard in the dining room.

"We have no information that they kept it (the knife) out of sight," Vogel says.

On Thursday more details about the crime were published, including confirmation regarding the stab wounds.

5 AM, it was possible they contained something incriminating. Taylor made a quick note to contact the dump.

Post carrier Charles Beherns had delivered their Tuesday afternoon paper around 4:30 PM. He confirmed seeing both his Monday paper and the Tuesday *Enquirer* on the Bricca front walk.

Taylor jumped on a tip from neighbor William Cullen. He thought Linda once worked for veterinarian Dr. Stanley Keller, rumored to now be in a hospital mental ward. This dovetailed with a report from a woman in the crowd after the discovery, who told a deputy that Linda worked for a vet now in a mental hospital.

Keller had an office on Glenway two miles south of the Bricca house, but apparently Linda never worked for him. Cullen's tip was closed – but this was not the last time Dr. Keller's name would appear in the case file...

VOGEL ASSIGNED ANOTHER TEAM to obtain statements from the nearest neighbors. Detective William Belbot was in his mid-40s, a lanky man who often wore flashy vests. He was street smart and relentless, a guy who closed virtually all of his cases. With him was Tom Pinkerton, a young West Side native burdened with the most famous detective surname in America.

With the husbands on the north end of Greenway back at work Thursday, Belbot and Pinkerton focused on the two housewives who knew Linda Bricca best – Betty Meyer and Joan Janszen, Distressed by the proximity of the crime, both were blunt about the perceived shortcomings of their young, good-looking neighbor.

Joan Janszen called Linda "a nice person with a fanatic love of animals. She never changed her mind and never complained about her home life." Yet she was "immature and cool towards Jerry sexually," and once confided that she did not want any more children "till Debbie was older."

Whenever Joan went to visit Linda the dogs were put in the family room before she entered. She'd last seen Linda on Saturday the 24th washing her car in the driveway around 3 PM. Joan didn't know Jerry as well, but he seemed like a "very nice fellow and a light drinker, who worked some very funny hours."

When asked, Joan Janszen stated that Linda "ran down to Dr. Leininger's office two to three times a week and sometimes three or four times a day." She described Leininger as mid-30s, six feet tall with a slender build, curly blonde hair and a long face.

Betty Meyer liked Linda but often regarded her with a jaundiced eye. Her neighbor was "gorgeous" and believed all the other husbands "were lusting after her." Betty knew all about the Florida "vacation", and was certain that Linda and Jerry were no longer having sex. Betty felt that Linda somehow resented Debbie, as if the child was "cramping her style."

She told the detectives about Linda's strange burial rituals for her pets, including the little coffins for the rabbits and her use of monogramed towels to bury a dead bird. Betty confirmed the dogs had "the run of the house and slept in bed with Linda every night."

To Betty, Linda Bricca was just "a child playing make believe in a doll house" instead of trying to be a good homemaker. She usually got her way with Jerry, who went along to avoid conflict.

Betty also saw Linda washing her car on that Saturday afternoon. She didn't mention the incident on Wednesday night before the murders – Linda coming to their house late and drunk to pick up Debbie, with Jerry becoming angry and making a threat.

But she gave detectives something to chew on. When asked about Dr. Leininger, Betty volunteered that Debbie often called him "Uncle Fred."

September 29th

The Thursday afternoon *Post* ran a feature headlined **FBI Lab to Check 30 Items Found at Scene of Triple Slaying**. It was the most detailed analysis of this inexplicable crime so far.

The missing carving knife had an elaborately carved wooden handle – the inscription on the blade read "Rajba Bros. India". At 6-1/2" long the blade matched most of the victim's wounds.

Items sent to the FBI included partial palm prints, hair samples, and bloody towels. Vogel downplayed it, knowing it was better to under promise and over deliver: "These are the bits and pieces found in the home. They represent only the thinnest of clues"

The logistics of this crime were puzzling. The family was killed sometime between 9 PM Sunday and 6:30 AM Monday, but based on digestion it appeared they died Sunday night. There were indications that ligatures were used on both adults, possibly adhesive tape that the killer removed. There was a large piece of tape dangling from Jerry's chin.

"I don't know who was killed first," Vogel admitted. "I don't know why there was no sign of a struggle."

When asked why Coroner Cleveland said Linda had been raped, Vogel replied that "the coroner told me that she had recent intercourse before the killing," meaning within 24-30 hours.

Vogel would not speculate on the identity of her sex partner – which ramped up the chatter all along the West Side.

BELBOT AND PINKERTON WERE still working close to the crime scene, ringing doorbells looking for worried housewives willing to talk.

Susan Day lived behind the Briccas on Greencrest Drive. Only 26, she became friendlier with Linda that summer when her daughter began playing with Debbie. Being close in age the two sometimes went shopping together – Linda "never carried much cash and charged everything." She sometimes complained about swelling in her legs. And naturally, Susan said she was "really funny over animals, loving them like children."

Helen Zambatis lived next to Sue Day and had known the Briccas for three years. She described Linda and Jerry as "friendly, light drinkers who seemed happily married." When the dogs were in their back yard at night Helen could see their floodlights on – the animals would bark furiously if anyone came near them.

The night of the murders Helen had glanced at the Bricca house just after 9 PM and could see their TV screen flashing in the lower room. After thinking about it, she realized their rear door must have been open for her to see the screen.

Helen also gave the detectives Cheryl Rehling's phone number and suggested they call her about Linda Bricca.

Gloria Weyman lived just around the corner on Lawrence Road. The 40-year-old wife and mother said they had known the Briccas for about three years but had not seen much of them this year.

Unlike others who'd visited the family, Gloria was certain the carving set was on the buffet in plain sight and not hidden in a drawer – suggesting that a stranger could have grabbed that knife.

Belbot leaned in as Weyman dished on Linda Bricca. Apparently the younger woman had confided about having a nervous breakdown sometime before she met Jerry. Linda also talked about a "male friend" she had been seeing in New York when she was a stewardess, and how he had showered her with expensive gifts and lavish dinners.

"Linda liked to project an attitude that she could handle any situation," Gloria said. "Yet she didn't make friends easily. I would describe her as immature yet very opinionated."

"Did she complain to you about anything in her marriage?"

"Only that they were not in a better financial situation."

Gloria offered up the obligatory "she was crazy about animals" and "Jerry worked odd hours." When asked if Linda Bricca had a boyfriend, Gloria pondered for several seconds before saying "No."

Gloria Weyman closed the interview by asking Belbot to check out her "strange" neighbor across the street. She said the guy would often stand in his yard grunting, groaning and waving his arms at passerby.

Their last interview of the day was the tip from Helen Zambatis. Cheryl Rehling, age 36 of Hyacinth Terrace, claimed to have seen Linda Bricca riding in a car with a man about 1 PM the day before the murders.

Since she lived almost a half mile from the Bricca house, they wondered how she could be sure it was Linda Bricca. Rehling said she met

Linda at a couple of neighborhood cookouts through Helen, and based on pictures in the paper she was certain the man driving the car was not Jerry Bricca. She described it as a light gray or green foreign car, and the driver was white, mid-30s, "light blond hair combed back," with a "long face but not skinny."

Her description struck a chord with Belbot, who promised to get back to her with a photo lineup so she could identify the driver.

Along with gaining insight into Linda Bricca, Belbot and Pinkerton had taken the pulse of the neighborhood. The housewives were petrified – phrases like "this is too close for comfort" and "how could it happen here" were no longer clichés when murder came home to roost.

As Thursday evening settled in, Vogel and Taylor knew their "first 48 hours" were up. Already hampered by the two day delay in finding the bodies, the next two days had borne little fruit.

They were looking to isolate people and circumstances that didn't fit – a startling concurrence that could not be explained. Most detectives believe there is no such thing as a coincidence. If you could pile five to ten of them on top of a suspect, chances are he was your killer.

Questions volleyed between them. What was under Linda's fingernails? Did they find anything in the house that didn't belong to the family? Did the intruders use a gun to intimidate the victims?

They believed the killer confronted Linda in the TV room while Jerry was upstairs putting Debbie to bed. He then became aware of a disturbance in the lower level, right below Debbie's room.

In the bedroom, perhaps Linda's protection of Jerry incites his rage. The impassioned killing of the two adults is followed by a cold blooded elimination of the child witness. Everyone was calling the Bricca murders a crime of passion, but Vogel wasn't so sure.

As night fell, they were left with the three motives Vogel had floated to the media that morning. Was it a revenge killing, a sex crime, or a botched burglary? Tomorrow they had a meeting with Sheriff Tehan, Captain Otting, and Prosecutor Rueger – Vogel hoped they had some answers.

Failure to find the motive could lead this investigation astray...

Friday, September 30th

The Cincinnati *Enquirer* editorial portrayed a city besieged by violence, under a simple, evocative title – **The Bricca Case:**

> **A crime eclipsing the chilling narrative "In Cold Blood" was committed the other night in a pleasant section of Bridgetown. A fiend – or fiends – stabbed to death Mr. and Mrs. Jerry Bricca and their four-year- old daughter and ransacked their home. Mrs. Bricca, a former airline stewardess, was raped.**
>
> **The triple murder may have no association with the year-long series of violent crimes involving women in this area. However, the brazenness of the assault, and its viciousness, provide new fuel for local concern about the rising rate of violence here. We have a long way to go in this cooperative effort. The savage wiping out of the Bricca family is only the latest and perhaps most horrible evidence of this.**

There were two articles contrasting the spike in crime with the new constraints on police. **County Area Crime Rate Climbs by 300%** allowed Sheriff Dan Tehan to lobby for more money and manpower. Of his 150 man squad, only 67 were assigned to county patrol in unincorporated areas.

In **Miranda Ruling Shackles Police,** William Boyers, special agent in charge of the Cincinnati FBI office, bemoaned that the new legislation was curtailing law enforcement powers:

> **Suppose county police today zero in on a suspect in the triple Bricca murder and in the initial throes of a guilty conscience he confesses it and even tells where the missing murder weapon is hidden.**
>
> **If his blurted confession came before the police had a chance to warn him of his Miranda rights against self-incrimination, not only would his confession be inadmissible – the prosecution could not even introduce the murder weapon.**

About 10 AM the "big meeting" broke up. Vogel had been in conference for two hours with Tehan, Otting, Rueger and Coroner Cleveland.

As he emerged an *Enquirer* reporter asked him "to comment on the persistent rumor that an adulterous romance was involved with this crime." The Lieutenant curtly denied it, saying everything they had so far indicated "the Briccas were a devoted, happily married couple."

Yet rumors about Linda Bricca's infidelity were eddying around the West Side. Word on the street presumed "the former airline stewardess" was fooling around, and it got her family killed...

AROUND NOON A FASCINATING suspect dropped into the case. He was a poignantly lost young man – two articles in the *Miami Herald* caught the eye of Dade County police and put him in the spotlight.

On September 28th a white male was brought to the Miami Missing Persons Bureau having been diagnosed with Hysterical Amnesia. He could not recall anything prior to 3:30 PM September 26th, when he found himself in the Greyhound Bus Station in Columbus, Ohio. He could not even remember his own name.

He boarded a bus for Miami after finding a ticket in his pocket, assuming someone would be waiting there for him. When no one met him, he took a taxi to the nearest police station and was then transported to a hospital.

The youth was identified as Ohio University student Jack Petersen after his father recognized his picture on TV. He was happily reunited with his parents and two brothers and taken back home. But not before his name surfaced in the Bricca investigation.

An officer in the Dade County Sheriff's office read two articles in the September 29th *Miami Herald* and thought he saw a connection. The piece about the missing Petersen boy from Ohio was directly opposite an AP Cincinnati story headlined **Young Engineer, Wife and Daughter Found Stabbed to Death in Ohio Home.**

The officer phoned Herb Vogel about the young amnesiac, and Petersen's fingerprints were forwarded for evaluation as a possible suspect in the Bricca murders.

By the end of the day, Jack Petersen was off the radar.

THAT AFTERNOON AN ANONYMOUS caller claimed "Linda Bricca hung around the Western Bowl quite a lot and drank pretty much." He insisted "she was quite a flirt." But detectives interviewed a Bricca neighbor working there who said she'd "never seen her in the place." They also showed Linda's picture to all the employees and no one remembered her.

Belbot and Pinkerton were interviewing people in the Bricca phone book. A General Electric repairman named Andrew Wulfeck told them he was last in their house in September 1965. Wulfeck said Linda had conducted herself "in a ladylike manner and was not forward with me like other women," some of who would "dress scantily and make suggestive remarks."

Shell station attendant Donald Sebastian responded to the Bricca home on Friday to jumpstart Linda's car, which she later brought in to have the battery terminals cleaned. She told Sebastian she had to take Debbie to an appointment, and they left the station about 11:30 AM.

Martha Olding had met Linda through the Monsanto wives club. Her impression of Linda was that she was quiet, dressed conservatively, wore little makeup, and was "a dear, sweet girl." She thought Jerry was "nice but outspoken" and "seemed to be religious." Martha couldn't imagine why Jerry didn't put up a fight, as "he was well built and rugged."

The detectives caught up with Nettie Caudell, a Bricca neighbor who lived on the Greenway corner and often served as a spontaneous babysitter. She discounted some things Linda would say, but Nettie had a soft spot for her and little Debbie, and was profoundly affected by this disaster just a few houses away.

"Could her love of animals have a bearing on this?"

"Maybe." Nettie paused. "I think it had taken over her life. I mean, she showed more affection for her dogs than her daughter. I've never even seen her hug Debbie."

"Did she share her personal problems with you?"

"She was peeved that Jerry told her they would have to have another child before she could get another dog. And she once told me that she was worried about who would take care of the dogs if something happened to her."

Belbot raised his eyebrows. *If something happened to her?* "When did you last see her?'

"Last Friday when I watched Debbie in the afternoon. Linda was late picking her up. She said something about her car not starting and the Shell attendant jumping it.

Pinkerton glanced at Belbot – they had just interviewed Don Sebastian, who said Linda's car trouble had been in the morning.

When asked, Nettie did not know if Linda had any "boyfriends."

Yet on a recent shopping trip to the Western Hills Plaza, when they passed the Glenway Animal Hospital Linda commented that Debbie had started calling Dr. Leininger "Uncle Fred."

When Nettie asked her why, Linda Bricca merely laughed...

September 30th

The *Post* ran a front page feature Friday afternoon under the headline **Slain Family's Neighbors Recall the 'Little Things'**:

> **Except for a solitary police cruiser parked outside 3381 Greenway Avenue to keep everyone away from the roped off house, the brutal stabbing of the Gerald Bricca family sometime Sunday night seemed like a bad dream... Kids on backyard swings, wagons in the driveways, and a lawnmower starting up down the block testified to the fact that life is going on in spite of the tragedy. But things aren't the same. Caution has become as tangible an object as the carpets, TV sets, and paintings found in every living room on this street.**

Babysitters were at a premium in Green Township, as teenage girls balked at staying in anyone else's home. Housewives who worked at nearby Western Bowl were no longer walking home alone at night. Screen doors and garages were now locked.

Suddenly neighbors couldn't watch each other without wondering – is the killer one of us?

Across the street from the crime scene, the Janszen children watched the investigation unfold. After staying home from school on Wednesday, Mary, Jim, Richard, and Jerry returned to the curious stares of classmates. At 12, oldest child Mary was peppered with questions like "What happened to the Bricca family?" When she answered truthfully with "I don't know," she was chided to "spill the beans" and "tell it all."

Kids on Greenway were bewildered. For every child this ghastly crime was like a monster movie come to life, and the Bricca killer became a cross between Dracula and Jack the Ripper.

The Bricca tragedy had permeated the whole West Side. At the dinner table or the water cooler, from the bowling alley to country club, the murders had sundered a crack in their world, exposing the evil poised to emerge...

VOGEL AND TAYLOR WERE revising the interview schedule when the directive came down from Captain Otting.

The meeting with the big brass hadn't gone well. Their case was pieced together with rumors – they were looking everywhere, but Otting didn't see it as productive. As the mistakes and false starts mounted, brainstorming turned into blame storming.

Emil Otting was in his mid-50s, and had risen through the ranks more as a politician than a policeman. He was a stickler for decorum – one former deputy told me Otting once upbraided him for not wearing his hat while helping an injured firefighter.

Otting reported to Dan Tehan, a bigger than life character. First elected Hamilton County Sheriff in 1949, he would hold the post until his retirement in 1972, quite a feat for a democrat running in a staunch republican region.

Affectionately called the "Part time Sheriff/Full time NFL referee," Tehan grew up on the West Side as a star athlete. He was an effective leader and an old school gentleman who personally attended any funerals involving his officer's families. And like Chief Schrotel with the CPD, Tehan engineered a complete overhaul of the department.

After the meeting, Tehan asked Otting to write up a protocol so they could get a handle on the unwieldy investigation. Vogel was grateful that some ground rules had been laid:

No one has a day off unless it is approved by Lt. Vogel.

Detectives Ron Taylor and McClaren will be charged with putting all materials, evidence, results of interviews, etc. into a master file and copy.

Detective Jerry Taylor shall assign all interviews and keep record of same. He shall also have assignments ready for the next day so there is no loss of time waiting around for same. All detectives give a telephone number to the dispatcher so we can reach you.

Sgt. Bell will work the evening shift with Detectives Bowman and Presnell.

One of these men shall stay at headquarters to receive calls and record same leaving a copy for detective Jerry Taylor for assignment.

The doors to the detective rooms shall be kept locked at all times... only official personnel shall be able to enter on official business... when completing business they are to leave.

This case shall not be discussed by anyone outside of the official family. Lt. Vogel shall give out all information to the news media... holding news briefings at his discretion.

Lt. Vogel shall be kept aware of all information coming to the patrol or detectives or headquarters pertaining to the Bricca case. He in turn shall keep the Captain aware of the progress of the case as it happens. All requests for added personnel or equipment shall be requested to Lt. Vogel who in turn shall notify the Captain for the OK.

Lt. Vogel and Captain Otting will be charged with keeping the sheriff informed of all information pertaining to this case. These rules shall apply at once...this being done for better efficiency and coordination so we can bring this case to a successful conclusion...

In the murder room insinuations and assumptions were overflowing. They had to winnow down the theories and separate them into three categories: unlikely, possible, and probable.

There was optimism about the upcoming FBI report. Murder cases are rarely elementary but always evidentiary – and physical evidence never lies.

Questions swarmed. Why didn't Jerry fight back? If he believed his family was in danger he should have fought like a tiger. If the killer entered through the rear door, why didn't the dogs go crazy? Neighbor Richard Meyer said the animals were particularly ferocious around strange men.

The press was hounding Vogel about the possibility of multiple perpetrators. Privately, he surmised the killer was known to the family, an ordinary man and a member of the community. If he held malice against the Briccas, where did he find someone irrational enough to share his rage?

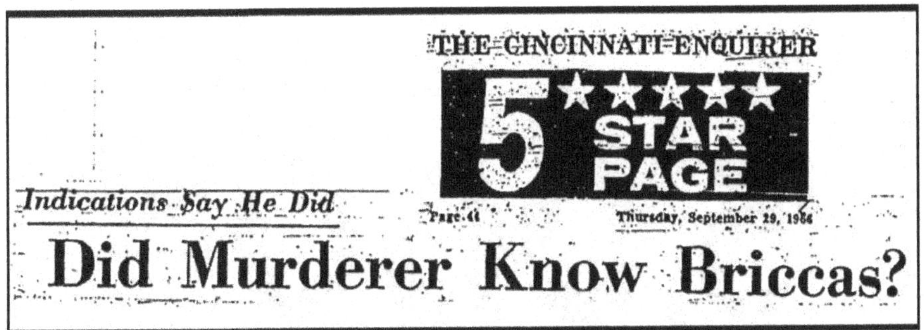
THE CINCINNATI ENQUIRER

5 STAR PAGE

Indications Say He Did

Page 41 Thursday, September 19, 1986

Did Murderer Know Briccas?

All the evidence suggested this was a personal cause homicide where the killer was emotionally entangled with the victim.

He believed Linda was the killer's target, but the motive of psychopathic hatred didn't ring true. For Vogel, this crime stank of fear – fear of exposure and loss of status.

What was Linda up to? A summer fling? Or was this a ripe affair, with love letters and clandestine trysts? Maybe it was just a red herring, and had no bearing on the crime.

The case consumed him. Vogel believed if he kept talking about it, a fresh angle would come to him. He had already spent countless hours studying those stark crime scene images, hoping some obscure detail would announce itself. Now he stared at them again, as if the murdered bodies could reveal the last events of their lives and expose their killer.

But what if this thing never made the closed file? Would he be endlessly running down leads and chasing across the country after every other family murder? Unless he found out what really happened, the Bricca case would always haunt him.

Herb Vogel yawned. It was too early in the game for these negative thoughts. Perhaps a rare confluence of actions would solve the crime. A persistent investigator might uncover a long buried clue. A merger of people and events could yield a forgotten connection. A guilty conscience may relinquish a shameful secret – a face, a name, a confession.

Or maybe they would just get lucky...

$5,000.00

REWARD

FOR INFORMATION LEADING TO ARREST AND CONVICTION OF THE MURDERER OR MURDERERS OF THE BRICCA FAMILY

THIS OFFER BEING MADE IN COOPERATION WITH THE HAMILTON COUNTY SHERIFF'S PATROL.

Supermarket chain Albers offered the first reward in the Bricca case.

CHAPTER EIGHT

DEAR UNKNOWN

"Commit a crime, and the earth is made of glass."
Ralph Waldo Emerson

OCTOBER 1ST – OCTOBER 8TH, 1966

Saturday, October 1st

The Saturday morning *Enquirer* provided the most public glimpse to date inside the Bricca Investigation with a front page feature headlined **Reconstruction of a Murder**. At yesterday's meeting Herb Vogel was given more latitude on releasing information to generate tips.

Vogel said the killer inflicted 23 wounds while snuffing out the lives of the young family. Denying that an affair was the motive, he insisted they had "some promising leads," and surmised the sequence of events in the triple slaying.

Shortly after 9 PM, the family was in the TV room watching the movie. Jerry's shoes were off as usual. Linda had laundry going and was folding some towels. It was likely that Jerry took Debbie upstairs to tuck her in – several friends confirmed that Linda rarely put Debbie to bed.

With Linda alone in the lower level, someone entered through the unlocked back door. When asked if he considered them an intruder or a friend, Vogel said it could "be one or the other, or maybe just an acquaintance. But I'm not saying either." He theorized that the intruder, bent on rape, grabbed the carving knife and forced Linda to the master bedroom, where he stabbed her and then killed Jerry when he intervened.

Yet the layout doesn't support it. If he's in Debbie's bedroom Jerry would be aware of someone forcing Linda into their bedroom. And Jerry was found beneath Linda, no doubt slain first because the killer feared his strength.

I believe the couple was herded upstairs, possibly at gunpoint. Jerry was put down with four stab wounds in the back, three in the neck and two in the head. His carotid artery was cut – the socks were stuffed in his mouth to stifle the hissing death rattle.

Linda was killed on the bed, stabbed six times in the chest and twice each on the head and neck. The chest wounds were delivered face to face between killer and victim, the six thrusts flashing in a harsh circle. There was speculation that the head wounds were made with an arrow, but their glancing nature were probably the result of the knife hitting skull bones.

Debbie was killed because she could identify the killer. She had been dragged from underneath her bed and stabbed four times in the back, the blade passing through her body each time.

Vogel was still waiting for the completed coroner's report, hoping it would shed more light on the positions of the bodies. "It might help us decide what was going on at the time of the attack." Vogel leaned toward the killer entering the back door, but wouldn't rule out the front door as the point of entry.

The young Lieutenant was clearly frustrated: "Anything is possible in this thing!"

OBSCENE PHONE CALLS KEPT cropping up during the interviews. Belbot and Pinkerton flagged one instantly – the woman's husband worked at Monsanto. Betty Haas said the man would always call when her husband was working the night shift, saying he liked her figure and inviting himself over. Then he would get filthy.

Bricca neighbor Mary Alice Baldwin was also being harassed on the phone by a caller who would just breathe hard and hang up.

Detective Ernest Nehrer conducted her interview that Saturday. Nehrer was in his early 30's, kind of a wheeler dealer who took pride in knowing something about everything. Yet he wasn't phony and was well liked, a bit of a partier who enjoyed his libations.

When a supervisor asked him if a report was ready, Nehrer gave the old school cop answer, pointing to his head. "In here."

"Ernie" could finagle a smile from even the most dismal person, and when interviewing someone he knew how to compromise instead of clash. His persona was perfect for putting a nervous witness at ease, especially one within twenty feet of the Bricca bedroom when the murders went down.

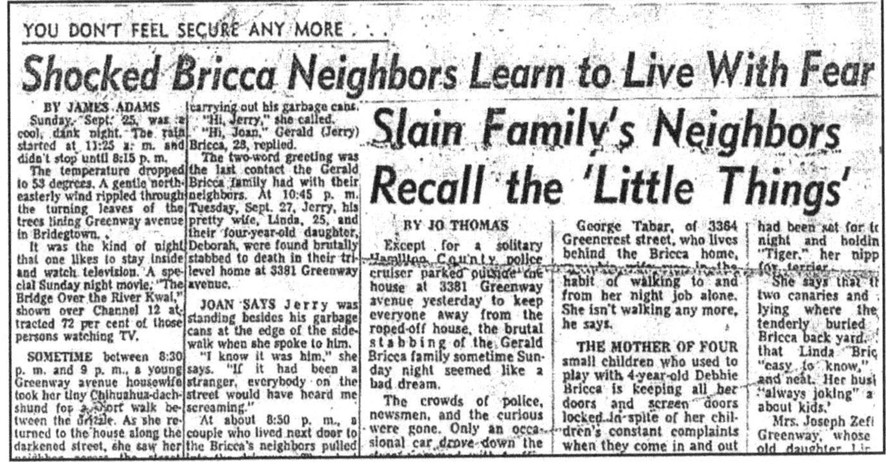

YOU DON'T FEEL SECURE ANY MORE . . .

Shocked Bricca Neighbors Learn to Live With Fear

BY JAMES ADAMS

Sunday, Sept. 25, was a cool, dank night. The rain started at 11:25 a. m. and didn't stop until 8:15 p. m.

The temperature dropped to 53 degrees. A gentle north-easterly wind rippled through the turning leaves of the trees lining Greenway avenue in Bridgetown.

It was the kind of night that one likes to stay inside and watch television. A special Sunday night movie, "The Bridge Over the River Kwai," shown over Channel 12 attracted 72 per cent of those persons watching TV.

SOMETIME between 8:30 p. m. and 9 p. m., a young Greenway avenue housewife took her tiny Chihuahua-dachshund for a short walk between the drizzle. As she returned to the house along the darkened street, she saw her carrying out his garbage cans.

"Hi, Jerry," she called.

"Hi, Joan," Gerald (Jerry) Bricca, 28, replied.

The two-word greeting was the last contact the Gerald Bricca family had with their neighbors. At 10:45 p. m. Tuesday, Sept. 27, Jerry, his pretty wife, Linda, 25, and their four-year-old daughter, Deborah, were found brutally stabbed to death in their tri-level home at 3381 Greenway avenue.

JOAN SAYS Jerry was standing besides his garbage cans at the edge of the side-walk when she spoke to him.

"I know it was him," she says. "If it had been a stranger, everybody on the street would have heard me screaming."

At about 8:50 p. m., a couple who lived next door to the Bricca's neighbors pulled

Slain Family's Neighbors Recall the 'Little Things'

BY JO THOMAS

Except for a solitary Hamilton County police cruiser parked outside the house at 3381 Greenway avenue yesterday to keep everyone away from the roped-off house, the brutal stabbing of the Gerald Bricca family sometime Sunday night seemed like a bad dream.

The crowds of police, newsmen, and the curious were gone. Only an occasional car drove down the

George Tabar, of 3364 Greencrest street, who lives behind the Bricca home, [illegible] habit of walking to and from her night job alone. She isn't walking any more, he says.

THE MOTHER OF FOUR small children who used to play with 4-year-old Debbie Bricca is keeping all her doors and screen doors locked in spite of her children's constant complaints when they come in and out

had been sat for [illegible] night and holdin[illegible] "Tiger," her nipp[illegible] fox terrier.

She says that [illegible] two canaries and [illegible] lying where the[illegible] tenderly buried [illegible] Bricca back yard. [illegible] that Linda Bric[illegible] "easy to know," and neat. Her hus[illegible] "always joking" a[illegible] about kids.'

Mrs. Joseph Zef[illegible] Greenway, whose old daughter [illegible]

As Bricca neighbors remembered the slain family, fear of the unknown killer was pervasive on Greenway Avenue.

Mrs. Baldwin heard some noises that night between 9-9:30 PM. First there was a sound like someone "bumping into a tree or a shrub", followed by a "thumping noise" a half hour later. Looking outside, she saw that the Bricca bathroom window was open.

Linda had once told Mary Alice about a circus man who let her feed the animals. This was a consistent theme – Linda connected to questionable men with roving carnivals featuring animal acts.

Nehrer saw she was a nervous wreck. The woman had been separated from the butchery next door by two walls and a narrow yard. As he reminded her to lock her doors, she surprised him.

"I've always locked my doors," replied Mary Alice Baldwin. "When Emmett and I were first married and living in South Carolina, a woman was stabbed to death across the street from our house. And she was the daughter of the county sheriff."

Ernie Nehrer left the interview in amazement. Most people are never touched by murder. Yet here was a woman who lived across the street from it AND next door to it...

Belbot and Pinkerton were also working the Greenway area. They had interviewed Gloria Weyman – now they were sitting down with her husband.

Edward Weyman didn't know the Briccas as well as his wife. He wondered about the money Linda spent for the custom built rabbit hutch, and he too had seen her treat the dogs as equals to her daughter. Ed felt Debbie received more discipline than love from her mother, as if she resented her child tying her down.

They interviewed Estelle Zeff, whose daughter Linda was the primary babysitter for the murdered family. Linda would watch Debbie at the Bricca house, and when she wasn't available Jerry brought his daughter to the Zeff house. Estelle last watched Debbie on Thursday before the murders, splitting time between her home that morning and the Bricca house that afternoon.

"How did the dogs behave?"

"Those dogs had been trained to mind her, and they got used Linda and me as well. Dusty was a cowardly dog – he would bark when someone first came in and then run and hide. Thumper would just keep barking and sniffing around their feet."

"Were the dogs ever vicious?"

"People in the neighborhood thought they were, but my daughter never had any problems."

Estelle Zeff saw no outward signs of trouble in the Bricca marriage, other than Linda's immaturity and her obsession with animals. She remembered her once taking money out of a red box in the dining room buffet where the missing knife was kept. Investigators had not found any money box there.

"When asked about Debbie, Estelle let out a bottomless sigh. "She was intelligent and very lovable."

"Mature for her age?"

"Very. She talked like a teenager." She wiped away tears. "That last time, out of the clear blue she asked me to call her Carol."

"Did she say anything else unusual that day?"

Estelle stared at Belbot. "She called the Vet Uncle Fred."

When the detectives asked to speak to Linda Zeff, Estelle went to her room but came back alone. "I'm sorry, but Linda is still too distraught," said her mother. "You'll need to come back another time."

Sunday, October 2nd

"Bricca Reward Swells, But Leads Remain Few" adorned the Cincinnati *Post* front page on Sunday. Local department store chain Albers offered a $5000 reward "for information leading to the arrest and conviction of the murderer or murderers of the Bricca family. This was quickly matched by the Monsanto Corporation.

Herb Vogel expressed impatience with the overdue FBI report, telling reporters "we have no strong leads and no suspects." He described a fruitless search of Rumpke's dump, where 15,000 tons of garbage was turned over by two bulldozers on the chance the killer had thrown the missing knife in the Bricca garbage can.

Over 300 miles to the north, a somber ceremony had commenced in Barrington, Illinois. After weltering in their own blood for two days and left naked on the coroner's gurney for two more, the slaughtered family was finally laid to rest.

After a service in the same church that hosted their wedding five years before, Gerald John Bricca, Linda Jayne Bulaw Bricca, and Deborah Ann Bricca were buried at Windridge Cemetery in front of an intimate group of family and friends. Windridge was a new facility, more like a nature sanctuary than a graveyard. Half the cemetery was wooded, and forest burials were allowed with natural stone markers. Next door was a pet cemetery – Linda's parents had picked their daughter's final resting place well.

Standing a short distance away was a man in an off the rack suit wearing sleek sunglasses. This county detective was looking for someone among the mourners who seemed out of place.

It would not be the first funeral of a murder victim attended by their remorseful killer...

BACK IN CINCINNATI, BELBOT and Pinkerton were interviewing Pat Subtelny, the wife of Jerry's friend and co-worker Dan.

At 35 Pat was 13 years older than Linda Bricca, and they never really clicked despite the rapport between their husbands. Pat was heavily involved with the Monsanto Wives Club, which Linda left earlier in the year.

"Why did she leave the club?"

"She thought we should be planning something more useful than bake sales and luncheon parties. We like each other well enough, but I enjoy bowling while all she cares about is animals. I've never met anyone who loved animals as much as her."

Pat told them about Linda getting special access to wild animals, including at the Shrine Circus when she wheedled herself into taking care of baby bears and elephants. Jerry had complained to Dan about being "stuck with babysitting."

Linda also talked about knowing someone at the zoo who would give her a job there, but with Debbie not yet in school it wasn't possible. Pat said she was "very unhappy about this."

"Did she rub people the wrong way?"

"She was an independent person, someone who would tell people to their face if she didn't like them."

Pat said Jerry was well-liked at Monsanto though somewhat of "a loner." Dan had told her about the problem with the pipefitters, which he felt had no bearing on the crime. Jerry was known to be blunt if workers were slacking off.

"Had anyone threatened Jerry?"

"Not that we know of. But I keep wondering why he didn't put up a fight that night. I mean, he was a husky guy." Pat frowned. "Dan said he had a special driver's license and might be epileptic."

Belbot made a note, wondering whether Jerry's condition might have hampered his ability to resist his killer. "Hear any rumors about Linda with other men?"

Pat gave him a long look. "Someone supposedly saw her at Walgreens with a strange man. She was buying sleeping pills."

Later in the day they crossed off three names from the Bricca's phone list. William Keener did some upholstery for Linda and Richard Kugile had done landscaping for the family.

Bob Schwartz owned Windcrest Kennels where Linda took Thumper to be groomed. Schwartz told them Linda Bricca had an appointment with him on Monday, September 26th, but didn't call or show, which surprised him. He had wondered about it until reading of the murders in the Wednesday paper.

Neither Keener nor Kugile had any contact with the family since 1964. Nevertheless, Vogel ordered criminal background checks on all three men, which came back clean. But they would have occasion to interview Schwartz again.

BY MIDAFTERNOON SUNDAY SOME promising leads surfaced.

Detective Ernie Nehrer took a call from Ray McAdams, who left Western Bowl around 10:30 PM the night of the murders and drove south on Greenway Avenue. As he passed the Bricca house he saw two men and a young woman getting into a car, which he described as "white or green in color."

McAdams gave him the phone number of another bowler who'd left moments before him and also saw the three strangers near the Bricca house. Ray Reicheld had turned down Greenway and saw the same car parked in front of the Bricca house. He'd seen saw a young white man entering the vehicle, and Reicheld described this subject as wearing a "frightened expression."

Both men were certain they were in front of the Bricca house. Reicheld described how the road takes a dip there, and he'd driven by after the murders to confirm the location.

McAdams and Reicheld gave solid witness statements, and they would be interviewed again. There was even discussion about having them hypnotized in order to enhance their recall.

The day ended with the Cincinnati Police gift wrapping two suspects for the county investigators. They would be the first in a long line of bad actors, salty dudes, and violent offenders who could be placed in Cincinnati on the night of the Bricca murders. All of these transient rogues had to be checked out.

Albert Hodges had been arrested for a strong arm robbery. A records check showed the 47-year-old white male had three convictions for assaulting young women from 1941-1955. CPD forwarded this to county because Hodges had been working construction at the Shillito's expansion on Glenway, a mile from the crime scene. His last day worked was September 30th.

The other suspect was more promising. A 44-year-old man named Leonard Deters had checked into the Veterans Hospital that morning claiming he had shot two people. The doctor had CPD take him to the crime bureau, where they found he was facing charges for setting his girlfriend's apartment on fire.

Deters told Cincinnati cops he made up the shooting story to get some free medical care. Still, Nehrer and Pinkerton went down to check him out. After talking to him they were ready to discount him – the guy was a gadfly, an annoying man trying to attract attention.

As they were leaving a Cincinnati detective showed them the file on the two-year-old unsolved murder of a young couple shot to death in their Camp Washington garage the day before Thanksgiving. The 1964 murder of Dennis and Evelyn Coby **(Queen City Gothic Chapter 9)** was the proverbial riddle wrapped in a mystery. CPD never got a whiff of a viable suspect.

Yet Leonard Deters had been interviewed as a person of interest in the Coby case before being released. So Nehrer had Deters finger printed, photographed, and interrogated.

Was he referring to the Coby double homicide when he claimed to have shot two people?

Monday, October 3rd

In a front page *Enquirer* story, Albers Supermarkets CEO Edwin Withers offered a compelling reason for his company's $5000 reward – he was "incensed over the murder of the child. It was merciless," Withers declared. "She could not have been a witness even if she recognized the murderer. It was utterly unnecessary even for a maniac."

County investigators didn't agree. This triple slaying was looking more like a personal cause murder leading to the elimination of a witness. Hot blood followed by cold blood. They were convinced the killer was no maniac and knew Debbie could identify him.

Fear Spurs Gun Sales – In Wake of Murders headlined page 18. The president of Brendamour's Sporting Goods said "the gun business has gone completely haywire at all our stores." Door chains, peepholes, and tear gas pens were also hot items.

Herb Vogel announced he was expecting the FBI lab results on Tuesday – he mentioned cigarette butts, palm prints, and hair samples that "may disclose the race of the assailant." Privately, he was certain they were looking for a white man.

They had used Benzedrine checks, luminal tests, and a black light probe to locate and analyze the bloodstains and blood spatter in both bedrooms. Jerry and Linda's driver's licenses indicated they were both type A, and samples were sent to a local lab to determine if there was any "foreign" blood on the victims.

Vogel admitted that "other evidence was being tested locally to determine the assailant's blood type." He didn't specify, but it had to be the semen found inside Linda Bricca. On the sixth day of their investigation, the words "rape" and "sex crime" were no longer being used – "recent intercourse" was now the polite term.

That test would prove that within 24 hours of her murder, Linda Bricca had sex with a man who was not her husband...

VOGEL HAD AUTHORIZED A check of the sewer system near the crime scene that morning, hoping to locate the murder weapon. Using special cameras and a closed circuit television, county engineers searched the sewers on Greenway, Lawrence, Werk, and Westbourne with no luck.

The weapon would never be found. Dozens of officers rooted through the neighborhood, prowling the yards, garages and porches. The bowling alley and a nearby park were also checked.

They also checked trip logs of the five major taxi companies in Cincinnati, but there were no fares either to or from the Woodhaven subdivision on the night of the crime.

Six days in, Vogel gave the impression they were on top of the investigation. Actually, they were drowning in a sea of information. The problem wasn't a lack of good leads, rather an overwhelming number of promising ones that begged to be checked out.

Could they breach the bottleneck? Even today, the logistics would be challenging – in the pre-computer age it was daunting.

Herb Vogel knew it would be a formidable investigation. The belief that "Murder Will Out" works fine for the TV shows, but in reality many cases were destined to remain unsolved...

THREE OF THE DOCTORS on the Bricca phone list were interviewed Monday. Dr. Mark Upson had last seen Linda on April 7th when he prescribed Cytomel for her thyroid disorder. She was also taking Tri-Presate for weight control and HydoDiuril for fluid retention.

Dr. White had treated Jerry for a lumbar disc displacement and prescribed Darvon. Debbie had also seen White to get corrective shoes for her flat feet and pigeon toe gait. White said Jerry had an appointment on Tuesday September 27th but didn't show.

Dr. Eugene Elam was treating Jerry Bricca for "convulsions" that had begun in 1960, confirming Pat Subtelny's prior statement that Jerry had a special driver's license because of epilepsy. Elam had prescribed Dilantin, a popular anti-epilepsy drug at the time.

There was a rumor Jerry quit taking his medication the week before the murders, causing Linda to become frightened of his renewed temper. Elam said his last seizure was in 1965, and insisted he was on his meds when he saw him in early September.

A sinister figure named Charles Lupo dropped into the case via an unknown tipster. Lupo was alleged to be some dangerous, playboy bartender at Western Bowl who was seen with Linda Bricca. A check of their records confirmed he'd never worked there.

Belbot and Pinkerton scored a live one late in the day. Richard Kissel was a Monsanto employee who had sometimes carpooled with Jerry. Kissel was quite expansive on the friction between Jerry Bricca and James Cannon.

"Cannon made a play for Linda at some dinner dance. He always flirts with the other wives when he's been drinking. Jerry got really pissed at him."

"Were there any threats exchanged?"

"Not that I heard, but they've been very cool towards each other at work."

"What's the deal with this Cannon guy?"

Kissel sighed. "He thinks he's some kind of movie star, you know, some great lover. In his world all women are in love with him, which gives him the right to annoy them at work or parties."

He said Cannon's transfer into Jerry's plant three weeks ago had aggravated the tension between the two men – men who could not be more different in efficiency and temperament.

On Wednesday September 28th Cannon had told Kissel about driving near Greenway and seeing the police lights Tuesday night. "He told me he saw Tom Olding and some other Monsanto people standing outside the Bricca house, and called them over to find out what had happened."

"How was Cannon acting on Monday and Tuesday?" Belbot considered that if Cannon was the killer, his behavior on those two days might betray guilt.

Richard Kissel stared at Belbot. "He wasn't here. He was on vacation from the Friday before the murders until Tuesday."

Tuesday, October 4th

It was day seven of the Bricca murder investigation. Herb Vogel was anticipating that FBI report: "It will tell us a lot – if we're lucky."

That morning there was an internal only meeting of the Bricca team. No sheriff, captain or prosecutor, just Vogel and his detectives. It was time to assess their game plan.

Imagine those 13 detectives in 1966. The case is a week old. What are you going to bring to the table for THIS meeting? More importantly, with limited time and manpower, are you going to waste county resources on brainstorming and conjecture? Can you afford to be running down every high risk/low reward lead?

Their only viable strategy would be exclusion rather than inclusion. They must find reasons to eliminate suspects, winnowing their list so precious hours aren't wasted on dead ends.

Meanwhile, the number of lead cards regarding suspicious men was growing. Even though they believed the killer knew the family, every report of "unknown subjects in the vicinity" was checked out. It was still possible that a psychopathic stranger passing through town murdered the Briccas for no discernible reason.

All week detective teams trekked out to take witness statements regarding dubious persons seen in the area and across the city. It was time consuming and ultimately frustrating.

Here are some of the interviews from October 4th thru October 8th, including the file number and distance from the crime scene.

#34 Virgil Rottert: He saw an unknown male parked and watching a house on Shadylawn Terrace (5 miles away) the weekend of the murders. He thought this was a man spying on his girlfriend with another man, but it turned out to be the other man waiting for the woman's husband to leave.

#42 Finley Duncan: An anonymous call stated that Duncan "hates all women." He was 53 years old with no record (1.5 miles). The caller insisted that Finley was a good suspect because "he hates any lady" and was "on vacation at the time."

#65 Ruth Walker: She told officers that her neighbor William Stamper (2.8 miles) once chased his late wife with a knife. Mrs. Walker was friends with the wife and had personal grudge against Stamper, a used car salesman known as a heavy drinker.

#70 Clarence Glener: He was asked by a man at a gas station on Victory Parkway (11 miles) what he would do if he "got hold of the man" who killed the Bricca family. This man then jumped in a white convertible and left in a hurry.

#71 Mrs. Donaldson: Don Menzi rented an apartment from her on Telford Avenue (7.4 miles) shortly after the murders. He kept looking out the window and seemed odd. His clothing was similar to a man seen on Greenway as reported in the paper.

#72 Anne Wippel: She was attending a wedding shower on Moonridge (0.6 miles) the night of the murders about 10:15 PM when a woman walked onto the porch and peered in at the party. She seemed frightened, and offered the hostess $5 to call her a cab. Two men talked to her and advised her to take the bus.

#95 Robert Hanson: He was on Greenway on October 1st delivering mail when a man asked him which house was the Bricca house. Hanson became suspicious when the man said he worked for WKRC-TV and got his license number. The car was registered to the stepfather of a man who worked for the station.

There was no end to it. Neighbors of an eccentric red-haired woman reported that she talked incessantly about the murders and filled her living room with newspaper clippings. Another woman on Greenway was observed scurrying and peering under bushes – turned out she was looking for her lost cat.

Most of these reports were remote at best. A few, like Anne Wippel, might glimmer for a day. Yet they all reveal something about the human condition.

Amateur sleuths were everywhere, eyeballs peeled. Fortune tellers and psychics relayed bizarre tips. People read the stars and conveyed solutions. Fanatics volunteered clues that had come to them in their dreams. All this flotsam had to be sifted.

And on Vogel's desk, the days died one after the other...

ANY MURDER INVESTIGATION WILL shine a light on those citizens living in that immediate vicinity. But a nasty triple homicide like Bricca insures that any questionable residents within close proximity will be exposed to the public eye.

Most neighborhoods have some borderline people living there. But without the bright beam of a murder probe, they usually remain in the shadows. It's always an innocuous character, one whom everybody knew yet no one noticed. These outliers probably had nothing to do with the crime, yet they can't be ignored.

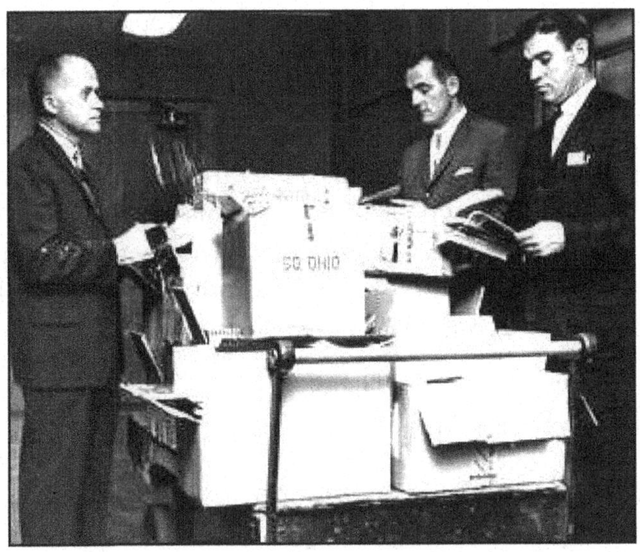

Prosecutor Mel Reuger (left) and Herb Vogel (not pictured) were awaiting FBI analysis of their 30 boxes of evidence.

Consider these men, living lives of quiet desperation until they were suddenly thrust into that scalding spotlight, a sampling of the peculiar people living within one mile of the Bricca crime scene:

- **The "Weirdo"** (0.2 miles away): The week of the murders, this 51-year-old man trapped a woman visitor in his house. He locked the doors and tried to make her drink his "special" wine.
- **The "Molester"** (0.8 miles away): This 27-year-old man was arrested for assault in 1958 for grabbing an 8-year-old girl from behind. He was known to annoy children in the neighborhood.
- **The "Ex-Con"** (0.4 miles away): A neighbor reported he was just released from prison. This individual was seen in the Western Bowl Parking lot around 7 PM the night of the murders.

The molester turned out to be the "somewhat retarded" son of a family on Moonridge. He had a 12/3/58 arrest after he grabbed a girl on Karen Avenue – she ran away, her mother called police, and the girl identified him. In 1966 he was 27 years old and still lived with his parents.

The ex-con was another dead end. He'd done some time, but the neighbor who called it in seemed to have a vendetta against his family. His alibi checked out.

The weirdo lived just around the corner on Lawrence – you could see the rear of the Bricca house from his backyard. He had genuinely frightened Mrs. Betty Hardig, who asked to use his phone, only to have him lock the door and refuse to let her leave. She finally talked her way out of there – later the man's sister-in-law told her he had a "mental problem."

This last interview would be filed away – only to resurface in January.

Wednesday, October 5th

Clues Lacking in Bricca Tri-Murder was the *Enquirer* headline on Wednesday. Despite the deluge of tips, letters, and allegations, the first week passed without any sign the killer would be caught.

Herb Vogel kept a positive spin – the FBI finally wired their preliminary report on the crime scene evidence. Telling reporters the investigation "is picking up speed," he promised to release details later that day.

A local psychiatrist had called Vogel that morning and hypothesized that the sexual assault of beautiful Linda was the motive for this murder. Vogel went back and forth on this one, but for now he preferred to conceal his uncertainty.

He could hear his men in the bullpen, and knew the sex angle wasn't going away. One detective conjectured that Jerry was fooling around on the side. Another was quizzing an anonymous caller who claimed Linda confessed to him about having an affair.

Yesterday the Personnel Manager at Monsanto had called about an employee who shared a babysitter with Linda Bricca. According to the sitter, the night before the murder she was supposed to watch Debbie because "Linda had a date."

Vogel knew they were spinning their web in too many directions. So what kind of perpetrator were they trying to snare?

Ernie Nehrer was visiting other West Side veterinarians. Their female victim was fanatical about her pets and their care. There was a budding feeling in the murder room that Linda's love of animals had a bearing on their case.

Vets at the Bridgetown Pet Hospital were shown pictures of Linda, but neither Dr. Henry nor Dr. Coleman had seen her before.

Nehrer's next stop was more interesting. Dr. Stanley Keller, longtime owner of the Western Hills Animal Hospital, was also shown pictures of Linda and the family. Keller vehemently insisted he didn't know them and knew nothing about them.

Nehrer had fielded a few stories about him already. One was that Linda DID work for him – another that Keller had spent time in a mental hospital. Sitting in front of him now, the always observant Nehrer noticed contradictions in the man's demeanor. His own effusive personality was falling flat with Keller, who seemed flighty. There was something askew about Dr. Keller, and Nehrer made a note for a full records check on him.

The guys in the bullpen were being inundated with tips about strange knives found around town.

#30 Boone County Sheriff: A knife was found in a Florence, KY mailbox on September 27th after some teenagers fought in the street. This knife was picked up for testing.

#92 Dan Blevins: He purchased a knife similar to the missing Bricca knife, but it did not match the murder weapon.

#103 Thomas Unger: The city transit worker found a knife on a bus at the Walnut Hills garage on October 5th. It was 7" long with white handle, and was being tested.

#139 Cliff Rockwell: A man sold him a knife at Rudy's Pony Keg. It was similar to the missing Bricca knife and had "India" on the handle, but was a lighter colored wood.

One young ruffian made a cameo appearance on two different tips regarding his possession of a knife. A temporary worker cutting grass at a cemetery named William Garling walked off the job on Thursday September 29th – his first and last day there. Before he left Garling showed a large knife to several workers and said he "wasn't afraid to use it."

The next day the 21-year-old Garling was sent on a job interview by his agency. When he learned he wasn't being hired, Garling flipped out and brandished a Bowie knife in front of the manager.

This hotheaded youth was soon eliminated as a suspect.

CGE meter man Harry McCarty said his last Bricca house reading was on September 12th. The meter was in the garage – if it was locked he would ring the bell, the dogs would bark and Linda would open it. McCarty had never been in the house itself.

There was a tip about another civil servant who had worked the Greenway area. William Nieman was identified as a Cincinnati Water Works meter reader who had disturbed a Sharonville woman on September 30th. The handsome, blonde 6-footer had bought her a gift of perfume. He also talked about the Bricca murders and claimed he "could move through any neighborhood without being noticed." He then made sexual advances and was rebuffed.

Nieman's supervisor placed him reading the Bricca meter one time in June. His last day of work was September 17th, and a background check showed no criminal record.

ANOTHER MAN WALKING A Greenway route reaped all the attention on this Wednesday. And detectives weren't even sure who he was.

A few weeks before the murders, Linda Bricca called her mother to complain about being rudely treated by the Jewel Tea and Spice salesman. She had tried to return a coffee pot, but the salesman blew up and cussed her out while standing on the Bricca front porch. Mrs. Bulaw remembered that Linda was very upset by it.

The Jewel Tea route man was 33-year-old Ernie Sipple. Detective Nehrer instantly recognized the name as a man he'd arrested six years ago for raping two women at knifepoint. But after pulling the records, Nehrer realized the Sipple rapist was actually Ernie's brother Allen.

After getting a list of local customers from the company, Nehrer showed pictures of the Sipple brothers to three women who lived on Greenway – two of them picked ALLEN Sipple as their route man!

Jewel Tea records showed Ernest Sipple was terminated on September 9th after checking into Veterans Hospital. Yet there was no record showing Ernest was admitted at that time.

Nehrer checked out the naval service records of the brothers, learning that Allen had used Ernie's identity previously to find work, which was difficult with his felony rape conviction.

Was it possible that a violent man like Allen Sipple pretended to be his brother and was actually the man who had the altercation with Linda Bricca? When the naval records came over, a comment by a doctor resonated with Nehrer: "Subject Allen Sipple is a paranoid schizophrenic who is capable of killing."

Nehrer began to wonder. What if sexual attraction was the cause but not the motive? Perhaps this horrific crime was a crazed act of retribution for a perceived slight or an imagined wrong...

October 5th

The Wednesday *Post* ran another somber feature headlined **Shocked Bricca Neighbors Learn to Live with Fear**.

It included an interview with neighbor Joan Janszen. She recalled walking her dog in the drizzle around 9 PM and being startled by Jerry standing beside his garbage cans. They briefly spoke before she watched him trudge back into his garage. She saw no strangers on the street or near the Bricca house.

Vogel had released more details. Jerry was found wearing a dark sport shirt, pants, and socks. They knew he liked to walk around the house in his stocking feet, indicating he was NOT attacked as he came in from taking out the garbage. Linda was found in a pale blue negligee and a blue housecoat trimmed in gold. Debbie was wearing a robe, panties and one red sock – the other sock was lying on the bed with the covers intact.

The barrage of interviews continued on this dreary Wednesday – 35 separate witness statements were taken on October 5th, the largest one day total of the entire investigation.

One promising tip fell flat by day's end. The Kissel Brothers Carnival was contacted about Linda Bricca possibly hanging out there and caring for animals. Yet the closest they'd been to Cincinnati in 1966 was Alexandria, KY over Labor Day Weekend – when Linda was in San Francisco.

Bill Belbot and Tom Pinkerton spent the afternoon at Monsanto. Gerald Taylor had conducted preliminary interviews on September 28th, and told Jerry's closest co-workers they would be back.

A week later the questions were sharper, the tone harsher, the shock giving way to suspicion.

Audrey Hummel did support work for Jerry. She said he was not the type "to bring personal problems to work," but he sometimes made joking remarks about his wife's love of animals. Audrey mentioned an obscene phone call she received two months before the murders. A man with a "hillbilly accent" wanted to "come over" – she hung up when he got vulgar. She thought the caller might be a Monsanto mechanic who worked for Jerry.

Pinkerton jotted down the name Ted Bowling and met Belbot's eyes. This was the fourth report of an obscene call received by a woman who either worked at Monsanto or had a husband who did.

Mary Bailey also worked in project engineering with Jerry Bricca, and noticed the tension between him and James Cannon. Jerry even put a reprimand letter in Cannon's file in mid-September – something about a project Jim messed up.

"Did he make any threats against Cannon?"

"No. But he told me he's 'put up with this stuff long enough.' Whenever Cannon's name was mentioned Jerry would groan."

"Does Cannon ever get fresh with you?"

"He gets familiar at times and will try to mess around, like if you're bending over while filing. But he's gotten better since they moved him to this office."

Ted Anderson came to Monsanto in 1964 from Procter and Gamble and was Jerry's boss. He considered Jerry and Linda to be "light drinkers." Linda was attractive, well dressed, and chatty, telling Anderson about her experiences as a stewardess. Jerry seemed proud of her and often deferred to her.

Anderson told about the problem with the pipefitters the week before the murders, when Jerry exchanged heated words with their supervisor. He said this "dispute was forgotten shortly afterwards."

"So what was his conflict with Cannon?"

"Jim never planned ahead – just saw what was in front of him."

"And Jerry had a problem with that?"

"He thought Cannon was careless. If Jerry thought there were problems with an installation he would stop and check the job. Jim just forged ahead no matter what."

Ted Anderson revealed that Jerry had unburdened himself on Thursday morning September 22nd. He attended a bachelor party with Anderson on Wednesday night, only to arrive home to an empty house. His wife was late picking up their daughter next door, and she showed up drunk. Jerry was extremely upset about it, and for the first time confided his domestic troubles to his boss.

Three days later he was dead...

Tom Olding had worked with Jerry since 1964. He liked him but didn't really know him – in his opinion Jerry was a private person with no interest in being social.

On Tuesday night September 27th, Art Nagel called Olding to tell him Jerry Bricca was dead. Olding and Nagel drove to Greenway and stood outside with the gathering crowd. After about an hour they saw Jim Cannon standing off to the side. They motioned him over and Cannon asked what had happened.

When Olding told him Jerry Bricca had been murdered, Cannon claimed not to know they were standing in front of the Bricca house. Yet Olding was certain he did know – he and Nagel found Cannon's manner at the crime scene to be odd.

But was there a standard of behavior when rubber-necking a triple homicide?

John Jarvis had worked with Jerry for two years and held him in high esteem. He was still distressed by the crime and became emotional several times. Jarvis admitted he emulated Jerry and copied how he did things at work.

"When did you last see him?"

"Sunday the 25th. I saw Jerry at the Monsanto gate and told him he forgot to sign in. We joked about his having to get up early and go to Nitro the next morning, which he didn't mind doing at all."

"Did you leave at the same time?"

"Yep, right around 8:30 that morning. I said see you next week and we both drove away." Jarvis flinched at the memory.

Belbot noticed some Monsanto men were dropping alibis into their comments – offhand remarks about where they were or who they were with that night. As the suspicion spread they were pulling away from each other, because who really knew what resided in the hearts and minds of their co-workers?

Dick Janszen called the homicide squad at 10:50 PM that Wednesday night. Janszen knew he and Richard Meyer were being looked at because of their proximity to the murdered family. He and his wife were upset about the tone of the questioning. Plus their phone was ringing off the hook after Joan was identified as the last person to see Jerry Bricca.

Janszen told them a private detective in Columbus contacted him, asking if the reward was growing and if Janszen "was interested in getting the case solved." This caller also claimed "he knew who did the job and that he lived on Greenway."

The mood on this Wednesday was captured by Joan Janszen's closing quote to that *Post* reporter.

"You just don't feel secure anymore. Even when your husband is home you still have doubt. Jerry was home when his family was killed and he was young and strong."

Joan Janszen had shivered with the first chill of autumn. "It gives you the creeps..."

Thursday, October 6th

The crime itself was already taking on a mythology, surpassing human motives of lust, greed, and hatred. It was like some force beyond the grasp of gravity. It had all the elements of a sensational case – nice neighborhood, attractive female victim, a whiff of sex, and an audacious killer.

But there was no mystique for Herb Vogel – only mystery. On Thursday morning he voiced frustration with the FBI crime lab. Yesterday's preliminary report isolated the hairs, fibers, and traces found at the scene, but didn't analyze or explain them.

"We are continuing to interview associates and acquaintances of the Bricca family," Vogel told the *Post.* "I wouldn't call them suspects but we eventually get around to asking them where they were on the night of September 25th."

Jerry Bricca's safe deposit box was checked and found to contain car titles and stock receipts. Cincinnati Bell provided a list of long distance calls made to and from Bricca house in September. Most were San Francisco and Barrington family members, but two calls to Columbus, Ohio could not be traced.

With each new day came more eccentric tips. A worker at a northern Kentucky auto dealer told several people that "all women should be killed," especially women who crave sex, because Jesus Christ told him to do this.

A woman was threatened by a man at Princeton Bowl. He had a full beard and "funny looking glasses", and grabbed her arm and said "you're not leaving!" When she rebuffed him he said, "You had better watch your mouth or I'll kill you".

She replied, "Do you like to kill people?"

He answered, "Yes, all the time."

Robert Marx had been arrested the night of the murders for stealing a car one mile from the crime scene. The timing and proximity necessitated checking him out, and he dished a tale about borrowing the auto from his friend. Detectives were satisfied this 20-year-old car thief had nothing to do with the murders.

Robert Windholz made an appearance after a Postal Inspector claimed one of his mailmen had information about the case.

Windholz believed he had an interaction with Jerry Bricca at Lakeview Tavern two weeks before the murders. He heard the barmaid ask the man sitting next to him "Hey Bricca, what do you want? Later this man had a whispered discussion with the barmaid, and Windholz was certain they were talking about him. He said Jerry's picture looked familiar.

Detectives soon dismissed Windholz as "immature or retarded", believing he came forward to cover up an altercation he had at the Groesbeck Frisch's.

But Janice Buell's tip was treated seriously. She was a high school senior who saw a brown car driving near the Bricca house on Saturday night September 24th around 9 PM. She was with two male classmates, and thinking it was her boyfriend following her she approached the car when it stopped.

It was not her boyfriend, and she observed two male subjects in the car who quickly drove away.

Kenneth Carr, owner of Tasty Food, called Vogel with information about the veterinarians along the Glenway corridor.

Carr spoke highly of Dr. Fred Leininger. "He's married with 5 or 6 kids. I think he's tops!"

"Why do you say that?"

"He has always been on the up and up with me."

"What about the people who work for him?"

"He had a man and wife working there who were Ohio State students. I believe they quit recently and went back to school."

Carr would not speculate about Leininger's personal behavior. But he did look askance at Dr. Stanley Keller. "The guy is flighty."

"You mean he's impulsive?"

"More like erratic. He tried to turn the garage next to his clinic into a pet shop last year. He stocked it with supplies but then shut it down after one day and sold everything back to the distributors."

"How is he with customers?"

"He is not very friendly to the people that he deals with."

Another tip regarding Leininger got Vogel's attention. Vera Richardson of the Western Hills Answering Service told investigators she took a call from Linda Bricca for Dr. Leininger on Thursday September 22nd at 7:15 PM. Linda had made an insistent request for Leininger to call her. Richardson stated that "the only time we mark a call in the doctor's book is if it is an emergency call."

Why was Linda trying so urgently to get a hold of Leininger on that night? This was the first time she had called his service – and she would be murdered with her family three nights later...

ANOTHER REPORT CAME ACROSS Vogel's desk that intrigued him. Jack Davis and his wife drove past the Monsanto plant at 9 PM on Saturday September 24th and saw two men having a fistfight in the parking lot. After seeing the picture of Jerry Bricca in the paper, Davis thought that he was one of the fighters.

He described the man as a white male in his late 20's, about 5-8 175 lbs with a dark crew cut wearing black pants and black shirt – the colors Jerry was wearing when he was murdered 24 hours later.

This echoed Dan Subtelny, Jerry's best friend at work. Dan told Belbot that some factory workers witnessed the parking lot fracas, but weren't sure who the combatants were in the dim lighting. Jim Cannon seemed to be one of the fighters. The other was either John Jarvis or Jerry Bricca.

Subtelny said "when Cannon gets boozed up he gets mean." He recalled a cookout when he and Linda Bricca argued about animals, and Jerry stepped in and "told Cannon to back off."

Both Jim Cannon and his ex-wife were in the interview schedule for Friday.

Woman's Screams End Attack Inside Elevator

A 48-year-old Walnut Hills woman was assaulted by a would-be strangler Thursday night, she told police.

The intended victim's screams routed the attacker. It happened in the Parkland Apartments, 2324 Park Ave., next door to the Verona Apartments in [illegible] elevator from the basement level and before she could start it up a man wearing a light brown or orange sweater opened the doors and entered.

Without a word, she said, he lunged at her with what she thought was a piece of plastic clothesline.

Whatever it was caught on her nose, scraping [illegible]

Screams Rout Attacker

A man tried to strangle a woman, 48, in an elevator at 2324 Park avenue last night, but her screams forced him to flee without harming her.

The woman, an office worker, was coming home from a beauty parlor at 7:45 p. m. She walked into the ele- [illegible] after parking her car. A man forced his way in with her.

She says he had a piece of rope in his hand and tried to put it over her head, but it caught on her glasses. She screamed and the man opened the elevator doors

Two more "Strangler" style attacks occurred at apartments in Walnut Hills in early October.

SINCE THE DISCOVERY ON September 27th, the Bricca case had pushed The Strangler off the front page. Cincinnati police were bracing for the next attack – and they didn't have to wait long.

On Tuesday night October 4th, a Walnut Hills woman was beaten and robbed as she entered her apartment building just before 9 PM. Mrs. Della Ernst, age 69, told police a "black youth dressed in a black suit" ran up behind her and yelled, "I want to talk to you!" As she turned around he hit her in the face and knocked her down, escaping with her purse containing $125.

On Thursday night, the phantom struck again. A 48-year-old Walnut Hills secretary was returning to her apartment on Park Avenue around 7:45 PM. Right next door were the Verona Apartments, where on October 12th, 1965 Elizabeth Kreco had been brutally assaulted in the basement. Kreco never recovered from the vicious rape, and had finally died on Monday, just nine days shy of the one year anniversary of the attack.

The woman parked her car in the basement garage and walked into the elevator. Without warning, a young black man forced his way in and lunged at her. He tried to loop a piece of cord around her neck, but it caught on her glasses. She let out a piercing scream, alerting the caretaker couple who lived in the basement.

They ran towards the elevator, but the assailant had escaped, his running footsteps echoing off the walls and fading into the night.

Friday, October 7th

The tip about the abrasive Jewel Tea route man, which looked so promising a few days ago, ultimately ran aground.

The possibility that violent offender Allen Sipple was working under his brother's identity had put a bounce in everyone's step. Allen raped two women at knife point in 1960, and Linda Bricca's mother remembered her daughter fretting about an altercation with her Jewel Tea man two weeks before the murders.

Some neighbors identified photos of Allen as their route man, even though his older brother Ernest was the employee assigned to Greenway Avenue. Yet a records check showed Allen Sipple was still incarcerated from his 1960 conviction at the Lebanon Prison Farm. He was often out on daytime work release programs, but he couldn't be placed near Greenway Avenue at any time.

It was playing like a broken record. The daily press updates became more contradictory and less optimistic. Every morning dawned with a new harvest of dramatic clues or possible suspects, only to have them quietly disowned by nightfall.

An *Enquirer* article summed up the county's exasperation. **Miranda Ruling Slows Probe into Bricca Family's Slaying** saw Herb Vogel vent about the recent Supreme Court ruling: "Two years ago we already would have brought people in here for questioning. Now we have to go out and gather 'backgrounds' that we could have gotten by direct questioning."

Vogel said persons "interviewed" so far have come in "voluntarily in the spirit of cooperation." But he issued this warning: "Criminals these days are thinking that even if they are caught, there is only a slim chance they will be convicted."

His fears were echoed by Judge William Keating, who predicted more confessions would be ruled out and plea deals rejected, resulting in more trials and acquittals. He mentioned "the triple murder in Bridgetown" and wondered "if their investigation leads them to a suspect how much will they be hampered by Miranda?"

Vogel had contacted the FBI about the tardy lab report. He tried a positive spin, saying "we are closer than we were a week ago, and we hope the laboratory will narrow the field a little more."

Friday's red herrings were dispensed with quickly. A report about a nude man seen on Greenway the afternoon of the murders was vague and seemed unbelievable. Another tip about a ""Foot Doctor" on Greenway being the suspect in a Kentucky cop shooting turned out to be bogus as well.

An anonymous caller told them to check out Prentice Glen Reynolds. He had a long police record, a history of mental illness, and was living in Cheviot with his stepfather. His mug shot was pulled with a notation to check his whereabouts on September 25th.

Joe Cella of the defunct Executive Modeling Agency was another name in the Bricca address book. Cella didn't recognize Linda Bricca but checked with his photographer, who gave investigators portraits of Linda and Debbie he took in April 1965.

Ernie Nehrer was assigned to canvas bars and taverns near Monsanto. He showed people Jerry's picture at the Lakeview, Lake Edwards and the Cozy Cottage, but no one recognized him except a Monsanto machine operator. This man had contact with Jerry on the job, calling him a reserved, quiet man "who did not kid around."

A hand drawn map found in the Bricca home of the Brower Road area was checked. It was a narrow lane that led to the river, and the only resident didn't know the family or any Monsanto people.

But one of his detectives told Vogel that this secluded road had a reputation as a "lover's lane."

Belbot and Pinkerton had three more Monsanto employees on their slate, but these interviews were not conducted at the plant.

Karen Campton left the company just before Labor Day, but she'd worked with Jerry Bricca and Jim Cannon for several years. Her husband was present during the interview at their home – Belbot felt she withheld information about Cannon because of this.

Karen said Jerry always spoke to everyone in the office but seemed incredibly busy, a "nose to the grindstone type of guy." She'd never heard any rumors about him "fooling around.

"Did he have problems with anyone?"

"Jerry got along with everyone, except maybe Jim Cannon."

"Describe Cannon for us."

Karen smiled. "He's the clown prince of the plant. A shameless flirt, but he makes up for it with a sense of humor."

"Did he make any of the women uncomfortable?"

"Well, one time when he bought a secretary some sexy underwear for her birthday. She opened the gift in front of everyone, and became very embarrassed."

"Did you ever date Cannon?" It was a blunt question with Karen's husband sitting there. She stammered that she "played golf with him several times" but did not date him.

Driving back to headquarters, Belbot turned to Pinkerton with a knowing grin. "She dated him, all right."

Two other Monsanto men were waiting there to be interviewed. The fact that they were requested to come to County headquarters was not lost upon them.

Arthur Nagel was the foreman who drew Jerry's ire when he caught two of his pipefitters "loafing" on the job. This incident took place on September 16th, and Nagel admitted Jerry was still steamed about it when they spoke on Friday, September 23rd.

But he and Jerry "talked it out," and he wasted no time shifting the attention to Jim Cannon. Nagel and Tom Olding were surprised to see Cannon in the crowd outside the Bricca house, and his explanation for being there puzzled them.

"We asked him if he'd heard about it on the radio. He claimed he was just driving by and saw the red lights from Glenway. But we didn't see them until we were on Lawrence."

"What time was this?"

"About 11:45 PM.

"How did he act?"

"Nervous. Everyone else was in shock. But he made sure to tell us that he'd been on vacation since Friday. And that he was out of town ALL day Sunday."

Their last interview was Theodore Bowling, a 31-year-old colleague of Jerry Bricca. A secretary already told detectives that she believed Ted Bowling was making obscene phone calls to her house. They also heard he went to the Bricca house in June and had spoken to Linda, which he emphatically denied.

To Belbot, Ted Bowling seemed like an odd duck, and he was restless during the interview. He rambled on about some letter Jerry put in a guy's file, and how he had played peacemaker between the two over a beer at Lake Edwards.

"Did you get along well with Jerry?"

"Oh yeah. Jerry was a real likable guy." Bowling took a long pull from his cigarette. "He was over all the outside work being done. Did a great job."

"Did you ever see Linda Bricca?"

"I saw Linda come to the plant a few times and pick Jerry up."

"When was this?"

"About three weeks ago, I guess." Then Ted Bowling stabbed out his cigarette and waved his hands. "Look, I'll do anything I can to help you. If you want to run me on the polygraph I'd be more than willing to have it done!"

Saturday, October 8th

An *Enquirer* editorial lauded the Crime Committee, noting that "Cincinnati is desperately eager to restore safety to its streets." They compared us with other troubled cities, showing why our unsullied mid-western values would see us through tough times.

> **Cincinnati is a stable community. Ours is not a transitory population, but largely a populace with old and deep roots in the Queen City. This means a widespread belief in law and order and a resolve to preserve them.**
>
> **Cincinnatians take considerable pride that their police department has been the object of nationwide respect and emulation. And out of that pride has grown a widely held inclination to cooperate in every possible way.**
>
> **No one can predict what the crime inquiry's upshot will be. But the citizens of Cincinnati clearly expect more than just another report to gather dust at City Hall, more than a list of scapegoats, more than an array of platitudes...**

The mood in the Bricca murder room was upbeat – today's interview schedule had three promising meetings. Jim Cannon and his ex-wife were on for separate interviews in the morning. And at 3 PM Herb Vogel and Gerald Taylor had an appointment with Dr. Fred Leininger at the Glenway Animal Hospital.

Of the 302 interviews listed on the official 1966 Information Sheet, 16 of them have their numbers highlighted as being crucial. These three would become the first to be so designated.

There were also routine inquiries on this day. Lead card 106 seemed tantalizing: *Find out which beauty salon Linda Bricca used and interview her operator as to what she may have told her about Mr. Meyer bothering her.*

Two detectives checked all the hair salons within proximity to the Bricca home. They flashed Linda Bricca's picture at four places in the Western Hills Shopping Center – Mabley & Carew, McAlpin's, Murray's Beauty Salon, and Don Sells, along with Mary Ellen's and Shillito's on Glenway

No one at these salons knew her or had seen her there before.

Cincinnati Zoo curator Ed Maruska walked Ernie Nehrer around to all the trainers so they could ID Linda's photo. Only one remembered talking to her, about a monkey she owned.

Harriett Lowe was Debbie's teacher at Happy Hours Nursery School from September 1965 until March 1966. She only knew Linda from chatting with her when she picked up Debbie.

Carla Burris was on the phone list and lived two doors down on Greenway. She was a former Bricca babysitter who hadn't talked to them in more than a year and knew nothing about the parents.

Bill Burkart was on the board of directors for Woodhaven Swim Club, and had approved he Bricca's application to join that summer. He'd met Jerry after playing in a poker group with him but didn't know him well. He said that "when they went to the swim club Mrs. Bricca always acted like a lady and dressed accordingly."

Ellen Dickinson, age 26, was a Monsanto wife who'd last seen Linda at the New Year's Eve party, where she complained about Florida and "the way married couples carried on down there."

Linda Bricca had told Ellen they "exchange keys and wives" and that she 'knew a lot of people in Fort Lauderdale that did it."

MARY ELLEN CANNON HAD been avoiding this interview. Belbot told Vogel "she acts like she doesn't want us to question her at all." Only after assuring her that Jim Cannon was also being interviewed right then did she consent to an 11 AM meeting at her apartment.

Her divorce from Jim had become final in June. After seven years of marriage and three kids, she was single again at age 28.

"When did he start stepping out on you?"

"About two years ago. He wasn't always at the plant when he said he'd be there. And he came home with lipstick and perfume on him. It might have been with Karen Campton."

Belbot glanced at Tom Pinkerton and smirked. "Did you two argue a lot?"

"Not really." Mary Ellen doused her cigarette. "He could hold his liquor pretty good. And I got used to him flirting with other women."

"Did his womanizing ever get him in trouble?"

She flinched. "He's never been in any trouble that I know of. He was very well liked in our neighborhood."

Cannon had stopped by on Friday the 23rd and told her he was driving to Indiana for the weekend. "He called me on Monday evening at five said he'd gotten back."

"Did you see him Tuesday?"

"Yeah, he brought a box of stuff over from his mother's house."

"How long did he stay?"

"Till our boys went to bed. I guess he left around nine." Belbot's notes showed Cannon was seen in the crowd outside the Bricca house around 11:45 PM that night.

Cannon called her about 7:30 PM Wednesday and they talked about the murders. Mary Ellen told him she was glad he didn't call her Tuesday night "because I wouldn't have slept."

"What did he say?"

"That he didn't sleep a wink."

Mary Ellen Cannon suggested they check out Marvin Brown. He worked with Jim at Monsanto and was a notorious hound – he had been pestering her for a date even before the divorce. She always put him off by mentioning the fact that he was married. Jim had told her Brown went out with a lot of women, both married and single.

She lit up a new cigarette. "Maybe he asked Linda Bricca out?"

Across Glenway Avenue another conversation was progressing. Herb Vogel and Gerald Taylor were at Jim Cannon's apartment, questioning the man who kept popping up on their lead cards.

Cannon lived on Janlin Court, less than a mile from the Bricca house. He was a rawboned, pallid six footer with a mane of dark hair and a roguish grin. Cannon knew exactly why the County's top homicide men were there and he was oozing alibi. He showed an amazing recall for his activities during the weekend in question.

The last time he saw Jerry Bricca was on Thursday the 22nd at work. Cannon was off the 23rd thru the 27th. He was in town on Friday but left

Saturday and drove to Evansville, Indiana to visit his brother. He spent the night and they played golf Sunday morning.

He then drove to Vincennes to visit his mother, arriving at 1 PM on the 25th. They visited until about 6 PM, and then went to his uncle's house a few blocks away. Around 7:30 they drove to nearby Frichton to visit some friends, arriving about 8:30 PM. They stayed to watch *The Bridge on The River Kwai*, left about 11 PM and returned to his mother's house where he spent the night.

Cannon got up around 7:30 AM Monday and had coffee with his mother before she went to work. He then drove to Vincennes University and saw a music student he knew. He returned to his mother's home at 11:30, had lunch with her and left when she went back to work, arriving in Cincinnati about 5 PM.

He spent the rest of Monday evening with a girl who worked for the Delta Airlines office, leaving her apartment around 2:30 AM.

Tuesday night he stopped at the Western Bowl and saw police cars and a crowd of people on Greenway, so he walked over to see what was going on. He met Tom Olding and Art Nagel standing outside, and they told him about the Briccas being murdered.

"Did you know it was the Bricca house when you walked up?"

"No. I've never been to their home. And those Greenway houses look alike."

"How long have you known Jerry?"

"Since he started there in '63.

"Did you two get along?" It was a loaded question.

"I've never had a close relationship with Jerry. We weren't friends or anything. But the only arguments we had were about work – never anything personal."

"Did you socialize with them?"

"Only at company parties." Cannon lit a cigarette. "One time I told them I called the SPCA to pick up a dog and I got an hour long sermon from Linda on why that was the wrong thing to do."

Taylor asked about his car, a clear suspect question. Cannon said he drove a 1965 Pontiac convertible.

If Cannon thought he was in the clear, their last question unnerved him. "Did you have a woman working for you at Monsanto named Betty Haas?"

When he said yes, Taylor zinged him. "Do you know anything about obscene phone calls being made to her residence?"

October 8th

Jim Cannon's detailed alibi deflated the earlier optimism.

Detectives couldn't get any traction. New names were drifting in and out, prospects who never became suspects and leads that got into the wind. Anticipation rose and fell like a cruel tide.

The pessimism wrought by so many lost trails was flagging their faith that a break was imminent. At this point they would welcome anything – a flicker, a nuance, a hand hold on this case.

Just after lunch, detective Robert McLaren took a call from a woman in Florida who knew Linda Bricca.

McLaren was desk bound in this investigation, typing up lead cards and reports while manning the phones. Known as "Mac", he was a big guy wearing a permanent scowl and a dark cigar. His gruff demeanor was affected from his years working undercover with biker gangs, and his stare could make you wilt.

The call was from Eva Evans, who lived next door to Linda Bricca's grandparents in Fort Lauderdale. They had met the family when Linda and Debbie came down in late February.

"Petie" Evans had heard about the murders from the Meyer family, and was calling to get more information. She told McLaren that Linda had visited with her "almost daily", using her swimming pool and helping with her dogs. Sometimes they went to the dog track with her husband and another man named Ed Clark.

When Vogel and Taylor returned from interviewing James Cannon, Marvin Melbourne Brown was there waiting for them. Belbot invited him to come in after Mary Ellen Cannon suggested that he might have known Linda Bricca.

Brown was 33, tall and lean with black hair and blue eyes. A foreman at Monsanto, he had around 100 men working under him. Brown had known Jerry Bricca for two years and met Linda at company functions. He was never out with them socially or in the Bricca home, but Brown admitted he knew the Cannons quite well.

"Did you ever go out with Mrs. Cannon?"

"Just once. We met at Western Bowl. She and Jim were splitting up, and I think she just needed a shoulder to cry on."

When asked where he was on Sunday night September 25th Brown didn't balk. He was at home in Cleves, watching TV with his wife and three children. He never left the house that night.

Two promising suspects had alibis for Sunday night that would hold up. Cannon had been particularly enticing. But Vogel had to admit it – even though he appeared to be loud, vulgar, and completely heedless of others, he was probably not their killer.

At 3 PM Vogel and Taylor arrived at the Glenway Animal Hospital to interview Dr. Fred Leininger. He had given a statement on September 28th regarding Linda Bricca's recent employment at his clinic. Since then they'd heard the rumors about Linda's romantic involvement with the Doctor.

Gerald Taylor conducted that first interview, and Leininger's demeanor raised some red flags. He was prepared for a confrontation this time.

For Herb Vogel, this was about gaining ground in a diminishing case. His men were wiped out. So he couldn't afford any distraction while they worked their most promising lead. Could they recover if a crime of this magnitude remained unsolved?

The clinic was closed when they arrived, and Leininger took them back to his office. Glancing at his watch, he said he had another appointment and was pressed for time. Taylor quickly advised him of his Miranda rights against self-incrimination – he said he understood, and voluntarily waived them for this interview.

The Doc was a six-footer with a solid build, lank, dirty blonde hair framing a long face and a mild chin cleft.

After some strained banter, they established that Frederick George Leininger lived on Zion Hill Road in Cleves with his wife Lynn and five children. He graduated from Hughes High School in 1949 before graduating Ohio State veterinary school in 1955. After serving in the army for two years, he worked for the Cincinnati Board of Health in 1957 as a meat inspector. In 1959 he opened his own vet office on Glenway Avenue.

He restated that he'd met Linda Bricca on November 9th 1963, when she brought her dogs in shortly after the family moved here.

"Were you ever inside the Bricca residence?"

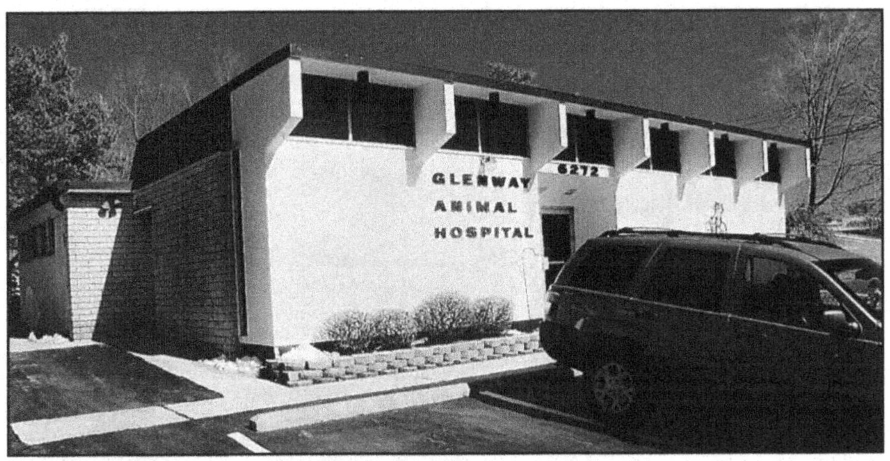

October 8th was marked on Herb Vogel's calendar for his 2nd interview with Fred Leininger at the Glenway Animal Hospital.

Leininger's eyes fluttered. "Once about a year ago...to treat her rabbits and pet bird."

"When did you last see Mrs. Bricca?

He hesitated a beat. "Wednesday evening the 21st. She worked that night until 9 PM."

Vogel and Taylor knew from Betty Meyer that Linda didn't pick up Debbie until 10:30 PM that night, and that she had walked in drunk. They let it pass for now.

"When was the last time you spoke to her?"

They noticed he was a little breathy, struggling to keep the tone easy and impersonal. "I called her Saturday morning the 24th to offer her a permanent job on Wednesdays. Jerry answered the phone, and we spoke briefly before Linda came on and agreed to work every Wednesday starting the 28th."

Vogel looked down at his notes. "Were you aware that Mrs. Bricca was trying to reach you Thursday night?"

Leininger's faint smile vanished. "I don't follow you."

"It's a matter of record with your answering service. Logged as an urgent call on Thursday September 22nd at 7:15 PM.

Leininger's shoulders hunched as if he'd caught a chill. "I was not aware of that."

"You didn't pick up the message?"

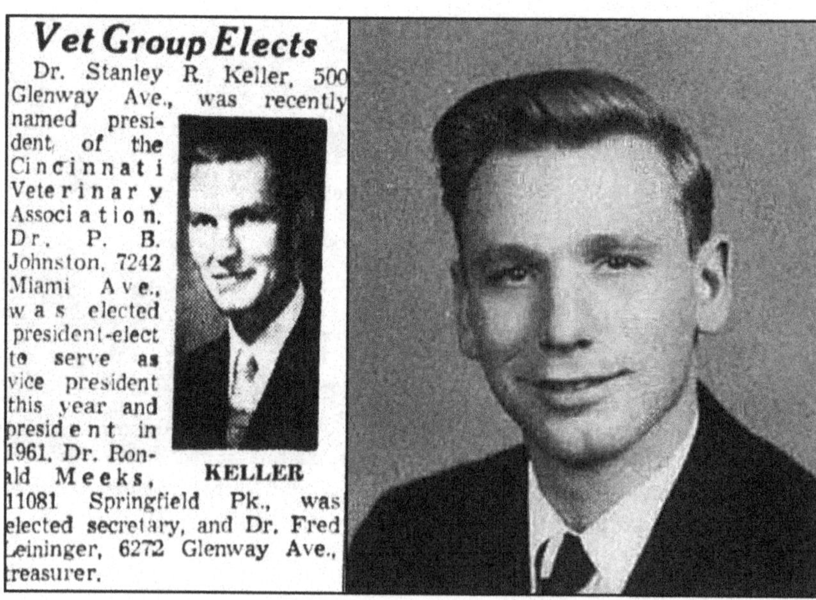

Vet Group Elects

Dr. Stanley R. Keller, 500 Glenway Ave., was recently named president of the Cincinnati Veterinary Association. Dr. P. B. Johnston, 7242 Miami Ave., was elected president-elect to serve as vice president this year and president in 1961. Dr. Ronald Meeks, 11081 Springfield Pk., was elected secretary, and Dr. Fred Leininger, 6272 Glenway Ave., treasurer.

KELLER

Dr. Stanley Keller was a close associate of and fellow CVA member with Dr. Fred Leininger (right, in 1955).

He thought for a moment, Taylor's pen etching notes in the silence. "I'm not really sure."

Vogel leaned in. "Are you unsure about whether she tried to reach you or whether you got the message and returned the call?"

"Both." Vogel blinked. Leininger eventually admitted it "was possible" Linda tried to call him on Thursday, and he "might have" talked to her. "I just can't remember."

After a weighty silence, Vogel shifted gears, asking Leininger about his hunting trip in Pennsylvania. Leininger said he'd left Cincinnati on Sunday morning October 2nd to meet friends in Potter County to bow hunt deer. They hunted Monday through Wednesday noon, before Leininger suddenly left to go home, arriving late that night. Taylor jotted down the names of his hunting companions.

Then they asked THE question. In hindsight, it's strange that Dr. Fred wasn't more prepared to account for his whereabouts on Sunday night September 25th.

"I'm sure I came into the office that night, because my help had quit the week before and I had to do the care and feeding."

Vogel pounced. "You told us during our first interview that you hired a new couple on the 22nd."

"Yes, that's true."

"So there was no reason to go unless you were called in?"

"Maybe I was called in." He offered a weak grin.

Vogel didn't return the smile. "Is there a record of that?"

"We don't keep any record of such calls." Vogel stared. The air had gone out of the room. Taylor recognized the familiar feeling of detectives with their baseball metaphors: 2nd out of the inning.

Caught in a thicket of questions, Leininger was tripping over his tongue. He said he may have come in that night to treat an animal but claimed they kept no such records of weekend treatments.

Vogel was incredulous. "You don't keep records?" When the doctor didn't respond, Vogel's tone was irritated. "But you have a record of Linda Bricca's first appointment in 1963? Leininger's shrug was not convincing. "So where were you that night?"

Leininger's confusion was palpable, his voice chalky. He offered that his in-laws may have visited, but Taylor had already checked and reminded Leininger that he was at their house on Saturday night and they had not seen him on Sunday.

Vogel's next question was a dagger. "What exactly was the nature of your relationship with Linda Bricca?"

Leininger had kept reminding them that he was pressed for time. Without answering the question, he abruptly terminated the interview at 4:00 PM, fifty minutes after it had begun. He stood up and smiled, making an ineffective attempt to shake hands. Vogel rose but did not extend his hand.

Once outside, Vogel and Taylor watched Dr. Fred Leininger drive away. Without saying as much, both detectives knew they had experienced "the moment." The moment when your case suddenly makes sense. It's like getting the third out.

Leininger had lied to them. From experience both men knew that beneath every smiling facade rolled a dark ocean, a human tide that could not be detected.

And within days, they would have corroborative statements that would put Leininger directly in the crosshairs of their investigation...

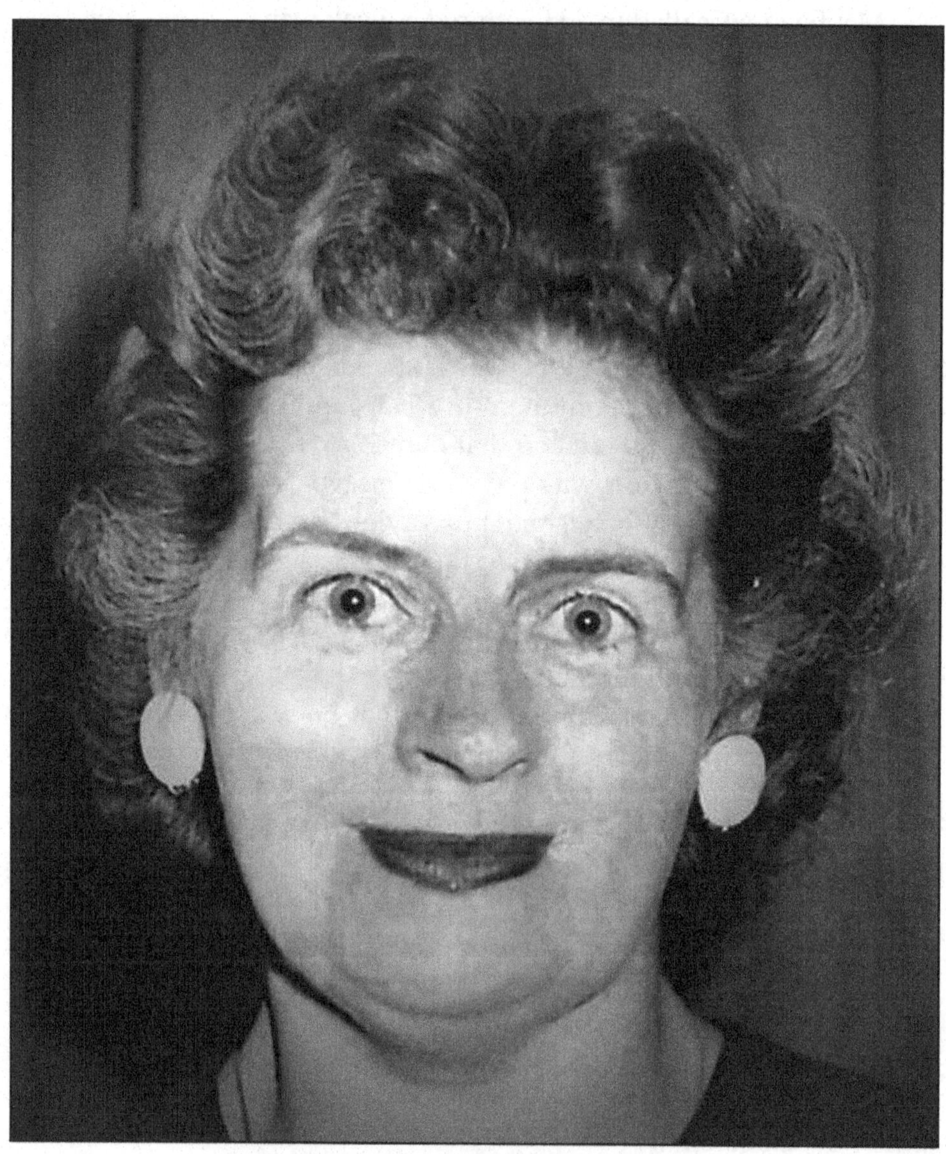

Alice Hochhausler would become the Cincinnati Strangler's most prominent victim.

CHAPTER NINE

GLIMMER OF GUILT

"A bad man can do a million times more harm than a beast."

Aristotle

OCTOBER 9TH – OCTOBER 20TH, 1966

Sunday, October 9th

The events of Saturday changed the dynamic in the murder room. On Sunday morning Herb Vogel called a meeting of his detectives to map out their new strategy and tactics.

The day's interview schedule was thankfully light, but yesterday's encounter with Fred Leininger expanded the playing field. Two of the doctor's hunting companions were on for today.

After the meeting Vogel sat with the Leininger transcript and considered some of the man's statements. During this interview Vogel got the feeling he would soon understand this crime. He hadn't felt it with any others. Now there was that glimmer.

He didn't like the guy. The vet's clinical indifference was laden with arrogance, like he was a gift to mankind. His answers were rife with disclaimers and bewilderment. Vogel remembered how Leininger's eyes tightened after certain questions, as if trying to gauge how much power they each had.

He and Taylor had played it well – Gerald the good cop taking notes, Vogel concentrating on the suspect. He had seen the man's Adam's apple twitch a few times – a sure sign of stress.

A good police interview integrates tactics (what the suspect sees) with strategy (what he doesn't see). Begin with short questions that demand long answers. Then ask the same questions in different ways to flush out contradictions – signs of deception that the criminologists call "consciousness of guilt."

People can lie. But behavior never lies...

SUNDAY'S TIPS FEATURED THE usual – suspicious black men, dubious white men, and wayward knives.

Of greater interest was an unfamiliar car seen on the night of the murders. A woman reported that her friend Eve Hall's husband had seen a red Chevy Impala in front of the Bricca house around midnight. The Hall family lived a quarter mile south on Greenway and was returning from the Ferguson Hills Drive In. Mrs. Hall was half asleep and did not see car.

Her husband mentioned it after the murders hit the paper. Amazingly, he told her the car's license plate number was either 8002CA or 8005CA. A quick check of both plates went nowhere, turning up a white Oldsmobile and a blue Chevy.

Detective Richard Bowman spoke with Ervin Hall later that day. "Pappy" Bowman was in his early 50's, and a former detective I interviewed called him "a guy who knew all the bad actors and locked most of them up. If you were a suspect, he would get you. You might as well give up."

He was on the backside of his career, yet Bowman possessed "bull dog determination" and "an encyclopedic memory of criminals."

Now Bowman was asking Hall the obvious question – why did he not report this car sooner? Here it was twelve days after the crime was discovered and he was sitting on a valuable tip.

Properly chastised, Hall claimed the license could have been any number between 8002CA thru 8009CA. He was positive the red car was a Chevy Impala, most likely a 1964 or '65 model, similar to his neighbor's car. And he was certain it was parked in front of Bricca house, fixing the time between midnight and 12:30 based on when the drive-in movie was over.

Sadly, this promising lead never panned out.

AN INTERVIEW WITH FRED Leininger's in-laws confirmed what was already known. Mr. and Mrs. Clinton Rau could not recall the last time they were at his house on a Sunday night. Leininger came to their house Saturday evening September 24th with three of his kids – the other two were sick and stayed home with his wife.

The Raus were certain they didn't go to the Leininger house on the 25th since they saw him the day before. They said their son-in-law seemed "very conscientious about his family and his work."

Belbot and Pinkerton hooked up with Leininger's hunting buddies in the early afternoon.

Larry Holt didn't know him well, having just met the doctor at the Crescent Bow Club earlier in the year, where Leininger was teaching him how to shoot. Holt would meet with Robert Girten, Oscar Kailholtz, and Leininger to have lunch at David's Buffett or the Gay Nineties – sometimes they would get take out and go to the archery club. About three months ago the four men had planned their Pennsylvania hunting trip for the first week of October.

Holt said Leininger traveled separately to their lodge, arriving Sunday night the 2nd and leaving to go back home on Wednesday, which was contrary to the group's plan. He had also veered away from their designated hunting areas and gone off by himself, which the others thought was odd.

Yet it was Robert Girten whose interview confirmed deception by Fred Leininger.

On Friday September 23rd, Girten and Leininger had taken their lunch out to the archery club range on Muddy Creek Road. As they were eating a blue station wagon pulled up and an attractive brunette got out and walked over to them.

Girten immediately sensed tension in Leininger. He introduced the woman as "the girl who is working for me now."

"How did his demeanor change?"

"He appeared to be real nervous at first that she was there."

"So what happened?"

"She asked Doc if she could follow us around on the course, which she did."

"How did he act during that?"

"Like he was bored or something."

Girten said after they'd finished the course he put his gear in the car and drove off, leaving Leininger there alone with the woman. He said Leininger was driving a red Buick station wagon with a black interior, confirming Holt's description of the doctor's vehicle.

"When did you realize the girl at the club was Linda Bricca?"

"About two days after the murders were in the paper Doc and I were having dinner at David's Buffett and he told me the dead woman was that girl who worked for him.

When Vogel was reviewed Girten's statement, he had to wonder: *Why did Leininger lie about the last time he saw Linda Bricca?* It wasn't Wednesday night at the clinic like he claimed.

Interview #188 was now the tipping point. Leininger had been caught in lies regarding the last time he saw Linda and his whereabouts on Sunday night September 25th. Vogel had actually felt him sweating when Leininger looked at his watch and terminated the interview.

His likely sexual involvement with Linda Bricca made him the prime suspect – and Leininger was very concerned with his image and standing in the community. He was somewhat of an elitist, and could not afford any hint of scandal in his cozy life.

Herb Vogel was determined to honor his policy of media cooperation. But he was not going to give Leininger to the press until after their third interview...

Monday, October 10th

By Monday the unsolved crime was moving off the front page.

Phone Clue Perused on Briccas" appeared on *Enquirer* page 32 and featured a "mystery number" on the Bricca's phone list assigned to the Executive Modeling Agency. Vogel announced his investigation of that former company.

He stressed that everything connected with the murdered family "has been carefully studied, including the dust from their floor." However, they were still waiting for the overdue FBI lab report.

The onslaught of tips was starting to diminish. The crackpots of those first feverish days were gone. The psychics, soothsayers, clairvoyants, mediums, and crystal ball gazers had been flushed out early, along with well-meaning amateur gumshoes.

With each passing day the odds were turning against them. Vogel understood that a killer not known to be at the crime scene has the best opportunity to cover his tracks.

A lack of physical evidence forced investigators to follow the 1966 detection playbook. They were locating witnesses and conducting interviews, piecing together movements and motives of various persons of interest before arriving at a hypothesis.

As one retired detective recently told me, "in our day fingerprints were DNA." But the dearth of clues rendered this case almost entirely circumstantial.

Yet Leininger had put a spring in Vogel's step – his instincts told him this was their guy.

Not that the doctor would spill just like that. He was a cocky suspect – a guy with "hubris" according to Taylor. Vogel saw how Leininger had fished for information during their Saturday session, almost like he was conducting a "reverse interview."

Was this man guilty because he had narrow eyes? Or was he innocent because he was a family man? Their third interview would be the deal breaker. Whether Leininger was calm or restless, cooperative or aloof, his guilt would leak through into his behavior.

The Monday interview schedule looked routine, with one exception. Vogel told Taylor and McLaren to drop in on Mrs. Leininger while her husband was at work. It would rattle Leininger, and they might learn something new about him.

Charlie Nagel and Robert Spraul drew the Paul Mendel interview. According to an anonymous tip, Mendel was a 29-year-old Monsanto worker who suffered a nervous breakdown around the time of the murders.

Bob Spraul was another "one of kind" detective, a 40ish "character" known for his sense of humor. He had been a fireman and worked for the salvage corps before becoming a cop, and he had a ton of "war stories" and liked "gallows humor."

Spraul was a department legend because of one case: "The Whitewater Township Panther." In the late 1950's there had been reports of a black panther roaming the Whitewater Forest and Spraul was assigned to find the animal. Years went by, and it became a running joke at county. Yet Bob Spraul never gave up looking for that elusive big cat.

Mendel proved to be an easier catch. The Harrison, Ohio native had never worked in Jerry's building at Monsanto, and didn't recognize his picture. His breakdown was caused by marital stress – Mendel knew almost nothing about the Bricca case.

McKinney and Hall continued canvassing businesses in the Bridgetown and Cheviot area, flashing pictures of Linda and Jerry at every tavern, restaurant, and store in the Glenway Avenue corridor. Yet no one remembered seeing the murdered couple.

A former employee of the Executive Modeling Agency called after reading that investigators were looking for them. Merriann Kirschner had looked through an old appointment book and found this notation on *4/21/65: Mrs. Bricca and daughter.*

Ernie Nehrer was at the county courthouse. The murdered family had not been involved in any criminal or civil litigation since they moved here in 1963. He also checked the employment record of Fred Leininger when he worked as a meat inspector for the Cincinnati Board of Health from 7/15/57 thru 1/4/59.

Unfortunately, there were no pictures or prints on file. Nor did Leininger have a criminal record or any traffic citations.

JUST AFTER 10 AM, Gerald Taylor and "Mac" McLaren turned onto Zion Hill Road, a wooded, winding section of Cleves where the houses and lots quickly swelled in size. Just past Tanglewood Park Drive they came upon 7781, the residence of Dr. Fred Leininger. Yet from the road they couldn't see the house.

McLaren let out a low whistle as they cruised up the long driveway. The place was imposing, set back from the road almost the length of a football field. The long driveway, the impressive spread, the forested acres – Leininger was living the good life. Taylor remarked that "the Doc must be doing pretty well."

They were dropping in on Lynn Leininger unannounced. Taylor was there with Vogel during the Saturday interview at Leininger's office, taking notes while taking the measure of the man. For Taylor, this veterinarian of good standing in the community was hiding something about his relationship with Linda Bricca.

Lynn Leininger met them at the door as if she'd been expecting them. A diminutive, wholesome looking mother of five, she held the door part way open and cut Taylor short.

"At this time we don't wish to discuss anything without our attorney present."

Taylor gulped. Leininger hadn't wasted any time. "You said we. What about you, Mrs. Leininger?'

"My husband advised me to do this." She handed Taylor a card. "Our lawyer is Richard Morr, and any communication is to go through him." She gave him a watery smile.

As Taylor and McLaren turned to leave, Lynn Leininger blurted out. "My husband was very upset by some of your questions."

Was this an opening? Taylor squinted back at her. "Such as?"

The faithful wife stammered. "I meant...um...that he, uh, was upset over not being able to remember where he was that night."

"Do YOU know where he was?" Taylor countered.

But Lynn Leininger had already closed the door...

Monday and Tuesday, October 10 – 11th

Taylor immediately called Vogel. "He lawyered up."

"Meet me at the clinic."

At 11 AM they converged on the Glenway Animal Hospital. But this third interview with their prime suspect wasn't happening.

Dr. Leininger was calm as they sat down in his office. Vogel assumed he was alerted by his wife, and Richard Morr must be on the way. Sure enough, there was a loud rap on the door two minutes into the interview. Morr entered and quickly shut it down.

"Gentlemen, why are you here?" Morr was 40, a handsome ex-marine who still looked fit and trim. His father was Fred Morr, a former state representative and current Hamilton County auditor. His brother Fred Jr. was the director of the Ohio Department of National Resources. Leininger could not have picked a more seasoned lawyer with better West Side connections.

Vogel would not be cowed. "We feel your client can supply us with information relative to an unsolved triple homicide."

Morr did not budge. "Are you going to charge him? Because if not I must ask you to leave the premises. "

"So we have to arrest him in order to speak with him?"

Morr offered his card, which Vogel did not take. "You are free to contact me at my office and discuss arrangements for any further discussion with Dr. Leininger." Vogel looked at the Doc, a smirk seeping over his lips.

Vogel motioned to Taylor with his head. "We'll be in touch. Count on it." And with that the Hamilton County detectives departed the Glenway Animal Hospital.

When they were outside, Vogel looked at Taylor. "I want surveillance on Leininger as soon as you can arrange it.

"24 hour?"

"No. Just have a uniform pick him up when he leaves for work and have another one put him to bed. If he goes out to lunch have someone in plain clothes at a nearby table."

ON TUESDAY THE *ENQUIRER* ran a piece headlined **300 Interviewed in Bricca Case.** Almost 200 of those had made their way into the case file.

"We know a lot about the Bricca family," Vogel told the press. The lieutenant said he hoped an "unknown fingerprint" might be isolated among the cartons of evidence being evaluated by the FBI.

Vogel discounted the modeling agency connection from the previous day. "Mrs. Bricca had entered her daughter in the agency's baby picture contest, which required the entry photo be taken by their photographer."

On Greenway Avenue Belbot and Pinkerton caught up with some neighbors they had missed. Marjorie Townsley lived 325 feet away from the Bricca house, and knew Linda just enough to chat on the street. She had heard a rumor that "the vet was down there the night before the murders and had a fight with Bricca."

Winnie Fisher lived on the corner of Greenway and Lawrence. Linda was at her Monte Carlo party in 1965 and the family had attended a few neighborhood gatherings that year. But she hadn't seen much of them this year. She said Linda was adamant about one thing – everyone on Greenway should take their dogs to Leininger's clinic because he had better prices and was "more friendly and understanding."

Pinkerton and Belbot also tracked down the couple who had left Leininger's employ the week before the murders. Robert Smatt was a grad student who began working there in June, got married in July, and had his wife join him in the clinic's furnished apartment.

"Was Dr. Leininger running around or seeing someone on the side?"

"I really don't know. But one time he told me that if he was going to play around it wouldn't be with one of his clients.

Belbot's eyes widened. "What brought this up?"

"Well, if a sharp looking girl came in we would wink at each other and make some comments after she left. You know, guy stuff."

"Do you know of any women he was friendly with?"

"The only one I remember was a dog breeder from Newport Kentucky named Charlotte."

Leininger's attorney Richard Morr (left) shut down the 3rd Interview and locked horns with Herb Vogel.

Neither Smatt nor his wife Nancy could remember seeing Linda Bricca at the clinic any more than two or three times.

"How did Dr. Leininger treat Mrs. Bricca when she was there?

"Doc treated her like any others. He was very cool toward most clients in the office."

Nancy Smatt remembered the blue station wagon but didn't know it belonged to Linda. They agreed that Leininger never went home for lunch, and that he usually ate at the Wagon Wheel or David's Buffet with Bob Girten or Oscar Kailholtz. Lunch hour was from 12-2 and the clinic closed at noon on Thursdays.

As the interview ended, Nancy Smatt suggested they talk to the girl she replaced. Her name was Ginny George, but he had no idea where she lived or worked now.

About 4:30 PM ON that Tuesday afternoon, a female resident in the Clifton gaslight district had an unsettling encounter.

Helene Muhsam, who lived on Evanswood Place, was parking her car when she sensed a presence nearby, as if "somebody was looking right through me." When she turned, a short black man was staring at her from about twenty feet away.

He smiled and bowed in her direction. She would later say "I knew this fellow didn't belong here." As Helene watched him saunter down Cornell Place towards Ludlow Avenue, she noted he was wearing a distinctive beret.

At 11:30 PM that night, Alice Hochhausler got in her station wagon and headed out to pick up her daughter. She was dressed for bed, wearing a bathrobe and slippers.

The 51-year-old mother of nine lived at the corner of Cornell and Evanswood, across from Helene Musham. Alice was a popular, vibrant housewife, active in the arts and charity work. Her husband was Dr. Carl Hochhausler, chief of surgery at Good Samaritan Hospital, where her eldest daughter Beth also worked as a nurse.

With an unknown killer on the loose, Alice was worried about Beth working 2nd shift and coming home at midnight. The Strangler's third victim, Jeannette Messer, had been struck down in nearby Burnet Woods, and Alice had a recent premonition that Beth could be in danger.

Now she was dropping Beth off at her apartment on Ludlow. As mother and daughter sat there, a two-tone Chevy pulled up behind them and stopped. There was a lone black man behind the wheel.

"I wonder what he wants." Alice frowned. "Do you think he's going to go around me?" After a few minutes the driver did just that. Even though the description of the Strangler car was out there, they didn't drive to the district five police station one mile west on Ludlow to report it.

Beth thanked her mother, crossed the street to her building and waved. Alice waved back, and turned onto Cornell towards home.

It was almost midnight as she pulled into her driveway. The moon was a pale sickle nestled among the clouds hovering over the Clifton gaslight district. Two yards over an outdoor barbeque was winding down as neighbors headed back to their homes.

Alice parked on the apron next to the garage. Rex, the family's German shepherd who usually slept in the garage at night, had been put in the basement so he wouldn't bark at the party goers. Inside, her husband and seven children were either asleep or bedding down. Her two teenaged daughters, talking in their room that overlooked the driveway, were not aware their mother had returned because the outdoor floodlights were off.

Alice walked down the driveway toward the gate. The warmth and safety of her stately Victorian house was a mere 40 feet away. Yet their neighbor's dog was barking furiously. Alice must have become aware, in her final moments, of someone whose approach meant deadly peril.

A crushing blow to her skull knocked her to the pavement, sending her car keys and partial denture flying down the driveway.

Panting in the darkness, the Strangler grabbed her legs and dragged the powerless woman back into the murky opening of the brick and stone garage...

Wednesday, October 12th

Dr. Carl Hochhausler awoke at 7:15 AM to find his wife was not in bed with him. He'd been asleep when she left to pick up Beth, but it appeared she'd never come to bed. He checked the laundry room before going out the back door.

Her car was parked in the usual spot, but when he saw one of her shoes lying in the driveway he froze. He found her lying spread eagled in the garage next to their old Triumph sports car, the belt of her red bathrobe knotted tightly around her neck.

It was the strangler signature – an improvised ligature and a victim left in a garish pose.

When the call came in to district five about a homicide on Cornell Place, half the on duty officers showed up. The Clifton gaslight district was one of Cincinnati's most historic districts, graced with lush trees and dignified homes. As shocking as the first four murders were, the killing of Alice Hochhausler mere steps from her back door had intensified the cliché: *How could this happen here?*

This crime would spawn the largest law enforcement mobilization in city history. The killer was now our unmitigated obsession. Every cop was engaged in the search and every citizen was consumed by it.

It was as if some killing entity had been loosed in the city, a mysterious beast lurking among us, like our childhood fear of wolves prowling the forest. Our youthful terrors had become a tangible, savage creature beyond the limits of our imagination.

Herb Vogel reviewed the specifics of this latest outrage with Sgt. Russ Jackson of the CPD, and was satisfied the Clifton killer was not his man. Still, Vogel marveled at the audacious nature of this latest murder, perpetrated a scant two weeks after the triple slaying in Bridgetown.

It was as if the Strangler was thumbing his nose at the police...

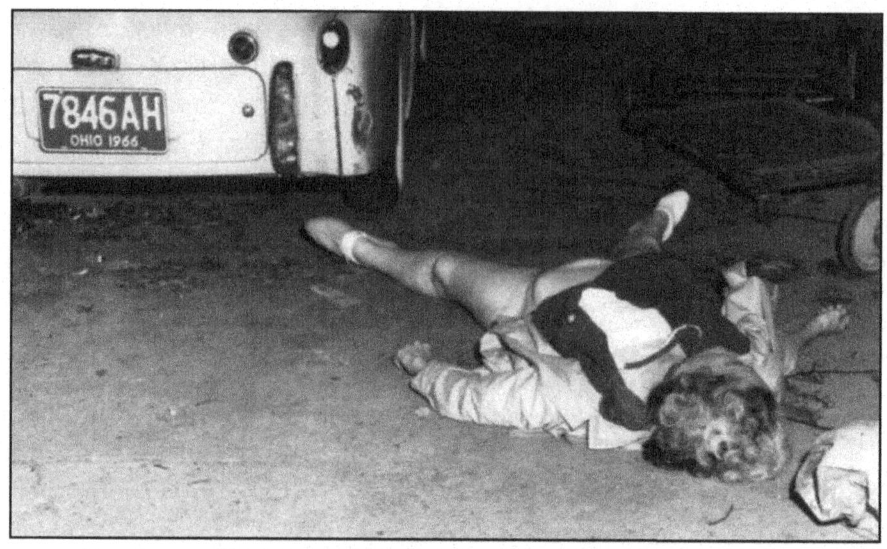

Alice was attacked on her driveway and dragged into the garage, where she was raped and strangled with her bathrobe belt.

VOGEL HAD FOUR TEAMS working the lead cards on this Wednesday, and Robert Hall and Rudy McKinney had three stops to make. Bob Hall was a big man, early 40's with a bald head and Vogel's ear. He was a talker – Bob could sling it with the best.

They checked out the original LaRosa's Pizzeria on Boudinot Avenue, since virtually every West Sider had eaten there at least once. Indeed, the manager had seen Jerry and Linda there on several occasions, and Jerry had picked up carryout orders. But neither Bricca was ever seen there in the company of anyone else.

Two doctors on Glenway had little to offer. Dr. Cassini had seen Debbie four times at his office for a sore throat and an allergy reaction. Dr. DeFranco treated Debbie three times in April 1966 for the same thing. Jerry had brought her in alone and once remarked that he was tired from working all night.

Ernie Nehrer had just left Lee Lutz Flowers, another entry in the Bricca phone list. Joe Lutz had done some business with Linda in the fall months, but knew her by sight and name only.

Nehrer next went to the local SPCA office, but no one there recognized pictures of Jerry or Linda. They told him that many people had

Alice Hochhausler was 40 feet from the safety of her back door when the Strangler struck. (2009 photos)

called wanting to adopt the Bricca dogs, a normal thing for crimes of this magnitude.

Belbot and Pinkerton were back on Greenway, catching up with neighbors who lived within sight of the murder scene. Four housewives said they only knew the Briccas well enough to wave.

But Rita Schroeder had numerous interactions with Linda, who often came over that summer to help Rita train her new dog. They would only talk about dogs and animals, and Rita never saw them have any

Bricca Slayer Scouted Home, Then Struck,

The killer of the Bricca family had the home under observation before he entered and stabbed the three to death, Lt. Herbert Vogel of the Hamilton County police believes.

"There was a little ground work, a little advance observation," Lt. Vogel said today. "I don't think the house was just chosen at random."

Lt. Vogel, who is heading the murder investigation for the county, says burglary as a motive for entering the house is "not much in consideration now.

"I THOUGHT it was a possibility, but it's not a strong factor in my mind now," he says.

The county detective says the FBI reported yesterday on one segment of evidence that had been sent to the laboratory in Washington for analysis.

"The FBI said a full report would follow soon," Vogel says. "The reply they sent us yesterday more or less confirmed our own belief in one area.

"The report was not complete enough to head us in any one direction," he said. "But I expect information to start coming in a little faster now."

Sounding optimistic over the progress his staff is making in the investigation, Vogel said:

"WE'RE ROLLING. We're not discouraged. One newsman said we have been at a standstill waiting for the FBI report.

"That's not true. We have been talking to friends and acquaintances of the family both in and out of town."

Vogel says he is not overlooking the possibility that Mrs. Bricca's love of animals might have a bearing on the case.

Neighbors are puzzled why the two Bricca dogs, who always roamed the entire house and would bark at strangers, were found in the first-level playroom when the murder was discovered at 10:45 p. m. Tuesday, Sept. 27.

Mrs. Bricca told a neighbor she once joined a circus just so she could feed the animals. She had started working part time for a Western Hills veterinarian only

Herb Vogel tried to assure residents that the Bricca crime was not random and that the family was targeted.

company. Linda seemed to have a lot of clothes, wore green often, and always dressed in style.

"What did she wear when she was washing her car?"

"Usually a one piece swimsuit or a tennis outfit. She wore sport clothes most of the time."

"Was she trying to dress sexy?

"Not on purpose. She seemed bashful to me. I only saw her in a dress one time."

Nagel and Spraul were leaving the J & J Food Market. Butcher Harry Caldwell certainly remembered his attractive customer, and had sold some rib eye steaks to Linda Bricca on Saturday the 24th around noon. He said she paid by check and Debbie was with her.

Their next lead looked hopeful. Nagel took a call from Oscar Martz, who lived almost 500 feet south of the Briccas and did not know them. But he had some compelling hearsay to dish.

Martz's friend had a daughter who went to school with a former Bricca babysitter, who allegedly made a suicide attempt shortly after the murders and was now in a hospital. But when Nagel called the number Martz gave him, the girl's mother assured him her daughter was fine and had never even met the Briccas.

The morning *Enquirer* quoted Herb Vogel as saying "the investigation is at a standstill." Now he gave the afternoon *Post* reporter his version. In an article headlined **Bricca Slayer Scouted Home, Then Struck,** Vogel speculated that the killer had the home under surveillance before the crime unfolded.

"There was a little groundwork, a little advance observation. I don't think the house was chosen at random." Vogel discounted burglary as a motive. Asked about the "standstill" quote, he bristled. "That's not true. We're rolling. We're not discouraged."

After admitting they were puzzled that the "aggressive dogs" were not a factor, he told the press what many on the West Side already knew – that Linda Bricca started working for a veterinarian only one week before her death.

Herb Vogel locked eyes on the reporter. "It's possible that Mrs. Bricca's love of animals might have a bearing on this case."

Wednesday, October 12th

News of Alice Hochhausler's murder swept through the city. **Strangler Takes 5th Victim! Mother of Nine Believed Raped** was the *Post's* deafening headline about his most daring crime yet.

People were stunned by the cruel irony of Alice's death. This devoted mother was outside at midnight only because she feared the Strangler would take her daughter! She had left the house in her bathrobe, knowing she could pick up Beth and drop her off without getting out of the car.

But that bathrobe belt ended up wrapped around her neck.

Neighbors escorting children to school in the gaslight district were greeted with a phalanx of flashing squad cars and EMT vehicles. Mouths gawked as startled questions were parried with terse details. As reporters gathered, one resident was heard to say "my God this is getting awfully close!"

"We are looking for a Negro, driving a cream and tan or bronze 1959 Chevrolet," Jake Schott told the press, which matched a car spotted in Burnet Woods before the Messer slaying in June.

Detectives believed the killer was the same man who parked behind Alice and her daughter on Ludlow. With Beth inside, the man followed Alice up Cornell, quickly parked on Evanswood, and ambushed her from the dense bushes lining her driveway. They found an empty can of malt liquor in those bushes, and there were several reports of prowlers nearby that night.

Her one shoe, partial dental plate, and car keys littered the driveway, mute testament to the force of the blow delivered to the back of her skull.

So now, an elegant Victorian home in a privileged neighborhood with charming gaslights was ground zero in the hunt for the Strangler. And this victim, the lovely, gregarious wife and mother of nine named Alice Hochhausler, would become the face of this unprecedented investigation...

IF HERB VOGEL HAD sympathy for his city counterparts he had no time to show it. Their afternoon interview schedule was promising.

Oscar Kailholtz was Leininger's barber and frequent lunch companion. He told detective Hall they usually talked about hunting and fishing, and confirmed he'd seen Leininger with other men at the Muddy Creek archery range next to his home.

Kailholtz swore Leininger never mentioned Linda Bricca. Hall took it in stride – the barber was a close friend of the doctor who kept insisting he "could not" shed any light on this case. Hall wondered if he meant "would not."

Ernie Nehrer was with Barbara Jean George and her husband Clyde, former employees of Fred Leininger. They had started working for him in June 1965 and lived in the clinic apartment until they moved out this past July. They both recognized Linda as a longtime customer from her picture – she came in frequently, usually with Debbie.

"Was she seeing the doctor on a social basis?"

"I don't think so," Barbara replied. "Every time she came in it was for a pet treatment or to ask for information."

"So they never went out?"

"If they did they never let on."

"What did you think of Linda Bricca?"

"She was well educated, kept herself dressed really well."

When asked her opinion of Dr. Leininger, Barbara replied that he was dedicated to his work and spent long hours at the clinic. He seemed more interested in the animals than the owners.

"Did he ever come in on Sunday?"

"He came in every Sunday Morning around 8 AM, checked the animals and was out of there by nine."

"Did he ever return later on a Sunday, like at night?"

"Only if there was an emergency – and during my 13 months there it never happened once."

"Did he ever discuss Linda Bricca with you?

"Not really. Once he said he wished she would take better care of her family than she did her pets. He complained she would bring them in for very minor reasons."

Barbara never heard any personal conversations between them. And she was certain he never made any house calls there.

Her husband Clyde thought Linda had worked for Leininger once before for about a week. Nehrer was doubtful but made a note. "Ever see anything out of the ordinary between Linda and the Doc?"

"Once last spring she brought in a rabbit in that died," Clyde remembered. "She was so upset that the Doc drove her home.

"What was your impression of her?"

"She made a pest of herself, calling after 9 PM for medicine or with silly questions."

BELBOT AND PINKERTON WERE interviewing Betty Meyer again, a follow-up from their first session on September 29th. This interview number was highlighted on the information sheet.

She had received a call from "Petie" Evans in Ft. Lauderdale asking for an update on the murders. Mrs. Evans told her the FBI questioned her and her husband, and wanted permission to open two letters from Linda. They had asked if Linda was "running around" while staying with her grandparents next door to the Evans.

Petie told Betty that when their dog was sick Linda called Dr. Leininger for advice. Linda also confided to her that she was "fed up with sex" and was going "to leave Jerry because I've had all I can take of him." Mrs. Evans had advised her to think it over before doing anything rash.

On June 8th Petie received a letter from Linda saying things had gotten worse with Jerry. She promised to write her a long letter with all the details, but was "too upset to begin to tell it now."

ACROSS TOWN AT COUNTY headquarters, Vogel and Taylor were interviewing Betty's husband. Richard Meyer knew he was considered a suspect, and his life was spinning out of control. Harassing phone calls at home prompted him to get an unlisted number, but now these cranks were calling him at work.

He heard the rumors – he was an alcoholic, he had been "bothering" Linda Bricca, he delayed checking on the family because he knew what had happened to them.

The GE employee was an army veteran, the father of four, and a Greenway resident since 1958. He was profoundly affected by the tragedy next door, and would do anything to help the investigators.

"Tell us what happened the night of September 21st at your house.

"I came home about 11 PM and Linda and Jerry were just leaving. Debbie was asleep and Jerry was carrying her.

"Had Linda been drinking?"

"She was about three sheets to the wind. My wife told me Linda showed up late to get Debbie and asked for a double shot as she was upset about something.

"Did you hear Jerry make any threat against Fred Leininger?"

"Not that I recall. But he did seem pretty upset with Linda."

Meyer said Linda had shown him a small tabloid she brought back from Florida, consisting of local gossip from Fort Lauderdale. At this time she told him she was "glad I came back when I did or I would have become an alcoholic."

Meyer confirmed that Linda's dogs did not like men. His wife and daughter went into their yard without trouble – "but if me or my son went there the dogs would get nasty."

On the night in question, Meyer went to Lou's Deli just before 9 PM, and when he returned the Briccas garbage cans were out but he didn't see anyone around the house. Meyer entered his house about 9:20 and watched the rest of the movie with his wife.

There was concern about the lack of activity next door on Monday and Tuesday, but he assumed they were out of town. On Tuesday night his wife insisted he go investigate, as the garbage cans were still out and the patio light still burning.

Both cars were there, so Betty called Linda Zeff, who was also concerned. He spoke with Richard Janszen, who suggested they call Monsanto, but no one could give them any information. As the two men walked across the street, they met Linda Zeff and her father coming up the street. Linda was certain something must be wrong, a fear confirmed when she looked in the back window and saw the dogs in the basement.

"What happened when you opened the front door?"

"Linda was behind me. I opened it at arm's length and exclaimed 'MY GOD someone is dead in there.'"

"Did you see something?"

"From there I could see a foot or a hand in the master bedroom. That was enough for me. I ran home and called the police."

Later, when reviewing the day's interviews, some things the George couple said flickered for Vogel. Clyde felt that Linda "was the type of person who had many associations with men."

His wife Barbara went further. "To me, Linda appeared to be a woman who if she ever had any trouble, she would go to a man to find the solution."

Thursday, October 13th

There are two prevalent myths about serial killers.

The first is that they won't stop killing until caught. But serial killers often quit without being apprehended, christened with shadowy sobriquets such as "Jack the Ripper", "Zodiac", the "Green River Killer", and "BTK." Albert DeSalvo, the alleged Boston Strangler, was never actually caught – he began confessing a year after the murders stopped while in a psych ward on another charge.

The second misconception is that they are always white males. While black serial killers before Atlanta's Wayne Williams were more obscure than infamous, Michael Newton's book *Hunting Humans* reveals that 15% of the 750 killers profiled were black, higher than the US black population of 13%.

Both of these fallacies would eventually surface during the Cincinnati Strangler saga.

The term serial killer wouldn't enter the lexicon until the late 1970's, but the slaying of Alice Hochhausler on her own driveway confirmed that these crimes were the work of one man.

With present day hindsight, we know that the Strangler was a disorganized offender. His crime scene's revealed a confusion of bodies, weapons and abandoned clues. A modern profiler would tag him as a socially inept loner with a prevailing sense of hostility and rage embedded in his personality.

He was the most elusive of criminals – a murderer of strangers...

ONLY A FEW SENIOR citizens were left to remember when the city had confronted such a mysterious killer. Variously called the "Cumminsville Ripper" or the "Murder Zone Killer", an unknown fiend terrorized the Queen City from 1904-1909, taking five female victims along the railroad tracks snaking through the squalid Cumminsville district **(Queen City Gothic Chapter 1).**

On Thursday morning the *Enquirer's* initial coverage of the Hochhausler murder was epic. Dueling headlines splashed across the front page – **City Police on Overtime as Strangler Strikes Again!** paired with **Grim Manhunt on for Mad Strangler**. The entire city police force was placed on emergency call, a first-time move that added one hundred uniformed officers under the control of the homicide squad.

Homicide Chief Jake Schott was blunt about how his men would investigate this latest slaying. "Our orders are to stop any suspicious looking person you see," he told the press. "If they don't give the right answers, bring them in. The department will back you 1000%. We need aggressive action!"

Schott dismissed any fears that the Miranda ruling or racial concerns would hamstring his detectives. "The city manager has given me a mandate to stop this reign of terror. Nobody likes to be stopped on the street. We will do it as tactfully as possible, but we must have freedom to pursue this investigation."

OVER AT COUNTY, MANPOWER was deflecting away from the Bricca case. A rash of burglaries was hammering them, yet incoming leads still needed attention.

Detective Nehrer was examining a list of long distance calls requested from Cincinnati Bell – their records only went back six months. Linda Bricca had made several calls from Ft. Lauderdale to her home number in March – obviously calls to Jerry

They also provided long distance calls from Fred Leininger's office in September 1966 which included three calls to Smithtown, NY, including one made at 10:30 PM on the night of the crime.

Based on a phone tip, Belbot obtained a list of employees at Western Hills Import Motors, only a quarter mile from the Bricca house. They did a criminal record check on terminated and current workers, but none could be connected to the murdered family.

He also looked at Linda's association with the local Animal Welfare League. Dorothy Morman had received a call from her two weeks before the murders, volunteering to help at their shelter.

Eleanor Zeisler, director of the Happy Hour Nursery, confirmed that Debbie Bricca left there in early March to go to Florida. Debbie attended three mornings per week – their van would pick her up and drop her off at the Lawrence corner.

Sgt. Herb Bell and detective Jim Presnell had four interviews for Thursday. Bell was an imposing figure, a nice guy who pretended to be "a hard ass." Presnell was an immaculate dresser with a blunt edge – some felt his candor was holding him back.

A waitress at Maury's Tiny Cove, a popular West Side eatery, recognized Linda's picture and said she'd been there but was uncertain if she was with someone. Presnell had a report claiming Linda was seen there with Arthur Chaney, who they were looking to interview. The waitress did not know Chaney.

A wannabe cop named Grigsby injected himself into the case with a tip about James Cannon. His wife worked at Monsanto, and apparently Cannon told her "he was glad the detectives didn't talk to him sooner because he had cuts on his face from a fight with his girlfriend," and knew this would be hard to explain in the wake of the murders. Yet no one else working with Cannon had seen any cuts.

John William McClain had been Jerry Bricca's ride to work when he first started at Monsanto Cincinnati. The 41-year-old said Jerry was living at the Travel Lodge Motel on Central Parkway while looking for a house. This carpool arrangement lasted for a month in October 1963. Other than a company dance in 1965, McClain had never socialized with Jerry and Linda.

Bell's notes show McClain to be "a quiet, shy type of person who speaks softly and is well mannered." He was calm, cooperative and "gave direct answers with no attempt at evasion."

Helen Wulsekuhl told Hall and McKinney that she was sent to the GAH to interview on for the receptionist job. When she arrived at 1 PM on Monday the 19th, Leininger came into the lobby with an attractive dark haired woman. The woman left with a child, and she was informed by Leininger that the position had just been filled.

When she saw the murdered family's pictures in the paper on Wednesday the 28th, Mrs. Wulsekuhl was certain the woman and child she saw were Linda and Debbie Bricca.

Their other interview was with Charlotte Ernst, a dog breeder identified by former employee Robert Smatt as a close friend of Leininger. She had known him for six years – he sold dogs for her and delivered some litters of puppies as well.

"When was the last time you saw the Doc?"

"About a month ago. I take my dogs in frequently."

"Did he ever get fresh with you?"

"Never, which is odd."

"Why is that?"

Mrs. Ernst, a handsome woman in her late 30's, pondered the question. "Most vets, in my opinion, think they're great lovers."

"But not Leininger?"

"Fred wasn't the type. He even introduced me to his wife, and we got along very well."

When she mentioned she used to breed dogs in Ft. Lauderdale Hall perked up, knowing Linda Bricca spent time there.

"Do you know any vets down there?"

"Dr, Leishore was a real lover. Thought he was God's gift. He worked at Kelly Hospital."

"Could Linda Bricca have known him?" McKinney handed over the picture of Linda.

"Yeah, I saw this in the paper. She's definitely his type."

"Did you ever see her at Leininger's clinic?"

"No." Charlotte Ernst shared a low chuckle. "I would have remembered someone like her..."

Friday, October 14th

The Friday *Enquirer* front page headline was monumental.

With a font rolled out for national disasters, Pearl Harbor, or the JFK assassination, **5000 Man Posse Beefs up Hunt for Sex Maniac** was the blood gorged depiction of a city engulfed in terror.

City Manager William Wichman and Safety Director Henry Sandman rounded up this unparalleled "posse" by calling for the formation of an auxiliary organization "to extend the eyes and ears of the 900-man police force." This was an all-out muster for an army of city and private sector employees to assist the cops.

NNATI ENQUIRER

AY MORNING, OCTOBER 14, 1966 PRICE 10 CENTS —HOME DELIVERED 50¢ A WEEK

5000-Man Posse Beefs Up Hunt For Sex Maniac

One meager clue developed Thursday as Cincinnati organized a 5000-man auxiliary group to help police in the search for the mad strangler.

The new clue—police now know the blood type of the man who raped and strangled Mrs. Alice Hochhausler, surgeon's wife, Tuesday night in the rear of her Clifton Hills home.

This clue bolstered police belief that the killer is the same man responsible for three other such deaths and one near-fatal attack in the city within the last year.

Meanwhile, in an unparalleled move, the city administration mustered an army of city and private industry employees to assist police.

City Manager William Wichman and Safety Director Henry Sandman set the wheels in motion for the auxiliary force "to extend the eyes and ears of the 900-man police force."

This was done at two meetings at City Hall. At the first, heads of all departments which have men circulating throughout the city were called—the Water Works meter readers, waste collection workers, building inspectors, etc.

Then representatives of

Reward Increased

The Clifton Kiwanis Club Thursday offered $100 to the $7000 previously announced reward fund for the capture and conviction of the murderer of Mrs. Hochhausler. The medical staff of Good Samaritan Hospital also announced it will contribute an amount to be later determined.

At the same time, the Kroger Co. announced that all of its stores will start this morning giving out free whistles to women.

Former Police Chief Stanley R. Schrotel suggested whistles as defense weapons earlier this week at a Council Crime Study hearing.

the Yellow Cab Co., Cincinnati Gas and Electric Co., Model Laundry, U. S. postal employees (1300 carriers), and French-Bauer and Sealtest dairies.

Carriers of both newspapers also were invited to join in the effort.

All were asked — and agreed willingly—to participate.

All will do two things:

• Primarily — seek out and report to police all tan and cream 1959 model automobiles. Police believe the killer may have driven a vehicle of this description.

• They also will report "anything of a suspicious nature."

In two other urgent moves, the administration ordered the police motor patrol bolstered by 30 more cars and also arranged for immediate delivery of 25 more two-way police radio sets which had been ordered for later this year. Hulbert Taft Jr., Taft Broadcasting Co., volunteered his private plane to fly to Chicago to pick up part of the radio order today.

Meanwhile, Mr. Wichman called Negro and white

Mrs. Alice Hochhausler
victim of vicious killer

The recruitment of an auxiliary "posse" made it official – this was the largest law enforcement mobilization in city history.

The mobilization for a manhunt had begun. Meter readers, mail carriers, garbage men, delivery drivers and anyone whose job kept them moving around the city was asked to join up, and all quickly agreed. Their mission was to spot and identify all cream and tan 1959 Chevys and "anything else of a suspicious nature."

The CPD assigned 23 detectives full time to the Hochhausler murder. A phone hot-line was put into action, and the operators at "Station X" logged 800 calls on the first day alone.

They were rounding up every known pervert, black or white, and the eager press viewed them in the sour smelling downtown lockup. There were ex-cons, drifters, and "pansies", twitchy little men with bloated, moist faces, the whisperers, the purveyors, the sex morons. The dregs of Cincinnati had never seen such a harsh light shined on their desperate, paltry lives.

A surge of anxiety washed over the city. Hardware stores ran out of locks. Self-defense classes were full. Anything resembling a guard dog was snatched up from the pound. Residents in the "Strangler Triangle" – Clifton, Walnut Hills, and Price Hill – kept their porch lights and driveway lamps burning all night.

On page nine a provocative feature asked the question: **Similarities Startling – All Point to One Man?** The four murders and one near fatal attack were similar. All of the victims were strangled with an improvised garrote. All were over 50 years old – all were struck a crushing blow to the head and then dragged. All but Alice Hochhausler were attacked in the daytime.

The wild card was Barbara Bowman – considered a Strangler victim by most of the detectives.

Acting Police Chief Guy York told a reporter the Strangler was a daring slayer "who glories in outsmarting the police. He must be pretty intelligent, because he gives his victims no time to scream and makes his getaway quickly and unobserved."

One year had passed since the attack on Elizabeth Kreco in Walnut Hills. But the savage killing of Alice Hochhausler on her own driveway had jolted the collective nerves of the city.

Finally, the shit had hit the fan...

ACROSS TOWN, THE COUNTY investigation into the Bricca murders was besieged by rumors about the arrest of a suspect.

The day before, an *Enquirer* piece headlined **No "One" Suspect in Bricca Murders** featured a frustrated Herb Vogel. "We have not yet zeroed in one any one person as a suspect." He said their interviews allowed them "to eliminate some possible suspects."

If Vogel thought this would quell the wild speculation he was mistaken. On Friday, a page one *Enquirer* headline stirred the pot again with **Rumors of Bricca Case Arrest Irk Authorities**. A wire service story was circulating about a man who'd been arrested and had confessed. Vogel firmly denied it: "You'd think we'd have heard the news first."

Captain Emil Otting jumped in. "I'm getting sick and tired of this. We did not arrest anybody, and Lt. Vogel and I have been busy all day telling people this. Just because a person comes in for an interview doesn't mean he's a suspect."

Yet there was nothing they could say to purge the allure of the betrayed workaholic husband and the beautiful cheating wife. The perfect narrative for innuendo – soon growing to a crescendo.

Bill Belbot took an interesting statement from Dr. Carroll Rolfes, who tried to take his dog to the GAH after it became violently sick on Monday September 26th, the day after the murders. Leininger had rebuffed him, "saying he was too busy and had no one to watch the dog." But Belbot knew the Westmans were working that day.

For Rolfes, this was completely out of character for his vet, who'd shown great compassion a year ago when he agreed to an emergency clinic visit for this same dog on a Saturday night.

Charlie Nagel was at Sears talking to the clerk who'd sold paint to Linda Bricca the week before the crime. Jerry Hicks said she bought a gallon of white and ordered special beige on Saturday September 17th, returning on Thursday to pick it up. Debbie was with her both times. Hicks knew the attractive brunette by sight, and Linda had casually mentioned that "her husband was doing some painting over the weekend."

A psychiatric case worker had called Vogel with a tip about a possible suspect. Ernie Nehrer was sent to interview a woman who had declared her ex-husband was a good Bricca suspect. When Nehrer asked why, she said that "he lives in Bridgetown, is very sadistic in nature, and is always picking up girls.

Nehrer sighed – another jealous wife trying to stick it to a former spouse.

With other detectives investigating garden variety crimes, Hall and McKinney took the lion's share of statements on Friday.

Melvin Bell was a Great Dane breeder and a client of Leininger's who'd known him for ten years. The doctor "was a nice person" and had "never made any advances towards my wife."

Rumors Of Bricca Case Arrest Irk Authorities

Confronted again Thursday with widespread rumors that a suspect had been arrested in the Bricca family murders, Lt. Herbert W. Vogel, in charge of the investigation categorically denied it.

"You'd think we'd have heard the news first," he commented.

HE SAID a radio station called him and quoted "an insurance wire service" to the effect that a man had been arrested and had confessed.

Capt. Emil J. Otting, in charge of Sheriff Dan Tehan's patrol, said:

"I'm getting sick and tired of this. We did not arrest anybody and Sheriff Tehan, Lieutenant V[illegible] and I have been bus[illegible] day telling people this. because a person com[illegible] for an interview do[illegible] mean he's a suspect."

They had intervi[illegible] three persons Wednesd[illegible] the New Burlington C[illegible] munication Headquarte[illegible]

There was some p[illegible] activity next door to

No 'One' Suspect In Bricca Murders

"We have not yet zeroed in on any one person as a suspect," Lt. Herbert W. Vogel of the Hamilton County Sheriff's Office said Wednesday in discussing widespread rumors that an arrest had been made in the Bricca murders case.

This was after county detectives interviewed 10 more persons in the murders of Mr. and Mrs. Gerald Bricca and their daughter, Debbie, four, 3381 Greenway Ave., Bridgetown. Their bodies were found in their home September 27.

THE questioning of three

home brought to about 350 the number of interviews by detectives since the bodies were discovered.

Although the interviews have not pinpointed one person, they have eliminated some possible suspects, the officer said.

Asked if any of his dozen

Cincinnati Enquirer

Page 14
Thursday, October 13, 1966

Vogel denied that there had been an arrest, but he couldn't stop the rumors that County was focusing on one suspect.

The president of the Animal Welfare League told them Linda came to her house in early August with rugs and supplies for the new animal shelter. Mrs. Robert Meyer said Linda mentioned their upcoming trip to California, assuring her that she would be available to volunteer on a regular basis any time after September 10th.

West Side resident Jerry Woebkenburg heard three men speculating at work that "the Dr. and Linda were having an affair, and when Jerry returned home the Doc killed him. Linda panicked and was killed along with Debbie to prevent them from talking."

Even though this theory was dominating the investigation, Hall's notes read "this seems to be just conversation among people. No basis for this."

Two veterinary clinics on Glenway were the final stops. At the Bridgetown Pet Hospital, they interviewed doctors Coleman and Henry about a Dr. Silk, who worked there until February before moving back to Canada. Dr. Henry stated that he has "been getting a lot of Dr. Leininger's business lately" and that "people are getting apprehensive about him."

Their last interview was a return trip to the Western Hills Animal Hospital, owned and operated by Dr. Stanley Keller since 1949. On October 4th Ernie Nehrer had spoken with Keller and came away wondering what he was hiding.

Now as Hall gathered some personal background, Keller again wilted under the pressure. He had met Dr. Silk but knew nothing about him, and he was adamant Linda Bricca had never worked for him. Keller made sure to inform them that he was a "former WWII fighter pilot" and "was a personal friend of Sheriff Dan Tehan."

This interview would be highlighted in the file, just like those of Fred Leininger and James Cannon. Something in Keller's manner had once again hoisted the red flags...

October 14th

Thousands Hunt Strangler – Schott Says Slaying a Crime of Chance was splattered across the front page of the Cincinnati *Post.*

"The slayer just happened to be in the area of the Hochhausler home and saw his opportunity to strike," Schott told reporters. "He prowls the city looking for the right opportunity – a woman alone at the right place and right time." He said the murder night was only the third time that Alice picked her daughter up from work, contrary to initial reports that this was her regular routine.

Schott confirmed they knew the blood type of the killer but would not disclose it. He also speculated that "someone out there knows who the strangler is but won't report him because of love or fear."

An *Enquirer* editorial quoted former chief Stanley Schrotel as he testified before the Crime Study Committee. No longer constrained by politics, Schrotel was direct and impassioned.

"We need more eyes, ears, and men," he reasoned. "Back up your officers and give them a sense of dignity. Then the headlines and attitudes will change." Schrotel also smacked the recent Miranda ruling, lamenting that "suspects are now advising policemen what to say."

The Hochhausler murder had rocked city hall. Today Councilman John Held proposed motions to eliminate door to door trick or treating and banning the wearing of Halloween masks.

The killing of lovely Alice had transformed quiet, tree-lined Cornell Place. Neighbors who just days before had admired the autumn-tinged trees were gathered in tight little groups, eyeing strangers and wondering if the murky ambiance of their historic gaslights was suddenly outdated...

A JUICY RUMOR WAS PHONED in to County that afternoon.

Allegedly a maid working across the street from the Bricca house encountered Linda Bricca there on Saturday evening September 24th. She told a friend that Linda "called her boyfriend" from that residence "to make a date for that night." But when interviewed, Maxine Woods declared she'd never worked in Bridgetown and failed to identify a photo of Linda Bricca.

Ernie Nagel followed up on another odd person in the Bricca neighborhood. Anthony Ree lived on Lawrence just around the corner from the Briccas, and had been treated for "an emotional illness" for ten years. Mrs. Ree suspected her neighbor called in the tip because Mr. Ree was jealous of the neighbor's husband.

Charlie Nagel had his own dead end to bury. A neighbor of Monsanto employee Russell Ashcraft in Miamitown heard him and his wife arguing on Wednesday morning September 28th – he had come home late with blood on his clothes. Ashcraft had worked on some projects managed by Jerry Bricca, but he could prove he was home on the night of September 25th.

Hall and McKinney were running background on Dr. Stanley Keller, the inscrutable, quirky vet who'd already been interviewed twice.

A supervisor at Good Samaritan Hospital pulled Keller's records, confirming he was admitted to their psychiatric ward three times in the last six years, most recently 8/15/65.

Keller suffered from depression and suicidal thoughts, yet there nothing to indicate any violence during these stays.

Hall had already pulled a police report from August 1966 concerning Dr. Keller. Thieves were hitting West Side vet clinics all year and stealing narcotics – Keller had reported $15 worth of drugs stolen during a Sunday night break in.

Vogel and Taylor took the plumb assignment. They interviewed Dr. Herman Rehder, who'd done relief work for Dr. Leininger on several occasions. The 36-year-old Rehder attended Ohio State Vet School with Leininger and the two remained friends.

Taylor received a tip that Rehder visited the Glenway Animal Hospital on Wednesday before the murders and spoke with Linda Bricca while she was working. They also learned he worked for the Cincinnati Health Department as a meat and dairy Inspector since 1959 – he had taken Leininger's old job there.

This year Rehder had worked at GAH on July 11th and 12th while Leininger attended a convention in Louisville. The last time he filled in was October 3rd thru 5th during Leininger's recent hunting trip.

During the interview Rehder mentioned a boy named Steve who'd worked at the clinic as an animal handler. Dr. Leininger thought highly of Steve, and had even sent him to school for additional training in the care of laboratory animals. He thought this boy would be about 19 or 20 now.

Asked why he mentioned Steve, Rehder said the boy was "strange". Yet Vogel was getting a strange vibe from Rehder, with his piercing eyes and restless disposition.

Taylor got to the meat of the interview. "Why did you stop at Dr. Leininger's clinic on September 21st?

"To find out if I was working for him during his hunting trip."

"Did you see Linda Bricca there?"

"Yes. They were talking when I arrived and he introduced us."

"Did you speak privately with her at that time?"

"Well, Fritz went to treat an animal, and we talked for about 20 minutes."

Taylor jotted down the nickname. "What did you talk about?"

"Mostly small talk. She was new on the job and I asked her how she liked it so far and she said 'very well' or something like that?'

"What else did you talk about?"

"How much Doc was paying for relief work, and how much more the pipefitters who worked for her husband at Monsanto made."

Dr. Rehder said this was the only time he'd seen Mrs. Bricca. He could not remember if he'd ever treated any of her animals.

Vogel saw the signs of anxiety. What was this man hiding?

They quickly found out. Rehder averted his eyes, and revealed something about his past. "When you check my background, you'll find I was committed to a mental hospital in Columbus shortly after I graduated Vet School in 1957.

"Which hospital"

"White Cross Hospital."

As Taylor made a note, Vogel ended the interview. "We'll be back in touch," he said, clinching eyes with Dr. Herman Rehder...

October 15th-16th

It was 3 AM, and the house on Harmony Lane was restless. 10-year-old Larry Foppe Jr. had been lying awake, knowing he could sleep in on Saturday. He heard his mother get up and go to the bathroom – his father was sawing logs, dead to the world.

His youthful thoughts drifted to the Bricca family, murdered in their house almost three weeks ago a quarter mile from the Foppe home. His dad was locking doors, which he'd never done before.

Then he heard it, the sound of someone rattling their front doorknob. Was he dreaming? No, because someone was pushing against the door of their modest brick split-level house.

As he sat up in bed, his mother's voice sliced through the silence. "Who's there?" she shouted. She yelled it twice more, the frightened question echoing down the hallway. And in the darkness young Larry heard running footsteps.

His father was quickly awake and down the stairs, but the intruder had vanished into the night.

His parents told him and his brothers to go back to sleep. Larry heard his mother talking in a tone he'd never heard before.

"Are you going to tell the police NOW?" she asked his father.

"You think it's something to do with..." his voice trailed off.

"You've waited long enough." Her manner softened. "What about your friend Dick Janszen finding those bodies. You think you're more haunted than he is?"

"Tell them what, exactly? Larry Sr. sounded almost afraid.

"About your last customer the night the Briccas were killed..."

THE *ENQUIRER* FRONT PAGE headline was perplexing: **Psychiatric Aid Asked in Hunt for Strangler.**

Homicide detectives are so consumed by the "WHO" that they rarely have time to consider the "WHY". They don't have to confirm motive as long as they can prove their suspect did the crime. Yet only a few days into the Hochhausler investigation, were Cincinnati Police turning to the head shrinkers?

"There is little doubt the man is a psychotic," Jake Schott said. "He may think he's in a duel with us. That last killing was almost an act of defiance." Schott had obtained records from Lima State Hospital for the Criminally Insane of all patients released up to a year before the October 12th, 1965 attack on Elizabeth Kreco.

That afternoon, top ranking detectives had a conference at General Hospital with their leading staff psychiatrists. But after the two hour meeting, cops and docs were at odds on "what makes the Strangler tick." There was no consensus on his physical appearance, his mental makeup, and his motivations to attack middle-aged women.

He was a phantom yet not a ghost...

NEHRER AND HALL TOOK two statements that afternoon. Lou Theuer owned Lou's Greenacres Food and Beverage at Lawrence and Glenway. He verified that Richard Meyer was a regular customer who stopped in between 9:00-9:30 PM on the night of the crime.

Ruby Grayson was one of the last people to see Jerry Bricca alive outside his house. The United Dairy Farmer's clerk was getting ready to close when Jerry came in at 8:45 PM that night.

He bought his usual three half gallons of milk and a quart of orange juice. She'd known him for several years, and on this rainy night

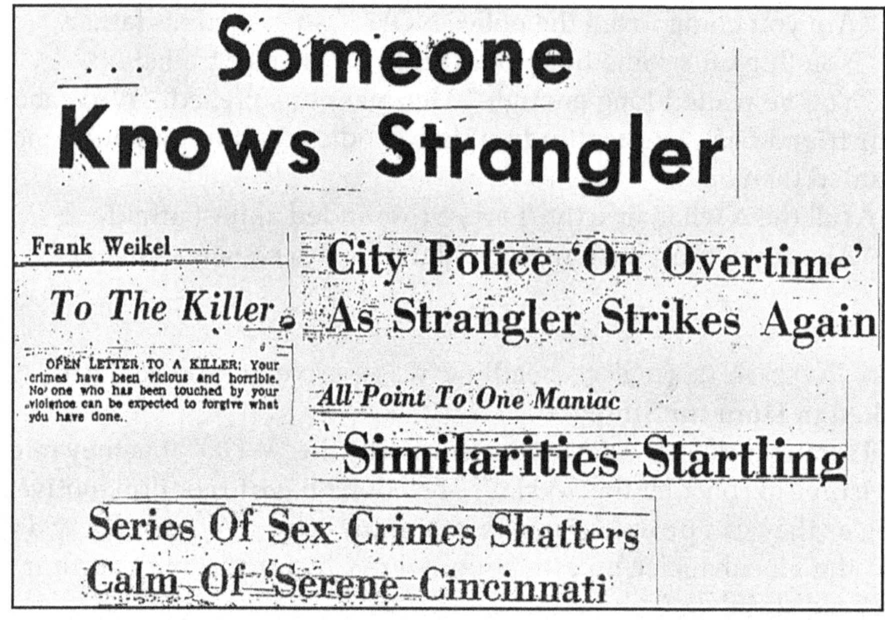

... Someone Knows Strangler

Frank Weikel

To The Killer

OPEN LETTER TO A KILLER: Your crimes have been vicious and horrible. No one who has been touched by your violence can be expected to forgive what you have done.

City Police 'On Overtime' As Strangler Strikes Again

All Point To One Maniac

Similarities Startling

Series Of Sex Crimes Shatters Calm Of 'Serene Cincinnati

The Hochhausler murder spawned a flurry of breathless headlines for anxious Cincinnati residents.

cheerfully chided him for forgetting his jacket before Jerry stepped out into the mist and headed home, less than a mile away.

Ruby broke down at one point – knowing what happened to Jerry after leaving her store was just too chilling. Tearfully, she said she'd never seen Linda Bricca and that Debbie was only with him once or twice.

"He was a gentleman and never did anything out of the way." She dried her eyes, and then fixed Nehrer with her gaze. "Was I the last one to see him?

Ernie Nehrer lowered his voice. "We think he put his garbage cans out as he arrived home from your store. A neighbor from across the street spoke to him at that time."

As they left, Nehrer saw the look on her face – somewhere between survivor's guilt and lingering horror...

LATE THAT AFTERNOON DETECTIVE "Pappy" Bowman took a call that roused him from his Saturday malaise. Listening intently to the caller, he held up his hand for quiet in the bullpen.

Larry Foppe was on the other end. The owner of the HiLo Beverage Depot was finally getting something off his chest. The abortive break-in at his house and his wife's insistence cinched it.

"The night the Briccas were killed, Dr. Fred Leininger came into my store about 10:30 PM to use the phone."

Realizing the HiLo was about a half mile from the crime scene, Bowman honed in. "What was his demeanor like?"

"I'm used to seeing him dressed up. He was wearing an odd sport coat, and he looked kinda shaggy, maybe from the rain."

"You're sure it was Leininger?"

"Oh yeah. He's a regular customer. Excuse me a second." Bowman heard Foppe waiting on someone. "OK...I can't really talk here. We're getting busy."

"What about this phone call he made?" Bowman waited as Foppe did another transaction.

"Well, he dialed, let it ring a few times, and then redialed. It sounded like there was no answer, but he said the line was busy. He also said he was on an emergency."

Bowman was furiously scribbling notes, other detectives pooling behind him. "When can you come in and give a formal statement."

"I work here seven days a week. But I can slip away tomorrow afternoon."

"Anything else you can tell me now?"

"He kept his left hand in his coat pocket, away from his body. His right hand seemed to be trembling."

"Did you see his car?"

"Yeah, he was driving the red station wagon."

"Have you seen him since then?"

"That's the funny thing. He used to come in three or four times a week. But the Doc hasn't been in here since that night."

Bowman exhaled. "Why have you waited so long to come forward with this information?"

"Check the police report I filed this morning. Then we'll talk."

ON SUNDAY THE 16TH, **Strange Fingerprints Found by FBI on Bricca Property** returned the Bricca case to the *Enquirer* front page. According to Herb Vogel, the FBI report had isolated prints "on items that would not be touched by the ordinary visitor."

"This doesn't mean those prints belonged to the killer," Vogel reminded. "They might have belonged to a recent house guest." The prints were being compared with known criminals on file.

Vogel believed "Mrs. Bricca's hands were bound with white adhesive tape," but that Jerry was trussed up "with a rope about ¼" thick." The killer had removed both ligatures.

Just past noon, detective Robert Hall arrived at 6595 Glenway to interview Larry Foppe. The owner of the HiLo locked his door and hung a temporary "Closed" sign. Bob Hall could sling the BS – just like Foppe. Both were garrulous men who still valued the truth.

Foppe reviewed his encounter with Leininger on the murder night – the odd appearance, furtive behavior, and failed phone call.

"Did he seem drunk?" Hall asked.

"Not really, but he looked like he hadn't shaved and his clothes were hanging loose. He's usually much neater than that."

"Was he afraid of something?"

"He appeared very nervous the whole time he was here." Foppe said Leininger's two attempts at making a call didn't go through and he "hung up the phone in disgust."

"I asked him what was the matter and he said he had an emergency call but he couldn't get a hold of the party." Foppe noticed Leininger had come from the direction of Western Bowl, and wondered why he didn't make the call from his office up the street.

He said Leininger "left quickly" and "acted like he didn't want to talk to me." Foppe then locked up and drove home, taking Greenway Avenue south. He passed the Bricca residence about 10:45 PM and saw "Mr. Bricca's car parked in front of their home." There was "a car in front of Mr. Bricca's but I didn't pay too much attention to it. It might have been a small blue car, possibly a Ford."

"Was it raining when you drove by?"

"Coming down pretty good. When I got home it was pouring."

"Did you see any other cars on Greenway?

"No. And there are usually a lot of cars around there. I drive it every night after I close up. I see things."

"Like what?"

"Lovers. Parked in cars on Greenway..."

October 17th – 20th

On Monday another witness came forward about a driver he saw near the murder scene. Shortly after 9 PM on September 25th, Charles Herbig was stopped on Glenway at the Lawrence corner when a dark blue car pulled up beside him to turn right. The driver was mid-30s, with short dark hair and appearing "very nervous." Herbig watched him for several seconds before the light changed and the driver turned right toward Greenway.

Two other interviews on this day would warrant having their numbers highlighted.

Phyllis Tenholder was a former Bricca babysitter who lived five doors south on Greenway. On Saturday night September 24th, the 16-year-old had observed a red car with a black hood parked on Greenway near the Bricca residence about 6:20 PM. The colors sounded like Leininger's car, but when shown their automobile mug book she picked out a 1958 Plymouth.

Phyllis worked for the Merle Norman Beauty Salon on Glenway, and was certain Linda came there to get her wig washed and set by Carol Sue Appleby.

Detective Bell was interested in the babysitting. "When was the last time you worked for Linda Bricca?"

"Spring and summer of last year."

"Did Linda ever say anything unusual to you?"

"One time she gave me her mother's phone number and said to call her 'if anything happened.'"

THAT AFTERNOON NEHRER AND Nagle paid a visit to a local celebrity.

A tip claimed one of Linda Bricca's rabbits had been featured on the "Skipper Ryle Show", a local television program on WKRC. After talking briefly with his secretary and producer, the detectives sat down with the star of the show himself, Glenn Ryle.

Born Glenn Schnitker on the West Side, Ryle was a former marine who fell into broadcasting by accident. Swarthy, hollow-eyed and powerfully built, Ryle had a resonant voice and a personality to match. He'd hosted the show for ten years, and it was 2nd only to WCPO's Uncle Al Show in popularity among kids.

Part of the show's appeal was that Ryle never just played to the children. It was a kid's show that adults could enjoy, and "Skipper" bantered inside jokes and innuendo aimed at a mature audience.

Ryle admitted having a rabbit on the show, brought there by his friend "Fritz" Leininger. As the interview progressed, Nehrer's notes showed his frustration: "In talking to Ryle we felt that he was a personal friend of Dr. Leininger."

Neither Ryle nor his staff recognized photos of Jerry or Linda. They hadn't met them or seen Linda at the studio.

"So how often did Dr. Leininger bring animals on your show?"

"Last spring we did four Sunday shows with live animals. Fritz came in on Thursdays to tape them."

"What did he talk about on these shows?"

"How to care for your pets and treat them if they became sick."

When they left Nehrer highlighted this interview number – one of 16 in the case file. Why did this one make the hot list?

Ernie Nehrer had a gut feeling about the "Skipper". Rumors would surface that the married Ryle was stepping out with other women. And he was a close personal friend of "Fritz" Leininger.

As the Hochhausler investigation entered its second week, *Enquirer* columnist Frank Weikel wrote an "open letter" to the killer:

> **It is more than possible that you can't even forgive yourself for these murders. Maybe your dreams are filled with the faces of your victims and their terrified voices pleading for mercy. Before another innocent person is killed please seek the help you need...**

Councilman John Held warned against any "vigilante" activity in the Strangler's wake. "This is no time to take the law into your own hands." With reports that residents were "arming themselves with crude weapons," he urged that no citizen "buy a gun without first consulting the police."

The next day, the Crime Commission voted unanimously to hold upcoming Halloween activities on Sunday October 30th in the daytime from 3-6 PM.

This was the most surprising example of the terror affecting the community. The chances that the Strangler might take a child seemed remote, but Cincinnati was now in zero-tolerance lockdown. Children with only a vague concept of murder finally understood that being out after dark could really be deadly.

The Bricca investigation seemed to be losing momentum as they chased lifeless leads. A former Cincinnati cop thought he saw Linda Bricca at the Carthage Fair in mid-August, but he could not identify her picture. A hospital orderly was overheard talking repeatedly about the Bricca case – a background check showed a guy with no criminal record but a real penchant for BS.

A Hamilton, Ohio woman called in about John Rooney, a representative for St. Anthony's Messenger who seemed obsessed with the case. Rooney had been working the area around Western Bowl for six years, and actually spoke to Jerry Bricca in June when he stopped his subscription.

He was just one more person with a peripheral connection to the crime, another bystander who had been profoundly affected by the specter of random, violent death...

NEHRER AND HALL VISITED the White Cross Hospital in Columbus to check out the case history of Dr. Herman Rehder, who admitted experiencing mental problems in their October 14th interview.

Neither detective was prepared for what they found.

Rehder had suffered a complete mental breakdown on May 31st 1957. Several days prior he tried to stab a man who asked his wife to dance at a social function. Then on the 31st Rehder DID stab a man at a tavern who he thought was trying to make time with the waitress – who happened to be Rehder's mother.

Admitted to White Cross later that day, intake notes describe Rehder as "hostile and uncontrollable... a raving maniac who destroyed hospital property." He was released in August but readmitted in January, then sent to Columbus State Mental Hospital in April 1958 because White Cross could no longer handle him.

Rehder had a high IQ but was dominated by his wife – they had rushed into marriage after she became pregnant. He manifested hyperactive behavior and had a history of threatening people with a knife. Final diagnosis was Manic Depression.

Herman Rehder's psychiatric history was a sexual minefield. His first sexual contact occurred with a prostitute at age 15. He later had

Glenn Ryle and Herman Rehder (1956) were close friends of prime suspect Fred Leininger.

homosexual relations with a horse trainer at a race track, and while at Columbus Receiving Hospital he seduced a female patient.

The next day Nagel and Taylor had their second interview with Dr. Rehder, who confirmed that everything in those reports was true. Rehder also admitted having an affair with a nurse he worked with at the Board of Health, even spaying her dog for free at the clinic while filling in for Dr. Leininger.

When asked, he did not remember if he ever treated the Bricca dogs, and insisted the only time he ever saw Linda was the Wednesday before her murder at the GAH.

"Did Leininger say anything to you about Linda Bricca?"

"No. But two days ago at the CVMA meeting he told me that he had spent that Sunday evening at home watching a movie on TV."

"Had you asked him about that night?"

"No, I hadn't."

Nagel made a note with a question mark. They then established Rehder drove a 1966 white Pontiac.

"Where were you on September 25th?"

"I was at Kissel Brothers on Colerain taking care of a horse I was boarding there. That was from about 4:30 to 6 PM.

"Where did you go after that?"

"I went home and watched TV with my wife and daughter before going to bed."

There were now three friends of Fred Leininger who had Herb Vogel's attention – Dr. Stanley Keller, Dr. Herman Rehder, and Glenn Ryle. They were solid citizens on the surface whose demeanor was suspect, with Leininger as the common thread.

Vogel looked at the Foppe interview again, reviewing some highlighted remarks:

- "I've known the doctor for some time, and he is a very strong man."
- "He told me if the Bricca dogs got to know you they weren't dangerous at all."
- "He hasn't been in since that night. The guy was a good customer, in three or four times a week. And all of a sudden he quits coming in."

Foppe hadn't held back. "He was a hard man to get to know. A cold, rigid guy who never let his feelings show. In my opinion he felt he was better than anybody else. He once said that he could get anything taken care of that he needed done."

It glinted for Vogel – "anything that he needed done?"

Detectives believe that every good mystery has a wild card. Was there a clue, a motive, a riddle dropping in out of the blue? Could they discover what spawned this terrible crime – and expose the hidden truths disguised as secrets?

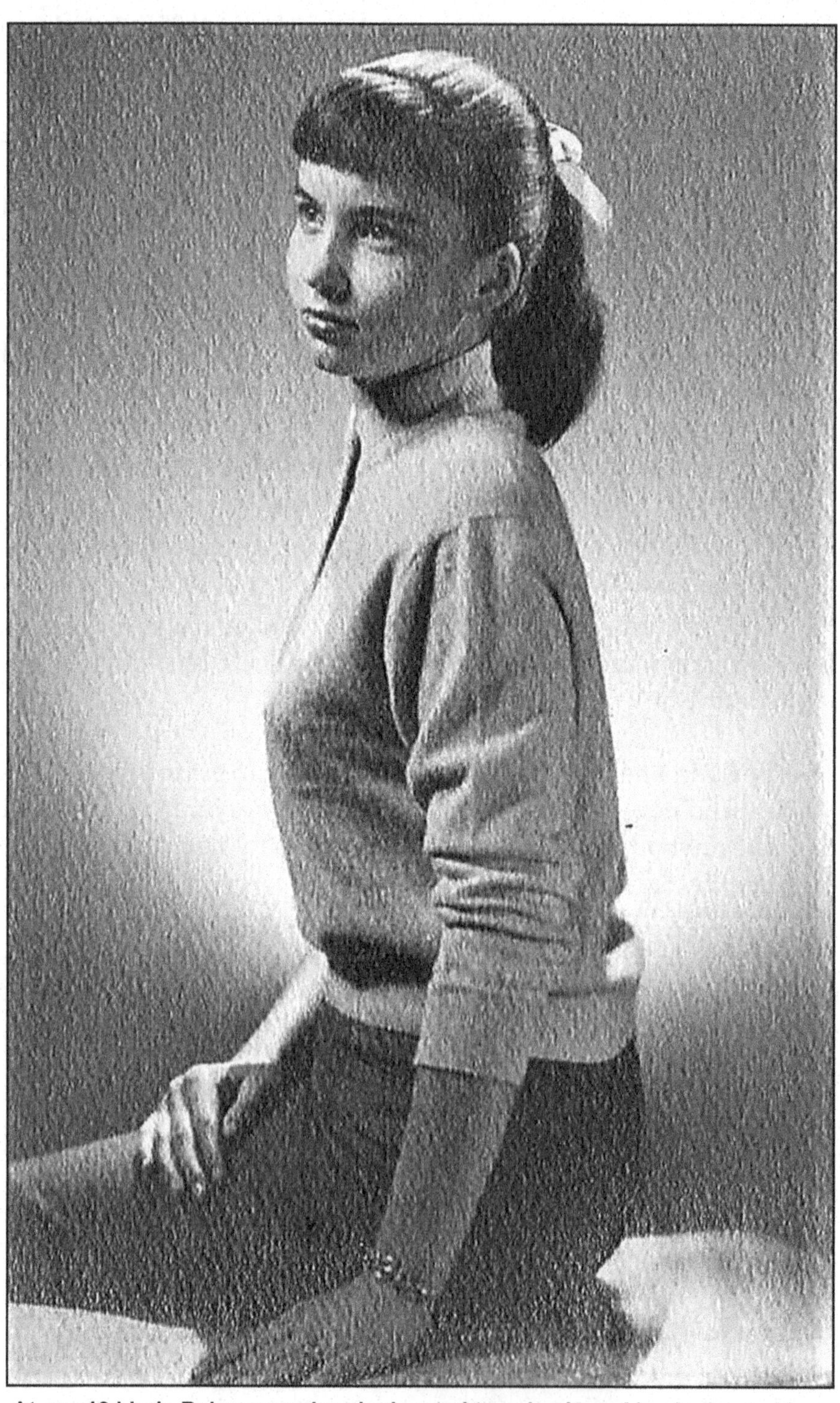

At age 13 Linda Bulaw was already devoted to animals and beginning to blossom into a beautiful young woman.

CHAPTER TEN

A FEW TOO MANY

"Once let a man be reasonably accused of murder, and all manner of evil is raked up, or invented, about him."

Edmund Pearson

OCTOBER 20TH – DECEMBER 9TH 1966

October 20th – 21st

Bricca returned to the front page of the *Enquirer* October 20th edition. **Police Mum on Report in Bricca Murder Case** heralded the arrival of the much anticipated FBI lab analysis.

Other than to say the report was "complete and detailed", Herb Vogel maintained a strict silence on its "top secret" contents, admitting only that there was microscopic examination of latent fingerprints found in the Bricca home. Vogel's standard answer became "there is nothing in the report I can comment on." When pressed for a clarification, he replied that "the Supreme Court is mighty funny these days."

The next day Vogel officially announced that "a white man killed the Briccas." He told a *Post* reporter that "we have nothing to indicate that the perpetrator of the Bricca homicide is of Negroid origin" and reiterated that "the Strangler did not murder the family."

That afternoon, the *Post* provided an update on the Alice Hochhausler murder: **FBI Agents Hope To Stack Evidence Against Killer Here**. The clothing taken from her pitifully defiled body was now piled on a laboratory table at FBI headquarters.

The bureau had over one hundred special agents assigned to their crime lab, most of them with advanced degrees and backed up by a staff of trained technicians. Previously examined were the clothesline taken from Emogene Harrington's throat, along with the nylon stocking and men's tie found around the necks of Lois Dant and Jeannette Messer.

They had already determined the Strangler had Type O blood. Now hairs and fibers were being scrutinized to determine the race of the killer. Using an electron microscope, the largest and most delicate instrument in the spectrograph unit, agents could magnify any evidence up to 100,000 diameters.

Normally FBI involvement would be limited – murder is not a federal crime unless it involves kidnapping, extortion, or interstate flight. But an FBI spokesman said Hoover was "concerned about crime conditions in Cincinnati" and had ordered an "all-out effort."

Queen City residents were apprehensive. On October 17th Stella Kraft had been attacked in her apartment hallway on Race Street. The 25-year-old housewife said a black man rushed at her and tore her blouse. Her screams drove him away, but not before he grabbed her purse. Two days later a 66-year-old woman was similarly assaulted on Auburn Avenue.

On October 19th, the Department of Safety had issued a projection for the next murder. Noting that none of the previous four strangulations had occurred after the 15th day of the month, they forecast the next crime to transpire around December 10th.

They could not have been more wrong...

FRANK WINSTEL WAS WORRIED about his aunt. He was unable to reach Rose Winstel by phone for several days – the 81-year-old woman lived alone in a small house at 2289 Vine Street in Corryville. Her brother lived with her for many years, but she had been alone there since his death in June.

Just after 8 PM on Thursday October 20th, Frank parked his car in front of the gaunt two decker where his aunt lived on the first floor. On either side, 15 feet away stood identical structures, narrow abodes that had seen better days. This was a seamy, crime infested sector across from Inwood Park, and Winstel never felt comfortable visiting here.

In the daytime, the steep hill behind her house seemed okay, but a closer look showed the beauty of the red and gold foliage was marred by a layer of debris and litter on the ground beneath. At night the heavily wooded knoll always looked foreboding to Frank.

At the side door his heart sank – the flimsy chain lock was ripped off the frame as if the door had been kicked in. Frank cautiously stepped inside the front room, which was ransacked.

He found Rose in the back bedroom. Her naked body was partially wedged under the bed. The cord from her heating pad was wrapped taut around her neck, and a blanket covered her face.

Police and reporters flocked to the site within five minutes of Winstel's frantic call. Coroner Frank Cleveland would confirm she died of strangulation and had been raped. She had been beaten severely around the head and face, more than the previous victims.

Cleveland estimated she had been dead between 16-24 hours. A neighbor saw Rose putting out her garbage can around 6 PM Tuesday, and no one had seen the elderly woman since. Cleveland speculated she had been killed Wednesday night.

A detective told an *Enquirer* reporter that "she looked exactly like the others. There's no doubt about it." Yet other investigators weren't so sure – this crime scene exhibited key distinctions from the Strangler's well known signature.

The forced entry was a first. "The killer must have thrown a shoulder block against the lock to force it open," said Jake Schott. Three of the other four victims sustained a single blow to the head, yet Winstel was bludgeoned repeatedly. Instead of leaving her spread eagled, the killer covered her face and tried to jam her body under the bed. And there were bite marks on her body, a detail Schott withheld from the press.

This crime seemed more personal. The killer made sure she was alone before breaching the door. He delivered a furious beating, then covered her up and tried to conceal the body, as if he was ashamed of what he'd done.

At 81, Rose Winstel was 25 years beyond the next oldest victim. She was a half blind semi-invalid, not a woman who would inspire such demented lust. Coverage of the 50-something victims had referred to them as "elderly" – now the age brackets were skewed by this latest atrocity.

As detectives scoured the dingy flat, a distressed Frank Winstel spoke to a *Post* reporter outside. "Rose had good reason to be afraid," he said. "She was definitely aware of the other stranglings and quite concerned. So was I. I cautioned her last week, the last time I saw her, to lock both locks on her door." She was "a very religious person", who was suffering from cataracts and "couldn't distinguish people until they got three or four feet away."

Ruth Wintstel's killer broke her door open. Frank Winstel leaves after he identified his aunt's body.

Frank shuddered as he contemplated his aunt's last moments. She was dragged from her bed with the covers still around her, then ravaged and desecrated by a maniac more beast than man.

Nearly blind, the last thing Rose heard was the horrifying sound of a human wolf blowing down her door....

October 22nd – 24th

The Cincinnati Strangler's rampage was covered by other Midwestern newspapers, but his crimes did not capture national attention the way another killer did a few years before.

Gerold Frank, author of bestseller "The Boston Strangler", told a local reporter that their killer, who allegedly murdered 13 women in 18 months, was more "cunning and daring" than his Cincinnati counterpart. The Boston slayer "only took victims in apartments where he was certain he would not be seen – while your strangler has taken chances in a basement, a park, and a driveway, where someone could have been watching."

But the murder of Rose Winstel finally landed the Queen City's phantom on the pages of *Newsweek Magazine*:

The chain latch gave easily in the decaying wood and the intruder was quickly inside the narrow old house on Cincinnati's seedy upper Vine Street. He found Miss Rose Winstel, an 81-year-old spinster, in her bedroom. If she screamed no one heard; not till next evening did a nephew find her body, bludgeoned, raped, strangled with an electric cord... Five such killings in ten months had made the signature fearfully plain to Cincinnatians – and yet hard for police to read...

No Suspect in Murder was the October 22nd *Enquirer* headline: Jake Schott was straddling the fence on the Winstel case – privately he wondered if they were dealing with a copycat killer.

There was an ironic twist to the murdered woman's last days. Concerned relatives, citing her age and solitary life, had recently made arrangements for her to enter a rest home. But Rose refused because she "didn't want to be crowded in with other women."

Violence Accepted as a Way of Life in Murder Locale painted an unflattering portrait of the Corryville neighborhood. Only 2-1/2 miles from the Hochhausler murder in the posh Clifton gaslight district, this ramshackle sector of lower Vine Street where Rose Winstel died might as well have been in another country.

Miss Winstel's home is in the midst of a racially mixed neighborhood where almost anything can happen – and often does. Residents have become almost calloused to the sounds of family fights and saloon brawls.

Just last week, a man was shot to death on the sidewalk outside the Peyton Place Café, located across the street from the house where Miss Winstel was raped, strangled, and brutally beaten...

That afternoon Jake Schott told the *Post* they believed the Winstel slaying was planned in advance. "We think the killer had to know she lived there alone and waited until he was sure there was no one about," Schott said, adding they were "certain that the killer is a Negro." Yet they knew almost nothing else about him.

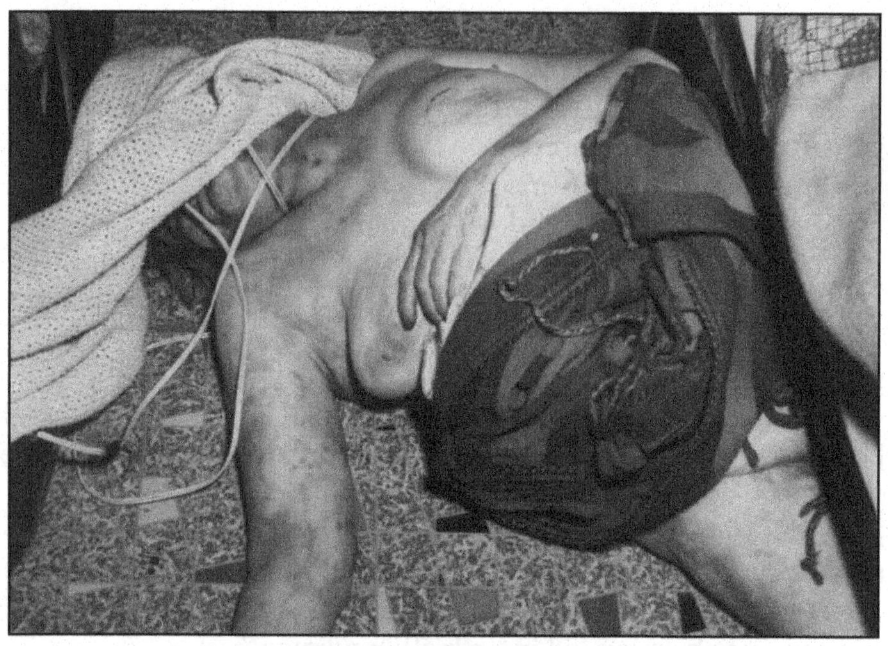

Unlike the other victims, Rose Winstel's body was partially jammed under the bed.

Cincinnati's black population was bristling at what they perceived was inflammatory coverage. An *Enquirer* letter to the editor from a 50-year-old woman captured the anger and dread:

> **An assailant is an assailant whether he is white or Negro and a woman is a woman... We value our lives as highly as the white women and deserve the same protection. We bleed and die when assaulted and raped just like a white woman does. If I sound bitter, I am.**
>
> **I'm human, and I'm scared...**

The next day, the *Enquirer* ran a provocative story: **Series of Sex Crimes Shatters Calm of Serene Cincinnati**. "Today apprehension covers the metropolitan area – a pall created by the slayings of women." The article was quick to point out that all female residents, black and white, were living in fear.

Roundup Of Suspects On

Another Woman Strangled

Cord Around Victim's Neck; Rape Verified

With a new strangulation-rape case—the fifth in 10 months—Cincinnati police late Thursday began a roundup of potential suspects.

One was arrested within two hours after the body of an 81-year-old widow, Mrs. Rose Winstel, was found in the first-floor bedroom of her home at 2280 Vine St., where she lived alone. The house is on Vine Street hill, half a block south of McMillan Street.

Police acknowledged they had no evidence to link the 23-year-old suspect to the murder other than he reportedly had been seen recently in the area.

The city's latest horror was discovered shortly after 8 p. m. by Robert C. Winstel, 1633 Trillium Ct., Newtown, a nephew of the victim. He told police he went to her home after he had been unable to reach Mrs. Winstel by telephone for several days.

Mrs. Winstel's body was found partly under her bed. The cord of a heating pad was taut around her neck. Her clothing from the waist down was in disarray.

Dr. Frank Cleveland, Hamilton County coroner, said autopsy showed she had died of strangulation. She had been raped. She had been severely beaten about the head and face.

The time of death, the coroner estimated, was 15 to 24 hours previously.

A neighbor, Mrs. Claudia Roper, 2287 Vine St., said she last saw Mrs. Winstel

Emergency Session

An emergency meeting of Cincinnati's Crime Study Committee will be held at 8 a. m. today in the office of City Manager William C. Wichman as the result of Mrs. Winstel's murder. Safety Director Henry Sandman, Acting Police Chief Guy York and Detective Chief Jacob Schott were instructed to be present.

of a retired railroad employe, was found raped and strangled April 4 in her Price Hill home.

Mrs. Jeanette M. Messer, 56, was raped and strangled early June 13 when walking her dog in Burnet Woods.

Mrs. Alice Hochhausler

Modest Vine St. Hill Home—Murder Scene

At age 81 Rose Winstel was much older than the other victims attributed to the Strangler.

A TRIPLE HOMICIDE IN FLORIDA caught Herb Vogel's attention.

On October 22nd Robert and Helen Sims and their 12-year-old daughter Joy were murdered in their Tallahassee home. The couple's oldest daughter came home from babysitting and found her family bound, gagged, stabbed, and shot. The father and daughter were dead – Mrs. Sims died later at the hospital.

Similarities to Bricca were there. Vogel winced when he read that almost 200 people had walked through the crime scene, including a cop who made coffee. Tallahassee detectives ruled out burglary and considered it a personal crime where the family was targeted. And neither the knife nor the gun had been found.

The owner of the Shell Station at Werk and Glenway was asked about the gas slip found in Jerry Bricca's car dated 9/25/66. He estimated the time of the sale as between 10-11 AM on the last morning of Jerry's life. Yet the attendant that morning did not remember waiting on him after viewing his photograph.

A young man in his early 20's was "mouthing off to a friend and bragged that he had killed the Briccas." Yet under questioning "he didn't have all the facts right" and "was just trying to be a big shot," according to Vogel. The boaster swiftly retracted his bogus confession and was released.

Carol Sue Appleby was identified by a babysitter as the hairdresser who took care of Linda's wig – she worked at the Merle Norman Beauty Salon on Glenway. Yet Carol didn't recognize Linda's photo and didn't believe she ever came in there.

Nehrer noticed she was nervous, as if she didn't want to get involved. He made a note to follow-up with her.

Richard Ernst knew Leininger though the Oak Hills High School Athletic Association – he had donated a small Scotty dog to the "Highlanders" as the mascot. Ernst did not socialize with Leininger, but his sister-in-law Charlotte Ernst, a dog breeder interviewed earlier, referred him to Leininger for treatment of his own dog.

Ernst gave them two more people to contact. He knew a teacher who was a personal friend of Linda Bricca. And the principal at West Harrison High was a close friend of Leininger.

Interview #238 was scheduled to obtain information and gather background on Dr. Robert Weadick, a veterinarian and a close associate of Dr. Stanley Keller. Keller had raised the hackles of some detectives with his strange behavior, and rumor had it that Linda Bricca had worked briefly for Weadick at his clinic.

Yet this entry on the interview control sheet was typed over with XXX's, and number 238 was assigned to the next one. There is no record that Dr. Weadick was ever interviewed.

October 25th – 26th

With Halloween approaching, the ghosts of murder and mayhem showed no signs of dispelling.

In the early morning hours of Sunday the 23rd, a postman ambushed his wife and shot her to death before killing himself in Kennedy Heights. Several neighbors saw Arthur Crowell attack Carol and heard her frantic screams, but no one helped her.

When a 47-year-old widow was found murdered in her Clifton apartment on Tuesday morning the 25th, fears that the strangler had taken another victim echoed around the city. But it was quickly determined that this one was personal.

Arrested for killing Virginia Wolpert was Cincinnati *Enquirer* copy editor Eugene Fiske, a divorced father of three and the erstwhile fiancé of the victim. Wolpert had been beaten to death during Fiske's jealous rage over her seeing other men. Fiske claimed to have no memory of the vicious attack, telling detectives he merely "slapped her around a little bit to straighten her out."

Later that night an elderly woman in Winton Place was attacked by a suspect who threw some sort of liquid in her eyes, temporarily blinding her as he escaped with her purse.

At the other end of Ohio, Sam Sheppard was again on trial for the 1954 murder of his pregnant wife Marilyn. Freed from prison two years earlier after his conviction was thrown out, the Cleveland retrial had a deliberately subdued media presence this time.

Despite new forensic evidence from Paul Kirk suggesting a third person was in the house the night of the murder, Cuyahoga County was not ready to let Dr. Sam off the hook, even though he had already served ten years in prison.

However, hot shot attorney F. Lee Bailey was handling the Sheppard defense this time. His youthful flamboyance was sure to create some fireworks as Ohio's most infamous murder case was beginning its third act.

Bricca investigators had a spate of interviews scheduled for October 25th and 26th. Each was an unknown quantity, and the currents of hope and despair eddied about the murder room. Would they get a big break today? Or just spin their wheels again.

A woman suggested they check out Elmer Stevenson – he had been "visiting" her for ten years, and she was scared of him. She claimed he had a bad temper, and would get close to people through their pets or kids. He turned out to be a harmless resident who liked to hang out at Western Bowl.

The former principal of Oak Hills High told Nehrer that he knew Fred Leininger through the school's athletic association. Despite others claiming they were close friends, Edward Kulstad insisted he knew nothing of the doctor's personal life. He'd known him for eight years, and saw him mostly at football games. Kulstad said Leininger was "a fine community man and dedicated civic leader."

As they left the interview, Ernie Nehrer wondered just how honest this man was being.

They went to the Harrison Elementary to speak with teacher Mary May, supposedly a close friend of Linda Bricca. Yet Mary barely knew her. Her husband was transferred to the Cincinnati Monsanto plant in January, but didn't know Jerry. For Mary, Linda was a casual acquaintance from the Monsanto Wives Club.

Swinging back by Greenway Avenue, they talked with Janet and George Ditullio, who lived across the street and two doors south of the crime scene. On the night in question they were attending a birthday party at the Burris residence. Around 8:50 PM George walked across the street to flip on his porch light and put his garbage cans out. Janet left the party moments before 9 PM.

Both were outside and within close visual distance of the Bricca house at the crucial time period – the killers were possibly watching the house or arriving during these minutes. Nehrer learned forward, waiting for the spark.

They had noticed Jerry's car parked in front of the house, yet neither one saw any strange autos or suspicious people nearby. The rain swept street was silent and barren...

Steve Saunders was a 19-year-old who had worked part time for Fred Leininger the last five summers, mostly as an animal handler and cage cleaner. Dr. Herman Rehder had suggested detectives should interview him, because Rehder thought the young man was "strange" and called him "a Norman Bates type" – an odd comment from someone with a troubled psychiatric history like Rehder.

Amazingly, Steve didn't recognize the picture of Linda Bricca, and claimed he never saw her at GAH. He knew nothing about the rabbit on Skipper Ryle's show, but said "the Doc and Skipper are good friends." Saunders denied Leininger was "a nervous type", insisting he was "a wonderful person and a family man."

On Wednesday the 26th, Taylor and Nagel interviewed Dr. Albert Weyman concerning his brother. Edward Weyman lived around the corner from the Bricca house, and they got a tip he had committed himself to a psychiatric ward 15 years earlier. But Doctor Weyman attributed his brother's nervous breakdown to the stress of leaving medical school, and assured them that Edward was released after six months and had no problems since.

Next stop was the Weyman home, where they followed up with Gloria Weyman about her "weird" neighbor. They didn't inform her they had just checked out her husband Edward.

She told them the neighbor used to watch her husband when he was mowing their lawn, changing positions to keep an eye on him. And he often waved his arms at people walking by for no reason.

"How often did you see Linda Bricca?"

"Frequently. She seemed to have all her work done by 10 AM and would come around for coffee."

"Did you see her much this year?"

"Not since spring. Ever since Jerry bought her that car."

October 26th – 30th

At 7 PM Wednesday night, babysitter Linda Zeff sat down for her first interview with Nehrer and Hall – 29 days after the Briccas were found murdered.

The 18-year-old was too distraught after being present when the bodies were discovered on September 27th. She'd seen her friend Linda's beloved dogs locked in the TV room lying in a stupor – and she had smelled death fanning out their front door. So they gently questioned the young woman who was perhaps the closest non-relative to the Bricca family.

Linda Zeff had been babysitting for them about three years. She was especially close to Linda Bricca – they were "like sisters" and she often went to their home just to talk to the older woman. And Jerry had been "a huge help" when she struggled with high school math. She mostly sat in the evenings, when the couple went out together for dinners or shows.

Linda Zeff mentioned that among the books Linda Bricca gave her was one about doctors.

"Why did she give you that book?"

"My boyfriend at the time was planning to be a veterinarian."

Nehrer perked up. "What did she think about that?"

"We talked about it. She told me 'don't ever go out with doctors, because they are only out for one thing.'"

"Did she explain this comment?"

"She just said 'believe me because I know.'"

Zeff said Jerry and Linda went to some nice restaurants, shows, and stage plays around Cincinnati – one time they went to a fancy dinner party at the home of a Monsanto executive.

"Did they ever go to Western Bowl?"

"Well I did, and I never saw them there. They didn't seem interested in sports like that."

"Did Linda ever go swimming?"

"They joined Woodhaven this past summer, but I only saw her there a few times."

When asked about the last time she saw Linda Bricca alive, Linda Zeff paused to compose herself. Ernie Nehrer took a fatherly tone and coaxed her along. She'd last seen her about 4:30 PM on Thursday, September 22nd, after she relieved her mother from babysitting at the Bricca house.

"How did she seem to you?"

"She was in a hurry and said she'd talk to me later."

Nehrer checked his notes. "Now did she call your mother later?"

"Yes. She asked if either of us could babysit from 7-9 PM as she had to work for the doctor."

Nehrer glanced at Hall, knowing the GAH wasn't open on Thursday nights. "But neither of you could?"

Linda Zeff nodded and then looked away. She did not mention her mother being afraid of the Bricca house, about her saying that there was "*something evil in there.*"

"Do you know who babysat for her that night?"

"When I was driving by I saw a really young girl at their door. She maybe had freckles. I'm not sure who it was."

Linda Zeff saw a few strange cars near the Bricca home that week, including a white Cadillac and a red Chevy convertible. She mentioned her friend Susan Keller, another babysitter who also saw the red car. Nehrer made a note to have her interviewed.

Finally, they showed Linda pictures from inside the Bricca home and asked her if everything seemed in order. She stared at them in silence for several minutes, shocked speechless by the ransacking of the rooms. When she finally spoke, voice parched and cracking, it was about two things.

"The knife is missing from the buffet set."

Nehrer was puzzled. "Wasn't it kept hidden away from Debbie?"

"No. They always displayed it with the knife crossed over the fork on top of the buffet."

"So even a stranger could have seen it?"

Linda nodded, tearing up a little. "That dog leash on the couch bothers me."

"Why is that?"

"The chains were always kept in the kitchen hanging on the cupboard door." Linda Zeff began to cry. She already expressed her sorrow over the dead family earlier in the interview. Now she broke down. "Those dogs loved me. Someone else must have taken them for a walk that night."

Ernie Nehrer had a different idea. Someone used the dog chain to truss up Jerry Bricca...

OCTOBER WAS BLEEDING AWAY, having leached every last ounce of fear from Cincinnati residents. The slaughter of the Bricca family had jolted the suburbs, while the murders of Alice Hochhausler and Rose Winstel shocked the city. The massive law enforcement mobilization and discriminatory roundup of black men had set everyone's teeth on edge.

On the 28th Herb Vogel had a lengthy phone conversation with Sheriff William Joyce about their respective triple homicides. Robert Sims, his wife, and 12-year-old daughter had been slain in Tallahassee on Saturday night the 22nd. The Florida Sheriff's Bureau would eventually request information on the Bricca investigation as well, but no connection was ever established.

The same day Jake Schott announced that 15,000 cars similar to the cream and tan Chevy seen near the Hochhausler murder had been checked out with no success. "The search has proved fruitless," he admitted.

On the bright Sunday afternoon of October 30th, thousands of dejected trick or treaters made their rounds in costumes not meant for daylight. Adults pronounced it a "big success," and there was talk of making daytime Halloween permanent. From enhanced safety to increased visibility, what was not to like?

Most children accepted the move grudgingly – for our youngsters, ghosts and goblins would always play better under cover of night with a sinister moon overhead.

The Cincinnati *Post* interviewed Cleveland Police Chief Richard Wagner, who had watched the Strangler saga with great interest. He called our killer "a Jack the Ripper type who strikes without warning," and advised that "in a series of crimes like this ordinary police procedures break down." Wagner also evoked Cleveland's "Mad Butcher of Kingsbury Run" – a torso killer who dismembered at least twelve victims in the 1930's and was never caught.

Meanwhile, the public library reported an increase in patrons boning up on self-protection, with research topics like "What's the best watchdog?" (German shepherd) and "what kind of door lock is most effective?" (Dead bolt)

On a more positive note, annoying political campaigners and pesky door to door salesmen all but vanished. Residents were being cautious about who might be on the other side of the door.

Yet this was strikingly out of character. The Queen City was like your maiden aunt with all the cats. She had always depended on the kindness of strangers...

10-5: October 31st – November 1st

Bricca investigators saw a flurry of activity as the month ended. More than thirty days in, they were feeling the pressure.

Herb Vogel sent an inquiry to the New Jersey State Police about Edward Clark, a handsome man from Point Pleasant NJ who had allegedly spent some quality time with Linda Bricca during her Fort Lauderdale hiatus. Both Linda's grandmother and her friend "Petie" Evans phoned in tips about Clark, but the records check came back clean – Clark was an ex-cop and a solid citizen.

During the frenzied hours after the bodies were found on Tuesday, September 27th, deputies and constables canvassed along the north end of Greenway and Lawrence. Officers asked neighbors if they'd seen anything unusual near the Bricca house on Sunday night. If nothing came

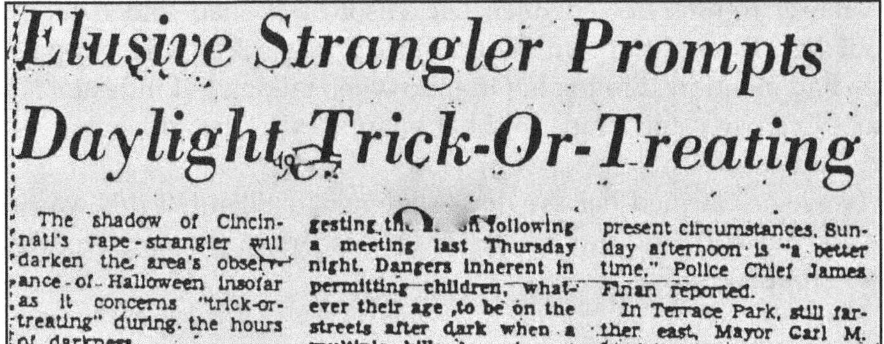

Elusive Strangler Prompts Daylight Trick-Or-Treating

The shadow of Cincinnati's rape-strangler will darken the area's observance of Halloween insofar as it concerns "trick-or-treating" during the hours of darkness.

gesting the [illegible] following a meeting last Thursday night. Dangers inherent in permitting children, whatever their age, to be on the streets after dark when a multiple-killer remains at

present circumstances, Sunday afternoon is "a better time," Police Chief James Finan reported.

In Terrace Park, still farther east, Mayor Carl M.

Concern that the Strangler might wear a mask to enter a house was one reason Halloween was moved to daytime.

to mind they were asked to recreate their activities that night and write down anything they remembered.

Yet most of these people lived 200-400 feet away from the crime scene, and only knew the victims to wave at them going by. On that rainy Sunday they had no reason to be watching for anything.

Jean Skinner had arrived home from her job at the Western Bowl Rodeo Room about 11:10 PM. She did not know the Briccas, and didn't see anything unusual on that end of Greenway.

Mrs. Gassner lived five houses away from the Briccas but never met them. On the murder night she was coming home from church around 11:30 PM and saw nothing curious in the area.

Pauline Hines lived 420 feet away and often said "Hi" to Linda Bricca. She saw Linda walking her dogs once in a while, but had never seen her in Western Bowl.

Oscar Martz walked his dachshund every night usually between 7:30-8 PM. He and his wife did their best to reconstruct the night in question – they were certain he walked the dog around 8 PM on Greenway up to Lawrence because he wanted to watch the movie. He did not see any strange cars or persons on north Greenway.

Ruth Hemmer lived five doors down from the crime scene and remembered her poodle acting strangely that night. She put the dog in their back yard at 10:30 PM and it began barking in a very excited tone, showing its teeth and looking in the direction of Bricca backyard. Ruth's visibility was poor because of the rain.

Nehrer re-interviewed Ellen Dickenson, who had told detectives about her conversation with Linda Bricca regarding wife swapping. Ellen had mentioned living in Orlando when talking to Linda at a New Year's Eve party and Linda told her about Key Clubs and swingers in Fort Lauderdale.

Now she clarified her previous statement – Ellen felt this was just idle conversation and did not believe Linda Bricca was involved with these groups.

THE FORMER OWNER OF the Executive Modeling Agency called Vogel about Linda Bricca's application. Joe Cella had taken it back on April 21st, 1965, and finally located it in his old files.

Vogel and Taylor studied their female victim distilled down to the black and white of physical dimensions and modeling potential:

- **Height:** **5'- 6-3/4"**
- **Weight:** **125 lbs.**
- **Bust:** **34**
- **Waist:** **24**
- **Hips:** **36**
- **Dress Size:** **10**
- **Hair:** **Brown**
- **Length:** **waist**
- **Eyes:** **Blue**
- **Complexion:** **Fair**

Under experience Cella wrote "modeled for photographer for five months while in high school. For Model Type he checked *Hands* but not *Feet, Facial* but not *Profile, Missus* but not *High Fashion,* and *Bathing Suit* but not *Cheesecake.* For Action he marked *Sophisticated,* but not *Vivacious,* and "*use for Publicity or Hostess.*"

Cella's remarks read "Pixy like face, nice personality. Could do something with her hair – it is very long. Not too much imagination but she has the will to work."

Vogel had to wonder. Did Linda really wish too model, or was she just looking for updated head shots for herself and Debbie? Then he stopped dead. There were three names listed as references. Dr. Mark Upson and Betty Meyer were the first two.

But it was the third name that jumped off the page: Dr. F. Leininger.

BABYSITTER SUSAN KELLER HAD a story to tell. The 19-year-old had recently married and was now working for a doctor's office. Detective Ernie Nehrer took her statement and later highlighted the number on the master sheet.

One encounter in April stood out for Susan, when she babysat most of the week for the family while alternating with Linda Zeff - Linda Bricca was attending the Shrine Circus every day.

On Saturday night Linda called home around 11 PM, telling her Jerry was due in on a plane but she couldn't pick him up. When he called Susan was to tell him to take a cab home.

"Did she say why she couldn't pick him up?"

"She was helping take down the tents and having car trouble."

"Who got home first, Jerry or Linda?"

"Jerry got home about midnight. I left about ten minutes later and saw Linda talking to a man parked on Greenway, who drove off when he saw me.

"Did Jerry see this?"

"Yes. He asked who it was and she said 'the man who started my car' and followed her home to see that she got there OK."

"How did Jerry react to this?"

"He seemed upset."

Susan hadn't received any strange phone calls while in their house, but she'd seen cars she couldn't recognize, like a red Chevy convertible and a white Cadillac parked in front of the Bricca home.

As the interview ended, Susan Keller gave Nehrer an incredulous look. "How could someone get into that house with those dogs? They were scary."

GERALD TAYLOR HAD A second interview with Cheryl Rehling, a 36-year-old housewife living on Hyacinth off Greenway. On September 29th she told detectives about seeing Linda Bricca in a car with a man the

Saturday before the murders. She described the car as light gray or green foreign car, and saw the same car parked in the Bricca driveway later that day.

Now Taylor was showing her a photo lineup – and Cheryl picked out the photo of Dr. Fred Leininger.

"Do you know this man?"

"No. But I'm certain he was the driver that day."

"How do you know it was Linda Bricca?"

"I met her at a cookout on Hyacinth last year. And then I saw her picture in the paper."

Without telling her who she'd identified, Taylor was ready to lock down her statement. "And you are certain this was the man you saw Linda Bricca with on Saturday September 24th around 1 PM?"

Cheryl didn't bat an eye. "Oh yes." She held the photo. "This is him. And I would tell him that face to face if you need me to."

November 2nd – 3rd

An 18-year-old student at Riverside City College in California was found brutally murdered on campus Halloween night. Cheri Jo Bates had been stalked, stabbed, and nearly decapitated while walking to her car after class.

Years later, San Francisco investigators would link her murder to the infamous Zodiac Killer, suggesting that Bates was his first victim. Zodiac would go on to kill anywhere from 7 (police tally) to 37 (Zodiac's boast) victims up until the mid-1970's. Although several good suspects were identified, including Arthur Leigh Allen, the crimes remain unsolved to this day.

And decades later, Zodiac would appear on a list of possible Bricca murder suspects.

Herb Vogel remained mum on the FBI lab report. He'd fenced with the media since October 20th, when he hinted about "unknown fingerprints" while suggesting Supreme Court rulings were hampering his investigation. Today he admitted the fingerprints "have yet to be identified."

There was also an FBI analysis on "an item connected with the case", but again he declined to specify. What they had found was traces of

Laminac resin from the piece of tape covering Jerry Bricca's face. Detective Hall had then gone to the American Cyanamid Company in Evendale to inquire about the uses of Laminac, and learned that Monsanto manufactured it for use in bows and arrows and other sporting goods equipment.

Vogel knew the unusual tape was their best piece of evidence. Tracing its origin just might lead them to their killer. Or killers...

ON GREENWAY AVENUE, MORE neighbors were being debriefed about the night of September 25th.

Elizabeth Kovac and Mary Anne Toerner lived slightly beyond a tenth of a mile from the crime scene, and both women were home watching the movie with their husbands. Both went to bed just after 11 PM, and neither heard anything unusual that night.

Betty Korty lived more than a football field away, but she and her husband had a nodding acquaintance with the Briccas. They had talked this over extensively – both were home that night and neither saw or heard anything.

None of these housewives knew anything about the Bricca family. Despite newspaper accounts calling the Woodhaven subdivision a "close-knit neighborhood," the street layout and merging of identical houses gave the area an impersonal feel. Next door and across the street neighbors usually knew each other, but beyond that in either direction stretched a grid of friendly strangers.

A persistent rumor that a former Bricca babysitter committed suicide after the murders was finally laid to rest. Not only had Yvonne Hays never sat for them, but she was alive and well, attending college in Kentucky.

Robert Schwartz was interviewed again, and Linda's dog groomer again confirmed she'd missed her appointment on 9/27/66 at the Windcrest Kennels. She had brought Dusty in for grooming five times between August 1964 and March 1966. Two employees of Schwartz were also checked out on this visit.

On November 2nd Vogel and Taylor had a second interview with Emmitt Baldwin, the Bricca neighbor to the north, regarding the man he saw walking up their driveway the night of the crime.

Baldwin could not positively identify him as Jerry, but he seemed certain the Bricca garbage cans were just put out and he assumed it was Jerry. Baldwin didn't recall seeing his car on the street.

He and his wife had discussed which window of the Bricca house was open that night, finally deciding it was the bathroom window. With their own bedroom just twenty feet from the Bricca bedroom, Baldwin said they heard a noise around 10:30 PM sounding like something falling.

But they were already in bed and he didn't investigate further.

ERNIE NEHRER WAS DOWNTOWN catching up with Joseph Zeff at his jewelry store. Zeff hadn't given a statement since the night the bodies were found, and seemed to be ducking detectives.

Discovering a multiple homicide where his daughter babysat had revived horrible memories of April 1961, when Joe Zeff found his sister Goldie and her husband James stabbed to death in their home in Price Hill **(Queen City Notorious Chapter 10)**.

He remembered taking a call from Betty Meyer asking if his daughter Linda had a key to the Bricca residence – she said something seemed to be wrong there. Within minutes he and Linda walked over to the Bricca house, meeting Richard Meyer and Dick Janszen standing out front.

"What did you do first?"

"Mr. Meyer, Linda and I walked around to the back. Linda became upset when she saw the dogs in the TV room."

"What did you and Meyer decide?"

"I suggested we try the front door to see if it was open."

"Where was Mr. Janszen at this time?"

"He was standing on the front sidewalk."

Zeff stated that Meyer opened the door slightly and called "Lin" three or four times, and then quickly shut the door "when he smelled the odor," and went to his house to call the police.

"Did you know the family at all?"

"Just Debbie from having her in our house. I wouldn't have known Jerry or Linda even if I'd seen them."

"How long did you stay?"

"Until the police came. I gave them a brief statement and then took my daughter home. She had become hysterical."

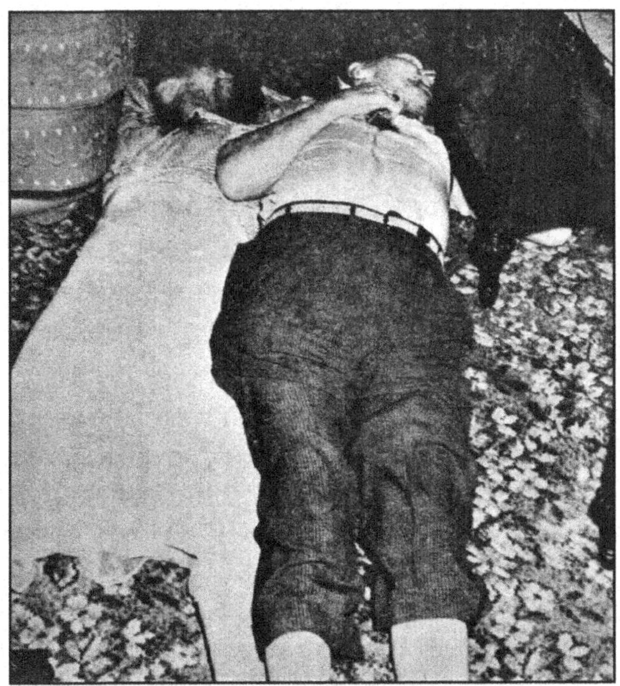

5-1/2 years before he discovered the murdered Bricca family, Joe Zeff had found his sister and brother-in-law slain.

THAT AFTERNOON A CINCINNATI *Post* "scoop" broke the Bricca case gridlock. A leak by a frustrated detective put Herb Vogel on the spot, and his denials became less convincing as rumors of a love triangle were again gusting through the investigation.

Bricca Family Slaying Probe Narrows to Single Slaying Suspect was splashed across the front page, leaving no doubt that County had zeroed in on a significant person of interest:

> **The hunt for the slayer of the Bricca family has narrowed to a single suspect.**
>
> **Investigators have refused to name a suspect, or admit they are even attempting to build a case around a specific person, but the *Post* has learned this is a fact.**

The suspect has employed an attorney to advise him. There is some indication investigators have not been able to get the suspect's fingerprints nor have they persuaded him to answer questions.

The long hours and intense investigation seems to have formed a noose of evidence which is slowly beginning to tighten around the neck of one man...

November 3rd – 7th, 1966

The prime suspect was not named.

Yet the onus landed on Fred Leininger from the moment Herb Vogel authorized his surveillance on October 10th. Leininger's evasive, contradictory answers in his October 8th interview had bumped him into the spotlight – a discrete, private spotlight.

Rumors about Leininger's involvement with Linda Bricca had been traveling along the Glenway corridor since shortly after the bodies were discovered. And a recent incident at a high school football game had exposed the doctor's predicament under the Friday night lights.

During the game, as Leininger moved around the home field bleachers, the detective shadowing him asked county deputies to move children and students away from their quarry. Witnesses would later describe an obvious, orchestrated movement of young spectators away from wherever Leininger happened to be standing.

From Vogel's perspective, they had a suspect with motive and without alibi whom they could place near the crime scene at zero hour. Their man claimed the last time he saw Linda Bricca was Wednesday evening at work, yet investigators could place him with her on Friday and Saturday as well.

On Thursday November 3rd Nehrer and Hall were back at Monsanto to interview Stan Drahman, a subcontractor who'd done work for Jerry Bricca.

They were following up on a "fight" the 54-year-old foreman for the Nagel Company supposedly had with Jerry over two of his workers slacking off . Drahman was upset that the detectives were still pestering

Bricca Family Slaying Probe Narrows to Single Suspect

One Bricca Suspect Remains, Police Admit

Hamilton County police admitted today that their investigation in the Bricca murder case centers on one man who has refused to answer any questions as reported in The Cincinnati Post and Times-Star Nov. 2.

When the story appeared in The Post, police refused to say they had a single suspect in mind.

LT. HERBERT VOGEL, who heads the sheriff's investigation, says the suspect has hired an attorney and now refuses to co-operate with police. Vogel already has had a 15-minute inter- [illegible]

man again that he refused to accept them.

There is some indication that the investigators have not been able to get the man's fingerprints to check against those found in the Bricca home.

Search for Fingerprint Evidence May Be Factor Delaying Move by Police

The hunt for the slayer of the Bricca family has narrowed to a single suspect.

Investigators have refused to name a suspect, or even to admit they are attempting to build a case around a specific persons, but The Post has learned this is the fact.

The suspect has employed an attorney to advise him.

There is some indication investigators have not been able to get the suspect's fingerprints nor have they been able to persuade him to answer questions.

Not all the fingerprints found in the Bricca home have been identified.

It is this inability to check fingerprints which apparently is keeping the investigation stalled at dead center for the time being.

THE PERSON around whom the investigation centers is white.

Investigators had said that they knew the slayer's blood type and that he was white.

Gerald Bricca, 28; his wife Linda, 23 and their daughter, Deborah, 4, were stabbed to death in their tri-level home at 3381 Greenway avenue, Bridgetown, apparently on the night of Sept. 25 or early Sept. 26.

THE CRIME that stunned the city was discovered at 10:45 p. m. Tuesday, Sept. 27. Two neighbor men, concerned because none of the family had been seen for several days, went to the Bricca home. The front door was unlocked. No one answered the door or responded to calls.

One of the men, trying to arouse the family, shined his flashlight through the half-open front door into a second-level bedroom. He saw what appeared to be a foot sticking through.

"Let's call the police," he said to his companion, backing out of the front door. "There's something wrong here."

County police found the bodies of Jerry and Linda Bricca on their bedroom floor. Jerry was wearing a dark brown, long-sleeve sport shirt, dark trousers and socks. He was not wearing any shoes.

Linda was clad in a pale blue negligee and a blue housecoat trimmed in gold. The unmade bed was spotted with caked blood. The bed covers were wrinkled. The pretty young mother, a former airline stewardess, had had intercourse. Police have been unable to determine whether she was raped.

DEBBIE WAS lying spread-eagle on her stomach on the floor of her bedroom next to her parents' room. A stuffed animal was about two feet from her outstretched right hand. She was wearing a terrycloth robe, panties and one red sock on her left foot. The covers on her bed were intact.

The silent killer made sure his victims would not survive. Reports from the Hamilton County coroner's office later revealed that Linda had been stabbed 19 times in the chest and neck, and Jerry four times in the back and three times in the neck. The slayer drove his knife through the body of Deborah four times as she lay [illegible]

In early November, the story broke that confirmed the Bricca investigation was focused on one man.

him about this – it was merely a work disagreement between him and Jerry pertaining to a project.

"When did this come to a head?"

"Friday the 16th on the overnight shift. Jerry told me he didn't like the way two of my pipe fitters were doing their work."

"What did you tell him?"

"Hey, I stood up for my guys. They had worked all day, and then Jerry came in after midnight to check up. It was close to 3 AM when we argued. My men and I were wiped out."

"How did you two resolve it?"

"When the shift was over Jerry and I went out for a cup of coffee. We patched it up. He even talked about his vacation in California."

"So you got along well with him after that?"

"Sure. This was just a work problem. Happens all the time. Jerry wanted it done one way and I told him it wasn't possible."

While at the plant, Nehrer tracked down two more workers who knew Jerry. Fred Flick was Jerry's age, lived only three blocks away, and would sometimes go swimming with him. Allan Nobel was a 31-year-old production supervisor who had twice socialized with Jerry and Linda. But neither man had anything to add.

Ernie Nehrer was talking to Dr. Mark Upson for the second time, because Linda's application to the Executive Modeling Agency had listed Upson as a personal reference.

The doctor was surprised – he knew nothing about her except treating her for excess body fluid – her last appointment was on May 13th. Upson insisted that she never made small talk with him.

Or so he said. That reference thing stuck in Nehrer's craw...

A CHECK OF FRED LEININGER'S high school records didn't turn over anything. He graduated from Cincinnati's Hughes High School in 1949 with good grades and attendance. There were no disciplinary notes – nor were any hobbies, clubs or sports mentioned.

On November 4th, Gerald Taylor was back at Glenway Animal Hospital to interview the young couple Fred Leininger hired the week before the murders. As he sat down with Valinda Westman, the doctor was noticeably out of the office.

"Did you work on Sunday September 25th?"

"No. We left at 8 AM that morning for northern Kentucky. Stephen preaches at a church there. We didn't get back until 7 PM.

"Did you see Dr. Leininger at the clinic when you returned?

"No, we did not."

Taylor asked if she ever talked to Linda on the phone. Valinda replied that Linda had called there on Friday morning the 23rd. "She said Debbie had left a book there and asked if the Doc could drop it off on his way home for lunch."

"And did he?"

"Yes. He was right there with the book when she called."

On Monday September 26th Leininger had asked them which day off they'd like during the week. Valinda thought this was odd, as she had already told him they had no preference.

"He suggested we take Wednesdays off."

"Did he say why?"

"He said he was going to train Mrs. Bricca to work there. He said she'd been after him to work there, and since she loved animals so much she could work on our day off."

On Monday November 7th, Gerald Taylor had a second interview with Robert Girten about his interaction with Leininger and Linda Bricca on that same Friday. For Taylor, Linda's call to the clinic that morning was a coded message for them to meet.

According to Girten, she showed up at the Archery Club on Muddy Creek Road around 1 PM.

"What was his demeanor like when she showed up?"

"There was very little conversation between them while I was there. It was like he was upset at first, and then bored that she wanted to watch us shoot."

"When you left, were they alone there?"

"Yes they were."

LATER THAT AFTERNOON, HERB Vogel received a large envelope from Coroner Cleveland's office. 41 days after the Bricca's were found murdered their morgue pictures were finally delivered.

These were stark, black and white images taken with a Speed Graphic, just like the crime scene photos. The victims were naked and pathetic, stripped of any vestige of life or humanity.

Even though he'd been dead for 60 hours, Jerry Bricca still looked physically imposing. The slow atrophy of his lifeless muscles contrasted harshly with his battered and contused face. Laying there on the slab his decaying body belied the strength still coiled within, the sinewy prowess that convinced Vogel one man alone could not have handled him.

Vogel glanced at the child and quickly looked away. Her nakedness was wretched and cruel, the blunt nature of murdered innocence. He had seen countless morgue photos, but this final image of little Debbie was obscene.

Linda's nude body did not escape his gaze. Was this once supple form what men were willing to cheat on their wives for – or kill for? The beauty of her past was now entombed within this husk. Still, almost three days after someone took her life, Linda's allure lingered like a silent echo.

The last photo caused Vogel to inhale sharply. It was a close-up of Linda, from her mid-section to the top of her head. Six knife thrusts had punctured her left breast in a crude circle, jagged, bloodless blemishes gouging her alabaster skin.

But it was her expression that would forever haunt him. Her eyes were half open, and her mouth was frozen into a scowl of pain. Or was it a smirk of recognition?

Go ahead, you gutless coward, Linda Bricca seemed to be hissing. *I knew you would do something like this...*

November 8th – 14th

Cincinnati Police had been craving one solid lead in the Strangler investigation after the Hochhausler and Winstel murders in October. Instead, the new month brought more false alarms.

A known predator named Eddie Phelps, who left Cincinnati the day after the Hochhausler slaying, was picked up in Indianapolis and grilled. They also looked at a former morgue attendant who had been discharged for molesting bodies in 1956.

A former convict refused to talk to police. Jake Schott said he'd been paroled in 1952 after serving 24 years for murder, and "clammed up because he was familiar with his constitutional rights".

On Tuesday the 8th twenty cops rushed to the scene of an attack on a 58-year-old woman. Mrs. Ruby Gore, a housekeeper for a residence in Elmhurst Place, was returning with groceries around 7:45 PM when she was accosted on the driveway.

"Hey, you remember me, don't you," a man called out. Then he moved toward her carrying a cord, and she started screaming. As several neighbors emerged from their houses, the stranger bolted – responding officers found a 15" length of rope in the street.

Ruby Gore was badly shaken up, and in the evening dusk her description was vague. "All she could remember was that he was very soft spoken and wore light clothing," a police sergeant told reporters. "The poor woman wasn't even sure whether he was a white man or a light–skinned colored man."

Elmhurst Place was an upper class East Side neighborhood, just a few blocks south of Grandin Road in Hyde Park, one of Cincinnati's most elite addresses. Violent crime was rare here, one notable exception being the 1956 unsolved murder of socialite Audrey Pugh **(Queen City Gothic Chapter 7)**.

As detectives investigated the incident, they became convinced this "frightener" was not their killer. The ritzy eastern location was not the Strangler's comfort zone.

On Wednesday morning two more distress calls went out. A Mt. Auburn housewife called police when a man "posing" as a Cincinnati Gas and Electric Company meter reader tried to enter her home. She said he "fled" after she called the utility company. It turned out he was a legitimate CGE employee, and instead of fleeing he'd just gone to his next stop.

An hour later police went speeding to Price Hill when a 75-year-old woman was found dead in her apartment. Had the Strangler struck again? Fears subsided when Elizabeth Gastenveld was promptly determined to have died of natural causes...

HERB VOGEL STAYED TIGHT lipped about his prime suspect, even as they were drilling deep into the life of Dr. Fred Leininger.

Gerald Taylor had already driven to Ohio State Vet School, but only came away with copies of Leininger's grades. And the secretary of the Northside Presbyterian Church confirmed that Leininger was married there in June 1952 and left the church in 1965 to join the Zion Evangelical Church near his home.

Janet Hyde had attended Hughes High School two years behind Leininger – her husband Charles was in the same class with "Fritz". She said Leininger had dated Lynn Nadine Rau all through high school, and never went with any other girls before their marriage. Janet hadn't socialized with the Leiningers since New Year's Eve, and admitted she didn't know them well.

Sylvester Kemper grew up next door to Leininger in Northside, and attended grade school with him. Kemper told detectives Leininger "always had strong feelings for any type of animal."

Most of this was routine. But a 72-year-old veterinarian gave them a glimpse of the inner Fred Leininger.

Dr. Carl Pleuger was listed as a reference for Leininger on his Ohio State Veterinary School application. Pleuger was still an active vet, who met Leininger in 1950 when he asked for the reference. As a result of the letter Leininger was admitted, but Pleuger hadn't seen him for 16 years.

When Ernie Nehrer asked him about Dr. Herman Rehder, the discussion intensified. Nehrer's pen started moving.

"When did you last speak to Dr. Rehder?"

"A couple of times last week. He said the police had been talking to him about Dr. Leininger."

"What did he say about that?"

"He wondered 'what the deal was' with Dr. Leininger. Apparently some drug salesman told him Leininger had a drinking problem."

"Did he tell Rehder anything more about this?

"Just that Dr. Leininger used to drink a lot of Vodka, and the salesman was wondering if he had overcome his problem."

Nehrer got a tour of Pleuger's operating room and he obtained a sample of veterinary tape to compare with the piece used to gag Jerry Bricca. Then he asked the doctor what drugs he would use to render an animal unconscious.

"Most of them have a phenobarbital base."

"Would these drugs leave a trace in the animal's bloodstream?"

"Definitely. But I have at least ten others that wouldn't."

Nehrer leaned in. "How long would it take to put out a small to medium size dog by injection?"

"No longer than fifteen seconds."

On November 12th, a story broke that would momentarily distract Queen City residents from their troubles.

The nation was still reeling from the crimes of Richard Speck and Charles Whitman that summer. Now, inspired by the media coverage of those unparalleled mass killings, an 18-year-old youth strolled into the Rose-Mar College of Beauty in Mesa, Arizona on that Saturday morning with a deadly purpose.

He forced five women and two children to lie down with their heads together like spokes in a wheel, and then calmly shot each one execution style.

A laughing Robert Benjamin Smith told the first policemen to arrive, "I shot some people. They're back there." The handsome, slightly

High school student Robert Smith was inspired by the crimes of Speck and Whitman to go on his own rampage.

built high school senior smiled as officers discovered the carnage – four women and a 3-year-old girl lay dead.

Another woman and a three-month-old baby were badly wounded but would survive. Told by one of his victims that 40 more people would arrive at the school shortly, Smith had replied "I'm sorry, but I didn't bring enough ammunition for them" and started shooting. After he shot Bonita Sue Harris, she pretended to be dead until the police arrived.

Voicing no remorse, Smith admitted that he'd felt "exhilarated" during the killings. He was described as "a kid that nobody knew" – until November 12th 1966.

At his trial Smith would be portrayed as a studious sociopath who surrendered to the violent fantasies lurking beneath his bland exterior. He considered killing the teachers at his high school, but decided instead on Rose-Mar as his target. Convicted in October 1967 and sentenced to death, Smith was given five life terms after the Supreme Court declared a death penalty moratorium in 1972.

Smith remains behind bars today, but the Rose-Mar massacre is largely forgotten. His 15 minutes of infamy were mercifully fleeting.

So how did this socially inept oddball become a mass murderer? "I wanted to make a name for myself," Robert Smith told police after his arrest. "I wanted people to know who I was..."

November 15th – 21st

Briccas' Neighbor Cleared By Police...Would Question 'Certain' Man. The *Enquirer* front page headline on November 15th spilled the secret the West Side already knew – the County had been shadowing their prime suspect since early October.

Neighbor Richard Meyer was finally cleared, even though he was never a serious suspect. The poor man had found his neighbors butchered, only to have crackpots besiege him with crank calls at his job and at home.

> **At the same time they acknowledged publically for the first time that there is one man they wish to question further. They did not identify him but said they have been unable to question him because he is "hiding behind his attorney..."**

Vogel admitted they had two interviews with the man – the first one a routine check of Bricca family background. But during a taped session at the man's workplace, he became flustered and was evasive about his relationship with Linda Bricca.

"I called the man and he verified he had hired a lawyer, "Vogel told the *Enquirer.* "I called the attorney, Richard Morr, but Mr. Morr stipulated certain conditions we had to meet before we could talk to his client that we could not accept."

In this article, Linda Bricca was described as "a housewife who worked September 19th through 21st as a temporary receptionist for Dr. Fred Leininger at the Glenway Animal Hospital."

The *Post* ran a similar article – **One Bricca Suspect Remains Police Admit** – reminding everyone THEY broke this story back on November 2nd with their "scoop" about the uncooperative suspect.

Investigators were staring at a hard truth – Linda had known Leininger for almost three years, but was murdered only AFTER she went to work for him. Had she stumbled upon some malfeasance at the clinic?

Would Question 'Certain' Man

Briccas' Neighbor Cleared By Police

Eight weeks after the Briccas were murdered, County admitted their investigation had narrowed to an unidentified suspect.

The inclusion of Leininger's name in an article about the unnamed prime suspect was either a veiled threat or honest exasperation. It aroused the whispers along the West Side.

Residents finally had a name to latch onto...

ON NOVEMBER 16TH DR. Samuel Sheppard finally heard the words "Not Guilty"! Convicted for killing his wife in 1954, in the 1966 retrial F. Lee Bailey won his acquittal by demolishing the forensic evidence that incriminated the doctor in the first trial.

Sheppard walked out a free yet broken man, his once promising life haunted by a scandalous murder.

Dr. Sam's nightmare began in the early morning hours of July 4th 1954, when 31-year-old Marilyn Sheppard was found bludgeoned to death in the bedroom of their Bay Village, Ohio home. The killer struck her 35 times with an unknown weapon, overkill that alluded to a crime of passion. An injured Sheppard told a disoriented story about grappling with a tall, bushy-haired intruder before being knocked unconscious, and he quickly became the prime suspect.

The Sheppard trial that fall was a national fixation, replete with sex, money, intrigue, and a pregnant, attractive victim. Three Cleveland newspapers titillated readers with gory details and rumors about Dr. Sam's infidelity. He was convicted of 2nd degree murder and sentenced to life in prison.

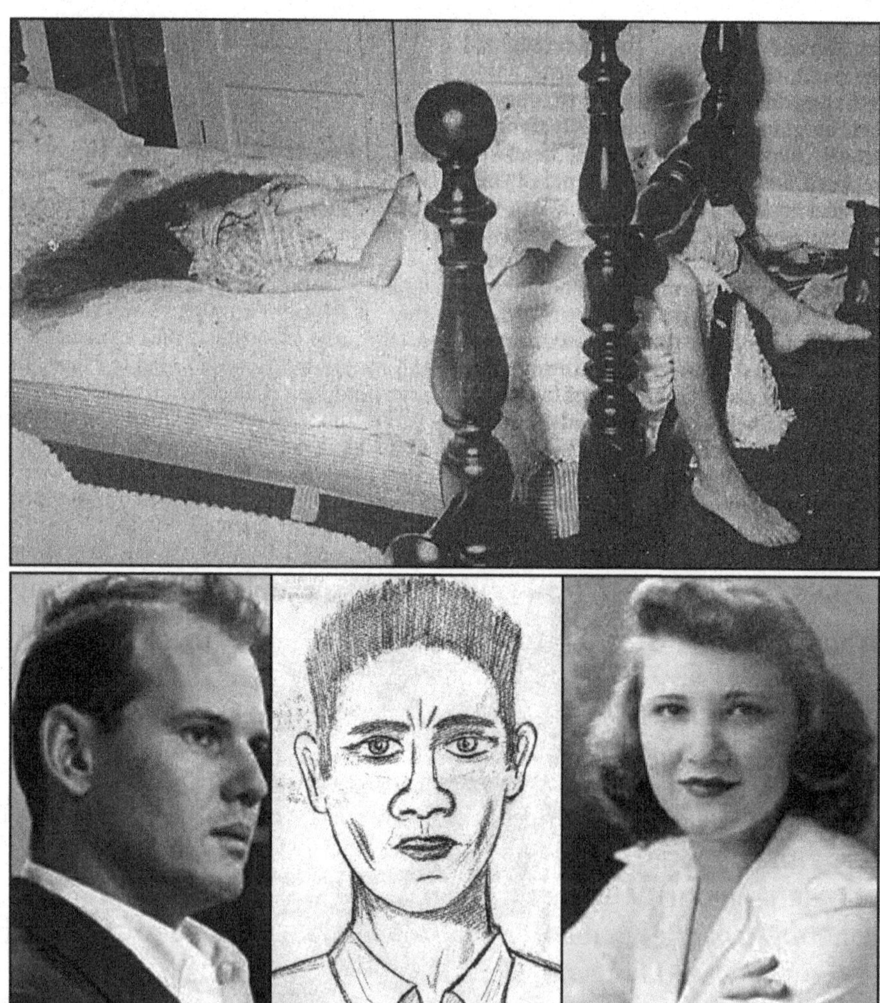

Sheppard said when his wife's screams awakened him he hurried up the stairs and was attacked by a tall, bushy haired intruder.

When Sheppard's lawyers were finally given access to the murder house, they engaged Dr. Paul Kirk, the father of modern blood spatter analysis, to inspect the crime scene. Kirk's stunning conclusion – the blood trail leading from the murder room, always assumed to be the victim's blood dripping from the weapon, was actually the killer's blood oozing from an open wound where Marilyn had bit him!

Sam Sheppard had no open wounds, and Kirk's new protocol for "blood grouping" did not match either him or his wife, proving that a third person bled at the murder scene that night.

In the 1990's, new DNA tests on this blood would eliminate Sam but point the finger at Sheppard window washer Richard Eberling, a convicted murderer suspected in the deaths of at least five women. That DNA profile did NOT exclude Eberling, a tall man known to wear bushy wigs, matching the description of a man seen by two witnesses near the Sheppard house the night of the murder.

These developments were too late to save Dr. Sam – never really exonerated in the public's eyes. He died in 1970 at age 46, a hopeless alcoholic claiming his innocence to the very end.

At 7 PM on the 16th, 18-year-old Linda Pierson left her Dayton, KY home to visit a girlfriend. A pretty high school dropout described as "a happy-go-lucky girl", Linda did not return home that night. Her partly nude body was found next morning in a wooded "lover's lane" near the river. She'd been raped and strangled.

Dayton is directly across the Ohio River from Walnut Hills, the scene of one murder and several attempts. Yet Campbell County officials declined to link the Pierson murder to the Strangler.

On November 19th, 12-year-old Frances Voils was found dead behind the high school in Nitro, West Virginia. She had been stabbed more than 50 times, but wasn't sexually assaulted. When police arrested Lennis Angel for the crime, they immediately sent his information to Herb Vogel. Angel was employed as a laborer at the Monsanto plant in Nitro, Jerry Bricca's destination for that ill-fated September 26th business trip.

It was a coincidence Vogel had to pursue, but no link to the Bricca murders was ever established.

Gerald Taylor obtained a program for the Shrine Circus held April 11th thru 16th at the Cincinnati Gardens, after several people claimed they saw Linda Bricca helping with the animals. A list was made of all Garden's employees working the circus.

Taylor interviewed Barney Rapp, whose agency booked Shrine's animal acts. Among those appearing were the Erik Adams Chimps, Tony Dianos Elephants, and Joe Frisco's Performing Wild Animals. All of their employees would be checked out as well.

Rapp didn't recognize a picture of Linda, but referred them to the liaison to the animal acts. Bob Allen remembered seeing her at the circus near where the trailers were parked, and said he'd try to determine which acts she was working for.

Charley Nagel followed up a tip that Linda brought an animal trainer home to dinner in October of 1964. Western Hills Plaza had booked the Hagen-Wallace Circus of Levittown PA that month. But the Plaza card file had no further information about them.

Taylor had another interview with Dick Janszen on the 15th. Janszen had been deeply affected by discovering and seeing the bodies. He repeated that he the last saw Jerry on Sunday morning as he came back from church. Janszen confirmed Jerry was wearing the same clothes he would be found in two nights later.

Taylor wanted a longer interview, but one look at Richard Janszen's haunted expression was enough. Sheer evil had come to dinner right across the street from his home and family.

And now his life was an evolving nightmare...

November 21st – December 5th

On Monday night November 21st the Strangler squad arrived at the scene of a fresh attack. A 55-year-old housewife had been dragged into a mud hole, beaten and then raped at a construction site near Reading Road and Elsinore Place.

The victim was walking home around 6:30 PM when a slender black man approached and spoke to her, but he seemed drunk so she walked across the street to tell a resident she was being followed. The man disappeared down the street, but grabbed her on the next block, punching her and pushing her into the excavation. He raped her, rifled her purse and then fled.

Responding officers confronted a familiar scenario – a woman walking in the Walnut Hills area attacked by a black man who asked her for directions.

On November 23rd Gerald Taylor interviewed Walter Burton, who took the portrait photos of Linda and Debbie in April 1965. Burton said it was his only contact with her, and he gave Taylor copies of all the photos he took that day.

Swede Johnson, nicknamed "Hunkie", dropped into the Bricca case a few days later via Bob Allen. Johnson, of Punta Gorda Florida, owned some animals that Linda was seen visiting at the Shrine Circus. Herb Vogel contacted the Florida State Sheriff's Bureau with a request for information on Johnson.

Either through her association with straying veterinarians or itinerant trainers, Vogel still felt that Linda Bricca's obsessive love for animals had led to the savage murder of her family.

The City Crime Study Committee ended its hearings on November 15th with few recommendations despite two recent Strangler murders. An *Enquirer* editorial called for stronger action: "Now the public probe is over. But still helpless, still waiting is a citizenry shocked by gruesome events."

Early parole for sex offenders had been evaluated by the committee and was a hot topic. Several rape victims told *Enquirer* crime reporter Margaret Josten that the Strangler "might be what is needed to wake up Ohio. You won't be able to find a single woman not in favor of keeping these men in prison."

Josten cited studies showing incarceration and treatment of sex offenders was not effective, quoting former prosecutor Carson Hoy, who wrote these scathing words in 1949:

> **They are almost certain to continue their criminal conduct, and since incarceration usually makes them worse, the release of such offenders is exactly the same as loosing a mad dog on the streets...**

Prosecutor Mel Rueger insisted that "today's sex-oriented advertising and entertainment" encouraged sex crimes, along with the "more permissive attitudes" of the 1960s. Most psychiatrists disagreed, arguing that rapists usually suffered from a hatred of women that was rooted in their childhood experiences.

The Strangler was skewing the crime rate – in a good way. Crime in Cincinnati plunged by 17.3% during the month of October, for no other reason than more police were on the streets.

On November 25th the Enquirer ran a feature headlined **Remember the Coby Case?** It was the second anniversary of the murders of Dennis and Evelyn Coby, whose bullet riddled bodies were found slumped in the back seat of their station wagon on Thanksgiving Eve of 1964 **(Queen City Gothic Chapter 9)**.

The Coby murders had become an unfathomable puzzle after two scant years. Not only were investigators baffled by the "who" and the "why", but the "when and where" were also a mystery.

A famine of clues and witnesses doomed this case from the get go. 53 years later, the Coby's killer remains at large...

THE PROBE INTO THE rape-murder of Linda Pierson was withering.

She was strangled and dumped in Dayton, KY near the Ohio River the morning of November 17th. Over 70 people had been interviewed, and polygraphs were given to four young men. Despite an arduous investigation, Pierson's killer was never caught.

The *Enquirer* acknowledged another grim anniversary on December 2nd. **Strangler Began Crimes Here One Year Ago** headlined a feature detailing six murders that began with the slaying of Emogene Harrington in Walnut Hills.

"We are looking for him, but to be honest, we don't have any good leads right now," said Jake Schott. In response to experts trying to predict when the Strangler would kill again, including one who believed his timing was linked to phases of the moon, Schott wearily explained that "he could strike at any time. There is no reason to believe he works according to any schedule."

A letter to the editor that same day described the irony of a city coming together while living in fear. The writer marveled at how Cincinnati was now "a brighter place to live...porch lights, yard lanterns, garage lamps, and house lights are ablaze throughout every neighborhood." But these homes were not extending a warm invitation – it was a safety precaution "against a year-long disease of Cincinnati society known as the Strangler."

The writer noted how "the fear of involvement has been abandoned" as residents were uniting in a "collective strength" and eschewing the politics of racial fear.

> **It is unfortunate that a series of murders must awaken the conscience of a community. But when the disease is finally cured and our city is once again at ease, the neighborhood lights will still be burning... this time as a symbol of warmth and invitation.**

How could this happen in our demure, bashful city of Cincinnati?

Each night the darkness approached, casting fear and friction across the city. And winter was impending, her icy fingers ready to freeze the horrors of our relentless imaginations...

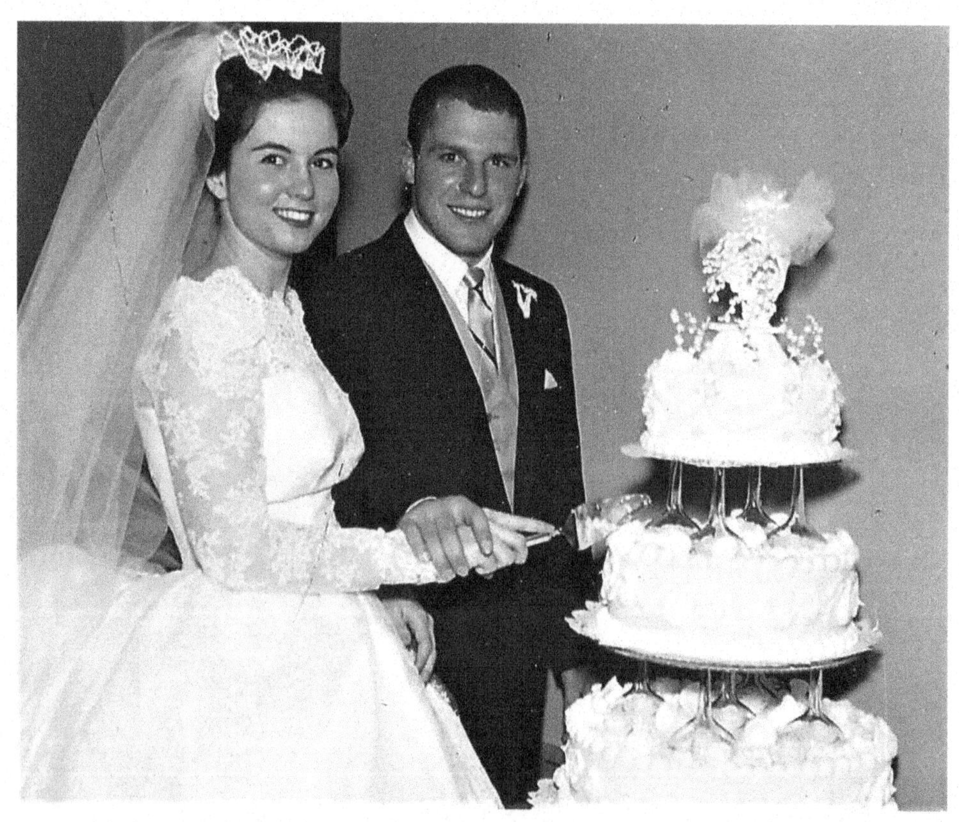

Linda and Jerry cut the cake as they embark on their new life together.

CHAPTER ELEVEN

HALFWAY TO HEAVEN

Man kills without ceasing, to nourish himself; but since in addition he needs to kill for pleasure, he has invented the chase..."

Guy DE Maupassant

DECEMBER 6TH, 1966 – FEBRUARY 2ND, 1967

December 6th – 9th

Gerald Taylor was on the West Coast.

Herb Vogel's top detective flew out on December 6th to interview relatives and friends of Jerry Bricca in San Francisco. Taylor focused on their recent trip for the wedding of Jerry's sister.

He first interviewed Jerry's father in his office. Dr. Elmer C. Bricca asked for a private meeting before Taylor saw the rest of his family. He was a respected Bay Area physician, and deftly balanced his cooperation with his privacy.

He admitted that Linda was pregnant when Jerry married her. "Jerry flew down from Seattle and told me she was expecting and they were going to be married."

"Did he say anything about being pressured to do it?"

"Never. He insisted he loved Linda and wanted to marry her. She had not pressured him in any way."

"Was he certain it was his child?"

"She told him he was the father but marriage wasn't necessary."

Dr. Bricca felt they had a happy union, and any difficulties were just normal growing pains of a young couple.

"Did Jerry ever complain about her?"

"He accepted her. My son did not like to argue and would go out of his way to avoid unpleasant situations."

"Do you know of anyone who held a grudge or would wish to harm them?"

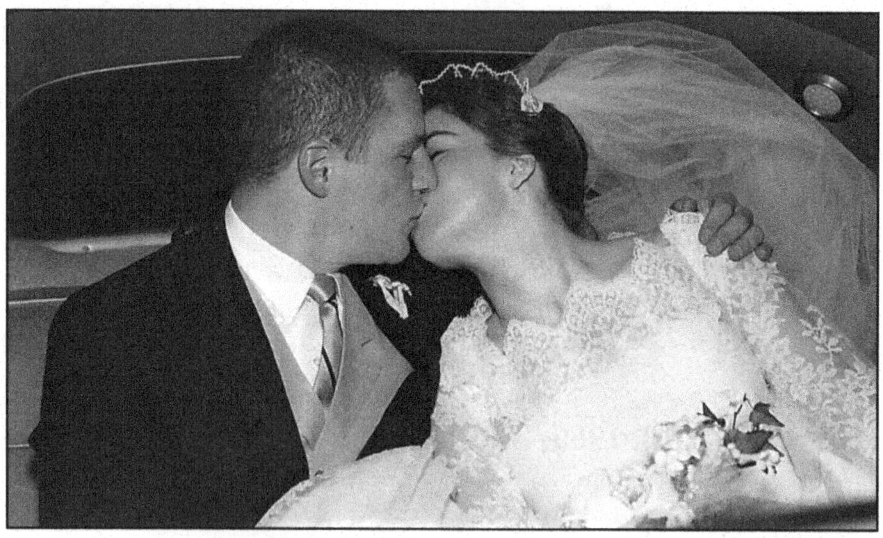

Dr. Elmer Bricca was certain that Linda didn't force his son into marriage even though she was pregnant.

"Certainly no one out here."

When Taylor was done, the Doctor asked him a pointed question. "Did the coroner's report show that Linda was pregnant?"

"Why do you ask?"

"Well, Linda blurted out to me that she might be pregnant, and was planning to see a doctor when they returned to Cincinnati."

"Did she seem concerned about it?"

"No. She told me they had decided to have another child and they'd been trying to conceive."

Later that day, Taylor spoke with Jack Liljeberg at the Standard Oil San Francisco branch. The Engineering VP interviewed had Jerry Bricca for a job in early September just before he returned to Cincinnati. Jerry told him that he wanted to move away from Cincinnati and return to his hometown.

Liljeberg said Standard Oil was impressed with Jerry and had drawn up an offer of employment beginning in October.

But three weeks later they heard about the murders...

TAYLOR HAD A FULL slate of interviews on December 7th, starting with Jerry's cousin and her mother.

Mrs. Marian Milani said Jerry, Linda and Debbie stayed at her house for three days when there was no more room at Dr. Bricca's house. She rarely saw them – they left early each morning and came back late in the evening. She got the impression Linda was upset about staying at her house and was bitter towards Dr. Bricca.

Marilyn Norton was the same age as Jerry, and they were very close before he left San Francisco. Other than her love for animals, she knew little about Linda – yet Marilyn's genuine affection for Jerry had her looking sideways at his wife.

"Was Jerry letting Linda push him around?"

"She took advantage of his personality. He wasn't confrontational – he'd rather side-step a problem than talk about it. For Linda, it was easier to ask forgiveness than permission."

"Did Jerry ever confide to you about any marital troubles?"

"He would never do that. But she seemed to be putting on an act that they were extremely happy."

"Would you know if either of them had been running around?"

"Probably not. But if one was my money would be on her."

Taylor next drove to Sunnyvale to interview George and Joyce Fox, who had hosted Linda and Jerry for dinner at their house – both men had graduated from Stanford in 1960.

Joyce met Jerry's wife previously. She felt Linda was withdrawn or shy and didn't mix easily with the group. Linda did tell her she was feeling better and was physically ready to have another child.

"Did she tell you she might be pregnant?"

"She didn't mention it. But she and Jerry wanted to return to San Francisco because they did not like Cincinnati."

"Did they say why?"

"Linda didn't like her neighborhood because the people were older and she had nothing in common with them."

George said the men traded college stories most of the evening. He saw no bickering between Jerry and Linda.

"Did she talk about animals or animal acts she'd seen?"

"She mentioned her dogs, and said they had a 'very good' veterinarian in Cincinnati." He also felt Linda seemed inhibited about talking much with people she didn't know.

"Did she and Jerry seem happy?"

"On the surface. But I tend to compare other married couples with my wife and me. They were not as happy as they tried to make other people believe."

FOR HIS LAST STOP that day, Gerald Taylor returned to Dr. Bricca's home to interview the rest of the family. Present were Elmer's wife Dolores, son Robert with wife Karen, and son Elmer Jr. Taylor sensed they had a private discussion about Jerry and Linda sometime after his interview with the doctor.

They agreed the only problems on this trip were between Linda and her father-in-law. Linda stalked out of the room during dinner after he refused to let Debbie speak at the table. She had expected everyone to listen, yet Dr. Bricca said at his table children would only speak when spoken to.

Dolores Bricca mentioned the argument about the hunting lodge. "Jerry always went hunting with Elmer and his brothers when he was visiting. But this time he balked at going because of Linda."

"What did she say?"

"That she didn't want to see animals hurt, especially by Jerry."

Dr. Bricca spoke up. "I told Jerry the caretaker of the lodge would be offended if he didn't see him on this trip – he'd known Jerry since he was a boy. I reminded him this was a family tradition. So I asked Linda if we could compromise on this one."

"What did she say?"

"She thought about it, and finally agreed Jerry could go. Since she wasn't going it would not hurt her."

They all thought Linda and Jerry were happy, but to Taylor it sounded rehearsed. The family admitted they knew very little about their married life in Cincinnati.

"Did you know about any sexual problems they may have had?"

"I know his medication created some issues," Robert Bricca replied. "But he didn't go into details about it."

"Do you know of anyone he would have confided in?"

"If Jerry did talk to anyone it would be George Fox." Taylor frowned. He spoke with Fox earlier that day but gained little insight.

None of them knew how Jerry and Linda had first met in Seattle. But they all agreed that Linda did NOT force Jerry into marriage.

Jerry's younger siblings (left) attended the wedding along with his parents Dr. and Mrs. Elmer Bricca (right).

"Did Linda say anything about being pregnant now?

"She mentioned it to me and Karen," Dolores replied. "She seemed happy about it."

"She told me she missed a period," Karen added. "But she said this was not the first time she'd had a false alarm."

"Did she say they'd been trying for another child?"

"Yes. Apparently she and Jerry had discussed it."

Again Taylor was perplexed, remembering interviews with Greenway neighbors who claimed Linda was adamant about not having a second child. "How did she act with Debbie on this trip?"

"Like a devoted mother," Karen smiled. "Showering her with love and affection.

Taylor blinked – this wasn't adding up. "Did either of them express a desire to leave Cincinnati?

Jerry's mother beamed. "Both Jerry and Linda told me they wanted to move back to San Francisco.

That night Taylor flew to Seattle. Next on the schedule were Jerry's co-workers and friends when he worked there for Monsanto. While on the plane he reviewed his San Francisco notes.

There was no indication that the murders were motivated by revenge toward the family. Yet his female victim had gotten some tough reviews. Maybe Linda was indeed "Hell on Wheels".

Or perhaps she was just a bored housewife who strayed one time – with the wrong guy...

Friday, December 9th

She felt his eyes all over her.

The black guy's stare cast a shiver down her spine. The young woman was leaving work at 12:30 AM, the Kenner Building towering behind her. He was sitting in a car at the corner of Ninth and Sycamore in downtown Cincinnati.

You had to deal with that down here. Long brown hair framing attractive, strong features made Sandra Chapas a favorite target of men. Lighting a cigarette, she hurried down the wide city sidewalk, coat open to the crisp December night. It was a two block jaunt to her apartment on Court Street – soon she would be safe at home. Besides, he was probably just picking up one of the black girls who worked on second shift.

But these days in Cincinnati, two darkened, deserted city blocks could be a long walk for a woman alone.

She glanced back. His car had pulled into the street and was crawling along about twenty feet behind her. Quickening her pace, she turned her head to watch him. Sandra knew cars – this one looked like a late 50's Chevy, a cream and something two-tone.

Anxiety heightened. They were saying "the Strangler was a Negro who drove a two-tone car." She looked back at Kenner but others leaving the shift had quickly dispersed.

Sandra tried to hush her racing thoughts. This was downtown and she was 22. Wrong place and age for the Strangler. Must be some guy who got shut out at the bars.

Still, for no logical reason she decided to react. A woman's instinct told her this one was bad news.

With a short block to go she bolted. Gasping the cold night air, she staggered into the doorway of her apartment building.

The man lurched the car into the curb and was coming after her. She pounded up the stairs to her 3rd floor flat, hearing him on the steps

Police got their big break when Sandra Chapas was chased into her building by a man who resembled the Strangler.

below. Terrified now, she fumbled for the keys as his urgent breathing filled the dank, narrow stairwell. Finally stabbing the key in the lock, Sandra Chapas just had to turn around and look.

He was right there. A short, dark man crouched just below the landing, reeking of alcohol and sweat. He was fondling his crotch and panting like a dog.

Their eyes locked, and in that indelible moment he became the bogeyman of her childhood, reaching out to grab her...

FOR 14 MONTHS THE Queen City had been living in the shadow of the Strangler. Ever since the attack on Elizabeth Kreco in October 1965, the sketchy description of the short, slightly built black man haunted Cincinnati police and left them hungering for one good tip.

With the Sandra Chapas incident, they got it.

Upon being spotted, the man chasing her vaulted down the stairs, nearly knocking down the husband of Sandra's neighbor. He jumped into the two-tone Chevy, and as his car roared away Lawrence Hall noted the license number. He repeated it to himself until he got to his apartment, where his wife got off the phone with Sandra and said, "Call the police."

Armed with the plate number of their suspect, police spent the early morning hours looking for him. They couldn't locate the man – and it cost them. Despite cops swarming the downtown area, the killer took another victim and slipped through the net to safety.

Friday December 9th dawned under a metal gray sky, one that began to press by mid-morning and issue an aimless drizzle. It was a reminder that the Ohio River valley's humid summers were often harbingers of icy, sullen winters.

An *Enquirer* headline got their reader's attention: **Psychiatrist Presents Theory on Strangler.** Dr. Charles Feuss theorized the killer "may very well be a necrophiliac – a lover of the dead. He has a tremendous hostility, perhaps growing from a bad mother relationship." Feuss called the killer a "sexual deviant."

As if on cue, the Strangler gave his reply...

AROUND 8:15AM ON NINTH Street, a Cincinnati police officer knocked on the door of the Brittany Apartments landlord. "There's a dead lady in your elevator," he advised them.

81-year-old Lulu Kerrick lay crumpled on the floor of the cramped lift, a stocking taut around her neck. The elderly resident had just returned home from St. Peter in Chains Cathedral at Eighth and Plum Street. The killer followed her into the elevator and quickly strangled her – this time there was no rape.

Miss Lulu Kerrick was a shy, deeply religious spinster in poor health, a woman who never could have imagined that in death she would become the object of the city's fascination and pity. "She never bothered anybody, she just wanted to be by herself," her horrified niece said after identifying the body.

Detectives arriving at the scene realized it was just two blocks over from where Sandra Chapas was terrorized seven hours earlier. They marveled at the killer's boldness – taking a victim during a downtown morning rush hour in a large building flush to the street with tenants bustling about on their morning routines.

Just after 9 AM cops converged on the Adam Wuest Company, a West End mattress manufacturer. There they arrested 29-year-old Posteal

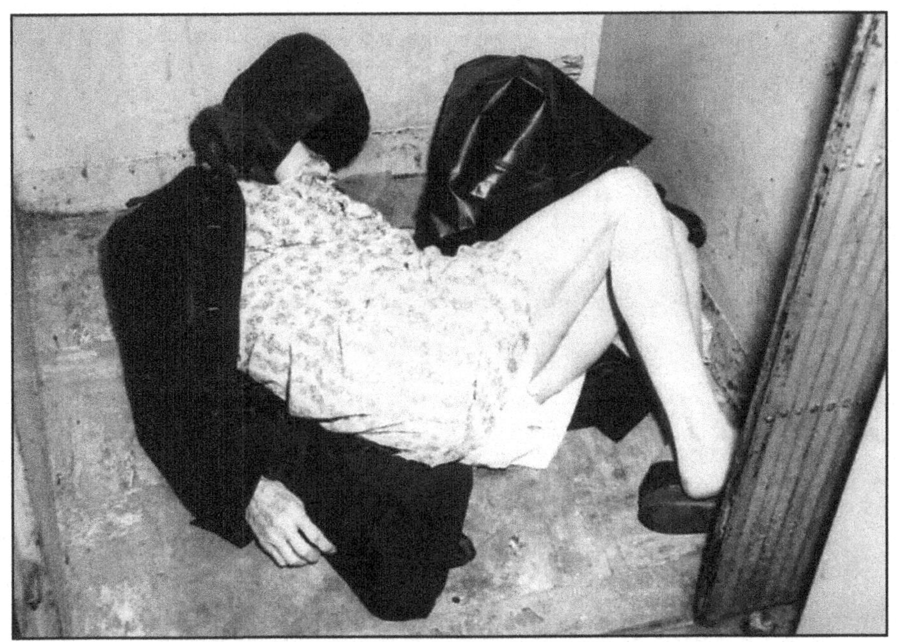

The murder of Lulu Kerrick was hit and run attack during a narrow window of opportunity – there was no time for rape.

Laskey Jr., whose license plate matched that of the black man fleeing the Chapas building.

Paul Morgan was one of the arresting officers. In a 1997 interview with this author, Morgan expressed surprise at the demeanor of a suspect who may have just committed murder: "He was pretty calm – he didn't try to resist."

Detective Morgan learned that Laskey left his rented room on Reading Road at 7:40 AM but had clocked in late at 8:07 AM. While driving Laskey back to headquarters, Morgan noted that his most likely route to work would have taken him past the Brittany Apartments at the time of the Kerrick slaying.

Laskey was one of the sex offenders quizzed earlier in the Strangler probe, and a former Yellow Cab driver checked out in theBowman slaying. His rap sheet revealed the part-time musician was no stranger to violence – there were four previous assault convictions, the first dating back to 1953.

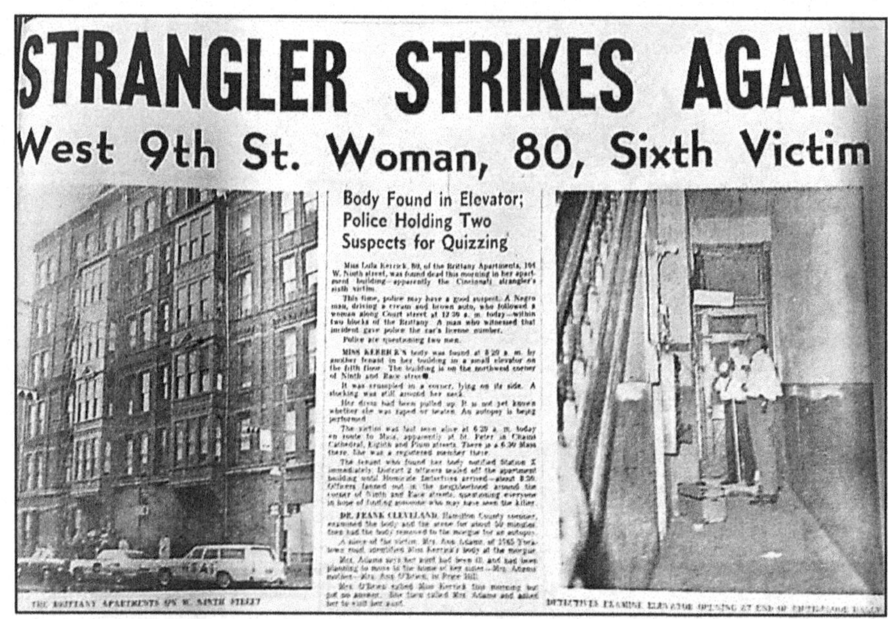

STRANGLER STRIKES AGAIN

West 9th St. Woman, 80, Sixth Victim

Body Found in Elevator; Police Holding Two Suspects for Quizzing

Miss Lula Kerrick, 80, of the Brittany Apartments, 104 W. Ninth street, was found dead this morning in her apartment building—apparently the Cincinnati strangler's sixth victim.

This time, police may have a good suspect. A Negro man, driving a cream and brown auto, who followed a woman along Court street at 12:30 a. m. today—within two blocks of the Brittany. A man who witnessed that incident gave police the car's license number.

Police are questioning two men.

MISS KERRICK'S body was found at 8:20 a. m. by another tenant in her building in a small elevator on the fifth floor. The building is on the northwest corner of Ninth and Race streets.

It was crumpled in a corner, lying on its side. A stocking was still around her neck.

Her dress had been pulled up. It is not yet known whether she was raped or beaten. An autopsy is being performed.

The victim was last seen alive at 6:20 a. m. today en route to Mass, apparently at St. Peter in Chains Cathedral, Eighth and Plum streets. There is a 6:30 Mass there. She was a registered member there.

[illegible]

As news of another murder spread, Cincinnati police arrested their suspect at his workplace.

Morgan and others engaged Laskey in an all-day interview session, and they slowly began to build their case against him.

Paul Morgan's excellent memory was making the Strangler connection. During the Bowman investigation, Laskey's photo was picked out by cab driver Sol Thompson as a possible match for the suspicious fare he picked up near the slaying scene. Thompson eventually eliminated Laskey's photo and picked a different man.

But it was something from the Hochhausler file that really glimmered for Morgan.

Posteal Laskey on the day of his arrest, shortly after the Kerrick murder, wearing the distinctive beret.

Eight hours before Alice was murdered on October 11th, her neighbor Helene Muhsam had a disturbing encounter with a strange man across from the Hochhausler driveway, a short, thin black man who was staring at her.

He had bowed in her direction and then strolled down Cornell Place. She couldn't give a good description, but she was certain of one thing. This man was wearing a distinctive beret.

Morgan grabbed the booking photos of Laskey taken that morning. Sure enough, the intake officer had Laskey wear his beret for the second of three pictures.

December 9th

On that momentous Friday in Cincinnati, Detective Gerald Taylor was in Seattle, interviewing Jerry's former co-workers and neighbors who knew Linda.

William Munro, personnel manager at Monsanto, confirmed Jerry began working there on 12/12/60 and was transferred to the Cincinnati plant on 7/9/63. He gave Taylor three addresses Jerry had listed with the company. Munro's assessment of Jerry was familiar – he was a likeable fellow who did a good job, and there were no reprimands in his file.

When his transfer came through Jerry was thrilled with the promotion and raise, and told Munro Linda was happy she would be closer to her parents in Chicago. No other Seattle workers had been transferred to the Cincinnati plant since Jerry Bricca.

"Do you know how Jerry and Linda met?

"I don't know anything about their personal life. I saw her twice – once at a Christmas party and then at Jerry's going away party."

"Did he ever confide any personal problems to you?

Munro weighed his words. "He told me Linda was three months pregnant when they were 'formally married' in Chicago. Apparently they had a secret ceremony so Linda could keep her airline job. He said the Chicago wedding was just to satisfy their parents."

Other employees agreed Jerry was popular and a capable worker. None knew of any clubs or organizations he belonged to, and no one stayed in contact with Jerry after his transfer.

Apparently things changed after Jerry got married. C.P. Miller said after that their only interaction was an occasional company party. Martin Berglund remembered that Jerry "bummed around with a few guys" from the plant prior to his marriage, but after he met Linda it was easier to reach him at her apartment.

Robert Ashley bowled with him for two years on the company team prior to his marriage. He remembered Jerry shared an apartment with a roommate, but he didn't know where it was. Ashley agreed that Jerry abandoned any afterhours partying with his co-workers after meeting Linda.

And so it went. No one knew anything about Jerry's personal life or visited him after he married Linda.

But William Smith knew Jerry better than the others. The factory foreman was a bowling teammate and "beer buddy" – Jerry often visited his house to help with projects or to grab a friendly meal. Smith helped Jerry and Linda move from their first house to a nicer one on Lakeside Avenue. This was also the last social thing he did with Jerry after the wedding.

The rest had a familiar ring. Jerry was a well-liked, dedicated worker with no adversaries at the plant. He would "go along to get along", always ready to avoid confrontation.

Even after four years, Smith was sincerely hurt by Jerry shunning him after marriage. "Helping them move was the only time I was ever in that house," he lamented, wiping away a tear.

ON FRIDAY AFTERNOON TAYLOR went to the Lakeside Avenue address and talked to Linda's former neighbors. He needed some insight into his female victim – then a 20-year-old bride saddled with an infant and stranded at home in an unfamiliar neighborhood.

Carl Hjert owned the house at 1415 Lakeside Avenue, which had a great view of Lake Washington. He rented the house to Jerry and Linda from 1962-1963, but only saw them when he collected rent or made minor repairs. Carl and his wife felt that they were a "nice young couple" but knew nothing about them.

An elderly couple across the street was friendly with Linda Bricca. Mary Hepworth said she would come over to talk quite often. Mary even corresponded with Linda after they moved to Cincinnati – she found three of Linda's letters but none were recent.

The Hepworths had two dogs, so Taylor asked who Linda used for vet care, but they were uncertain since she rarely left the house or went anyplace alone. While admitting the young couple had few visitors, Mary said Jerry and Linda always seemed very happy, "at least on the surface."

Mrs. Betty Westenberg was just two years older than Linda and her closest friend on that street. Linda would come over with the baby during the day to visit.

Betty's backyard bordered the lake and they had a boat. Jerry and Linda enjoyed boating and swimming, and Jerry would sometimes water ski. She said Linda didn't seem to have any other friends, and she knew nothing about Linda's veterinary care.

"Did she talk a lot about her pets?

"Not at all. I can't ever remember her dominating a conversation with animals."

"Did she pay an unusual amount of attention to the dog?

"She never seemed worried about it. I took it for granted that she kept up to date with all the shots. They also had a rabbit, and Jerry had an aquarium for his fish."

Betty said the only time Linda went out by herself was on Saturdays when she would go grocery shopping while Jerry was home with the baby.

"Did she ever tell you she felt trapped always staying home?"

"Never. Once I told her I would be glad when my son was in school so that I could get out of the house and go places. She seemed surprised and asked me where I would go. She said she had no desire to go out and was 'perfectly happy' with her home."

Betty knew of no trouble between Jerry and Linda – with one exception. "She said she needed to visit a psychiatrist and asked if I could watch Debbie one day a week when she went to see him.

"How often did she go?"

"That's what's odd about it. She changed her mind and never went to my knowledge."

"Did she say why she had wanted to go?"

"I asked. But she wouldn't tell me what her problem was or why she felt she needed psychiatric help."

December 10th – 11th

With Posteal Laskey in custody Cincinnati Police were working overtime to keep him there. Already a suspect in the Lulu Kerrick slaying, an indictment in the August 14th stabbing death of Barbara Bowman seemed imminent.

Laskey was a former Yellow Cab taxi-driver, a connection that prompted them to bring the Bowman witnesses in for a lineup on Saturday morning. All six identified Laskey as the cab driver who picked up Bowman at the Lark Café that night.

A deeper look at Laskey's record triggered anger and frustration among the detectives.

Already a violent four-time felon, he was arrested on October 9th, 1965 in the brutal beating of a 16-year-old Clifton girl earlier that day. He quickly posted bond and was back out on the street. After five continuances he was finally convicted of assault and battery on November 30th. Yet despite his despicable history, Judge William Matthews sentenced him to three years' probation!

Paul Morgan couldn't believe what he was reading. Here was a career predator with multiple assault convictions, in and out of prison since 1953, yet some bleeding heart judge slapped his wrist, gave him probation and let him walk.

Morgan noted that three days after posting bond, Elizabeth Kreco was attacked at her Walnut Hills apartment. And three days after Laskey was gifted his probation, Emogene Harrington was raped and strangled in her Walnut Hills apartment on December 2nd.

Laskey's troubles multiplied as the day wore on. The couple who witnessed the Chapas incident identified him as the intruder – this new charge violated his probation. Virginia Hinners, who survived a traumatic September attack at the New Thought Unity Church in Walnut Hills, also recognized Laskey as her assailant and he was charged with that crime as well.

Still pending were the six rape-strangulations. The Sunday *Enquirer* front page headline, **Jailed Suspect in Spotlight of Seven Murder Probe**, forced Jake Schott to admit that Laskey was a suspect in all the crimes.

Especially the murder of young Barbara Bowman. Readers around the city were waiting to exhale. If Laskey was Barbara's killer, would the stranglings end?

Jailed Suspect In Spotlight Of 7-Murder Probe

JONES, WALTER LEE	3/8/35	5'6"	151 ✓
✓ JORDEN, FRED DANIEL (Committed to workhouse 5/66, does not get out until 9/67)	12/13/35	5'6"	150 ✓
LASKEY, POSTEAL (NMN) (CK'd by Lt. Mac.)	6/18/37	5'6"	135 ✓
LEMON, JIMMIE LEE	5/11/33	5'6"	155
LEWIS, FRED (NMN)	7/19/35	5'6"	146

As police tried to link Laskey to the strangulations, they learned he'd already been checked out in the Bowman slaying.

On Saturday December 10th Gerald Taylor was still in Seattle, checking out addresses for Jerry Monsanto had given him.

At his first stop, the owner bought the building after Jerry moved to Cincinnati, and there were no previous tenant records. One resident suggested checking at the bar across the street, but the owner did not recognize pictures of Jerry or Linda.

The second address was a derelict two-family with a high turnover rate. No one ever lived there for more than a few months.

Taylor next checked out six veterinary offices near the Bricca's Lakeside address, but none recognized Linda's picture or had any record of treating her animals. Linda was a memorable woman, and he was puzzled by her lack of contact with any local vets.

Sally Watts was the Supervisor for United Airlines Stewardesses flying out of Seattle. She wasn't working there in 1961 and didn't know

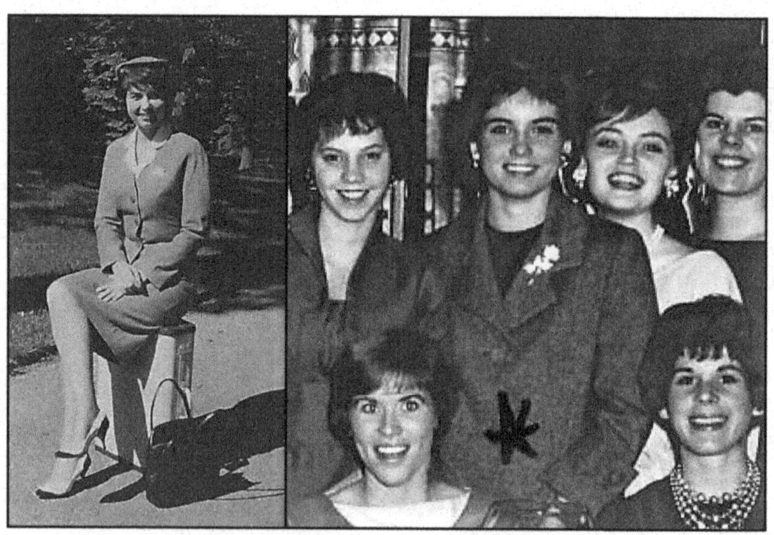

Linda flying the friendly skies in July 1961 (left), and at a United Airlines party several months later (marked with a star).

Linda Bulaw. Watts said she heard that two stewardesses recognized Linda's picture after reading about the murders. She promised to identify them and have the Seattle police notify Taylor.

"Why was her employment terminated?"

Watts checked their records. "On 11/4/61 she experienced muscle spasms and air sickness on a flight."

Taylor knew this was morning sickness but said nothing. "Did she leave a forwarding address?"

"Monsanto Chemical Company in care of Jerry Bricca."

Mrs. Carol Karrigan had contacted Taylor through the Seattle Police, and she looked like a promising interview – she dated Jerry's roommate in 1961 and she'd known Linda Bulaw.

Her boyfriend at the time was Harry Cain, nicknamed Buzz, who now lived in Maryland. Karrigan said while she was going with Cain, Jerry often hung out with them, even coming to her apartment with Cain for supper.

"Did he ever bring a date?"

"Never once until Linda."

"How did he meet her?"

"I have no idea. All of a sudden she was just there."

"He never told you or Buzz how he met her?

"He never said. But she was always there. She would be at the apartment cleaning or doing laundry, even when he wasn't there."

Karrigan thought Jerry was "a rather strange person," amiable yet shy. "He just didn't make friends easily and often kept to himself. I never met any of Linda's girlfriends either."

"Did she have any roommates?"

"I don't know. She never spoke of them. I didn't even know where she lived."

After Jerry and Linda got married, they stayed for several months in a house owned by Jerry's friend who was visiting Europe for a year. Karrigan was only there one time – she did not remember the friend's name or the address.

"Did Linda mention anyone she dated before Jerry?"

"I never heard either of them say anything about it."

"After the marriage did you hear any rumors that Linda was running around?"

"Not at all. She seemed devoted to Jerry."

Taylor learned little on this day. Friends had established that Linda was about three months pregnant when they were married. Apparently she and Jerry lived together in a Seattle house for at least one month prior to the wedding.

The one thing he nailed down was hauntingly familiar. No one knew anything about the inner life of Jerry and Linda...

TAYLOR'S LAST SEATTLE STOP was at the office of Dr. Sheldon Biback, Linda Bricca's obstetrician. The Doctor was on vacation, but Taylor reached him by phone at his residence.

He had delivered Debbie on June 6th, 1962 at the King County Hospital. But without his records handy he could offer no details. This became a pattern during the phone interview – Dr. Biback made some tantalizing remarks but wasn't able to give specifics.

He would be back in his office on the 13th, but Taylor was leaving tonight for Chicago. Biback promised to make copies of his records and forward them.

"Did you treat her for anything besides her pregnancy?"

"I remember I counseled her for frigidity. She was having a problem with sex."

Taylor's eyes widened as he checked his notes – someone in San Francisco said she had mentioned a long delivery. "Did this condition come about because of her difficult labor having Debbie?"

"There were no difficulties delivering Debbie. She had this problem a long time before she married Jerry."

Taylor was intrigued. "So it wasn't from the pregnancy or birth?"

"Not this birth." Biback's voice sounded tinny over the line. "I think it developed from her first pregnancy."

Taylor was floored. "Her first pregnancy?" He was almost shouting. "I thought Debbie was her only child!"

"I can't confirm it without my records. I have a great number of patients."

"I understand. But you believe she was pregnant before?"

"I am quite sure she had a prior pregnancy," the doctor droned. "Debbie was the second time around for Linda..."

December 12th

On Monday Gerald Taylor called on Phil Herriott, Supervisor at the UAL School for Stewardesses in Elk Grove, Illinois.

His records showed Linda Bulaw was in training from March 27th through April 27th 1961 at their Cheyenne, Wyoming School – she began flying on the 28th, and her employment was terminated on November 4th. Her class roster of 17 showed two other members who went to Seattle with Linda upon their graduation. Herriott provided a copy of her training report with personal observations, but Linda's personnel records were no longer available.

Next Taylor went to the Winnebago County Sheriff's Office to interview burglary suspect Edward Marlow Struss. Herb Vogel had called him in Seattle with information that Struss was seen on the Cincinnati's West Side on Sept. 25th and was worth checking out.

Struss was cooperative with Taylor. The tall, good-looking 26-year old couldn't recall where he was on the 25th, but denied any knowledge of the Bricca crime and provided fingerprints, palm prints and hair samples. Taylor was satisfied Struss wasn't their guy.

He then visited the Chicago Police Department to pick up information on animal acts that toured the Cincinnati area in 1966. This was in response to Vogel's letter requesting names of local booking agents in the Chicago area.

Taylor had one more interview scheduled in Chicago that day – Mr. and Mrs. Adolph Bulaw, parents of Linda Bricca. Perhaps they could shed some light on their mercurial daughter...

BACK IN CINCINNATI THE interview schedule dried up. Leads were wilting with the investigation now almost three months old.

Attempts to arrange another interview with Fred Leininger were being stonewalled by lawyer Richard Morr. Vogel had a meeting scheduled with Prosecutor Rueger to discuss that situation.

Ernest Nehrer and Bob Hall were cleaning up a few loose ends. A tip that a waitress at Maury's Tiny Cove had seen Linda Bricca there was groundless. She huffily informed them she knew nothing about it. A barmaid at David's Buffet called "Crazy Janie" also did not recognize Linda's picture.

Charley Nagle interviewed yet another veterinarian. Based on a tip that Linda Bricca had interacted with the Cincinnati Zoo, Dr. Jerry Theobald met him there. He checked his files and couldn't find a Bricca reference, nor did he did not recognize her picture.

Nagel wouldn't give up that easily. "Are you certain you never talked to her?"

Dr. Theobald, a 34-year-old married man, seemed suddenly uneasy. "It's possible she may have called me about her parakeet. That rings a bell."

"Why would she call you about a parakeet?"

"That is my special area of expertise."

"What kind of car do you drive?" This was a suspect question, and Theobald knew it. He gave Nagel the color and model of his 1965 Chevy and a 1964 Ford.

Nagel knew Linda had a thing for veterinarians, yet Theobald proved to be overly helpful. This respected doctor, like so many others, moved to the back of the case file.

Murder would touch him again eleven years later, in a more personal way. Dr. Theobald's 18-year-old daughter Nancy was abducted on

November 16th, 1977 while leaving her job at the Calhoun Street Arby's in Clifton. Her body was found in Butler County December 28th – she'd been raped and strangled.

A Hamilton County task force linked her murder with a series of abductions and strangulations of 15 other young women found dumped in remote areas from 1974-1978. There were eventually arrests and convictions in some those cases.

But the murder of Nancy Ann Theobald remains unsolved...

GERALD TAYLOR SAT DOWN with Linda Bricca's parents in their tasteful Barrington, Illinois home for his final interview on this trip. Within a week he had visited San Francisco, Seattle, and the Chicago area. Now he was hoping Linda had confided some family secrets to her mother.

Mr. and Mrs. Adolph Bulaw were still coping with their daughter's death. The shock and grief had mercifully played out, but the ache of loss was still evident on their faces.

The former June Miller was starving for closure. She knew of no one with anything against Jerry or Linda. And Adolph was certain there were no business enemies who would harm them for revenge.

June admitted Linda had revealed details about her marital problems. There seemed to be a sexual incompatibility from the moment they were married. She got the impression Jerry was always worn out from working long hours and was "too tired for romance when he got home." It sounded more like a "quickie."

"Did she ever say she wanted to leave him?"

"Just before she went to Florida last March she called me and said she was considering leaving Jerry."

"Was that Florida visit a trial separation?"

"She never said that, but I believe it was."

"So what happened?"

"She called me after three weeks down there and said she was going to stay with Jerry no matter what."

June did not think her daughter was running around on Jerry. Linda had always gone with one boy at a time and stayed faithful while they dated, so June believed Linda would leave Jerry first rather than cheat on him.

"Do you know Dr. Fred Leininger?"

June Miller Bulaw attending to daughter Linda on her wedding day, just before leaving for the church.

"Yes. I was under the impression he was very close to both Linda and Jerry. Debbie called him Uncle Fred."

Taylor made a note that June was the third person to say that about Debbie. "Did she tell you about working for him?"

"When we last spoke on that Saturday night she went on and on about it."

"That was Saturday night September 24th, correct?"

"Yes." June Bulaw paused, her eyes growing misty. "She was going to work on Wednesdays at his clinic. She told me about the operations she helped him perform and her other duties. She sounded quite excited by all of it."

"What days did she say she worked that week?"

"Monday, Tuesday and Wednesday."

Mrs. Bulaw could not provide names of any of Linda's close friends. On her June visit to Chicago she spent all the time with her mother – she did not see anyone else or go anywhere by herself.

Taylor discounted this last statement but said nothing. He knew Leininger owned property in Barrington – there easily could have been a rendezvous on this trip.

"Was Linda dating anyone in Seattle before Jerry?"

"Not that I know of. Her work schedule kept her busy. Then one trip home she suddenly began talking all about Jerry."

"How did you learn she was pregnant?"

Adolph Bulaw spoke up. "Jerry wrote me a letter saying she was pregnant and that he loved her and wanted to marry her."

"Did he say Linda was pressuring him?

June was puzzled. "Just the opposite. Linda was here the week before we got the letter but didn't tell me she was expecting."

They called Linda and spoke to her and Jerry about it, and they decided to come to Chicago and be married. The wedding took place on Nov 25th, 1961, and Debbie was born 6-1/2 months later.

Both parents confirmed her lifelong love of animals. Mr. Bulaw told Linda that if she got enough experience and wanted to open her own clinic, "she could hire her own vets" and he "would finance it at a as a business venture." Taylor made another note.

"Did she ever talk with you about seeing a psychiatrist?"

June hesitated. "She was thinking about it in Seattle. But she told me she found another solution."

Taylor let that go. "Did Linda express any fear to you the last week of her life?"

June Bulaw eyed at him. "Yes. She was afraid of Jerry."

"Did she say why?"

"She found out several months before that Jerry was an epileptic. She learned it by accident and was very upset that he hadn't told her before."

"So they fought about this?"

"Worse. Linda told me Jerry stopped taking his medication the week before the murders..."

December 13th – 23rd

Cincinnati Police put Posteal Laskey under their microscope, and it was not a flattering close up. Detectives were happy he was off the street and confident he'd never see another day of freedom.

Laskey was released in August 1965 after serving an 18 month sentence in the Kentucky Reformatory. He'd been convicted of the December 1963 robbery and assault of a Covington KY woman. The record showed he followed her into her apartment building and grabbed her legs on the stairway – she screamed, he ran off with her purse but was quickly caught.

His vicious October 9th 1965 assault of a Clifton teenager had only resulted in probation, and Elizabeth Kreco was attacked three days later. Paul Morgan believed a career assailant like Laskey was tired of being identified and had progressed to murder.

Jake Schott took his case to the grand jury in the Bowman slaying. Six witnesses identified Laskey as the driver who picked up Barbara, and cabbie Sol Thompson also fingered him as his suspicious passenger after the murder. That bootleg driver was using "186" on his radio calls to the Yellow Cab dispatcher, which was Laskey's call number when he drove for them in 1962.

Yet the city was still restless. With Laskey in custody, on Tuesday night December 13th 79-year-old Anna Scales was beaten in the basement of her Walnut Hills apartment building by a short, slightly built black man who said he was looking for the caretaker.

LEGAL MANEUVERS WERE CHURNING around Posteal Laskey. On Friday the 16th the Grand Jury indicted Laskey for the murder of Barbara Bowman. Jake Schott stayed close lipped, but future indictments seemed possible for some of the six strangulations.

Two other indictments were handed down for the Walnut Hills attacks against Virginia Hinners on September 21st and Delle Ernst on October 4th. Both women had identified Laskey as the man who assaulted and robbed them.

In a surprise move, County Prosecutors Burton Signer and Donald Roney resigned on December 12th and agreed to represent Laskey. Roney had a long history as a prosecutor, and had investigated two of Cincinnati's most infamous crimes – the sensational 1956 slaying of Audrey Pugh in Hyde Park and the brutal 1963 bludgeoning of Patty Rebholz in Greenhills **(Queen City Gothic Chapters 7 and 8)**.

Meanwhile, an *Enquirer* editorial took local law enforcement to task for their interpretations of the recent Supreme Court decision protecting the rights of suspects.

Laskey was given probation after a 10/9/65 assault (left), yet after his arrest on 12/9/66 he never saw another day of freedom.

Prosecutor Mel Rueger had bypassed a preliminary hearing and taken evidence against Laskey directly to the Grand Jury because of "the great amount of publicity given to the case". He cited the overturned conviction of Dr. Sam Sheppard. Yet Sheppard was freed because of trial misconduct, not pre-trial publicity.

The *Enquirer* also believed that County investigators "displayed what we regarded as an unwarranted reluctance to discuss the investigation into the deaths of three members of the Gerald Bricca family." Herb Vogel had not provided any further information about the unidentified prime suspect since admitting their investigation had "narrowed to one man" in mid-November.

Up until then Vogel had been accessible when dealing with the press. Now it was suggested he was not "complying with the public's right to know about official proceedings" in the Bricca case.

Yet neither Rueger nor Vogel showed any inclination to back down from their positions – a testament to the complex and sensational nature of the parallel investigations into these crimes.

On Monday December 19th, Cincinnati finally had a new Police Chief to fill the void left by Stan Schrotel's September retirement. Lt. Colonel Jacob W. Schott, head of the Homicide Squad, was elevated to the top job after achieving the highest score on the promotional examination given to four candidates.

He had been in training for this since he joined the force in 1937. Tall and rugged, Schott had been described as "looking like a Cary Grant who had to work for a living." He possessed a soft, mannerly style of speaking with definite Mid-western undertones.

Schott made it clear in his first press conference that "apprehension of the Strangler" was his top priority.

Privately, he was hoping they already had him in custody...

POSTEAL LASKEY WAS FACING a six month sentence for his "assault" of Sandra Chapas, even though he never actually touched her. Now his alibi witness for that crime, a "shapely go-go dancer" named Brenda Jackson, was missing. Burton Signer claimed she failed to show for a hearing because she was in police custody.

Jackson did appear in court the next day and testified before the grand jury, along with three members of Laskey's family. All were subpoenaed by Mel Rueger, who wanted more information on Laskey even though he already had the Bowman indictment.

Enquirer columnist Frank Weikel wrote three columns in three days about the Strangler suspect. On the 20th he quashed a rumor that an "all-white" grand jury had returned the murder indictment against Laskey, pointing out that three black women and one black man had been serving on that panel since early December.

The next day Weikel wrote about a phone call he received from the mother of a Laskey victim. Her 16-year-old daughter was attacked by him on October 9th 1965, yet Laskey was released on bond and back on the street that same day. Despite her warning that Laskey could repeat an attack like the one on her daughter, he was placed on probation in November 1965.

Now 14 months later, the victim was still receiving medical treatment for a blow to the head inflicted during Laskey's assault. Her mother told Weikel that she called police in August after the Bowman murder and told them Laskey was a likely suspect, because her daughter "knew Miss Bowman and they looked somewhat alike." But her warning had "fallen on deaf ears."

Weikel's third column identified Laskey as the man who walked into the Avondale Branch of the Hamilton County Legal Aid Society in late November and announced "I need help." When told he could talk to

New chief Jake Schott said the capture of the Strangler was his top priority.

an attorney, the man changed his mind. As he walked out, he said "The help I need isn't from a lawyer. It's from a doctor."

After Laskey's picture was in the paper, employees at that office recognized him as their visitor.

Signer and Roney continued to fight the indictment against their client. Filing a motion to suppress the evidence, Signer charged that Laskey was "unlawfully and surreptitiously removed" from the "Cincinnati Workhouse" and "placed in a wire cage" for viewing by the Bowman witnesses – who all identified Laskey as that driver.

On December 23rd, after the motion to suppress was denied, Posteal Laskey pled "not guilty" to the Bowman murder charge, as well as the Hinners and Ernst assaults. Chief Schott was confident his men had built a solid case against Laskey as Bowman's killer.

Yet something was bothering him. Based on semen found in the Strangler victims, their killer was apparently blood type O. Schott knew this type of testing was not always reliable, especially when the semen was mixed with bodily fluids from the victims.

But he couldn't ignore that Laskey's blood was type A...

December 28th – 31st

As 1966 came to a close, the national media looked back on what was truly a momentous year for all the wrong reasons.

The equanimity of the early 60's had slipped away, and there were few bright spots. Dark clouds like Vietnam, race riots, the nuclear threat had rained a quandary of confusion, anger, and fear. There was upheaval and innovation, and it crossed all boundaries. Liberal and conservative, radicals and reactionaries – everyone was getting whiplash from the torrid pace of relentless change.

So the pundits ignored reality and focused on pop culture. It was a breakthrough year for Motown, now rivaling the Beatles runaway success. Hair was longer, love songs were discarded, and social consciousness took root. Music, art, film, and television were moving so swiftly that cultural norms were shattered.

When nationally syndicated gossip columnist Earle Wilson recalled the best of 1966, he kept the tone predictably light.

Girl of the Year was Mia Farrow, who in July at age 21 married singer Frank Sinatra, 30 years her senior. And of course, "the best father/ daughter duo was Frank and Mia... I mean NANCY Sinatra."

The rest was equally tongue in cheek. Biggest book was of course Jaqueline Susann's "Valley of the Dolls" – the "best sexpots" were Raquel Welch and Sharon Tate. Wilson's "Most Uplifting Sight" was "Jackie Kennedy in a short-short dress". His "Biggest Eye-opener" was "my cataract operation and topless waitresses."

The Cincinnati *Post* ran a feature titled **Best of Zany News Locally in 1966,** countering the anxiety perched on city shoulders over the murders of ten citizens. Blunders and bloopers made for relaxing reading just before the New Year.

Under the heading "Best Errors" was an event from December 1965 that still rankled many local sports fans as the greatest crime ever: "Bill DeWitt's trade of Frank Robinson for what's-his-name and who's-this..."

It was New Year's Eve at the Bulaw home in Barrington, Illinois. June Miller Bulaw was sitting in her daughter's old room in the late afternoon, feeling the hollow throb of her first holiday season without Linda.

She looked out the window at the gray, lonely landscape. The winter trees were skeletal against an ashen sky. Everything in her world was frozen – movement, time, love.

She was still shaken by the cemetery that morning. She and Adolf had only visited a few times after the October 2nd burial. It was too fresh, too painful. June felt ready today, until she saw the cigarettes. Jerry and Debbie's graves were clear, but there was a ring of nine Marlboro butts circling Linda's marker.

June shivered at the memory. Was this a friendly memorial, or a message from the killer? She would have to call Lt. Vogel about it. He'd told her about finding Marlboro butts at the crime scene, and she had assured him neither Jerry nor Linda smoked.

So here she sat in Linda's old room. Jay had come over on Christmas with his new wife, and at ten Brian still had that childlike joy. But Adolf was taking it hard – she'd heard his laments of naked pain as he contemplated the empty chair at the table.

By the time she entered Linda's room and closed the door, the living and the dead were seamlessly mingled in her mind. She allowed the peace and stillness to seep into her soul.

The room was just as Linda left it when she moved to Seattle in 1961. June rejected her son's opinion that she was creating a shrine – Jay and Linda were never that close. No, this was about vowing that her dead daughter would not disappear.

She gazed at the framed picture of handsome Erwin Seegers, the longtime family friend who started dating Linda when she was 16 and he was 30. They had gotten serious too quickly. The age difference disturbed June more than Adolph – should she have stopped it early on?

Erwin's marriage proposal ten months later was a pleasant shock. But when he called it off Linda had become violently sick. Erwin came to check on her yet Adolph threw him out of the house, which infuriated Linda. She didn't speak to her father for months.

Linda began to accelerate her life, starting college right after graduation in an effort to close the age gap with Erwin. But then he married someone else, and she went into another funk.

Adolf, June, Linda, and Jay Bulaw out to dinner in 1959, shortly before Linda met 30-year-old Erwin Seegers.

The next nine months were a blur. Linda started dating a young man in college, and they were getting serious when he was killed in a car crash. Linda suffered a breakdown, and June pulled her out of school and took her to Florida to recuperate. When they returned in the spring of 1961, Linda went to work for United Airlines.

June turned Erwin's picture face down.

Could she dispel this eclipse that blotted out their lives? It was a cruel spike in their timeline – other events were marked "before or after the crime." Burying your child was overwhelming enough. Yet Linda was horrifically murdered, along with her daughter and husband. Can anyone really recover from such devastation?

June picked up a picture of Linda at age six with the family dog. She had always been very watchful over animals – she didn't even want to see a fly killed.

Once again the memory came flooding back, the irony unsettling. The dog had died a few months later, and every time Adolph buried it Linda dug it up and put it on the back steps. Finally June cradled her daughter in her arms and whispered "We have to leave him in the ground so he'll go to heaven."

The image of her answer would never subside, her blue-eyed girl staring at her in stunned disbelief. "Would you leave me in the ground if I died?"

June Miller Bulaw, six days past Christmas, felt like a marooned survivor of some unseen wreckage. Sorrow had imprisoned her – she could not be touched, nor could she flee...

January 1st – January 14th, 1967

The Bricca case took an intriguing turn on January 5th 1967, when a suspect reeled into the center of the waning investigation.

Around 3 AM on that Thursday, Huntington, West Virginia police responded to a call about a woman screaming in a downtown apartment. They found Ruth Marie Fliehman stabbed to death in her bedroom – the autopsy would reveal 17 wounds in her chest, neck, and head. The 20-year-old was wearing only her underwear, a phone clasped in her hand as if she'd tried to call for help.

Cops on the scene noticed a blood trail leading to a motel across the street. Astoundingly, it led right to the killer's room. They arrested Richard Tucker after finding a knife they believed to be the murder weapon. The 24-year-old salesman for the Sun Oil Company was in West Virginia on a business trip.

Police found a card in his wallet showing five visits to a Cincinnati psychiatrist between May and September of 1966, which prompted Huntington PD to contact Herb Vogel.

County detectives quickly dug into the life of Richard Tucker, looking for any link to Bricca. His rap sheet showed a 9/8/65 arrest in the Hartwell neighborhood as a Peeping Tom. And he'd admitted to Huntington police that he'd been "peeping" for some time.

Vogel's hopes rose when they verified that he was back in Cincinnati on September 24th and 25th. And Tucker also drove a white Plymouth convertible, similar to one seen in the Bricca neighborhood the week before the murders...

ON JANUARY 7TH GERALD Taylor conducted an extensive interview with Pamela Tucker at the office of her attorney.

She was afraid of her ex-husband. Tucker owned a hair trigger temper, had struck her several times, and sometimes the littlest aggravation would set him off. She finally left him in July.

Salesman, 24, Held On Murder Charge

A Cincinnati salesman was charged Thursday in Huntington, W. Va., with the murder of a young part-time waitress. She was found stabbed to death in the bedroom of her apartment.

Huntington police arrested Richard L. K. Tucker, 24, 2493 Wenatchee Ln., Mt. Washington, in his room at a motel across the street from the murdered woman's apartment.

The victim was identified as Ruth Marie Fliehman, about 20, formerly of Lawrence County, Ohio. Police said she had been employed in Huntington at the Peo-

Richard L. K. Tucker

. . . arrested at 4 a. m.

police said a trail of blood spots led from the woman's apartment to Tucker's motel room. Tucker was arrested at 4 a. m., a little more than one hour after police responded to a call that a woman was screaming in the building where Miss Fliehman lived.

The victim was stabbed in the neck, but police would not say how many wounds she suffered. Tucker suffered a cut wrist but it was not certain whether it was incurred during a struggle or self-inflicted.

POLICE SAID a knife, believed to be the murder

Bricca Slaying Link In Stabbing?

A possible link between the triple murder of the Gerald Bricca family last September 25 and the slaying last Thursday of a Huntington, W. Va. waitress was being investigated Monday by the Hamilton County Sheriff's Patrol.

A Mt. Washington salesman, Richard Lynn Koontz Tucker, 24, 2493 Wenatchee Ln., has been charged with murder by Huntington police in the fatal stabbing of Ruth Marie Fliehman, about 20.

THE VICTIM, found dead in her bedroom, had worked for a canvas manufacturer and was a part-time waitress at a drive-in restaurant a few blocks from her apartment.

Lt. Herbert Vogel, who heads the investigation into the stabbings of the Gerald Bricca family, said times. An Oriental carving knife, believed to be the murder weapon, is missing from the home.

THE BRICCA family's bodies were found in two bedrooms late September 27.

West Virginia killer Richard Tucker was a Cincinnati native who could be placed there the weekend of the Bricca murders.

She said he had a habit of taking long walks in the evening and sometimes wouldn't return until 3-4 AM.

"How did he look when he came back?"

"He wasn't messy or anything like that."

"Did he bring anything home with him?"

"No. But he told me he snooped around people's yards and peeked in their windows while he was out."

Pamela believed he had several friends who were homosexual – Tucker told her that he'd had a gay experience when younger.

"Do you remember him being home in September?"

Pamela took a deep drag off her cigarette. "He was working in Philadelphia, but he flew home every weekend and rented a car."

"So he wasn't driving his white Plymouth?"

"I never paid attention to what car he had." She knew nothing about Richard seeing a psychiatrist. But while visiting her and their son a week before Christmas, he showed her a hunting knife he'd bought. He said he "was going to use it." From the description it was the same one that he used to stab Marie Fliehman to death.

Within days of this incident, their divorce became final.

Gerald Taylor called Tucker's psychiatrist for additional information. Dr. Glen Weaver knew about the violence, but expressed surprise at his peeping and his murder arrest. Nor did he know anything about the homosexual activity alleged by his wife.

Taylor made an appointment to meet him on January 13th, but when he arrived Weaver said he'd been advised by Tucker's attorney not to talk. Yet by this time his client's known movements on the weekend of the Bricca murders were exonerating him.

His supervisor verified that Tucker bought an airline ticket on September 23rd and flew to Cincinnati on that date. His return flight left Cincinnati at 5:46 PM on September 25th 1966 – more than three hours before the Briccas were murdered. TWA did not keep records after 60 days and could not verify if he took the flight. But an agent at Hertz confirmed Tucker rented a 1966 Tempest LeMans on September 23rd and returned it to their Greater Cincinnati Airport office at 4:15 PM on the 25th, proving he was at the airport 90 minutes before his flight. And Sun Oil records showed Tucker was at work on Monday morning September 26th.

Another promising suspect had eliminated himself. Richard Tucker would be convicted of murder, but was somehow pardoned by the West Virginia governor in 1972 and paroled to Ohio.

AS JIM DELL'AIRA SAT there, he thought this must be the strangest job interview he'd ever been part of.

What the hell was going on here?

It was Saturday morning January 14th at the Cincinnati Monsanto Plant in Addyston. Jim had been sent there by an agency to interview for an open position in plant engineering. The 36-year-old from Delaware was looking to better himself by transferring to another city – much like Jerry Bricca's September meeting with Standard Oil in San Francisco.

The two men interviewing him today were in bad moods. There was no humorous banter to break the ice, and neither one would make more than random eye contact. They were stiff, formal and obviously wished they were someplace else.

They told Jim this was their first Saturday after the Monsanto strike ended. As supervisors, both men worked in the plant during the strike and experienced friction crossing the picket line. Now on their first free Saturday in two months they had to come in to interview Jim, and they were not happy about it.

Jim had also once worked during a strike, and empathized with them over dodging strident strikers and running production with a skeleton crew of office workers. That seemed to break the ice.

Jim was well qualified, and they offered him the position on the spot. They seemed anxious to have this search over with. But when Jim asked them about the man he was replacing, they averted their eyes. One of them mumbled "he left."

Jim departed Monsanto, eager to call his wife and discuss the generous offer he was certain to take. But he also wondered why the demeanor of the interviewers had been so peculiar.

Only when he started the new job in February did he learn that the man he replaced at Monsanto was the murdered Jerry Bricca.

January 15th – January 31st

On Sunday, January 15th, the Green Bay Packers defeated the Kansas City Chiefs 35-10 in the first ever Super Bowl. Its doubtful prosecutors scrutinizing Laskey or detectives shadowing Leininger took time off to watch the football game.

On January 19th Gerald Taylor travelled to Flemingsburg KY, prompted by a tip Herb Vogel received from their county Sheriff. A woman named Jane Wallingford apparently knew who was in possession of the Bricca murder weapon!

Wallingford had a friend named Bonnie Tolver, who claimed her boyfriend had slain the Bricca family. The killer was Perry Dieterich of Maysville KY – he told Tolver he'd been to the Bricca house, had seen the bodies, and knew where the murder knife was.

As Taylor listened for details only the killer would know, his hopes were quickly dashed. Dieterich told Tolver both "Linda and Debbie were gutted, their insides were thrown against the wall, and one of Jerry's arms was cut off," along with his genitals.

Further investigation showed Dieterich was a delusional alcoholic who kept dynamite in his house. He was well known to the Maysville Police – the chief told Taylor he was "liable to tell a girl anything to impress her."

Taylor also interviewed Dr. Philemon Dill, a 25-year-old vet who interned with Leininger at GAH and remained a close friend. Shown pictures of the Bricca family, he did not recognize them or remember treating their animals.

"Did Dr. Leininger say anything to you about us?"

"Only to expect a visit from county detectives."

Taylor smirked. "Did he prep you?"

Dill took no offence. "He told me to be completely truthful with you, because if I lied you would find out and not give him any rest."

"So why won't he cooperate with us?"

"I don't know." Dill smiled dutifully. "But I'll speak with him and try to convince him that he should talk to you."

OSWALD ASSASSIN JACK RUBY'S sudden death on January 3rd had played out when the next big story of 1967 broke on January 27th.

A flash fire during a launch rehearsal test at Cape Kennedy killed three Apollo 1 crew members – Command Pilot Virgil "Gus" Grissom, Senior Pilot Edward White, and Pilot Roger Chaffee. The fire was of electrical origin, exacerbated by combustible nylon material – a faulty door hatch also prevented a quick rescue.

That week saw a brief flurry of Bricca interviews. Even with Fred Leininger as the focus, they were still looking at other suspects.

Lee Casper Schaible lived just around the corner from the Bricca house. In October, Betty Hardig had complained about her 58-year-old neighbor to investigators. She had entered Schaible's house to use his phone, but he locked her in with him and made weird, suggestive comments before finally opening the door.

Gerald Taylor interviewed Schaible and his wife at their home on January 24th – he offered Taylor peanuts and some of the "special wine" he'd offered Hardig. His wife said since he hurt his back he rarely left the house, and that he always locked the door when others were there.

Schaible's doctor confirmed the injury, calling him "a nut, but a harmless one."

William Nieman was a part-time meter reader who worked Greenway Avenue in June 1966. A complaint from a female customer in Sharonville resulted in a follow up interview where he claimed the incident was "just a misunderstanding" after he made "an awkward pass at her."

He did not recognize pictures of the Bricca family, and records showed he'd only worked the southern end of Greenway that summer. Nieman was open and cooperative during the interview, and gave his palm print voluntarily.

Walter Garling had already appeared in two previous statements when he brandished a knife while working temporary jobs in September. The 22-year-old had a long record of car thefts, and was first committed to Longview Mental Hospital at age 12. He lived in Westwood, about five miles from the Bricca house.

On January 26th a check of Longview records eliminated Garling. He was admitted on September 1st, 1966, escaped September 10th, returned on the 21st, and released on September 27th. Garling was present for all three bed checks on the night of September 25th.

ON JANUARY 31ST TAYLOR was questioning Judy Schreiber about her ex-boyfriend Joseph Bach Jr.

A car seen near the Bricca house on the murder night was identified as Bach's 1963 Chevy based on the license plate. Yet he lived 11 miles away – so what was he doing in Bridgetown?

Schreiber had a specific memory of that night, because it was the first Sunday they'd been together since his recent stint in the navy. The 21-year-old lived on Ebenezer Road, and Bach picked her up earlier that Sunday and took her to 6 PM Mass. He brought her back home between 9:00 and 9:30 PM.

Taylor frowned – the timeline seemed to clear Bach. "Did you two have any reason to be on Greenway Avenue that night?

Judy Schreiber blushed. "It's possible. We would sometimes park there and fool around a little before going home."

Taylor flashed on Larry Foppe's comment: *I see things. Lovers, parked in cars on Greenway.* "Would you have both been visible to anyone driving by?"

"Unless I was laying down across the front seat."

"Why did you break up with Joseph Bach?"

"No special reason. He wasn't mean or anything. I was looking for someone who wanted to settle down and he wasn't the one."

Schreiber then told Taylor about a regular customer at the UDF where she clerked, a man about 24 who came in every Sunday between 10 AM and Noon. After the Bricca murders, she had remarked to him about what a terrible thing it was.

"He said he lived a few houses away from them. Then he whispered he was home alone that evening without an alibi."

"How did you respond to that?"

"I said I was sure he had nothing to worry about."

"What did he say?"

"I could have done it for all the police know..."

February 1st – February 2nd

Carol Appleby was not helpful when interviewed in October. She was supposed to be Linda's hairdresser, yet failed to identify her picture. On February 1st she was still wary.

Gerald Taylor wasn't buying it. Today Carol was saying Linda's picture looked familiar but she didn't remember doing her hair. She asked them to talk to her manager at the Merle Norman Salon.

Janet Schum recognized Linda's picture immediately and recalled doing her hair about three times.

"Did you ever have any personal conversations with her?"

"Not that I can remember."

"Did she ever say anything about one of her neighbors bothering her?" This question was based on hearsay about Richard Meyer.

"Not to me. But I'll check with some of the other girls."

Later that day Taylor had a follow up interview with Robert Reicheld. In September he gave a statement describing three persons he saw entering a car in front of the Bricca house at 11:30 PM the night of the murders.

There was talk about having Bob and Ray McAdams, driving behind him as they left Western Bowl, hypnotized to enhance their recall of that night. Taylor settled for a second interview, yet Reicheld couldn't illuminate his fleeting glimpse of the strangers.

Taylor was certain Reicheld and his wife saw them in front of the Bricca house – he cited the dip in the road and had checked the location after reading about the murders. He again described the light green Falcon parked facing south and a young white male getting into the driver's side who appeared "startled or frightened" as his headlights swept over the car.

Reicheld said there were only two cars parked together on that end of Greenway. Taylor knew the other car was Jerry's.

His final stop that day was a chat with Sally Heine, a 19-year-old who knew the girl supposed to babysit for Linda Bricca the night of the murders. But Taylor was skeptical of this hearsay story.

"So who told you about this?"

"A girl I bowl with named Nancy Siegert."

"What exactly did she say?"

"Something about the babysitter being a friend of her cousin." She warned him not to expect much.

Taylor grimaced. "Why is that?"

"Nancy told me the babysitter won't say anything because she doesn't want to get involved."

THE NEXT DAY TAYLOR located Nancy Siegert. The 19-year-old Cincinnati Bell operator recalled telling the story about the babysitter to Sally Heine, yet couldn't remember who told her. Taylor sensed Siegert was being evasive, yet she continued to plead ignorance on the baby sitter and the source of the story.

Next was a 2nd interview with Glenn Ritchie, Jerry Bricca's travel partner for the September 26th West Virginia trip.

Taylor wanted clarification about the trip he and Jerry took to Danville, Illinois on September 19th. Bad weather had cancelled their flight home, so Ritchie rented a car and they drove back. He had dropped the other men off and Jerry was his last stop at around 10:20 PM before going home.

"Were there any lights on at his house."

"None. Not even the porch light."

Ritchie had seen another car parked on the street behind Jerry's in front of 3381 Greenway. He couldn't identify it in the gloom other than it being a dark colored station wagon.

"Did your wife know you were going to be late?"

"I called her from the road and asked her to call the other three wives. She got hold of Mrs. Hackworth and Mrs. Kilkenny."

"But not Jerry's wife?"

"She didn't call Mrs. Bricca. I don't know why."

TAYLOR'S NEXT STOP WAS Dan and Sandra Baldwin, the son and daughter-in-law of the Bricca's next door neighbors to the north. The young couple was visiting his parents on Saturday night September 24th and had seen a light green Falcon parked in the Bricca driveway around 9 PM.

When they left Greenway another vehicle followed them all the way to Cleves Warsaw Avenue. The driver was a lone white male driving fast and seemingly trying to get them to stop. They described his vehicle as a 1950 Plymouth that was a pinkish color.

Taylor had seen a report from Ray Hoffbauer, an off duty County Deputy who followed a car near the Bricca house the night before the murders. It seemed that Hoffbauer was tailing the Baldwins.

Dan Baldwin had also heard the story from Sally Heine's brother about the Bricca babysitter on the murder night. The still unidentified sitter had arrived around 10 PM, but was concerned about two men sitting in a car in front of the Bricca house. When they got out of the car she began to walk away – she saw one man enter the residence while the other paced back and forth out front.

Taylor was unconvinced by this odd hearsay. The mysterious babysitter never materialized, and he chalked it up to the rumor mill.

He spoke with Ray McAdams, who was driving behind Robert Reicheld on the murder night and also saw several people in front of the Bricca house.

"How far behind Reicheld's car were you?

"About five or six car lengths. The other car was in front of the Bricca residence. It was light Green or possibly white."

"And you saw someone getting in the driver's side?

"It looked like a young girl, maybe about 20 with light brown hair. She looked frightened, but maybe because my car startled her."

Taylor knew Reicheld had described the same subject as a man, but otherwise they matched. "Were there others in the car?"

Bricca Case Still Open Investigator Insists

Is the sheriff's investigation now at a standstill in the brutal stabbings of the Bricca family in Bridgetown?

"No;" declared Lt. Herbert Vogel Wednesday. "We still have an investigation going although the number of de-

Triple Homicide

Bricca Case Probe Stymied

In early February Vogel vented about the lack of cooperation from Fred Leininger and his attorney.

"I saw a shadow that looked like two people sitting close together on the passenger side. But I can't be sure about that."

Taylor asked Richard Meyer about a discrepancy that troubled him. Monsanto secretary Mary Bailey told detectives Meyer called there on Monday September 26th and left a message for Jerry to call him back. Yet Meyer continued to deny this, saying the only time he called Monsanto was when he and Dick Janszen spoke to the guard at the gate just before they discovered the bodies.

As he was leaving the Meyer house, Betty Meyer stopped him. "You know, I think when they were in Florida Dr. Leininger had a key to their house and was checking on the dogs."

Taylor's eyes flashed. "Leininger had a key to their house?"

She gave him a uneasy look. "I think so. But I'm not positive."

ON THAT THURSDAY HERB Vogel spoke to the media for the first time since November. His quotes in an *Enquirer* article headlined **Bricca Case Still Open** volleyed between defiance and defeat.

Vogel denied their investigation was at a standstill. "We still have an investigation going although the number of detectives on it has been reduced from 10 to 2. We can't afford to use more men full time because burglaries are knocking us cold."

Indeed, other crimes were flourishing as tips and interviews diminished. And their prime suspect had fashioned a stalemate.

> **One man who detectives would like to question further has hired a lawyer who has set terms for the interview which police will not accept. "This is still an obstacle," the lieutenant said, "until we find a way to circumvent it."**

Vogel and Coroner Frank Cleveland were still at odds over the alleged rape of Linda Bricca. Vogel maintained there was "evidence of recent sexual relations before the killing," but nothing to indicate definitely to me that it was rape." He clarified "recent intercourse" as 24 to 36 hours before the family was slain.

This strongly implied that their female victim was having an affair that may have turned deadly. They could link their suspect to Linda Bricca, but he continued to reject all requests for blood, hair, and fingerprint samples for comparison.

Their case was slipping into darkness – like the dashing, diminishing wail of midnight trains echoing past a ghost town...

Linda with bridesmaids and entire wedding party.

Known to their neighbors as "the kids," Gerry and Linda were a popular couple.

THE BRICCA MYSTERY

...AND NOBODY IS TALKING

"The most beautiful child you could imagine."

CINCINNATI, OHIO, APRIL 6, 1967

■ For two days the neat house on the quiet street in the suburb where the Briccas lived had been strangely quiet. So quiet that at the close of the second day, a worried neighbor went to the front door and opened it. He saw a foot lying on the floor at the top of the stairs, too still to calm his fears. Opening that door was the act that launched an investigation into the slaughter of the Bricca family, man, wife and child. This was on September 27, 1966. And in the seven month investigation that followed, the problem of getting at the truth has been a problem of opening the right door. In that time, the police have, by their own count, talked to more than 400 people. No one has been able to tell them anything that has brought them closer to a solution.

But there is one man whose story they would like to hear. They don't say that the solution to the Bricca massacre hinges on what this man

The July 1967 issue of *Front Page Detective* confronted the wall of silence surrounding the Bricca case.

CHAPTER TWELVE

PHANTOM FOOTSTEPS

"The man who never alters his opinion is like standing water, and breeds reptiles of the mind."

William Blake

FEBRUARY 3RD, 1967 – DECEMBER 31ST, 2017

February 3rd – March 28th

Crime stories dominated the national news in February and March of 1967.

On February 20th, the trial of Richard Speck for the murder of eight student nurses began in Peoria, Illinois after a change of venue from Chicago was granted. Actual testimony wouldn't begin until April, after a flurry of pre-trial motions contesting Speck's sanity resulted in a six week evaluation by a panel of psychiatrists.

Four days later, alleged Boston Strangler Albert DeSalvo escaped from Bridgewater State Hospital with two other inmates. Women of Boston cowered behind locked doors until he was recaptured the next day.

That same day, an AP story revealed the coincidental deaths of 16 persons connected to the JFK assassination whose testimony contradicted the Warren Commission conclusions. And there'd been several mass shootings that week, including four persons gunned down by an Illinois resort lake.

In March a Cincinnati *Enquirer* headline announced **Murder Spree Hits Local Area**. There had been 14 murders so far in 1967, but publicity was scant, since most were domestic killings, drunken shootings or black on black crimes.

With Posteal Laskey's murder trial approaching, the local chapter of the Black Nationalists began distributing leaflets in black neighborhoods that read: "Will we stand by as we have in the past and see one of our BLACK BROTHERS sacrificed?"

On March 17th, Laskey's lawyers tried to have Judge Simon Leis Sr. removed from the trial for bias and prejudice. While sentencing Laskey for an assault conviction in 1958, Leis had told him that "Men like you should be put out of society for life." A district court judge ignored his history with the defendant and denied the motion.

Signer and Roney then filed for a change of venue, arguing that Laskey couldn't get a fair trial because of the "climate of fear", citing news reports and detective magazines linking him "with some unknown person called the Cincinnati Strangler."

Judge Leis denied the motion, and set the trial for March 27th.

JIM DELL'ARIA SAT IN his cubicle in Monsanto's Building 7, thinking about the extraordinary circumstances that brought him to Cincinnati for this particular job. He began work there in February, and his family was moving out in April. Jim had yet to tell his wife about the secret kept from him during his first weeks at Monsanto.

It was subtle at first – that awkward job interview, the silence about his predecessor, nervous looks when he approached whispering co-workers. Plus the previous fellow's desk was all wrong. It wasn't organized like an engineer leaving the company.

Jim was a process engineer, like this "Jerry" guy who apparently departed rather suddenly. This was the pursuit of efficiency in manufacturing methods to save time and money, and Jim was a logical, methodical planner who dealt with tangible measures. But to his eyes something was dreadfully wrong in his department.

It all came out when he asked John Jarvis how to get in touch with Jerry Bricca. Jim had a problem he was certain only the former project manager could answer. Jarvis became flushed, drew him aside, and told him about the murders.

So that was why the interview in January was so strange! The man he replaced was slain along with his family, and they hadn't caught the killer yet. It was a rare, shocking situation with no prototype for polite discussion.

Now it was March, and John Jarvis was talking about it often. Jim could see he had been profoundly affected by the crime. John admitted he practically "worshiped" Jerry Bricca – he shadowed him, watched how he worked, and strove to emulate him.

Even six months later Jarvis was fidgety about it, still stressed over having aggressive questions hurled at him by suspicious detectives. Jim could picture Jarvis being interrogated – the guy was probably a basket case as the cops grilled him about the murder of his closest co-worker and good friend.

When Jim asked about his theory of the crime, Jarvis surprised him again. People at Monsanto seemed to know who did it.

"So who was it?" Jim wasn't sure he wanted to know.

"The feeling around here was that the vet did it. Guy by the name of Fred Leininger."

"Why would he kill the whole family?"

John Jarvis lowered his voice. "Jerry's wife was vivacious. A real knockout. She was having an affair with Leininger."

ON MARCH 28TH THE *Enquirer* front page headline seemed to sound the death knell for the Bricca investigation: **Bricca Case Probe Stymied.** The lead was unambiguous:

> **Sheriff's deputies want to question a man in the Bricca murder case, but his attorney says, 'NO!' They have offered to meet several conditions set by attorney Richard Morr, yet he says the police offer is 'only half' of what he wants for his client.**

Herb Vogel was at the end of his tether. "We feel as if we are being hindered even though we agree to most of the conditions laid down by Mr. Morr. We feel his client could supply us with information that may prove important to an ultimate solution to this triple homicide."

Once again he failed to identify their suspect, but by now half the West Side knew it was Fred Leininger.

After interviewing over 400 people, Morr's client was #1 on a short list of those not yet eliminated. Yet county detectives had not spoken to him since October 8, 1966.

In February, Vogel had made substantial concessions to Morr in order to facilitate the meeting. Morr never responded, despite repeated phone calls to his office. On March 21st Gerald Taylor "bumped into" the lawyer at the County Courthouse, and Morr asked for the tape recording of the October interview – without promising another session with his client.

According to Vogel, these seven questions were sent in advance to Morr – the same ones asked of any other person of interest:

- **When did you last see Linda Bricca alive?**
- **Did you see Linda Bricca on Thursday, September 22.**
- **When did you last visit the Bricca residence?**
- **For what reason did you last visit the Bricca residence?**
- **Did Linda Bricca ever discuss with you any of her personal problems?**
- **Were you ever out with Linda Bricca socially?**
- **Where were you on Sunday, September 25, between 9 PM and midnight?**

But through his attorney, the suspect declined to answer any questions about his relationship with Linda. Or any other questions, for that matter.

Predator and prey retreated into a lingering psychological stalemate, evocative of Dostoyevsky's classic novel *Crime and Punishment*, yet enduring much longer...

March 27th – April 7th

It was only a matter of time before the national crime tabloids swooped in to cover the trials and tribulations of the Queen City.

The March issue of *Inside Detective Magazine* contained the feature **If This is Barbara's Killer, Will the Stranglings End?**

> **During this year of multiple horrors, fear has become as common as air. Most women would not dream of venturing out alone at night and all Cincinnati slept behind double-locked doors... The murders are the prime matters for debate in**

> **bars, conversation pits, coffee klatches and in city council... Cincinnati for the past year has been the home and hunting ground to someone known only as the Cincinnati Strangler. In one year he has slain six or seven women and raped five of them...**

On Monday March 27th, Posteal Laskey went on trial for the killing of Barbara Bowman. Prosecutor Melvin Rueger would wait for this verdict before considering charges in the other murders.

An all-white pro-death penalty jury was seated, and as testimony began on Monday April 2nd, members of Cincinnati's Black Muslim sect began observing the proceedings. Rumors were spreading through the black community that Laskey was being railroaded as the Strangler in a trial not connected with those crimes.

With little physical evidence the prosecution relied heavily on eyewitness testimony. Three patrons at the Lark Café identified him as the driver who picked up Bowman. They had admittedly been drinking, and their descriptions of the man's facial hair and clothing were not consistent. Laskey's goatee was a bone of contention – his sparse chin whiskers were only obvious in profile.

Several passengers, including two black men, identified Laskey as their driver in cab #870 that night. Sol Thompson, the cabby who picked up a drenched fare near the crime scene, identified Laskey as the man who entered his cab around 3 AM.

Especially damning was the Yellow Cab dispatcher who testified that call #186 used by the killer was Laskey's number when he worked there in 1962. This blunder actually proved the Bowman slaying was a crime of chance. If Laskey had planned to kill a female passenger that night, he would never have used a call number that could be linked to him.

Over strong defense objections, Virginia Hinners was allowed to describe her harrowing assault the previous September in the New Thought Unity Center. She left no doubt that Laskey was her assailant during the lengthy encounter. Hinners told how he first asked to see the janitor, but then choked her, threw her around the room, and threatened her with "what the others got."

Two surprise witnesses delivered dramatic testimony. These women testified they drove by a cab parked near the murder scene and stopped

State Witness Places Laskey Near Death Scene

A description of a Negro man rising from the back seat of a taxicab and crawling to the front seat, while a white woman rose from the same back seat, was given Thursday at the first degree murder trial of Posteal Laskey Jr.

Mrs. Irene Aultz, 3821 Boudinot Ave., identified that man as the 29-year-old Laskey. She is the first wit-

It was after she said they came abreast of a taxicab to ask directions that she described the scene. Mrs.

Key eyewitness testimony linked Laskey with Barbara Bowman in the stolen cab at the crime scene.

to ask directions from a black man sitting in the rear seat. Signer and Roney wore blatant expressions of disgust as the witnesses drove a spike into their defense.

Both were married with husbands serving in Vietnam, and they were driving around at 2:30 AM looking for a party they knew about. Mrs. Eileen Aultz swore that after she spoke to the driver, someone else rose up in the back seat beside him.

"My God, that's a white woman!" she exclaimed. They drove off, assuming they had interrupted a romantic encounter.

Despite slanting rain and dismal darkness, Aultz identified that man as Posteal Laskey.

GERALD TAYLOR WAS DOING paperwork when the phone rang. The caller said he was an amateur sleuth who could break the deadlock in the

Bricca case. He wouldn't reveal his name, but his voice was authoritative, like an ex-cop might sound.

Taylor fed him some line. "Why haven't you called us earlier?"

"You guys are helpless with that lawyer protecting him. No way to force a confession."

"So why are you calling me now?"

"I'm hoping you will give my story to the press, so the publicity will force your suspect to come forward."

"And who is our suspect?"

"Fred Leininger. The vet Linda worked for that last week."

Taylor winced. "And what was his motive?"

"It's clear as day. Leininger was stuck on her, made advances, was rejected, and then sought revenge." The caller said Leininger was a good sized man, a "vicious man who was not insane."

"So how did the crime go down?"

"He saw them all in the basement, so he came in the front door and waited in the bedroom. First he hit Jerry over the head with a blackjack, and then Linda. He choked the child to death, and then slashed them up to make it look like a maniac had done it."

Taylor sighed. "So if we publish his name as the prime suspect he'll be forced to cooperate?"

"Let me repeat," the mystery caller droned. "He is a brutal man but not a maniac."

SIX MONTHS AFTER THE murders, only Herb Vogel and Taylor were working the case. Vogel was focused on a piece of evidence that intrigued the FBI – the tape attached to Jerry Bricca's face. He had received their analysis on March 22nd, and immediately fired off a letter to the 3M Company, the Fortune 500 godfather of pressure sensitive tape manufacturers.

He indicated that their tape fragment was used to gag a victim in a triple homicide. Could they identify the company that manufactured the tape, and whether the unusual 1-7/8" width was made for a particular use?

3M's top tape engineer responded quickly, insisting that despite the FBI analysis they needed to see the actual tape sample. He agreed the width was "unusual but not unknown," and supplied a list of companies that "possibly could have produced it." He also provided Vogel with names of all the American companies that produced cloth tapes.

As April slid into its second week, Vogel and Taylor began the mind-numbing task of contacting every one of those companies.

April 8th – May 30th

The prosecution in the Laskey trial rested their case on Saturday April 8th. The defense opened on Monday morning, called only 11 witnesses, and was done by mid-afternoon.

Laskey's mother, brother and three family members corroborated his alibi for the Bowman slaying, swearing that "Junior" was home in bed on the night of August 14th, 1966. But none could explain why they remembered that particular night.

In a mild surprise, the defendant took the stand to proclaim his innocence. Prosecutor Melvin Rueger spent an unbelievably short 17 minutes on his cross-examination of Laskey. Yet there were several heated exchanges.

Q: Didn't you use cab number 186 in 1962?

A: I think perhaps I did.

Q: You know very well you did, don't you, Laskey?
Mr. Signer: Objection. He is arguing with the witness.
The man answered the question for him.

Q: Have you got a goatee now?

A: Yes, sir.

Q: Got a moustache now?

A: Yes, sir.

Q: Look at the judge. Turn all the way around.

A: Pardon?
Mr. Signer: Objection.
Mr. Rueger: Just to see if it's visible from all angles.
Mr. Signer: This is not a lineup.

Rueger even asked him to walk across the courtroom, because some Lark Café witnesses said the cab driver had a distinctive gait. Signer's objection was sustained, and Rueger broke off his cross.

After another spate of defense motions, the case went to the jury late Wednesday. They deliberated for eight hours before finding him guilty of first degree murder with no recommendation for mercy.

Laskey flashed a grim smile. "I expected it," was his only comment. The *Post* headline that afternoon thundered the verdict: **Laskey Guilty, Must Die!**

Prosecutors and police were vague on whether the Bowman conviction closed the six strangling cases. When asked if those murders were now solved, City Manager William Wichman would only say "I've got a smile on my face."

True Detective Magazine ran a **Special Double Length Feature! Exclusive Report on Cincinnati's Phantom Slayer** in their April issue. Their conclusion echoed the sound of a city ready to finally breathe:

> **For a full year, the city's women lived in terror as a short dark man committed rape after rape and killed without warning or mercy. With brazen audacity, he even killed a woman in a neighborhood where he knew a score of policemen were hunting for him...**
>
> **But now the tension has been broken. And once more women are seen in the city's streets after the fall of night...**

Local Civil Rights groups assailed the verdict and death sentence. The NAACP called it "circumstantial evidence of white witnesses versus Negro witnesses." The Congress of Racial Equality condemned "the wanton desire for blood which led to selection of an all-white jury," and "a trial held in an atmosphere where fear reigned and desire to kill a nigger held sway..."

On Saturday April 15th, a few protestors appeared outside the courthouse, carrying signs saying "Laskey is Innocent – We Know It!" One of them was Laskey's cousin Peter Frakes.

LASKEY'S ATTORNEYS FILED A motion for a new trial, citing 27 alleged errors. Most compelling was Judge Leis not recusing himself despite showing previous bias toward Laskey with his "men like you should be put out of society for life" remark in 1958.

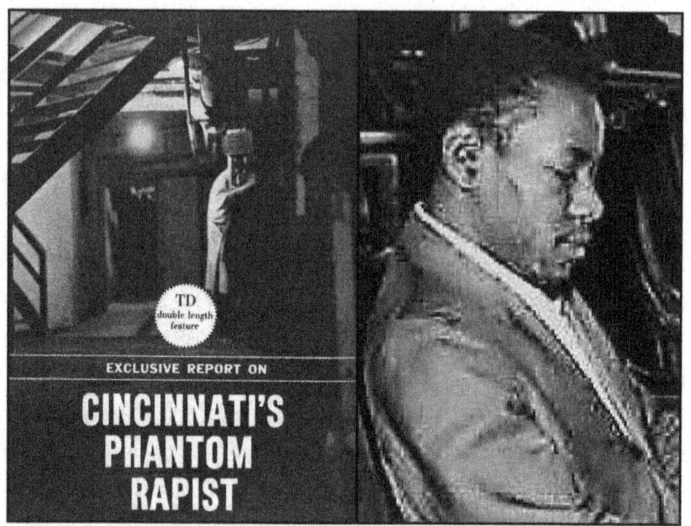

***True Detective* ran a feature on the Strangler and speculated whether Laskey's conviction would end the terror.**

That same day in Peoria, Illinois, Richard Speck was found guilty of killing the eight student nurses and sentenced to death, closing the book on one of the most horrific mass murders of all time. The national media reveled in the Speck conviction while completely ignoring the Laskey verdict.

Ominous clouds were forming as spring continued its journey towards the "Summer of Love." A proposed visit by Black Power advocate Stokely Carmichael stirred up racial tension when a group of local ministers denounced him. The NAACP remained neutral, with local chairman Dr. Bruce Green saying "We feel he has a right to speak but we do not have to agree with him."

Carmichael did speak at an Avondale church on April 29th to a mostly black audience of a thousand people. He told them that "the struggle is under way and there can be no turning back." He lauded boxer Mohammed Ali, the former Cassius Clay, who the day before had refused induction into the US Army. "He is the man of the hour for the Negro race...by standing up to the white man."

In early May, Judge Leis set Posteal Laskey's date with the Ohio electric chair for September 15th. Laskey told the judge that "You will be passing sentence on an innocent man."

In an interview on May 17th, Dr. Martin Luther King predicted "a very dark summer" of racial rioting, citing "the intolerable conditions that cause Negro despair that are still here." King did not sanction the violence, calling it "an endless reign of meaningless chaos," but he believed that "a riot is the language of the unheard."

International news was no better. As Israeli and Arab soldiers were squaring off in the Gaza Strip for the start of the "Six Day War", the Pentagon announced that US troops suffered their worst week of the Vietnam War, as Vietcong rocket and mortar attacks in the DMZ killed 337 soldiers and wounded 2282. The heavy losses brought our casualties in Vietnam to 10,253 killed since 1964.

By the end of May Laskey had gained a groundswell of support. A Cincinnati delegation went to Columbus and asked Governor Rhodes to review Laskey's conviction. They charged that Laskey "was also convicted of being the alleged Cincinnati Strangler... the very air in Hamilton County was electrified with the desire to convict any Negro because of the strangler scare."

On the final day of May, Peter Frakes was back at the courthouse, bearing a new placard that read "Laskey is Innocent, but Cincinnati is Guilty!"

June 1st – June 28th

June came rumbling in on rumors of impending strife. Nationally and locally, newspapers warned that the "long, hot summer" of racial discontent was simmering.

J. Edgar Hoover denounced some black leaders, saying they were inviting "hotheads and rabble rousers" to riot in specific cities this summer. "It's an open invitation to move into action on cue. It puts them on notice that they are expected to riot."

An NAACP spokesman in New York City seemed to agree, saying portentous signs were emerging and "there are some small groups talking about the possibility of violence." Stokely Carmichael chimed in, saying "If we don't get justice we're going to tear this country apart." Moderate black leaders criticized him for this statement, but the fuse was lit.

On June 5th the *Enquirer* AP ran this fateful headline: **Nation Braced for Summer Race Riots**. The same day, violence flared in Boston and

Clearwater, Florida. Across the nation people held their breath as civil rights crusaders called for peaceful protests.

A June 8th letter in the *Enquirer*, Reverend Samuel Wright asserted that "Posteal Laskey was tried in a climate of fear, frustration, and suspicion...because this city had been seized with an awesome fear by the Strangler." And he wondered "how was it humanly possible in such a prejudiced and hysterical environment for Laskey, a Negro, to receive a fair trial?"

On June 10th, Peter Frakes was on an Avondale corner with his picket sign. He was asked to "move along" by a police officer because the crowd around him was blocking pedestrian traffic. When he refused Frakes was arrested on a charge of "loitering".

Cincinnati's loitering statutes had long been imposed with bias toward black men, and this selective enforcement riled the black communities and their leaders.

With omens of unrest hovering over Cincinnati, Dr. Martin Luther King stepped into the fray. On Sunday morning June 11th, he preached non-violence at churches in Lockland and Avondale. Eschewing the radical "Burn Baby Burn" rhetoric of extremists like Carmichael, Dr. King urged his brethren to "Learn Baby Learn!" And he warned them that "hate and violence can destroy us all."

King left Cincinnati that afternoon confident he had spanned a bridge over troubled waters. This man of peace, whose anti-Vietnam fervor equaled his passion for civil rights, could never have imagined what turmoil the next day would bring to the Queen City...

FRAKES HAD WARNED THE arresting officers that "if you try and move me, there'll be a riot." Yet on Monday night June 12th, a peaceful protest was scheduled at the site of his arrest.

The meeting began at 7 PM, and progressed nonviolently as citizens marched near the corner of Reading and Rockdale until 9 PM. Donald Spencer and Clyde Vinegar, two local civil rights leaders, addressed the crowd but soon began to admonish the conduct of some young black males who showed up. "This is the kind of behavior we don't need!" shouted Vinegar.

The youths started booing the speakers and throwing things, while another roving band began throwing firebombs through windows.

Within ten minutes around 200 police officers showed up and further incensed the crowd. The epicenter at Reading and Rockdale exploded with the force of a human earthquake.

The city was under siege for five days as disorder flared through Avondale and other black neighborhoods. Youths would loot stores, destroy cars, set fires and pelt first responders with rocks and bottles. Emergency calls tumbled over each other as they spewed from police and fire radios. Before the week was out, the litany of violence was long – vandalism, rock throwing, window smashing, arson, assault, shooting, looting, and Molotov cocktails.

Only the deployment of 1000 Ohio National Guard helped the overmatched Cincinnati police quell this insurrection – or revolution, depending on which side you were on. The final tally: 1 dead, 63 injured, 362 arrests, and millions of dollars in property damage.

An *Enquirer* editorial on June 15th tried to bring perspective to the tumult of the last four days. While not condoning the violence, they reasoned that "such an outburst of venom could only be triggered" by longstanding frustration and despair.

> **As the ashes are sifted for the causes and as conviction of the guilty is sought, citizens of good will, both black and white, must remember not to condemn a whole race for what some have done.**
>
> **However one looks at it, though, these are sad days for the Queen City...**

WAS THE POSTEAL LASKEY verdict responsible for the riot? Two Government studies would eventually link his conviction and death sentence to the June race riots.

The tableau of events in 1966 had brewed a wicked concoction for the sedate Queen City.

It began with police telling the media that the strangler was a black man. Eventually they apprehended a black suspect, and the pressure to convict was tremendous. For a large segment of the Cincinnati's German/Appalachian population, there was no greater crime than a black man raping and murdering white women.

The black community saw a rush to find a scapegoat. White justice was hurtling off the tracks. There is no physical evidence against him as the "Strangler", yet they watched the prosecutor build a circumstantial case in an unrelated stabbing death of a young woman. They witnessed a trial marked by prejudice, politics, innuendo, and guilt by inference.

The dilemma was peace vs. justice. Law Enforcement officials clamored for a conviction based on damning testimony and their belief that the city's safety and sanity were in the balance. Black people could argue for an acquittal based on reasonable doubt and their belief that Laskey's prosecution was politically motivated.

Everyone wanted the strangler's reign of terror to end, but no one was blind to the ramifications of a guilty verdict.

Cincinnati's hangover from the June riot never faded. When Martin Luther King was assassinated the following April, the city's second riot in ten months left two dead, countless injured, and forever splintered Cincinnati's image as the serene and majestic Queen City of the Midwest...

July 1st – September 2nd

On June 29th Posteal Laskey was granted an indefinite stay of execution. Mandatory appeals would easily give him several more years of life, and perhaps beyond.

Louis Jose Monge was executed in the Colorado gas chamber on June 9th for murdering his wife and three of his children. The pace of capital punishment in this country had slackened in the 1960's, but no one could have guessed that Monge would be the last inmate legally put to death for the next ten years.

In early July, *Front Page Detective* ran a tantalizing feature titled **The Bricca Mystery...and Nobody is Talking.** Although Bricca was mentioned in some pulp treatments of the Strangler saga, this was the genre's first story devoted entirely to this crime.

The article confronted the prime suspect in a way the Cincinnati papers wouldn't dare:

> **Police have, by their own count, talked to more than 400 people. No one has been able to tell them anything to bring them closer to a solution.**

> **But there is one man whose story they would like to hear. They don't say the solution to the Bricca massacre hinges on what this man could tell them, but this is a door they haven't been able to open. This man stands on his constitutional right not to answer any questions the police put to him, and as a result the investigation into three brutal and sadistic murders may grind to a halt...**

There was no legal way to force his answers. Nor was there a penalty for exercising his rights, and his silence could not be cited in court as grounds for suspicion.

The *FPD* article played fast and loose with some of the "facts." Jerry and Linda were "stabbed so many times that much of the autopsy consisted simply of counting the knife thrusts. Witnesses saw the Briccas working on a "backyard project" that rainy Sunday and Linda walking the dogs between 8:30-9:00 PM.

Yet the writer did evoke the sense of anxiety and outrage: "These crimes, savage and unspeakable, have had a profound effect on the suburban community where the Bricca family lived... the details that trickled out stimulated the feeling of fear."

The crime's magnitude forced people to overcome their restraint and get involved: "The cooperation was excellent. It was that kind of crime. No one wanted to go on record as being unwilling to assist in the apprehension of the man who slaughtered the Briccas."

His conclusion exposed the lingering frustration over an investigation that had become a stalemate:

> **What is a police officer entitled to think when one man out of 400 refuses to cooperate? Four hundred people saw it as their responsibility to assist in every way to find the killer at large among them. One man has elected to use his constitutional privileges to flaunt the good will and best interests of an entire community.**
>
> **And the man who slaughtered three people without regard to their constitutional rights to summer nights around the barbeque pit along Greenway Avenue – running the dogs, raking the leaves, or just growing up – will never be brought to justice...**

On July 29th, Lieutenant Herb Vogel submitted his Bricca investigation summary to Captain Otting and Sheriff Tehan. The five page report concentrated on three areas – testing of the tape from Jerry's face, interviews of animal trainers who were at the April 1966 Shrine Circus, and the standoff with Dr. Fred Leininger.

Vogel first reviewed investigational parameters including manpower, canvassing, lead cards, interview schedules, and forensic testing. Approximately 400 lead cards were issued and 18 packages sent to the FBI lab.

After sending out letters to every tape manufacturer on the list provided by the 3M Company, a local rubber company confirmed the evidence tape was a "high-grade waterproof medical tape" as opposed to an industrial tape. The tape analysis itself reads like today's DNA jargon, and would cause even the most an ardent detective's eyes to glaze over.

Gerald Taylor then went to the Johnson and Johnson Research Center in New Jersey for a consultation. None of the companies on their list had records of selling this unusual 1-7/8" wide product. But tapes of similar composition had been sold to, among other outlets, veterinarians and distributors of veterinary products.

A chart of infra-red curves on the adhesive gave them a prospective match – the Kendell Company in Barrington, Illinois. Taylor traveled there to pick up some samples.

Herb Vogel could not hide his astonishment – Barrington was where both Linda's parents and Fred Leininger owned property...

On April 2nd Vogel had travelled to Columbus, Ohio to interview Marion Earl Grubbs about his animal act at the Shrine Circus. Grubbs was shown pictures of Linda – he denied ever seeing her and insisted he'd never allow any outsider near his elephants. He gladly gave up the names of Johnnie Harriott and Joe Frisco, two other trainers at the Shrine Circus who were "friendly with the girls" and would allow them to "ham around with their animals."

Harriott had a jealous wife who would not appreciate someone like Linda playing up to her husband, while Frisco employed "two white males at the Cincinnati Gardens" who were of questionable character. Both men had elephants in their acts, and Frisco kept a little apartment with a couch and a bed set up in a semi-trailer outside the Gardens.

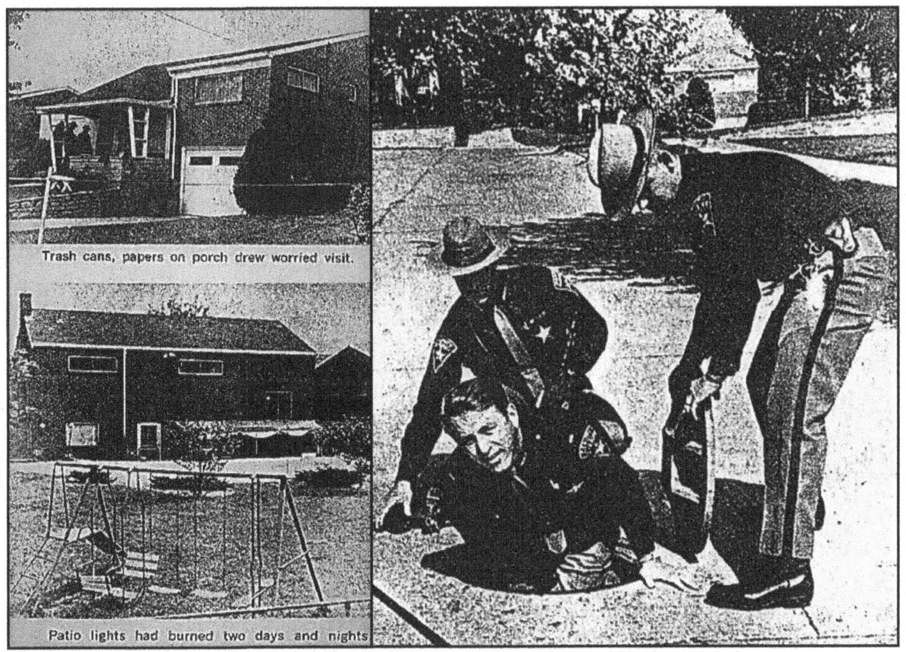

The *Front Page Detective* article showed pictures of the crime scene and police searching the sewers for the missing weapon.

This animal trainer scenario was favored by Captain Otting, who believed "at least three people" participated in the murders. And it tallied with two witnesses who saw three subjects in front of the Bricca house around the time of the murders.

Finally, Vogel reviewed their February meeting with Richard Morr, attorney for Fred Leininger. Morr had asked for the interview questions to be submitted to him in advance, and also requested a copy of the tape recording from his client's October 8th interview. Plus he wanted this next interview at a place of his choosing that was convenient for both him and his client.

Yet even with those concessions granted, Morr did not reply to their certified letter.

The final paragraphs of the report left no doubt about the obstacle they faced with their prime suspect:

Repeated attempts have been made to come up with some sort of agreement with Richard Morr, attorney for Fred Leininger,

> **and all have failed, even though we did comply with the lawyer's request of submitting a record of the questions prior to our interview with his client.**
>
> **It now appears that Mr. Morr will not allow us to interview his client under any circumstances.**

I spoke with former Hamilton County Prosecutor Mike Allen to ask if HE would have done anything different to breach the 1966 stalemate between Richard Moor and Melvin Rueger:

> ***Morr was holding all the cards. But any suggestion that Mel Rueger would have backed off to protect a prominent suspect is ludicrous. Mel was by the book, a boy scout, and everyone knew it.***
>
> ***Once the stalemate was confirmed, I would have identified the suspect to the press. I would hope the media would have found out his name and reported it first. Because identifying a legitimate suspect would not be slanderous or libelous.***
>
> ***If the suspect is in custody, under interrogation, not free to leave, but not under arrest, all Miranda rules would apply. In 1966, this would be more open to interpretation. So Rueger was walking the line, trying not to run afoul of Miranda.***
>
> ***A Grand Jury could have issued a subpoena. The suspect would have to appear by himself in the jury room, but a good lawyer would have advised him to plead the 5th whenever he was uncomfortable with a question or in doubt about an answer.***

So Fred Leininger could have been forced in front of a Grand Jury – where he would again exercise his constitutional right to remain silent.

September 3rd – October 24th

The Bricca investigation flickered to life on September 3rd, when Ernie Nehrer sent a letter to the Houston, Texas PD about a triple stabbing there the previous morning.

An intruder had knifed a young girl to death and attacked her parents, who were in critical condition from multiple wounds. The mother was raped, and the parents were bound with ropes and found on top of each other in a closet.

A suspect who lived near the victims was arrested a few days later, and any tenuous connection to Bricca evaporated when he could be placed in Houston on September 25th 1966.

A Cincinnati *Post* front page feature on September 22nd allowed the County to fire off a final salvo in the Bricca case: **Prosecutor Believes He Knows Who Killed Bricca Family... A Year Goes By – Still No Arrest**. As the one year anniversary of the crime approached, Rueger insisted he knew the Bricca killer's identity.

> **How can a murderer kill a family of three and vanish without a trace? Hamilton County officials don't think he has. They're convinced they know who the killer is.**
>
> **"This is a classic case where Supreme Court rulings thwart law and justice," says Rueger. "Here is a case where a man kills three persons, there are no living witnesses and he doesn't leave behind any evidence."**
>
> **"The only chance law enforcement has is to talk to the suspect, because we have insufficient evidence to go to the grand jury. But we can't question the man because the Supreme Court says that would be infringing on his constitutional rights."**

An unidentified detective was blunt: "You would tear a guy apart if it was ethical, but you're prevented by law from doing some things." Then he voiced what repulsed the entire city. "There was only one reason he would have to kill the little girl," he spat. "She knew him too well."

Another official revealed that Linda had known the suspect since 1963, and that they were seen together "several times on a lonely road." Motive for the triple murder was the suspect's fear of scandal. If their affair was exposed, it would jeopardize his marriage, his family, and his business.

Rueger had the last word. "We could use psychology and sales talk to get our suspect to confess. Now we have been deprived of those two tools by the Supreme Court, and men are walking around free who should be behind bars."

A YEAR GOES BY—STILL NO ARREST, ALTHOUGH . . .

Prosecutor Believes He Knows Who Killed Bricca Family

BY JAMES ADAMS

It will be a year Monday since a killer entered a tri-level home in Bridgetown and stabbed to death Gerald (Jerry) Bricca, 28; his wife, Linda, 25, and their daughter, Deborah, 4.

How can a murderer kill a family of three and then vanish without a trace?

Hamilton County officials don't think he has. They're convinced they know who the killer is.

Then why don't they make an arrest?

THIS IS THE QUESTION that angers Melvin G. Rueger, Hamilton County prosecutor.

"This is a classic case where recent Supreme Court rulings thwart law and justice," says Rueger. "Here is a case where a man kills three persons, there are no living witnesses and he doesn't leave behind any evidence.

"The only chance the law enforcement official has is to talk to the suspect, because we have insufficient evidence to go to the grand jury.

"But we can't question the man because the Supreme Court says that would be infringing on his Constitutional rights."

COUNTY OFFICIALS say they now know the suspect became acquainted with Mrs. Bricca shortly after the family moved here from Seattle.

Police also say the couple was seen together several times on a lonely road.

Here's how county officials reconstruct the crime:

Jerry Bricca worked long and odd hours at Monsanto Co. plant in Addyston where he was an engineer. He went to the plant Saturday morning, Sept. 24, and worked through the night. On Sunday morning, he attended 10 o'clock Mass at St. Aloysius Church in Bridgetown. He went back to work and didn't get home until late that evening.

JERRY PARKED his car in front of his home and then walked into the garage to carry out the garbage cans for next morning's pickup. He was seen alive by a neighbor between 8:30 p. m. and 9 p. m. Sunday.

Authorities now theorize that Jerry surprised the suspect by coming home at an unexpected time. The suspect heard Jerry carrying out the garbage cans and was prepared for him.

"I think the man in the house hit him as he walked in," one official says.

This particular official believes that the suspect killed Bricca because he was afraid of a scandal. Mrs. Bricca then was killed, too.

"There was only one reason he would have had to kill the little girl," the official says. "She knew him too well."

THE BODIES of Jerry and Linda Bricca were found on their bedroom floor. Debbie was on the floor of her bedroom next to her parents' room. Jerry had been stabbed seven times and Linda 10 times. The slayer drove his weapon through the body of Deborah four times as she lay on the floor.

A carving knife missing from the Bricca home has never been found, but officials now believe the killer might have used an arrow instead of a knife to stab his victims.

The bodies were not found until 10:45 p. m. Tuesday, Sept. 27. By this time decomposition made it difficult to determine whether the weapon was a knife or some other kind of sharp-pointed instrument.

"We always have informed suspects of their rights before questioning them," Rueger says, "but we could use psychology and sales talk to get them to confess.

"Now we have been deprived of those two tools by the Supreme Court, and men are walking around free who should be behind bars."

On the one year anniversary of the murders, Prosecutor Mel Rueger left no doubt that he knew the killer's identity.

The Bricca case was poised to pass into legend, a blending of history and myth that would seep into the West Side conscience like an invisible shadow, until the actual events would become blurred.

Because any good legend is nurtured by that old adage – the fewer the facts, the stronger the opinion...

THE ONE YEAR ANNIVERSARY article read like a last gasp for justice.

Except for sporadic mentions over the next few years, the Bricca investigation went into a deep freeze. Phone tips straggled in, mostly from citizens who just wanted to help. The cranks were still out there, berating detectives for not cracking the case or spinning wild conjectures to help them solve it.

A few were officially concerned – homicide detectives from other jurisdictions burdened with similar crimes. The magnitude of Bricca persistently aroused investigators from far-flung states.

Vogel was exhausted. HIS case might go on forever, and he hadn't taken a break for over a year. But the deck was stacked against them. They were dealing with a rational perpetrator who had committed a bizarre crime, a cunning killer or killers with a calculated yet inexplicable motive.

Even with a prime suspect under surveillance there was no "smoking gun", no single clue conclusive of guilt. Rumors highlighted some suspicious circumstances, yet they needed to link these stubborn coincidences with provable allegations.

And a smart lawyer like Richard Morr could sever a few links and destroy their fragile chain so that no Grand Jury would act on it.

The Bricca case jacket officially has 302 interviews, which does not include the 28 statements Gerald Taylor took in San Francisco, Seattle, and Chicago. Vogel also questioned some animal trainers in Columbus and Taylor had talked with several tape experts.

Interview #302 was completed on February 7th 1967, which is the last item one on the "Information Sheet." Yet there are some unnumbered entries of enticing material that didn't make the case file. Here are some examples:

- Mr. Yankowski, a Monsanto employee, was interviewed regarding a letter written by Jerry Bricca and placed in his file.
- They compared the unknown fingerprints with those of Posteal Laskey in Cincinnati PD custody. Fingerprints did not match.
- A Volkswagen dealer was interviewed regarding a sale made to Fred Leininger. His Oldsmobile was wholesaled to Potts Auto Sales, but it had already been cleaned up by their lot boys. The title for his "trade-in" was taken to the Post Office Inspector for a Ninhydrin process to lift any latent fingerprints.
- Mr. & Mrs. Bulaw went to see Dr. Leininger at the Glenway Animal Hospital. The discussion was taped and insight was gained regarding Leininger's psychological condition. *There is no date for this meeting and the tape is not in the case file.*

Three other entries caught my attention – none of these incidents were dated either.

Some head hair clippings and the "local suspect's" hat were sent to the FBI lab for comparison with the hair sample found clutched in Linda Bricca's hand. Phyllis Vogel told me that a detective lifted Leininger's hat from the cloak room of David's Buffet while the doctor was eating there.

They were toying with their suspect, and if Leininger knew who took the hat he never complained. Although this evidence was obtained without a warrant, County was willing to chance it to break the logjam. If they were lucky enough to go to trial, they would take their chances on admissibility at that time.

In December Herb Vogel showed up at the Glenway Animal Hospital with his dog for treatment. Leininger spoke to him, asking "aren't there any good vets near where you live? " The two were cordial at first, with Leininger saying that "we can get together after the holidays to discuss the Bricca matter, on a social level."

Yet Phyllis Vogel assured me this conversation ended badly, with Leininger angrily ordering Vogel to leave the premises. The notes claim this meeting was also "monitored and recorded", just like the Bulaw's discussion with Leininger referenced earlier. Was Leininger aware he was being recorded during these interactions? Or were the Bulaws and Vogel wearing a wire?

It was a report from Mrs. Bulaw that truly glistens for me.

In late December June Bulaw called Vogel to tell him she'd found cigarette butts arranged in a circle on Linda's ground marker. It unnerved her – the grave was on a private estate and not easy to locate. Someone made a point of leaving the butts that way.

This dovetails with a 2010 email I received from a Bulaw relative:

> ***The parents stated to me that upon a visit to the cemetery, someone had outlined only Mrs. Bricca's grave, with Marlboro cigarette butts. It is entirely possible that the suspect did this as well, since he owned property in Barrington Hills at this time.***

Leininger did own property in Barrington. And while Linda Bricca didn't officially smoke, I've interviewed neighbors who said she liked a cigarette when she was out walking with Debbie.

So was this a gesture from Leininger to his murdered lover? Perhaps it was a sign of remorse – without a hint of regret...

October 25th, 1967 – October 31st, 1969

On October 25th *Enquirer* Columnist Frank Weikel wrote a provocative update on the Bricca case: **Police Keep Tabs on Killing Suspect**. Weikel's police connections landed an interview with "a high ranking Hamilton County police official," who spoke about the surveillance of their prime suspect.

> **We're just about living with him. A policeman checks on him from the time he leaves his home in the morning and stays**

nearby until he returns for bed. One of our men even has lunch in the same restaurant where the suspect eats.

Weikel suggested their stalking was having an adverse effect on the suspect's drinking – "his normal one martini lunch has now tripled." He also revealed that Jerry Bricca's father was "in town recently and tried to talk with the suspect but was unable to get an appointment."

Weikel took another shot at the unnamed suspect on January 11th, 1968 with **The Bricca Case – No Co-Operation:**

The mystery is nearly 16 months old. County police are still watching the man they call a 'prime' suspect. Word has it that this suspect was confined to a hospital recently for treatment of nerves...

So Fred Leininger was being tailed. But was he being legally harassed? A friend of Bricca neighbor Joan Janszen told me that County detectives stayed in touch with her for years after the crime.

From her we learned that the police were making their presence known to Mr. Leininger. One quote I remember was that they would find him out somewhere and would say to him "Sure is terrible what was done to that little girl. How could anybody who did something like that to a little girl live with themselves?" She said it would usually be a couple of uniformed officers together whenever they would do this.

At this point in the investigation there was no strategy – it was all tactics, anything flagrant to set Leininger's teeth on edge. County walked up to the legal limit but did not cross it. Anytime Leininger used a restaurant glass or got a haircut he had to be careful. And if confronted by surly officers while leaving his favorite West Side watering holes the doctor had to stand there and take it.

This would be the last mention of the Bricca case in any local paper until May 1977.

But the Bricca case didn't disappear just because calendar pages flipped off like in an old newsreel. The shock, the anger, the pain, and the questions were still unreconciled.

SEVERAL FRONT PAGE CRIMES would transpire during 1969, including a mysterious East Side triple homicide and a West Side robbery "massacre."

On Sunday May 25th, Dr. Jane Shutt was found murdered in the basement of her spacious home in the Clifton gaslight district **(Queen City Notorious chapter 13)**. The prominent, attractive 43-year-old psychiatrist had been shot three times and struck 17 blows to the head with a fireplace poker.

Cincinnati detectives learned the victim was separating from her 75-year-old husband. Yet within hours the focus shifted to 23-year-old adopted daughter Barbara Jean Shutt, a volatile waif whose odd demeanor betrayed awareness of guilt. She confessed the next day, only to recant by claiming she was protecting her father. But Charles Shutt was proven to be in church with the couple's natural children when his wife was killed.

Barbara Jean was found guilty in a trial tainted by lurid accusations of adultery and lesbianism. One reporter even wrote "Who's being tried here – the murderer or the victim? The inscrutable, enigmatic woman child would serve 15 years in prison before being paroled into obscurity.

An appalling mass murder would rock the West Side in September. On Wednesday the 24th, Delhi police checking out a possible robbery at the Cabinet Supreme Savings and Loan stumbled upon a scene of appalling horror – four dead women stacked in the bank vault, riddled with gunshots. They were identified as teller Lillian DeWald and three unfortunate customers who walked in on the botched holdup.

The violence of the crime was matched only by the stupidity of the killers. Their actions when "casing the joint" days before had drawn attention, and all three were in custody by the 28th. In separate trials, John Leigh, Watterson Johnson and Raymond Kassow were sentenced to be executed on September 24th, 1970, one year from the date of the massacre.

Yet none of them would ever sit in Ohio's electric chair.

THE QUEEN CITY HAD barely recovered from the Cabinet Supreme atrocity when a baffling triple murder staggered the city – and revived restless memories of the three-year-old Bricca mystery.

The horror began on the Indian summer morning of October 23rd, when the bodies of Martin Dumler, his wife Patricia, and her mother

Frank Weikel

Police Keep Tabs On Killing Suspect

WHAT'S NEW in the murder investigation surrounding the brutal killings of Gerald Bricca, his wife and daughter?

This was a question I put to a high ranking Hamilton County police official. His answer follows:

"We're just about living with the suspect. A policeman checks on him from the time he leaves home in the morning and stays nearby until he returns for bed. One of our men even has lunch in the same restaurant where the suspect eats."

Thursday, Jan. 11, 1968
Page 15

Frank Weikel

The Bricca Case –No Co-Operation

BACKGROUND: Let's take a look at the progress—or lack of progress —in the still unsolved murder of Jerry Bricca, his wife and four-year-old daughter.

County police are still watching a man they call a "prime" suspect. Word has it that this suspect was confined to a hospital recently for treatment of nerves.

Frank Weikel's columns highlighted Mel Rueger's frustration over the stalemate with the prime suspect.

Mary Wilson were discovered in the master bedroom of their East Side Mt. Lookout home **(Queen City Gothic Chapter 12)**. All three had been shot in the head at close range, and the Dumlers were also stabbed in the chest. Their two children, ages 4 and 5, slept through the slaughter and alerted neighbors when they couldn't get into their parent's bedroom.

Mt. Lookout was one of Cincinnati's elite neighborhoods, abounding with lovely homes and verdant lawns. The idyllic setting, along with the victim's social standing, guaranteed this investigation would be rigorous and painstaking. Police insist that every homicide is investigated equally, but catching the killer of three affluent citizens in this prime location became their top priority.

The Dumler killer was poised and efficient, gunning down the three adults with murderous accuracy. He was also comfortable enough to remain in the house long enough to search it without waking the children. The coroner said the stab wounds were post-mortem, meaning the killer knifed Martin and Pat at least an hour after he shot them.

A police report filed two days before the murders glimmers for me. A Dumler neighbor reported his .38 caliber revolver with four "wad cutter" rounds had been stolen from his unlocked car. The weapon, the ammo, and the number of shots match the slugs in the victim's bodies.

The murder of Martin and Patricia Dumler, along with her mother in Mt. Lookout, remains unsolved almost 50 years later.

A killer lifting this weapon was familiar with the street and knew the gun would be there.

Pat Dumler was an attractive and buxom 27-year-old housewife, yet the investigation kept delving into the private life of her husband Martin. At age 29 he was the sales manager of a company run by his father, but he was rumored to have some shady gambling connections. The day before the murders, he was seen engaged in a heated discussion with a stranger on his father's driveway.

Lead investigator Paul Morgan, the man who arrested Posteal Laskey in December 1966, concluded Martin and Pat knew their killers. Mary Wilson was collateral damage – wrong place, wrong time. Morgan theorized the killer or killers arrived around 11 PM, and were let into the house by Martin.

Electrical cords in the home had been cut and were missing. Based on lividity, the cords had been used to bind the victims and were removed at least an hour after they died. Whoever killed the adults didn't seem concerned about the sleeping children.

A number of good suspects hovered on the radar, including a family member and a Dumler neighbor. Yet despite one of the most intensive investigations in Cincinnati Police department history, whoever killed the Dumlers was never caught. As with the Bricca murderer, his identity remains a mystery to this day.

And just like Bricca, the Dumler case still survives on rumors and undertones...

November 1969 – December 1981

Just over four years later, the Bricca tragedy claimed another life. On October 13th, 1970, former neighbor Richard Janszen died at their new home on Falconbridge Drive at the age of 41.

His wife Joan and their four children saw his final agony. Richard had gone to the doctor that day, complaining of indigestion and heartburn. He came home feeling better, only to have a massive heart attack that night on their living room floor – he died before the ambulance got there.

The Janszen's had moved away from the haunting memories of Greenway Avenue in 1969, but Richard never recovered from his gruesome tour of the Bricca murder scene. The shock and horror of seeing his neighbors butchered in their own home had broken something inside him.

His children told me the father they knew slowly faded away after that night. Unlike his wife, Richard never spoke of about the murders. A cheerful family man with a passion for bowling became a shell of his former self, plagued by phantom images of the appalling violence he'd viewed.

Now 50 years later, the Janszen children consider their father to be the fourth victim of the Bricca killer...

On October 3rd, 1971, a man was shot to death at the north entrance to Spring Grove Cemetery on Gray Road. As fate would have it, he would become the third person murdered that night between 10 and 11:30 PM **(Queen City Gothic chapter 13)**.

First a woman was shot to death while pulling into her apartment parking space just after 10 PM. Second to die was a UC grad student hacked to death while walking home around 10:30 PM. Coverage of these two crimes was in depth, with Cincinnati Police promising to bring their killers to justice.

Yet the third person murdered that night was forgotten by the press and prompted nothing but silence from the police.

Like the other two murders, the slaying of 33-year-old Paul Robert Mueller was destined to be unsolved. The separated father of four was sitting in his car around 11:30 PM, chatting on the pay phone outside the cemetery gate when someone pumped two bullets into his head.

One tip mentioned a group called the "Black Legion", who may have killed Mueller over a bad drug deal or some other nefarious connection. Decades later, this same faction resurfaced with from several anonymous leads linking them to the Bricca murders.

In June 1972, the United States Supreme Court dropped a legal bombshell when their Furman v. Georgia decision struck down all existing state death penalty statutes as unconstitutional.

The Furman decision caused all pending death sentences to be commuted to life imprisonment with chance of parole. Hundreds of condemned inmates were sprung from death row, including Richard Speck, the Manson Family, Robert Kennedy's assassin Sirhan Sirhan, and the Cabinet Supreme killers mentioned earlier.

There was one more – alleged Cincinnati Strangler Posteal Laskey, who would never be executed for killing Barbara Bowman.

As Laskey vacated death row, the Bricca investigation was a glacier. New detectives were given the file, Herb Vogel hoping a "new pair of eyes" would spot something they had missed.

May across the West Side believed Fred Leininger was the unnamed prime suspect, but his practice at the Glenway Animal Hospital wasn't suffering. If his colleagues heard the whispers about his past it didn't faze them – in 1974 they elected Leininger president of the Cincinnati Veterinarian Medical Association.

One of the most lethal shootings inside a private home in American history went down on Easter Sunday, March 30th, 1975, when James Ruppert murdered 11 family members in his mother's house in Hamilton, Ohio. Press coverage of this slaughter was epic – it quickly became known as the "Easter Sunday Massacre."

Despite his insanity plea, Ruppert was convicted of murdering his brother and mother and is now serving two life sentences.

Veterinarian Named

DR. FRED G. LEININGER will replace Dr. Ray Jacobsen as president of the Cincinnati Veterinary Medical Association. Dr. Leininger operates the Glenway Animal Hospital, Westwood, and has been active in the veterinarians' group since 1958. He will be inducted at the group's annual Christmas party at the Beverly Hills Supper Club.

Despite being followed by a cloud of suspicion, Fred Leininger was named president of the CVMA in 1974.

The Bricca case returned to the local papers in May 1977 after a nine year absence when the *Enquirer* ran a brief article headlined **Update... Triple Murder**. Herb Vogel, now a captain, was quoted saying the County was "not actively working the case" and will resume "only if something new comes in."

He admitted the probe had "narrowed to a single suspect", but was "dropped because there wasn't sufficient evidence to go on."

Murder nostalgia continued in August 1977, when *Enquirer* crime reporter George Hahn responded to the "Son of Sam" killings with a feature headlined **Terror in New York Brings to Mind Fearful Days of Cincinnati Strangler**.

It was a basic review of the murders and the city engulfed in terror, but there was one surprise. Retired Sgt. Russ Jackson, who headed the homicide squad during the Strangler investigation, told Hahn "there was no doubt in my mind" that Barbara Bowman's murder was tied to the other six. Jackson insisted that "we could have proved it in court if we had to."

With the Bricca murders more than ten years past, an employee of Fred Leininger described him as "always being on his guard" and careful around new clients.

A client I interviewed had this to say about Leininger in the early 1980's:

> ***I remember him wearing glasses. He was older, very very quiet. He seemed more farm-boyish. He didn't seem like he was a super healthy individual...tall and thin. He did not look imposing.***
>
> ***My parents thought he was a bit backwards, kind of a 'weirdo'. He was also heavy handed with treatments. My mom compared him to Lurch, but she can be catty...***

I can see him – he likes animals better than people. I picture him collecting insects as a child and serenely using his "killing jar".

His physical movements are not instinctive – they evoke a monitoring system, always on watch. He is precise, hooded. He tilts his head to conceal his eyes.

In reality, he is sentenced to a visible life in the present, in a world where he must sometimes dread the sound of his own name.

Yet all secrets were safe with him – because none were more deadly than his own...

January 1982 – February 2004

In January 1982, *Cincinnati Magazine* revisited the Bricca murders. With Lincoln Stokes as the Sheriff, the County's position on the case had shifted from the Dan Tehan regime, most notably when asked about the "prime suspect."

> **Rumors abounded. Police questioned a local businessman witnesses claimed to have seen with Mrs. Bricca when her husband was at work. But Captain Henke dismissed those ancient suspicions.**

Leads were drifting when detectives caught the case. "You might be able to pin a witness's memory down to the last 24 hours, but not 48," Henke reasoned. "What did you have for breakfast two days ago? How many people can remember details like that?"

Henke turned the crime scene pictures face down so the magazine writer couldn't see them. "It's hard to imagine how anyone could do what they did to that little girl... you don't even want to see these photos."

"Could the case still be solved?"

"At his point we'd need the spoken word," Henke replied. "Someone's conscience would have to get the better of them." Or perhaps another criminal might try to cut a deal on his own sentence by giving up the killer.

So 16 years later it was a total mystery? Yet coverage from 1966-67 proved the investigation had narrowed to "one man", one who was connected to Linda Bricca and refusing to cooperate.

Starting with Lincoln Stokes and continuing through the tenure of Simon Leis Jr., the County's stance cast Bricca as a whodunit – completely at odds with the West Side word on the street.

In December 1991 the Cincinnati *Post* ran an update on the Bricca case. Facts were rendered vague, including the absurd summation that "authorities never came up with any suspects."

Author George Stimson included a Bricca chapter in his excellent 1998 **The Cincinnati Crime Book**. And I wrote my first Bricca feature for the March 2002 *Snitch Magazine*: **Unsolved Bricca Case Haunts West Side.**

But beyond Stimson and Townsend, the Bricca murders had seemingly dropped off the local true crime radar.

It was late morning on Monday, February 23rd, 2004 when EMT Bill Hauer and his partner made a run to the Omni Netherland hotel in downtown Cincinnati. The call was coded "unknown trouble, possible injuries" in one of the hotel rooms.

As Hauer got off the elevator on the 10th floor, they could already smell death in the hallway. Entering the room in question, they found an older couple lying on the bed in bathrobes, plastic bags tied around their heads and an empty bottle of morphine nearby. They appeared to have been dead for more than 24 hours.

Yet as they approached the bed they heard shallow breathing. The woman was still alive, lying across the man's arm, which had turned black. He was definitely dead – she was in a coma. Their identification

Fred and Lynn Leininger (far right) are shown at an Opera Board meeting in Sarasota, Florida in 2001.

was laying on the nightstand, next to a generous tip for the maid, showing them to be husband and wife.

After the woman was removed, Hauer looked around the room. There was a man's suit hanging in the closet with a note attached: "Please bury me in this." There were other instructions concerning final arrangements for the couple, including monetary birthday gifts for their grandchildren. This was a planned suicide pact.

He glanced again at their driver's licenses. Dr. Fred Leininger, the deceased, was 72. His wife, Lynn Rau Leininger was 73, still hanging on but critical. She would linger for another ten months, dying on December 7, 2004.

They had driven up from Sarasota, Florida on Saturday the 21st and checked into the hotel. The catalyst was apparently Lynn Leininger's failing health. Fred also had heart trouble, and was depressed over losing money in the 2001 Enron financial scandal.

There was a brief note, but it made no mention of the man's notorious past. And the bizarre death of the prime Bricca suspect didn't make a ripple in the Cincinnati media.

But rumors about "the Vet's" suicide were already flourishing...

WHAT BECAME OF POSTEAL Laskey, the alleged Cincinnati Strangler?

Spared the electric chair when the death penalty was declared unconstitutional in 1972, Laskey was rejected for parole five times

Strangler' goes to grave; '60s saga conclude

an Horn
n@enquirer.com

osteal Laskey Jr. never nitted he was the "Cincin- Strangler," one of the 's most notorious serial ers.

His accusers were frustrat- for years by Laskey's deni- because they believed he ed and killed as many as en women in 1965 and 6.

They wanted him to admit t he'd done.

Laskey

Now that he's dead, they hope he has no choice.

"He's going to have to answer to God for what he did," said Hamilton County Prosecutor Joe Deters.

Prison officials confirmed Tuesday that Laskey died of natural causes May 29 at the Pickaway Correctional Institution in Orient, Ohio.

They did not disclose the cause of death but said Laskey, who was 69, had been sick for some time.

"He'd been in failing health," said prison spokeswoman Andrea Dean.

Laskey had been in prison for 40 years and was serving a life sentence for the murder of Barbara Bowman, a 31-year-old woman who was found strangled, raped and stabbed in Price Hill on Aug. 14, 1966.

See LASKEY, Page B5

Posteal Laskey was convicted of killing Barbara Bowman in 1966, but authorities say he was the serial killer known as the Cincinnati Strangler. Police believe these are the other victims:

Emogene Harrington, 56, strangled and raped Dec. 2, 1965, in her apartment building on East McMillan Street.

Lois Dant, 58, strangled and raped April 4, 1966, in her Price Hill apartment.

Jeanette Messer, 56, strangled and raped June 10, 1966, while walking her dog in Burnet Woods.

Alice Hochhausler, 50, strangled and raped Oct. 11, 1966, as she got out of her car in the driveway of her Cincinnati home.

Rose Winstel, 81, strangled and raped Oct. 20, 1966, in the bedroom of her Vine Street home.

Lelia Kerrick, strangled Dec. 9, 1966, in an elevator in her Ninth Street apartment.

Enqui

Posteal Las Jr., then 2 hours afte December 1966 arre

Posteal Laskey went to his grave protesting his innocence of the Bowman murder and the six strangulations.

beginning in 1984. Before each hearing, the board would be flooded with letters pleading that the "Strangler" not be released.

Yet after the Bowman conviction, no charges were ever brought against Laskey in the six murders attributed to the Strangler. Those cases remain "officially" unsolved a half a century later.

Laskey died in prison on May 29, 2007, and took his secrets to the grave. So was he really the Strangler?

He certainly murdered Barbara Bowman. The eyewitness testimony was compelling, and the rope found in the stolen cab was matched to his workplace. Giving his former call number to dispatchers was not only foolish, but indicated Laskey had no intention of killing anyone that night. He saw an opportunity with a younger victim and took it, but Barbara did not go down without a fight, and Laskey could not erase the trail he left.

Laskey fits the profile of a disorganized serial killer – a territorial offender who briefly stalked his victims before killing them and leaving their bodies at the crime scene. Laskey had a history of attacking women, but got tired of being identified. He matched the Strangler's description, and the murders DID stop after his arrest.

I like him for Emogene Harrington, Jeannette Messer, Alice Hochhausler, and Lulu Kerrick. The location and audacity of the Lois Dant murder might point in another direction, but more likely it was Laskey getting lucky. Only the slaying of Rose Winstel doesn't fit the pattern – it's a 50-50 proposition that he killed her.

While researching my 1997 *Cincinnati Magazine* feature on the Strangler, I reached out to Laskey. He wrote back that he would "like to have my side of the story told if it is done in an even handed way." But even an impartial rendering of the Cincinnati Strangler saga always leads back to Laskey.

The killer will always leave something at the crime scene and take something from it. Posteal Laskey left many infamous landmarks around the city – and took the Queen City's legacy of shelter from the storm of madness...

February 2004 – December 2017

With Fred Leininger secure from the judgement of any earthly court, the Bricca case slowly returned to life. The internet and advances in DNA testing not only refreshed this mystery on-line, but the possibility of a forensic solution was now gleaming.

After 40 years, detectives were beginning to look at old evidence in a new way. Cigarette butts found at the crime scene, hair clutched in Linda's hand and semen taken from her body formed a DNA tripod that would be useful in eliminating suspects.

Optimism was tempered. Detectives in 1966 had no concept of a genetic fingerprint, although they preserved what they had as best they could. But the evidence was four decades old, and DNA will degrade when exposed to the ravages of moisture and time.

Yet scientific advances were moving at light speed. The process of extracting DNA from sweat, blood, or saliva was improving every year, and law enforcement could see the potential for DNA sequencing in cold cases. And with the introduction the FBI's combined DNA indexing system (CODIS), there was the possibility the Bricca sample could draw a hit from a known offender.

The Bricca case was reconsidered in the April 2008 issue of *Cincinnati Magazine* with **Death on a Quiet Street**. Writer Jack Heffron, a West Side native, confronted the Bricca legend with an intriguing revisionist slant and some eloquent prose:

> **Ask anyone of a certain age who grew up in this part of town if they remember it. They do. In fact, just say the name "Bricca." The hard snap of consonants, the novelty of it, especially in this German-Irish part of town, possess a charge that will spark a memory...**

Heffron linked Linda Bricca to the Valerie Percy killing, writing that a Chicago investigative reporter told him "odds are they knew each other." However, they grew up in Chicago suburbs that were 28 miles apart and went to different schools. It's doubtful that Adolph Bulaw, who owned a mid-sized welding firm, ever hob-knobbed with the Percy family.

The connection to the Lonnie Trumbull/Lisa Wick attack in Seattle is even more stubborn. A former Bricca neighbor told Heffron that "Linda said she'd worked with and lived with the two women." Yet during Linda's eight month stint with United Airlines in 1961, murder victim Trumbull and survivor Wick were 15-year-old high school students living in Oregon. June Bulaw also confirmed to investigators in 1966 that her daughter did not know them.

Heffron wrote that none of the neighbors he spoke to "believe the killer was having an affair with Linda," and that the county "contradicts the claim by Melvin Rueger that law enforcement had narrowed the investigation to a single suspect." But the media coverage and internal reports in 1966 left no doubt that a prime suspect was stonewalling Herb Vogel's efforts to interview him.

Heffron was skeptical that this was a crime of passion with a single killer: "Why does someone bent on murder tie up his victims first? And how does someone holding a knife tie up two adults?" His scenario suggests calculated planning, perhaps a conspiracy or maybe a professional killer.

But the nature of this crime, despite the icy control of the organized offenders, confirms this was indeed a personal cause homicide, where one of the killers was obsessively entangled with the alluring female victim...

Queen City Gothic was published in 2009. My first book was a true crime anthology of classic murder mysteries in Cincinnati history. My Bricca chapter was the longest essay published on the case and the first to identify Fred Leininger as the prime suspect.

Yet if I were writing that chapter today it would be different. I had tried for years to access the Bricca case file without success, so most of my research was secondary sources, and I was guilty of perpetuating unfounded rumors and tenuous connections.

In October 2012 a local news station ran some promos promising "a new theory on the Bricca murders". Instead, they foisted the bizarre speculation that the Briccas were killed by "The Zodiac". Not only were the 1969 time frame and west coast location all wrong, but the Zodiac's MO was shooting couples in parked cars, not stabbing families.

In March 2013, Ohio Attorney General Mike DeWine spotlighted the Bricca murders to further his efforts in cracking cold cases. "This gruesome triple homicide happened nearly five decades ago, but we still have hope that someone out there knows something," said DeWine, whose Unsolved Homicides Initiative created a statewide database of 5,000 unresolved Ohio murders.

NOVEMBER 3RD, 2014 WAS a watershed moment in my long obsession with the Bricca murders. On that day I was granted access to the case file by Sheriff Jim Neil's administration. I walked into county headquarters and was transported back to 1966.

The crime scene photos were a revelation. Jerry Bricca's muscular build screamed out for two killers. Linda's negligee was extremely low cut, not your typical attire for a Sunday night of watching TV. So what was really going on that evening?

Debbie was obviously the last victim. Her four wounds were almost surgical in precision – my feeling was that whoever killed her did not stab her parents. Other photos showed the ransacking of the house, which appeared staged.

After the ill-advised Zodiac story, several other Bricca features were run by the local media, including my own WLWT appearance on March 29th, 2013. During the interview I said that the chances for a break in the case were much better now.

With DNA advances and the emergence of CODIS, optimism ran high that the Bricca murders could be solved...

BUT THE MOMENTUM HAS stalled. On September 27th 2016, WCPO ran the story **Who killed Bricca Family?** This marked the first time the local media had publically identified Dr. Fred Leininger as the suspect. It only took them a half century to do it.

Hamilton County detectives Douglas Todd and Brian Williams, who weren't even born when the Briccas were slain, had inherited the case. "I think the answer is in that box," Todd told reporters as he gestured

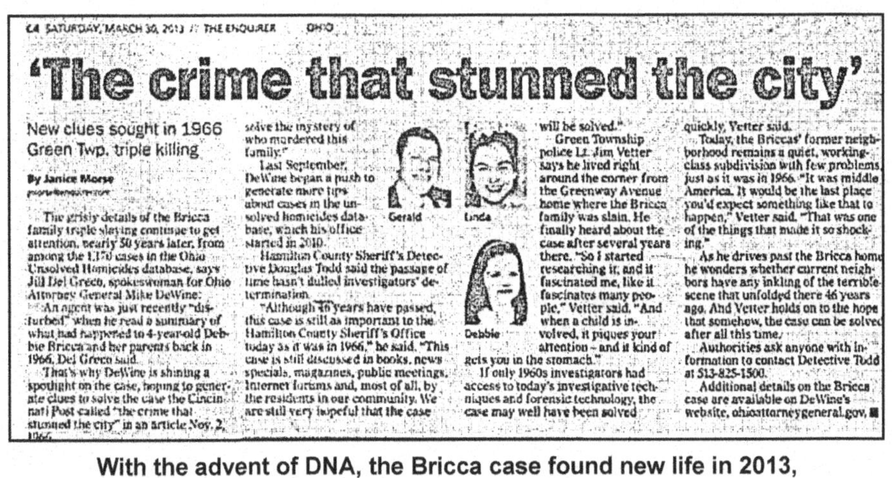

C4 SATURDAY, MARCH 30, 2013 // THE ENQUIRER OHIO

'The crime that stunned the city'

New clues sought in 1966 Green Twp. triple killing

By Janice Morse

The grisly details of the Bricca family triple slaying continue to get attention, nearly 50 years later, from among the 1,170 cases in the Ohio Unsolved Homicides database, says Jill Del Greco, spokeswoman for Ohio Attorney General Mike DeWine.

An agent was just recently "disturbed" when he read a summary of what had happened to 4-year-old Debbie Bricca and her parents back in 1966, Del Greco said.

That's why DeWine is shining a spotlight on the case, hoping to generate clues to solve the case the Cincinnati Post called "the crime that stunned the city" in an article Nov. 2, 1966, solve the mystery of who murdered this family."

Last September, DeWine began a push to generate more tips about cases in the unsolved homicides database, which his office started in 2010.

Hamilton County Sheriff's Detective Douglas Todd said the passage of time hasn't dulled investigators' determination.

"Although 46 years have passed, this case is still as important to the Hamilton County Sheriff's Office today as it was in 1966," he said. "This case is still discussed in books, news specials, magazines, public meetings, Internet forums and, most of all, by the residents in our community. We are still very hopeful that the case will be solved."

Gerald

Linda

Debbie

Green Township police Lt. Jim Vetter says he lived right around the corner from the Greenway Avenue home where the Bricca family was slain. He finally heard about the case after several years there. "So I started researching it, and it fascinated me, like it fascinates many people," Vetter said. "And when a child is involved, it piques your attention – and it kind of gets you in the stomach."

If only 1960s investigators had access to today's investigative techniques and forensic technology, the case may well have been solved quickly, Vetter said.

Today, the Briccas' former neighborhood remains a quiet, working-class subdivision with few problems, just as it was in 1966. "It was middle America. It would be the last place you'd expect something like that to happen," Vetter said. "That was one of the things that made it so shocking."

As he drives past the Bricca home he wonders whether current neighbors have any inkling of the terrible scene that unfolded there 46 years ago. And Vetter holds on to the hope that somehow, the case can be solved after all this time.

Authorities ask anyone with information to contact Detective Todd at 513-825-1500.

Additional details on the Bricca case are available on DeWine's website, ohioattorneygeneral.gov. ■

With the advent of DNA, the Bricca case found new life in 2013, when the Ohio AG spotlighted the notorious cold case.

toward the case file. "And it's going to take a phone call...somebody knows something who didn't speak up."

> **Tips from callers have slowed to a trickle, and the detectives are concerned that people who might have information they need don't know it or have been withholding it. And they will take it to the grave.**
>
> **"Those in their 20s and 30s are in their 70s and 80s now, and someone who might have good information they're holding onto may never get to tell it. So why not now?" Williams said. "It may be just a little piece of information that you thought was not worth saying at the time or you didn't want to smear anyone's name. Whatever it is, it's worth hearing."**

The Bricca case is now over 50 years old, and the killer or killers have vanished down an endless corridor of yesterdays. The passage of time has withered the crime down to its tangents and nuances – shades of yellowed gray that have no objective import and carry the dust of another era.

Can we unravel this mystery – or face a future of red herrings?

And what of my own obsession with Linda Bricca? Gazing at her black and white images, I see the memory of her radiance and feel her ruined dreams. Her luminous eyes reach through me to some haunted past.

Our restless ghosts are languishing not from old age – but from eternal broken hearts...

Dr. Fred Leininger is the mystery man of the Bricca case,
a soft blur who never came into focus.

CHAPTER THIRTEEN

NIGHT OF A THOUSAND LIES

"When seven or eight clear items of circumstantial evidence point directly to the guilt of a person, that person is innocent nowhere but in a detective novel."
Edmund Pearson

The Armchair Detective

The Bricca case is murder with only the first act – no arrest, trial, or conviction. No TV show ending, snap of handcuffs or dank cell. The veil never lifted, and the aftermath remains unwritten.

Some talk about "The Case" as an elusive thing, like a tattered memento or a macabre relic. But the undercurrents never subside, and as time withered the public perspective, this mystery became a maze with many dark corners.

In 1966, the famine of physical evidence forced investigators to focus on rumors of infidelity. Yet after more than 50 years, this crime transcends human motives of lust, greed, and hatred.

The players are dying every year – investigators, witnesses, friends and foes. With each death the answers are buried deeper. Is there anyone still out there with private, pertinent information?

Perhaps there IS someone who never realized they had something to offer the investigation. Until now...

ENTER THE ARMCHAIR DETECTIVE. By definition, he or she is an amateur investigator who doesn't visit crime scenes or interview witnesses. All their information comes from secondary sources perused in the comfort of their den.

The phenomenon began in the 1920's with the advent of detective magazines, those pulp monthlies where sex and violence fused so that our greatest desires and worst fears were simpatico. This genre provided a refuge for eager readers to sample the range of human depravity while pandering to scandalous voyeurism. Pinup girls meeting wicked guys spawned the True Crime phenomenon.

Most importantly, in these tabloids the police detective's skills took a back seat to the reader's own investigative prowess. Finally, WE became the sleuth.

How do you know if you are one? I'll quote from The Moonstone by Wilkie Collins, one of the first great detective novels: "Do you feel an uncomfortable heat at the pit of your stomach…and a nasty thumping at the top of your head? I call it the detective-fever."

My detective chops were honed in my youth. After reading "Ten Little Indians" by Agatha Christie I was hooked, breeding obsessions with Lizzie Borden, Jack the Ripper, the Lindbergh baby, and yes, the Bricca murders. I have no law enforcement background, but the depth and breadth of my research into the fine art of murder knows no boundaries.

It consumes me to this day. I cannot resist the seductive lure of a mystery. I savor the luscious twists of a conundrum. I listen to enigmas that go bump in the night. They all take shape in my mind's eye, and naming the killer becomes my obsession.

For the armchair detective, there is no presumption of innocence or reasonable doubt. ALL evidence is admissible – hearsay and rumor can't be disregarded. I have no bias, no agenda, and no stock in the outcome other than determining the truth. And I accept my own irrelevance to whatever murder case I'm working.

Besides the vast amount of knowledge and fact assimilation required, what other tools do we use? As with any investigation, a certain amount of luck is necessary. To quote legendary baseball GM Branch Rickey: "Luck is the residue of design..."

How does an armchair detective cultivate lady luck? Here are five useful tools:

- Develop and nurture a network of friends and connections.
- Amplify your speculations and quickly admit your mistakes.
- Be aggressive and take risks with your theories that survive.
- Always view complex interpretations with strong pessimism.
- Play precise hunches with fact assimilation plus experience.

In this chapter I will attempt to arrive at the most likely hypothesis for the big question: Who Killed the Bricca Family?

The Bricca house sits forever in sunshine and shadow...so what happened here on the night of September 25th 1966?

RATHER THAN BORE YOU with the standard ten steps to hypothesis formulation, I'll introduce my own creation: **Rules for Armchair Detectives**. I've compiled over 100 of them through my decades of crime exploration – most my own invention, others from movies or books, and some are quotes from retired investigators.

Here are ten rules to consider in solving the Bricca mystery.

- **Murder is always about passion or gain.** Murders are usually what they seem, and the simplest explanation is preferred.
- **Objectivity has never solved a crime.** A heart of darkness is full of riddles, and only subjectivity can uncover the secrets.
- **Physical evidence never perjures itself.** Only its collection, preservation, or interpretation can be in error.
- **A rumor is often a premature fact.** Consider the source, but usually the whispers and gossip revolve around a core truth.
- **There is no such thing as a coincidence.** They are rare, so learn to understand the cold logic of seemingly random events.
- **Your only loyalty is to the evidence.** Your correct conclusion has to be consistent with every known fact of the case.

- **Never outsmart your gut instinct.** It's more than playing a hunch – it's not over analyzing or thinking too much.
- **People can lie, but behavior never lies.** The suspect's guilty conscience will always ensnare him in his own thicket.
- **Every mystery has a wild card.** You never see the startling consequence or the surprise suspect coming out of left field.
- **You can't solve a mystery.** It's called a mystery when the pieces don't fit, so turn it into a PUZZLE and put them together.

Lastly, please remember this. NEVER read your own thoughts or actions into the plans of a murderer. Even if you never take a risk, killers often succeed because of THEIR audacity...

The Crime

The logistics of the Bricca murders remain as challenging today as they were in 1966. Was this a crime of passion, or a strategic murder masquerading as an eruption?

A recent news program referred to the Bricca killings as a "savage frenzy," although crime scene photographs don't support this. There is no "back spatter" of blood to indicate the killer was wildly plunging his knife it into the victims. With the exception of the two facial wounds each on Jerry and Linda, the placement and depth of the other 17 wounds shows a degree of precision.

Jerry was beaten about the face, trussed up and forced on his belly before the fatal attack began. After four thrusts to his back, his jugular was sliced open and he began choking on his own blood – the killer taped the socks in his mouth to muffle the death rattle. So there are elements of passion and control in Jerry's murder.

All of Linda's wounds were from the front as she lay on the bed, the killer facing her. There's a ring of six knife thrusts to the left of the sternum. A glancing wound to the corner of her mouth gave it ghastly clownish effect. It was personal – this whole mess was her fault, after all. Yet it was also restrained.

Debbie did not receive the brunt of the attack. The wounds bisected her thin body, but she was collateral damage – removal of a witness. The only emotion the killer felt toward her was fear.

Two witnesses saw three people getting into a car where this car is located – odds are these were the killers. (2016 photo)

Why would an enraged killer commit a "crime of passion" by first binding the adult victims, then remove the ligatures and spend time at the scene searching the house? How did one man manage to control three people, including a burly male, and two aggressive dogs? If the killer was armed with only a knife, it's hard to believe Jerry Bricca wouldn't have made a move to regain control.

Could there have been two or three killers at the Bricca house that night, friends who lived the rest of their lives entwined in a deadly conspiracy of secrecy and guilt?

Consider the two witnesses leaving Western Bowl who saw the same trio of subjects entering a car in front of the Bricca house on the murder night. These bowlers did not know each other – yet their independent statements offer corroboration.

It's a rainy Sunday night just before 11:30 PM. No one in that neighborhood had a good reason to be out on the street. There were no other cars parked on that section of Greenway. So these three people were undoubtedly leaving the Bricca house, skewing the odds against the lone killer theory.

A review of the crime scene analysis in chapter 7 supports this:

- **Probability of an "organized" offender:** only one of them needed to keep a cool head.
- **Control of the two adults:** Jerry was outnumbered and quickly neutralized.

- **Control of the two dogs:** much easier if one of them was familiar with the animals.
- **Use of and removal of ligatures:** one covers them while the other binds them.
- **Lack of defensive wounds or struggle:** much harder to overcome two assailants.
- **Killers remained at the scene:** one stayed calm enough not to panic or hurry.
- **Staging of robbery:** removal of a personal connection to one of the killers.

Could one man have accomplished all this? It's a dicey proposition given Jerry's impressive physique and preemptive nature. He would certainly try to protect his family against a solo killer armed only with a carving knife.

But a partner with a gun solves that.

ONE YEAR AFTER THE crime, an unnamed "official" told a reporter that "Jerry surprised the suspect by coming home at an unexpected time. I think the man in the house hit him as he walked in."

Yet despite newspaper reports that Jerry came home from Monsanto just before 9 PM, he actually leaves at 4:30 PM, picks up Linda's prescription, and is home to take Glenn Ritchie's 6:45 PM call about their flight to West Virginia the next morning.

Jerry makes a run to UDF around 8:30 PM to buy milk, putting the garbage cans out when he returns home. I don't think the killers enter during this time frame – but they probably have the family under observation shortly after Jerry comes back.

Jerry puts Debbie to bed, and when he leaves the TV room the killers enter the unlocked rear door and confront Linda. Upstairs, Jerry removes one red knee sock from Debbie, laying it on the bed. Then some disturbance draws him back to the lower level.

Friends of the family said they ALWAYS put the dogs in the lower level TV room when they had visitors. That is exactly where the dogs were found – another sign the victims knew the killer. If the killers entered through the back door, then the catalyst for the crime occurred in THIS room before moving to the bedrooms.

How are the dogs controlled? That's a wild card, unless one of the killers is well acquainted with Dusty and Thumper. Possibly after being drugged, the dogs are shut in the TV room. Jerry and Linda are bound, Jerry probably trussed up with the dog chain later found out of place. Then they are walked upstairs to the bedroom.

Jerry is neutralized with thrusts to the back and neck, probably while resisting. Linda stares down her killer as the knife impales her flesh. Debbie is dragged from underneath the bed and killed quickly and coldly.

The killers remain in the house for several hours, opening every drawer and looking in every nook. Yet the ransacking looks a little too frenzied. Was it pure staging? Or the removal of a personal association, like love letters or private gifts.

What sort of man is our prime mover? Without looking at possible accomplices, what type of profile can we draw of our killer?

Working within FBI parameters, a personal cause murder of this magnitude requires a perpetrator near the top of the food chain. Someone supremely confident with his status and his abilities.

- **Above average intelligence**
- **Socially competent**
- **Sexually competent**
- **Likely to be a skilled worker**
- **Living with partner**
- **Controlled mood during crime**
- **Alcohol use associated with crime**
- **Precipitating situational stress**

The Bricca killers were no ordinary street criminals or aspiring hoodlums. There was a level of sophistication and control, even as emotions flared at the scene. These guys had been partners before, married men who enjoyed the thrill of the chase and pilfered moments of illicit sex.

Neither of them could have killed alone. Because like Richard Loeb and Nathan Leopold slaying Bobby Franks in Chicago, or Perry Smith and Richard Hickock slaughtering the Clutter family in Kansas, these two men, neither capable of murder, had unhinged into a single murderous entity proficient enough to kill...

The Investigation

Two rumors about the Bricca investigation ran wild in 1966 and still reverberate today. Did the cops "screw up" and/or "cover up" to such an extent that justice was denied?

The better question might be this. Were county detectives brilliantly cunning with the cover-up AND absurdly incompetent with the screw-up? Can you have it both ways?

On the night of September 27th, 1966, there was almost a two hour gap between Green Township constables discovering the bodies and Herb Vogel arriving at the crime scene. During that interlude the house was not locked down – there were police from different jurisdictions, overlapping first responders, and curious off-duty personnel wandering through the rooms.

All of them made decisions, took actions, and raised questions that were second guessed under the glare of media publicity. People who aren't actively working the crime scene don't need to be there. Yet with a major crime like Bricca, nonessential personnel often manage to gain access.

First responders are often tending to a live victim, so they're not focused on scene preservation. They may inadvertently leave fingerprints, footprints, and DNA evidence behind. Detectives must account for it and get samples from each person for elimination.

The protocol for working a homicide scene was different in 1966 than it is today. There was no log of who entered and when, and those gathering evidence didn't wear gloves or shoe covers.

Back then, fingerprints were the DNA for homicide investigators, and a crowded scene could jeopardize their integrity. The myth of fingerprints is at they're easy to leave, when actually a clean, hard surface must be available to receive them.

ALL crime scenes from the pre-DNA area were compromised to a certain degree. But that didn't stop cases from being solved.

Dr. Edmond Locard, the forensic pioneer who coincidentally died in 1966, formulated the fundamental theory that "every contact leaves a trace." His principle of exchange states that "when a person comes into contact with an object or another person, a cross transfer of physical evidence can occur." Unfortunately, this standard applies equally to the criminals and the cops.

Volunteer fireman Bob Sweeney told me that some first responders were wandering through the house picking up items and touching surfaces. They all brought traces into the scene with them, from clothing fibers to soil on their shoes. If anyone sneezed there might be a used facial tissue – if someone spruced up there could be random hairs left. Even a carelessly discarded cigarette could skew the evidence.

Green Township had jurisdiction over the scene until Herb Vogel arrived. When Vogel got the call, he had just brought his wife and daughter home from the hospital after their car accident earlier that day. Plus he lived on the east side of Anderson Township. By the time he arrived sometime after midnight and took charge, any cross contamination had already occurred.

Obviously investigative procedure should have been followed better in those first two hours. Yet it was no different than many other crime scenes of the 1960s – these detectives were not specialists trained in evidence collection. However, the key evidence in the two murder rooms was protected well enough to eventually yield a DNA profile of the killer.

I do NOT believe that Hamilton County Sheriff's officers "screwed up" the Bricca crime scene to the extent that it prevented a resolution to this case.

ADDRESSING SPECULATION ABOUT A "cover up" to protect the prime suspect is much easier. Because it never happened.

Rumors that Mel Rueger and/or Herb Vogel were bribed are pure fantasy. Rueger was a stickler when it came to ethics, and Vogel maintained surveillance on the suspect for years afterwards. Besides, there was no "smoking gun" in this case that demanded a bribe to make it vanish.

Theorizing that the victims knew their killer, investigators started close and worked outward, interviewing all primary and secondary persons who had contact with the family. Looking for time gaps between the lead card and the interview dates, it's obvious the high priority tips were followed up immediately, while complaints about a woman's suspicious boyfriend would linger for several days.

The night the bodies were found officers went door to door on north Greenway and east Lawrence, asking residents to write down anything they remembered seeing on Sunday night. There were delays with some of these "proximity" interviews. Yet anyone who saw something came forward immediately – the rest were inside watching the movie with their windows closed against the rain.

The 48 hour delay in discovering the murders hampered the investigation. Asking residents with no reason to be watching what they remembered from two nights ago is a losing proposition. It would have been a whole new ball game if the bodies had been found shortly after the murders were committed.

Despite these constraints, Herb Vogel brought the investigation to the doorstep of the prime suspect, whose attorney proved to be a bigger obstacle than the recent Miranda decision. And Vogel made concessions to facilitate a third interview – and a possible arrest stemming from it.

We don't know what discussions he had with the prosecutor about the stalemate. Apparently Rueger felt they didn't have sufficient evidence to move forward. Yet I am certain Vogel tried every tactic to break the case open, from furtive shadowing to brazen mind games.

Lastly, Phyllis Vogel assured me that her husband was always burdened by not cracking the biggest case of his career. So the notion that Hamilton County law enforcement got in bed with the suspect and covered up his involvement in the Bricca murders remains as ludicrous today as it was in 1966.

After everyone else is done, the detectives still own the case.

When the evidence is collected, photographs taken, autopsy completed, and any relevant toxicology, ballistics, or psychology is finished, detectives take the evidence and try to fit it into a scenario. They sift through leads, meet with witnesses, and try to match the physical evidence with a viable theory.

In the initial phase of any investigation, brainstorming is essential. There are no stupid questions and no improbable theories – you need to get the ideas out there and on the board.

Deduce, determine and decide – that's what a murder investigation is. The detective must overcome chaos in the pursuit of watertight facts. If any theory is contradicted by a proven fact that theory must be wrong.

Investigators must also guard against confirmation bias. The human mind is prone to select and interpret facts according to its emotional needs. Failure to follow the evidence spawns hasty, biased theories, with selectively chosen evidence to buttress them. Conflicting facts are discarded, and the case begins a dying crawl to the unsolved file.

The key is to keep it simple. Murders are usually what they appear to be. If you hear hooves, think horse – not zebra.

So I won't second guess the Hamilton County detectives. As depicted in earlier chapters, this team of 13 veteran cops was laser focused on apprehending the Bricca killer. Their main tools were lip service, shoe leather, and informants.

But perhaps investigators should just throw the book out the window when they catch a case like Bricca. There's no template to compare it to, and the stakes are too high.

They were certain of one thing: *If we solve this case, no one will remember us. If we don't, no one will ever forget us...*

Evidence and Victims

Sometimes police fail to think small. Obvious physical evidence Is often absent, but minute clues are always there.

The power of this evidence lies in its obscurity. Investigators and perpetrators alike tend to overlook it. Even a cunning criminal risks leaving traces of blood, hair, and fibers. These silent bystanders remain at the crime scene for months and even years.

Bricca investigators were hoping the FBI microscopic analysis could link a suspect to the crime scene, or at least assist with a reconstruction. Even with compelling circumstantial evidence, direct evidence always carries more weight.

Forensic Scientist Paul Leland Kirk, the pioneer of modern blood spatter evidence, was mentioned earlier in a reference to the Sam Sheppard case. His 1953 book, **Crime Investigation: Physical Evidence and the Police Laboratory**, was on the shelf of every homicide commander in 1966, including Herb Vogel.

Kirk was a disciple of the Locard exchange principle – that every contact leaves a trace. Dr. Locard was the father of modern forensic analysis, and Kirk expressed his basic principle as follows:

> **Wherever he steps, whatever he touches, whatever he leaves, will serve as a silent witness against him. Not only his fingerprints**

> **or his footprints, but his hair, the fibers from his clothes, the glass he breaks, the tool marks he leaves, the paint he scratches, the blood or semen he deposits or collects. All of these and more bear mute witness against him.**

Kirk was adept at finding facts that eluded police and errors in evidence analysis. We'll never know what effect he may have had on the Bricca investigation if he'd been called in to consult.

THEIR BEST PIECE OF physical evidence was the tape used to help gag the dying Jerry Bricca. Analysis showed it to be an unusual 1-7/8" width medical tape often distributed to veterinarians, but it couldn't be conclusively linked to any suspect.

Other evidence is problematic. The seminal fluid from Linda Bricca's "recent intercourse" provides blood type and little else. The cigarettes and palm prints could be from some innocent visitor. The hair found clutched in Linda's hand was never identified, although one detective told me it was "most likely from a relative."

So there could be an innocent explanation for everything at the scene – except that tape over Jerry's mouth.

Victim toxicology came back clean except for prescription drugs in the adults. But when Linda's parents took the dogs back to Chicago a chance to test them for recent sedation was lost.

With the new millennium came the Bricca DNA profile, derived from the butts, hair, and semen. I've been told the profile would never register an "OJ Simpson number like 1 in 17 million." It's more like 1 in 30 men, which are not good odds in the DNA game. The Bricca profile was checked against the CODIS database of known felons and predictably came up empty.

Lacking physical evidence, Bricca became a circumstantial evidence case. This could be any combination of occurrence, coincidence, demeanor, observation, patterns, or facts.

Compiling a list of interview candidates was integral to the Bricca investigation. Despite the outbreak of CSI fever, murder cases are usually cracked with insight from people who knew the victims...

How well do we know the people in our lives? Think of crime programs where friends and family are shocked by the allegations against their loved ones – accusations that turn out to be true.

Men keep more secrets than women, because they don't have as many close friends, and were raised to believe that confessing their secrets makes them look weak. Just like with Jerry Bricca.

So what was going on with him the last week of his life?

The young engineer was clearly distracted by something – he finally opened up to his boss on that Thursday. There is hearsay evidence that Jerry threatened to "beat up" Fred Leininger the night before while in the Meyer living room. Couple this with a statement made to me by one of Jerry's co-workers: "He had a temper."

Jerry was no wimp – he was athletic enough to become an award winning college swimmer. His Stanford pictures show a virile, iron-jawed determination combined with a hint of menace.

The wild card is Jerry's epilepsy medicine. According to Linda's brother Jay, she complained to their mother that last week that Jerry quit taking his medication and his anger issues had returned. And someone told detectives Jerry Bricca might have been in a fistfight at the Monsanto parking lot the night before his murder.

People spoke of his cheerful disposition and avoidance of confrontation. But maybe his cork was in too tight.

It's hard to see beyond Debbie Bricca's picture – she's the forever four-year-old, a child whose precocious nature doomed her.

Linda Zeff told me Debbie "talked like she was ten," and "impressed everyone who met her." She understood that adults liked to fuss over her, cooing she that was so beautiful AND smart. She could speak in sentences and recognize specific people.

If Debbie knew a man well enough to call him "uncle", then she could tell a detective when this man had visited her house...

"Linda was like a big girl playing house... she did not want any more children and he did...she wasn't happy about having sex with him...she was the type who would lead him on and then say forget it...she was gorgeous and knew it."

Comments from female neighbors who thought they knew Linda were politely catty. She was prettier, slimmer, and younger than the other wives, some of whom no doubt caught their husbands mooning after Linda as she washed her car in those shorts. Whether she cared about these amorous hubbies is immaterial – but their wives' reaction to winsome Linda was swift and certain.

Judith Bush Hemmer, a young housewife who lived with her in-laws at 3355 Greenway, had several encounters with Linda when she was out walking with Debbie, who would sing "Twinkle, Twinkle Little Star" to Judy:

> ***If I was on the porch Linda would stop and talk. She appeared older than she was, very self-confident, but something wasn't right. If you were to take a still shot of her, she would appear to be relaxed, but even the shortest video would have proved that wrong. She was restless, bored, and searching. For what?***

A comment by Linda's Seattle obstetrician glimmers for me – "Debbie was not her first pregnancy." After being jilted by Erwin in June 1960, Linda supposedly had a nervous breakdown that September when her new boyfriend was killed in a car accident.

But suppose Linda's mother taking her to Florida for six months was actually to hide her "first" pregnancy? She could give birth away from the local Barrington gossip, secretly give the child up for adoption, and return home to lie about her age and become an 18-year-old airline stewardess.

It's mere supposition at this point, but if true it could explain many things about our enigmatic female victim...

Marriage did not free Linda from the tyranny of her own beauty. She felt a responsibility to look striking going back to her airline stewardess days. Striding through airports in her fitted navy blue uniform, perky beret and high-heels, she could feel the male heads turning. And for the first time in her life it was intoxicating.

Soon enough she knew the rules, reducing all men to the obvious. A coy smile and a flip of her dark hair often triggered a dinner invitation. Or more.

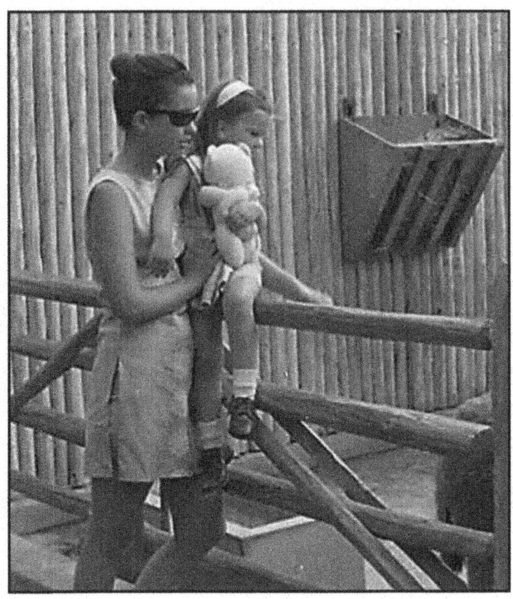

Linda Bricca and Debbie at the Cincinnati Zoo in 1965.

It was fun to play with lonely males' responses. She could flirt outrageously, yet at evening's end deliver nothing beyond a chaste kiss. Then she could disappear, pleading an early morning flight. She had power over them, which gave her the right to refuse sex.

She'd always sailed through life, assured that her pretty face and jaunty figure would attract yet protect her from this type of man.

Recalling those heady, ego-boosting days provided an antidote for her predictable existence as a housewife and mother. Her marriage was stale, but Debbie was so breathtakingly beautiful. People stopped her on the street to comment on it, only to gasp at something her child said that everyone else had missed.

As an attractive woman, Linda may have resented her daughter receiving more attention than she did.

Rumors and Motives

The mythology of the Bricca case is laden with hearsay, gossip, whispers, and undertones. Bizarre, untenable suspects have been linked by innuendo and irrationality for over the last half century.

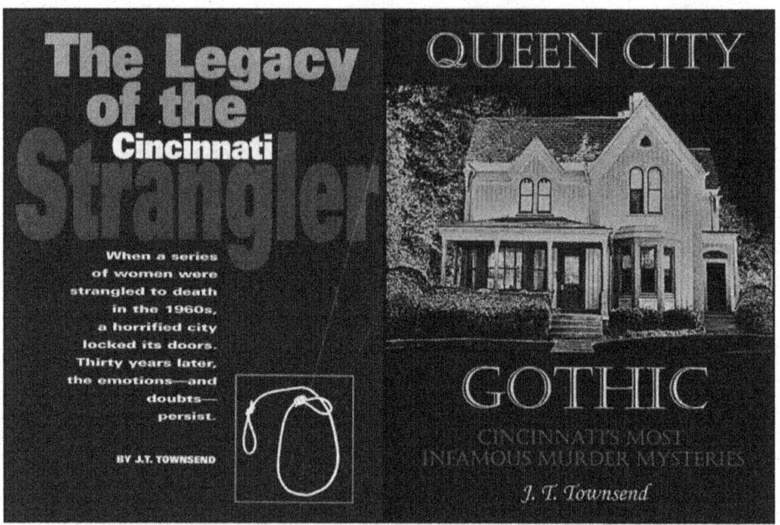

Townsend's first free-lance crime article appeared in Cincinnati Magazine in August 1998. QCG came out in October 2007.

Those who persist with this shadow narrative are often misled, misinformed, and mistaken.

A woman spoke to me after a Bricca program once and told me the "real story." It seems someone at County told her uncle that they found Linda's "call girl book" with all her clients' phone numbers at the crime scene – this was from her stewardess period in 1961. If that wasn't enough, the night of the murders a country detective broke into the Glenway Animal Hospital and found bloody clothes and other evidence that incriminated Leininger.

This is an urban legend on steroids. Linda was a stewardess for just eight months, and dated Jerry for four of them. She was NOT a high class hooker at age 18.

The Westmans were living at GAH and didn't report a break-in that night. And how would police know to force entry on the murder night when the bodies were not discovered for two more days?

The rumor that Jerry was castrated is tenacious, and I repeated it in **Queen City Gothic**. Having viewed the crime scene photos, I know Jerry was fully dressed and there were no genital mutilations.

Bernard Tigges, the SPCA officer who took charge of the dogs that night, told me he did not think they had been drugged – "they were just hungry, dehydrated and scared." Yet the drugging rumor is still pervasive.

The fewer the facts the stronger the opinion. It has been 130 years since an unknown subject with the "killer" sobriquet of Jack the Ripper terrorized the slum streets of London. Yet each passing decade spawns more wild theories and bogus claims about the first ever psycho-sexual serial murderer.

British writer Lucy Worsley explains how the 1888 killings of a few gin-sodden prostitutes have evolved into our greatest murder mystery and a true crime cottage industry:

> **In 1888 a serial killer was terrorizing the East End of London. The few undisputed facts about him are rather grubby and shop-soiled from so much handling and the identity of the murderer is still a complete mystery. Over the summer and autumn, several killings of prostitutes on the streets of Whitechapel became linked – at least in the public's imagination – with a single perpetrator... The final touch came from a hoax letter, purporting to be from the killer but probably written by a journalist aiming to stir up the story. He signed it with the name that still stands today as shorthand for the whole ragbag of half- facts and inferences: the assumption that there was a single killer, who called himself JACK THE RIPPER...**

Bricca has seen the same evolution on a regional basis. As Cincinnati's most notorious cold case, it has generated more rumors than the other 12 chapters of **Queen City Gothic** combined.

This eccentricity of the human mind can be found in the narrative of any notorious crime. People will discard stubborn facts yet swallow any juicy hearsay or backstairs prattle. Throw in a sketchy conspiracy and you have their full attention.

This makes great conversation – but doesn't solve a murder...

LET'S USE PROCESS OF elimination with the FBI murder classifications to illuminate the motive for the Bricca murders.

Sociopathic killings are random or planned stranger murders that may involve multiple victims. Several serial killers have been identified as Bricca suspects, but everything points to the victims knowing their murderer.

A **sexual homicide** or lust murder seems possible. The reporting about Linda's "beauty" and her "rape" make it a logical motive. But the crime scene photos show her panties in place, and the autopsy only referred to "recent intercourse." There was a sex angle to this case, but sexual assault was not the objective.

Did an unlawful enterprise like a bungled burglary mutate into a **felony murder**? Jerry's empty wallet was on the bed, and drawers had been rifled. But the Bricca family had neither the money nor the means to be targeted for a "big score." Despite the rumors, no credible drug connection turned up either.

What about a **contract killing**? Richard Meyer saw the bodies and told reporters the killers were "professional." Perhaps a third party did eliminate the victims for personal reasons. This case has been dogged by rumors of a "mafia hit," which always remain unsolved and no one ever talks – just like Bricca.

This theory involves Adolph Bulaw's business or Jerry's Monsanto activities. Yet Jerry was not involved in product design, making it unlikely he was a "whistle-blower" about Agent Orange or other despicable Monsanto products. If he went to the Feds about company malfeasance, the hit man would have put a bullet in his brain some dark night in the company parking lot, rather than needlessly taking out the whole family.

There is no discernable connection between Mr. Bulaw's welding company and the mob, and I'm puzzled why this rumor still thrives. But if he's late with a payoff they would shoot him near his business – not drive five hours to slaughter his daughter and her family.

There is no evidence that Bricca was a professional hit. If this WAS a contract killing, it is virtually unique in true crime history.

Group cause murder includes group excitement homicide, where multiple offenders feed off each other's rage and take turns attacking the victim. The Manson cult murders come to mind – also jealous teenagers killing a classmate in a secluded location. Torture is often used to escalate the group toward lethal violence.

Though not ringing with the same verve as Linda's affair, rumors of group involvement still resonate. I've received information through the years about a faction of West-Side residents linked to the crime. Corroboration has come from six different respondents, all of them unknown to and independent of each other...

Bricca has all the footprints of a **personal cause murder**.

The violence stems from aggression between people emotionally entangled with each other. A prime example would be domestic violence. Not every mistreated wife is murdered by her husband – but nearly all wives killed by their husbands were abused previously.

Surprisingly, homicide is the leading cause of death among pregnant women. But another equal opportunity stressor on any relationship is cheating.

Adultery can ignite a personal cause murder. Defense lawyers say that just because their client was having an affair doesn't mean they killed their spouse or lover. Yet infidelity is often at the heart of sensational crimes. Here are five that have stood the test of time:

- **1906 Stanford White:** The famous architect was shot by millionaire Harry Thaw over White's relationship with his wife Evelyn Nesbit Thaw.
- **1922 Halls Mills Case (The minister and the choir singer):** The unsolved killings of two married lovers who were slain during a tryst in New Jersey.
- **1927 Ruth Snyder/Judd Gray:** The lovers murdered her husband, and both were executed after a spectacular trial.
- **1954 Marilyn Sheppard:** Husband Sam had several affairs, which swayed his murder conviction in his first trial.
- **2002 Laci Peterson:** Husband Scott was leading a double life with another woman when he killed his pregnant wife.

A recent FBI victimology study identified "adultery as a risk factor for homicide." A glut of emotions – hate, envy, revenge all rear their heads when illicit sex is involved.

Monogamy is still a strongly held moral ideal, even when not adhered to. But affairs are perceived differently by men and women, as illustrated here:

"Waiting to have someone's stolen seconds can burn you alive... Also there are certain times you have no other choice – not honoring this fascination, this car crash of desire, is also a

lie. There is power in having someone risk everything for you. There is nothing more frightening than being willing to take this freefall..."

Daphne Gottlieb

A traitor serpent sleeps below
Who rises at a glance, a play
Of light upon a curve, a sway
Of flesh, deliberate and slow...

Ray Russell

This is the Mars and Venus of intimacy.

Men give love to get sex, and women give sex to get love. Women may use sex to get what they want, but not men. Because sex IS what men want.

A woman who loves multiple men may feel she has betrayed them all, while a man who only loves one woman may believe he has betrayed himself.

Yet no human is ever above temptation. And those who flee temptation often leave a forwarding address.

Cheating on a spouse is not just about sex – the excitement of planning the rendezvous rouses emotions long stifled by a sour or troubled marriage. Grabbing purloined hours can engorge the heart with passion or undermine the psyche with depression.

And those highs and lows can turn on a dime...

Possible Suspects

Among the over 300 interviews in the case file lurks our killer.

He was most likely known to the family, an ordinary man and a member of the community. Yet beneath his professional persona there coiled a dark, secretive man.

It's time to evaluate the suspects, from the ridiculous to the sublime. Some inclusions are almost comical, but they still hold currency in the public imagination. The fewer the facts a wannabee sleuth has at his fingertips, the wilder his conjectures become. And it's always a cavernous leap to embrace reckless gossip while eschewing stubborn truths.

The internet age of true crime has perpetuated a flawed obsession – the premise that links unsolved murders to available or proximate serial killers. These suspects are products of inductive reasoning, a bottom up method akin to profiling:

- **Theories move from the specific to the general**
- **It establishes probability but not certainty**
- **It allows that the conclusion could be false**

An example of inductive reasoning might say this: Kidnappers in the 1930's were gangsters. The Lindbergh baby was kidnapped in 1932. Therefore gangsters kidnapped the Lindbergh baby.

Inductive reasoning works if you're a profiler, but it can often embody a killer prototype rather than a solid prospect.

There is a website dedicated to the proposition that Uni-Bomber Ted Kaczynski was not only the Zodiac Killer, but that he also murdered Valerie Percy and the Bricca family. Yet Kaczynski was at the University of Michigan in 1966 getting his doctorate in mathematics. And serial killers do not begin with the hands on "wet work" of the Percy and Bricca murders only to become content with sending bombs through the mail.

A Cincinnati news station once ran a feature linking the Bricca murders to the Zodiac Killer. Yet the Zodiac operated on the West Coast three years after Bricca with a completely different MO – he liked to shoot people in cars, not stab them in homes. Yet these inconvenient facts don't seem to bother the conspiracy buffs.

Because Ted Bundy is a suspect in the July 1966 attack on the two stewardesses in Seattle, his name pops up in the Bricca case. Yet Linda Bulaw didn't know Lonnie Trumbull and Lisa Wick. When she began training with UAL in April 1961, Lonnie and Lisa were Oregon high school freshmen. Bundy himself was just 18 when the Briccas were killed, and he's never been placed in Cincinnati.

Della Sutorius was a teenager in 1966 and lived within a mile of the Bricca house. She was convicted of murdering husband Dr. Darryl Sutorius in 1996, but perhaps her homicidal instincts were honed by the Bricca murders. In *Della's Web*, author Aphrodite Jones writes that "the Bricca case had become rather infamous in Western Hills...16-year-old Della taunted her sister that she did it."

Serial killers such as Ted Bundy (left) and The Zodiac have been erroneously linked to the Bricca murders.

Based on proximity alone, she is ranked above our three serial killers. But Della's many husbands had more to fear from this "black widow" than did a middle class family 30 years earlier.

The killings of Valerie Percy and Linda Bricca one week apart spun a web of rumors connecting these two young women from upscale Chicago suburbs. Yet this formerly intriguing coincidence falls apart under close scrutiny.

They were allegedly embroiled in some drug scheme while they were UAL stewardesses together – ignoring the fact that Valerie was still a high school student during Linda's brief stint as a flight attendant. They didn't attend the same schools, and there is no evidence that they ever met or their fathers knew each other.

Valerie was beaten and stabbed during what appeared to be a botched home invasion burglary. Yet Linda was stabbed to death with her family by killers who targeted her due to a personal connection that imploded. The two crimes are not even similar.

It's possible that a random criminal or unhinged person killed the Bricca family. Yet every bad actor or wandering felon known to be on the west side that weekend was checked out and cleared.

The Jewel Tea route man who argued with Linda glimmered for several days on the premise that Allen Sipple was working his brother's route – he had raped two women at knifepoint six years earlier. But detectives could never place him on Greenway Avenue.

All murder cases have guys like him. Plenty of smoke but no fire...

THE LAST OF OUR implausible suspects is the most fascinating.

As mentioned previously, Jack Rauss was convicted of 2nd degree murder and manslaughter in the killing of James and Goldie Cunningham of Price Hill in 1961 (**Queen City Notorious Chapter 10**). The 28-year-old former football star, described as the "All-American Boy", became "the killer next door" when he erupted over derogatory remarks Goldie made about this mother.

Rauss's connection to Bricca is tenuous yet intriguing. In March 1961, his mother was injured in a bus accident while on a trip with Goldie. She'd been widowed for a year and a half, and Rauss didn't like her traveling with Goldie, who was 15 years younger than her invalid husband and liked hanging out with other men.

Two weeks after the crash, Rauss showed up at the Joseph Zeff house on Greenway Avenue. Zeff was Goldie Cunningham's brother, and his wife Stella was in the kitchen when Rauss suddenly appeared, clearly agitated and looking for James Cunningham, who was staying there while Goldie was in the hospital. But Stella was frightened by Rauss and denied knowing where he was.

When James and Goldie were found stabbed to death on April 17th, it was Stella who told investigators about her disturbing encounter with Jack Rauss and his animosity towards Goldie. Rauss was picked up for questioning and soon confessed to killing the couple, who had babysat him as a child.

Rauss was released in early September 1966, and he allegedly still carried a grudge against the Zeff's, who lived two doors down from the Briccas in an identical brick tri-level. In the darkness Rauss got the wrong house and killed the Bricca family in a panic.

Yet Joe Zeff, whose daughter Linda was the Bricca's primary babysitter and who was present when their bodies were found, lived at 3313 Greenway – 13 doors south of the murder house.

That Jack Rauss would nurse a five year hatred for the Zeffs, enter a house a tenth of a mile from them, and brutally kill three strangers

Convicted of two West Side murders in 1961, former football star Jack Rauss became an intriguing Bricca suspect decades later.

seems ludicrous. And Rauss had a clean record after his release until his death in 1994.

Probable Suspects

Using deductive reasoning instead of inductive allows us to go top down rather than bottom up. Instead of drawing broad generalizations from specific observations, the goal is to formulate a particular hypothesis that fits the wide-ranging facts.

- **Theories move from the general to the specific**
- **It links the premises with the conclusions**
- **Both the premise and conclusion must be true**

An example of deductive reasoning might say: Lizzie Borden was known to dislike her stepmother Abby Borden. Lizzie was alone in the house with Abby when she was murdered. Therefore Lizzie Borden killed her stepmother.

Consider the trench coated man seen walking on Greenway by the teenage girl mailing a letter. We can't prove he did NOT kill the Briccas, because you can't prove a negative. Anything IS possible. But a good detective deals in probabilities, not possibilities.

There is nothing to suggest random selection of the Bricca house by a mysterious maniac. Yet Mr. Trench Coat, along with others seen on Greenway Avenue the night of the murders, are better suspects than the known serial killers for one reason –proximity to the crime scene provided him an opportunity.

Investigators looked closely at Monsanto personnel. Were there any snakes lurking behind those nice suits or sharks prowling under those blue collars?

Twenty employees who worked closely with Jerry Bricca were interviewed between September and December of 1966 – some of them twice. One name stands out: James Cannon. Cannon was the irascible, inappropriate engineer who thought he was God's gift. He was rough and erratic, often at odds with the smoothly competent Jerry, who scowled at Cannon's outrageous flirting.

Jim Dell'Aria, hired to replace the murdered man, became Cannon's supervisor in July 1967 and expressed strong opinions about him to me. "Cannon was an independent guy, brash but sharp. He was reckless in his job sometimes and hard to control."

"Did Cannon ever talk about the murders like your other co-workers did?"

"He never once spoke of the murders to me."

Cannon's interview is marked with the tell-tale asterisk on the control sheet, as was that of his ex-wife Mary Ellen. His meticulous alibi for the murder weekend attracted suspicion, as did his sudden appearance outside the Bricca house the night the bodies were found. Cannon even told some co-workers that "they will try to pin this thing on me" because of some scratches he received in a "fight with his girlfriend."

20 people at the sprawling Monsanto complex along the Ohio River in Addyston were interviewed by investigators.

If Cannon was the killer, at least seven people he supposedly saw on his weekend junket to Indiana were lying. His mother and brother may have covered for him, but it's doubtful other relatives and their friends would claim he was with them when he wasn't – and maintain that lie in the face of a triple murder investigation.

James Cannon was a babe hound, and fit the profile of a killer who had a thing for Linda. Throw in the tension with Jerry at work and it's easy to see why detectives drilled so deep on him.

But like many other excavations in this baffling case, this one was a dry well...

Rumors that a local celebrity was involved still resonate today. Consider this 2010 email I received:

> ***I think the reason so many people thought "Skipper" Ryle could be guilty was because he rode a distinctive motorcycle and it was parked in front of the Glenway Animal Hospital a lot.***

Pet Care	Narcotics Thieves Are Busy Again
Dr. Fred Leininger, Cincinnati veterinarian, is now a regular featured guest of Skipper Ryle's Sunday morning show. Dr. Leininger discusses how to care for your pets.	Thieves who have been burglarizing local doctors' and veterinarians' offices of narcotics have struck again. Dr. Stanley Keller, owner of the Western Hills Animal Hospital reported to police that sometime between 9 p. m. Sunday and 8:30 a. m. Monday burglars forced open a locked medicine cabinet in his offices and took narcotics valued at $15.

Glenn Ryle had Dr. Leininger as a guest on his show.
Stanley Keller had narcotics stolen from his office.

The thought was that Dr. Leininger was covering up for the Skipper. The rumor was so strong that many of us young mothers would not let our kids watch Skipper Ryle's program anymore.

Another email talked about Ryle "hanging out at the corner of Woodhaven and Greenway in the summer of 1966. He would park and just sit there – he never got out of the car. Our parents told us not to worry since he was on TV."

Still another resident recalled how Ryle would "sit on his motorcycle outside the Woodhaven Swim Club and eyeball the women in their bathing suits."

And a woman who walked home from school on Greenway in the spring of 1966 told me she sometimes saw a motorcycle parked in the Bricca side yard. Her description matched Ryle's bike.

Glenn Ryle was questioned by Bricca detectives about his relationship with Fred Leininger. They left feeling that Ryle was "a close friend" of Leininger and they should not expect him to cooperate. Was Ryle worried about his friend being accused of the murders? Or more concerned about being implicated himself?

It is plausible that Linda Bricca met Ryle through Leininger. He had a reputation as a married man who strayed, opening up the possibility that Linda was having more than one affair. Ryle also had a military background in Special Forces and martial arts – a "bad dude" who had been trained to kill.

If Leininger had a problem with Jerry Bricca, Glenn Ryle would be on a short list of friends to back him up...

Bricca neighbors had proximity with a chance of motive. Dick Meyer, who with Dick Janszen alerted police to the bodies, was the last neighbor cleared. Both were profoundly affected by seeing their gruesomely slain neighbors. Janszen died three years later at age 41, never recovering from the horror he encountered that night.

There was a rumor Linda told her hairdresser Meyer was "bothering" her. Like other husbands on Greenway, Dick Meyer probably ogled his fetching neighbor when she was washing her car in a bathing suit. County detectives should have "officially" cleared Meyer long before November 14th, 1966.

Judith Hemmer Bush, who lived five doors down from the Briccas in 1966, told me about a neighbor who aroused her suspicions. The man's wife was interviewed – yet he was not.

In the 1970's Judy found herself working in the same office with him. He "had a terrible temper, and talked a lot about Linda Bricca being hot and sexy." Judy felt he was a "Jekyll and Hyde personality." Her mother's friend allegedly saw Linda enter his house a few times that summer when his wife wasn't home.

Yet this neighbor, who I won't name but sounds like a better suspect than Richard Meyer, never made the case file...

Conjecture that the family was killed by drug dealers thrived alongside the Mafia hit allegations. Linda allegedly told a neighbor about helping break up a drug ring. This is an astounding thing to tell someone, even if she was making it up.

Knowing her passion for animals, perhaps they were veterinary drugs. There was a rash of break-ins at West Side animal clinics that summer, including several at Dr. Stanley Keller's location. The drug connection could have involved "animal tranquilizers."

There is a website linking the Church of Satan to a number of cold cases from 1966-1969, including Bricca. Three other 1966 murders in this book made the list – Valerie Percy, the Sims Family in Florida, and Cheri Jo Bates in Riverside CA.

A satanic cult killed the Briccas? It seems ridiculous. At least I thought so until receiving this bombshell email in 2011:

> ***I witnessed a murder by the same group of criminals who killed the Briccas. I have lived in fear of them for many years... an organized crime/satanic cult group existed in the area. It may sound off, but satanic cults were a big problem in Southern Ohio for decades. They had a hit man who was a Cincinnati Police officer. He killed the Bricca's because Linda had found out too much. She worked for a veterinarian named Leininger who was supplying the group with drugs they used to sedate animals during sacrifices.***

As I read on, this group sounded more like the "Black Legion", possibly involved in the ambush killing of Paul Mueller at Spring Grove Cemetery in 1971 **(Queen City Gothic chapter 13)**. This group was suspected of several murders that year, including a woman tortured and slain at the Brass Boot Bar.

There were rumors that a CPD car was parked near the Bricca house that night. And I learned the officer identified as the group's "hit man" committed suicide in Mount Echo Park in 1984. Six other people have confirmed his identity to me since the original email, all independently of each other. The same name keeps coming up.

I also interviewed a woman who claimed to have been sexually molested by this group as a child. Listening to her heart wrenching story, I concluded she was either the Meryl Streep of actresses or was actually re-living this shocking event in front of me.

Was this her bizarre false memory – or just the wicked truth?

HERB VOGEL SPENT A whole page of his July 1967 Bricca status report on animal trainers he investigated.

Linda Bricca attended the Shrine Circus at the Cincinnati Gardens in April and she was the only non-Gardens employee allowed access behind the scenes with the animals. Some detectives would later question what she may have done to earn it.

Vogel dived into the seedy, itinerant world of traveling animal acts and their owners, questioning Marion Earl Grubbs and some of his associates. Their demeanor was mostly evasive – perhaps because some of them were rumored to have sex in their trailers with women visiting the circus.

Did Linda offer sexual favors for the chance to ride the elephants, feed the bears, and groom the monkeys?

There were rumors she gave them oral sex and their wives found out and wanted to teach her a lesson. These were hard faced "carny" women with no qualms about getting tough. Only this time it got of hand.

Captain Otting wrote a scenario for this theory, concluding that "as many as three people committed this crime," with two men killing the adults while a woman controlled the child. This scenario was validated by witnesses who saw two males and one female in front of the Bricca house around 11:30 PM on the murder night.

The workaholic, brooding husband and the pretty, ex-stewardess wife – a soap opera cliché, or the catalyst for adultery? Obsessive affairs of the heart often lead to crimes of passion. If Linda WAS having an affair, her lover would be a "person of interest."

According to Linda's brother, she called their mother the week of the murders and begged to move back home with Debbie, saying Jerry had quit talking his epilepsy pills and was becoming volatile. We know he was angry at Linda when she arrived late and drunk at the Meyer house after working for Leininger Wednesday night. Jerry even made a muffled threat against the doctor, and then strangely confided some of it to his boss.

Other than money problems, infidelity is the likely culprit for this kind of marital friction.

GIVEN HER AFFINITY FOR veterinarians, our list just got shorter. Rumor has it that Dr. Herman Rehder was getting complaints from female clients. He was a tantalizing suspect – Rehder's psychotic history and personal failures were the perfect cocktail for misplaced aggression. Had Leininger ever considered that his friend and colleague was an emotional time bomb?

Because just four days before the murders, this disturbed man with a violent past had materialized directly in front of Linda Bricca. Yet when

Both Stanley Keller and Herman Rehder were colleagues and friends of Leininger, and met Linda Bricca through him.

interviewed by detectives, Rehder appeared to have a solid alibi, watching TV at home with his wife and child.

Rumors have swirled around Dr. Stanley Keller for decades. He had already spent three previous stints in a psychiatric ward before 1966. And his odd demeanor during two interviews hoisted red flags for incredulous detectives. The guy was more than "flighty" – there was something "off" about him.

I've heard weird stories from former clients about pets dying under Keller's care after going in for routine checkups or minor surgery. But while giving a Bricca program in 2015, a woman stood up and volunteered a most disturbing story about Keller.

During that fateful summer of 1966, Stanley Keller had stopped at her isolated house on River Road while she was alone and asked to use the phone. She knew him only as a member of her husband's bowling team but nevertheless let him in.

Once admitted, his behavior alarmed her. He made suggestive comments and demanded to know if she were alone – she lied and claimed their "boarder" was asleep in the spare room. At that point Dr. Keller abruptly left, leaving her scared and shaken...

The Leininger Interviews

On October 8th, 1966 Fred Leininger submitted to a 45 minute taped interview with lead investigator Herb Vogel. It was the pivotal moment of the Bricca investigation.

Leininger was vague about his relationship with Linda Bricca, lied about when he'd last seen her, couldn't account for his whereabouts on the night in question, became flustered and finally terminated the interview. When Vogel returned two days later with more questions, he was blocked by attorney Richard Morr. Leininger then exercised his right to remain silent. Forever.

Frederick George Leininger casts a long, potent shadow over the Bricca case file. Interview number #188 is marked with the telltale asterisk, and it is the ONLY interview typed in all CAPS, the modern social media equivalent of shouting.

Leininger was never identified as the suspect until this author did so in the Bricca chapter of **Queen City Gothic**. Yet Vogel's July 1967 status report was the first official confirmation that he was the unnamed "man" who hired Morr and spurned cooperation.

Glenway Animal Hospital was owned by Fred Leininger from 1958 until 1995. Linda Bricca had known him since November 1963, even using Leininger as a reference on her Executive Modeling Agency application in April 1965.

Yet she was murdered ONLY AFTER working three days for Leininger – Monday thru Wednesday September 19-21st 1966...

Good interrogators look for two things. A "tell" is body language indicative of guilt. "Leakage" is partial information that suggests the suspect knows more than he's telling.

One retired police detective I interviewed gave me this great quote: "Always look for inappropriate affectation during interrogation. A bad lie is as good as a confession." He also insisted that "Miranda never stopped us from getting a confession."

He described how during an interview a witness could be "nibbled, squirreled, or flipped." When encountering a cocky suspect, he would say "the guy has hubris." He told me that brash, narcissistic suspects are the ones "most likely to leak guilt while trying to show you how smart they are."

When I asked if he took notes during an interrogation I was surprised – he never wrote anything down. Taking notes would distract the suspect and hinder their chances of building a rapport.

At 4 PM on Wednesday September 28th, 1966, Detective Gerald Taylor was sitting across from Dr. Fred Leininger. Taylor had just left Monsanto and Jerry's shocked co-workers, and this visit to the GAH was ostensibly to interview Linda's employer.

She'd only worked there three days – and less than 24 hours after the crime was discovered rumors were hovering about Leininger's relationship with the slain woman.

Leininger was half handsome, a lone wolf wearing an edgy melancholy, like a perpetual five o'clock shadow. Here was a man who would feel compelled to prove his superiority to all those who came against him.

Taylor asked short questions and gave the Doc room to banter. He established that Linda worked the first three days of the previous week. "How did she get the job?"

"She came here on Monday the 19th to pay a bill. The couple working here had just left to go back to school." Leininger smiled ruefully. "She was bothering me about working here."

Bothering? Taylor let it go. "So you hired her?"

"Yes, to fill in until I hired another couple. Then she would just work on Wednesdays."

Taylor locked eyes on him. "When did you meet Linda Bricca?"

Leininger consulted his notes. "Her first appointment was November 9th, 1963 for her two dogs. They had just moved here."

"Did you make any house calls? Taylor saw it again, that furtive, distracted look.

Without checking his notes, Leininger answered. "It was one time, in November 1965 for her rabbit and parakeet.

"That's the only time you've been in the Bricca home?"

Leininger stared, contemptuous of this leading question. "Yes."

As Taylor rose to leave, Leininger stopped him. "There's one more thing. Last Friday I dropped a book off at the Bricca house that Debbie left here."

Taylor regarded him balefully but said nothing.

"Debbie was in the yard," the Doc announced. "I just handed her the book. I didn't see Mr. or Mrs. Bricca at that time."

As Gerald Taylor left Leininger's clinic, he thought of something his father, also a cop, once said to him. "Beware of the man who answers the question before it's asked."

TEN DAYS LATER TAYLOR was back at the GAH with his boss.

Vogel's inquiries into his background had not escaped the Doctor's notice. They must have something. But he had acquitted himself well during that first interview. Leininger's feeling of superiority was like a confirmation of his code.

If he expected them to go right after him he was mistaken. The two detectives spent at least 15 minutes on his background, information they could have gleaned elsewhere. For Leininger it was a dead giveaway – they were just fishing and hadn't caught anything. The outcome was in his hands.

There was no reason to panic. He was a respected citizen, a businessman sitting in his own office. There were no glaring lights or blustering cops. These investigators were deferential, asking his help to clear up an astonishing crime. They were doing their job to throw light on the murders.

As Leininger casually answered questions about the clinic, he relished his power. But he knew this situation wouldn't stand still.

The question about Linda calling him Thursday night came out of nowhere. *Why hadn't he gotten that message?* He stared back at Vogel. Certainly he was superior to this county errand boy?

Now he would have to prove himself, and show that he was in another orbit from their pedestrian trajectory.

Yet he stumbled over his alibi for that night, and the questions came with an accusatory tone meant to embarrass him. *Don't lose your cool. And be polite to them.* He wondered if being courteous would count for something.

Maybe it would keep him from getting caught...

DURING ONE OF THE silences, Herb Vogel regarded the man in front of him. A well-built six footer, about 210 pounds with strong arms, he was a skillful bow-hunter yet a compassionate veterinarian. What other contrasts would be exposed today?

Vogel knew that killers who aren't seasoned criminals will show consciousness of guilt. Eventually the struggle of reconciling your deception leaks out. Only a sociopath can hide it.

Yet this man sitting here was in a different league, deftly avoiding questions about the crime and maneuvering into a personal conversation. He must be careful not to reveal too much.

Vogel's voice was fluid and soft, but it could quickly turn cold and lethal, like a gun. For now he kept his speech holstered. He believed he could tell what this guy was thinking, just by scrutinizing his verbal cues and body language.

Once the questions veered toward Linda Bricca, Vogel got what he was looking for. Leininger's replies became shifty, his tone stilted, his gestures ever more expansive.

When Vogel asked about the message she left with his service the man's face underwent a visible reaction. His Adam's apple bobbed and a cluster of veins darted across his forehead.

Vogel had seen it before – the subject forfeits his composure when thrown a curveball question.

Leininger's confusion was tangible, his words chalky, like a dream where your voice is parched. As he floundered for an alibi, Vogel felt something between contempt and pity. The poor bastard.

By the time Leininger terminated the interview, Vogel saw this crime for what it truly was. This guy was overpowered by his fixation with Linda, and it took a wrong turn into rage. It was the evil of passion AND the fear of public exposure, of shame and disgrace.

And now the spider was caught in his own web.

Herb Vogel believed that the "perfect crime" was a myth. Perhaps the mistake was that this killer believed he could carry the deadly secret for the rest of his life...

Fred Leininger

Who was Frederick George Leininger?

Larry Mentrup worked at the Glenway Animal Hospital for 27 years, beginning in 1969. He consented to an interview in 2013.

"Were you nervous about working for him?"

"No, because it never entered my mind that he did it."

"Did clients ever ask questions about him?" Or was Linda Bricca ever mentioned?"

"Never."

Mentrup was a loyal employee and beneficiary of the doctor's largesse. Leininger paid for Larry's disabled son to get special treatment at a California clinic, including air fare for the whole family. He remembers that Leininger "had a passion for his job", and "often treated animals for nothing." The "Doc" would mentor Ohio State vet students every year, and was "a great teacher."

Mentrup admitted Leininger was "standoffish until he got to know you." And he agreed it was "strange for a veterinarian" to be such an avid bow hunter.

"Did he ever seem like he was under stress?

"He was always on his guard, mainly with new clients. He realized they would put him under the microscope."

"In what way?"

"He was run through the meat grinder grapevine."

According to Larry Mentrup, Glenn Ryle was a "regular client" – he and Leininger were "close friends". He also told me that if a friend needed help Leininger would "do it no questions asked."

A GAH CLIENT HAD A different take on the doctor, describing two odd incidents he witnessed:

> *There was a wall between the two front treatment rooms, and one time he literally fell into the wall. It was obvious he was intoxicated with something... you'd have to be to fall into the wall like that. It looked funny. My first thought was that he was trying to medicate away his guilt.*
>
> *The other time my brother and I had a hold of our dog but when Dr. Leininger tried to give him a shot the dog growled and tried to get at him. We held onto him, yet Leininger jumped back into the wall, knees buckling and hands pulled up near his neck. A cowardly pose – he looked petrified. The hypodermic was*

> ***hanging in our dog's hip, bouncing up and down as he growled. The shot was never administered. This guy seemed such a coward that I wondered how in the world he could have gotten up the courage to kill three people...***

During a Bricca program a woman stood up and announced that she was "shocked to learn Dr. Leininger was the prime suspect."

She told the audience that Leininger was their family vet and "we all loved him." A year after the murders, when she was 15, her precious new kitten got outside and was never found. She was bereft – until a week later when "Doc showed up at our door with an almost identical kitten" and gave it to her.

There was this 2013 email from a veterinary technician at a surgical clinic, where they did procedures beyond the expertise of regular vets:

> ***Fred Leininger did not send many referrals to our clinic. He did the surgery himself, although in my opinion he was not capable of doing so. To me, this is like a general practitioner doing brain surgery. It is accepted practice to refer cases that are beyond your expertise. Leininger had a reputation for having a big ego and being something of a pervert with the young female techs. No one wanted to work for him and didn't for long.***

I interviewed a woman who met Leininger in the early 1990s and stayed friends with him until his death. She'd heard a few rumors about his past but nothing concrete – she was stunned when I informed her that he was the prime suspect in a triple homicide.

> ***He was cultured, extremely respectful and sensitive. I feel SO certain that man could not harm a child. I can see where someone might see him as creepy but I think he was just shy and goofy. Perhaps he never grew up all the way emotionally?***
>
> ***He never, EVER mentioned the murders to me. There was no need. I never questioned him. He gave me no reason to.***
>
> ***He used to tell me about exploring in the woods as a kid being the best times of his childhood. Doc spoke often of being a geeky kid who loved to observe wildlife and experience nature.***

> ***He was extremely compassionate, and a true animal welfare supporter. He never wanted anything to suffer. If a veterinarian sees something suffering and they can't fix it, they put it to sleep...***

The image of young Fred discovering a wooded sanctuary while other boys were playing baseball is pleasing to me – a lonely, awkward lad who realized early on what his true calling would be.

Yet Leininger's zeal for hunting seems incompatible for a "compassionate" vet. I once asked a veterinarian friend who hunted how he reconciled killing animals with his profession. He told me that "the killing becomes incidental to the hunt..."

A CHILDHOOD FRIEND OF THE Leininger children told me that whenever she went there to visit, her sister would say "So you're going over to the killer's house?" Once she came home and told her parents "I think Mr. Leininger looks down on us." They replied, "Oh, the KILLER looks down on US?"

This echoes Larry Foppe, who saw a distraught and disheveled Leininger in his Pony Keg the night of the murders.

> ***The doctor is spoiled, with the attitude that I got mine you get yours. Most of the time he feels he could get anything he needed taken care of. In his opinion he was better than anybody else... he was a very cold, hard man. He didn't seem to have many feelings or didn't appear to show any...***

I spoke with a woman who described an unsettling encounter with Leininger in 1975. Knowing the rumors about him, she left a bar where Leininger was hitting on her. She said he trailed her to two other bars, followed her home in his car, and only drove away when her husband came outside.

The woman who claimed to be molested by a shadowy group of West Side Satan disciples told me this: "Linda was killed by the cult because she was about to turn them in for animal sacrifices. And Leininger was supplying drugs to this group..."

INSTEAD OF INDUCTIVE OR deductive, we'll employ abductive reasoning when evaluating suspect Fred Leininger.

Abductive reasoning begins with a set of observations and ends with the most probable explanation. When there is no clear answer, theories are tested and a presumption is made. Abductive reasoning is often used by jurors based on evidence they've heard.

Say you come home and find torn up papers all over the floor, and the only living creature known to be in the house is your dog. Even though a family member or an intruder could be responsible, you conclude the dog did it because it is the most likely scenario.

Here are 13 coincidences that Fred Leininger has pointing at him – the ONLY Bricca suspect to be this unlucky:

- **The murderer knew the family, and 300 such people were interviewed – Leininger knew them.**
- **Jerry and Linda were victims of a personal cause homicide and Leininger knew them personally.**
- **He was seen alone with Linda Bricca on the Friday and Saturday afternoons before the crime.**
- **Leininger was observed in the vicinity of the crime scene at the time of the murders.**
- **His appearance, conduct, and demeanor that night were indicative of someone in a panic.**
- **Rumors linked him romantically with Linda Bricca within the first hours of the investigation.**
- **He lied to police about his alibi, and become flustered and confused during the second interview.**
- **He lawyered up after his second interview and refused all requests for further interviews.**
- **He was the #1 suspect in a small group of suspects who could not be eliminated completely.**
- **Debbie was murdered only because she was a witness who knew their killer.**
- **Two friends and Linda's mother said Debbie had called Leininger "Uncle Fred".**

- **The tape on Jerry's chin was determined to be a high grade medical or veterinary tape.**
- **Leininger killed himself and his wife attempted suicide in Cincinnati in February 2004.**

This is not enough to bring an indictment, much less a guilty verdict. But it illustrates how a set of circumstances can diminish the probability that an innocent suspect could be this ill-starred.

Because in the court of the armchair detective, where ALL evidence is admissible, this set of circumstances confirms Fred Leininger's involvement in the Bricca murders...

THE KEY TO SOLVING this case may be buried with Fred Leininger. Bodies can be exhumed by judicial authority for a DNA match under the "prime suspect" provision. But it's an unpleasant and costly undertaking, and would surely meet familial resistance.

While compelling, the circumstantial case against Leininger never passed the legal threshold to arrest a prominent citizen. Our prime suspect didn't "walk" – because he was never in custody.

But more than a half century later, it all comes back to Fred Leininger. The man was a paradox, possessed of unselfish generosity and compassion for his friends, countered by shallow charm and disdain for those he considered beneath him.

And after September 25th, 1966, confidence and trust were no longer within his province. He had to learn to live without them.

For the last 38 years of her married life, Lynn Leininger's husband was the prime suspect in a triple homicide. How did she even begin to process this? Someone she loved and respected was believed capable of committing a horrible crime. Could his judgment, wisdom, and kindness be cancelled out in the heat of passion? How could this man be so rational, yet so ruthless?

She had to believe him innocent, or else go mad. But something was different about him. That bland agitation about his sense of entitlement was missing. Why wasn't he demanding his rights or mocking the cops? Instead, he told her "everything was fine." Knowing him so well, his calmness was unsettling for Lynn. Could he be guilty of something?

After graduating from high school (1949), Fred Leininger (1974) would become a triple murder suspect 17 years later.

One fact speaks volumes – Lynn Leininger did not provide an alibi for her husband on the night in question. Perhaps she could not do so without lying.

And what about Fred himself? If he was guilty, in what part of his brain did he bury the truth for almost four decades? What were those years like for him?

Someone once said that the damned don't die – they just have nightmares that never cease. Did Fred Leininger live out his days in the contempt and loathing of his own heart?

Or did the avid hunter track down his conscience and find his own punishment?

The Explanation

All week long Linda had suffered from restless nights and a sensation of foreboding – a creepy-crawly feeling that something terrible was about to happen. It was like a dark wing beating far back in her mind, never coming into focus.

It was an ornery day, with tufts of rain and fissures of light throttling her senses. Splinters of a dream clung to her, but Linda couldn't quite grasp it – something about her mother dying.

It had been a watershed week in so many ways. Linda told herself it wasn't that momentous – just a series of small things, small mistakes, small lies. She had said just enough to everyone, yet told everything to no one.

Fred had showed his true colors Wednesday night. He crossed the line and didn't even flinch. Instead of pride she saw vast conceit, arrogance without appreciation. A liar with a slick tongue, all promises and no delivery, just like most men.

She had told Jerry that the affair was over, nothing more. Now they were locked into strained silences and awkward decorum, an embarrassed gloom settling over them. Could their marriage recover? Neither of them knew for sure. But as they began to watch the movie on Sunday night, Linda felt encouraged.

Still, that familiar feeling of dread wouldn't go away...

AN ADULTEROUS AFFAIR IS at the heart of this crime. Nothing I encountered in the file has swayed me from that. Our killer's means and opportunity were variables, but his motive was fixed.

Questions abound. Did Linda say she was carrying his child? Did he promise to leave his wife and help her start her own clinic? Did she learn about some illegal activities at GAH?

Was he truly lusting after her? Had passion led to obsession? Had she forced his hand and driven him into survival mode?

He stood to lose his family, his business, his status.

Perhaps even HIS life...

HE WAITED UNTIL THE neighbors had put their garbage cans out. By 9:15 PM the rain sluiced street was desolate and darkness bled away all color. His vision became like a grainy black and white image from a frayed photo album.

He was a hunter, blending with the landscape, not hidden, but a natural blur as your prey comes whirring out of a grove. Sitting quietly in the car, he became part of the street. Approach each thicket anticipating the ambush. Never go downwind.

He had fortified himself with several shots, yet courage was oozing out of his fingertips, like the quivering excitement when you catch your balance on the edge of the abyss.

The sky was milky with mist. He saw his shadow scurry across the lawn and leap into the night. Now he was just a fog, a wraith attracted by other shadows.

SHE drove him to this. One side silk and the other sandpaper, her kiss voracious yet hollow, her eyes sublime and unreadable.

He felt the failure of the whole thing – the woman who glowed for you turns out to be a whore, and you realize love is just a delusion.

Their passion was consummated and even consecrated – yet now it was ugly and acrid.

All that was left tonight was his belief in his own precision, the dynamic friction of gaining control and letting go at the same time.

Like his partner said..."always make sure the juice is worth the squeeze. If it isn't, then burn your bridges from both ends..."

LONG BEFORE CELL PHONES and social media tracked our every move, Linda Bricca's interactions the week before her murder are like a trail of breadcrumbs in a deep, dark forest.

On Monday she goes to work for Dr. Fred Leininger. Taking this job with this man set the stage for her murder.

On Tuesday she works again, yet Leininger hires another couple, putting Linda's new job in jeopardy. But he relents and gives her part time hours on Wednesdays.

On Wednesday she comes home from work late, drunk, and distraught. Whatever occurred between her and the doctor between 9-10:30 PM, the spark of murder is kindled.

On Thursday she doesn't work at GAH, but places an "urgent" call to Leininger that evening. Jerry is working, and Linda tries hard to get Linda Zeff or her mother to babysit Debbie that night.

On Friday Linda shows up at the archery range while Leininger is with his friend. It becomes awkward and uncomfortable, and when he leaves Linda and Fred are alone in a secluded location.

On Saturday morning Leininger calls the Bricca house and speaks to both Jerry and Linda. That afternoon Linda is twice seen riding in a car with a man who looks like Leininger. On this day Linda also has sex with a man who is not her husband.

In a personal cause murder, always look for someone who interacted with the victim in the days before the crime. Assuming Linda saw Leininger Thursday night, she had personal contact with him every day that week.

Linda was inflicting an emotional toll on Leininger, and he must preserve his wealth and status at all cost. Suddenly the value of murder is escalating while the expense diminishes. Motive is looking for opportunity, and he will seize that moment.

The killer instinct is still our most primal urge. In nature, every creature is either predator or prey. Life feeds on death. The thrill of the hunt and the lure of the kill – violence is part of our human DNA, and no one is immune.

It's survival of the fittest. Kill or be killed...

IT BEGINS IN WRANGLING and confusion. After the confrontation in the TV room, Jerry is trussed with the dog chain. Yet even bound and with a gun on him, the guy is seething, ready to spring.

His partner pummels Jerry to keep him quiet – soon his face looks like a badly dressed steak. But the young husband's lips writhe as he mutters some venomous threats.

The woman is holding the child in the next room. Fred's partner whispers "Leave them alive and we're going down on a felony."

Jerry is still struggling. He's almost free of the chain when his partner suddenly plunges the knife four times into his back, and then cuts his throat! The room is filled with a rasping sound as Jerry chokes on his own blood.

His partner takes the gun and hands him the knife. Linda is on the bed petrified, a blue vein in her throat throbbing. And something else is in her eyes, like contempt for his weakness.

Somehow, his father's words skim through his mind. "You can't get the core of the apple without breaking the skin". His mind flickers to the woods and fields of his childhood, to the freedom and idleness of those vanished years.

Linda watches him, her breasts heaving under the skimpy negligee. She smells deeply of some kind of woozy perfume. He feels himself quickening, a terrible and insufferable rush. Her nearness is overpowering.

His partner's voice is far away. "Swallow her, or spit her out."

He flashes on their first time together, her eyes darting, hipbone jutting, limbs askew, hair fanning out in a field of grass. The sweet, musky writhing of flesh. Seeing that orgasmic flush spread over her pale flesh, the aura of sex sweeping into him with a dreadful scent of thrill and fever.

He thrusts, and she becomes clenched, rigid, her body convulsing with her effort to break through. Her tendons are taut as fine wires against his willing blade.

He feels the dark power within, growing toward release, eruption, violently flaring out. He hears someone screaming, like they were submerged, drowning in blood.

He billows with a throbbing frenzy, almost unbearable, until it bursts, blotting out his mind in a decisive moment of release. His climax is liquid fire, flowing, plummeting. He is not empty, but endless, carrying her into eternity.

There is a frozen moment before she dies, knowing he has won. But now she has the power, and her glassy, lifeless stare will forever haunt him.

"I defy you to ever forget me."

He staggers out the front door, into the frantic rain and the moist, lingering odor of the dark green night. Behind the houses he sees the Western Bowl neon glaring and blinking into the night, turning into a reddish-orange glow, like the skyline of Hell...

MURDER IS ALWAYS ABOUT **passion or gain.** Detectives determined early that the killer was no stranger, and there was nothing tangible to gain from this young family. Yet Debbie was murdered in cold blood, so different from the passionate carnage in the other bedroom. This articulate child was one witness too many.

A rumor is often a premature fact. Whispers about Linda and "the vet" began soon after the bodies were discovered and never ceased. A rumor this vibrant HAS to be driven by a core truth. Even with the clot of gossip clogging the case, Linda's affair with Leininger breaks through as the MOST probable motive for murder.

There is no such thing as a coincidence. There is logic to the random events linking Leininger to the murders. What are the odds he becomes distraught by an unrelated medical emergency around the same time the Briccas were being killed only a half mile away? And as coincidences continue to pile up, there comes a point where it's improbable that any innocent suspect could be that ominous.

People can lie, but behavior never lies. Leininger unraveled during that second interview. The question about Linda's urgent call to his answering service unnerved him, and his demeanor and his body betrayed him when he lied about where he was on the murder night. Compelling your suspect into "consciousness of guilt" is the objective of any interrogation. But Leininger was perceptive enough to know he was on the brink – his termination of the interview was timely.

Every good mystery has a wild card. This card is the identity of Leininger's partner or partners. Who would he turn to if he was afraid of Jerry physically and Linda emotionally? Jerry allegedly threatened violence against Leininger to Betty Meyer on Wednesday night. And by Friday Linda was making him uncomfortable, showing up unexpectedly at his archery club.

Glenn Ryle was a close friend who Leininger could confide in. Men rarely have more than one of these. Ryle was interviewed about his association with Leininger – it was one of the 16 that were highlighted. Apparently Ryle raised more questions than answers.

Dr. Stanley Keller and Dr. Herman Rehder are on the short list as well. These colleagues were longtime friends of Leininger, men with psychological skeletons in their closets who came across as evasive during their interviews.

If Leininger WAS supplying drugs to a satanic cult doing animal sacrifices, a rumor more credible than it sounds, the second man at the crime scene could be from this group. Perhaps a woman came along to control Debbie, which would account for the three people seen outside the Bricca house around the time of the murders...

CONSIDER FRED LEININGER. HE married his high school sweetheart while in college, and has five children under ten by 1966. He is neither good-looking nor charming, and is raw and unsophisticated with women. Linda Bricca's physical splendor and sexual allure must have been an irresistible cocktail.

But if beauty is only skin deep, why are men so obsessed with it? Beauty is a fragile thing, always on the verge of being lost. Maybe some things are more exquisite because they are fleeting.

Did Fred keep pictures of her? Secreted in his attic or basement, haunting, enigmatic little touchstones of the most exciting and terrible time of his life.

He probably rationalized that divine fate had let him get away with it. Now he could find out who he would become.

He became a vampire, a Dracula like villain, caught up in an extraordinary predicament – a form of criminal immortality. Once he was just a man. Now he is haunted by the pain of knowing that he is different, and it will always follow him on earth.

Did Fred Leininger take his secrets to his grave?

But he never accepts responsibility for having killed them. In his methodical mind she took an action, he had a reaction, and there was a consequence, which was neither punishment nor reward. Just like in nature.

So he must live on, without ever telling it. But he will bear the burden. And it won't matter how much he lies.

Because in truth, he is a murderer...

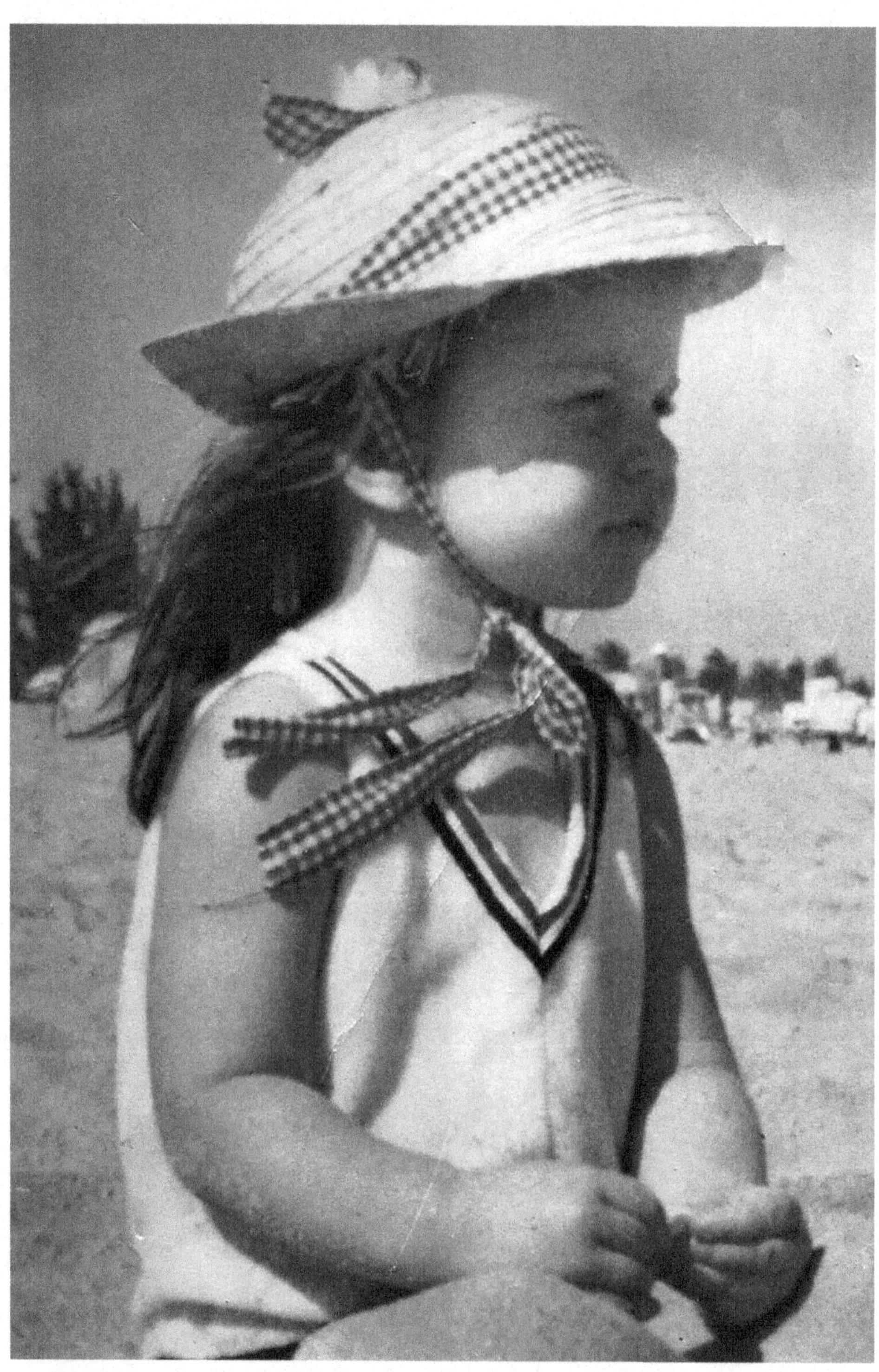

Debbie Bricca on the beach during Linda's Florida "vacation" in March 1966, looking out across the ocean to a future that would never arrive for her...

FINAL EXIT: LOOSE ENDS

They are not long, the weeping and the laughter,
Love and desire and hate;
I think they have no portion in us after
We pass the gate...

Ernest Dowson

NOTHING HAUNTS LIKE AN unsolved murder.

From the first investigator to the last armchair detective, a crime buried without reconciliation is never really laid to rest.

Will there ever be a solution to the Bricca mystery? Do we need to name the killer? Or just choose our favorite ending?

After more than a half century, the chances for a legal resolution in the Bricca case are DOA. The killers are no longer bound by any earthly court, and beyond the pangs of conscience.

With this book, I wanted to drive a stake through the heart of this undead case and banish my childhood nightmare of a sinister slayer come to life. I haven't answered every question here, because as with all mysteries there are still loose ends eluding me. But my hope is that neither the crime nor the killer will ever hold that power over me again.

A cold case detective once said to me, "Let no victim's ghost say we didn't try." It resonates to this day.

I see them everywhere now. Jerry pushing 80, sporting a cane yet still strong and swimming laps, his gray crewcut gliding through the water. Linda lovely and lissome at 75, a feisty animal rights activist with stunning white hair, running her own no-kill shelter. And brilliant, captivating Debbie, a corporate VP pondering retirement at age 56 while expecting her first grandchild.

I feel this beautiful slaughtered family in the pulse of my mind, on their deserted street at twilight, with summer almost gone. I seek them in the shadows – but they are always just beyond my reach.

Our souls are destined to abide in mystery, forever surrounded by ghosts.

We must learn to live with them...

TIMELINE OF BRICCA AND STRANGLER 1961-PRESENT

11/25/61 Jerry Bricca and Linda Bulaw married in Chicago
06/06/62 Deborah Ann Bricca born in Seattle, WA
07/09/63 Jerry Bricca transferred to Cincinnati by Monsanto
11/09/63 Linda Bricca takes her dogs on her first visit to the GAH
08/21/65 Posteal Laskey released from LaGrange Reformatory
10/09/65 Laskey arrested for Clifton assault and released on bail
10/12/65 Elizabeth Kreco assaulted at Verona Apts. Walnut Hills
10/21/65 Teenage girl assaulted on Windsor Avenue, Walnut Hills
10/21/65 Woman assaulted on Lennox Avenue, Walnut Hills
10/25/65 Margie Helton assaulted, robbed on Gilbert Ave., Walnut Hills
11/30/65 Posteal Laskey placed on probation for 10/9 assault
12/02/65 Emogene Harrington murdered on E. McMillan, Walnut Hills
01/16/66 Digna Canales, 32, survives strangling attempt in N. Avondale
04/04/66 Lois Dant murdered on Rutledge Avenue, Price Hill
04/30/66 Attempted rape of woman by young black man at her door
06/04/66 Mary Teppe, 61, choked & robbed on E. McMicken, Downtown
06/10/66 Jeannette Messer murdered in Burnett Woods, Clifton
06/26/66 Police announce a "Negro" is the killer of all three women
08/14/66 Barbara Bowman murdered on Ring Place, Price Hill
08/17/66 The Bricca family flies to SF for Jerry's sister's wedding
08/24/66 Woman, 35, raped & assaulted on Mulberry St., Downtown
08/29/66 Rose Thompson, 40, attacked by black man, Price Hill
09/06/66 Police Chief Stanley Schrotel resigns to take another job
09/07/66 The Bricca family returns from their San Francisco trip
09/12/66 Woman, 25, attacked on Victory Parkway, Walnut Hills
09/19/66 Linda Bricca begins work at the GAH for Dr. Fred Leininger
09/21/66 Virginia Hinners attacked and robbed E. McMillan, Walnut Hills
09/21/66 Linda Bricca works her last day at GAH, comes home drunk
09/25/66 Bricca family apparently murdered between 9-10:30 PM
09/27/66 Two women, 27 & 61, are assaulted Downtown by black men

09/27/66	**Bricca family found slain on Greenway Ave., Bridgetown**
09/28/66	Lead investigator Herb Vogel holds his first press conference
09/28/66	Fred Leininger interviewed about Linda' employment at GAH
09/29/66	Newspapers speculate the Bricca killer knew the victims
09/29/66	Thirty boxes of Bricca evidence are sent to the FBI for analysis
10/04/66	Delle Ernst assaulted Edgecliff Dr. Walnut Hills by black man
10/06/66	Woman, 48, assaulted on Park Ave. Walnut Hills by black man
10/08/66	Fred Leininger's 2nd Bricca interview makes him prime suspect
10/10/66	Vogel orders daytime surveillance on suspect Leininger
10/11/66	**Alice Hochhausler murdered on Cornell Place, Clifton**
10/12/66	Enquirer Headline – "5000 Man Posse Hunts For Sex Maniac"
10/18/66	Woman, 25, assaulted Race St., Downtown by black man
10/20/66	Woman, 66, assaulted Auburn Ave., Downtown by black man
10/20/66	**Rose Winstel murdered on Vine Street, Corryville**
10/21/66	Vogel announces the Bricca family was killed by a white man
10/30/66	Halloween is held during daylight hours because of Strangler
11/15/66	County confirms one Bricca suspect has not been cleared
11/21/66	Woman, 55, raped Gilbert Ave. Walnut Hills by black man
12/06/66	Gerald Taylor flies to west coast to interview Bricca relatives
12/09/66	Sandra Chapas, 22, menaced on Court St. by black man
12/09/66	**Lula Kerrick, murdered on 9th Street, Downtown**
12/09/66	Posteal Laskey arrested, charged with Sandra Chapas assault
12/11/66	Posteal Laskey charged with 9/21 assault on Virginia Hinners
12/12/66	Gerald Taylor returns from SF/Seattle/Chicago interview trip
12/14/66	Anna Scales, 79, assaulted on Kemper Lane in Walnut Hills
12/15/66	Grand Jury Indicts Posteal Laskey for Bowman murder
12/22/66	Colonel Jacob Schott is sworn in as new Police Chief
01/05/67	Cincinnatian Richard Tucker arrested for murder in WVA
02/02/67	County announces that the Bricca case is still open
03/19/67	Motion denied removing Judge Simon Leis from Laskey trial
03/23/67	Motion denied for change of venue in the Laskey trial
03/27/67	Murder trial of Posteal Laskey starts in County Courthouse
03/28/67	County announces that the Bricca case probe is "stymied"
04/02/67	Herb Vogel travels to Columbus OH to interview animal trainers
04/08/67	Prosecution rests their case in the Laskey trial
04/10/67	Prosecution and defense rest in Laskey trial and case goes to jury
04/13/67	Laskey found guilty with no recommendation for mercy

04/14/67	Prosecution says Laskey won't be tried for the six stranglings
05/05/67	Posteal Laskey sentenced to be executed on 9/15/67
06/11/67	Martin Luther King preaches non-violence at local churches
06/12/67	Riot breaks out in Avondale after Laskey's cousin is arrested
06/17/67	Riot ends and National Guard pulls out after 362 arrests
06/29/67	Posteal Laskey is granted indefinite stay of execution
07/29/67	Herb Vogel submits Bricca status report to Sheriff Tehan
09/22/67	Melvin Rueger confirms he knows the identity of Bricca killer
1977	Posteal Laskey's death sentence commuted to life in prison
1980	Laskey denied parole; also in 1982, 1984, 1987, 1997, 2002
June/95	Fred Leininger sells GAH and moves to Sarasota FLA
Aug/97	Townsend article on Strangler published in *Cincinnati Magazine*
02/23/04	Bricca suspect Fred Leininger commits suicide in Cincinnati
05/29/07	Posteal Laskey dies in prison after serving 40 years for murder
10/12/09	*Queen City Gothic* published with longest Bricca essay to date
03/29/13	Ohio AG Mike Dewine requests information on Bricca murders
03/29/13	Townsend appears on WLWT news for Bricca case feature
04/30/13	Coroner sends Bricca evidence to FBI for DNA testing
11/03/14	Townsend granted access to Bricca file by Hamilton County
Sept. 2018	*Summer's Almost Gone* published by JT Townsend

INTERVIEW SCHEDULE CHRONOLOGY (PRIORITY BOLDED)

September 28, 1966

#1 William Klein: Personnel Manager of Monsanto Company.
#13 Walgreen's Pharmacy: Mr. Neisel stated Linda called at 10 AM Sunday, for RX. Husband came in store between 4 PM – 5 PM to pick it up.
#14 Glenn Ritchie: Monsanto, states arrangements were made on Sept. 21, 1966, for flight to Charleston West Virginia, with Jerry Bricca.
#17 Cecile Fox: Travel Agency regarding Airline tickets.
#23 National Carpet: determine if any carpet was sold to Briccas.
#122 Dan & Pat Subtelny: on phone list at Briccas (also on 10/1 & 10/5).
#129 Ted Anderson: Jerry Briccas boss at Monsanto (also 10-5).
#131 John Jarvis: worked with Jerry Bricca (also 10-5).
#155 Will Rist: rode back and forth to work with Bricca.
#12 Phyllis Keller: neither Keller girl was scheduled to babysit.
#8 Fred Leininger: about Linda's employment at Glenway Animal Hospital.

September 29, 1966

#6 Meter Reader: Al Shelton of Cincinnati Water Works.
#7 Dr. White: Jerry had appointment for 4:30 PM Sept. 26, 1966.
#9 Bob Holzschu: Enquirer delivery man.
#16 William Cullen: regarding Dr. Keller and previous hospital record.
#24 Elmer Bauer: Information on Lou Vannavitch bothering his wife.
#26 Western Bowl: Interview employees white and Negro.
#31 Lt. Armstrong, Dade County, Florida. Regarding amnesia victim picked up at the bus station in Miami, name is Jack Bruce Peterson.
#112 Joan Janszen: on telephone list at Briccas.
#113 Betty Meyer: on telephone list at Briccas. (also 10-12)
#114 Sue Day: on phone list at Briccas.
#116 Art and Helen Zambatis: on phone list at Briccas.
#123 Gloria Weyman: on phone list at Briccas. (also 10-26)
#126 Cheryl Rehling: saw man with Linda on Saturday 24th. (also 10-27)
#156 Interview with Gale Griswald: reference man standing in rain.
#157 Mrs. Robert Herche: subject seen on Bridgetown Rd.

September 30, 1966

#19 Betty Haas: Obscene phone calls (Mr. Haas employed at Monsanto).
#32 Middletown Police Dept: regarding a William L. Mille, M/W/46.

#52 Mrs. Kesse: Information involving her babysitter and a prowler.
#63 Harry Rechtin: a subject near Moonridge and Eula, supposedly retarded.
#115 Nattie Caudell: Also Donald Sebastian on phone list at Briccas.
#120 Andrew Wulfeck: on phone list at Briccas. GE repairman.
#121 Martha Olding: on phone list at Briccas. Monsanto wife.

October 1, 1966

#36 Art Tenhundfeld: regarding suspicious unknown male who came into his station looking like he was in a fight, has car and license number.
#37 Kay Foegle: Black man going through garbage on Monday in area.
#44 Betty Hardig: Information on subject on Lawrence Road, Lee Schaibel frightened her. (also 1/24/67)
#45 Mrs. Ed Weyman: Good friend of the Briccas, information in reference to the carving set on Briccas buffet.
#61 Mrs. Emmitt Baldwin: reference Bricca Case and obscene phone calls.
#100 David Bierley: reference male black eating in restaurant at Shillito's.
#111 Estelle Zeff: on phone list at Briccas, daughter Linda interviewed 10/26.

October 2, 1966

#22 Ray McAdams: he saw two white males and one female running from area of homicide. (also 2-6-67)
#29 Robert Reichalt &McAdams: Both men saw a light green Falcon parked on Greenway at 11:30 P.M. Sunday. (also 1-31-67)
#34 Virgil Rottert: Reported M/W subject hanging around the area at night questioned the subject who stated he was spying on his girlfriend.
#35 Bob Gramke: saw blue 1964 truck parked in the area Saturday evening. #42 Anonymous Call: Information on a Finley Duncan as a suspect.
#47 Mr. Kiefler: Information reference to a man near the Bricca Home.
#48 Mr. Bachman: Someone walking a dog in the area of the Bricca home. #49 Charles Lucas: Information about car in area of Bricca Home.
#50 Mike Mayer: Information about man burying something.
#51 Mr. Schobert: Information regarding car.
#53 Mr. Bode: Information on prowler in area of Greenway.
#59 Cincinnati PD: Reference subject picked up for Strong Arm Robbery.
#60 Veterans Hospital: Reference a subject who stated he shot two people.
#62 Bert Potts: Information on truck in area of Greenway.
66 Donald Frank: Reference to suspicious subject in McFarlands Woods.
#117 Zelma Clark: On phone list at Briccas. Owns Pet store.
#118 William Klener: On phone list at Briccas. (also 1-27-67)
#119 Mr. Kugile: On phone list at Briccas. (also 1-31-67)
#124 Bob Schwartz: Windcrest Kennels on phone list at Briccas.

October 3, 1966

#2 Mr. Beach: Insurance Agent for Bricca Family.
#10 Charles Behrens: Post-Times Star delivery man.
#11 Patrolmen Anderson: Reference a woman who states has received obscene phone calls when her husband was working at Monsanto.
#55 Arthur Miller: Reference a subject in the area on 9-23-66.
#74 Check all taxi companies, reference fares to or from area.
#78 Pick up Charles Lupo and bring him in.
#125 Richard Kissel: On phone list at Briccas. Monsanto employee.
#162 Information from Cincinnati PD about call made to Indiana State Police.

October 4, 1966

#3 Dr. Eugene Elam:
#4 Dr. Nabors.
#5 Dr. Upson: Had appointment with Linda 4:30 PM April 7, 1966.
#72 Anne M. Wippel: suspicious person night of homicide on Woodhaven.
#75 Dr. Keller: if he knew Briccas or treated any of their animals.
#79 Interview Meter Man from CG&E working Greenway area.
#81 Mr. Walsh: information on person burning items.
#88 Bill Holub: Information reference Mrs. Bricca having date.

October 5, 1966

#15 Mrs. Green: Furnace company salesman at her door.
#18 Charles Lupo: Former bartender at Western Bowl.
#25 Tom Fleming: Reference hitchhiker with fresh cut on face.
#32 Sheriff Henderson, Boone County: received a call about disturbance in front of her house. Next morning she found knife in her mail box.
#38 Detective Hall: Anonymous call that Linda Bricca hung around Western Bowl quite a lot and drank pretty much. Also that she was quite a flirt.
#40 R. H. Dougherty: unknown M/W applied for a job and had a bowie knife.
#41 Helen Johnson: Information on a water meter reader. M/W/28 stopped at her home on Wednesday, 9/28/66, and made advances. He also talked about the Bricca murders. Subject is Bill Newmer.
#64 Paul Fagin: Subject worked with Bricca at Monsanto.
#67 Donna Nixon: Babysitter for Mrs. Kesse reference to prowler incident.
#68 Retha Morgan: Reference to a subject she believes could be suspect.
#69 Edward Walter: Reference suspicious black person.
#73 Earl Henry Koch: In Bricca phone book.
#76 Jewel Tea Company: Identify route man and check him out. (also 10-7)
#80 Kissel Bros: Check with animal trainer to see if he knew Mrs. Bricca.
#82 Betty Runk: Walgreens employee saw someone burying something.

#83 Check Sewers in the Greenway area assisted by County Engineers.
#85 Mrs. Scott: Reference subject claiming to be building inspector.
#86 Mrs. Ora Nix: Information on suspicious person.
#87 Flo Hine: Information from Betty Runck. (also 10-26)
#89 Mrs. Melvin Enderle: obscene phone calls and a black man in the area.
#91 Joe Schoenberger: Information on vehicle in the area.
#92 Dan Blevins: Reference knife he has like the one we are looking for.
#101 Cincinnati Bell: Check calls received Bricca residence past two months.
#103 Thomas Unger: See subject about a knife he found and pick it up.
#105 Detective Rutledge: Meet at the CPD to pick up information on Bricca.
#108 Ellen Dickinson: anything she can tell about Linda Bricca. (also 10/27)
#110 Detective Groppe CPD: Reference hunting knife found downtown. Also get information about Garling who is wearing a knife in his belt.
#127 Audrey Hummel: Worked with Jerry Bricca. Obscene calls.
#128 Mary Bailey: Worked with Jerry Bricca and Jim Cannon.
#130 Tom Olding: On phone list at Briccas. Regarding Jim Cannon.
#132 Glenn Richie: Worked with Jerry Bricca (also 2-1-67)
#133 Phone call received information from Carolyn Snodgress
#141 Kenneth Carr: reference Fred Leininger and Stanley Keller.
#142 Joe Lamb: reference a knife found on Burton St. in Avondale.
#143 Dick Janszen: received phone call from John Dillon who stated he was a Detective and has info on the Bricca case. (also 11-14)

October 6, 1966

#7 Auto stolen from Werk Road registered to Bonnie Meadows.
#28 Janice Buell: Reference suspicious person in car.
#58 Vera Richards: phone call from Mrs. Bricca to Fred Lininger on 9-21-66.
#94 Jack Davis: Saw two men fighting in the Monsanto parking lot on 9/24/66, one man looked like Jerry Bricca.
#97 Mrs. Broering: Reference black man in '58 Plymouth a melon color.
#96 Robert Merk: Reference vehicle parked in the area on 9/27/66.
#98 Mary Ellen Cannon: her background and any other information on her ex-husband James R. Cannon.
#99 Shell Station at Werk & Glenway: Interview attendant about Jerry Bricca being in station on the night of September 25, 1966.
#102 Robert Windholtz: Check subject reference report by Floyd Osborne.
#106 Find which Beauty Salon Linda Bricca used, and interview her operator as to what she may have told her about Mr. Meyers bothering her.
#107 Robert Marks: Reference auto he stole at Werk & Glenway on 9/25/66.
#109: Received information from FBI about Marvin Brown at Monsanto.
#134 Vernice Tankersley: pick up a knife her children found on Monday.
#135 Ted Bowling Interview: Worked with Jerry Bricca at Monsanto.
#136: Dave Maur: reference Bricca case and Janice Buell.
#137 Larry Abbott: friend of Dave Maur.
#139 Rudy's Pony Keg: Cliff Rockwell reference man trying to sell him a knife.

#144 Gene Knoerl: Robke Chevrolet Covington KY reference Bricca case.
#147 Call Oxford PD to check on the call received from Mrs. Bacholt.
#148 Check Bricca safety deposit box belonging at 5/3rd bank Western Hills.
#149 Det. Rutledge CPD: take clothing to Kettering, check for blood stains.

October 7, 1966

20 Susan Ray: reference knowledge of nude man seen on Greenway.
21 Investigate possibility of "Foot Doctor" on Greenway, looks like suspect wanted in Kentucky for shooting Campbell County Officer.
#33 Charlene Collins: Reference man she met in a bar who seemed to know a lot about when Bricca arrived home on Sunday.
#39 Robert Guill: reference two M/W subjects at the "Guest House Motel".
#56 Petie Evans: Ft. Lauderdale, Florida. Jim & Petie Evans address found in Bricca address book and also a letter.
#57 Executive Modeling Agency: in address book. (also 10-28 & 11-23)
#65 Ruth Walker: has information regarding William Stamper.
#70 Clarence Glener: Reference person renting trailer.
#71 Mrs. Donaldson: Reference strange subject renting from her.
#90 Harry Pierce: Reference subject on a bus with blood on him.
#137 Check out bars in the Monsanto area and see if Jerry Bricca went to these often. Lakeview, Lake Edward, Cozy Cottage.
#146 Check out Prentiss Fisher and back ground, also where he was on 9/25 & 26/66. Known burglar, was picked up, interviewed, and eliminated.
#150 Karen Camton: friction between James Cannon and Jerry Bricca.
#154 Interview people at Woodhaven Swim Club Reference Linda and Jerry.
#160 Check the area of the hand drawn map found in the Bricca residence, and see if anyone there knew them.
#161 Arthur Nagel: Worked with Jerry Bricca, infor about arguments.
#191 James Cannon: Reference Bricca homicide and friction with Jerry.

October 8, 1966

#77 Cincinnati Zoo Ed Maruska: check to see if he knew the Briccas.
#84 Mr. Schobert: Reference truck in area and a suspicious person at door.
#93 Ontario Store: Check for MW 27 5'6" selling jewelry on Saturdays.
#140 Checker Taxi: Reference driver stated he had a fare a few weeks ago named Bricca, who was taken to address in the Bridgetown area.
#145 Joe Vetere. Information on young MW in area. Molestation case.
#151 Olan Mills Photo: check if Bricca Family used service. Also check an employee James O'Banion for a record.
#158 Find church the Briccas went to and if Linda & Jerry went together.
#164 Bill Burkart: recommended Briccas membership Woodhaven Swim Club.
#165 Thomas C. Obrien: found in the Bricca phone list.
#167 Carla Burris: On Bricca phone list. (also 10-27)
#168 Janet and Dean Albright: On Bricca phone list.

#169 George Barry (refinisher): On Bricca phone list.
#170 Harriett Lowe: On Bricca phone list.
#188 Dr. Fred Leininger: Reference Linda Bricca and Bricca Homicide.

October 9, 1966

#52 Mr. Haseneier: two subjects at his Lawrence home on 9/25/66.
#54 Mr. Schiering: subject in area of Greenway at 7 AM 9/26/66.
#153 Check out Paul Mendel works at Monsanto, had a nervous breakdown.
#173 Check with Larry Holt, and Bob Girten reference Dr. Leininger hunting trip with them Oct 1st to Oct 7th. (also Girten 11-7)
#174 Leiningers father-in-law Clinton Rau: Check what Sunday they visited Leininger, how long they stayed dates Sept 18th, 25th and Oct 2nd.
#175 Clarence Flick: Chevrolet Impala 0/L 8002CA parked in front of the Bricca residence at Midnight 9/25/66.
#176 Fenton Schaller: 1965 Red Chevy Impala O/L 8005CA parked in front of the Bricca residence at midnight 9/25/66.
#177 Mrs. Gehling: 1965 Red Chevy Impala parked in front of the Bricca residence at midnight on 9/25/66.
#183 Ken Wallace: Reference a knife found in an auto at the Colerain Sales.
#184 Mr. Hall: vehicle parked in front of the Bricca residence on 9/25/66.

October 10, 1966

#159 Check Court House for any Bricca family litigation in the past three years.
#180 Lynn Leininger: 7788 Zion Hill Road. Refused to be interviewed.
#182 Check bowling Alleys, bars, and restaurants in the area Re Bricca case.
#186 Check former employment record Fred Leininger at Cincinnati City Hall.
#189 Marge Birch: phone call about a vehicle in the area of her home.
#190 Merriann Kirschner: Reference the Executive Modeling Agency.
#192 Alma Kendrich: Reference to John McClain.

October 11, 1966

#185 The Schmatts: Interview former employees of Dr Leininger.
#196 Marjorie Townsley & Winnie Fisher: Reference neighbors.

October 12, 1966

#95 Robert Hanson: driver in the area asked where Bricca house was.
#163 Harry Caldwell: J&J Food Market reference Linda and Jerry.
#171 LaRoss'a Pizza: On phone list in Bricca residence.
#172 Lee Lutz Flowers: On phone list in Bricca home.
#178 Dr. Casinni On phone list in Bricca home.
#179 Dr. James De Franco: On phone list in Bricca home.
#181 Oscar Kailholtz : Reference information about Dr. Leininger.

#187 Roy Streicher (Roy's Tree Service): His card found in Bricca home.

#193 Interview residents at 3354, 3376, 3344, 3349, and 3380 Greenway reference the Bricca homicide.

#194 Oscar Z. Martz: reference Bricca Case. (also 10-13)

#196 Interview the people at the SPCA reference Linda Bricca.

#199 Jeanie George: Reference Linda Bricca working for Dr. Leininger.

#251 Richard Joseph Meyer: next door neighbor of Briccas. (also 2-6-67)

October 13, 1966

#104 John McClain: reference an argument in the Monsanto parking lot between Jerry Bricca and John Jarvis. (also 1-31-67)

#152 Loren Smalle: Monsanto employee has been in Rollmans Psychiatric Hospital 3 times, stays 3 months at a time.

#197 Sara Oyler: Reference Linda Bricca.

#198 Gayle Szempruch: Her aunt was sentt to GAH for job interview 9/19/66.

#200 Cincinnati Bell: long distance calls made from Dr.Leininger's phone.

#201 Western Hills Import: On Glenway, get a list of all of employees.

#202 Vernon Ward: J&J Market, reference the Bricca Case.

#203 Elinore Zeisler: Director of the Happy Hour Nursery re the Bricca case.

#204 Mrs. Moorman: Reference Linda Bricca.

#205 Charlotte V. Ernst: Reference Dr. Leininger and Linda Bricca.

#209 Get back ground and check on Albert James Benedetti possible suspect.

#210 Check out Arthur Chaney, information he was seen with Linda Bricca.

#211 Check out Joseph L. Bach, his 1963 Chev O/L 5828 EC was seen near the Bricca residence at 11:30 PM on 9/25/66.

#215 Jerry Grigsby: He has information about the Bricca Homicide.

#216 Patrolmen Rusch: subject he arrested and knives that he found.

#217 June Emmich: David's Buffet Restaurant reference the Bricca homicide.

October 14, 1966

#207 Melvin D. Bell: Reference Linda Bricca and Dr.Leininger.

#208 Mrs. Ivan McKinley: information which may help on the Bricca case.

#212 Mrs. Robert Meyer: was a former neighbor of Linda Bricca and her sponsor for the League for Animal Welfare.

#213 Dr. Carrol Rolfe: reference information about Dr. Leininger.

#214 Sears Clerk: reference Linda Bricca buying paint there on 9/24/66.

#218 Jerry Woebkenberg: report he made to District 3 CPD on Bricca case.

#219 R.E.Coleman And J.W. Henry: Bridgetown Pet Hospital, reference the Bricca case and see if they know a Dr. Silk.

#220 Dr. Stanley Keller: At the Western Hills Animal Hospital reference Bricca case and see if he knows a Dr. Silk.

#221 Mrs. Wood: she was working across the street from Bricca home on 9/25/66 and Linda made a phone call to her boyfriend from that residence.

#222 **Dr. Herman Rehder: City Employee worked with Dr. Leininger and may have information about the Briccas. (also 10-20)**
#223 Anthony Re: patient of Dr. McDevitt for emotional illness.
#224 Kevin Healy: subject was going with Anthony Re's wife. (also 11-7)
#225 Dotty Emnerd: Find girlfriend in Miamitown and ask what she saw.
#226 Rodger Weseli: Good Samaritan Hospital: Stanley Keller mental record.
#227 **Larry Foppe: Owner of HiLo Beverage Depot, has information about seeing Dr. Leininger 9/25/66. (Also 10-16)**

October 15, 1966

#228 Lou's Greenacres Food & Beverage: owner reference the Bricca Family.
#229 United Dairy Farmer on Glenway: reference the Bricca Family.

October 16, 1966

#46 Mrs. Bryant: Reference knife supposed to be similar to Bricca knife.
#230 **Phyllis Tenholder: 3354 Greenway Ave, reference a vehicle parked near the Bricca residence on 9/24/66.**

October 17, 1966

232 Charles Herbig: Reference a car he saw at Lawrence and Glenway on night of September 25th, 1966.
#235 **WKRC TV: Interview Glenn Ryle reference animals used on his show and his friendship with Fred Leininger.**

October 19, 1966

#233 **White Cross Mental Hospital: get background on Dr. Herman Rehder, former patient there.**
#234 John Rooney: St. Anthony Messinger. Sold it to Jerry Bricca.

October 20, 1966

#231 Carol Sue Appleby: Merle Norman Beauty Salon, she took care of Mrs. Bricca's wig. (also 1-24)
#236 Mr. Boller: reference Mrs. Bricca possibly being at Carthage Fair.
#239 St. Mary's Hospital: Check on subject orderly supposed to be good friends with and live near Bricca Family.

October 21, 1966

#206 Richard Ernst: Reference Dr.Leininger and Linda Bricca.
#237 Shell Station at Werk and Glenway: Check what time Jerry Bricca was in station on 9/25/66, reference gas slip in car, also reference exact time and date he worked on Volkswagen.

October 25, 1966

#238 Elmer Stevenson: Subject has a bad temper, bowls at Western Bowl.
#240 West Harrison High School: Mr. Kulstad, good friend of Leininger.
#241 Mary May: Friend of Linda Bricca.
#242 Mrs. Eleanor Knierim: Information on the Bricca Case.
#244 Steve Saunders: Worked for Leininger. See what he knows about him.

October 26, 1966

#166 Jean and John Farr: On Bricca phone list. Husband is Jerry's cousin.
#249 Dr. Albert Weyman: Reference brother Edward L. Weyman.
#250 Janet and George Ditullio: Neighbors, reference whether they saw anything on the night of Sept. 25th in or around the Bricca house.
#111 Linda Zeff: Bricca primary babysitter.
#243 Mr. Baldwin: Liberal Savings & Loan, reference if he knows Jerry Bricca.

October 28, 1966

#248 Contact New Jersey State Police reference to suspect Edward Clark.
#57 Joe Cella: former operator of Executive Modeling Agency. Pick up a picture of Linda Bricca and determine circumstances surrounding the picture.
#245 Donna Andersen: She used to baby sit for the Briccas.

October 31, 1966

#254 Mr. & Mrs. Hemmer: Reference if they knew the Briccas or anything about them, and if they saw anything that night.
#255 Mr. & Mrs. Skinner: Reference if they knew the Briccas or saw anything.
#256 Mrs. Shearer: Reference if she knew the Briccas or saw anything abo.
#257 Mr. & Mrs. Joseph Hines: if they knew Briccas or saw anything that night.
#258 Mr. Toedt: Reference if he knew the Briccas or saw anything that night.
#259 Mrs. Gassner: Reference the Briccas and what she knows about them.
#260 Oscar Martz: walking his dog on Greenway and if he saw anything.
#261 Carl Pabst: Why was he driving area of Robinette and Brater at night?

November 1, 1966

#252 Mr. Zeff, 3313 Greenway: What he knows of the Bricca family.
#253 Susan Keller: former babysitter, what she knows about Briccas.
#262 KY State Police: check out Yvonne Hayes if she attempted suicide.
#266 Mr. & Mrs. John Kovac: if they knew Briccas or saw anything that night.
#267 Marian Toerner,: Reference what they can tell about Briccas or that night.
#268 American Cyanamid Company: usage for Laminac, reference FBI Report.
#269 Robert Schwartz, Windcrest Kennels: find out who worked for him.

November 3, 1966

#247: Emmitt Baldwin: Reference did he see Jerry Bricca on night of Sept. 25th.
#263 Mr. & Mrs. John Georgeton: reference what they know about Briccas.
#264 Mr. & Mrs. Frank Korty: Reference what they can tell about Briccas.
#270 Stan Drahman: works for the Nagel Company at the Monsanto Plant, reference the trouble he had with Jerry Bricca on 9/16/66.

November 4, 1966

#246 Dr. McDevitt: Reference Anthony Re and his condition.
#272 Hughes High School: get all background information on Dr. Leininger.
#273 See Mr. Brown at the Cincinnatian Hotel and get information.
#274: Valinda Westman: worked at GAH, reference if she knew Linda Bricca.

November 7, 1966

#271 Dr. Mark Upson: Linda Bricca used him as a personal reference.
#275 Opal Havens: Reference to what she knows of Albert Vincent.

November 9, 1966

#276 Dr. C.A. Pleuger: What he knows about of Dr. Fred Leininger.
#277 Sylvester Kemper: What he knows about Dr. Fred Leininger.

November 10, 1966

#278 Mrs. Donald Young: reference background on Dr. Fred Leininger.
#279 Ohio State University: get background on Dr. Fred Leininger.

November 12, 1966

#282 Janet Hyde: Reference what she knows about Dr. Fred Leininger.
#265 3323 Greenway: whoever lives there to see if they knew Briccas.

November 15, 1966

#283 Syrian Temple: get list of animal acts with the Shrine Circus at Cincinnati #284 Western Hills Plaza: what animal act was there in October 1964.

November 18, 1966

#280 Richfield Construction: Reference work they did on or around Greenway In September and October 1966. Canvas Greenway also.
#281 Mrs. Preston: Reference Homer Anderson may be Bricca suspect.

November 23, 1966

#57 Walter Burton: circumstances of photographing of Linda Bricca.

#285 Florida State Sheriff's Bureau: get information on Swede Johnson and Helen Haag regarding their whereabouts in September 1966.

December 6, 1966: San Francisco

SF 6-1: Dr. Elmer C. Bricca: San Francisco, before meeting with the entire family.

SF 6-2: Dr. Rafael Bricca: Jerry's cousin in SF. he did not know Jerry that well.

SF 6-3: Jack W. Liljeberg: he works for Standard Oil in SF and offered Jerry Bricca a job after an interview in early September.

December 7, 1966: San Francisco

SF 7-1 Jerry's father and his children: at Bricca family residence, mostly about Jerry's marriage to Linda.

SF 7-2 Joyce and George Fox of Sunnydale CA: about having dinner with Linda and Jerry during the SF trip for the wedding.

SF 7-3: Jerry Reinhart and Jack McCullough, about that same dinner.

SF 7-4: Marilyn Norton: Jerry's cousin, her insight into their marital relationship.

SF 7-5: Mrs. Marian Milan: Jerry's aunt and Marilyn's mother. Jerry and Linda stayed with her for three days of their trip.

December 9, 1966: Seattle

SE 9-1: William Munro: Plant Manager of Monsanto and Jerry's employer.

SE 9-2: Martin Berglund: Production Manager at Monsanto, worked with Jerry.

SE 9-3: C.P. Miller: Personnel Manager at Seattle Monsanto.

SE 9-4: Wilfred Bowers: hourly employee at Monsanto, worked with Jerry daily.

SE 9-5: William Smith: hourly employee at Monsanto knew Jerry a little better.

SE 9-6: Robert Ashley: nothing different from what other employees said.

SE 9-7: Dorothy Warfield: neighbor of Jerry and Linda Bricca when they lived on Lakeside Avenue in Seattle.

SE 9-8: James & Mary Hepworth: older neighbors, Linda helped with their dogs.

SE 9-9: Mrs. Betty Westenberg: Neighbor and close friend who said Linda rarely went out or visited any friends.

December 10, 1966: Seattle

SE 10-1: Taylor went to two of Jerry's Seattle addresses looking for anyone who knew him or remembered him, interviewed three people.

SE 10-2: Taylor went to six veterinary clinics near the Bricca's Seattle address but none remembered Linda or had records showing her as a client.

SE 10-3: Sally Watts of UAL: She confirmed Linda's termination on 11/4/6.

SE 10-4: Carl Hjert: Bricca on Lakeside Ave., saw them only for rent and repairs.
SE 10-5: Carol Karrigan: She was dating Jerry's roommate when Jerry met Linda.
SE 10-6: Dr. Sheldon M. Biback: Linda's obstetrician, said he treated her for frigidity and that she had a pregnancy previous to Debbie.

December 12, 1966: Chicago

CH 12-1: Phill Herriott: Supervisor UAL School for Stewardess in Elk Grove, Illinois. Verified her training and gave names of two Seattle classmates.
CH 12-2: Edward Marlow Strus: Jailed burglar supposedly in Cincinnati 9/25/66.
CH 12-3: Mr. & Mrs. Adolph Bulaw, Barrington, Illinois: Long interview, she told of the Erwin relationship and other problems Linda had while dating.

December 15, 1966

#289 Theobald Animal Hospital: see if Dr. Theobald knew Linda Bricca or had consulted her. He was associated with the Cincinnati Zoo.
#286 Tiny Cove Restaurant: Ellie the barmaid to see if she remembers Linda Bricca being in Tiny Cove at any time.
#287 David's Buffet: Crazy Janie", barmaid at David's, reference Linda Bricca being there. Report of Linda there with another man was incorrect.
#288 Pasquales Pizza: Cliff Newman, reference his knowing Jerry Bricca, may have been bowling with him on several occasions.

#301 **1/6/67:** Call Huntington WV and check out Richard Tucker. Check with his former wife living in Cincinnati. (also 2-6-67)
#293 **1/13/67**: Dr. Phil Dill: What does he know about Dr. Leininger?
#300 **1/19/67**: Jane Wellingsford: what she can tell us about Perry Dieterich.
#290 **1/26/67**: Dr. Muegeik: Reference Lee Casper Schaible.
#295 Longview Hospital: check out Walter Danny Garling, when he was there.
#294 William Nieman: Reference his reading meters and having trouble with women or acting suspicious. Also get his palm prints.
#291 **1/21/67**: Janet Schum: Reference her doing Linda Briccas Hair.
#292 Judy Schreiber: Reference what she knows of Joe Bach and the Briccas.
#296 Sandra Baldwin: Were they on Greenway September. 25, 1966?
#298 George Heine: Also Sally Heine to see what they know of a baby sitter from that night who saw something.
#297 2/1/67: Daniel Baldwin: Reference his being on Greenway on Sept. 25, 1966 and also about a License # he may have.
#299 Nancy Siegert: Reference what she knows about the baby sitter story.
#302 **2/6/67**: pick up Bricca medical records from Drs. Heil, Amann and Custer.

AUTHOR INTERVIEWS

Personal Interviews

Interview with Jay Bulaw	2/15/2013
Interview with Phyllis Vogel	7/31/2013
Interview with Larry Mentrup	11/8/2013
Interview with Peggy Doerger	10/10/2014
Interview with Larry Foppe Jr	3/30/2015
Interview with Jim Dell'Aira	12/26/2015
Interview with Bob Sweeney	12/28/2015
Interview with Bob Weitzel	12/30/2015
Interview with Jim Janszen	1/7/2016
Interview with Bob Frazier	1/13/2106
Interview with the Janszen Children	1/16/2016
Interview with Ginny Meyer Schardine	1/18/2016
Interview with Ruth Bernhard	1/22/2016
Interview with Ray Hulgin	2/18/2016
Interview with Linda Zeff Batson	8/19/2016
Interview with William Hauer	10/15/2016
Interview with Dan Baldwin	10/21/2016
Interview with Mike Allen	10/24/2016
Interview with Ray Hoffbauer	11/10/2016
Interview with Judith Bush Hemmer	1/10/2017
Interview with Susan Keller	6/21/2018

Email Interviews

Interview with Marilyn Kelley	2010
Interview with Steve Veid	2010
Interview with Eric Luo: (Bulaw relative)	2010
Interview with Linn Conyers	2010
Interview with Joe Stallkamp	2011
Interview with Helen Hofman	2012
Interview with Kaitlyn Jacobs	2012
Interview with Carol Budd	2013
Interview with Bernard Tigges: (Cary Robers)	2013
Interview with LizAnne Kubicki	2013
Interview with Dee Ehrhardt	2016
Interview with Kristi Crawley Van Tuyl: (Julie Ress)	2016
Interview with Joan Bricca Freeman	2018

Anonymous

Interview with Confidential Informant (Leininger)	2009
Interview with Confidential Informant (Suspect)	2010
Interview with Conspiracy Theorist	2011
Interview with Leininger Friend	2014
Interview with Confidential Informant (Leininger)	2014
Interview with Confidential Informant (Keller)	2015
Interview with other psychics	2016

NEWSPAPER CITATIONS

Scientist's Wife Found Slain – Victim of Strangler
Cincinnati Enquirer 12/03/1965 1:3
Strangler Struck in Dim and Dusty Basement
Cincinnati Enquirer 12/03/1965 7:2
Grim Hunt If On For Strangler
Cincinnati Enquirer 12/04/1965 1:4
Slayer Believed Man Wanted In Other Cases
Cincinnati Post Times Star 12/04/1965 1:7
Trucker May Be Witness Was Rape Killer Seen
Cincinnati Enquirer 12/05/1965 1:2
Reward Pushed In Rape Slaying
Cincinnati Enquirer 12/17/1965 26:5
Man Quizzed In Slaying Of Scientists Wife
Cincinnati Post Times Star 12/20/1965 1:5
Woman Strangled With Stockings-Body Found In Her Price Hill Apt
Cincinnati Post Times Star 04/04/1966 1:7
Killer Strikes Again, Housewife Raped, Slain In Price Hill
Cincinnati Enquirer 04/05/1966 1:6 pic
Strangulation Shocks Victim's Neighborhood
Cincinnati Enquirer 04/05/1966 10:5
Strangler May Have Called On Victim Twice-Cousin Tells Of Call Interrupted
Cincinnati Enquirer 04/06/1966 1:4
FBI Examines Hair, Other Murder Clues
Cincinnati Post Times Star 04/06/1966 1:7
Six Questioned In Sex-Slaying, Meager Clues Prove Worthless
Cincinnati Post Times Star 04/07/1966 1:1
Sex-Slaying Investigation at Standstill
Cincinnati Post Times Star 04/08/1966 10:7
Clues To Price Hill Murder Sought In Other Major Cities
Cincinnati Enquirer 04/09/1966 36:1
Reward Up To $883-Dant Killer Still Hunted
Cincinnati Enquirer 04/10/1966 6a:8
Third Woman Raped, Slain, Body Found in Burnet Woods
Cincinnati Post 06/10/1966 1:4
Mad Strangler Catches Widow Strolling Alone
Cincinnati Enquirer 06/11/1966 1:2
The Strangler... Who, What, Why?
Cincinnati Enquirer 06/11/1966 9:2
Anyone See Slayer in Park Police Quiz Motorists Pedestrians
Cincinnati Post Times Star 06/11/1966 1:5

A Dog, A Walk, No Fear—Then Death
Cincinnati Enquirer 06/11/1966 40:2
Rape Slaying Tipsters Flood Police Phones
Cincinnati Enquirer 06/13/1966 1:7
Little Learned In FBI Study of Rape Killing
Cincinnati Post Times Star 06/14/1966 1:8
Fear Gripping Women While Strangler Roams
Cincinnati Enquirer 06/14/1966 23:3
Negro Killed Three Women, Police Say
Cincinnati Enquirer 06/15/1966 13:3
8 More Policemen Added To Those Working On Messer Case
Cincinnati Post Times Star 06/15/1966 1:5
Veteran Sleuth Has Own Views On Woods Crime Patrick H Hayes
Cincinnati Enquirer 06/16/1966 14:7
Hospital Employee Quizzed In Slaying Was In Park On Day Of Murder
Cincinnati Post Times Star 06/23/1966 1:8
Mrs. Messer Slain By Negro FBI Finds
Cincinnati Post Times Star 06/24/1966 1:7
FBI Finding Adds Clue in Rapist Murder Hunt
Cincinnati Enquirer 07/07/1966 4:5
Strangler Clue in Sunday Murder Victim...
Cincinnati Enquirer 08/15/1966 1:7
Killers Methods Called Most Bizarre In City History
Cincinnati Enquirer 08/15/1966 31:1
Woman Fatally Stabbed Hit by Cab After Strangling Fails,
Cincinnati Enquirer 08/16/1966 1:2
Past Present Cab Drivers Quizzed In Hunt for Killer
Cincinnati Enquirer 08/16/1966 1:1
Illicit Cabbie May Be Killer of Secretary
Cincinnati Post Times Star 08/16/1966 1:7
Seeking Killer, Aroused Cabbies Offer Police Aid
Cincinnati Enquirer 08/17/1966 1:4
Burnet Woods Clue Cab Sighted Before Slaying
Cincinnati Post Times Star 08/17/1966 1:4
Police Think Robbery Was Killers Plan
Cincinnati Enquirer 08/18/1966 1:4
Illicit Cabbie Asked Fares Before Killing
Cincinnati Post Times Star 08/18/1966 1:1
Cab Drivers Quizzed Again In Slayer Hunt
Cincinnati Post Times Star 08/19/1966 1:4
Picture of Suspected Killer Being Compiled
Cincinnati Post Times Star 08/20/1966 1:4
Taped Voice Eyed As Murder Clue
Cincinnati Enquirer 08/22/1966 14:1
Police Armed With Pictures Comb Area For Slaying Clues
Cincinnati Enquirer 08/24/1966 1:6

Family of 3 Knifed To Death Bridgetown Ohio
Cincinnati Enquirer 09/28/1966 1:4
Neighbors Think Bricca Killer No Stranger
Cincinnati Enquirer 09/29/1966 1:1
FBI Lab to Check 30 Items Found At Scene of Triple Slaying
Cincinnati Post Times Star 09/29/1966 1:5
Many Sign Petitions; Murders Spur Plea for Police
Cincinnati Enquirer 09/29/1966 44:4
Slain Family's Neighbors Recall the Little Things
Cincinnati Post Times Star 09/30/1966 38:4
Reconstruction of A Murder Solution Worth $7000
Cincinnati Enquirer 10/01/1966 1:3
No Solid Lead Yet In Bricca Probe
Cincinnati Post Times Star 10/01/1966 1:6
Bricca Reward Swells, But Leads Remain Few
Cincinnati Post Times Star 10/02/1966; 1:6
Reward Upped In Bricca Case Total $12,000
Cincinnati Enquirer 10/03/1966 1:8
Bricca Lab Report May Come Today
Cincinnati Enquirer 10/04/1966; 1:1
Shocked Bricca Neighbors Learn To Live With Fear
Cincinnati Post Times Star 10/05/1966 42:4
Miranda Ruling Slows Probe into Bricca Family's Slaying
Cincinnati Enquirer 10/07/1966 40:1 1966
Phone Clue Perused On Briccas
Cincinnati Enquirer 10/10/1966; 32:7
Bricca Employer Gives $5000 for Murder Hunt
Cincinnati Enquirer 10/12/1966 1:1
Bricca Slayer Scouted Home Then Struck Vogel Says
Cincinnati Post Times Star 10/12/1966 4:3
City Police on Overtime As Strangler Strikes Again
Cincinnati Enquirer 10/13/1966 1:3
Grim Manhunt on for Mad Strangler
Cincinnati Enquirer 10/13/1966 1:5
Someone Knows Strangler – York Asks Help
Cincinnati Post 10/13/1966 1:4
Citizens Cooperate With Police in Mobilizing Against Killer
Cincinnati Post 10/13/1966 12:2
No "One" Suspect In Bricca Murders
Cincinnati Enquirer 10/13/1966; 14:6
Rumors Of Bricca Case Arrest Irk Authorities
Cincinnati Enquirer 10/14/1966; 1:2
5000 Man Posse Beefs Up Hunt for Sex Maniac
Cincinnati Enquirer 10/14/1966 1:1
Similarities Startling – All Point to One Man
Cincinnati Enquirer 10/14/1966 10:1

Thousands Hunt Strangler
Cincinnati Post 10/14/1966 1:2
Psychiatric Aid Asked In Hunt for Strangler
Cincinnati Enquirer 10/15/1966 1:6
Strange Fingerprints Found By FBI on Bricca Property
Cincinnati Enquirer 10/16/1966 1:6
Prints Found In Bricca Home Considered Very Slim Clue
Cincinnati Post Times Star 10/17/1966; 8:3
Minute Check Given Bricca Rug
Cincinnati Post Times Star 10/18/1966; 10:7
Police Mum On Report In ... Murder Case
Cincinnati Enquirer 10/20/1966 1:5
FBI Agents Hope To Stack Evidence Against Killer Here
Cincinnati Post Times Star 10/20/1966 20:1
Bricca Slayer Believed White
Cincinnati Post Times Star 10/21/1966 1:3
Miss Rose Winstel, 81, Raped, Badly Beaten in Vine Street Slaying
Post 10/21/66 1:4
Another Woman Strangled – Rape Verified
Cincinnati Enquirer 10/22/1966 1:6
Police Think 5th Slaying Planned
Cincinnati Post 10/22/1966 1:3
Violence Accepted as a Way of Life in Murder Locale
Enquirer 10/22/66 22:5
Rose Winstel Knew – And Feared for her Life
Enquirer 10/22/66 22:3
No Suspect in Murder
Enquirer 10/22/66 5:2
Professed Killer Found Boasting
Enquirer 10/23/66 1:3
Bricca Case Confession Retracted
Cincinnati Post Times Star 10/24/1966 1:3
500 Cars Checked by Police Investigating Hochhausler Slaying
Cincinnati Post 10/27/66 1:5
Self-Protection Study Spurred by Local Strangler Murders
Cincinnati Post 10/28/66 11:3
Prober Mum on Bricca Report
Cincinnati Enquirer 11/02/1966 10:4
Slayings Reward Fund Reaches $26,105 Total
Cincinnati Post 11/2/66 1:4
Bricca Family Slaying Probe Narrows to Single Slaying Suspect...
Cincinnati Post Times Star 11/02/1966 1:2
Florida Seeks Bricca Details
Cincinnati Enquirer 11/05/1966 4:3
Woman Accosted; Was It Strangler?
Cincinnati Enquirer 11/8/66 1:4

Neighbor of Bricca Cleared: Police Want Certain Man
Cincinnati Post 11/14/66 1:2
Briccas Neighbor Cleared By Police
Cincinnati Enquirer 11/15/1966 1:5
One Bricca Suspect Remains Police Admit
Cincinnati Post Times Star 11/15/1966 1:7
Bricca Murder Probers Seek Link With Girls Slaying In WV
Cincinnati Post Times Star 11/22/1966 6:5
Bricca Clue Held Faint
Cincinnati Enquirer 11/23/1966; 8:5
Strangler Began Crimes Here One Year Ago
Cincinnati Enquirer 12/2/66 1:5
Psychiatrist Presents Theory on Strangler
Cincinnati Enquirer 12/9/66 1:4
Strangler Strikes Again! Body Found in Elevator
Cincinnati Post 12/09/1966 1:1
Strangler's Victims—6 or 7?
Cincinnati Enquirer 12/10/1966 28:3
Suspect Quizzed In Taxi Slaying Questioned In Death of Lula Kerrick
Cincinnati Enquirer 12/10/1966 1:5
Ex-Cabbie, Quizzed in Slaying, Jailed After Assault Hearing
Cincinnati Post 12/10/66 1:6
Jailed Suspect in Spotlight of Seven Murder Probe
Cincinnati Enquirer 12/11/1966 1:1
Faces New Charge Virginia Hinners At New Thought Unity Center Identifies
Cincinnati Post Times Star 12/12/1966 1:7
Bowman Case Murder Charge Looms Today
Cincinnati Enquirer 12/13/1966 1:1
Laskey Has Alibi at Same Time of Alleged Assault Faces Bowman Slaying
Cincinnati Post Times Star 12/14/1966 1:7
Laskey case goes to Grand Jury
Cincinnati Enquirer 12/15/1966 1:3
On Deaf Ears; Mother of Daughter Reported To Police About
Cincinnati Enquirer 12/15/1966 7:1
Jury Indicts Laskey in Bowman Slaying
Cincinnati Post Times Star 12/16/1966 1:8
I Need Help ... Asked At Branch Office of the Hamilton County Legal Aid
Cincinnati Enquirer 12/21/1966 7:1
Laskey Enters Not Guilty Plea to Murder Robbery Indictments
Cincinnati Post Times Star 12/23/1966 1:6
Bricca Slaying Link in Stabbing?
Cincinnati Enquirer 01/10/1967 6:1 1967
Bricca Case Still Open Investigator Insists
Cincinnati Enquirer 02/02/1967 41:1
Laskey Trial Opens Monday
Cincinnati Enquirer 03/26/1967 1:4

Triple Homicide Bricca Case Probe Stymied
Cincinnati Enquirer 03/28/1967 1:7
State, Defense Statements to Jury Open Laskey Trial
Cincinnati Enquirer 04/04/1967 1:3
State Witness Places Laskey Near Death Scene
Cincinnati Enquirer 04/07/67 1:4
Worker at New Thought Unity Center Says Laskey Attacked Her
Cincinnati Post 04/08/1967 1:2
5 Defense Witnesses Back Up Laskey Alibi
Cincinnati Enquirer 04/11/1967 1:1
Laskey Guilty, Must Die
Cincinnati Post Times Star 04/13/1967 1:1
Judge Leis studies Laskey appeal, attorney lists major arguments
Cincinnati Post Times Star 04/21/1967 34:3
Defense fund set for Laskey
Cincinnati Post Times Star 04/21/1967 34:5
Year Goes By No Arrest, Prosecutor Believes He Knows Who Killed Briccas
Cincinnati Post Times Star 09/22/1967 1:3
Laskey Death Sentence Upheld In Ruling by Appeals Court
Cincinnati Post Times Star 02/13/1968 1:1
Laskey Case Started Reign of Fear In City
Cincinnati Enquirer 03/03/1968 11a:1
Posteal...Is Granted Stay Of Execution
Cincinnati Post Times Star 03/26/1970 45:6
Update ... Triple Murder
Cincinnati Enquirer 05/06/1977 D1:1
Terror in New York Brings To Mind Fearful Days Of Cincinnati Strangler
Cincinnati Enquirer 08/12/1977 A13:1
Leis Fights Parole for Man Jailed As 'strangler' In '67
Post 01/04/1980 9:4
Parole Denied For Alleged City Strangler
Post 01/10/1980 12:1
Prospect of Laskey Parole Enrages Mother Of Victim
Cincinnati Enquirer 04/09/1982 A1:5
Laskey's Conviction Touched Off A Tinderbox Of Racial Tensions
Cincinnati Enquirer 04/09/1982 C1:4
Living With the Cincinnati Strangler-Panic Was City's Reaction To Strangler
Cincinnati Enquirer 10/06/1985 E1:2
Serial Killers In Local History
Cincinnati Enquirer 03/24/1991 B3:1
Unsolved Murders (Bricca Family 09-27-1966)
Post 12/24/1991 5a:4
Strangler Up For Parole (30 Years After City Was Terrorized)
Post 01/24/1997 1a:4 Pic +
A Reign Of Terror (Cincinnati Strangler)
Post 02/08/1997 1a:2+ Pic

Strangler to Remain Locked Up; Parole Board Rejects Laskey
Post 02/10/1997 1a:1+
Cincinnati Strangler is Denied Parole: He Must Serve 10 More Years
Cincinnati Enquirer 02/14/2007 B2:1
'Strangler' Goes to Grave; '60s Saga Concludes
Cincinnati Enquirer 06/13/2007 B1:2+ Pic
Strangler Terrorized Cincinnati in 1960s
Cincinnati Enquirer 12/06/2010 C5:1 pics
The Crime That Stunned the City
Cincinnati Enquirer 3/30/13 C4:1 pic

Magazine Citations

Exclusive Report on Cincinnati's Phantom Slayer
True Detective Magazine. October, 1966.
The Bricca Mystery...And No One is Talking
Front Page Detective. July, 1967.
Will The Stranglings End?
Inside Detective. March 1967.
Getting Away with Murder
Cincinnati Magazine. January, 1982.
The Legacy of The Cincinnati Strangler
Cincinnati Magazine. 08/01/1997 31+ Pic
Unsolved Bricca Case Haunts the West Side.
Snitch Magazine. March, 2002
Cases Of The Century: The 10 Top Cases Of Cincinnati's Legal Legacy
Cincinnati Magazine. 08/01/2001 Sup
Death On a Quiet Street
Cincinnati Magazine. 04/01/2008 116:1+ pic
Unsolved mysteries: 19 local crimes, conundrums phenomena—explained!
Cincinnati Magazine. 04/01/2013 54:1+ pic

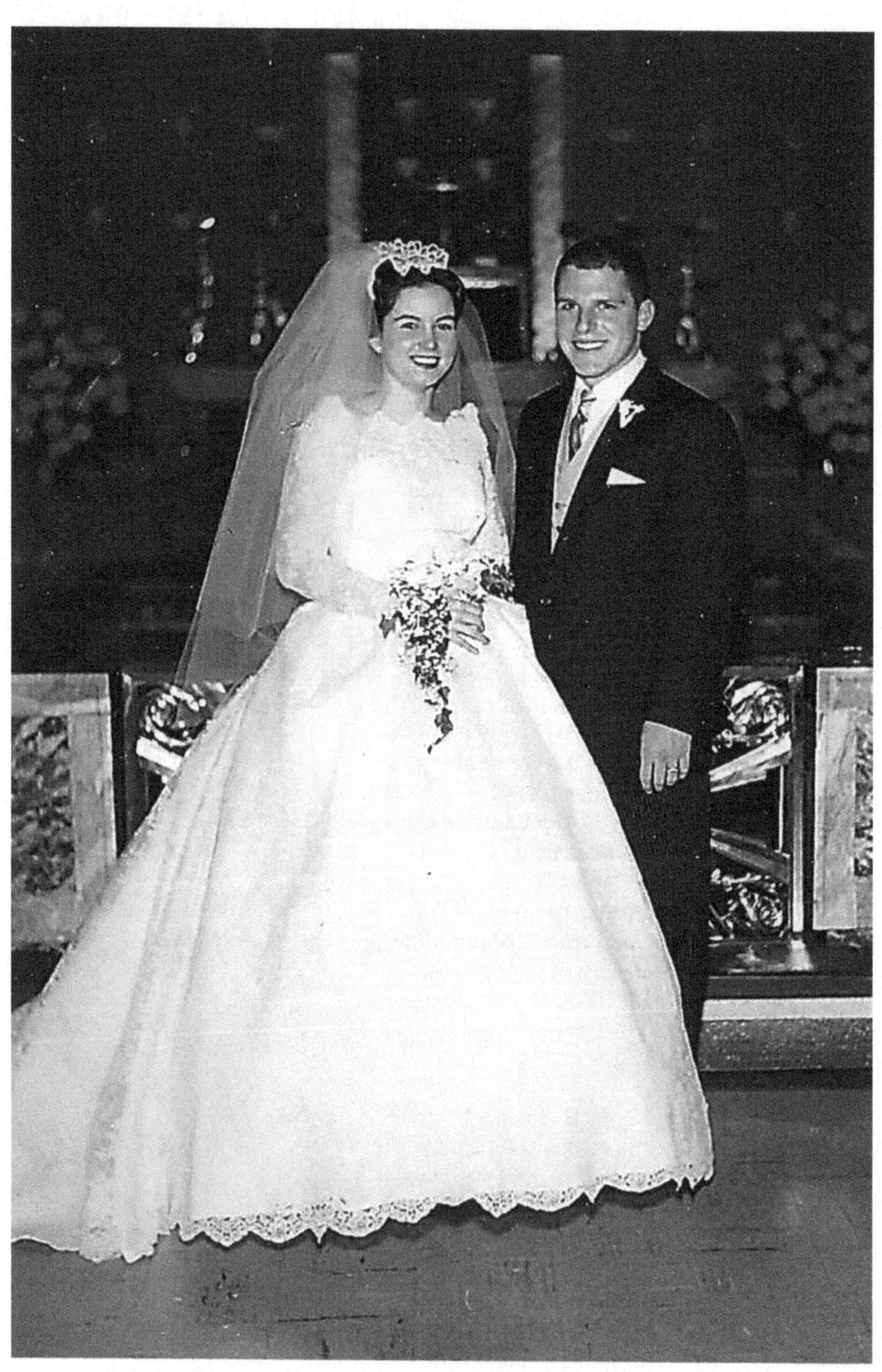

Jerry and Linda, man and wife, courtesy of Jay and Mona Bulaw.

PHOTO AND IMAGE CREDITS

Dedication: Author's Collection
Contents: Jay and Mona Bulaw
Maps: Author's Collection
A Preface: Author's Collection
A Prelude: Author's Collection

Chapter 1:	Page : 10	Jay and Mona Bulaw
	Page : 15	Author's Collection/*Cincinnati Enquirer*
	Page : 16	Author's Collection/*Cincinnati Enquirer*
	Page : 21	Author's Collection/*Cincinnati Enquirer*
	Page : 23	Author's Collection
	Page : 24	Author's Collection
	Page : 25	*Cincinnati Enquirer*
	Page : 31	*Cincinnati Post;* 04/05/66 1:5
	Page : 34	Jay and Mona Bulaw
	Page : 36	Author's Collection
	Page : 39	Author's Collection
Chapter 2:	Page : 42	Elgin Illinois High School Yearbook 1959
	Page : 46	Author's Collection
	Page : 47	*Cincinnati Post;* 06/10/1966 1:4
	Page : 50	Jay and Mona Bulaw
	Page : 53	*Life Magazine;* September 16, 1957
	Page : 55	*Cincinnati Enquirer;* 06/11/1966 1:2
	Page : 57	Idaho State Journal, 06/24/1966 9:2
	Page : 60	*Cincinnati Enquirer;* 06/15/1966 13:3
	Page : 64	*Time Life Books; True Crime,* 1993
	Page : 65	*Time Life Books; True Crime,* 1993
	Page : 71	*Time Life Books; True Crime,* 1993
	Page : 72	*Life Magazine;* August 12, 1966/Author
	Page : 77	Author's Collection
Chapter 3:	Page : 80	Jay and Mona Bulaw
	Page : 83	Jay and Mona Bulaw
	Page : 85	*Cincinnati Enquirer;* 07/16/1966 1:3
	Page : 86	Author's Collection
	Page : 89	Author's Collection
	Page : 92	Author's Collection
	Page : 96	Jay and Mona Bulaw
	Page : 102	Author's Collection

	Page : 104	*In Cold Blood;* Random House, 1966
	Page : 111	Author's Collection
Chapter 4:	Page : 114	Jay and Mona Bulaw
	Page : 117	Author's Collection
	Page : 120	Author's Collection
	Page : 125	Author's Collection/Enquirer
	Page : 130	*Cincinnati Enquirer;* 09/21/1966 8:1
Chapter 5:	Page : 142	Author's Collection
	Page : 144	Author's Collection
	Page : 147	Author's Collection
	Page : 151	Author's Collection
	Page : 153	Author's Collection
	Page : 154	*TV Guide Magazine;* Week of 09/24/1966
	Page : 158	*Cincinnati Enquirer;* 06/13/1966 17:1
	Page : 159	Author's Collection
	Page : 162	Author's Collection
	Page : 165	Author's Collection
Chapter 6	Page : 170	*Cincinnati Enquirer;* 09/29/1966 44:4
	Page : 177	Author's Collection
	Page : 183	Author's Collection/**Post**
	Page : 184	Author's Collection
	Page : 190	*Cincinnati Enquirer;* 09/28/1966 1:4
	Page : 195	Hamilton County Sheriff's file photos
Chapter 7	Page : 200	*Cincinnati Enquirer;* 09/29/1966 1:1
	Page : 203	*Cincinnati Enquirer;* 09/28/1966 1:1
	Page : 204	*WCPO.com;* 09/29/2016
	Page : 207	*WCPO.com;* 09/29/2016
	Page : 211	*Cincinnati Enquirer;* 09/29/1966 1: 2
	Page : 215	*Cincinnati Post;* 09/28/1966 1:1
	Page : 216	Author's Collection
	Page : 222	*Cincinnati Post;* 09/30/1966 1:3
	Page : 233	*Cincinnati Post;* 09/29/1966 44:3
Chapter 8	Page : 234	*Cincinnati Post;* 10/02/1966 2:4
	Page : 237	*Cincinnati Post;* 10/05/66 42:4
	Page : 247	*Cincinnati Enquirer;* 10/1/1966 1:4
	Page : 257	*Cincinnati Enquirer;* 10/7/66 1:7
	Page : 267	Author's Collection
	Page : 268	*Cincinnati Enquirer;* 01/21/60/Author
Chapter 9	Page : 270	*Cincinnati Enquirer;* 10/13/1966 1/4
	Page : 279	*Enquirer;* 01/19/1971 17:1/Phyllis Vogel

	Page : 282	Author's Collection
	Page : 283	Author's Collection
	Page : 284	*Cincinnati Post;* 10/12/1966 4:3
	Page : 293	*Cincinnati Enquirer;* 10/14/1966 1:1
	Page : 296	*Cincinnati Enquirer;* 10/13/1966 14:1
	Page : 302	Cincinnati Enquirer; various
	Page : 308	Author's Collection
Chapter 10	Page : 310	Jay and Mona Bulaw
	Page : 314	Author's Collection
	Page : 316	Author's Collection
	Page : 317	*Cincinnati Enquirer;* 10/22/1966 1:6
	Page : 325	*Cincinnati Post;* 10/20/1966 1:8
	Page : 331	*Inside Detective Magazine;* April 1962
	Page : 333	*Cincinnati Post/Enquirer* 11/2-3/18 1:1
	Page : 339	*Timeline.com;* 11/16/2016
	Page : 341	*Cincinnati Enquirer;* 11/2/66 1:1
	Page : 342	Infamous Murders; Treasure Press, 1985
Chapter 11	Page : 348	Jay and Mona Bulaw
	Page : 350	Jay and Mona Bulaw
	Page : 353	Jay and Mona Bulaw
	Page : 355	Author/*Enquirer* 12/10/1966 28:3
	Page : 357	Author's Collection
	Page : 358	*Cincinnati Post;* 12/09/1966 1:1
	Page : 358	Author's Collection
	Page : 363	*Enquirer* 12/11/1966 1:1/Author
	Page : 364	Jay and Mona Bulaw
	Page : 369	Jay and Mona Bulaw
	Page : 372	Author's Collection
	Page : 374	*Inside Detective Magazine;* March 1967
	Page : 377	Jay and Mona Bulaw
	Page : 379	*Cincinnati Enquirer;* 01/06/1967 41:4
	Page : 387	*Cincinnati Enquirer;* 03/28/1967 1:7
	Page : 389	Jay and Mona Bulaw
Chapter 12	Page : 390	*Front Page Detective;* July 1967
	Page : 396	*Cincinnati Enquirer;* 04/07/1967 1:5
	Page : 400	*Inside Detective Magazine;* March 1967
	Page : 407	*Front Page Detective;* July 1967
	Page : 410	*Cincinnati Post;* 09/22/1967 1:3
	Page : 415	*Cincinnati Enquirer;* 10/25/67 & 01/11/68
	Page : 416	Author's Collection
	Page : 419	*Cincinnati Enquirer;* 1974
	Page : 422	Author's Collection

	Page : 423	*Cincinnati Enquirer;* 06/13/2007 B1:2
	Page : 427	*Cincinnati Enquirer;* 03/30/2013 C4:1
Chapter 13	Page : 428	Author's Collection
	Page : 431	Author's Collection
	Page : 433	Author's Collection
	Page : 443	Jay and Mona Bulaw
	Page : 444	*Cincinnati Magazine;* August 1997/Author
	Page : 448	Author's Collection
	Page : 450	Time Life Books, True Crime, 1993
	Page : 452	*Inside Detective Magazine;* April 1962
	Page : 454	City of Addyston/Kelly Cross Mansu
	Page : 455	Author's Collection
	Page : 459	Author's Collection
	Page : 469	Author's Collection
	Page : 475	Author's Collection
	Page : 476	Jay and Mona Bulaw
Final Exit	Author's Collection	
Image Credits	Jay and Mona Bulaw	
Ackn/Author	*Front Page Detective;* July 1967/Author	

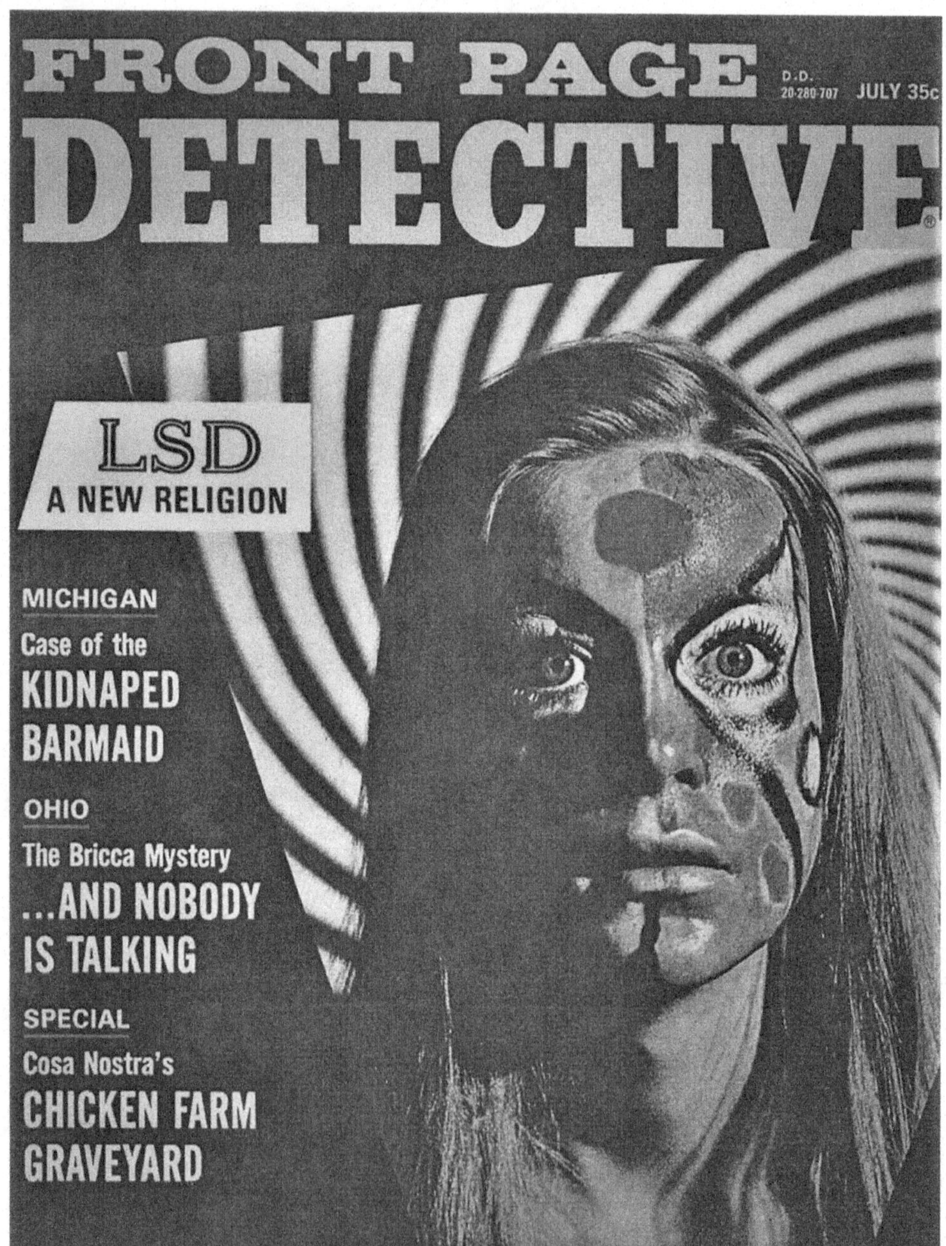

Front Page Detective July 1967 is the only known pulp magazine feature on the Bricca case.

ACKNOWLEDGMENTS

THERE ARE THREE PEOPLE who were integral to the creation of *Summer's Almost Gone.*

A huge thank you to **Doug Todd** of the Hamilton County Sheriff's Office, whose passion for justice and selfless initiative finally opened up the files after almost 50 years.

Thank you to **Shawn Glover**, whose pursuit of pictures and creative talents propelled the quality and quantity of the imagery embellishing this book.

And my sincere appreciation to my good friend **Dannyn Qualls-Gibeau**, affectionately known as "Dash the Ripper", for stepping into some big editing "shoes" and filling them splendidly.

There is a diverse group of people who tagged along with me on this obsessive journey.

Kim Ryan, my partner in crime, who has worn many hats while propelling me on my passage from Jeffrey Tesch to JT Townsend.

Tricia Huff, my superb genealogist, who located the missing witnesses and forgotten connections to this ancient crime.

Victoria Norman, my microfilm editor with the PLCHC, who saved me countless hours of trouble and aggravation.

Mona and Jay Bulaw, who dug through their archives to supply the wedding pictures and other personal photos of the family.

Paula Holmes Payne, who founded Historical True Crime Cincinnati and showed me the power of Facebook groups.

Ken Lippert and Joe Diana, who became the emergency supply chain team for True Crime Detective Press.

John Farnham, so instrumental for my first book, and who's never lost faith in my ability to be a crime writer.

Eric Ford, a true friend, and the kind of buddy every guy should have but that hardly any do.

Those with a connection to the Bricca case who consented to be interviewed are the lifeblood of this book.

My thanks to Phyllis Vogel and Ray Hulgin, for taking me inside a 50- year-old investigation with no surviving participants.

Also to Bob Sweeney and Bob Weitzel, for taking me inside the most infamous crime scene in Cincinnati history.

And especially Linda Zeff, who opened up a painful chapter of her life and made this beautiful, murdered family come alive for me.

As always, there are the Bricca fanatics – the few and the faithful who never let this murdered family stray far from their thoughts.

Brian Bolten, an insightful blogger/historian who gave me the idea for the "Kwai concept" on the murder night.

Judith Bush Hemmer, a delightful new friend who reincarnated the sights and sounds of the West Side in 1966.

Kelly Cross Mansu and Connie Healey, who were able to locate the final key images at the 99th hour.

Julie Ress, my "amazing friend" who grew up near the Bricca house and gave me her Cousin Kristy Krawley's story.

And to all the rest my hardcore Bricca minions...people like "zaftig" sisters Chris Grimm & Angie Reverman,"Inspector" Jim Ammann, David Gray, Crystal Lay Freeland, Steve Berninger, Alan March, Jerry Smith, Susu Cecile Freemond-Brown, and George Stimson... just to name a few.

To all my friends and family, acknowledged in the back of my two previous books, who can now breathe a sigh of relief that I've finally put this obsession in the ground.

To my wife Sheryl, who patiently reads all my work and knows all about the highs and lows of living the creative life.

And finally, to my late, great editor and friend **Coleen Armstrong,** who started me on the journey of free-lance writing back in 1997. Another irreplaceable person in my life gone too soon. But you made me the writer I am today...

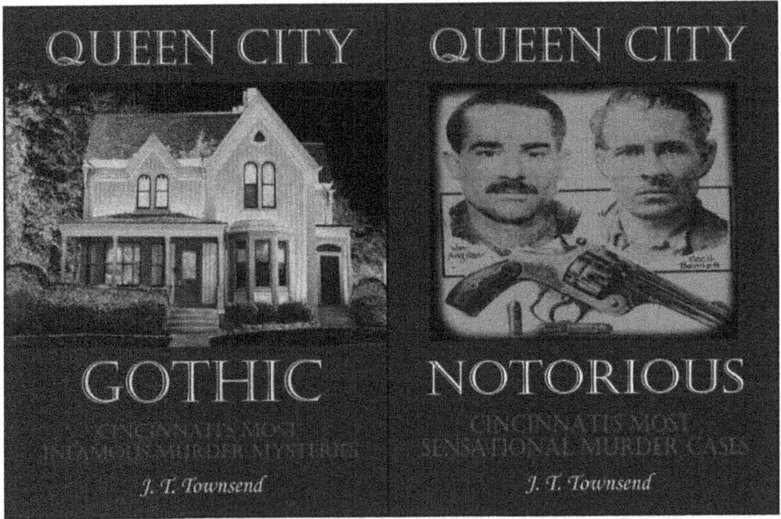

J. T. Townsend is a freelance writer, armchair detective, and lifelong resident of Cincinnati. He is the author of the 2009 regional true crime best seller **Queen City Gothic**, and 2014's **Queen City Notorious**. His work has appeared in the *Cincinnati Enquirer, Cincinnati Magazine, Word Magazine, Crime Traveler* and *Clews*. He has presented over 300 programs in the Cincinnati area as part of his **True Crime Lecture Series**, including Jack the Ripper, Lizzie Borden, the Lindbergh Kidnapping and the Lincoln Assassination.

Visit his website at www.jttownsend.com

Like his Facebook page: www.facebook.com/TrueCrimeDetective/

JT's 50 year Bricca journey from 1966-2016.